The Ships and Aircraft of the U.S. Fleet

The Ships and Aircraft of the U.S. Fleet

THIRTEENTH EDITION

By Norman Polmar

Naval Institute Press
Annapolis, Maryland

Frontispiece: Submarines have an increasingly important role in naval warfare, with expanded mission opportunities being offered by anti-ship and land-attack cruise missiles, over-the-horizon targeting systems, and satellite navigation and communications. The attack submarine LA JOLLA (SSN 701) is seen during a brief moment on the surface with the submarine's traditional enemies—a carrier and ASW ship, the RANGER (CV 61) and BAGLEY (FF 1069). (1983, Giorgio Arra)

For George H. Miller

Contents

Preface

This thirteenth edition of *The Ships and Aircraft of the U.S. Fleet* describes the U.S. Navy of the mid-1980s as the fleet undergoes an almost unprecedented peacetime buildup. This edition continues the effort begun with the eleventh edition to provide a new order of coverage of the U.S. Fleet. The breadth and depth of data on the fleet—its ships, aircraft, weapons, electronics, personnel, organization, and shipyards—are significantly greater than available in any other single volume. (This same concept and format have been adopted for the reference work *Guide to the Soviet Navy*, also published by the Naval Institute Press.)

This volume gives increased emphasis to naval aviation, electronics, nuclear weapons, the Marine Corps, Rapid Deployment Force, Navy organization, and shipyards. All of these are of major importance to the effectiveness of the U.S. Fleet.

The organization of the ship and aircraft listings have been devised by the author; they are intended to help the lay reader as well as the professional to quickly locate ships and aircraft. (The official Navy order of ship listings is provided in Chapter 9.) Also, a more simplified means of listing ship status is used. The official Naval Vessel Register uses a more detailed—and complex—method. For example, RECU is used to indicate that the ship is "Inactive, in commission, in reserve, undergoing conversion." In this edition of *Ships and Aircraft* the boldface **AA** and **PA** are used to indicate active ships in the Atlantic and Pacific fleets, respectively, while boldface **IO** indicates ships that normally operate in the Indian Ocean region. The lighter letters AR and PR indicate ships in naval reserve; and NDRF for National Defense Reserve Fleet (under the cognizance of the Maritime Administration). Operational ships assigned to the Naval Reserve Force are indicated by NRF-A or NRF-P while the Navy's Military Sealift Command are listed as MSC-A or MSC-P, the suffix letter indicating assignment in the Atlantic and Pacific areas, respectively; the simple listing MSC for status indicates unassigned ships or ships on worldwide routes. The status note Building indicates ships under construction and the term "Yard" indicates those ships in long-term modernization or conversion.

This edition contains expanded chapters on Navy and Marine organization and personnel. This material is in response to requests, partially from non-American readers, for more of a perspective on the current strength and organization of the Navy and Marine Corps. It is hoped that this material will help those readers seeking such information and not detract from the book's use by readers who have other sources. In general, the information in this volume is current through mid-1984.

Once again I am in debt to many individuals and organizations for their help in preparing this, the 13th edition, of *The Ships and Aircraft of the U.S. Fleet*. Special thanks are due to the advice, assistance, and tolerance of Fred Rainbow, managing editor of the Naval Institute *Proceedings*, and to Dr. Norman Friedman, former deputy director of national security studies at the Hudson Institute. Also helpful has been A. D. Baker, editor of *Combat Fleets*.[1]

A large number of the photographs in this edition was taken by my friend and colleague Dr. Giorgio Arra. In addition, several photographs of Mr. and Mrs. L. van Ginderen, W. Donko, and Stefan Terzibaschitsch have been used. Many of their photos that do not appear in the edition were invaluable in determining the current weapon and electronic installations of U.S. ships. Robert L. Lawson and JOC Kirby Harrison, outstanding aviation photographers, have provided several of the aircraft photos used in this edition. Most U.S. Navy photographs were provided with the help of Robert A. Carlisle, Head, still photography, Office of the Chief of Navy Information (CHINFO), and his assistants JO1 David Kronberger and Domingo Cruz.

Most of the ship drawings were prepared by M. Simoni for *Flottes de Combat*.

Among the many persons who have contributed to this edition have been W. J. Armstrong, historian of the Naval Air Systems Command; Timothy J. Beecher, McDonnell Aircraft; Lt. Carl R. Begy, USS Blue Ridge; Capt. H. J. Bernsen, USS Lexington; Lt. L. H. Bradshaw of VX-1; Scott Brinckerhoff of United Technologies/Norden; Jim Bright, Newport News Shipbuilding; Robert G. H. Carroll III of Sikorsky Aircraft; Lloyd F. Carter, Naval Research Laboratory; "Blade" Chapman; Lt. (jg) Joseph F. Coble III of HC-1; Ross S. Dessert, Boeing Marine Systems; Lt. Comdr. M. W. Doubleday, Fleet Public Affairs, CinC Pacific Fleet; Marianne Elmore, Gould Electronics; Capt. J. C. Farrar of Division of Public Affairs, Headquarters, USMC; Robert C. Ferguson of Lockheed-California Company; Susan Y. Flowers of McDonnell Douglas Astronautics; William M. Frierson, NAS Patuxent River; Lou Granger of the Military Sealift Command; Robert P. Harwood and Brian R. Salisbury of Grumman Corp.; Harry Gann, McDonnell Douglas; Nancy H. George, Bell Aerospace Textron; Lt. Mike Gault of VC-8; Capt. Robert V. Gooloe, Jr., of HM-12; Col. John Greenwood, editor of the *Marine Corps Gazette*; A. C. Hagelberg, General Dynamics/Pomona; Ray Hagen, Office of the

---

[1] This is the English-language edition of *Flottes de Combat* by Jean Labayle-Couhat.

Oceanographer of the Navy; Comdr. T. P. Hayes, USS MOUNT WHITNEY; James Hessman, editor of *Sea Power* (Navy League); J. F. Isabel of General Dynamics/Convair; Kohji Ishiwata, editor of *Ships of the World*; G. W. James, Jr., of Lockheed Shipbuilding; Paul R. Kelleher of the Military Sealift Command; Loretta Kelly, Cessna Aircraft; Comdr. R. A. Killion of Submarine Development Group 1; Dennis P. Klauer, Naval Military Personnel Command; Capt. Richard K. Knott, head, aviation periodicals and history for the Deputy CNO (Air); John Kvasnosky of Boeing Aerospace; T. C. Lackey of HC-11; Rear Adm. Julian Lake, electronics expert *par excellence*; PH1 David Lister of the USS L. Y. SPEAR; Jerry Littman of General Dynamics/Pomona Division; Lt. M. E. Livingston of the USS LA SALLE; Tony Marchitelli and Tony Conway, Naval Sea Systems Command; Comdr. Tyrone G. Martin; Paul Martineau of Litton/Ingalls Shipbuilding; Comdr. R. A. McDaniel of HC-4; Comdr. E. C. McDonough, Headquarters, U.S. Marine Corps; Lt. Comdr. Peter Mersky of *Approach* magazine; Rear Adm. Wayne Meyer, deputy commander, Naval Sea Systems Command; Rear Adm. J. Brad Mooney, Chief of Naval Research; Lt. (jg) C. J. Mullarkey of VC-10; James J. Murphy of General Dynamics/Marine Operations; Donald J. Norton and Nicholas F. Pensiero of RCA; Capt. D. J. O'Shea, USS POINT LOMA; PH3 R. Olson; John Patrick of LTV-Vought; Michael Pollock and Dan Reeder of Hughes Aircraft; Rear Adm. Donald P. Roane, project manager, Aegis Shipbuilding Project; Comdr. A. E. Rypka, commanding officer, VC-1; Chris Schildz of McDonnell Aircraft; Lt. A. R. Schmid, HC-3; Col. E. E. Shoults, project manager T-AKRX, Naval Sea Systems Command; Dick Spivey, Bell Aerospace Textron; Lt. Roger Still and Anna C. Urband of CHINFO; J. W. R. Taylor, editor of *Jane's All the World's Aircraft*; Lt. Comdr. N. B. Thompson, Naval Postgraduate School; B. B. Toole, HC-6; Dr. Scott Truver of Information Spectrum Inc.; Judy Van Benthuysen of CHINFO; Dolph M. Veatch, editor of *Surface Warfare*; Lt. Cdr. Gregory Warneford, VX-1; Theodore R. Wieber, Jr., Raytheon Marine Company; and Ens. Helen A. Zeppenfeld of VC-5. Also, appreciation is given for the help from Scott Brinckerhoff, United Technologies/Norden; Vincent Malcolm, General Dynamics/Electric Boat; Brian Salisbury, Grumman Aerospace; and Brad Veek, Hughes Aircraft.

Ted Minter has provided an invaluable backup on much of the data in this volume.

Finally, this book could not have been produced without the encouragement and help of Thomas Epley, director, Naval Institute Press; Cynthia Barry, who edited the manuscript; Beverly Baum, who did the layouts; and Patty Maddocks and Mary Sprawls who assisted in photo research.

The Ships and Aircraft of the U.S. Fleet is planned for publication every third year by the Naval Institute Press. Work on the next edition begins almost immediately, hence comments, additional data, and illustrations are most welcome. Material should be addressed to the author in care of the Naval Institute Press, Annapolis, Md. 21402.

Norman Polmar

The Ships and Aircraft of the U.S. Fleet

1 State of the Fleet

The decline of the U.S. Fleet in the post-Vietnam era—which led to a nadir of some 450 active, Navy-manned ships in 1980—has been reversed. Although Secretary of the Navy John Lehman has called for a 600-ship fleet, by 1990 the U.S. Fleet will have some 700 *operating* ships. The turn-around has been qualitative as well as quantitative: The congressional funding of two aircraft carriers in a single fiscal year is unprecedented since World War II, and the battleship recommissionings have been pressed forward with almost unbelievable enthusiasm and political support from Congress as well as the Administration.

While serious questions have arisen over the ability of the Navy to maintain and man a fleet of this size, the fact is that by 1990 there will be at least half again as many ships in U.S. naval service as there were ten years earlier. (Of course, the overwhelming majority of the ships in the fleet in 1990 will have been built or were on order prior to the Reagan Administration taking office.)

Secretary Lehman has become one of history's few naval leaders to significantly change the direction of a major fleet in peacetime. He has been able to do so because of close ties with the leadership of the Reagan Administration as well as with several influential members of Congress, and his own knowledge and strong feelings about the Navy. Many Americans viewed the presidential election of November 1980 as a call for a military buildup. That election came in the wake of seizure of the American embassy in Tehran late in 1979 by Iranian terrorists, the Soviet invasion of Afghanistan, the threat of Soviet military action against Poland, and major Soviet advances in strategic and conventional weapons.

Upon entering the White House in January 1981 the Reagan Administration proposed three major areas of defense buildup: (1) strategic offensive forces; (2) rapid-deployment conventional forces for crisis reaction; and (3) "naval superiority."

When named Secretary of the Navy, Lehman immediately put forward a plan for a "600-ship" fleet, a plan that would reverse the decline of the Navy that had reached a high of almost 1,000 active, Navy-manned ships during the Vietnam War. Equally significant, Lehman proposed the immediate construction of two additional NIMITZ (CVN 68)-class nuclear aircraft carriers and reactivation of all four IOWA (BB 61)-class battleships from the reserve (mothball) fleet.

Secretary Lehman was able to gain the first objective, the authorization in fiscal 1982 of two new carriers. Proposals to reactivate one of the mothballed HANCOCK (CV 19)-class ships as a temporary means of increasing carrier strength was, however, rejected by Congress. When this edition of *Ships and Aircraft* went to press the dreadnoughts IOWA and NEW JERSEY (BB 62) had been returned to active service, with the MISSOURI (BB 63) in a shipyard being rehabilitated; reactivation of the fourth ship, the WISCONSIN (BB 64), is planned.

These 15 carrier battle groups and 4 battleship-centered surface action groups are the centerpieces of the proposed 600-ship fleet. However, the question must be raised: "What is a ship?" The *actual* goal is not 600 ships, but something more than 700 ships. Secretary Lehman has changed the method of ship counting; however, his counting scheme is more realistic for today's naval forces.

What is a ship for counting purposes? The Navy has recently introduced the term "battle forces" and this is the 600-ship fleet now planned. The 600-ship number excludes strategic missile submarines and their support ships as well as certain types of auxiliary ships; however, the 600 ships do include some—but not all—ships in the Naval Reserve Force and civilian-manned auxiliaries of the Military Sealift Command. Also, there are new types of ships, such as the T-AGOS towed-array surveillance ships, with 12 being built and more proposed.

Thus, the new counting method and hence the 600-ship number have little relationship to previous counting methods and fleet totals.

Table 1-1 lists the composition of the active U.S. Fleet over the past two decades. The term Total Operating Forces includes all operational ships manned by active Navy personnel, Naval Reserve Force, and Military Sealift Command; active ships are those in active service with Navy crews; and Battle Force Ships are those that comprise and support the planned 15 carrier Battle Groups (CVBG) and battleship-centered Surface Action Groups (SAG). Note that ships of the Naval Reserve Force (NRF) and Military Sealift Command (MSC) are included. For probably the first time since just after World War II, beginning in the late 1970s the naval reserves have been provided with first-line amphibious ships and, under the Reagan Administration, with the fleet's newest combatant ships and aircraft (see Chapter 7). Similarly, despite strong opposition from segments of the uniformed Navy, beginning in the 1970s several replenishment ships have been civilian manned under the aegis of MSC. These ships are now fully integrated in the operating fleet and have proved highly successful in supporting the high tempo of fleet operations.

Although the Kitty Hawk (CV 63) and her air wing of some 85 high-performance aircraft are becoming increasingly vulnerable to Third World as well as to Soviet weapons, aircraft carriers continue to provide the most effective means of projecting U.S. military power into many forward areas. (1984, U.S. Navy)

FLEET READINESS

Beyond the procurement of ships and aircraft, emphasis is also being given to increasing readiness for combat. The improved personnel situation coupled with the increased purchase of munitions and other expendables, and efforts to increase ship steaming and aircraft flight time, have contributed to an improvement in fleet readiness. According to Secretary Lehman,

> The fleet is more ready to go in harm's way than at any time in peacetime history. In the past three years, surface ship combat readiness has improved by 14% and aviation readiness by 24.2%. Three years ago only five of our twelve aircraft carriers could be deployed with the required aviation spare parts support. During the past year [1982] we had eight of our thirteen carriers simultaneously deployed with the required spare parts.[1]

There are, however, differences of opinion over the degree to which the combat readiness of the fleet has been improved. And there is still a severe shortfall of munitions. Secretary Lehman has called special attention to the frustrations over the Navy's Operations and Maintenance (O&M) funding:

> There are two frustrations. O&M cuts [by Congress] *always* come, even though Congress lately has been saying, "We musn't cut readiness." But they end up doing just that. It was done last year—substantial cuts in the O&M account. We pay a price in readiness, in training, and in infrastructure.
> But the taxpayers also pay a long-term penalty that is very substantial. Why? Because when those cuts are taken, we end up losing second-source competition, as we did on the HARM missile program. We end up reducing the buys for sustainability items and spares so that the prices go way up.[2]

The current shortfall of weapons means that the Navy simply does not have enough weapons to fill up all ships, especially carriers, with weapons. In some critical munition categories a deploying carrier must take aboard missiles from a carrier returning from deployment. A related problem is the shortfall of munitions limits the amount of test and practice done with weapons. Some F-14 crews fire a single Phoenix missile once a year—or less often. One officer has addressed this problem in the following terms:

> "Daily Practice with Guns": Technology has dealt a cruel blow. As our weapons get better, their cost, range, and other characteristics have made it too difficult to carry out Thomas Truxtun's dictum. We are riding around with a load of silver bullets with which we have little fleet experience.
> Harpoon, Tomahawk, Mk 46 torpedo, ASROC, SUBROC, Standard, Phalanx, Sea Sparrow, Phoenix—nobody shoots enough of these weapons to know if they are any good with them. Nobody shoots enough to close the design loop with fleet experience. Nobody shoots enough to learn enough to drive tactics. Acceptance testing and evaluation firings tell us the weapon works, but they do not tell us about the readiness and effectiveness of the entire weapon system, including ship, crew, and tactics.[3]

Still, Congress generally finds it easier to cut back on the procurement of munitions, fuel, and other consumables because their deletion from the budget is not as visible or politically sensitive as the loss of ships and aircraft.

[1] Secretary of the Navy John F. Lehman, Posture Statement, 23 March 1983, p. 4.
[2] Interview with Secretary Lehman, "By Every Measure, a Tremendously Improved Force," *Sea Power* [Navy League], April 1984, p. 16.
[3] Commander John L. Byron, USN, "Sea Power: Opportunities," U.S. Naval Institute *Proceedings*, February 1984, p. 70.

MAINTAINING A 600-SHIP FLEET

The planned 600-ship fleet is shown in the last column of Table 1-1. The ability to maintain the "600-ship fleet" is, however, questionable. Three factors can be expected to contribute to the failure to maintain the planned force levels.

Political. The initial support of the Reagan Administration's defense buildup has dissipated somewhat, as the president's party has lost seats

TABLE 1-1. FLEET STRENGTH (End of Fiscal Year)

	1964	1968	1972	1976	1980	1984	1990
Total Operating Forces	1,003	1,055	713	555	531	552	750+
Active Ships	917	976	654	476	456	492	500+
Battle Force Ships	—	756	520	367	384	426	606
Active Ships							
Submarines							
SSBN	21	41	41	41	41	35	33
SSN/SSGN	20	33	56	64	73	95	100
SS/SSG/LPSS	86	74	39	10	6	4	—
AGSS/SSAG	13	12	2	1	1	1	1
Aircraft Carriers							
CV	14	14	13	11	9*	9*	8
CVN	1	1	1	2	3	4	7
CVS	9	8	3	—	—	—	—
Surface Combatants							
BB	—	1	—	—	—	2	4
CA	2	4	1	—	—	—	—
CAG	2	—	—	—	—	—	—
CG/CLG	18	25	24	21	18	20	37
CGN	2	3	3	6	9	9	9
CC (command ships)	2	2	—	—	—	—	—
DDG	31	37	38	38	37	37	38
DD/DDR/DL	179	181	83	31	43	31	31
FFG	—	6	6	6	12	43	40
FF/FFR/AGFF	40	44	61	59	59	51	50
Patrol Combatants							
PHM	—	—	—	—	1	6	6
Other	6	9	16	8	3	1	—
Mine Warfare	85	84	31	3	3	3	—
Amphibious Warfare							
LCC	5	5	3	2	2	2	2
LHA/LHD/LPH	6	8	7	8	12	12	} 60+
Other**	120	142	66	52	46	48	
Fleet Auxiliaries							
Underway Replenishment	72	75	59	40	32	38	n.a.
Tenders	33	35	27	25	24	25	n.a.
Tug-type ships	71	70	47	39	15	14	n.a.
Other	74	59	18	10	2	2	n.a.
Naval Auxiliary Force							
Auxiliary Ships	1	4	6	19	25	22	n.a.
Naval Reserve Force							
DD	13	16	31	30	16	1	1
FF/FFG	27	19	4	—	—	10	26
Patrol Combatants	9	6	—	5	—	—	—
Mine Warfare	13	12	18	22	22	18	25
Amphibious Warfare	—	—	—	3	6	2	5
Auxiliary Ships	—	—	—	2	6	7	10

n.a. = not available.
*Plus one CV in yard for modernization (SLEP).
**Includes LPDs employed as flagships (AGF).

The current U.S. fleet buildup includes several classes of auxiliary ships as well as support aircraft, both vital for sustained effectiveness in peace as well as in war. Here a CH-46 Sea Knight from Helicopter Combat Support Squadron 6 transports supplies to the destroyer tender PUGET SOUND (AD 38) at Gaeta, Italy. (1982, U.S. Navy, PH1 Douglas Tesner)

in the 1982 congressional election with more losses expected in 1984. Similarly, other issues have taken precedence over defense programs, an anticipated situation as we move farther away from the events in Iran and other issues predominate our national psyche.

Personnel. The large-scale manpower shortages of the Navy in the late 1970s have been largely corrected through pay increases and the general improvement in morale. The quality of Navy and Marine manpower is exceedingly high with most enlisted and officer recruitment and retention quotas being met (see Chapter 6). There is concern, however, that the improving economy, the decline in that fraction of the population of military entry age, and the increasingly high technical skill levels needed to operate the modern Navy cannot continue to be met.

Service Competition. The emphasis on naval-related defense issues by the Reagan Administration has led to major criticism by the leadership of the Army and Air Force, who perceive that their programs have suffered because of the Navy. There will be increasing pressure from the Army and Air Force, and from their supporters, for a more balanced approach to defense expenditures.

The Navy has already been forced to decommission several ships earlier than had been planned and to defer the construction of others in order to fund higher-priority programs. Destroyers of the FORREST SHERMAN (DD 931) class and dock landing ships of the THOMASTON (LSD 28) class have been retired ahead of schedule to save their operating costs.

There have also been major cutbacks in the planned construction of surface combatants. Table 1-2 shows the surface combatant ships requested in the three five-year shipbuilding plans put forward by the Reagan Administration. (The last two five-year programs of the Carter Administration are included for comparative purposes.) Note that during

TABLE 1-2. SURFACE COMBAT PROGRAMS

	FY1981	1982	1983	1984	1985	1986	1987	1988	1989
Nuclear Missile Cruisers (CGN 42)									
January 80 (Carter)	—	—	—	1	—				
January 81 (Carter)		—	—	—	—	—			
January 82 (Reagan)			—	—	—	—	1		
January 83 (Reagan)				—	—	—	—	—	
January 84 (Reagan)					—	—	—	—	—
Actual authorized		(none)							
Aegis Missile Cruisers (CG 47)									
January 80 (Carter)	2	3	3	4	4				
January 81 (Carter)		2	2	4	4	4			
January 82 (Reagan)			3	3	3	4	4		
January 83 (Reagan)				3	3	3	3	2	
January 84 (Reagan)					3	3	3	2	2
Actual authorized	(2)	(3)	(3)	(3)					
Guided Missile Destroyers (DDG 51)									
January 80 (Carter)	—	—	—	—	1	—	(3)	(5)	(5)
January 81 (Carter)	—	—	—	—	—	1	—	(3)	(5)
January 82 (Reagan)			—	—	1	—	3	(5)	(5)
January 83 (Reagan)				—	1	—	3	5	(5)
January 84 (Reagan)					1	—	3	5	5
Actual authorized		(none)							
ASW Destroyers (DD 963)									
January 80 (Carter)	—	—	—	—	—				
January 81 (Carter)		—	—	—	—				
January 82 (Reagan)			—	—	—	2	1		
January 83 (Reagan)				—	—	—	—	1	
January 84 (Reagan)					—	—	—	—	—
Actual authorized		(none)							
ASW Frigates (FFG 7)									
January 80 (Carter)	6	4	2	4	—				
January 81 (Carter)		3	2	—	—	—			
January 82 (Reagan)			2	2	2	3	3		
January 83 (Reagan)				—	—	—	—	—	
January 84 (Reagan)					—	—	—	—	—
Actual authorized	(6)	(3)	(2)	(1)					
Net changes in fiscal 1985–1987 shipbuilding programs					deleted 14 of 27 surface combatants				

TABLE 1-3. FIVE-YEAR SHIPBUILDING PROGRAM

Ship/Class		FY 1984 (Actual)	FY 1985	FY 1986	FY 1987	FY 1988	FY 1989
SSBN 726	Trident Submarine	1	1	1	1	1	1
SSN 688	Attack Submarine	3	4	4	4	4	4
SSN	New Design	—	—	—	—	—	1
CG 47	Aegis Cruiser	3	3	3	3	2	2
DDG 51	Missile Destroyer	—	1	—	3	5	5
FFG 7	Missile Frigate	1	—	—	—	—	—
LHD 1	Helicopter Carrier	1	—	1	—	1	1
LPD 16	Amphibious Ship	—	—	—	—	2	2
LSD 41	Dock Landing Ship	1	2	2	2	—	—
MCM 1	Mine Countermeasure	3	4	4	1	—	—
MSH 1	Mine Hunter	1	—	4	4	4	4
AE	Ammunition Ship	—	—	1	1	1	1
T-AGS	Surveying Ship	—	2	—	—	—	—
T-AGOS	Surveillance Ship	—	3	3	—	—	—
T-AO	Oiler	2	3	3	3	3	2
AOE	Combat Support Ship	—	—	1	—	1	1
AR	Repair Ship	—	—	—	—	—	1
Total New Ships		16	23	27	22	24	25
Conversions/Acquisitions							
CV	Carrier modernization (SLEP)	—	1	—	1	—	—
BB	Battleship reactivation	—	1	—	1	—	—
LPD 4	Amphibious Ship mod. (SLEP)	—	—	—	1	3	3
T-ACS	*Crane Ship acquisition	—	2	—	—	—	—
T-AFS	Combat Store Ship acquisition	1	—	—	—	—	—
T-AGM	Range Ship acquisition	—	—	—	1	—	—
T-AGS	Sound Barge acquisition	—	—	1	—	—	—
T-AH	Hospital Ship acquisition	1	—	—	—	—	—
T-AK	FBM Cargo Ship acquisition	—	1	—	—	—	—
T-AKR	Fast Cargo Ship acquisition	4	—	—	—	—	—
AO	Oiler conversion (JUMBO)	—	—	—	—	1	2
T-AVB	Aviation Ship acquisition	—	1	1	—	—	—
Total Conversions/Acquisitions		6	6	2	4	4	5

*T-ACS is a merchant ship modified to an auxiliary crane ship; the conversions will not be assigned Navy hull numbers; they will be laid up in ready reserve for rapid reactivation with merchant crews. One T-ACS was modified in fiscal 1984 using operations and maintenance funds.

TABLE 1-4. FIVE-YEAR AIRCRAFT PROCUREMENT PROGRAM

Aircraft		FY 1984 (Actual)	FY 1985	FY 1986	FY 1987	FYF 1988	FY 1989
A-6E	Intruder	6	6	—	—	—	—
AV-8B	Harrier II	27	32	46	47	48	60
C-2	Greyhound	6	8	8	9	—	—
C-9B	Skytrain II	4	—	—	—	—	—
UC-12B	Huron	—	12	24	12	—	—
KC-130T	Hercules	2	—	—	—	—	—
E-2C	Hawkeye	6	6	6	6	6	6
E-6A	TACAMO	—	—	3	3	3	3
—	EW Aircraft	1	—	—	—	—	—
EA-6B	Prowler	8	6	6	6	6	6
—	Adversary Aircraft	4	8	12	—	—	—
F-14A/D	Tomcat	24	24	24	12	12	24
F/A-18A	Hornet	84	84	102	120	120	120
P-3C	Orion	6	9	9	9	9	9
RP-3D	Orion	—	—	—	—	1	1
T-34C	Mentor	—	—	114	—	—	—
T-44A	—	—	—	—	15	—	—
T-45A/B	Hawk	—	—	—	—	8	24
JVX	(tilt-rotor aircraft)	—	—	—	—	—	18
AH-1T	SeaCobra	—	22	22	—	—	—
SH-2F	LAMPS I	6	6	—	—	—	—
CH-53E	Super Stallion	11	10	14	14	14	14
TH-57C	SeaRanger	21	36	—	—	—	—
SH-60B	Seahawk/LAMPS III	21	18	18	18	18	18
Total Aircraft		237	291	408	271	245	294

the three fiscal years covered by all three plans (1985–1987) there has been a reduction of 14 ships—1 nuclear missile cruiser, 2 Aegis missile cruisers, 3 ASW destroyers, and 8 frigates. Thus, just over half of the surface combatants in the three fiscal years have been dropped from the Reagan budgets.

Further, the long-awaited missile destroyer class, now the ARLEIGH BURKE (DDG 51) class, may be cut back severely—*if* Congress approves construction at this time. The Navy's DDX study of the late 1970s had proposed building more than 60 anti-air missile destroyers to replace cruisers and destroyers that would be retired in the 1980s and 1990s. The Carter Administration had proposed construction of 49 ships; the Reagan Administration initially called for 61 of these ships (see Chapter 15 for requirements for the class). By 1984 the Navy was asking for an initial buy of only 29 BURKE-class destroyers—to take the Navy through the fiscal year 1994 or 1995 program, after which the cruiser-destroyer situation will be reevaluated.

A related factor in the Navy's future will the the Navy's leadership. At this writing it appeared likely that John Lehman would remain SecNav for perhaps two more years, at least until mid-1986. This would insure continuation of on-going programs and enable him to influence selection of the next Chief of Naval Operations. The current CNO, Admiral James Watkins, who will serve until mid-1986, has become an effective, hard-line spokesman for the Navy. But there are differences of opinion between the Navy's military and civilian leadership, and few admirals have enjoyed close and influential relationships with Congress and administrations.

STRATEGIC MISSILE SUBMARINES

The Navy's strategic missile submarines, armed with the Poseidon C-3 and Trident C-4 missiles, provide the most survivable portion of the nation's so-called Triad of strategic forces—land-based missiles, land-based bombers armed mainly with cruise missiles, and submarine-launched missiles.

The Trident submarines of the OHIO (SSBN 726) class are being built at the rate of one per year, initially to supplement and eventually to replace 31 older missile submarines. Under the terms of the 1972 Strategic Arms Limitation Treaty (SALT) the United States has an upper limit of 44 strategic missile submarines with 710 missiles.[4] At the end of 1984 the U.S. Navy had 35 operational submarines with 592 missiles. The construction of OHIO-class SSBNs, each with 24 missiles, means that the upper limit of 710 weapons will be achieved in the mid-1990s with perhaps 17 OHIO-class submarines (408 missiles) and 19 older submarines (304 missiles). After that the number of submarines will decline rapidly as the remaining ex-Polaris boats are retired, resulting in a strategic missile force of some 20 OHIO-class submarines and 480 missiles.

While the number of boats will be small, the introduction of the Trident II or D-5 missile in 1989 will provide significant advances in missile accuracy and range.

ATTACK SUBMARINES

The Navy is seeking to reach a force level of 100 nuclear attack submarines by 1990. The mission potential of these submarines has increased significantly with the development of the Harpoon and Tomahawk cruise missiles, which can be launched from standard 21-inch torpedo tubes, over the horizon targeting systems, and satellite reconnaissance and communications.

The Navy should be able to reach the 100-submarine goal by about 1990, if the current four-per-year construction rate continues. Again, the retirement of older submarines earlier than planned or a slowdown in construction would have an effect on the 100-boat goal. (In the 1970s the Navy was not able to reach the goal of 90 attack submarines, both nuclear and diesel.)

The Navy is planning a new class of attack submarines, now designated as the SSN-21 design. This submarine will be larger and slightly faster than the LOS ANGELES (SSN 688) class, now in production. The SSN-21 will also have other features lacking in the LOS ANGELES, such as under-ice and mining capabilities.[5]

The diesel submarine issue continues; the U.S. Navy refuses to consider the construction of new diesel submarines for any mission, training or combat. Advocates of such craft believe they would be valuable for ASW training (to simulate Soviet and Third World diesel undersea craft) and for certain combat roles in restricted and congested areas, such as the Sea of Japan and Mediterranean Sea. The great attractiveness of diesel submarines is their low cost (about one-third of a nuclear submarine), low manning requirement, and the reduced training needed

---

[4] The Soviet limitations under SALT I are 62 nuclear submarines with 950 missiles.
[5] These features are being fitted to the later LOS ANGELES-class submarines.

for diesel crews in comparison with nuclear submarines. The diesel submarine issue will not go away.

AIRCRAFT CARRIERS

The aircraft carrier continues to be the centerpiece of U.S. naval strategy. While justified primarily for potential conflict with the Soviet Union, the carrier has continually demonstrated that it provides the most flexible and most capable response to crises in the Third World. Indeed, despite increased U.S. anti-air and anti-missile capabilities, the probability of a carrier surviving against a Soviet missile attack when within range of land-based strike aircraft has probably been declining.

The recent authorization of two additional nuclear-propelled carriers, the ABRAHAM LINCOLN (CVN 72) and GEORGE WASHINGTON (CVN 73), may provide a force of 15 carriers in the early 1990s—eight large conventional and seven nuclear carriers plus the older MIDWAY (CV 41) and CORAL SEA (CV 43). But the probability of an operating force of 15 carriers is questionable; at least one ship will be in long-term modernization, the CORAL SEA will be employed as a training ship, the propulsion plant of the ENTERPRISE (CVN 65) may not be suitable for upgrading, and fiscal constraints could cause full retirement of the MIDWAY and/or CORAL SEA.

While the procurement of the AV-8B Harrier VSTOL attack aircraft for the Marine Corps and the development of the tilt-rotor/JVX VSTOL aircraft primarily for the Marines has forced wide acceptance of VSTOL, the Navy continues to advocate an all-large carrier force. The significant number of helicopter carriers in service do, of course, have a VSTOL capability, but the ships lack the speed, support, and command facilities for use in a VSTOL combat role. There are no specific plans to procure any VSTOL aircraft for Navy combat use, although Secretary Lehman has said the JVS has obvious utility for providing airborne sensors and flying other missions from surface combatants. (The Navy recently purchased an Israel-produced reconnaissance drone for use from battleships; see page 104.)

SURFACE COMBATANTS

Few naval programs have captured the imagination of the American public as has the recommissioning of the battleships. President Reagan spoke at the NEW JERSEY commissioning ceremonies on 28 December 1982 and Vice President Bush at the IOWA ceremonies on 28 April 1984. The NEW JERSEY's initial deployment saw her operating in troubled waters off Central America and Lebanon supporting American interests in Third World crises; the provision of Tomahawk land-attack missiles in these ships provides the potential for use in a U.S.-Soviet conflict.

The MISSOURI (BB 63) is being returned to active service; reactivation of the fourth ship of the class, the WISCONSIN (BB 64), is planned.

The future for the remainder of the Navy's surface combatant program is less sanguine. The highly successful Aegis cruisers of the TICON-DEROGA (CG 47) class are in series production; although being criticized in Congress and in the press for alleged shortcomings, the two ships in commission have demonstrated their capability in extensive trials. Further, their having been adopted from the SPRUANCE (DD 963) design reflected an imaginative and cost-effective approach to putting the Aegis anti-war warfare system to sea. The TICONDEROGA class can be considered the most effective anti-air *and* anti-submarine surface ship at sea today. The provision of a vertical-launch missile system in most ships of the class will further enhance their effectiveness in the anti-air, anti-ship, and strike roles.

Criticism is also directed against the planned ARLEIGH BURKE-class destroyers, which are to have a derivative of the Aegis system. As noted above, the number of ships initially proposed under the Reagan Administration has been reduced by half. The opposition focuses on the ship's high cost and inferior capabilities compared with the TICONDEROGA-class

O'BANNON at Antwerp (1984, L. & L. van Ginderen)

Aegis cruisers. The BURKE class has no helicopter hangar (the CG 47 has facilities for two) and the BURKE carries 90 vertical-launch missiles (the CG 47 carries 122).

In an effort to garner support for the program, the Navy named the lead ship for Admiral Arleigh Burke, at the time the most respected of the Navy's living flag officers, who had served as the Chief of Naval Operations for an unequaled six years, 1955–1961.

Should the BURKE class be delayed, or should the number of destroyers built in the 1990s be reduced, the situation for the Navy's surface combatant forces could become critical.

Production of the OLIVER HAZARD PERRY (FFG 7)-class frigates is coming to an end. This class represents the largest surface combatant program of any Western navy since World War II, with several ships being assigned to the NRF. The Reagan Administration has dropped plans to continue construction into the 1990s, although congressional pressure to help the depressed shipbuilding industry may keep the program alive for a few more years. These ships are being used in many non-frigate roles because of the shortfall in destroyers, but they lack some features needed for fleet operations and they have little potential for upgrading.

AMPHIBIOUS WARFARE

The Reagan Administration's commitment to increasing amphibious lift from just over one Marine Amphibious Force (MAF) to an MAF plus one Marine Amphibious Brigade (MAB)[6] is proceeding apace. Construction has begun on the WASP (LHD 1)-class helicopter carriers, a refinement of the TARAWA (LHA 1) class. Similarly, the long-delayed WHIDBEY ISLAND (LSD 41) class is in production with a derivative LPD class also planned.

Amphibious assault will also be enhanced by the deliveries of the Landing Craft Air Cushion (LCAC) to the Navy and large CH-53E helicopters to the Marine Corps. During the 1990s the Marines expect to take delivery of a new tilt-rotor assault aircraft (now designated JVX) to replace the aging CH-46 Sea Knights, the mainstay of the Marine air assault force.

Like all other naval forces except possibly submarines, the amphibious warfare community can expect to feel the results of any major cutback in naval funding. As noted above, older LSDs are being retired ahead of schedule and the LCAC is a candidate for reduction.

MINE WARFARE

A final area of naval warfare to which the Reagan Administration has made a major commitment is the mine countermeasure forces. These have been largely neglected for the past 25 years with the only important development in that period being the production of 30 RH-53D minesweeping helicopters; that force, with limited mine countermeasure capability, lost seven helicopters in the aborted Tehran embassy rescue in 1980. This neglect occurred as the Soviet Union continued its extensive developments in mine countermeasures and offensive mine warfare, and with an emerging threat from the Third World in this area.

After several years of discussion as to what kinds of mine countermeasure forces should be developed, the Navy is now constructing two types of minesweepers, and producing the MH-53E, a more effective minesweeping helicopter.

But the development of offensive mine warfare has fared less well. Production of the long-touted CAPTOR (Encapsulated Torpedo) has been on-again, off-again, and often offered up as an early budget sacrifice. The intermediate-depth mine, which has undergone several name changes, has been cancelled completely. On the plus side, the Navy and Air Force have experimented of late with a variety of platforms for minelaying, including B-52 bombers, C-130 cargo planes, frigates, and replenishment ships.

AUXILIARY SHIPS

A significant number of auxiliary ships are being built, especially underway replenishment ships to help ensure the mobility of the battle forces. Note that these latter ships are counted as part of the battle forces whether civilian or Navy operated.

MARITIME PREPOSITIONING SHIPS

Not included in the 600-ship fleet are the Maritime Prepositioning Ships. Described in detail in Chapter 5, the Maritime Prepositioning Ships (MPS) are part of the concept of a rapid-deployment force to provide weapons and material afloat for "marrying up" with troops to be flown into a crisis area. A number of merchant-type ships are now employed in this role.

Thirteen ships are being converted for the "ultimate" MPS force, which will carry material for three Marine brigades. In addition, the Navy is converting two hospital ships, two aviation base/supply ships, and other ships to complement the MPS force.

Also, eight high-speed cargo ships have been modified to carry ground combat equipment. Four of these ships will be based on the U.S. East Coast and four on the West Coast, ready to be loaded rapidly with vehicles, munitions, and other supplies and to transport them to crisis areas.

Thus, a major naval buildup is taking place in the United States. As Admiral Watkins has noted, "Peace, crisis, conflict: often in today's world there are no clear demarcations. The Navy must be prepared to act any day, every day, along the entire spectrum of conflict potential—to ensure national security while limiting crisis, controlling escalation or terminating conflict."[7]

The extensive use of naval forces—Navy and Marine—during the post-World War II period has demonstrated the continuing importance of the fleet. While there are questions about specific programs, and whether the rate of development can be continued, the fact remains that the decision has been made at the highest levels of government to provide an improved naval posture to help carry out national policy in a troubled world.

---

[6] See Chapter 4 for composition of the MAF and MAB.

[7] Admiral James D. Watkins, USN, Report to Committee on Armed Services, House, U.S. Congress, 8 February 1984, p. 1.

2 Navy Organization

There are four military services under the Department of Defense—the Army, Air Force, Navy, and Marine Corps. (In addition, the Coast Guard is a military service under the Department of Transportation; see Appendix A.)

ESTABLISHMENT

The American Navy can be traced to the Continental Navy of March 1776, when seven small ships converted from merchant vessels sailed from New England to the Bahamas to capture guns for George Washington's army. These and subsequent Continental ships had surprising successes against the British during the American Revolution.

With the adoption of the Constitution in 1788 naval affairs were placed under the jurisdiction of the War Department. Ten years later, an Act of Congress of 30 April 1798 formally established a Navy Department. An act of 11 July of the same year established the Marine Corps as a separate service within the Navy Department.

As originally established the Secretary of the Navy exercised direct control over the Navy's shore establishment as well as the operating forces. From 1842 onward, Congress established a series of bureaus to provide effective procurement of ships and supplies, to manage personnel, and to operate the shore activities. These bureaus, commanded by naval officers, also reported directly to the Secretary of the Navy.

The position of Aide for Operations was established from 1909–1915 to provide a flag officer (rear admiral) on the staff of the Secretary of the Navy. The aide would be responsible for ship operations and training, planning, intelligence, and logistics and would recommend fleet appointments. In 1915, because of the conflict in Europe, the position was changed to Chief of Naval Operations (admiral). However, the Chief of Naval Operations (CNO) did not direct forces afloat. Rather, various squadron and, from 1906, fleet commanders exercised command of ships, with their commands based on geographic areas. In 1919 the position of Commander-in-Chief U.S. Fleet (CinCUS) was established as overall commander of forces afloat—reporting to the Secretary of the Navy, independent of the Chief of Naval Operations.[1]

These positions remained independent until Admiral Ernest J. King, who became Commander-in-Chief U.S. Fleet in 1941, was additionally named CNO in 1942. Beginning at that time the CNO *de facto* had operational command of forces afloat. The CinCUS position was abolished in October 1945, immediately after World War II.

The National Security Act of 1947 created the Department of Defense, established the subordinate Department of the Air Force, changed the War Department to the Department of the Army, and retitled the Navy Department. With the establishment of the Department of Defense the Joint Chiefs of Staff (JCS) was formalized, having been set up in 1942 to provide liaison with the British Combined Chiefs of Staff. The Chief of Naval Operations, in addition to serving as military head of the Navy, became the Navy member of the JCS.

There were continuous organizational changes within the Navy. Among the more significant, in 1963 the technical bureaus were incorporated under a central Naval Material Command headed by the Chief of Naval Material (admiral). This had the effect of increasing the influence of the CNO over the bureaus. Then, in 1966 the Secretary of the Navy placed the Naval Material Command (and hence the system commands) under the Chief of Naval Operations, giving him full responsibility for material, personnel, and medical support of the operating forces. (The current system commands are Air, Sea [ships, weapons, etc.], Electronic, and Facilities.)

The Bureau of Naval Personnel and Bureau of Medicine and Surgery survived with those titles but were shifted from the Secretary to the CNO in 1966. These organizations became the Naval Military Personnel Command and Naval Medical Command, respectively, in 1978 and 1982.

OPERATIONAL ORGANIZATION

Almost from its outset the Navy has had a bilinear organization with the squadron and later fleet commanders (and after 1942 the CNO) exercising military command over the operating forces while the Secretary of the Navy, through civilian assistants and the chiefs of bureaus and offices, directed the business and support activities.

The establishment of the Department of Defense in 1947 was followed by amendments in 1949 that created the bilinear military structure that forms the basis of the current Defense structure.

The President, under the Constitution, is the Commander-in-Chief of the U.S. Armed Forces. The Secretary of Defense, the President's immediate subordinate, serves as the day-to-day decision maker in defense matters. Together, the President and Secretary of Defense—and designated alternates—constitute what is called the National Command

---

[1] The position of Commander-in-Chief U.S. Fleet (CinCUS) was not active in 1920–1921.

Secretary of the Navy John Lehman
(DOD, Helene Stikkel)

Admiral James D. Watkins, Chief of Naval
Operations (U.S. Navy, PHCS J. D. Haynes)

General Paul X. Kelley,
Commandant of the Marine Corps

Authority (NCA), empowered to command all U.S. combat forces. (The President and Secretary of Defense also supervise the administration of U.S. military forces, the procurement of supplies and equipment, and the development of future military systems.)

The President is advised by a National Security Council (NSC), which has the Vice President, the Secretaries of Defense, State, and Treasury, the Chairman of the Joint Chiefs of Staff, and the Director of Central Intelligence as regular members. The official who coordinates NSC activities, and reports directly to the President, is his National Security Advisor.

Under the President the operational chain-of-command goes through the Secretary of Defense to the Specified and Unified Commanders. Virtually all operational U.S. military forces are assigned to these commanders, who are four-star officers. The Unified Commands, which are based on geographic areas, control forces from more than one service; the Specific Commands generally have forces from only one service (see Figure 2-1).

The Joint Chiefs of Staff is usually placed between the Secretary of Defense and the operating commands in organizational diagrams. Although technically correct from a communications viewpoint, this is somewhat misleading because the role of the JCS is strictly advisory, and it is not part of the National Command Authority.

The Specified Commands are the Aerospace Defense Command, Military Airlift Command, and Strategic Air Command, all commanded by Air Force generals. The Atlantic, Pacific, European, and Southern Commands are responsible for operations in their respective geographic regions (the Southern Command encompassing Central and South America). The recently established Central Command is responsible for planning operations in Southwest Asia, employing the Rapid Deployment Joint Task Force (see Chapter 5). The Readiness Command is a noncombat organization set up to control a central reserve of U.S. Army and Air Force combat units in the United States.

The CinC of a Unified Command is customarily from the service that makes the largest contribution to the theater. Thus, admirals command the Atlantic and Pacific Commands, with headquarters in Norfolk, Virginia, and Pearl Harbor, Hawaii, respectively.

The four principal unified commands—Atlantic, Pacific, Europe, and Central—are task oriented and are assigned whatever mix of service components that are required by their missions. Within each of these commands are component commanders who direct specific service participation, and other operational tasks as assigned (see Figure 2-2).

The Atlantic Command has primarily naval components. The admiral who serves as Commander-in-Chief Atlantic (CinCLant) is additionally his own naval component commander, with the title CinC Atlantic Fleet (CinCLantFlt). Also, he serves as a NATO theater commander with the title Supreme Allied Commander Atlantic (SACLant), for which he has a separate, multinational staff. All three headquarters are co-located in Norfolk.

Reporting to CinCLantFlt are the Commander Second Fleet, who directs most fleet operations in the Atlantic; the Commander Submarine Force Atlantic Fleet (ComSubLant), who controls most submarine operations in the Atlantic; and certain specialized subordinate commands. The separate operational command arrangement for submarines, which is similar in the Pacific region, reflects their strategic attack role and the unique command and control problems associated with coordinating their operations with surface and air forces.

The arrangement in the Pacific Command is different, although the Pacific Command also has primarily naval components. The naval component of CinCPac is the CinC Pacific Fleet (CinCPacFlt), also an admiral with headquarters at Pearl Harbor. He coordinates activities of the Commander Second Fleet (Pearl Harbor), with responsibilities for the eastern Pacific, and Commander Seventh Fleet (aboard a command ship home ported in Yokosuka, Japan), with responsibilities for the Western Pacific and Indian Ocean areas. In addition, the submarine

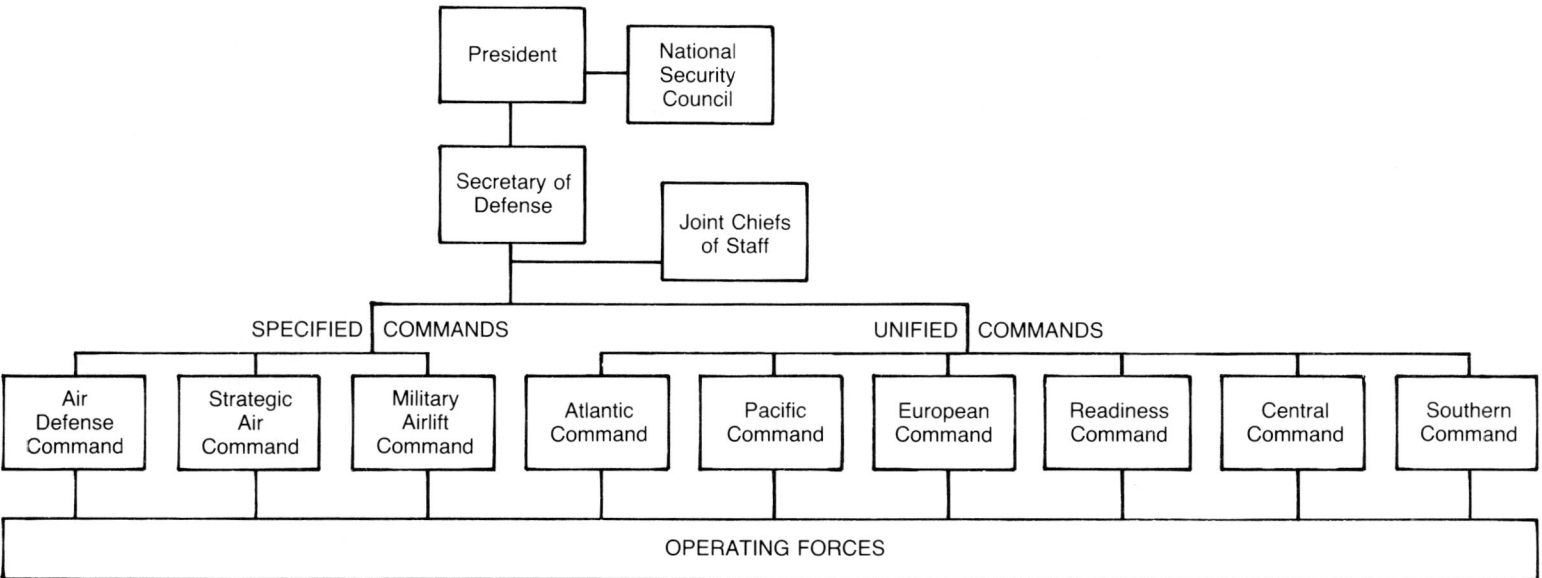

Figure 2-1. U.S. National Defense Command Structure

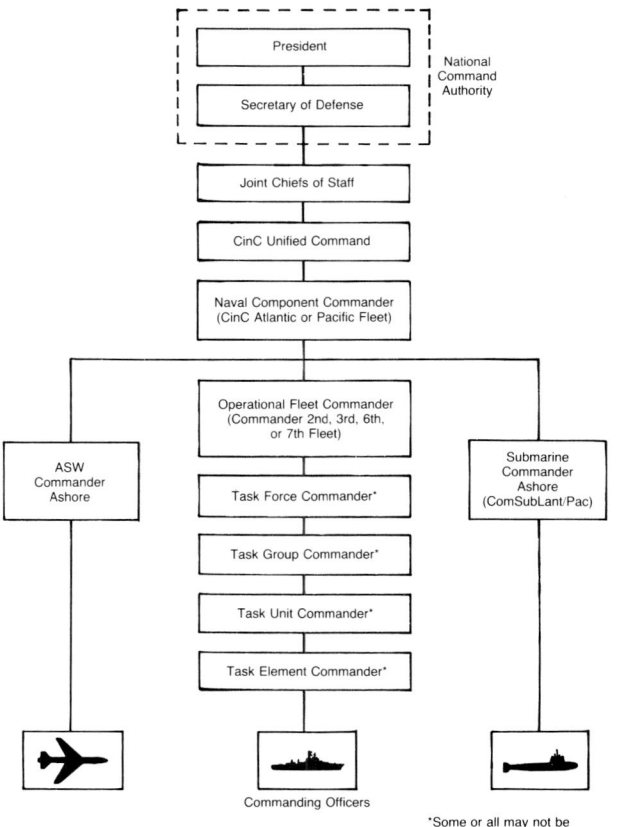

Figure 2-2. Operational Chain of Command

force commander (ComSubPac) controls all submarine operations in the Pacific-Indian Ocean areas under the direction of the fleet commander.

The European Command embraces a greater number of service components and a greater variety of forces than any other major U.S. command. Moreover, the European Command is closely integrated with the NATO alliance with many commanders holding posts in both the national and NATO chains of command. The Commander-in-Chief U.S. Forces Europe, an Army or Air Force general, is also the NATO Supreme Allied Commander Europe.

His naval component commander is the CinC U.S. Naval Forces Europe (CinCUSNavEur), an admiral based in Naples, Italy, with his deputy in London (vice admiral). Most U.S. naval forces in European waters operate in the Mediterranean under the U.S. Commander Sixth Fleet. CinCUSNavEur also holds the NATO position of CinC Allied Forces Southern Europe.

Below the four numbered fleets—the Second, Third, Sixth, and Seventh—naval operating forces form task forces, task groups, task units, and task elements. These are generally organized and assigned forces to accomplish specific objectives. The current Navy task organizations are described in Chapter 3.

Under this operational concept the Chief of Naval Operations does not command combat forces or plan naval campaigns, except when he is specifically assigned to do so by the Secretary of Defense or by the JCS. The CNO is, however, directly involved in the administrative chain of command.

ADMINISTRATIVE ORGANIZATION

The administrative organization of the Navy begins with the Secretary of Defense, but then goes through the Secretary of the Navy and the Chief of Naval Operations, as shown in simplified form in Figure 2-3. The CNO is essentially a manager, with the primary task of supporting operational commanders. He is responsible for logistics, maintenance, personnel management, training, procurement of naval systems and supplies, and research and development.

To accomplish his tasks the CNO has a large staff known as the Office of the Chief of Naval Operations (OpNav), and he directs the large shore establishment with both his own staff and through the Chief of Naval Material. His principal deputies and assistants within the OpNav staff are:

OP-09   Vice Chief of Naval Operations (****)[2]
OP-090 Director Navy Program Planning (***)
OP-091 Director Program Resource Appraisal Division (**)
OP-092 Director Fiscal Management Division (**)
OP-093 Director of Naval Medicine/Surgery Division (***)[3]
OP-094 Director Command and Control (***)
OP-095 Director Naval Warfare (***)
OP-098 Director Research, Development, Test & Evaluation (***)
OP-007 Chief of Information (*)
OP-008 Naval Inspector General (**)
OP-009 Director of Naval Intelligence (**)
OP-01   Deputy CNO (Manpower, Personnel & Training) (***)[4]
OP-02   Deputy CNO (Submarine Warfare) (***)
OP-03   Deputy CNO (Surface Warfare) (***)
OP-04   Deputy CNO (Logistics) (***)
OP-05   Deputy CNO (Air Warfare) (***)
OP-06   Deputy CNO (Plans, Policy & Operations) (***)

The two fleet Commanders-in-Chief (CinCLantFlt and CinCPacFlt) report to the CNO in the administrative chain of command and have responsibility for the readiness of their forces. This includes both material readiness—the maintenance and logistics that enable naval forces to operate as required—and training. Thus, the Commanders-in-Chief of the Atlantic and Pacific Fleets, in addition to their operational duties, share the responsibility for administrative support of forces afloat, including certain shore bases and activities.

Each of the two fleet commanders have four subordinate type commands to supervise specific categories of forces: Naval Air Force (which includes aircraft carriers as well as aviation units), Surface Force, Submarine Force, and Fleet Marine Force. These "type" commanders are based ashore. While the type commanders—except for ComSubLant and ComSubPac—do not normally have operational responsibilities,

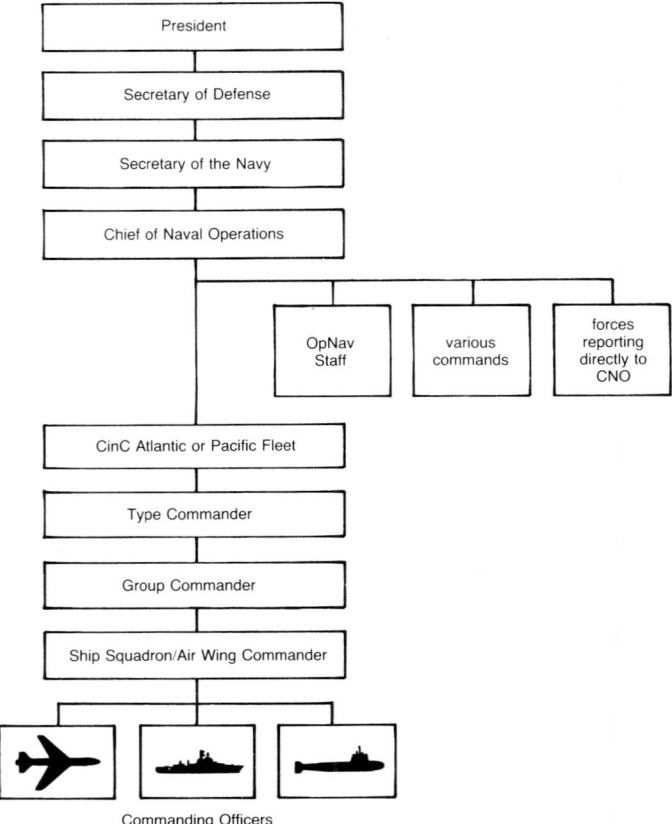

Figure 2-3. Administrative Chain of Command

they do maintain continuous personnel, logistics, and other forms of support with their ships and often have actual control when the ships are at their home port or in a shipyard or are not otherwise assigned to operational commanders. Similarly, carrier air wings and other air units not aboard ship or forward deployed come under their respective type commanders.

Below the type commanders in the administrative chain of command are officers in charge of groups (e.g., cruiser-destroyer groups) and their subordinates who command ship squadrons and aircraft wings. At this level some commanders are in the operational as well as administrative chains of command. At sea this distinction becomes somewhat blurred, and existing command links and staffs may be called upon to simultaneously handle operational and administrative matters.

[2] Stars indicate grade of current incumbent.
[3] Also Commander Naval Medical Command.
[4] Also Commander Naval Military Personnel Command.

3 Fleet Organization

The U.S. Navy's operational forces—ships, submarines, aircraft, Marine units, construction battalions (Seabees), and certain other units—are simultaneously under two organizational structures: administrative and tactical.

The administrative organization of the Navy is responsible for the training and readiness of naval forces. This organization is based on "type" categories, with similar forces grouped together to facilitate training, overhaul, repair, logistics, and other aspects of readiness. Within the Navy, the administrative organization begins with the Secretary of the Navy and continues through the Chief of Naval Operations and the Commandant of the Marine Corps, to the commanders-in-chief of the Atlantic and Pacific Fleets.

Within each fleet there are air, surface, and submarine "type" commanders responsible for their respective forces. In addition, commanding generals of the respective Fleet Marine Forces also function as type commanders. The type commanders have cognizance over the air wings and squadrons, and ship and submarine groups, squadrons, and divisions, as well as the individual aircraft, surface ships, and submarines, and their crews and equipment.

While the type commands are similar in both fleets, the components of those type commands differ considerably. Further, in the surface forces the organizations are not always homogeneous; for example, a destroyer squadron will often include frigates and both missile-armed and all-gun destroyers; some squadrons have both active ships and Naval Reserve Force ships. In the Atlantic Fleet the higher-numbered destroyer squadrons do not have ships assigned; the lower-numbered squadron commanders to whom ships are assigned are responsible for the ships' training, maintenance, and logistics. When the ships go to sea, the higher-numbered squadron commanders are their tactical commanders and assume task force or task group designations. In the Pacific Fleet the destroyer squadron commanders have both functions, i.e., readiness and deployment as operational commanders.

The operating forces of the Navy are concentrated in the Second Fleet in the Atlantic, the Third Fleet in the eastern Pacific, the Sixth Fleet in the Mediterranean, and the Seventh Fleet in the western Pacific-Indian Ocean regions. As noted in Chapter 2, the *operational* control of the fleets is exercised through the unified commands. Thus, these fleets are commanded through unified commands and their naval component commanders:

Component Commander	Operating Fleet
CinC U.S. Atlantic Fleet	Second Fleet
CinC U.S. Naval Forces Europe	Sixth Fleet
CinC U.S. Pacific Fleet	{ Third Fleet { Sixth Fleet

Thus, the Atlantic and Pacific Fleet commanders function in both the administrative and tactical chains of command. The fleets' tactical organizations are based on task forces with the TF designation based on the relevant numbered fleet designation. When appropriate, subgroupings are designated as task groups and smaller task units. Accordingly, TF-62 in the Sixth Fleet could have TG-62.2 and that, in turn, TU-62.2.1.

Within both the Atlantic and Pacific Fleets are contingency task forces that can be rapidly activated for specific missions and operations. Within the Pacific Fleet these are assigned Fifth Fleet TF designations.

In the following tables, stars are used to indicate the grades of commanders: **** for admiral, *** for vice admiral or Marine Corps lieutenant general, ** for rear admiral or Marine Corps major general, and * for commodore or Marine Corps brigadier general. In the Atlantic Fleet, TF-44 Commander Coast Guard Forces, when activated, consists of assigned Coast Guard units under the Coast Guard flag officer commanding the Atlantic area.

In the following tables of administrative organization the ships assigned to type commanders are indicated. Such assignments change regularly, as new ships are commissioned, older ships are stricken, ships are reassigned for overhauls or modernization, etc. Aircraft carriers and command ships are identified by hull number.

More detailed organization of the fleet aviation units are provided in Chapter 28 of this volume.

UNITED STATES FLEET DEPLOYMENTS[a]

Pacific Fleet		Atlantic Fleet	U.S. Naval Forces Europe	
Seventh Fleet (Western Pacific)	**Third Fleet** (Eastern Pacific)	**Second Fleet** (Atlantic)	**Sixth Fleet** (Mediterranean)	**Middle East Force** (Persian Gulf)
6 attack submarines	28 attack submarines	40 attack submarines	4 attack submarines	2 surface combatants
1 transport submarine	4 aircraft carriers	5 aircraft carriers	2 aircraft carriers	1 flagship (AGF)
2 aircraft carriers	60 surface combatants	60 surface combatants	14 surface combatants	
18 surface combatants[b]	24 amphibious ships	1 flagship (LCC)	5 amphibious ships	
1 flagship (LCC)	38 auxiliary ships	26 amphibious ships	12 auxiliary ships	
8 amphibious ships		40 auxiliary ships		
15 auxiliary ships		3 minesweepers		
Aviation units:[c]	Aviation units:	Aviation units:	Aviation units:	
2 CVW	4 CVW	4 CVW	2 CVW	
4 VP	8 VP	10½ VP	1½ VP	
1 VQ	1 VQ[d]	1 VQ[d]	1 VQ	
Marine units:	Marine units:	Marine units:	Marine units:	
1 Division	1 Brigade	1 Division	1 Marine Amphibious	
1 Air Wing	1 Division	1 Air Wing	Unit	
	1 Air Wing			

[a] Nominal assignment of active ships and squadrons; strategic missile submarines are not indicated. Ships assigned to the Indian Ocean are drawn from both the Atlantic and Pacific areas.
[b] Surface combatants are cruisers, destroyers, and frigates.
[c] See Chapter 28 for aviation abbreviations.
[d] VQ squadrons assigned to the Second and Third Fleets are strategic communications units; the others are electronic surveillance squadrons.

COMMANDER-IN-CHIEF U.S. NAVAL FORCES EUROPE (****)

Sixth Fleet[a] (***)		TF-66	Area ASW Force
TF-60	Battle Force (**)	TF-67	Maritime Surveillance and Reconnaissance Force (**)
	TG-60.1 Battle Group 1 (**)		TG-67.1 Maritime Patrol Air Group Sigonella (Sicily)
	TG-60.2 Battle Group 2 (**)		TG-67.2 Maritime Patrol Air Group Rota (Spain)
	TG-60.5 Screen Group		TG-67.3 Maritime Patrol Air Group Suda Bay (Crete)
	TG-60.7 Flagship		TG-67.4 Air Reconnaissance Group[d]
TF-61	Amphibious Force	TF-68	Special Operations Force
TF-62	Landing Force	TF-69	Attack Submarine Force[c]
TF-63	Service Force[b]		TG-69.7 Submarine Refit and Training Group (La Maddalena, Sardinia)
TF-64	FBM Submarine Force[c] (**)	TF-109	Middle East Force (**)

[a] Also Commander Naval Striking and Support Forces Southern Europe (NATO).
[b] Commander Service Squadron 6.
[c] Commander Submarine Group 8.
[d] Fleet Air Reconnaissance Squadron (VQ) 2.

COMMANDER-IN-CHIEF ATLANTIC FLEET[a] (****)
Administrative

Naval Air Force[b] (***)	Norfolk, Va.	CV 43, CV 59, AVT 16
Carrier Group 2 (**)	Naples, Italy	—
Carrier Group 4 (**)	Norfolk, Va.	CV 62, CV 67
Carrier Group 6 (**)	Mayport, Fla.	CV 60
Carrier Group 8 (**)	Norfolk, Va.	CV 66, CVN 68, CVN 69
Naval Surface Force (***)		
Flagships (departing Sixth Fleet)		AD 38
(Middle East Force)		AGF 3
(arriving Sixth Fleet)		AGF 11
(Second Fleet)		LCC 20
Cruiser Destroyer Group 2 (**)	Charleston, S.C.	1 AD
		2 CG
Destroyer Squadron 4[c]	Charleston, S.C.	6 DDG
		6 FF
Destroyer Squadron 6[c]	Charleston, S.C.	7 DD
		6 FFG
		2 FF
Destroyer Squadron 20[c]	Charleston, S.C.	—
Destroyer Squadron 36[c]	Charleston, S.C.	—
Cruiser Destroyer Group 8 (**)	Norfolk, Va.	5 CGN
		6 CG
Destroyer Squadron 2[c]	Norfolk, Va.	11 DDG
		1 FFG
		2 FF
Destroyer Squadron 10[c]	Norfolk, Va.	2 DDG
		8 DD
		7 FF
Destroyer Squadron 22[c]	Norfolk, Va.	—
Destroyer Squadron 26[c]	Norfolk, Va.	—
Destroyer Squadron 32[c]	Norfolk, Va.	—
Cruiser Destroyer Group 12 (**)	Mayport, Fla.	1 AD
		1 CG
Destroyer Squadron 8[c]	Mayport, Fla.	18 FFG
Destroyer Squadron 12[c]	Mayport, Fla.	4 DDG
		1 FFG
		8 FF
Destroyer Squadron 14[c]	Mayport, Fla.	—
Destroyer Squadron 24[c]	Mayport, Fla.	—
PHM Squadron 2	Key West, Fla.	6 PHM
Surface Group 4 (**)	Newport, R.I.	1 DD (NRF)
		2 FF
		2 FF (NRF)
Service Group 2 (**)	Norfolk, Va.	2 AD
		1 AR
Service Squadron 2	Earle, N.J.	5 AE
		2 AOE
Service Squadron 4	Norfolk, Va.	3 AFS
		5 AO
		3 AOR
Service Squadron 8	Little Creek, Va.	3 ARS
		1 ARS (NRF)
		2 ATF (NRF)
		1 ATS
Amphibious Group 2 (**)	Norfolk, Va.	LCC 20
		2 LHA
		1 LKA
		1 LST
Amphibious Squadron 2	Norfolk, Va.[d]	1 LPH
		1 LPD
		1 LSD
		3 LST

Amphibious Squadron 4	Norfolk, Va.[d]	1 LPH
		1 LPD
		1 LSD
		2 LST
Amphibious Squadron 6	Norfolk, Va.[d]	1 LPH
		1 LPD
		1 LSD
		2 LST
Amphibious Squadron 8	Norfolk, Va.[d]	AGF 11
		1 LPH
		1 LKA
		3 LPD
		3 LSD
		2 LST
Mine Group 2	Charleston, S.C.	3 MSO[e]
Mine Division 121	Newport, R.I.	2 MSO (NRF)
Mine Division 123	Little Creek, Va.	3 MSO (NRF)
Mine Division 125	Charleston, S.C.	7 MSB
		1 LCU
Mine Division 126	(various)	4 MSO (NRF)
Special Warfare Group 2	Little Creek, Va.	(various)
Submarine Force (***)		
Submarine Development Squadron 12	Groton, Conn.	5 SSN
Submarine Group 2 (*)	Groton, Conn.	4 SSN
Submarine Group 6 (**)	Charleston, S.C.	1 AS
		11 SSBN
Submarine Group 8 (**)	La Maddalena, Sardinia	1 AS
Submarine Squadron 2	Groton, Conn.	1 ASR
		9 SSN
		NR 1
Submarine Squadron 4	Charleston, S.C.	1 AS
		2 ASR
		12 SSN
		1 SS
Submarine Squadron 6	Norfolk, Va.	1 AS
		1 ASR
		9 SSN
Submarine Squadron 8	Norfolk, Va.	1 AS
		13 SSN
Submarine Squadron 10	New London, Conn.	1 AS
		5 SSN
Submarine Squadron 14	Holy Loch, Scotland	1 AS
		7 SSBN[f]
Submarine Squadron 16	Kings Bay, Ga.	1 AS
		9 SSBN
Submarine Squadron 18	Charleston, S.C.	1 AS
		4 SSBN
Fleet Marine Force (***)	Norfolk, Va.	
II Marine Amphibious Force[g] (**)	Camp Lejeune, N.C.	
2nd Marine Division (**)	Camp Lejeune, N.C.	
2nd Marine Aircraft Wing (**)	Cherry Point, N.C.	
2nd Force Service Support Group (*)	Camp Lejeune, N.C.	

[a] Also Commander-in-Chief Atlantic (unified command of all U.S. air, land, sea forces); Supreme Allied Commander Atlantic (NATO); CinC Western Atlantic Area (NATO).
[b] See Chapter 28 for subordinate aviation units.
[c] Squadrons with ships assigned are readiness squadrons and do not deploy but provide material and personnel support; squadrons without ships are tactical squadrons that deploy with the ships.
[d] Some ships are home ported at Little Creek, Va.
[e] One ship home ported at Panama City, Fla.
[f] The SSBNs are home ported in the United States.
[g] Also Commanding General 2nd Marine Division.

Operational

Commander-in-Chief Atlantic Fleet (****)		TF-87	Tactical Development and Evaluation and Transit Force
TF-40	Naval Surface Force (***)	TF-88	Training Force
TF-41	Naval Air Force (***)	TF-89	Coastal Defense Command
TF-42	Submarine Force (***)	TF-134	Naval Forces Caribbean (**)
TF-43	Training Command (**)	TF-137	Eastern Atlantic (**)
TF-44	Coast Guard Forces (**USCG)	TF-138	South Atlantic Force
TF-45	Fleet Marine Force (***)	TF-139	Multilateral Special Operations Force
TF-46	Mine Warfare Force (**)	TF-142	Operational Test and Evaluation Force (**)
TF-47	Naval Construction Battalions (**)	Commander Second Fleet (***)	
TF-49	Poseidon Operational Test Force[a]	TF-20	Battle Force[d] (***)
TF-80	Naval Patrol and Protection of Shipping	TF-21	Sea Control and Surveillance Force[d] (***)
TF-81	Sea Control and Surveillance Force	TF-22	Amphibious Force[e] (**)
TF-82	Amphibious Task Force	TF-23	Landing Force[b] (***)
TF-83	Landing Force[b]	TF-24	ASW Task Force[f] (**)
TF-84	ASW Task Force	TF-25	Mobile Logistics Support Force[g] (**)
TF-85	Mobile Logistic Support Force	TF-26	Patrol Air Force[c] (**)
TF-86	Patrol Air Task Force[c] (**)	TF-28	Caribbean Contingency Force

Note: Most of the task forces reporting directly to the CinC Atlantic Fleet do not exist in peacetime but are activated by the fleet commander when appropriate.
[a] Commander Submarine Force.
[b] Commander II Marine Amphibious Force.
[c] Commander Patrol Wings Atlantic.
[d] Commander Second Fleet.
[e] Commander Amphibious Group 2.
[f] Deputy Chief of Staff (Operations), CinC Atlantic Fleet.
[g] Commander Service Group 2.

COMMANDER-IN-CHIEF PACIFIC FLEET[a] (****)
Administrative

Naval Air Force[b] (***)	North Island, Calif.		Destroyer Squadron 17	San Diego, Calif.	1 DDG	
Carrier Group 1 (**)	North Island, Calif.	CV 63			1 DD	
		CV 64			1 FFG	
Carrier Group 3 (**)	Alameda, Calif.	CVN 65			2 FF	
		CVN 70	Cruiser Destroyer Group 5 (**)	San Diego, Calif.	4 CG	
Carrier Group 5 (**)	Cubi Point, Philippines	CV 41[c]	Destroyer Squadron 9	Long Beach, Calif.	1 DDG	
Carrier Group 7 (**)	North Island, Calif.	CV 61			2 DD	
Naval Surface Force (***)	Coronado, Calif.[d]	4 AD			6 FFG	
		1 AR	Destroyer Squadron 21	San Diego, Calif.	1 DDG	
		1 BB[e]			1 DD	
Surface Squadron 1	Long Beach, Calif.[d]	1 ARS			1 FFG	
		3 ATF			2 FF	
		1 AVM	Destroyer Squadron 31	San Diego, Calif.	2 DDG	
		2 FF			2 DD	
		1 LKA			3 FFG	
		1 LST			3 FF	
Cruiser Destroyer Group 1 (**)	San Diego, Calif.	5 CGN	Service Group 1	Oakland, Calif.[d]	2 AFS	
Destroyer Squadron 5	San Diego, Calif.	1 DDG			2 AOE	
		2 DD			3 AOR	
		1 FFG			1 AR	
		1 FF	Service Squadron 3	Vallejo, Calif.[d]	7 AE	
Destroyer Squadron 13	San Diego, Calif.	2 DD	Surface Group Western Pacific (*)	Subic Bay, Philippines[d]	LCC 19	
		1 FFG			2 AFS	
		4 FF			2 CG	
Destroyer Squadron 23	San Diego, Calif.	1 DDG	Destroyer Squadron 15	Yokosuka, Japan	1 DDG	
		2 DD			4 FF	
		1 FFG	Mine Squadron 5	Seattle, Wash.		
		2 FF	Mine Division 51	Tacoma, Wash.	2 MSO (NRF)	
Cruiser Destroyer Group 3 (**)	San Diego, Calif.	4 CG	Mine Division 52	San Francisco, Calif.	2 MSO (NRF)	
Destroyer Squadron 7	San Diego, Calif.	2 DDG	Mine Division 53	Seattle, Wash.	3 MSO (NRF)	
		3 DD	Mine Division 54	San Diego, Calif.	2 MSO (NRF)	
		1 FF				

Surface Group Long Beach (*)	Long Beach, Calif. (Est. 1985)	—
Surface Group Mid-Pacific (**)	Pearl Harbor, Hawaii	2 AO
		1 AR
		1 CG
Destroyer Squadron 25	Pearl Harbor, Hawaii	2 DDG
		2 FF
Destroyer Squadron 33	Pearl Harbor, Hawaii	1 DDG
		2 FF
Destroyer Squadron 35	Pearl Harbor, Hawaii	1 DDG
		5 FF
Service Squadron 5	Pearl Harbor, Hawaii	2 ARS
		2 ATS
Amphibious Group 1 (*)	White Beach, Okinawa	—
Amphibious Group Eastern Pacific (*)	San Diego, Calif.	1 LSD
Amphibious Squadron 1	San Diego, Calif.	1 LHA
		1 LPH
		2 LPD
		1 LSD
		2 LST
Amphibious Squadron 3	San Diego, Calif.	1 LPH
		1 LKA
		2 LPD
		1 LSD
		2 LST
Amphibious Squadron 5	San Diego, Calif.	1 LHA
		1 LPH
		2 LPD
		2 LSD
		3 LST
Amphibious Squadron 7	Long Beach, Calif.	1 LHA
		1 LKA
		1 LPD
		2 LSD
		2 LST
Special Warfare Group 1	Coronado, Calif.	—

Submarine Force (**)	Pearl Harbor, Hawaii	—
Submarine Squadron 1	Pearl Harbor, Hawaii	8 SSN
		1 SS
Submarine Group 5 (**)	San Diego, Calif.	1 AS
		5 SSN
Submarine Squadron 3	San Diego, Calif.d	1 AS
		8 SSN
Submarine Development Group 1	San Diego, Calif.d	1 AGDS
		2 ASR
		1 AGSS
		3 SSN
		3 DSV
		2 DSRV
Submarine Squadron 7	Pearl Harbor, Hawaii	10 SSN
Submarine Group 9	Bangor, Wash.	1 SS
Submarine Squadron 17	Bangor, Wash.	3 SSBN
		2 SSN
Submarine Group 7	Yokosuka, Japan	1 AS
		1 SSe
Fleet Marine Force (***)	Camp Smith, Hawaii	
I Marine Amphibious Force f (**)	Camp Pendleton, Calif.	
1st Marine Division (**)	Camp Pendleton, Calif.	
3rd Marine Aircraft Wing (**)	El Toro, Calif.	
III Marine Amphibious Force g	Okinawa	
3rd Marine Division (**)	Okinawa	
1st Marine Aircraft Wing (**)	Okinawa	
1st Marine Brigade (*)	Kaneohe Bay, Hawaii	
1st Force Service Support Group (*)	Camp Pendleton, Calif.	
3rd Force Service Support Group (*)	Okinawa	

a Also Naval Component Commander, U.S. Pacific Command.
b See Chapter 28 for subordinate aviation units.
c The MIDWAY is home ported at Yokosuka, Japan.
d The ships are home ported at various West Coast bases.
e DARTER (SS 576) has moved from Subic Bay, Philippines, to Sasebo, Japan
f Also Commanding General 1st Marine Division.
g Also Commanding General 3rd Marine Division.

Operational

Commander-in-Chief Pacific Fleet (****)
  Commander Third Fleet (***)
    TF-30 Battle Force (as assigned)
    TF-31 Combat Support Force a (***)
    TF-32 Patrol and Reconnaissance Force b (**)
    TF-33 Logistic Support Force c
    TF-34 Submarine Force d (**)
    TF-35 Surface Combatant Force (as assigned)
    TF-36 Amphibious Force e (*)
    TF-37 Carrier Strike Force (as assigned)
    TF-39 Landing Force f (**)
  Fifth Fleet
    TF-50 Battle Force
    TF-51 Command and Coordination Force g (****)
    TF-52 Patrol and Reconnaissance Force
    TF-53 Logistic Support Force
    TF-54 Submarine Force
    TF-55 Surface Combatant Force
    TF-56 Amphibious Force
    TF-57 Carrier Strike Force
    TF-59 Landing Force
  Commander Seventh Fleet (***)
    TF-70 Battle Force h (**)

    TF-71 Command and Coordination Force i (***)
    TF-72 Patrol and Reconnaissance Force j (*)
    TF-73 Logistic Support Force k (*)
    TF-74 Submarine Force l
    TF-75 Surface Combatant Force (as assigned)
    TF-76 Amphibious Force m
    TF-77 Carrier Strike Force h (**)
    TF-79 Landing Force n (**)

Note: Most of these task forces reporting to the CinC Pacific Fleet under the Fifth Fleet do not exist in peacetime but are activated by the fleet commander when appropriate. Unlike the Atlantic Fleet's task forces, the commanders of the Fifth Fleet units are not normally assigned in peacetime.

a Commander Third Fleet.
b Commander Patrol Wings Pacific Fleet.
c Commander Service Group 1.
d Commander Submarine Force Pacific Fleet.
e Commander Amphibious Group Eastern Pacific.
f Commanding General I Marine Amphibious Force.
g CinC Pacific Fleet.
h Commander Carrier Group 5.
i Commander Seventh Fleet.
j Commander Patrol Wing 1.
k Commander Naval Surface Group Western Pacific.
l Commander Submarine Group 7.
m Commander Amphibious Group 1.
n Commanding General III Marine Amphibious Force.

4 Fleet Marine Force

The Marine Corps is an integral part of the U.S. Fleet with the combat elements of the Marine Corps being assigned to the Atlantic and Pacific Fleet commands. In addition, the Navy operates more than 60 amphibious assault ships and almost 20 maritime prepositioning ships carrying Marine equipment in support of the Rapid Deployment Force.

With a strength of more than 197,000 men and women, the U.S. Marine Corps is the world's largest such force, being larger than the armies of most NATO nations and compares with Britain's Royal Marine strength of 7,750, and the Soviet Union's Naval Infantry strength of some 13,000.

The Marine Corps also has a large air arm of fixed-wing aircraft as well as helicopters. No other nation's marines are believed to operate fixed-wing aircraft although the British, Soviet, and some other marines do fly a small number of helicopters. (See Chapter 28 for a discussion of Marine Corps aviation.)

ESTABLISHMENT

The Marine Corps was established on 10 November 1775 by the Continental Congress, with two battalions being raised of men who were "good seamen, or so acquainted with maritime affairs as to be able to serve to advantage by sea, when required." Subsequently, Marines have fought at sea and ashore in almost all American conflicts. The Corps reached a peak strength of 485,000 men and women during World War II, with six divisions and four aircraft wings (plus numerous separate squadrons).

From its beginning, the Marine Corps has been a separate service within the Navy Department. The senior Marine officer is the Commandant with the rank of full general. He is a member of the Joint Chiefs of Staff (JCS) and while responsible for the readiness and training of the Marine Corps, he does not have operational command of Marine combat forces except as specifically assigned by the JCS or Secretary of Defense. Rather, the senior organizational commands of the Marine Corps—Fleet Marine Force (FMF) Atlantic and Pacific—are type commands within the Atlantic and Pacific Fleets.[1]

Further, the Navy provides direct support to the Marine Corps with medical personnel, chaplains, and special warfare units (see below).

Marine representatives serve on all appropriate Navy staffs, including in the office of the Secretary of the Navy and the Office of the Chief of Naval Operations.

In addition to combat (and support) components of FMF Atlantic and FMF Pacific, the Marine Corps provides:
- security detachments for aircraft carriers and battleships
- security detachments for selected Navy shore installations in the United States and abroad
- security detachments for U.S. embassies and diplomatic missions.

ORGANIZATION

The basic Marine Corps organization consists of three infantry divisions, three aircraft wings, and three force service support groups.

The Marine divisions are the largest ground combat divisions of any nation, each with some 16,000 officers and enlisted men. (By comparison, the largest U.S. Army division has about 15,000 men while the largest Soviet divisions have 11,160 men.) The Marine divisions have a triangular organization, each consisting of three infantry regiments, one artillery regiment, and several combat support battalions. Each infantry regiment, in turn, has three infantry battalions, each with three rifle companies. Navy personnel perform all medical and chaplain duties within the divisions and subordinate units.

Marine Division Organization

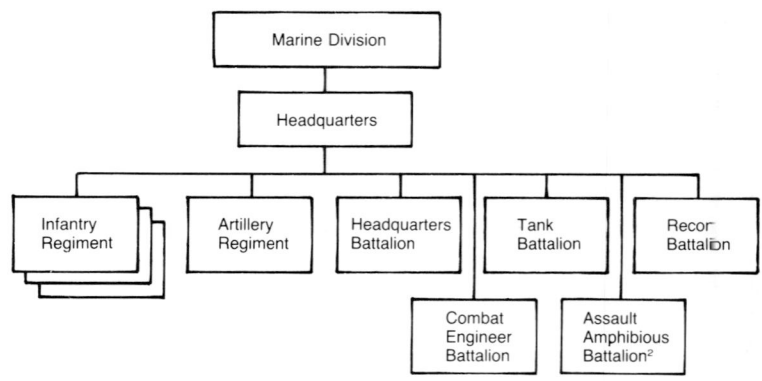

---

[1] The fleets' other type or administrative commands are Naval Air Force, Surface Force, and Submarine Force.

[2] Amphibian tractors; see Chapter 21 for details on these battalions.

Marines on duty in Beirut: These Marines from the 32nd Marine Amphibious Unit that served with the multi-national force in Lebanon keep a lookout during a lull in the civil war. Marines have historically been employed in limited conflicts and crises where the use of air power or army forces would have led to a greater national involvement. (U.S. Navy; PH3 R. D. Fitzgerald)

In the future each division will be provided with a battalion of light armored vehicles.

Marine divisions, first formed in 1941, fought as such in World War II, the Korean War, and the Vietnam War.[3] During the 1950s the United States began the practice of maintaining battalions afloat on board amphibious ships in the Mediterranean (Sixth Fleet), Western Pacific (Seventh Fleet), and at times in the Caribbean area (Second Fleet).

These were generally Battalion Landing Teams (BLT), consisting of a rifle battalion plus an artillery battery, tank platoon, engineer platoon, and composite helicopter squadron (if a carrier-type amphibious ship were available) plus supporting units. Thus, the infantry battalion of about 1,200 men was reinforced to about 1,800 to form a BLT.

By the 1960s the reinforced battalions were being organized as Marine Expeditionary Units (MEU) and the regiments as Marine Expeditionary Brigades (MEB) for specific operations and exercises. Subsequently, the Marines have formally organized combat units into Marine Air-Ground Task Forces (MAGTF) for operations and exercises. These are combined air-ground combat teams based on the existing battalion, regimental, and divisional organizations. The composition of specific MAGTFs will vary with their mission, the available Marine units, and the available amphibious shipping. The following table provides the nominal composition of the air-ground task forces:

MARINE AIR-GROUND TASK FORCES

Structure	Marine Amphibious Unit (MAU)	Marine Amphibious Brigade (MAB)	Marine Amphibious Force (MAF)
Ground combat element	Battalion landing team	Regimental landing team	Marine division
Aviation combat element	Composite aircraft squadron	Composite aircraft group	Aircraft wing
Combat service support element	MAU service support group	Brigade service support group	Command support group
Total Personnel			
Marine	2,350	15,000	48,200
Navy	156	670	2,400
Amphibious Shipping	4–6 ships	21–26 ships	approx. 50 ships

[3] Prior to 1941 the largest Marine combat organization was a brigade, with two brigades fighting in France in 1917–1918.

The Marine Corps is still primarily an amphibious assault force, and regularly exercises this capability. (Top left) Marines deploy from an amphibious tractor during a landing on the western coast of Denmark; (top right) the Marines still use conventional landing craft and pontoon causeways, as this one at Beirut, to bring ashore heavy vehicles and equipment; (bottom) but increasingly the Marines are using helicopters for landing operations, as these Marines boarding CH-46D Sea Knights on the TARAWA (LHA 1). (U.S. Marine Corps and, bottom, U.S. Navy)

In addition to the Navy personnel assigned to the Marine units listed above, in an amphibious assault the Navy would provide specialized support units such as Sea-Air-Land (SEAL), Explosive Ordnance Disposal (EOD), and Underwater Demolition Teams (UDT) in direct support of the Marines.

The personnel listed above and their weapons, vehicles, other equipment, and supplies compose the assault echelon of the various MAGTFs. These forces would be carried in the amphibious ships indicated. For sustained operations ashore the assault echelon would require the follow-on support that would have to be carried in commercial merchant ships.

A Marine Amphibious Force with nine rifle battalions in theory could provide several MAUs or two MABs. However, there are sufficient combat and service support units for the MAF to simultaneously provide two or three MAUs or one MAB.

AMPHIBIOUS ASSAULT

All Marine units are intended for amphibious assault. There is currently sufficient amphibious lift, with eight Navy amphibious squadrons, for the simultaneous lift of the assault echelon of one MAF. The Reagan Administration plans to increase this lift capacity by 1994 to one MAF plus one MAB.

The constraints on amphibious lift have necessitated that Marine amphibious units be divided into an Assault Echelon (AE), an Assault Follow-On Echelon (AFOE), and Fly-In Echelon (FIE). Only the assault echelon is normally carried in specialized amphibious ships. Commercial merchant ships would be employed to carry the follow-on echelon.

The current Marine doctrine is to conduct amphibious landings with helicopters, amphibian tractors, conventional landing craft, and—in the future—air cushion vehicles. These several types of landing vehicles coupled with the different types of amphibious ships that carry them complicate amphibious lift and assault planning. Also, the potential need for RH-53D/MH-53E minesweeping helicopters and AV-8A/B Harrier light attack aircraft in an amphibious assault could reduce the deck space available for assault/cargo helicopters. And, at present there are only three Marine helicopter squadrons that fly the CH-53E Super Stallion, which is needed to lift the M198 155-mm howitzer, the light armored vehicle, and other Marine heavy equipment. This helicopter force is inadequate for many potential amphibious situations and while more of these 16-ton-capacity helicopters are planned, they will probably not be available until well after Marine units "heavy up."

OPERATIONAL

Within FMF Atlantic are the 2nd Marine Division and the associated 2nd Marine Aircraft Wing and 2nd Force Service Support Group located on the U.S. East Coast. These units constitute the II Marine Amphibious Force.

The II MAF forward deploys a MAU afloat in the Mediterranean on a continuous basis, and from August 1982 until February 1984 provided the Marine amphibious assault unit that served ashore in Lebanon. (U.S. Marines were put ashore on 25 August 1982 to assist in the evacuation of terrorist leader Yassir Arafat and his followers from Beirut; the Marines were then withdrawn but returned to Lebanon a few weeks later as part of a multi-national peacekeeping force.) Since late 1979 the afloat MAU in the Mediterranean has periodically sailed into the Indian Ocean to support U.S. interests in conjunction with the Persian Gulf crises.

Additionally, the II MAF periodically deploys a MAU or MAB to Northern Europe for training and joint/combined exercises and on occasion deploys a MAU to the Caribbean area. Equipment and supplies for a MAB are being prepositioned ashore in Norway with the II MAF assigned to provide troops to marry up with this equipment for the defense of the area. These troops would be airlifted from the United States.

Finally, in July 1983 the headquarters was activated for a brigade to use equipment that will be prepositioned aboard ships in the Atlantic region or the Indian Ocean as part of a Rapid Deployment Force (RDF). This headquarters, for the 6th MAB, consists of some 200 Marine and Navy personnel. It would command the regiment, air group, and support forces flown overseas to marry up with the prepositioning ships.

Under FMF Pacific the 1st Marine Division, 1st Force Service Support Group, and 3rd Marine Aircraft Wing form the I MAF on the U.S. West Coast. The I MAF and II MAF rotate combat elements to the III MAF in the Western Pacific, including the afloat MAUs. The I MAF also has responsibility for developing plans for the employment of Marines in the Indian Ocean region in conjunction with the Rapid Deployment Force program. The 7th MAB was established in May 1980 as the first Marine organization dedicated to being airlifted to marry up with the equipment aboard prepositioning ships in the Indian Ocean.

The III MAF—also part of FMF Pacific—includes the 3rd Marine Division on Okinawa, with its 1st Brigade permanently based on Oahu, Hawaii, with associated Marine Aircraft Group 24 from the 1st wing. The remainder of the 1st wing and the 3rd Force Service Support Group are based in Japan and Okinawa.

The I and III MAFs normally have one MAU and one BLT afloat in the Western Pacific-Indian Ocean region.

MARINE CORPS RESERVE

The Marine Corps Reserve consists of the 4th Marine Division and the 4th Marine Aircraft Wing. These units generally parallel active units in organization, but in some categories have older equipment and lack several service support components.

Marine reservists have training sessions on a weekly or monthly basis, and for two weeks during the summer. The latter periods include participation in exercises with active units in the United States and, on an increasing frequency, overseas.

5   Rapid Deployment Force

The present concept of a Rapid Deployment Force provides for the airlifting of U.S. troops to a crisis area where they would be married to weapons and other equipment carried to the area by pre-loaded merchant-type ships. The use of Navy/Military Sealift Command ships and the assignment of Marine Corps units to the Rapid Deployment Force require their consideration in any discussion of the U.S. Fleet.

The RDF program was developed because of the inability of the United States to project ground combat forces into the Persian Gulf region after the fall of the Shah of Iran in late 1979 and the subsequent capture of the American embassy in Tehran.

The initial U.S. program to airlift troops to forward areas and marry them to equipment in forward-deploy or preposition supply ships dates to the early 1960s. Mr. Robert S. McNamara, the Secretary of Defense under Presidents Kennedy and Johnson, had proposed such a program using the large C-5 Galaxy cargo aircraft and Forward Deployed Logistic (FDL) ships. Congress refused to fund the FDL ships for fear that the prepositioning of military supplies would lead to U.S. involvement in conflicts.

Still, the Department of Defense did have the Navy load three Victory-type merchant ships with military equipment and munitions and moor them in the Far East. Designated T-AG 172–174, these ships were operated by the Military Sea Transportation Service with civilian crews. Their cargoes were used in the early phases of the Vietnam conflict and the ships were subsequently engaged in general cargo operations under MSTS control.

ESTABLISHMENT

The concept of prepositioning military material afloat in potential crisis areas was again put forward in the late 1970s. President Carter directed the National Security Council in 1977 to review U.S. military capabilities. The resulting studies indicated that the United States was not prepared for military responses to crises in the Third World, particularly in the Persian Gulf area—a serious deficit as the area's oil fields are of major importance to the West.

President Carter directed that a mobile strike force be established for use in non-NATO areas. Soon referred to as the Rapid Deployment Force (RDF), this plan was handled with a high degree of secrecy because of the fear of public reaction based on the American military failure in Vietnam. Plans for an RDF were well advanced when, in

November 1979, the U.S. embassy in Tehran was seized by Iranian terrorists in the aftermath of the fall of the Shah's government.

The subsequent hostage crisis created renewed public and congressional support for military forces that could intervene in the Third World. On 5 December 1979, Marine Major General Paul X. Kelley provided a detailed account of RDF planning at a Pentagon press conference.[1] The RDF would consist of a headquarters staff that would undertake contingency planning but would not have military forces permanently assigned. Rather, when required the RDF would be assigned combat and support forces from the Army, Navy, Marine Corps, and Air Force.

In peacetime the RDF would be subordinate to the U.S. Readiness Command, which had responsibility for readiness of all ground forces in the United States. When operational, the RDF would be under the Joint Chiefs of Staff, in a manner similar to the various unified commands. (The U.S. Army strongly opposed this situation, proposing instead that the RDF be a part of the Readiness Command at all times.)

Subsequently designated as the Rapid Deployment Joint Task Force (RDJTF), the command was formally established in December 1979. The combat forces indicated for probable assignment in a crisis were the Army's XVIII Airborne Corps, consisting of the 82nd Airborne Division (parachute) and 101st Airmobile Division (helicopter), plus an Army mechanized infantry division and available units of the I and II Marine Amphibious Forces. Of significance, all of these forces except the mechanized division are "light" combat units, considered to have limited combat capabilities against Soviet tank or even motorized infantry forces, which are superior in tanks and artillery to comparable-size U.S. airborne/air mobile or Marine units.

After extensive consideration and debate, the RDJTF was elevated to the level of a unified command on 1 January 1983 and renamed the U.S. Central Command.

MARITIME PREPOSITIONING

The principal area of concern in the establishment of the RDF was the Persian Gulf and adjacent areas, generally referred to as Southwest Asia by U.S. military planners. The region is politically unstable and is

---

[1] Later in December he was named commander of the Rapid Deployment Joint Task Force. General Kelley subsequently was appointed Assistant Commandant of the Marine Corps in 1981 and the Commandant in 1983.

Maritime prepositioning ships ride at anchor off Diego Garcia in the Indian Ocean, part of the massive U.S. effort to provide a rapid military response to crises in Southwest Asia. In the foreground are the vehicle cargo ships Mercury (T-AKR 10) and Jupiter (T-AKR 11), with a heavily laden tanker in the distance. (U.S. Navy; PH3 P. Ricci)

the primary source of oil for several Western European nations and Japan. And the United States lacks military bases there.

After the fall of the Shah, the U.S. Navy deployed carrier battle groups to the region as well as an amphibious squadron carrying a Marine Amphibious Unit (see Chapter 4). The capabilities of this force for ground combat in the region could be considered as minimal.

Accordingly, several merchant-type ships—MSC operated and commercial ships under contract—were loaded with Marine equipment and munitions and deployed to Diego Garcia, a British-controlled island in the Indian Ocean, some 2,000 miles from the Persian Gulf. These ships began loading at U.S. ports in May 1980 and all were in place at Diego Garcia by mid-July. These ships became the Near-Term Prepositioning Force (NTPF).

The ships consisted of two ships already in MSC service, the Meteor (T-AKR 9) and Sealift Pacific (T-AOT 168); two ships that were acquired specifically for the role, the Mercury (T-AKR 10) and Jupiter (T-AKR 11); and three commercial merchant ships under charter, the American Champion, American Courier, and Zapata Patriot. Together these seven ships carried sufficient equipment, ammunition, spare parts, food, fuel, and potable water to support a 12,500-man Marine Amphibious Brigade (MAB) plus several Air Force tactical squadrons for two weeks of sustained combat.[2] Some of the initial seven ships have been replaced; the NTPF at the end of 1983 consisted of six ships carrying

material for the MAB plus three ships loaded with Army ammunition, one ship with medical supplies, and several ships with fuel and potable water—a total of 17 ships.[3] One other prepositioned ship was based in the Mediterranean in 1983.

The basic NTPF (i.e., material for one MAB) is now being supplemented and will later be replaced by Maritime Prepositioning Ships (MPS) that are being built or converted specifically for the RDF program. The current plan is for a force of 13 prepositioning ships in the Atlantic region or Indian Ocean carrying material for three MABs with a total of some 46,000 troops.

The MTPF-MPS transition is planned on the following schedule:

RAPID DEPLOYMENT FORCE PREPOSITIONING SHIPS
(Brigade Equivalents/Prepositioning Ships)

	Fiscal 1983	Fiscal 1984	Fiscal 1985	Fiscal 1986
NTPF	1/6	1/6	1/6	0/0
MPS	0/0	1/4	2/9	3/13

The ultimate MPS force will consist of five new construction ships and eight former merchant ships that have been extensively converted. All will be MSC-operated with civilian crews; see Chapter 24 for characteristics and details.

[2] A MAB normally consists of 11,200 troops in the assault echelon; this was increased to 12,500 men for the Indian Ocean RDF.

[3] The break-bulk cargo ship with medical supplies carries two 400-bed Army field hospitals and one 200-bed combat support hospital.

CONCEPT LIMITATIONS

The RDF/MPS concept has severe limitations. The transport aircraft carrying troops from the United States may require overflight rights and, in some situations, overseas refueling locations. Upon arrival in the crisis region, the aircraft must have secure airfields on which to land, with those airfields near a port facility with road access between the two.

The prepositioning ships, currently anchored at Diego Garcia, must transit to the airfield-port location. During their passage the ships could be vulnerable to hostile air, surface, or submarine attack and hence some protective forces will have to be provided. Upon arrival at the airfield-port location the ships must have a safe anchorage and piers for unloading.

The marrying up of airlifted troops and sea-based material must thus occur in a friendly or at least benign environment that is able to meet stringent requirements for airfield and port facilities. Once the troops are prepared for ground combat, their inter-theater mobility is severely restricted. The Marines cannot be reembarked in the prepositioning ships for transit or amphibious assault. (The 327 amphibian tractors being embarked in the prepositioning ships are for ground transport, not amphibious assault.)

PREPOSITIONING SHIPS

The following ships have served in the NTPF. Those listed as charter ships were assigned hull numbers by MSC for accounting purposes. They are not standard designations and the ships do not appear in the Naval Vessels Register.

All ships are unarmed and have civilian crews, with some ships carrying Navy communications detachments and Army or Marine maintenance teams.

Military Sealift Command Ships

Number	Name
T-AKR 9	METEOR
T-AKR 10	MERCURY
T-AKR 11	JUPITER
T-AOT 168	SEALIFT PACIFIC

Marine M60A1 tanks and other vehicles await loading on board the vehicle cargo ship MERCURY at Wilmington, N.C., prior to the ship's departure to join the Near-Term Prepositioning Force (NTPF) in the Indian Ocean. The preposition ships do not have an amphibious assault capability. (U.S. Navy; PH3 George Bruder)

The chartered container ship AMERICAN CHAMPION rides at anchor as part of the NTPF. Note the cranes that will permit offloading without the need for port facilities. Most military cargo is carried in break-bulk and vehicle cargo ships. (U.S. Navy; PH3 P. Ricci)

Commercial Ships Under Charter

Number		Name	Type
T-AKR	112	LYRA	(German design)
T-AOT	1001	PATRIOT	T6-S-98a
T-AOT	1002	RANGER	T6-S-98a
T-AK	1003	AMERICAN SPITFIRE	C4-S-69
T-AK	1004	AUSTRAL LIGHTNING	C8-S-81b (LASH)
T-AK	1005	AUSTRAL RAINBOW	C8-S-81b (LASH)
T-AOT	1006	ROVER	T6-S-98a
T-AOT	1007	AMERICAN COURIER	T6-S-98a later T-AO 2015
T-AK	1008	AMERICAN TITAN	C4-S-69
T-AK	1009	AMERICAN SPARTAN	
T-AK	1010	AMERICAN TROJAN	C4-S-69
T-AK	1011	AMERICAN MONARCH	C4-S-69
T-AOT	1012	THE SPIRIT OF LIBERTY	
T-AK	1013	DEFIANCE	
T-AK	1015	AUSTRAL WYTHE	C8-S-81b (LASH)
T-AOT	1201	NEW YORK SUN	
T-AOT	1202	TEXAS TRADER	T2-SE-A1
T-AOT	1203	OVERSEAS ALICE	
T-AOT	1204	OVERSEAS BALDEZ	
T-AOT	1205	OVERSEAS VIVIAN	
T-AK	2005	TRANSCOLORADO	C4-S-B1
T-AK	2006	TRANSCOLOMBIA	C4-S-B1
T-AK	2011	AMERICAN CHAMPION	C4-S-57a
T-AK	2031	BUILDER	C3-S-46a
T-AK	2032	BAY	C3-S-46a
T-AK	2033	BUYER	C3-S-46a
T-AK	2034	DAWN	C4-S-58
T-AK	2035	GULF SHIPPER	C3-S-37d
T-AK	2036	GULF TRADER	C3-S-37d
T-AK	2037	MALLORY LAKES	C4-S-66
T-AK	2038	MASON LYKES	C4-S-66

RAPID RESPONSE SHIPS

Separate from the NTPF/MPS ships are the 8 high-speed merchant ships of the SL-7 type that the Navy is converting to carry the equipment of an Army armored (tank) or mechanized infantry division. The ships will be capable of other sealift missions as well. Four of these ships are to be maintained on the U.S. Atlantic coast and four on the Pacific coast to provide a rapid-reinforcement capability. (These converted SL-7s are T-AKR 287–294; see Chapter 24.)

Follow-on material for these units and those of the RDF would be carried by merchant ships in Ready Reserve Force (RRF) which are laid up under Maritime Administration jurisdiction. These ships, some with special features for carrying military equipment, are to be broken out of the mothball fleet and ready to steam within a few days' notice. In 1983 the RRF contained 30 merchant ships with a goal of 77 ships consisting of 61 dry cargo ships and 16 tankers. Some of the cargo ships will be configured as Auxiliary Crane Ships (T-ACS), being fitted with heavy cranes to unload their own and other ships' cargo without the need for port facilities.

Two merchant ships are being converted to serve as hospital ships to support the RDF (T-AH 19 and 20).

Finally, the Marine Corps has proposed the conversion of two merchant ships to provide aviation support in forward areas (these would become T-AVB 3 and 4).

6 Naval Personnel

The U.S. Navy has an active duty strength in late 1984 of 68,500 officers and 496,000 enlisted men and women—a total of approximately 564,500.[1] An increase of almost 14,000 occurred in fiscal 1984 with additional increases planned for the near future to man the increasing size of the active fleet. These numbers do not include almost 75,000 reservists on active duty (see Chapter 7).

The quality of U.S. naval personnel is very high, with the current record-level recruiting and retention rates providing naval leaders with the ability to select the people they want in many categories.

ENLISTED PERSONNEL

The U.S. military establishment is an all-volunteer force. During the late 1970s the Navy as well as the other services had major recruiting and retention problems. In 1981, some 13 percent of the Navy's ships and 25 percent of the aviation squadrons were considered not combat ready because of personnel shortages.

There was a turnaround in recruiting in 1980 and since then Navy enlisted recruiting has reached 100 percent of goals. More importantly, almost 90 percent (60,000) of the non-prior service male enlistees were high school graduates, well above the number expected. Recruit aptitude test scores continue to increase and are, overall, 11 percent above original recruiting goals. This change in recruiting and retention can be attributed to the improved morale of the military services and to increases in salary and certain special pay and bonuses. The current high morale reflects the improvement in the national attitude toward the military over the past few years, partly attributable to the Reagan Administration attitude. It is also due to several internal Navy measures, such as allowing a commanding officer to discharge undesirable personnel in certain categories.

Progress in the retention of Navy personnel has been equally impressive during the early 1980s, with first term, second term, and career enlisted retention rates all surpassing goals since 1980. As a result, the Navy has been able to reduce the shortage of senior petty officers from an estimated 22,000 in 1981 to the current shortage of 9,300 in 1983. This reduced shortfall has occurred even as the need for petty officers has increased in line with the increasing size of the active fleet. The

[1] This compares with a Soviet naval strength of some 348,000 (not including the Naval Infantry or Marines) and a British naval strength of 64,000. The U.S. Navy's midshipmen are included in the enlisted category for accounting purposes.

TABLE 6–1. ENLISTED RETENTION

	Fiscal 1981	Fiscal 1982	Fiscal 1983	Fiscal 1984 (Goal)
1st Term (4–6 yrs)	41.7%	50.3%	55.7%	50%
2nd Term (8–10 yrs)	56.9%	63.0%	65.4%	65%
3rd Term (10 + yrs)	94.1%	95.3%	96.6%	95%

petty officer shortfall will be eliminated completely by 1989 if current trends continue.

These trends will be difficult to maintain. A decreasing pool of men and women of military recruiting age and an improving civilian economy will pose obstacles to the recruiting of quality personnel. Quality is particularly important because of the high technology of modern ships, aircraft, weapons, and sensors.

OFFICERS

Officer recruiting and retention in all of the "warfare communities"—air, surface, and submarine—have improved during the past few years. But shortfalls remain in the mid-grade ranks of surface warfare, pilot, and submarine officers. These shortages are the result of earlier difficulties in officer recruiting and retention.

The Navy has an annual recruiting goal of some 4,600 officers per year. Current efforts meet or exceed the goals in all officer categories except for nuclear officers. In that category just over 70 percent of the goals are being reached. The Navy requires some 670 nuclear submarine officers per year. During the past few years the Naval Academy quota (about 225) has been met as have the Nuclear Propulsion Officer Candidate (NUPOC) program (625); the Naval Reserve Officer Training Corps (NROTC) input has been slightly less than the quota (185). Neither the total requirement nor the Naval Academy proportion had ever been achieved until Naval Academy midshipmen were, for a brief period in the early 1980s, "drafted" into the nuclear program.

Subsequently, a combination of special payments and a general change in policy have contributed to an improvement in nuclear recruiting. An applicant accepted into the nuclear program receives a bonus of $3,000 before reporting to initial training; after completing nuclear power training there is another $3,000 bonus; and after the obligated six years of service there is an annual continuation bonus of $6,000.

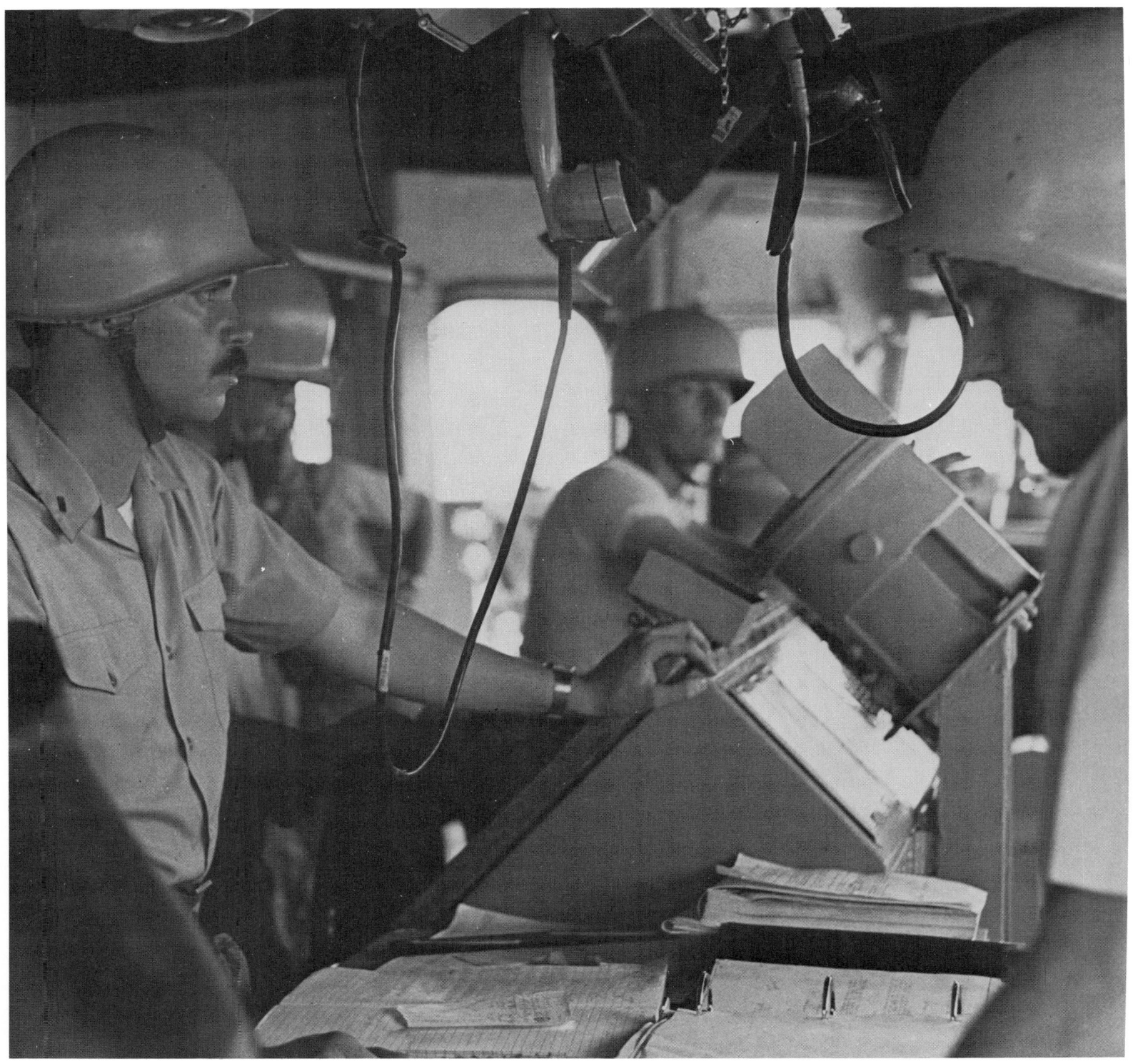

The Navy provides the opportunity for command and responsibility at a relatively early age, as this watch officer demonstrates in the guided missile destroyer DEWEY (DDG 45) during exercises in the South Atlantic. Too often, however, naval service also means vast amounts of administrative work. (1979, U.S. Navy)

Changes in procedures for interviewing midshipmen and junior officers candidates for the nuclear program also account for recent increases in personnel. Admiral Kinnaird McKee became head of the nuclear propulsion program in March 1982; with previous experience as Superintendent of the Naval Academy and Commander Third Fleet, he brought to the position a new, more realistic approach to nuclear personnel selection and handling.

As shown in the following chart, officer retention has increased dramatically during the past few years.

TABLE 6-2. OFFICER RETENTION

	Fiscal 1980	Fiscal 1981	Fiscal 1982	Fiscal 1983
Surface Warfare	39%	42%	43%	45%
Pilot	30%	42%	49%	58%
Flight Officer	71%	65%	73%	74%
Nuclear Submarine	36%	33%	39%	46%
General Line	n.a.	46%	44%	60%

NOTE: n.a. = not available.

Nuclear submarine officer retention has greatly improved, but because of previous recruiting problems, the shortage of mid-grade nuclear qualified officers (i.e., lieutenant commander through captain) will worsen.

The data in Table 6-3 are based on early 1984 estimates—one year earlier the shortfall was predicted at 538 in fiscal 1986 and 555 in fiscal 1989. The Navy is hoping to "control" the widening gap by minimizing losses from the existing mid-grade group, meeting retention goals for junior officers, and maintaining the flow of new officers into the program. Money, nuclear officer scholarships, concern at the highest levels of the Navy, more time ashore for junior officers as the nuclear population increases, a depressed civilian nuclear community, and other factors

TABLE 6-3. MID-GRADE NUCLEAR OFFICER SHORTAGE

	Fiscal 1983	Fiscal 1986	Fiscal 1989
Deficit	495 of 1,886 required	635 of 1,995 required	689 of 2,065 required
Percent	26%	32%	33%

Naval service is highly attractive at this time, according to recruiting and retention data. The officer ranks of the submarine service, however, continue to have shortages—a situation expected to worsen in the future despite the financial incentives, the high morale of submarine service, and the depressed civilian nuclear industry. These Navymen are aboard the Trident submarine OHIO (SSBN 726) at Bangor, Wash. (1982, U.S. Navy, PH2 Shayna Brennan)

Many Navy jobs lack the technology and glamour shown in television recruiting spots. The job of a boiler technician in the guided missile cruiser HORNE (CG 30)—and hundreds of others—are seldom discussed outside the Navy but are vital to the operation of the fleet. (1977, U.S. Navy)

indicate that there will be continued improvement in this area after two decades of severe problems.

The shortage of experienced, mid-grade nuclear qualified officers is the Navy's most serious manpower problem. The submarine force remains short about 900 officers, meaning that officers are currently spending 14 years at sea and 6 years ashore in a 20-year career. The Navy's goal is to reduce the nuclear officer's time at sea to 11 years in 20— a goal that will be difficult to achieve. (The enlisted submariners spend 5 years at sea for 2 years ashore.)

In all other areas but one, the overall Navy officer retention rate is improving. The major exception is of surface warfare officers, which continues to have shortfalls in retention.

WOMEN IN THE NAVY

The number and role of women in the Navy are increasing rapidly. There are currently more than 47,500 women on active duty—approximately 6,500 officers and 41,000 enlisted women, representing about 9 percent of the active naval personnel. The total number of women is expected to increase to almost 52,000 in the near future.

Women are currently assigned to a large number of noncombat aircraft units and surface ships on a permanent basis, and may be assigned to combat units for temporary duty. While no women are assigned to submarines, there are several women in nuclear instructor assignments. Almost 40 ships—mostly fleet auxiliaries—now have a total of some 3,000 women in their crews.

7 Naval Reserve

The U.S. Naval Reserve has approximately 108,700 officers and enlisted men and women in the Selected Reserve or Category A. These "ready reserve" personnel normally train 48 days per year plus two weeks on active duty and receive pay for their services. Their strength is planned to increase to a goal of 110,000 men and women by the fall of 1985.

Approximately 14,500 additional reservists are on full-time duty with a planned increase to about 15,500.[1] In addition, there are about 80,000 reservists in the category of Individual Ready Reservists, some of whom attend drills but are not paid.

The Selected Reservists regularly participate in Navy day-to-day activities. For example, reserve patrol squadrons routinely conduct ASW patrols from bases in the United States and overseas during their training periods. (In fiscal 1983 these P-3 Orion squadrons flew 800 hours in support of the national drug interdiction program.) Other reserve squadrons fly regular support missions for the active Navy and, with reserve surface ships, participate in fleet exercises when possible.

Also, selected reservists have served in the battleships IOWA (BB 61) and NEW JERSEY (BB 62) since their recommissioning, most on a two-year recall to active duty. Beyond those crewmen assigned to the NEW JERSEY, another 135 selected reservists were flown from the United States to the Middle East to go aboard the ship during the 1983 year-end holidays to permit regular crew members to take holiday leave. The success of this program led to the subsequent rotation of reservists to the ship before her return to the United States. Some consideration was given to operating the fourth reactivated battleship, the WISCONSIN (BB 64), with mostly reservists; however, the ship will be manned by active personnel when recommissioned.

The Naval Reserve is undergoing a massive modernization program. Traditionally, in peacetime the reserves were provided with "cast off" equipment—the oldest types of ships and aircraft still used by the active Navy or material discarded by the active Navy. Today front-line ships and aircraft are being provided to the Naval Reserve as part of a reorganization of U.S. reserve forces from a "vertical" to a "horizontal" relationship with the active forces. According to Secretary of the Navy John Lehman, "That means essentially that the reserves must provide immediate augmentation to the active force in time of emergency across the entire spectrum of warfare."

[1]These are either part of the TAR (Training and Administration of Reserves) or special recall to active duty programs.

ESTABLISHMENT

The naval reserve concept can be traced to the American Revolution when several of the colonies employed armed merchant ships to resist British military activities within their states' waters. By the time of the Declaration of Independence in 1776 there were 11 colonies with some form of navy.

During the next century there were various forms of state volunteers with a volunteer force establishment in the Union Navy during the Civil War. Then, beginning in 1888 several states established naval components as part of their state militias. These naval militias were intended for harbor and coastal defense; they had no federal standing and rules for applicants and level of competence varied considerably from state to state.

Beginning in 1891 the Navy offered to all state militias to participate in some naval exercises and there was soon federal cooperation in a number of training areas. Two years later the training ship NEW HAMPSHIRE (launched in 1864 although laid down 45 years earlier!) was transferred from the Navy to the New York State Naval Militia.

By the eve of the Spanish-American War of 1898 there were more than 4,000 men in state naval militias. When the conflict erupted the militias were used to patrol the coasts (there was a perceived threat of a Spanish assault) while thousands more militiamen were taken into the Navy. Their outstanding service in the war led to Navy Department recommendations for the creation of a national Naval Reserve. This was opposed—mostly by state interests—until 1914 when Congress passed legislation that largely placed the naval militias under supervision of the Navy Department. In time of war they would become part of the Navy (as the state National Guard units would become part of the Army). A year later, in 1915, the U.S. Naval Reserve was established, a reserve force to be composed of men honorably discharged from the active Navy. The state militias continued to exist.

With U.S. entry into World War I in April 1917 the militias were mobilized as the National Naval Volunteers, with almost the total strength of just over 10,000 men coming onto active duty in the Navy. By September their ranks had grown to almost 17,000 men. These volunteers were consolidated with the Naval Reserve in July 1918, creating the current U.S. Naval Reserve organization. (The states of California, Illinois, and New York continue to maintain state naval forces, whose members are additionally in the Naval Reserve.)

Under the Navy's "total force" concept the Naval Reserve has many of the forces and capabilities required for a multimission fleet. Most of the Navy's special warfare capabilities are vested in the Naval Reserve, as these riverine patrol boats of Special Boat Unit 22, shown during an exercise in the Panama Canal Zone. (1983, Department of Defense)

ORGANIZATION

The Chief of Naval Reserve (rear admiral) manages the Naval Reserve Programs. He also serves on the staff of the Chief of Naval Operations as the Director of Naval Reserve (OP-09R).

The Naval Reserve Force (surface ships) report directly to the active fleet commanders and the Naval Air Reserve Force (tactical air units) report through the Commander Naval Air Reserve Force to the Chief of Naval Operations. The Chief of Naval Reserve has certain administrative and recruiting functions that support these forces.

The headquarters of the Chief of Naval Reserve and the Commander Naval Air Reserve are located in New Orleans, La.

Those Naval Reserve activities that report directly to the Chief of Naval Reserve are:

Naval Reserve Air Centers
Naval Reserve Air Units
Naval Reserve Anti-Submarine Warfare Training Center
Naval Reserve Construction Force/First Naval Construction Brigade
Naval Reserve Intelligence Program
Naval Reserve Readiness Regions

There are 23 Naval Reserve Air Centers, most located at Naval Air Stations with tactical air units assigned. The Reserve Air Units are also based at those stations.

The First Naval Construction Battalion Brigade consists of 17 reserve Mobile Construction Battalions—the famed "seabees." These provide two-thirds of the Navy's total construction battalion force.

The Naval Reserve Intelligence Program provides one-third of the Navy's intelligence personnel.

SURFACE FORCES

At the end of 1984 the Naval Reserve Force (NRF) was to consist of:

　1 Destroyer (DD)
　9 Frigates (FF/FFG)
　2 Amphibious Ships (LST)
　18 Minesweepers (MSO)
　4 Fleet Tugs (ATF)
　2 Salvage Ships (ARS)

　4 Special Boat Units (numerous craft)
　16 Mobile Inshore Undersea Warfare Units (numerous craft)

Destroyers. The single NRF destroyer, the EDSON (DD 946), is also employed as a school ship at the Surface Warfare Officers School; the ship is based at Newport, R.I. No additional destroyers are planned for the Naval Reserve.

Frigates. Up to 26 frigates are currently scheduled for transfer to the NRF in accordance with the following tentative schedule. These ships will carry the SH-2F LAMPS I helicopter, flown by reserve squadrons.

Amphibious Ships. During the later 1970s four amphibious cargo ships (LKA) were transferred to the Naval Reserve. However, they have been returned to active service because of fleet requirements. Two LSTs are the only amphibious ships planned for the NRF operation during the 1980s.

Tentative plans call for the transfer of three amphibious ships to the NRF in the early 1990s—one additional LST, one LSD, and one LPD.

Minesweepers. One of the outdated MSOs assigned to the NRF will be discarded in 1984–1985, with the remainder to be phased out as the

The Navy's decision to provide the reserves with modern aircraft—as this F/A-18 Hornet—and ships will give the reserves an almost unprecedented combat capability relative to active forces. The reserve phase in of the F/A-18 includes reservists first supporting and flying F/A-18s of fleet readiness squadron VFA-125. (Northrop)

Ship	Homeport	Transfer to NRF
FFG 7 O. H. Perry	Newport, R.I.	May 1984
FFG 9 Wadsworth	Long Beach, Calif.	1985
FFG 10 Duncan	Long Beach, Calif.	21 Jan 1984
FFG 11 Clark	Newport, R.I.	1985
FFG 12 Geo. Philip	Long Beach, Calif.	1986
FFG 13 S. E. Morison	Newport, R.I.	1986
FFG 14 John H. Sides	Long Beach, Calif.	1986
FFG 15 Estocin	Newport, R.I.	1986
FFG 16 Clifton Sprague	Newport, R.I.	Aug 1984
FFG 19 John A. Moore	Long Beach, Calif.	1987
FFG 20 Antrim	Newport, R.I.	1987
FFG 21 Flatley	Newport, R.I.	1987
FFG 22 Fahrion	Newport, R.I.	1988
FFG 23 Lewis B. Puller	Long Beach, Calif.	1987
FFG 25 Copeland	Long Beach, Calif.	1988
FFG 27 M. S. Tisdale	Long Beach, Calif.	1988
FF 1054 Gray	Long Beach, Calif.	15 July 1982
FF 1055 Hepburn	Long Beach, Calif.	1985
FF 1058 Meyerkord	Long Beach, Calif.	1985
FF 1060 Lang	Long Beach, Calif.	15 Jan 1982
FF 1061 Patterson	Newport, R.I.	15 June 1983
FF 1072 Blakely	Newport, R.I.	15 June 1983
FF 1091 Miller	Newport, R.I.	15 Jan 1982
FF 1096 Valdez	Newport, R.I.	14 Aug 1982

(two additional FFGs to be designated)

entire force of 17 MSH and 14 MCM mine countermeasure ships are turned over to the NRF.

Auxiliary Ships. The NRF will discard the four fleet tugs (ATF) and one salvage ship (ARS) in 1984–1985. Subsequently, five Cimarron (AO 177)-class fleet oilers and two repair ships (AR) will be assigned to the reserves. The latter ships, one on each coast, will support intermediate maintenance requirements for the reserve frigates.

AVIATION

The Naval Air Reserve Force currently operates more than 400 aircraft organized into six wings with the following squadrons:

2 Reserve Carrier Air Wings
    4 Fighter Squadrons (VF)
    1 Strike-Fighter Squadron (VFA)
    5 Attack Squadrons (VA)
    1 Light Photographic Squadron (VFP)
    2 Carrier Airborne Early Warning Squadrons (VAW)
    2 Tactical Electronic Warfare Squadrons (VAQ)
    2 Aerial Refueling Squadrons (VAK)

2 Reserve Patrol Wings
    13 Patrol Squadrons (VP)
1 Reserve Helicopter Wing
    2 Helicopter ASW Squadrons (HS)
    2 Light Helicopter ASW Squadrons (HSL)
    1 Helicopter Combat Support Squadron (HC)
    2 Helicopter Light Attack Squadrons (HAL)
1 Fleet Logistics Support Wing
    2 Fleet Composite Squadrons (VC)
    12 Fleet Logistic Support Squadrons (VR)

These squadrons are listed, with their bases and aircraft, in Chapter 28 of this edition.

The Naval Air Reserve began an extensive modernization in the early 1980s in most aircraft categories.

Fighter Aircraft. VF-301 was preparing to transition from the F-4S Phantom to the F-14A Tomcat when this edition went to press, the first reserve unit to fly that aircraft. VF-302 will follow while VF-201 and VF-202 will shift from the F-4N to the more-capable F-4S variant.

Attack Aircraft. The trouble-plagued engines of the A-7B have accelerated the transition to other attack aircraft. VA-203 has received the later A-7E while VA-303 changed to VFA-303 in 1984 and began receiving F/A-18A Hornets in June. VA-205 will receive the A-7E and VA-304 will shift to the F/A-18 in 1985.

Airborne Early Warning. VAW-78 has begun to exchange E-2B Hawkeye AEW aircraft for the E-2C with VAW-79 to follow shortly.

Patrol Aircraft. The P-3A and P-3B Orions flown by the reserves are receiving a Tactical Navigation (TacNav) modification that will significantly enhance their ASW capability.

Helicopters. The helicopter portion of the Naval Air Reserve is being provided with SH-2F LAMPS I helicopters for use aboard the newly acquired frigates. HS-84 began flying the SH-2F in early 1984, being changed to HSL-84, followed in 1985 by HS-74 changing to HSL, and HSL-94 to be formed in 1986. The remaining helicopter ASW squadrons (HS) will continue to fly SH-3 Sea Kings for the foreseeable future.

Transports. The transition from the venerable C-118 to the C-9B Skytrain II is almost completed for all reserve fleet logistic support squadrons (VR).

Medium Attack/Electronic Warfare/Reconnaissance/ASW/Tanker aircraft. There are no plans to modernize the reserve reconnaissance (RF-8G Crusader), electronic warfare (EA-6A Intruder) or tanker (KA-3B Skywarrior) units; there are no near-term plans to provide the reserves with a medium attack (A-6 Intruder) or ASW (S-3 Viking or ASW helicopter) capability. One RF-8G squadron was decommissioned in the fall of 1984, to be replaced with the TARPS-configured F-14s of the fighter squadrons.

8 Glossary

AA	Anti-Aircraft
AA	Atlantic (Fleet) Active
AAW	Anti-Air Warfare
ABL	Armored Box Launcher (Tomahawk)
Academic	Navy-owned ship operated by academic or research institution
AMCM	Airborne Mine Countermeasures
AEW	Airborne Early Warning
AR	Atlantic Reserve (Fleet)
ASMD	Anti-Ship Missile Defense
ASROC	Anti-Submarine Rocket
ASUW	Anti-Surface Warfare
ASW	Anti-Submarine Warfare
beam	extreme width of hull
bhp	brake horsepower
BPDMS	Basic Point Defense Missile System (Sea Sparrow)
CGR	Coast Guard Reserve
C&GS	Coast and Geodetic Survey
CIWS	Close-In Weapon System (Phalanx)
COD	Carrier On-board Delivery
Comm.	Commission
DASH	Drone Anti-Submarine Helicopter
displacement	*light* (ship) is displacement of the ship and all machinery without crew, provisions, fuel, munitions, all other consumables, or aircraft
	standard is displacement of ship fully manned and equipped, ready for sea, including all provisions, munitions, and aircraft, but without fuels
	full load is displacement of the ship complete and ready for service in all respects, including all fuels (aircraft as well as ship)
DP	Dual-Purpose (for use against air and surface targets)
draft	maximum draft of ship at full load, including fixed projections below the keel, if any (e.g., sonar dome)
DWT	Deadweight Tonnage (the ship's carrying capacity)
ECM	Electronic Countermeasures
EW	Electronic Warfare
extreme width	maximum width at or about the flight deck, including fixed projections (e.g., gun "tubs")

FBM	Fleet Ballistic Missile
FCS	Fire Control System
fiscal	Fiscal Year (FY); from 1 October of the calendar year until 30 September of the following year (since 1976; previously from 1 July through 30 June); S in front of the FY indicates a supplemental authorization
flag	special accommodations for fleet commander and staff; lesser unit commanders and their staff are included in ship's manning data
FRAM	Fleet Rehabilitation And Modernization
FRESCAN	Frequency Scan (radar)
FY	Fiscal Year
GFCS	Gunfire Control System
GL	Great Lakes
gross	ship's tonnage measured in total cubic contents expressed in units of 100 cubic feet or 2.83 cubic meters
HTS	High Tensile Steel
HY	High Yield (steel)
IO	Indian Ocean (active)
IOC	Initial Operational Capability
IW	Inland Waters
LAMPS	Light Airborne Multi-Purpose System (helicopter)
Lant	Atlantic
lbst	pounds static thrust
length	*wl* indicates length on waterline (this is the length between perpendiculars [bp] in naval practice)
	oa indicates length overall
manning	the number of personnel assigned to the ship or craft; the term *complement* is no longer used by the U.S. Navy
MarAd	Maritime Administration
MCLWG	Major Caliber Lightweight Gun (8-inch Mk 71)
MCM	Mine Countermeasures
Mk	Mark
Mod	Modification
MPS	Maritime Prepositioning Ship
MSC	Military Sealift Command (changed from MSTS in 1970)

The MSB 16 showing her array of MCM gear. (1983, Giorgio Arra)

MSTS	Military Sea Transportation Service (from 1949 to 1970)
NDRF	National Defense Reserve Fleet
n.mile	nautical miles
NOAA	National Oceanic and Atmospheric Administration
NOSC	Naval Ocean Systems Center
NFAF	Naval Fleet Auxiliary Force (UNREP ships operated by Military Sealift Command)
NRF	Naval Reserve Force (suffix A indicates Atlantic Fleet; suffix P indicates Pacific Fleet)
NSRDC	Naval Ship Research and Development Center
NTDS	Naval Tactical Data System
NTPS	Near-Term Prepositioning Ship
OSP	Offshore Procurement (ship built overseas with U.S. funding)
OTH	Over-The-Horizon (targeting)
PA	Pacific (Fleet) Active
Pac	Pacific
PR	Pacific Reserve (Fleet)
psi	pounds per square inch (boilers pressure)
reactors	the first letter of a reactor designation indicates the platform (A = Aircraft carrier, C = Cruiser, D = frigate (DL, now cruiser), S = Submarine); numeral indicates sequence of reactor design by specific manufacturer; and second letter is manufacturer (C = Combustion Engineering, G = General Electric, W = Westinghouse)
RFA	Royal Fleet Auxiliary (British)
RDF	Rapid Deployment Force
SAM	Surface-to-Air Missile
SATCOM	Satellite Communications
SCB	Ships Characteristics Board's sequential numbering of all Navy ship designs reaching advanced planning stage; numbered in a single sequential series from 1947 (SCB No. 1 was the NORFOLK, CLK 1/DL 1) through 1964 (SCB No. 252 was the FLAGSTAFF, PGH 1); from 1964 on numbered in blocks: 001–009 cruisers, 100 carriers, 200 destroyers/frigates, 300 submarines, 400 amphibious, 500 mine warfare, 600 patrol, 700 auxiliary, 800 service craft, 900 special purpose. The latter numbers have suffix of fiscal year of prototype ship, as 400.65 being the AGC/LCC of fiscal 1965 design.
SEAL	Sea-Air-Land team
shp	shaft horsepower
SLEP	Service Life Extension Project
SSM	Surface-to-Surface Missile
STOL	Short Take-Off and Landing
SUBROC	Submarine Rocket
SURTASS	Surveillance Towed Array Sensor System
TACAN	Tactical Aircraft Navigation
TACTAS	Tactical Towed Array Sonar
TARPS	Tactical Air Reconnaissance Pod System
T-ASM[1]	Tomahawk Anti-Ship Missile
T-LAM[1]	Tomahawk Land-Attack Missile
TRA	Training
troops	accommodations for troops
UNREP	Underway Replenishment
USCGC	United States Coast Guard Cutter
USNS	United States Naval Ship (civilian-manned ship operated by the Military Sealift Command)
USS	United States Ship (Navy-manned)
VDS	Variable Depth Sonar
VLS	Vertical Launch System
VERTREP	Vertical Replenishment
VOD	Vertical On-board Delivery
VSTOL	Vertical/Short Take-Off and Landing

[1]From about 1983 the Navy has begun using simply TASM and TLAM without the hyphens.

9 Ship Classifications

U.S. Navy ships and small craft, with a few specific exceptions, are classified by type and by sequence within that type. The list of classifications (Secretary of the Navy Instruction 5030.1) is issued periodically, updating a system that began in 1922. The U.S. Navy's current list, based on a format developed in 1977, seeks to better define ship types and missions and to facilitate comparisons with Soviet ship types.

The following are those classifications on the current list, last updated in 1983.

Letter prefixes to the basic symbols are used to indicate:

E in experimental or development status
F being constructed for foreign government
T- assigned to Military Sealift Command (formerly Military Sea Transportation Service)
W Coast Guard cutter

The suffix N denotes nuclear-propelled ships. For service craft, the suffix N indicates the non-self-propelled version of a similar self-propelled craft. The letter X is used unofficially as a suffix to indicate new designs or classes, as DDX, SSNX, LHDX, ARX.

More formal designations often exist for several years in official documents and usage before they appear in the ship classification instruction, as MSH (added to the list in 1982) and LHD (added in 1983).

Warships

Aircraft Carriers
CV	Multi-purpose Aircraft Carrier
CVN	Multi-purpose Aircraft Carrier (nuclear)
CVS	ASW Aircraft Carrier

Surface Combatants
BB	Battleship
CA	Gun Cruiser
CG	Guided Missile Cruiser
CGN	Guided Missile Cruiser (nuclear)
DD	Destroyer
DDG	Guided Missile Destroyer
FF	Frigate
FFG	Guided Missile Frigate

Submarines
SS	Submarine
SSG	Guided Missile Submarine
SSN	Submarine (nuclear)
SSBN	Ballistic Missile Submarine (nuclear)
SSAG	Auxiliary Submarine

Other Combatants

Patrol
PG	Patrol Combatant
PHM	Guided Missile Patrol Combatant (hydrofoil)

Amphibious Warfare
LHA	Amphibious Assault Ship (general purpose)
LPH	Amphibious Assault Ship (helicopter)
LPD	Amphibious Transport Dock
LHD	Amphibious Assault Ship (multi-purpose)
LKA	Amphibious Cargo Ship
LPA	Amphibious Transport
LSD	Dock Landing Ship
LST	Tank Landing Ship
LCC	Amphibious Command Ship

Mine Warfare
MSO	Minesweeper—Ocean
MCM	Mine Countermeasures
MSH	Mine Hunter

Auxiliary Ships

Mobile Logistics Ships
AE	Ammunition Ship
AF	Store Ship
AFS	Combat Store Ship
AO	Oiler
AOE	Fast Combat Support Ship
AOR	Replenishment Oiler
AD	Destroyer Tender
AR	Repair Ship
AS	Submarine Tender

Support Ships
ARS	Salvage Ship
ASR	Submarine Rescue Ship
ATA	Auxiliary Ocean Tug
ATF	Fleet Ocean Tug
ATS	Salvage and Rescue Ship
AG	Miscellaneous
AGDS	Deep Submergence Support Ship
AGEH	Hydrofoil Research Ship

AGF	Miscellaneous Command Ship
AGFF	Frigate Research Ship
AGM	Missile Range Instrumentation Ship
AGOR	Oceanographic Research Ship
AGOS	Ocean Surveillance Ship
AGP	Patrol Craft Tender
AGS	Surveying Ship
AGSS	Auxiliary Research Submarine
AH	Hospital Ship
AK	Cargo Ship
AKR	Vehicle Cargo Ship
AOG	Gasoline Tanker
AOT	Transport Oiler
AP	Transport
APB	Self-Propelled Barracks Ship
ARC	Cable Repairing Ship
ARL	Repair Ship, Small
AVM	Guided Missile Ship
AVT	Auxiliary Aircraft Landing Training Ship

Combatant Craft

Patrol

PB	Patrol Boat
PCF	Patrol Craft (fast)
PGH	Patrol Gunboat (hydrofoil)
PTF	Fast Patrol Craft
ATC	Mini-Armored Troop Carrier
PBR	River Patrol Boat

Amphibious Warfare

AALC	Amphibious Assault Landing Craft
LCAC	Landing Craft, Air Cushion
LCM	Landing Craft, Mechanized
LCPL	Landing Craft, Personnel, Large
LCU	Landing Craft, Utility
LCVP	Landing Craft, Vehicle, Personnel
LWT	Amphibious Warping Tug
SLWT	Side Loading Warping Tug
LSSC	Light Seal Support Craft
MSSC	Medium Seal Support Craft
SDV	Swimmer Delivery Vehicle
SWCL	Special Warfare Craft, Light
SWCM	Special Warfare Craft, Medium

Mine Warfare

MSB	Minesweeping Boat
MSD	Minesweeping Drone
MSI	Minesweeper, Inshore
MSM	Minesweeper, River (converted LCM-6)
MSR	Minesweeper, Patrol

Service Craft

AFDB	Large Auxiliary Floating Dry Dock
AFDL	Small Auxiliary Floating Dry Dock

AFDM	Medium Auxiliary Floating Dry Dock
ARD	Auxiliary Repair Dry Dock
ARDM	Medium Auxiliary Repair Dry Dock
YBD	Bowdock
YFD	Yard Floating Dry Dock
YTB	Large Harbor Tug
YTL	Small Harbor Tug
YTM	Medium Harbor Tug
YO	Fuel Oil Barge
YOG	Gasoline Barge
YW	Water Barge
YC	Open Lighter
YCF	Car Float
YCV	Aircraft Transportation Lighter
YF	Covered Lighter
YFN	Covered Lighter
YFNB	Large Covered Lighter
YFNX	Lighter (Special Purpose)
YFR	Refrigerated Covered Lighter
YFRN	Refrigerated Covered Lighter
YFU	Harbor Utility Craft
YG	Garbage Lighter
YGN	Garbage Lighter
YOGN	Gasoline Barge
YON	Fuel Oil Barge
YOS	Oil Storage Barge
YSR	Sludge Removal Barge
YWN	Water Barge
APL	Barracks Craft
DSRV	Deep Submergence Rescue Vehicle
DSV	Deep Submergence Vehicle
IX	Unclassified Miscellaneous
NR	Submersible Research Vehicle (nuclear)
YAG	Miscellaneous Auxiliary
YD	Floating Crane
YDT	Diving Tender
YFB	Ferry Boat or Launch
YFND	Dry Dock Companion Craft
YFP	Floating Power Barge
YFRT	Covered Lighter (Range Tender)
YHLC	Salvage Lift Craft, Heavy
YM	Dredge
YNG	Gate Craft
YP	Patrol Craft
YPD	Floating Pile Driver
YR	Floating Workshop
YRB	Repair and Berthing Barge
YRBM	Repair, Berthing, and Messing Barge
YRDH	Floating Dry Dock Workshop (Hull)
YRDM	Floating Dry Dock Workshop (Machine)
YRR	Radiological Repair Barge
YRST	Salvage Craft Tender
YSD	Seaplane Wrecking Derrick

MARITIME ADMINISTRATION CLASSIFICATIONS

The U.S. Maritime Administration classifies its ships by their design characteristics. This classification scheme is included in *Ships and Aircraft* because of the large number of Maritime Administration (previously Maritime Commission) ships that remain on the Naval Register in the amphibious warfare and auxiliary ship categories. (During World War II escort aircraft carriers and patrol frigates also were built to Maritime Commission designs.) NOAA ships are also built to MarAd design.

Explanation of symbols:

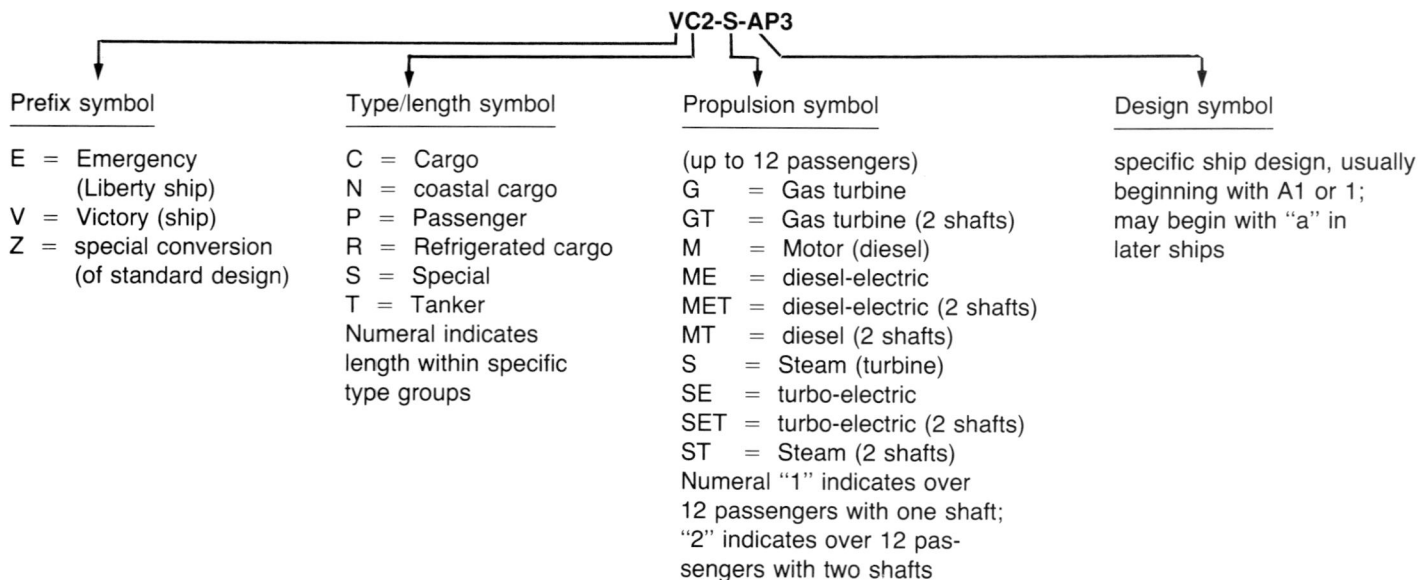

VC2-S-AP3

Prefix symbol	Type/length symbol	Propulsion symbol	Design symbol
E = Emergency (Liberty ship)	C = Cargo	(up to 12 passengers)	specific ship design, usually beginning with A1 or 1; may begin with "a" in later ships
V = Victory (ship)	N = coastal cargo	G = Gas turbine	
Z = special conversion (of standard design)	P = Passenger	GT = Gas turbine (2 shafts)	
	R = Refrigerated cargo	M = Motor (diesel)	
	S = Special	ME = diesel-electric	
	T = Tanker	MET = diesel-electric (2 shafts)	
	Numeral indicates length within specific type groups	MT = diesel (2 shafts)	
		S = Steam (turbine)	
		SE = turbo-electric	
		SET = turbo-electric (2 shafts)	
		ST = Steam (2 shafts)	
		Numeral "1" indicates over 12 passengers with one shaft; "2" indicates over 12 passengers with two shafts	

10 Ship Names

For most of this century the naming of U.S. Navy ships had been based on a style developed in the early 1900s. There were periodic exceptions and, of course, new name sources were added as new ship types were developed in response to more complex naval warfare and an increased need for specialized ships. Since the 1970s, however, the "traditional" sources for ship names have been largely ignored, mostly for overriding political reasons. Thus, today several ship types have multiple name sources.

The following discussion is arranged in the format of ship listings in this volume.

SUBMARINES

The 41 strategic missile submarines (SSBN) completed from 1960 to 1967 were named for "famous Americans," although several were, in fact, named for "foreigners." The subsequent Trident submarines built from the early 1970s onward have been named for the States of the Union, beginning with the OHIO (SSBN 726). Previously, state names were assigned to battleships.

An exception to the latter name source for SSBNs was made in 1983 when the RHODE ISLAND (SSBN 730) was renamed for Senator Henry M. (Scoop) Jackson immediately prior to launching.

Attack submarines have had several names sources. The U.S. Navy's first submarine was the HOLLAND (later SS 1), named for its designer, John P. Holland, who was alive when the craft was commissioned in 1900. Subsequent U.S. submarines were given "fish" names until 1911 when class letters and numerals were assigned (such as A-2). This scheme continued until 1931, at which time fish names were again used in addition to the class designations (and hull numbers). The class designations were discarded in the late 1930s.

After World War II the class letter-number names were again used for the small T (training) and K (hunter-killer) submarines, but they were soon given fish names. Postwar submarines continued the use of fish or marine-life names until 1971 when Admiral H. G. Rickover, then head of the Navy's nuclear-propulsion program, instituted naming of attack submarines for deceased members of Congress who had supported nuclear programs. Only four SSNs were so named.

The name source for attack submarines was changed to city names in 1974, with the first being LOS ANGELES (SSN 688). In 1983, however, Secretary of the Navy John Lehman directed that the then-building SSN 705 be named HYMAN G. RICKOVER, for Admiral Rickover whom he had forced to leave the Navy in January 1983. (This was the second recent U.S. Navy ship to be named for a living person, the first being the CARL VINSON/CVN 70.)

AIRCRAFT CARRIERS

Aircraft carriers have traditionally been named for American battles and older warships. The first U.S. carrier, however, the converted collier LANGLEY (CV 1), was named for American aviation pioneer Samuel P. Langley. Subsequent carriers were named for battles and older ships, as LEXINGTON (CV 2 and later CV 16) and RANGER (CV 4 and later CV 61). The CV 38 was named SHANGRI-LA for the mythical location of James Hilton's novel after President Franklin D. Roosevelt told the press, for security reasons, that the Doolittle carrier raid against Japan on 18 April 1942 had come from Shangri-La.

The CV 42 was renamed before completion for President Roosevelt, who died in office on 12 April 1945. Subsequently, the CV 67 was named for President John F. Kennedy, assassinated while in office in 1963. All subsequent carriers have been named for persons, with the CARL VINSON named while the congressman was still living.

BATTLESHIPS

Battleships (BB) have been named for States of the Union, except that the KEARSARGE (BB 5) carried the nickname of Vermont. Subsequently, state names have been assigned to cruisers and Trident strategic missile submarines.

CRUISERS

Cruisers were historically named for American cities, beginning with the ATLANTA and BOSTON completed in 1887. A notable exception was the CANBERRA (CA 70/CAG 2), named for the Australian capital and an Australian cruiser of that name sunk while operating with U.S. forces off Guadalcanal in 1942.

The 1975 changes in frigate (DLG/DLGN) designations led to 20 ships named for Navy and Marine personnel becoming cruisers (CG/CGN 16 through 35). The next six cruisers (CGN 36-41) were assigned state names.

The name source for cruisers was changed again, to American battles, with the Aegis program. The lead ship was the TICONDEROGA (CG 47) completed in 1983. However, the fifth ship of the class (CG 51) has been named THOMAS S. GATES, for a late Secretary of the Navy.

DESTROYERS

U.S. destroyers have traditionally been named for naval heroes and leaders, including Secretaries of the Navy, and inventors who have benefited the Navy. In 1983, the not-yet-started DDG 51 was named ARLEIGH BURKE for the former Chief of Naval Operations (1955–1961), "Thirty-one-knot" Burke, a sobriquet earned for his destroyer's exploits in World War II.

FRIGATES/ESCORTS

The frigate ship type evolved from the World War II-era destroyer escort (DE) and thus have destroyer-type names. The HAROLD E. HOLT (DE/FF 1074) remembers the deceased Australian prime minister who supported U.S. policies in the Vietnam War.

COMMAND SHIPS

Amphibious command ships (LCC/AGC), which evolved from the World War II amphibious force flagships (AGC), are named for mountains and ranges.

AMPHIBIOUS SHIPS

Amphibious assault ships (LHA/LPH) are named for battles fought by Marines.

Amphibious cargo ships (LKA/AKA) and amphibious transports (LPA/APA) are named for counties.

Amphibious transport docks (LPD) are named for cities that honor explorers and pioneers.

Dock landing ships (LSD) are named for historic sites and cities.

Tank landing ships (LST), named from 1955, are named for counties and parishes.

PATROL SHIPS AND CRAFT

Hydrofoil missile craft (PHM) are named after mythological characters.

Patrol combatants (PG/PGM) were named for small cities and towns.

MINE WARFARE SHIPS AND CRAFT

The ocean minesweepers (MSO) were all given adjectival names, a scheme continued with the MCM type. The new MSH type will have the bird names previously carried by coastal minesweepers.

AUXILIARY SHIPS

Destroyer tenders (AD) generally are named for geographic areas, except for the SAMUEL GOMPERS (AD 37), which honors an American labor leader.

Ammunition ships (AE) carry the names of explosives and volcanoes.

Store ships (AF) are named for star constellations.

Combat store ships (AFS), fast combat-support ships (AOE), and replenishment oilers (AOR) have city names.

Missile range instrumentation ships (AGM) carry a variety of names, including cities (WHEELING/T-AGM 8), "range" names (RANGE SENTINEL/T-AGM 22), and missile project names (REDSTONE/T-AGM 20), while the former Air Force ships honor generals (GENERAL H. H. ARNOLD/T-AGM 9).

Oceanographic ships (AGOR) and surveying ships (AGS) are generally named for oceanographers.

Ocean surveillance ships (T-AGOS) have attribute names.

Hospital ships (AH) have been assigned "mercy" names.

Cargo ships (T-AK/AKR) mostly have star and other cellestial names.

A helicopter touches down on the deck of the SES-200 during evaluation of the craft for possible naval use. After Coast Guard trials with the craft, that service purchased three similar surface effect ships. (1982, Bell Halter)

An amphibious squadron at anchor in Hong Kong: The BELLEAU WOOD (LHA 3), her flight deck crowded with Marine helicopters; the THOMASTON (LSD 28); and the TUSCALOOSA (LST 1187) demonstrate the three basic types of amphibious ships in the fleet today. (Giorgio Arra).

Oilers (AO/T-AOT) historically have been named for rivers with Indian names. The lead ship of the latest class, the HENRY J. KAISER (T-AO 187), however, honors American industrialist and World War II master of mass-producing ships.

Transports (T-AP) carry the names of deceased generals and admirals.

Repair ships (AR and ARL) and cable ships (T-ARC) are assigned mythological names.

Salvage ships (ARS) are named for terms related to salvage activity.

Submarine tenders (AS) carry a mixture of names—mythological (PROTEUS/AS 19) and submarine pioneers (SIMON LAKE/AS 33), with the HOWARD W. GILMORE (AS 16) having been named for a World War II submarine hero.

Submarine rescue ships (ASR) have historically had bird names, with the first ASRs having been converted World War I-era minesweepers of the Bird class.

Tugs (ATA/ATF) have Indian names.

Salvage and rescue ships (ATS) carry the names of American towns with English namesakes, a reasonable scheme for ships that were built in England.

Seaplane tenders (AV, with the AV 11 now AVM 1) had bay and sound names.

11 Strategic Missile Submarines

The submarine "leg" of the U.S. strategic offensive forces—often referred to as the "triad"—consists of 31 older strategic missile submarines (SSBN), armed with the Poseidon C-3 or Trident C-4 missile, and a small number of new, very large submarines carrying the Trident C-4 missile. The new submarines are being built at the rate of about one SSBN per year, with four ships in commission at the end of 1984.

Strategic missile submarines are at sea about 55 percent of the time on deterrent patrol with their missiles targeted at the Soviet Union and Eastern Europe. Since the USS GEORGE WASHINGTON began the first so-called deterrent patrol on 15 November 1960, U.S. SSBNs have conducted more than 2,000 such patrols, most of approximately 60 days duration.[1] The new Trident SSBNs operate in the Pacific while the 31 older submarines of the LAFAYETTE class, armed with Poseidon or Trident missiles, operate in the Atlantic-Mediterranean areas.

The number of SSBNs in commission will increase gradually into the early 1990s. At that time the 31 older submarines of the LAFAYETTE class will begin to reach the end of their expected 30-year service life. The SSBN force is then expected to decline rapidly, to perhaps a nadir of 15 to 17 new Trident submarines by about 1997. There will then be an increase to the expected force of 20 Trident submarines—10 operating in the Pacific, based at Bangor, Wash., and 10 in the Atlantic, based at Kings Bay, Ga.

The new Trident submarines carry 24 Submarine-Launched Ballistic Missiles (SLBM) compared with 16 missiles in earlier U.S. missile submarines. And, beginning with the ninth Trident SSBN, these submarines will have the improved D-5 missile (which will later be backfitted into the first eight Trident submarines after about ten years of service). The decision to provide the D-5 missile will cause some delays in the SSBN 734 and 735.

The basis for the Trident program was the STRAT-X study undertaken by the Department of Defense in 1967–1968 to determine future strategic weapon requirements. The study proposed a new class of missile submarines about the same size as the SSBN 616 class, with very-long-range (circa 6,000-n.mile) ballistic missiles carried external to the pressure hull.[2] The submarine was to have a relatively slow speed. This submarine—designated Underwater Long-range Missile System (ULMS)—evolved into the SSBN 726 class, with the reactor plant being the principal determinent of the submarine's size.

Members of Congress and DOD officials have periodically proposed the construction of smaller SLBM submarines to complement the SSBN 726 program; these efforts have been strongly resisted by the Navy's submarine community, and no progress has been made in this context.

Type	Class	Comm.	Active	Building	Reserve	Notes
SSBN 726	OHIO	1981—	4	7	—	24 Trident C-4 missiles
SSBN 616	LAFAYETTE	1965–1967	12	—	—	16 Trident C-4 missiles
SSBN 616	LAFAYETTE	1963–1964	19	—	—	16 Poseidon C-3 missiles

[1] These do not include the several Regulus strategic missile submarine patrols made from 1957 to 1964 in the Western Pacific by five submarines, the TUNNY (SSG 282), BARBERO (SSG 317), GRAYBACK (SSG 574), GROWLER (SSG 577), and HALIBUT (SSGN 587).

[2] This has been done in the U.S. and Soviet navies with cruise missiles.

The lead Trident submarine OHIO on the surface at high speed. The strategic missile submarines or "boomers" rarely steam on the surface and generally operate at slow speeds to reduce the probability of detection. U.S. submarines rarely have their hull numbers painted on their sail. (1983, U.S. Navy)

4 + 16 NUCLEAR-PROPELLED STRATEGIC MISSILE SUBMARINES: "OHIO" CLASS

Number	Name	FY/SCB	Builder	Laid down	Launched	Commissioned	Status
SSBN 726	OHIO	74	General Dynamics/Electric Boat	10 Apr 1976	7 Apr 1979	11 Nov 1981	**PA**
SSBN 727	MICHIGAN	75	General Dynamics/Electric Boat	4 Apr 1977	26 Apr 1980	11 Sep 1982	**PA**
SSBN 728	FLORIDA	75	General Dynamics/Electric Boat	9 June 1977	14 Nov 1981	18 June 1983	**PA**
SSBN 729	GEORGIA	76	General Dynamics/Electric Boat	7 Apr 1979	6 Nov 1982	11 Feb 1984	**PA**
SSBN 730	HENRY M. JACKSON	77	General Dynamics/Electric Boat	19 Jan 1981	15 Oct 1983	1985	Building
SSBN 731	ALABAMA	78	General Dynamics/Electric Boat	27 Aug 1981	19 May 1984	1985	Building
SSBN 732	ALASKA	78	General Dynamics/Electric Boat	9 Mar 1983	1984	1986	Building
SSBN 733	NEVADA	80	General Dynamics/Electric Boat	8 Aug 1983	1985	1986	Building
SSBN 734	. . . . . .	81	General Dynamics/Electric Boat		1986	1989	Building
SSBN 735	. . . . . .	83	General Dynamics/Electric Boat		1987	1989	Building
SSBN 736	. . . . . .	83	General Dynamics/Electric Boat		1988	1990	Building
SSBN 737	. . . . . .	84	General Dynamics/Electric Boat		1989	1991	Building
SSBN	(5 submarines)	85–89					Planned
SSBN	(3 submarines)	90–92					Planned

Displacement:	16,764 tons standard		Manning:	160 (15 officers + 145 enlisted)
	18,750 tons submerged		Missiles:	24 tubes for Trident C–4 SLBM in SSBN 726–733
Length:	560 feet (170 7 m) oa			24 tubes for Trident D–5 SLBM in later submarines
Beam:	42 feet (12.8 m)		Torpedo tubes:	4 21-inch (533-mm) tubes Mk 68 (amidships)
Draft:	36 ½ feet (11.1 m)		ASW weapons:	Mk 48 torpedoes
Propulsion:	2 steam turbines (General Electric); 1 shaft		Radars:	BPS–15 surface search
Reactors:	1 pressurized-reactor S8G (General Electric)		Sonars:	BQQ–6 bow mounted
Speed:	28 knots surface			BQR–15 towed array
	approx. 30 knots submerged		Fire control:	1 Mk 98 missile FCS
				1 Mk 118 torpedo FCS

These are the largest submarines yet built in the United States (the Soviet Typhoon SSBNs are almost half-again as large). The OHIO was laid down nine years after completion of the previous U.S. strategic missile submarine, the WILL ROGERS.

While the exact number of ships to be constructed has not been determined, current planning provides for between 15 and 17 submarines to be in service by the late 1990s when the last of the LAFAYETTE-class submarines are retired. An eventual force of 20 Trident submarines (480 missiles) is currently planned.

Class: The Trident program is considerably behind the schedule established in May 1972 when the weapon system was approved for development. The lead submarine was funded in FY 1974 with a schedule put forward at that time for constructing an initial series of 10 Trident SSBNs at an annual rate of 1-3-3-3, with these 10 submarines to have been completed by 1982.

The first Trident submarine was ordered on 25 July 1974 with a planned delivery of 30 April 1979. The shipyard agreed, however, to attempt to make delivery in December 1977 because of the high priority of the program. Subsequent delays caused by the Navy and problems at the shipyard have resulted in late deliveries of the early submarines, with authorizations for the first 10 submarines covering a 10-year period vice 4 years. The FY 1984–1988 five-year defense plan provides for the construction of 5 submarines at the rate of one SSBN per annum.

Cost: The SSBN cost in FY 1985 is $1,755 million plus $14.7 million for outfitting, and $24.2 million for post-delivery costs, a total of $1,793.9 million.

Design: SCB No. 304.74. The largest submarines yet built in the West, the size of these craft was determined primarily by their reactor plant. These submarines have a conservative design with the bow sonar dome and amidships torpedo tubes of later attack submarine designs. These are the only 24-tube strategic missile submarines built by any nation, with the Soviet Typhoon-class SSBNs each having 20 tubes.

The ships have comfortable accommodations for their crews, which is about the same size as in previous American SSBNs. Three logistic hatches, in the forward (control-accommodation section), center (missile), and after (engineering) compartments have escape trunks that can be removed when in port to provide large, six-foot-diameter logistic hatches. These provide for the rapid transfer of supply pallets, equipment replacement modules, and even machinery components, permitting a significant reduction in the time required for replenishment and maintenance. (The standard U.S. submarine hatches are 26 inches in diameter.)

Engineering: The S8G reactor plant was originally intended to provide up to 60,000 shp, having been based on an earlier design for a large, high-speed cruise missile submarine. Its actual horsepower is publicly reported as being in excess of 30,000 shp, but significantly less than the 60,000 goal.

The S7G reactor plant, a land-based prototype of the OHIO plant, is installed at West Milton, Conn.

Reportedly, the OHIO is significantly quieter than the ship's design goals for self-quieting, and at low speeds (i.e., when using natural convection rather than pumps for the circulation of pressurized water in the primary loop) the OHIO may be the quietest nuclear submarine yet constructed.

Manning: These submarines, as all other U.S. SSBNs, have alternating "blue" and "gold" crews; while one crew is at sea, the other is engaged in training, mostly with system simulators, leave, medical treatment, and other shore activities. The officer complement of these submarines includes a medical officer, but, as with earlier SSBNs, he will probably be deleted from the crew after sufficient experience is developed for the special medical problems related to Trident SSBN operations.

Missiles: These submarines are initially being fitted with the Trident C-4 missile. Beginning with the ninth ship they will be fitted with the Trident D-5 missile, which will be backfitted into the earlier craft. The completion of the SSBN 734 and 735 is being delayed about one year to provide them with the D-5 missile.

The OHIO fired the first Trident C-4 to be launched from this class on 17 January 1982.

Names: SSBN 730 was originally named RHODE ISLAND; renamed for Senator "Scoop" Jackson, long-time supporter of nuclear and defense programs, following his death in September 1983.

Operational: The OHIO made her first operational deployment from 1 October 1982 to 10 December 1982. The first squadron of nine or ten submarines will operate in the Pacific, based at Bangor, Wash., in Submarine Squadron 17, established on 5 January 1981. The second squadron will be formed in the Atlantic, based at Kings Bay, Ga.

These submarines are intended to conduct 70-day patrols interrupted by 25-day overhaul/replenishment periods, during which time the blue/gold crews change over. Under this schedule the submarines undergo a lengthy overhaul and reactor refueling (and conversion of the first eight submarines to the D-5 missile) every ten years.

Sonar: The BQQ-6 sonar is similar to the BQQ-5 in attack submarines less the active sonar elements. A towed array is provided in the BQQ-6 system.

The OHIO is pushed to her berth at the Bangor submarine base by the tugs MANHATTAN (YTB 779), forward, and OTTUMWA (YTB 761), aft, while other tugs stand by. The turn-around phase of SSBN operations is undertaken as rapidly as possible to obtain maximum on-patrol time. (1982, U.S. Navy; PH1 Harold Gerwien)

The MICHIGAN underway in the Atlantic with all masts and periscopes retracted into the sail structure. (1982, General Dynamics/Electric Boat)

The OHIO undergoing a nighttime degaussing at submarine base in Bangor. (1983, U.S. Navy)

The OHIO in the dry dock at the new Trident base at Bangor, Wash. A small deck structure covers the aftermost logistics hatch; the sheath along the port side houses the towed array sonar; the side plates house sonar antennas on the after diving planes. (1982, U.S. Navy; PH2 R. Hayes)

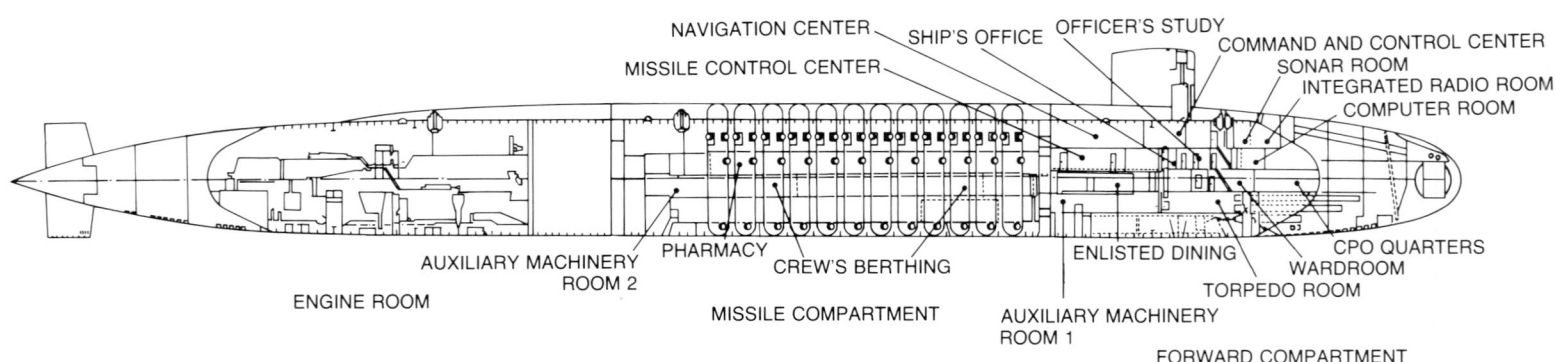

A high-oblique view of the OHIO on sea trials. She has two periscopes and an antenna mast raised. The Tridents are the largest submarines built in the West, but they are dwarfed by the Soviet Typhoon-class SBBNs, which are about the same length, but with a 76-foot beam and a displacement of some 25,000 tons submerged. (1981, U.S. Navy; PH2 William Garlinghouse)

31 NUCLEAR-PROPELLED STRATEGIC MISSILE SUBMARINES: "LAFAYETTE" AND "BENJAMIN FRANKLIN" CLASSES

Number	Name	FY	Builder	Laid down	Launched	Commissioned	Status
SSBN 616	LAFAYETTE	61	General Dynamics/Electric Boat	17 Jan 1961	8 May 1962	23 Apr 1963	**AA**
SSBN 617	ALEXANDER HAMILTON	61	General Dynamics/Electric Boat	26 June 1961	18 Aug 1962	27 June 1963	**AA**
SSBN 619	ANDREW JACKSON	61	Mare Island Naval Shipyard	26 Apr 1961	15 Sep 1962	3 July 1963	**AA**
SSBN 620	JOHN ADAMS	61	Portsmouth Naval Shipyard	19 May 1961	12 Jan 1963	12 May 1964	**AA**
SSBN 622	JAMES MONROE	S61	Newport News Shipbuilding	31 July 1961	4 Aug 1962	7 Dec 1963	**AA**
SSBN 623	NATHAN HALE	S61	General Dynamics/Electric Boat	2 Oct 1961	12 Jan 1963	23 Nov 1963	**AA**
SSBN 624	WOODROW WILSON	S61	Mare Island Naval Shipyard	13 Sep 1961	22 Feb 1963	27 Dec 1963	**AA**
SSBN 625	HENRY CLAY	S61	Newport News Shipbuilding	22 Oct 1961	30 Nov 1962	20 Feb 1964	**AA**
SSBN 626	DANIEL WEBSTER	S61	General Dynamics/Electric Boat	28 Dec 1961	27 Apr 1963	9 Apr 1964	**AA**
SSBN 627	JAMES MADISON	62	Newport News Shipbuilding	5 Mar 1962	15 Mar 1963	28 July 1964	**AA**
SSBN 628	TECUMSEH	62	General Dynamics/Electric Boat	1 June 1962	22 June 1963	29 May 1964	**AA**
SSBN 629	DANIEL BOONE	62	Mare Island Naval Shipyard	6 Feb 1962	22 June 1963	23 Apr 1964	**AA**
SSBN 630	JOHN C. CALHOUN	62	Newport News Shipbuilding	4 June 1962	22 June 1963	15 Sep 1964	**AA**
SSBN 631	ULYSSES S. GRANT	62	General Dynamics/Electric Boat	18 Aug 1962	2 Nov 1963	17 July 1964	**AA**
SSBN 632	VON STEUBEN	62	Newport News Shipbuilding	4 Sep 1962	18 Oct 1963	30 Sep 1964	**AA**
SSBN 633	CASIMIR PULASKI	62	General Dynamics/Electric Boat	12 Jan 1963	1 Feb 1964	14 Aug 1964	**AA**
SSBN 634	STONEWALL JACKSON	62	Mare Island Naval Shipyard	4 July 1962	30 Nov 1963	26 Aug 1964	**AA**
SSBN 635	SAM RAYBURN	62	Newport News Shipbuilding	3 Dec 1962	20 Dec 1963	2 Dec 1964	**AA**
SSBN 636	NATHANIEL GREENE	62	Portsmouth Naval Shipyard	21 May 1962	12 May 1964	19 Dec 1964	**AA**
SSBN 640	BENJAMIN FRANKLIN	63	General Dynamics/Electric Boat	25 May 1963	5 Dec 1964	22 Oct 1965	**AA**
SSBN 641	SIMON BOLIVAR	63	Newport News Shipbuilding	17 Apr 1963	22 Aug 1964	29 Oct 1965	**AA**
SSBN 642	KAMEHAMEHA	63	Mare Island Naval Shipyard	2 May 1963	16 Jan 1965	10 Dec 1965	**AA**
SSBN 643	GEORGE BANCROFT	63	General Dynamics/Electric Boat	24 Aug 1963	20 Mar 1965	22 Jan 1966	**AA**
SSBN 644	LEWIS AND CLARK	63	Newport News Shipbuilding	29 July 1963	21 Nov 1964	22 Dec 1965	**AA**
SSBN 645	JAMES K. POLK	63	General Dynamics/Electric Boat	23 Nov 1963	22 May 1965	16 Apr 1966	**AA**
SSBN 654	GEORGE C. MARSHALL	64	Newport News Shipbuilding	2 Mar 1964	21 May 1965	29 Apr 1966	**AA**
SSBN 655	HENRY L. STIMSON	64	General Dynamics/Electric Boat	4 Apr 1964	13 Nov 1965	20 Aug 1966	**AA**
SSBN 656	GEORGE WASHINGTON CARVER	64	Newport News Shipbuilding	24 Aug 1964	14 Aug 1965	15 June 1966	**AA**
SSBN 657	FRANCIS SCOTT KEY	64	General Dynamics/Electric Boat	5 Dec 1964	23 Apr 1966	3 Dec 1966	**AA**
SSBN 658	MARIANO G. VALLEJO	64	Mare Island Naval Shipyard	7 July 1964	23 Oct 1965	16 Dec 1966	**AA**
SSBN 659	WILL ROGERS	64	General Dynamics/Electric Boat	20 Mar 1965	21 July 1966	1 Apr 1967	**AA**

Displacement:	6,650 tons light
	7,250 tons standard
	8,250 tons submerged
Length:	425 feet (129.6 m) oa
Beam:	33 feet (10.06 m)
Draft:	31½ feet (9.6 m)
Propulsion:	2 steam turbines; 15,000 shp; 1 shaft
Reactors:	1 pressurized-water S5W (Westinghouse)
Speed:	approx. 20 knots surface
	approx. 25 knots submerged
Manning:	143 (13 officers + 130 enlisted)
Missiles:	16 tubes for Poseidon C-3 except
	16 tubes for Trident C-4 in SSBN 627, 629, 630, 632–634, 640, 641, 643, 655, 657, 658
Torpedo tubes:	4 21-inch (533-mm) Mk 65 (bow)
Torpedoes:	Mk 48
Radars:	BPS–11/11A
Sonars:	BQR–7
	BQR–15 towed array
	BQS–4
Fire control:	Mk 113 torpedo/missile FCS

These submarines were built to carry the Polaris SLBM, with all subsequently being modified to carry the Poseidon C-3 missile and the last 12 submarines later being upgraded to fire the Trident C-4 missile. All 31 submarines are operational in the Atlantic-Mediterranean areas.

Class: The last 12 submarines of this design are officially the BENJAMIN FRANKLIN class (see Design notes). Four additional submarines were proposed in the fiscal 1965 shipbuilding program to complete the then-planned 45 submarine program (five squadrons of nine submarines each); the additional submarines were cancelled by Secretary of Defense Robert McNamara.

Design: SCB No. 216. These submarines are enlarged and improved versions of the previous ETHAN ALLEN class. Like the ETHAN ALLEN class, the pressure hulls are constructed of HY-80 steel.[3]

The last 12 submarines of this class have quieter machinery installations and other minor differences. The DANIEL WEBSTER has bow-mounted diving planes instead of sail planes (as in all other U.S. SSBNs).

Missiles: The first 8 submarines initially deployed with the Polaris A-2 missile and the 23 later units with the Polaris A-3 missile. All were converted during 1970–1978 to launch the Poseidon C-3 missile. Subsequently, 12 of these submarines were selected for modification to launch the Trident C-4 missile. Their dates of conversion are listed below; those modifications made at Cape Canaveral, Fla., were undertaken by technicians from the Norfolk Naval Shipyard. The more lengthy modification periods indicate the work being accomplished during an overhaul.

[3] HY-80 indicates High Yield steel capable of withstanding pressures of 80,000 pounds per square inch.

The VON STEUBEN at high speed. This submarine initially carried the Polaris A-3 strategic missile; subsequently updated to carry the Poseidon C-3 with multiple, independently targeted warheads. The last 12 submarines of this design have been again refitted to carry the Trident D-4 missile. (1983, Giorgio Arra)

VON STEUBEN (1983, Giorgio Arra)

The tug TOMAHAWK (YTB 789) nudges the HENRY L. STIMSON alongside the FRANCIS SCOTT KEY, which is moored to the submarine tender SIMON LAKE (AS 33) at Kings Bay, Ga. These and other SSBNs of Submarine Squadron 16 have been rearmed with the Trident C-4 missile. The squadron shifted from Rota, Spain, to Kings Bay in 1979.

The FRANCIS SCOTT KEY made the first Trident C-4 deployment beginning in October 1979.

SSBN	FY	Yard	Conversion
627	79	Newport News Shipbuilding	Aug 1979–Feb 1982
629	80	Cape Canaveral, Fla.	Apr 1980–May 1980
630	80	Cape Canaveral, Fla.	June 1980–Aug 1980
632	80	Newport News Shipbuilding	Jan 1980–May 1982
633	80	Newport News Shipbuilding	July 1980–Dec 1982
634	81	Cape Canaveral, Fla.	Sep 1981–Nov 1981
640	80	Portsmouth Naval Shipyard	Nov 1979–Sep 1981
641	79	Portsmouth Naval Shipyard	Mar 1979–Dec 1980
643	80	Portsmouth Naval Shipyard	June 1980–Mar 1982
655	80	Cape Canaveral, Fla.	Dec 1979–Feb 1980
657	79	Cape Canaveral, Fla.	Sep 1978–Dec 1978
658	79	Cape Canaveral, Fla.	Sep 1979–Nov 1979

Operational: All 31 submarines are assigned to the Atlantic Fleet, operating out of New London, Conn.; Charleston, S.C.; Kings Bay, Ga.; and Holy Loch, Scotland.

These submarines were designed originally for a 20-year service life, but the Navy has determined that they will be able to operate successfully for 30 years.

"ETHAN ALLEN" CLASS

Five ballistic missile submarines of the ETHAN ALLEN (SSBN 608) class were built, being completed in 1961–1963. All were withdrawn from the strategic role in 1980–1981 and employed briefly in the attack submarine role. (See Chapter 12 for details and status.)

"GEORGE WASHINGTON" CLASS

The U.S. Navy's first five ballistic missile submarines were based on the SKIPJACK (SSN 585) design, lengthened to provide space for 16 Polaris missile tubes and related equipment. These submarines were completed in 1960–1961 after a remarkably rapid design and construction period. Three of these submarines were withdrawn from the strategic missile role and changed to SSNs (see Chapter 12). The two others were stricken while still in a missile submarine status: THEODORE ROOSEVELT (SSBN 600) and ABRAHAM LINCOLN (SSBN 602), both stricken on 1 December 1982.

The DANIEL BOONE departing the naval base at Charleston, S.C. Note the raised, mast-mounted BPS-15 radar on the starboard side of the sail. A safety track zigzags between the missile tubes; the track permits men to work on deck with safety lines while at sea. (1983, Giorgio Arra)

The WILL ROGERS, last of the 41 Polaris-Poseidon submarines to be completed, arriving at Groton, Conn. (1980, L. & L. van Ginderen)

The DANIEL WEBSTER, the only U.S. SSBN with bow-mounted diving planes, maneuvers in the Thames River off New London with the help of a pair of YTBs. (1975, U.S. Navy)

SSBN STUDY CONCEPTS

Several alternative SSBN designs were considered by the Navy during the 1970s because of the rapidly increasing costs of the Trident program. In general, these were for smaller submarines, generally with fewer than 24 missiles. Included was a proposal to construct additional LAFAYETTE-class submarines with minimal updating. All of these proposals were eventually rejected by the Navy, primarily on the basis of being less "efficient" than the Trident design.

The latest proposal for a smaller SSBN came from President Reagan's Commission On Strategic Forces, chaired by General Brent Scowcroft. In its final report, dated 6 April 1983, the commission recommended:

Consistent with the long-term program recommended for the ICBM force . . . to reduce the value of individual targets, the Commission recommends that research begin now on smaller ballistic missile-carrying submarines, each carrying fewer missiles than the Trident, as a potential follow-on to the Trident submarine force. The objective of such research should be to design a submarine and missile system that would, as much as possible, reduce the value of each platform and also present radically different problems to a Soviet attacker than does the Trident submarine force. This work should proceed in such a way that a decision to construct and deploy such a submarine force could be rapidly implemented should Soviet progress in anti-submarine warfare so dictate.

12 Submarines

The U.S. Navy operates just over 90 nuclear-propelled attack submarines (SSN) and 4 diesel-electric attack submarines (SS). The roles of the Navy's attack submarines are increasing in importance, in part because of the recent developments in attack submarine weapons (undersea-launch Harpoon and Tomahawk) and the availability of advanced sensors to provide enhanced targeting capabilities (e.g., towed-array sonars, satellites).

In peacetime these submarines undertake a variety of missions, among the most important being intelligence collection and anti-submarine training of air, surface, and other submarine forces. In wartime the primary mission of U.S. attack submarines would be operations against Soviet "attack" and strategic missile submarines as well as anti-surface ship, land attack (with Tomahawk), and mining operations. The ASW activities would center on establishing "barriers" across probable routes of Soviet submarines and directly supporting carrier battle groups and possibly other surface forces.

The current U.S. Navy force goal is 100 SSNs. Some Navy authorities have estimated that requirements in the 1990s and beyond could be as high as 140 submarines. The Navy is now building SSNs at the rate of 4 of the Los Angeles class per year, a rate to sustain a force of more than 100 SSNs. The retirement of older SSNs as they reach a nominal service life of about 25 years, however, will probably hold the force at just over 90 submarines. (Ninety attack submarines was the Navy's force goal from 1973 to 1981—that goal was never achieved; before that a force of 120 attack submarines, both diesel and nuclear, was authorized.)

An advanced attack submarine is being designed for construction in the 1990s (see below). It will follow the trend of U.S. SSN classes of being larger than the previous design, but the next class is planned to have significant improvements in combat capability. The previous SSN 594, 637, and 688 classes have had essentially the same weapons and sensors (with upgrade) with the major changes in design being in the "after end"—the propulsion plant.

In addition to the attack submarines, one nuclear submarine, the SEAWOLF, is employed for research, and two former Polaris submarines, the JOHN MARSHALL and SAM HOUSTON, are being converted to special-mission submarines. The latter will serve as swimmer/commando transports and possibly in other roles. (The transport submarine GRAYBACK/SS 574 was stricken in 1984.)

Four diesel-electric attack submarines of 1950s construction remained in service when this edition went to press. These craft have been highly successful in exercises despite their age and limited capabilities. Intensive efforts by several members of Congress, naval analysts, and even naval officers to initiate development of a small number of advanced diesel undersea craft for ASW training and limited combat operations have met with strong opposition from the Navy's leadership. This opposition is based on a fear of losing SSN funding in favor of the diesel craft.

Finally, the Navy operates one diesel research submarine, the deep-diving DOLPHIN. She conducts research in a number of fields, including, most recently, tests of laser devices for communications with submerged submarines.

(The Navy's research submersibles, including the nuclear-powered NR-1, are listed in Chapter 27.)

Type	Class/Ship	Comm.	Active	Building	Reserve	Notes
SSN 688	Los Angeles	1976–	29	15	—	class in production
SSN 685	Lipscomb	1974	1	—	—	
SSN 671	Narwhal	1969	1	—	—	
SSN 637	Sturgeon	1967–1975	37	—	—	
SSN 594	Permit	1962–1967	13	—	—	1 additional submarine lost
SSN 608	Ethan Allen	1961–1963	2*	—	2	ex-Polaris missile type
SSN 598	George Washington	1959–1961	—	—	3	ex-Polaris missile type
SSN 597	Tullibee	1960	1	—	—	no longer first line
SSN 587	Halibut	1960	—	—	1	ex-Regulus missile type
SSN 586	Triton	1959	—	—	1	ex-radar picket
SSN 585	Skipjack	1959–1961	5	—	—	1 additional submarine lost
SSN 578	Skate	1957–1959	3	—	1	
SSN 575	Seawolf	1957	1	—	—	research submarine
SSN 571	Nautilus	1954	—	—	1	memorial
SS 580	Barbel	1959	3	—	—	
SS 576	Darter	1956	1	—	—	
AGSS 555	Dolphin	1968	1	—	—	research submarine

* In conversion to special-mission submarines.

A new attack submarine goes to sea. The SAN FRANCISCO leaves her building yard and steams down the James River into Hampton Roads. The U.S. Navy has sought to build quality submarines to overcome the Soviet Union's quantitative lead of almost 3-to-1 in undersea craft. (1981, Newport News Shipbuilding)

ADVANCED SUBMARINE DESIGN: "SEAWOLF" (SSN 21)

Displacement:	
	approx. 10,000 tons
Length:	approx. 350 feet (106.7 m) oa
Beam:	
Draft:	
Propulsion:	2 steam turbines; 30,000 + shp; 1 propulsor
Reactors:	1 pressurized-water
Speed:	
	30 + knots submerged
Manning:	approx. 130
Missiles:	Harpoon and Tomahawk SSMs launched from torpedo tubes
Torpedo tubes:	8 30-inch (760-mm) (amidships)
ASW weapons:	Mk 48 torpedoes
	ASW Stand-Off Weapon
Radars:	
Sonars:	
Fire control:	

The Navy plans to construct a new class of nuclear-propelled attack submarines to succeed the Los Angeles class. The emphasis in this class will be on: (1) improved machinery, (2) quieting, and (3) improved combat systems, both sensors and additional weapons. These submarines are expected to be slightly faster than the Los Angeles class and to have more torpedo tubes and internally stowed weapons. There will be no external Tomahawk VLS tubes.

The Navy has designated this class as SSN-21, indicating an attack submarine for the 21st century. For a brief period the Navy considered assigning the hull number SSN 21 to the lead submarine; that number was previously carried by the submarine F-2 (initially named Barracuda), completed in 1912.

Estimates for the construction of about 30 submarines beginning in fiscal 1989, at an eventual production rate of three or four submarines per year, is $36 *billion*. Navy cost criteria for the fiscal 1985 budget was $1.8 *billion* for the lead ship and $1.2 *billion* for follow-on ships.

The lead submarine is expected to be requested in the fiscal 1989 shipbuilding program.

The decision to construct a new SSN class was made in 1982. This followed a Navy decision one year earlier *not* to construct a new SSN. The Commander, Naval Sea Systems Command, Vice Admiral Earl B. Fowler, Jr., told a congressional committee on 30 July 1981, that

We are not designing one [an advanced SSN]. We reviewed back in early 1981, all the design efforts that we had going on in Electric Boat, and decided to stop the design efforts on all the new classes of submarines and to proceed on a course of upgrading the 688 class as the attack submarine.

No conspicuously cost-effective candidate to follow the SSN 688 class emerged from the studies of alternative attack submarines. The CNO directed that effort toward the design of the Fleet Attack Submarine (a smaller, less capable submarine) and the SSNX (a larger, more capable submarine) should be discontinued. The CNO also directed that highest program priority be placed on improving the capability of the SSN 688 class and existing ASW weapons.[1]

Subsequently, in the summer of 1982, at about the time of the change of CNO, the Navy decided to seek development of a new SSN class (tentatively designated SSNX).

Design: The new submarine will be slightly shorter in length than the Los Angeles class but will have a greater diameter to provide a displacement almost one-third greater than the previous class.

As indicated in the drawing, the new SSN will be fitted with bow torpedo tubes, retractable bow diving planes vice sail-mounted planes, a more streamlined sail structure, a three-surface tail configuration, and a propulsor (similar in concept to the Mk 48 torpedo) vice conventional propeller.

The torpedo tubes will be of 30-inch diameter to provide for quiet "swim-out" of Mk 48 torpedoes and, eventually, the possible launching of larger-diameter torpedoes. (Modern Soviet SSNs are reported to carry torpedoes of 650 mm.)

The submarine will have internal stowage for about twice the number of tube-launched weapons now carried by U.S. submarines, i.e., about 50 weapons in the new SSN including those carried in torpedo tubes.

Improved machinery will be fitted to provide increased speed, and improved sonar will be installed.

Name: The lead ship was assigned the name Seawolf in 1985, with the expectation that the SSN 575 with that name, the U.S. Navy's second nuclear-propelled submarine, will be retired before the SSN-21 is completed. The previous USS Seawolf (SS 197) was sunk by U.S. forces during World War II.

[1] See page 78 for the characteristics of these alternative submarine designs.

Advanced submarine design, artist's concept.

29 + 33 NUCLEAR-PROPELLED ATTACK SUBMARINES: "LOS ANGELES" CLASS

Number	Name	FY	Builder	Laid down	Launched	Commissioned	Status
SSN 688	LOS ANGELES	70	Newport News Shipbuilding	8 Jan 1972	6 Apr 1974	13 Nov 1976	**PA**
SSN 689	BATON ROUGE	70	Newport News Shipbuilding	18 Nov 1972	26 Apr 1975	25 June 1977	**AA**
SSN 690	PHILADELPHIA	70	General Dynamics/Electric Boat	12 Aug 1972	19 Oct 1974	25 June 1977	**AA**
SSN 691	MEMPHIS	71	Newport News Shipbuilding	23 June 1973	3 Apr 1976	17 Dec 1977	**AA**
SSN 692	OMAHA	71	General Dynamics/Electric Boat	27 Jan 1973	21 Feb 1976	11 Mar 1978	**PA**
SSN 693	CINCINNATI	71	Newport News Shipbuilding	6 Apr 1974	19 Feb 1977	10 June 1978	**AA**
SSN 694	GROTON	71	General Dynamics/Electric Boat	3 Aug 1973	9 Oct 1976	8 July 1978	**AA**
SSN 695	BIRMINGHAM	72	Newport News Shipbuilding	26 Apr 1975	29 Oct 1977	16 Dec 1978	**AA**
SSN 696	NEW YORK CITY	72	General Dynamics/Electric Boat	15 Dec 1973	18 June 1977	3 Mar 1978	**PA**
SSN 697	INDIANAPOLIS	72	General Dynamics/Electric Boat	19 Oct 1974	30 July 1977	5 Jan 1980	**PA**
SSN 698	BREMERTON	72	General Dynamics/Electric Boat	6 May 1976	22 July 1978	28 Mar 1981	**PA**
SSN 699	JACKSONVILLE	72	General Dynamics/Electric Boat	21 Feb 1976	18 Nov 1978	16 May 1981	**AA**
SSN 700	DALLAS	73	General Dynamics/Electric Boat	9 Oct 1976	28 Apr 1979	18 July 1981	**AA**
SSN 701	LA JOLLA	73	General Dynamics/Electric Boat	16 Oct 1976	11 Aug 1979	24 Oct 1981	**PA**
SSN 702	PHOENIX	73	General Dynamics/Electric Boat	30 July 1977	8 Dec 1979	19 Dec 1981	**AA**
SSN 703	BOSTON	73	General Dynamics/Electric Boat	11 Aug 1978	19 Apr 1980	30 Jan 1982	**AA**
SSN 704	BALTIMORE	73	General Dynamics/Electric Boat	21 May 1979	13 Dec 1980	24 July 1982	**AA**
SSN 705	CITY OF CORPUS CHRISTI	73	General Dynamics/Electric Boat	4 Sep 1979	25 Apr 1981	8 Jan 1983	**AA**
SSN 706	ALBUQUERQUE	74	General Dynamics/Electric Boat	27 Dec 1979	13 Mar 1982	21 May 1983	**AA**
SSN 707	PORTSMOUTH	74	General Dynamics/Electric Boat	8 May 1980	18 Sep 1982	1 Oct 1983	**PA**
SSN 708	MINNEAPOLIS-SAINT PAUL	74	General Dynamics/Electric Boat	20 Jan 1981	19 Mar 1983	10 Mar 1984	**AA**
SSN 709	HYMAN G. RICKOVER	74	General Dynamics/Electric Boat	24 July 1981	27 Aug 1983	8 Sep 1984	**AA**
SSN 710	AUGUSTA	74	General Dynamics/Electric Boat	1 Apr 1982	21 Jan 1984	Feb 1985	Building
SSN 711	SAN FRANCISCO	75	Newport News Shipbuilding	26 May 1977	27 Oct 1979	24 Apr 1981	**PA**
SSN 712	ATLANTA	75	Newport News Shipbuilding	17 Aug 1978	16 Aug 1980	6 Mar 1982	**AA**
SSN 713	HOUSTON	75	Newport News Shipbuilding	29 Jan 1979	21 Mar 1981	25 Sep 1982	**PA**
SSN 714	NORFOLK	76	Newport News Shipbuilding	1 Aug 1979	31 Oct 1981	21 May 1983	**AA**
SSN 715	BUFFALO	76	Newport News Shipbuilding	25 Jan 1980	8 May 1982	5 Nov 1983	**AA**
SSN 716	SALT LAKE CITY	77	Newport News Shipbuilding	26 Aug 1980	16 Oct 1982	12 May 1984	**PA**
SSN 717	OLYMPIA	77	Newport News Shipbuilding	31 Mar 1981	30 Apr 1983	Sep 1984	**PA**
SSN 718	HONOLULU	77	Newport News Shipbuilding	10 Nov 1981	24 Sep 1983	Feb 1985	Building
SSN 719	PROVIDENCE	78	General Dynamics/Electric Boat	14 Oct 1982	2 June 1984	1985	Building
SSN 720	PITTSBURGH	79	General Dynamics/Electric Boat	9 Apr 1983	Dec 1984	1986	Building
SSN 721	. . . . . .	80	Newport News Shipbuilding	5 Jan 1983	Nov 1984	1986	Building
SSN 722	. . . . . .	80	Newport News Shipbuilding	6 July 1983	1985	1986	Building
SSN 723	. . . . . .	81	Newport News Shipbuilding		1985	1987	Building
SSN 724	. . . . . .	81	General Dynamics/Electric Boat		1986	1987	Building
SSN 725	. . . . . .	82	General Dynamics/Electric Boat		1986	1988	Building
SSN 750	NEWPORT NEWS	82	Newport News Shipbuilding	3 Mar 1984	1986	1987	Building
SSN 751	. . . . . .	83	General Dynamics/Electric Boat		1986	1988	Authorized
SSN 752	. . . . . .	83	General Dynamics/Electric Boat			1988	Authorized
SSN 753	. . . . . .	84	Newport News Shipbuilding			1990	Authorized
SSN 754	. . . . . .	84	General Dynamics/Electric Boat			1990	Authorized
SSN 755	. . . . . .	84	General Dynamics/Electric Boat			1990	Authorized
SSN	(4 submarines)	85					Planned
SSN	(4 submarines)	86					Planned
SSN	(4 submarines)	87					Planned
SSN	(4 submarines)	88					Planned
SSN	(4 submarines)	89					Planned

Displacement:	6,200 tons standard		Torpedo tubes:	4 21-inch (533-mm) tubes Mk 67 (amidships)
	6,900 tons submerged		ASW weapons:	Mk 48 torpedoes
Length:	360 feet (109.7 m) oa			SUBROC in SSN 688–699
Beam:	33 feet (10.1 m)		Radars:	BPS–15A surface search
Draft:	32⅓ feet (9.85 m)		Sonars:	BQQ–5 bow mounted
Propulsion:	2 steam turbines; approx. 30,000 shp; 1 shaft			BQR–15
Reactors:	1 pressurized-water S6G (General Electric)			BQR–26 in some submarines
Speed:	_____			BQS–13
	30+ knots submerged			BQS–15
Manning:	133 (13 officers + 120 enlisted)			towed array
Missiles:	Harpoon and Tomahawk SSMs launched from torpedo tubes		Fire control:	1 Mk 113 torpedo FCS in SSN 688–699 (to be refitted with Mk 117)
	12 vertical launch tubes for Tomahawk SSM in SSN 719 and later submarines			1 Mk 117 torpedo FCS in SSN 700 and later submarines

This is the world's largest class of nuclear-propelled submarines with 64 submarines planned through the fiscal 1989 program. These are large attack submarines, developed to counter the Soviet Victor fast-attack submarines that were first completed in 1967–1968. The LOS ANGELES submarines are about five knots faster than the previous U.S. STURGEON class, the higher speed being the principal advantage over the earlier class; however, the LOS ANGELES class is about half again as large in terms of displacement and considerably more expensive (see Cost notes). According to official statements, with the LOS ANGELES "the speed threshold which had been established by SKIPJACK 18 years earlier was finally surpassed."

The Soviet Alfa SSN and possibly Papa and Oscar SSGNs are significantly faster than the LOS ANGELES class.

Construction of this class continues, with an improved version of the LOS ANGELES being planned for later ships. From SSN 721 these submarines will have their control planes moved from the sail to the bow and made retractable, and will be provided with other features for under-ice operations. There will also be improvements in sonar and ship quieting.

Class: This is the largest class of nuclear submarines yet constructed by any nation (followed in numbers by the 37 STURGEON-class SSNs and about that number of Soviet Delta-class SSBNs). Twenty additional submarines of this class are planned for construction in the FY 1985–1989 defense plan; these would bring the total class to 64 submarines.

Classification: Submarine hull numbers 726 through 749 were reserved for Trident SSBNs.

Cost: The average cost of each SSN in the FY 1985 program is to be $720 million plus $10.5 million for outfitting, and $10.9 million for post-delivery costs, i.e., a total of more than $741 million per submarine. While cost comparisons of ship classes are difficult, the last (37th) STURGEON cost $186 million compared with the 32nd LOS ANGELES which had an estimated cost of $343 million in same-year dollars.

Design: SCB No. 303. This was the first U.S. nuclear submarine design for which Newport News Shipbuilding was the lead yard; Electric Boat or the Portsmouth yard was the lead for all previous "nukes." These are large SSNs, the increase in size over the STURGEON class being due primarily to the installation of the larger, more capable S6G reactor plant in an effort to regain the speed loss of the PERMIT and STURGEON classes.

The LOS ANGELES also has improved sonar and fire control systems (that are being retrofitted to the STURGEON class) compared with previous classes. Most units will be backfitted with 12 vertical-launch Tomahawk missile tubes (see below). The class is not fitted, however, to carry mines.

These submarines have berthing for only 95 enlisted men; the remainder use sleeping bags in available space or "hot bunk." The ships are considered to be quite crowded in comparison with other SSNs.

Electronics: The large towed-array passive sonar is carried in a sheath-like housing fitted to the upper starboard side of the hull.

The submarines fitted with the Mk 113 (analog) fire control system cannot carry the Tomahawk missile, while those with the Mk 117 (digital) cannot carry the SUBROC. All will be refitted with the Mk 117 and are to be armed eventually with the ASW Stand-Off Weapon (SOW).

The SAN FRANCISCO at high speed with one of her periscopes in the fully extended position. The sheath of her towed array runs along the starboard side of her hull with the safety track on top. Modern submarines have limited deck space. (1981, Newport News Shipbuilding)

Engineering: The S6G reactor is estimated to have an initial fuel core operating life of 10 to 13 years.

Missiles: The Harpoon and Tomahawk missiles can be launched from the torpedo tubes in this class, with the latter limited to ships with the Mk 117 fire control system. The SSN 719 and later units will have 12 vertical launch tubes for Tomahawk missiles fitted forward, between the pressure hull and sonar sphere, in space previously used for ballast tanks. (Under current plans 33 of the proposed 64 submarines would have VLS Tomahawk.) The ATLANTA became the first ship operationally armed with the T-ASM version in November 1983.

Names: The SSN 705 was originally to be named CHICAGO; changed while under construction to CORPUS CHRISTI for the Texas city by that name. The name was previously borne by the frigate PF 44 (launched in 1943) while the seaplane tender ALBERMARLE (AV 5) was converted to a helicopter repair ship (ARVH 1) during the Vietnam War and re-named CORPUS CHRISTI BAY (she was operated by the Military Sealift Command for the Army). After protests from Catholic groups, the SSN 705 was commissioned as the CITY OF CORPUS CHRISTI.

The MINNEAPOLIS-SAINT PAUL honors the "twin cities" in Minnesota, that are actually named Minneapolis-St. Paul.

The SSN 719 was named PROVIDENCE in September 1983 to honor the state of Rhode Island after the SSBN 730 was renamed HENRY M. JACKSON.

LA JOLLA (1983, Giorgio Arra)

A low-oblique view of the SAN FRANCISCO (1981, Newport News Shipbuilding)

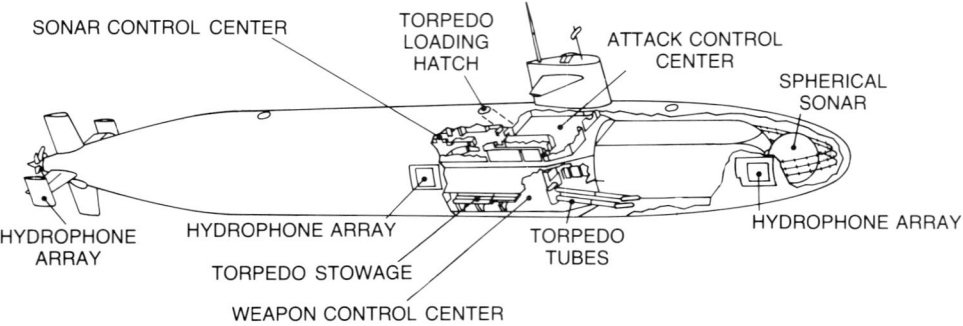

SONAR CONTROL CENTER

TORPEDO LOADING HATCH

ATTACK CONTROL CENTER

SPHERICAL SONAR

HYDROPHONE ARRAY

HYDROPHONE ARRAY

TORPEDO TUBES

HYDROPHONE ARRAY

TORPEDO STOWAGE

WEAPON CONTROL CENTER

LA JOLLA (1983, Giorgio Arra)

JACKSONVILLE (1983, Giorgio Arra)

1 NUCLEAR-PROPELLED ATTACK SUBMARINE: "GLENARD P. LIPSCOMB"

Number	Name	FY	Builder	Laid down	Launched	Commissioned	Status
SSN 685	GLENARD P. LIPSCOMB	68	General Dynamics/Electric Boat	5 June 1971	4 Aug 1973	21 Dec 1974	**AA**

Displacement:	5,800 tons standard
	6,480 tons submerged
Length:	365 feet (111.3 m) oa
Beam:	31¾ feet (9.7 m)
Draft:	31 feet (9.5 m)
Propulsion:	turbo-electric drive (General Electric); 1 shaft
Reactors:	1 pressurized-water S5Wa (Westinghouse)
Speed:	approx. 18 knots surface
	approx. 25 knots submerged
Manning:	128 (13 officers + 115 enlisted)
Missiles:	Harpoon SSM
Torpedo tubes:	4 21-inch (533-mm) tubes Mk 63 (amidships)
ASW weapons:	Mk 48 torpedoes
	SUBROC
Radars:	BPS–15
Sonars:	BQQ–5 bow mounted
	BQS–14
	towed array
Fire control:	1 Mk 117 torpedo FCS

The LIPSCOMB was constructed to evaluate a Turbine Electric Drive (TED) propulsion plant. Speed was sacrificed to reduce machinery noises. The TULLIBEE, constructed more than a decade earlier, was in part a similar effort to replace reduction gear with electric drive. No additional submarines of this type were built because of a decision to make the faster LOS ANGELES class the standard SSN design.

The LIPSCOMB is considerably larger than the contemporary STURGEON class.

Design: SCB No. 302. The propulsion plant makes the LIPSCOMB a significantly larger submarine than the STURGEON design.

Fire control: The Mk 117 torpedo fire control system has been installed in place of the original MK 113.

Missiles: The LIPSCOMB will be fitted to launch the Tomahawk from torpedo tubes.

Sonars: The original BQQ-2 sonar system has been upgraded to the BQQ-5 configuration. An additional, not publicly identified sonar was fitted to the forward edge of the LIPSCOMB's upper sail structure in June 1977 (see photo).

The GLENARD P. LIPSCOMB—sometimes referred to as the "Lipscomb fish"—returns to home port, New London. Note the YTB on the port side, small sonar dome on the bow, bitts and cleats (that retract when at sea), and bulge at the top of the sail for special sonar installed in 1977. (1979, U.S. Navy; Jean Russell)

The GLENARD P. LIPSCOMB off Portsmouth, England. (1980, L. and L. van Ginderen)

1 NUCLEAR-PROPELLED ATTACK SUBMARINE: "NARWHAL"

Number	Name	FY	Builder	Laid down	Launched	Commissioned	Status
SSN 671	Narwhal	64	General Dynamics/Electric Boat	17 Jan 1966	9 Sep 1967	12 July 1969	**AA**

Displacement:	4,450 tons standard
	5,350 tons submerged
Length:	314 feet (95.75 m) oa
Beam:	38 feet (11.6 m)
Draft:	26 feet (7.9 m)
Propulsion:	2 steam turbines (General Electric); approx. 17,000 shp; 1 shaft
Reactors:	1 pressurized-water S5G (General Electric)
Speed:	approx. 25 knots surface
	approx. 30 knots submerged
Manning:	128 (13 officers + 115 enlisted)
Missiles:	Harpoon SSM
Torpedo tubes:	4 21-inch (533-mm) tubes Mk 63 (amidships)
ASW weapons:	Mk 48 torpedoes
Radars:	BPS–15
Sonars:	BQQ–5 bow mounted
	BQS–8
	towed array
Fire control:	1 Mk 117 torpedo FCS

The Narwhal was constructed to evaluate the natural-circulation S5G reactor plant. Weapons, sensors, and other features of the Narwhal are similar to the Sturgeon-class SSNs.

Design: SCB No. 245.

Fire control: The Mk 117 torpedo fire control system has been installed in place of the original Mk 113.

Missiles: The Narwhal will be fitted to launch the Tomahawk missile as well as Harpoon from torpedo tubes.

Reactor: The S5G reactor plant uses natural convection rather than pumps for heat transfer/coolant transfer at slow speeds, thus reducing self-generated machinery noises. This concept is used in the subsequent Los Angeles and Ohio (SSBN 726) classes. A land-based prototype of the S5G plant was built at Arco, Idaho.

Sonar: The BQQ-2 has been upgraded to a BQQ-5 configuration.

Narwhal (1982, Giorgio Arra)

Narwhal (1969, General Dynamics/Electric Boat)

37 NUCLEAR-PROPELLED ATTACK SUBMARINES: "STURGEON" CLASS

Number	Name	FY	Builder	Laid down	Launched	Commissioned	Status
SSN 637	STURGEON	62	General Dynamics/Electric Boat	10 Aug 1963	26 Feb 1966	3 Mar 1967	**AA**
SSN 638	WHALE	62	General Dynamics, Quincy, Mass.	27 May 1964	14 Oct 1966	12 Oct 1968	**AA**
SSN 639	TAUTOG	62	Ingalls Shipbuilding	27 Jan 1964	15 Apr 1967	17 Aug 1968	**PA**
SSN 646	GRAYLING	63	Portsmouth Naval Shipyard	12 May 1964	22 June 1967	11 Oct 1969	**AA**
SSN 647	POGY	63	Ingalls Shipbuilding	4 May 1964	3 June 1967	15 May 1971	**PA**
SSN 648	ASPRO	63	Ingalls Shipbuilding	23 Nov 1964	29 Nov 1967	20 Feb 1969	**PA**
SSN 649	SUNFISH	63	General Dynamics, Quincy, Mass.	15 Jan 1965	14 Oct 1966	15 Mar 1969	**AA**
SSN 650	PARGO	63	General Dynamics/Electric Boat	3 June 1964	17 Sep 1966	5 Jan 1968	**AA**
SSN 651	QUEENFISH	63	Newport News Shipbuilding	11 May 1965	25 Feb 1966	6 Dec 1966	**PA**
SSN 652	PUFFER	63	Ingalls Shipbuilding	8 Feb 1965	30 Mar 1968	9 Aug 1969	**PA**
SSN 653	RAY	63	Newport News Shipbuilding	1 Apr 1965	21 June 1966	12 Apr 1967	**AA**
SSN 660	SAND LANCE	64	Portsmouth Naval Shipyard	15 Jan 1965	11 Nov 1969	25 Sep 1971	**AA**
SSN 661	LAPON	64	Newport News Shipbuilding	26 July 1965	16 Dec 1966	14 Dec 1967	**AA**
SSN 662	GURNARD	64	Mare Island Naval Shipyard	22 Dec 1964	20 May 1967	6 Dec 1968	**PA**
SSN 663	HAMMERHEAD	64	Newport News Shipbuilding	29 Nov 1965	14 Apr 1967	28 June 1968	**AA**
SSN 664	SEA DEVIL	64	Newport News Shipbuilding	12 Apr 1966	5 Oct 1967	30 Jan 1969	**AA**
SSN 665	GUITARRO	65	Mare Island Naval Shipyard	9 Dec 1965	27 July 1968	9 Sep 1972	**PA**
SSN 666	HAWKBILL	65	Mare Island Naval Shipyard	12 Dec 1966	12 Apr 1969	4 Feb 1971	**PA**
SSN 667	BERGALL	65	General Dynamics/Electric Boat	16 Apr 1966	17 Feb 1968	13 June 1969	**AA**
SSN 668	SPADEFISH	65	Newport News Shipbuilding	21 Dec 1966	15 May 1968	14 Aug 1969	**AA**
SSN 669	SEAHORSE	65	General Dynamics/Electric Boat	13 Aug 1966	15 June 1968	19 Sep 1969	**AA**
SSN 670	FINBACK	65	Newport News Shipbuilding	26 June 1967	7 Dec 1968	4 Feb 1970	**AA**
SSN 672	PINTADO	66	Mare Island Naval Shipyard	27 Oct 1967	16 Aug 1969	29 Apr 1971	**PA**
SSN 673	FLYING FISH	66	General Dynamics/Electric Boat	30 June 1967	17 May 1969	29 Apr 1970	**AA**
SSN 674	TREPANG	66	General Dynamics/Electric Boat	28 Oct 1967	27 Sep 1969	14 Aug 1970	**AA**
SSN 675	BLUEFISH	66	General Dynamics/Electric Boat	13 Mar 1968	10 Jan 1970	8 Jan 1971	**AA**
SSN 676	BILLFISH	66	General Dynamics/Electric Boat	20 Sep 1968	1 May 1970	12 Mar 1971	**AA**
SSN 677	DRUM	66	Mare Island Naval Shipyard	20 Aug 1968	23 May 1970	15 Apr 1972	**PA**
SSN 678	ARCHERFISH	67	General Dynamics/Electric Boat	19 June 1969	16 Jan 1971	17 Dec 1971	**AA**
SSN 679	SILVERSIDES	67	General Dynamics/Electric Boat	13 Oct 1969	4 June 1971	5 May 1972	**AA**
SSN 680	WILLIAM H. BATES	67	Litton/Ingalls Shipbuilding	4 Aug 1969	11 Dec 1971	5 May 1973	**PA**
SSN 681	BATFISH	67	General Dynamics/Electric Boat	9 Feb 1970	9 Oct 1971	1 Sep 1972	**AA**
SSN 682	TUNNY	67	Litton/Ingalls Shipbuilding	22 May 1970	10 June 1972	26 Jan 1974	**PA**
SSN 683	PARCHE	68	Litton/Ingalls Shipbuilding	10 Dec 1970	13 Jan 1973	17 Aug 1974	**PA**
SSN 684	CAVALLA	68	General Dynamics/Electric Boat	4 June 1970	19 Feb 1972	9 Feb 1973	**PA**
SSN 686	L. MENDEL RIVERS	69	Newport News Shipbuilding	26 June 1971	2 June 1973	1 Feb 1975	**AA**
SSN 687	RICHARD B. RUSSELL	69	Newport News Shipbuilding	19 Oct 1971	12 Jan 1974	16 Aug 1975	**PA**

Displacement:	29 units:
	4,250 tons standard
	4,780 tons submerged
	SSN 678–684, 686, 687:
	4,460 tons standard
	4,960 tons submerged
Length:	291¹¹/₁₂ feet (89.1 m) oa
	except last 9 ships 302¹/₁₂ feet (92.1 m) oa
Beam:	31⅔ feet (9.65 m)
Draft:	29½ feet (9.0 m)
Propulsion:	2 steam turbines; 15,000 shp; 1 shaft
Reactors:	1 pressurized-water S5W (Westinghouse)
Speed:	approx. 20 knots surface
	approx. 30 knots submerged
Manning:	128 (13 officers + 115 enlisted)
Missiles:	Harpoon SSM
Torpedo tubes:	4 21-inch (533-mm) tubes Mk 63 (amidships)
ASW weapons:	Mk 48 torpedoes
	SUBROC in submarines with Mk 113 torpedo FCS
Radars:	BPS–15
Sonars:	BQQ–2 or BQQ–5 bow mounted
	BQR–26 in SSN 666
	BQS–8/12 in SSN 637–639, 646–653, 660–664
	BQS–13 in later submarines
	towed array
Fire control:	1 Mk 113 in SSN 637, 650, 653, 661, 672, 675–678, 683, 687
	1 Mk 117 in other submarines

These submarines are improved versions of the PERMIT class, the principal visible difference being the taller sail structure and under-ice operational capability (see Design notes). After the LOS ANGELES class, this is the largest U.S. series of nuclear-propelled submarines.

The GUITARRO sank alongside a pier at the San Francisco Naval Shipyard on 15 May 1969, while still under construction because of faulty ballasting; there were no casualties. She was rebuilt.

The CAVALLA was modified about 1983 to support the development of swimmer-delivery concepts and equipment; a hangar structure has been fitted.

Builders: The POGY was begun by the New York Shipbuilding Corp., Camden, N.J. The contract for her construction was terminated on 5 June 1967, and the unfinished submarine was towed to the Ingalls yard for completion.

Design: SCB No. 188A (through SSN 664) and subséquently SCB No. 300 in the new series. These submarines are similar to the previous PERMIT class, but with several deficiencies of the earlier design being corrected. An improved electronics suite was provided as well as a larger sail structure that provides more space for masts, under-ice operational features, and depth keeping when near the surface. Again, this resulted in a larger submarine which, with the S5W reactor plant, resulted in a further loss of speed over the PERMIT and SKIPJACK classes.

The under-ice features include upward- and forward-looking navigational sonars, strengthened sail and rudder caps, and provision for the sail-mounted diving planes to rotate 90° for breaking through ice.

Since 1978 the SSN 679 and 687 have had a communication buoy housing aft of the sail.

Fire control: This class was built with the Mk 113 analog fire control system; being replaced by Mk 117 digital system during overhauls.

Missiles: The Tomahawk cruise missiles will be provided for launch from torpedo tubes; the GUITARRO was trials ship for the submarine-launched Tomahawk.

Names: The SSN 680 was originally to be named REDFIN; renamed on 25 June 1971 for a deceased member of Congress.

Operational: The WHALE was the first of several submarines of this class to conduct extensive operations under the Arctic ice pack. She first voyaged to the North Pole in April 1969.

Sonar: The original BQQ-2 system is being upgraded to BQQ-5 configuration during overhauls. The HAWKBILL has a protruding BQR-26 sonar fitted in the forward part of her sail structure.

Many, if not all, of these submarines have an acoustic device known as GNAT, fitted just forward of the upper rudder fin.

The RICHARD B. RUSSELL was refitted after completion with a housing aft of the sail for an emergency communications buoy designated Bustle. (1978, U.S. Navy)

The SEAHORSE shows the basic design of modern U.S. nuclear attack submarines. These boats have taller sails than the previous PERMIT class, providing more space for masts and better depth control when at periscope depth. (1983, Giorgio Arra)

The PUFFER prepares to enter port; her towed array sheath is visible along the port side as are small sonar domes on after deck and navigation light atop rudder post. (1980, Giorgio Arra)

The HAWKBILL with her masts and scopes raised. Her BPS-15 radar is just visible below the American flag; raised are her No. 1 attack scope (Type 2F) with IFF/UHF antenna next to it; the No. 2 attack scope (Type 2) with loop radio antenna mast barely raised; and the BRA-21 radio antenna mast. Retracted into the sail are the ECM mast, snorkel induction mast, and BRD-6 antenna mast. (1979, Giorgio Arra)

The GURNARD surfaced at the North Pole displays the vertical position of the sail-mounted diving planes for breaking through polar ice. This feature is found in all STURGEON-class submarines. Because of renewed U.S. Navy interest in the Arctic an under-ice capability will be provided in later LOS ANGELES-class boats. (1976 U.S. Navy)

13 NUCLEAR-PROPELLED ATTACK SUBMARINES: "PERMIT" CLASS

Number	Name	FY	Builder	Laid down	Launched	Commissioned	Status
SSN 594	PERMIT	58	Mare Island Naval Shipyard	16 July 1959	1 July 1961	29 May 1962	**PA**
SSN 595	PLUNGER	58	Mare Island Naval Shipyard	2 Mar 1960	9 Dec 1961	21 Nov 1962	**PA**
SSN 596	BARB	58	Litton/Ingalls Shipbuilding	9 Nov 1959	12 Feb 1962	24 Aug 1963	**PA**
SSN 603	POLLACK	59	New York Shipbuilding	14 Mar 1960	17 Mar 1962	26 May 1964	**PA**
SSN 604	HADDO	59	New York Shipbuilding	9 Sep 1960	18 Aug 1962	16 Dec 1964	**PA**
SSN 605	JACK	59	Portsmouth Naval Shipyard	16 Sep 1960	24 Apr 1963	31 Mar 1967	**AA**
SSN 606	TINOSA	59	Portsmouth Naval Shipyard	24 Nov 1959	9 Dec 1961	17 Oct 1964	**AA**
SSN 607	DACE	59	Litton/Ingalls Shipbuilding	6 June 1960	18 Aug 1962	4 Apr 1964	**AA**
SSN 612	GUARDFISH	60	New York Shipbuilding	28 Feb 1961	15 May 1965	20 Dec 1966	**PA**
SSN 613	FLASHER	60	General Dynamics/Electric Boat	14 Apr 1961	22 June 1963	22 July 1966	**PA**
SSN 614	GREENLING	60	General Dynamics/Electric Boat	15 Aug 1961	4 Apr 1964	3 Nov 1967	**AA**
SSN 615	GATO	60	General Dynamics/Electric Boat	15 Dec 1961	14 May 1964	25 Jan 1968	**AA**
SSN 621	HADDOCK	61	Litton/Ingalls Shipbuilding	24 Apr 1961	21 May 1966	22 Dec 1967	**PA**

Displacement:	3,750 tons standard except SSN 605, 613–615 3,800 tons 4,300 tons submerged except SSN 605 4,500 tons; SSN 613–615 4,600 tons
Length:	278½ feet (84.9 m) oa except SSN 605 296¾ feet (90.5 m); SSN 613–615 292⅛ feet (89.1 m)
Beam:	31¾ feet (9.7 m)
Draft:	29 feet (8.8 m)
Propulsion:	2 steam turbines (General Electric in SSN 603–605, 612; De Laval in SSN 606, 613–615; Westinghouse in others)
Reactors:	1 pressurized-water S5W (Westinghouse)
Speed:	approx. 20 knots surface approx. 30 knots submerged
Manning:	128 (13 officers + 115 enlisted) in most units; some have more
Missiles:	Harpoon SSM being fitted
Torpedo tubes:	4 21-inch (533-mm) tubes Mk 63 (amidships)
ASW weapons:	Mk 48 torpedoes SUBROC in submarines with Mk 113 torpedo FCS
Radars:	BPS–5/9/11/15
Sonars:	BQQ–2 or BQQ–5 bow mounted BQS–14 towed array
Fire control:	1 Mk 113 torpedo fire control in SSN 604–606, 612–615 1 Mk 117 in other submarines

These submarines established the basic design for subsequent U.S. Navy SSNs and SSBNs, having a deep-diving capability, quiet machinery, large bow-mounted sonar, and torpedo tubes mounted amidships.

Builders: The GREENLING and GATO were launched by the Electric Boat yard in Groton, Conn., and then towed to the General Dynamics yard at Quincy, Mass., for completion. The later submarines of this class were delayed for inspection and modification after the loss of the THRESHER.

Class: Originally a class of 14 submarines, the lead ship, USS THRESHER (SSN 593), was lost during deep-diving trials off the New England coast on 10 April 1963. All 112 naval personnel and 17 civilians on board at the time were lost in what remains history's worst submarine disaster as well as the first nuclear submarine loss.

Following the loss of the THRESHER these submarines have been officially called the PERMIT class.

The SSN 594–596 and 607 were originally ordered as Regulus cruise missile submarines (SSGN with same hull numbers); they were reordered as attack submarines after the Regulus II program was cancelled in December 1958.

POLLACK (1983, Giorgio Arra)

Design: SCB No. 188. While propelled by the same S5W reactor plant as the SKIPJACK class and having a modified "tear-drop" design based on the previous SKIPJACK class, these submarines represented a radical development in submarine design with a significantly greater depth capability, achieved with the use of HY-80 steel (vice High Tensil Steel of previous U.S. submarines), and a high degree of machinery quieting. These features resulted in a much larger submarine with a related reduction in speed over the SKIPJACK class. In an effort to reduce underwater drag, the sail structure was kept to minimum size, resulting in a reduction of masts and intelligence-collection capabilities.

In addition, they have the large, bow sonar installation of the smaller TULLIBEE, which requires that the torpedo tubes, reduced to four, be positioned amidships, angled outboard two per side.

The later submarines were modified (and enlarged) after loss of the THRESHER.

The JACK has a modified propulsion system with a direct-drive (ungeared) turbine. She is fitted with a large-diameter, sleeve-like outer propellor shaft housing a smaller-diameter inner shaft, providing an arrangement of counter-rotating propellers on essentially a single shaft. The scheme was used to increase efficiency and reduce turbulence. There was no increase in speed and the machinery spaces are ten feet longer than in other units of the class. The concept has not been repeated in other submarines.

Fire control: The original Mk 113 analog torpedo FCS is being replaced during overhauls with the Mk 117 digital system.

Missiles: Harpoon SSM is being fitted to this class. They will not carry the Tomahawk cruise missile.

Names: The names of three submarines were changed during construction: SSN 595 ex-POLLACK, SSN 596 ex-POLLACK and ex-PLUNGER, and SSN 603 ex-BARB.

Sonars: During overhaul the original BQQ-2 sonar is being upgraded to BQQ-5.

POLLACK (1983, Giorgio Arra)

The GUARDFISH rolls gently to port as she maneuvers among sailing craft off San Diego. Her portside towed array housing is readily visible. These submarines had the same S5W propulsion plant of the previous SKIPJACK class, but they introduced a new sonar design and interior "front-end" arrangement that was followed in succeeding SSN classes as well as in the Trident SSBN. (1983, Giorgio Arra)

2 NUCLEAR-PROPELLED ATTACK SUBMARINES
2 NUCLEAR-PROPELLED SPECIAL OPERATIONS SUBMARINES } "ETHAN ALLEN" CLASS

Number	Name	FY	Builder	Laid down	Launched	Commissioned	Status
SSN 609	SAM HOUSTON	59	Newport News Shipbuilding	28 Dec 1959	2 Feb 1961	6 Mar 1962	Yard
SSN 610	THOMAS A. EDISON	59	General Dynamics/Electric Boat	15 Mar 1960	15 June 1961	10 Mar 1962	PR
SSN 611	JOHN MARSHALL	59	Newport News Shipbuilding	4 Apr 1960	15 July 1961	21 May 1962	Yard
SSN 618	THOMAS JEFFERSON	61	Newport News Shipbuilding	3 Feb 1961	24 Feb 1962	4 Jan 1963	AR

Displacement:	6,955 tons standard
	7,900 tons submerged
Length:	410½ feet (125.2 m) oa
Beam:	33 feet (10.1 m)
Draft:	30 feet (9.1 m)
Propulsion:	2 steam turbines; 15,000 shp; 1 shaft
Reactors:	1 pressurized-water S5W (Westinghouse)
Speed:	approx. 20 knots surface
	approx. 25 knots submerged
Manning:	SSN 609 136 (12 officers + 124 enlisted)
	SSN 611 137 (13 officers + 124 enlisted)
Missiles:	removed
Torpedo tubes:	4 21-inch (533-mm) tubes Mk 65 (bow)
ASW weapons:	Mk 48 torpedoes
Radars:	BPS-15
Sonars:	BQS-4
	BQR-15
	BQR-19
	towed array
Fire control:	1 Mk 112 torpedo FCS

These submarines were built as ballistic missile submarines (SSBN) and after extensive service in that role were modified for use as attack submarines. As SSNs these submarines suffered from their relatively large size, limited torpedo reloads (eight), lack of SUBROC or tactical missile capabilities, limited sonar effectiveness, and slow speed compared with other attack submarines.

The EDISON and JEFFERSON were decommissioned and laid up in reserve on 30 September 1983 and 30 September 1984, respectively. The HOUSTON and MARSHALL are being converted to special-mission submarines, to carry frogmen or commandos, and conduct other operations. They are in the Pacific and Atlantic, respectively.

Class: Originally a class of five submarines (SSBN 608–611 and 618). The ETHAN ALLEN (SSN 608) was decommissioned on 30 September 1982 and stricken on 31 March 1983.

Classification: SAM HOUSTON changed to SSN on 10 November 1980, THOMAS A. EDISON to SSN on 6 October 1980, JOHN MARSHALL to SSN on 20 June 1981, and THOMAS JEFFERSON to SSN on 11 March 1981.

New classifications are not known for the two special-mission conversions. They may remain as SSNs.

Design: SCB No. 180. These were the first U.S. submarines designed from the outset as SSBNs, the previous GEORGE WASHINGTON class having been converted during design/construction from attack submarines. These submarines are constructed of HY-80 steel (as the PERMIT and later SSN classes).

As SSBNs their manning was 12 officers and 129 enlisted men.

Missiles: These submarines were initially armed with the Polaris A-2 missile. All were later modified to launch the Polaris A-3.

The SAM HOUSTON at high speed on the surface off Apra Harbor, Guam, shortly before being reclassified as an SSN. (1979, U.S. Navy; PH2 Edward O'Brien)

The attack submarine nee Polaris missile submarine SAM HOUSTON underway in the Hood Canal off the Trident submarine base in Bangor, Wash. These submarines lacked effective sonar, quieting, and torpedo reloads to serve effectively in the SSN role. (1981, U.S. Navy)

3 NUCLEAR-PROPELLED ATTACK SUBMARINES: "GEORGE WASHINGTON" CLASS

Number	Name	FY	Builder	Laid down	Launched	Commissioned	Status
SSN 598	George Washington	S58	General Dynamics/Electric Boat	1 Nov 1957	9 June 1959	30 Dec 1959	PR
SSN 599	Patrick Henry	S58	General Dynamics/Electric Boat	27 May 1958	22 Sep 1959	9 Apr 1960	PR
SSN 601	Robert E. Lee	59	Newport News Shipbuilding	25 Aug 1958	18 Dec 1959	16 Sep 1960	PR

Displacement:	6,000 tons standard
	6,685 tons submerged
Length:	381⅔ feet (116.4 m) oa
Beam:	33 feet (10.1 m)
Draft:	29 feet (8.8 m)
Propulsion:	2 steam turbines; 15,000 shp; 1 shaft
Reactors:	1 pressurized-water S5W (Westinghouse)
Speed:	approx. 20 knots surface
	approx. 25 knots submerged
Manning:	139 (12 officers + 127 enlisted) as SSBNS
Missiles:	removed
Torpedo tubes:	6 21-inch (533-mm) tubes Mk 59 (bow)
ASW weapons:	Mk 48 torpedoes
Radars:	BPS-15
Sonars:	BQS-4
	BQR-19
Fire control:	1 Mk 112 torpedo FCS

This was the first class of Western strategic missile submarines (SSBN). These three submarines were modified for brief service in the attack role, but they suffered from the same limitations as the Ethan Allen class, although they had six torpedo tubes and 11 reloads. (Two other submarines of this class were laid up in reserve after being partially dismantled; they were not modified to the SSN configuration because of insufficient core life.)

The George Washington was decommissioned on 30 September 1984, the Patrick Henry on 25 May 1984, and the Robert E. Lee on 1 December 1983. The George Washington served in the Atlantic as an SSN; she sailed from Groton, Conn., in April 1984 for decommissioning and laying up with other ex-SSBNs at Bremerton, Wash.

Class: The first five submarines of this class (SSBN 598–600) were authorized in the fiscal 1958 supplemental shipbuilding program, signed by President Eisenhower on 11 February 1958. In anticipation of this action, the Navy had shortly before redesigned two attack submarines of the Skipjack class as missile submarines; they were the Scorpion (SSN 589) and the then-unnamed SSN 590. These were completed as the SSBN 598 and 599, respectively. Two additional submarines were authorized in fiscal 1959 (SSBN 601 and 602).

The Theodore Roosevelt (SSBN 600) and Abraham Lincoln (SSBN 602) were decommissioned on 28 February 1981 and their missile systems and reactor plants were dismantled. Both were stricken on 1 December 1982.

Classification: SSBN 598 changed to SSN on 20 November 1981; SSBN 599 on 24 October 1982; and SSBN 601 on 1 March 1982.

Design: SCB No. 180A. These submarines established the basic design for all later U.S. and foreign SSBNs until the construction of the Soviet Typhoon class in the late 1970s.

The redesign of the Skipjack class provided for the addition of almost 130 feet in length to accommodate two rows of eight missile tubes, auxiliary machinery, and missile fire control and inertial navigation.

Missiles: Upon completion, these submarines were armed with the Polaris A-1 missile, being later upgraded to fire the Polaris A-3. The George Washington began the first Polaris "deterrent" patrol on 15 November 1960. The Robert E. Lee completed the final Polaris patrol on 1 October 1982.

The high "turtle back" necessary to house the Polaris missile in the Skipjack-class hull diameter is visible in this view of the Patrick Henry, taken during the submarine's brief career as an SSN. (1983, Giorgio Arra)

1 NUCLEAR-PROPELLED ATTACK SUBMARINE: "TULLIBEE"

Number	Name	FY	Builder	Laid down	Launched	Commissioned	Status
SSN 597	TULLIBEE	58	General Dynamics/Electric Boat	26 May 1958	27 Apr 1960	9 Nov 1960	**AA**

Displacement:	2,317 tons standard
	2,640 tons submerged
Length:	273 feet (83.25 m) oa
Beam:	23⅓ feet (7.1 m)
Draft:	21 feet (6.4 m)
Propulsion:	turbo-electric drive with steam turbines (Westinghouse); 2,500 shp; 1 shaft
Reactors:	1 pressurized-water S2C (Combustion Engineering)
Speed:	approx. 15 knots surface
	15+ knots submerged
Manning:	94 (12 officers + 82 enlisted)
Missiles:	none
Torpedo tubes:	4 21-inch (533-mm) tubes Mk 64 (amidships)
ASW weapons:	Mk 48 torpedoes
Radars:	BPS-12
Sonars:	BQQ-2 bow mounted
Fire control:	1 Mk 112 torpedo FCS

The TULLIBEE was designed as a small, hunter-killer submarine intended to operate off enemy ports and in narrow waterways (as were the earlier diesel-electric submarines of the SSK 1 class). The construc-tion of additional submarines of this design was halted in favor of the larger and more versatile PERMIT class.

Classification: While being planned the TULLIBEE was sometimes referred to as a hunter-killer submarine (SSKN), but that designation was never officially assigned.

Design: SCB No. 178. This was the first U.S. submarine to have bow-mounted sonar with the torpedo tubes fitted amidships, angled out to port and starboard. This sonar arrangement, followed in later SSNs and the OHIO (SSBN 726) class places the acoustic detection equipment in the best position with respect to ship movement and machinery noises. The TULLIBEE was not fitted to fire SUBROC as well as later SSNs.

Engineering: The nuclear power plant is smaller and less powerful than in other U.S. submarines, with turbo-electric drive used in place of steam turbines and reduction gear to reduce self-generated noise.

A prototype of this reactor (designated S1C) was built at Windsor, Conn.

Sonar: The BQG-4 PUFFS fire control sonar (three vertical-fin antennas) has been deleted.

The TULLIBEE is the smallest nuclear submarine constructed by the U.S. Navy. The Soviet high-speed (43-knot) Alfa SSN is shorter but has a greater diameter and displacement, and the new French RUBIS-class SSN has smaller dimensions than the TULLIBEE. The three-fin BQG-4 PUFFS shown here has been removed. (1968, U.S. Navy)

1 NUCLEAR-PROPELLED RESEARCH SUBMARINE: "HALIBUT"

Number	Name	FY	Builder	Laid down	Launched	Commissioned	Status
SSN 587	HALIBUT	56	Mare Island Naval Shipyard	11 Apr 1957	9 Jan 1959	4 Jan 1960	PR

Displacement:	3,850 tons surface
	5,000 tons submerged
Length:	350 feet (106.7 m) oa
Beam	29½ feet (9.0 m)
Draft:	21½ feet (6.5 m)
Propulsion:	2 steam turbines (Westinghouse); approx. 7,500 shp; 2 shafts
Reactors:	1 pressurized-water S3W (Westinghouse)
Speed:	15.5 knots surface
	15+ knots submerged
Manning:	120 (12 officers + 108 enlisted)
Missiles:	removed
Torpedo tubes:	6 21-inch (533-mm) tubes (4 bow Mk 61 + 2 stern Mk 62)
ASW weapons:	torpedoes
Radars:	SS-2
Sonars:	BQS-4
Fire control:	1 Mk 101 torpedo FCS

The HALIBUT was designed and constructed as a guided missile submarine (SSGN) to launch the Regulus II strategic cruise missile. After that weapon was cancelled in December 1958, the ship was armed with the Regulus I missile, carrying that weapon on deployments to the Western Pacific from 1960 to 1964.

After deletion of her missile equipment, the HALIBUT was reclassified as an attack submarine (SSN) on 15 August 1965 and subsequently served as a research submarine until decommissioned on 30 June 1976. In the latter role, the HALIBUT's forward missile hangar was modified for research equipment, a ducted bow-thruster was provided for precise control and maneuvering, and provisions were made for carrying submersibles on the after deck (mated to the after escape hatch).

She is laid up in reserve at the Bremerton Naval Shipyard, Wash.

Class: No additional submarines of this design were built. An improved Regulus II-armed SSGN class was planned, but those submarines were reordered as PERMIT-class SSNs.

Design: SCB No. 137A. The HALIBUT has a large hangar forward, faired into the hull. It was capable of carrying two Regulus II or five Regulus I missiles. In her SSGN role the HALIBUT was fitted with a trainable launcher fitted between the hangar and sail structure.

Engineering: The reactor plant is similar to that of the SKATE-class SSNs. The HALIBUT is slower because of her larger size and hull shape. The HALIBUT was originally ordered as a diesel-electric submarine, but on 27 February 1956 the Navy announced that she would be provided with nuclear propulsion.

HALIBUT (1970, U.S. Navy)

The HALIBUT in San Francisco Bay while serving in the underwater research role. A deep submergence vehicle is on the submarine's stern, mated to the aftermost hatch to permit crewmen to pass between the two while they are submerged. The HALIBUT could launch and recover the submersible while she was at depth. The "hump" on her forward deck is her hangar hatch. (1970, U.S. Navy)

1 NUCLEAR-PROPELLED ATTACK SUBMARINE: "TRITON"

Number	Name	FY	Builder	Laid down	Launched	Commissioned	Status
SSN 586	TRITON	56	General Dynamics/Electric Boat	29 May 1956	19 Aug 1958	10 Nov 1959	AR

Displacement:	5,940 tons standard
	6,670 tons submerged
Length:	447½ feet (136.5 m) oa
Beam:	37 feet (11.3 m)
Draft:	24 feet (7.3 m)
Propulsion:	2 steam turbines (General Electric); approx. 34,000 shp; 2 shafts
Reactors:	2 pressurized-water S4G (General Electric)
Speed:	27 knots surface
	20+ knots submerged
Manning:	172 as SSRN (16 officers + 156 enlisted)
	159 as SSN (13 officers + 146 enlisted)
Missiles:	none
Torpedo tubes:	6 21-inch (533-mm) tubes Mk 60 (4 bow + 2 stern)
ASW weapons:	torpedoes
Radars:	SPS-26 3-D (see notes)
	SS-2
Sonars:	BQS-4
Fire control:	1 Mk 101 torpedo FCS

The TRITON was designed to serve as a radar picket submarine (SSRN) to provide early warning of air attack against a carrier task force. The rationale for her construction, however, was Admiral Rickover's desire to test a two-reactor nuclear plant in a submarine, in part as a precursor to multi-reactor surface warships.

The Navy phased out the radar picket submarine program in the late 1950s because of the greater effectiveness of Airborne Early Warning (AEW) aircraft. The TRITON was reclassified as an SSN on 1 March 1961 and employed in general submarine operations until decommis-sioned on 3 May 1969 and placed in reserve. She is laid up at the Naval Shipyard, Norfolk, Va.

The TRITON was the longest U.S. submarine prior to the SSBN 726 class.

Design: SCB No. 132. The TRITON was designed for high speed sur-face operations to operate with aircraft carriers. A large, retractable air search radar was fitted in the sail structure. A large Combat Information Center (CIC) was provided as well as extensive communications equip-ment.

Engineering: This is the U.S. Navy's only two-reactor submarine, with a total shaft horsepower not approached until the LOS ANGELES-class SSNs were built. A single-reactor prototype of the TRITON plant was built as the S3G at West Milton, N.Y.

Operational: Between 16 February and 10 May 1960 the TRITON trav-elled around the world submerged, cruising 41,500 n.miles in 84 days in an effort to enhance national prestige. (The submarine did broach the surface once to allow an ill sailor to be taken off of the sail structure by small boat.) A crew of 175 plus 8 scientific personnel were on board for the cruise.

Radar: The SPS-26 is an electronically scanned, three-dimensional search radar that was the forerunner to the SPS-39 radar (see Chapter 31). The only other ship to carry the SPS-26 was the large frigate NORFOLK (DL 1). The TRITON's large radar antenna fully retracted into the sail structure (retracted at 90° to port, see photograph).

The large TRITON was built as a test bed for a two-reactor propulsion plant. She did not serve in the radar picket role and was unsuccessful as an SSN. In this view she has scopes and masts raised from her sail structure with her SPS-26 air search radar retracted. Proposals to employ the TRITON as an under-ice tug and rescue ship or national command ship were never developed, and she was laid up after less than a decade of service. (1963, U.S. Navy)

5 NUCLEAR-PROPELLED ATTACK SUBMARINES: "SKIPJACK" CLASS

Number	Name	FY	Builder	Laid down	Launched	Commissioned	Status
SSN 585	SKIPJACK	56	General Dynamics/Electric Boat	29 May 1956	26 May 1958	15 Apr 1959	**AA**
SSN 588	SCAMP	57	Mare Island Naval Shipyard	22 Jan 1959	8 Oct 1960	5 June 1961	**AA**
SSN 590	SCULPIN	57	Ingalls Shipbuilding, Pascagoula, Miss.	3 Feb 1958	31 Mar 1960	1 June 1961	**AA**
SSE 591	SHARK	57	Newport News Shipbuilding	24 Feb 1958	16 Mar 1960	9 Feb 1961	**AA**
SSN 592	SNOOK	57	Ingalls Shipbuilding, Pascagoula, Miss.	7 Apr 1958	31 Oct 1960	24 Oct 1961	**AA**

Displacement:	3,075 tons standard
	3,500 tons submerged
Length:	251¾ feet (76.8 m) oa
Beam:	31½ feet (9.6 m)
Draft:	28 feet (8.5 m)
Propulsion:	2 steam turbines (Westinghouse in SSN 585; General Electric in others); 15,000 shp; 1 shaft
Reactors:	1 pressurized-water S5W (Westinghouse)
Speed:	approx. 20 knots surface
	30 + knots submerged
Manning:	120 (12 officers + 108 enlisted)
Missiles:	none
Torpedo tubes:	6 21-inch (533-mm) tubes Mk 59 (bow)
ASW weapons:	Mk 48 torpedoes
Radars:	BPS-12
Sonars:	BQS-4 (modified)
Fire control:	1 Mk 101 torpedo FCS

The SKIPJACK-class submarines were the first to combine nuclear propulsion with the high-speed, "tear-drop" hull design of the experimental submarine ALBACORE. These were the fastest submarines in the U.S. Navy when built; their speed was not equalled until the LOS ANGELES class.

The SKIPJACKS remain in first-line service although they lack the quieting and sonar, as well as advanced cruise missile capabilities of later SSNs.

Class: The SCORPION (SSN 589) of this class was lost with all 99 men on board in May 1968 while some 400 miles southwest of the Azores.

Design: SCB No. 154. The tapered stern with a single propeller shaft prevented the installation of stern torpedo tubes. This design was the basis for the U.S. fleet ballistic missile submarines constructed during the late 1950s and 1960s. See GEORGE WASHINGTON class for details.

Engineering: At the time of their completion these submarines were credited with an endurance of about 140,000 n.miles or more than 4,000 hours of operation before refueling. The S5W reactor, which was used for two decades in U.S. SSNs and SSBNs, as well as the British submarine DREADNOUGHT, was a refinement of the previous pressurized-water reactors, with significantly increased power. No land-based prototype was constructed.

The SCAMP, second ship of the highly successful SKIPJACK class. They were the Navy's first high-speed SSNs; later U.S. submarines can dive deeper, are quieter, and have improved sonar, but have fewer torpedo tubes and, until the LOS ANGELES class, were slower. The SKIPJACKS were the last of several postwar submarine classes to have names beginning with the same letter, the practice before World War II. (1976, Giorgio Arra)

4 NUCLEAR-PROPELLED ATTACK SUBMARINES: "SKATE" CLASS

Number	Name	FY	Builder	Laid down	Launched	Commissioned	Status
SSN 578	SKATE	55	General Dynamics/Electric Boat	21 July 1955	16 May 1957	23 Dec 1957	**PA**
SSN 579	SWORDFISH	55	Portsmouth Naval Shipyard	25 Jan 1956	27 Aug 1957	15 Sep 1958	**PA**
SSN 583	SARGO	56	Mare Island Naval Shipyard	21 Feb 1956	10 Oct 1957	1 Oct 1958	**PA**
SSN 584	SEADRAGON	56	Portsmouth Naval Shipyard	20 June 1956	16 Aug 1958	5 Dec 1959	PR

Displacement:	2,570 tons standard
	2,861 tons submerged
Length:	267⁷/₁₂ feet (81.7 m) oa
Beam:	25 feet (7.6 m)
Draft:	21 feet (6.4 m)
Propulsion:	2 steam turbines (Westinghouse); approx. 7,500 shp; 2 shafts
Reactors:	1 pressurized-water S3W in SSN 578 and 583; S4W in SSN 579 and 584 (Westinghouse)
Speed:	15.5 knots surface
	20 + knots submerged
Manning:	121 (12 officers + 109 enlisted)
Missiles:	none
Torpedo tubes:	8 21-inch (533-mm) tubes (6 bow Mk 56 + 2 stern Mk 57)
ASW weapons:	Mk 48 torpedoes
Radars:	BPS-12
Sonars:	BQS-4
Fire control:	1 Mk 101 torpedo FCS

This class was the first U.S. effort to develop a nuclear-propelled submarine for series production. These are no longer considered first-line submarines, with the SEADRAGON decommissioned on 12 June 1984.

The SEADRAGON was home ported in Sasebo, Japan, from November 1964, the first U.S. nuclear submarine to be based overseas.

Design: SCB No. 121. These submarines have a conventional design.

Engineering: The nuclear plant of the SKATE class is similar in arrangement to that of the NAUTILUS, but smaller and simplified. The differences between the S3W and S4W are primarily in plant arrangement.

Operational: All of these submarines except the SWORDFISH have operated extensively under the Arctic ice pack. The SKATE was the world's first submarine to surface at the North Pole, doing so for the first time on 17 March 1959. (The SKATE had been the second submarine to reach the pole, in August 1958, immediately after the NAUTILUS.) In July-August 1962 the SKATE and SEADRAGON became the first craft to conduct multi-submarine operations at the North Pole.

SKATE (1980, Giorgio Arra)

The SKATE-class submarines, the lead ship shown here, are being decommissioned after a service life of about 25 years. These twin-shaft submarines have operated extensively in the Arctic. Their bow diving planes retract when not in use, a feature planned for future SSNs to facilitate under-ice operations. (1980, Giorgio Arra)

▌ NUCLEAR-PROPELLED RESEARCH SUBMARINE: "SEAWOLF"

Number	Name	FY	Builder	Laid down	Launched	Commissioned	Status
SSN 575	SEAWOLF	53	General Dynamics/Electric Boat	15 Sep 1953	21 July 1955	30 Mar 1957	**AA**

Displacement:	3,720 tons standard
	4,280 tons submerged
Length:	337½ feet (102.9 m) oa
Beam:	27¾ feet (8.5 m)
Draft:	22 feet (6.7 m)
Propulsion:	2 steam turbines (General Electric); approx. 15,000 shp; 2 shafts
Reactors:	1 pressurized-water S2Wa (Westinghouse)
Speed:	19 knots surface
	20 + knots submerged
Manning:	122 (10 officers + 112 enlisted)
Missiles:	none
Torpedo tubes:	6 21-inch (533-mm) tubes Mk 51 (bow)
ASW weapons:	Mk 48 torpedoes
Radars:	BPS-5A
Sonars:	BQS-4
Fire control:	1 Mk 101 torpedo FCS

The SEAWOLF was the world's second nuclear-propelled submarine. She was designed to evaluate a competitive nuclear plant to that of the NAUTILUS (see Engineering notes). She is no longer considered a first-line submarine and has been engaged in research activity since 1969.

Design: SCB No. 64A. The SEAWOLF has been fitted with four side thrusters, two forward and two aft, for the research role. She is configured to carry a submersible on her after deck.

Engineering: The SEAWOLF was built with a liquid-metal (sodium) reactor plant (S2G). After almost two years of limited operations the original plant was shut down in December 1958 and a modified NAUTILUS-type plant was installed. The submarine was recommissioned on 30 September 1960.

A land-based prototype for the SEAWOLF plant (S1G) was built at West Milton, N.Y.

The SEAWOLF with special markings on her sail to assist the underwater recovery of submersibles. Although used as a dedicated research submarine, she still carries an SSN designation. (1974, William Whalen, Jr.)

The SEAWOLF off San Francisco about 1977. The openings for her thrusters are visible forward and aft. (U. S. Navy)

1 NUCLEAR-PROPELLED SUBMARINE: "NAUTILUS"

Number	Name	FY	Builder	La d down	Launched	Commissioned	Status
SSN 571	NAUTILUS	52	General Dynamics/Electric Boat	14 June 1952	21 Jan 1954	30 Sep 1954	Memorial

Displacement:	3,530 tons standard
	4,040 tons submerged
Length:	319⁵⁄₁₂ feet (97.4 m) oa
Beam:	27½ feet (8.4 m)
Draft:	22 feet (6.7 m)
Propulsion:	2 steam turbines (Westinghouse); 15,000 shp; 2 shafts
Reactors:	1 pressurized-water S2W (Westinghouse)
Speed:	18 knots surface
	23.3 knots submerged
Manning:	120 (10 officers + 110 enlisted)
Missiles:	none
Torpedo tubes:	6 21-inch (533-mm) tubes Mk 50 (bow)
ASW weapons:	torpedoes
Radars:	BPS-5A
Sonars:	BQS-4
Fire control:	1 Mk 101 torpedo FCS

The NAUTILUS was the world's first nuclear-propelled submarine (proceeding the first Soviet nuclear-propelled surface ship, the icebreaker LENIN, and the November-class nuclear submarines by about five years). The NAUTILUS got underway on nuclear power for the first time on 17 January 1955.

Always based on the East Coast, her home port was changed from New London, Conn., to the Mare Island Naval Shipyard in May 1979 in preparation for decommissioning. She was formally decommissioned on 3 March 1980 and moored at Mare Island prior to being towed back to the East Coast for establishment as a memorial. The Navy had decided to moor the ship at the Washington Navy Yard in the nation's capital. President Carter, however, directed that the ship be moored at New London.

Design: SCB No. 64. The NAUTILUS and five succeeding nuclear attack submarines have conventional hull forms based on the German Type XXI submarine of World War II. Although intended to evaluate nuclear propulsion in a ship platform, the NAUTILUS was a fully armed and combat-capable submarine, unlike the unarmed diesel-electric research submarines ALBACORE (AGSS 569) and DOLPHIN.

Engineering: The land-based prototype of the NAUTILUS plant was the S1W reactor at Arco, Idaho.

Operational: The NAUTILUS became the first ship to reach the North Pole, sailing under the ice pack at the top of the world on 3 August 1958.

The NAUTILUS arriving at the Mare Island Naval Shipyard for defueling and decommissioning. She was to be towed back to the East Coast and preserved as a memorial. (1979, U.S. Navy)

NAUTILUS (1975, General Dynamics/Electric Boat)

3 ATTACK SUBMARINES: "BARBEL" CLASS

Number	Name	FY	Builder	Laid down	Launched	Commissioned	Status
SS 580	Barbel	56	Portsmouth Naval Shipyard	18 May 1956	19 July 1958	17 Jan 1959	**PA**
SS 581	Blueback	56	Ingalls Shipbuilding, Pascagoula, Miss.	15 Apr 1957	16 May 1959	15 Oct 1959	**PA**
SS 582	Bonefish	56	New York Shipbuilding, Camden, N.J.	3 June 1957	22 Nov 1958	9 July 1959	**AA**

Displacement:	2,145 tons standard
	2,895 tons submerged
Length:	219½ feet (66.9 m) oa
Beam:	29 feet (8.8 m)
Draft:	28 feet (8.5 m)
Propulsion:	3 diesels (Fairbanks Morse); 4,800 bhp
	2 electric motors (General Motors); 3,150 shp; 1 shaft
Speed:	15 knots surface
	25 knots submerged
Manning:	82 (8 officers + 74 enlisted) except 87 (8 officers + 79 enlisted) in SS 581
Missiles:	none
Torpedo tubes:	6 21-inch (533-mm) tubes Mk 58 (bow)
ASW weapons:	Mk 48 torpedoes
Radars:	BPS-12
Sonars:	BQS-4
Fire control:	1 Mk 101 torpedo FCS

The Bonefish at anchor. When not underway, U.S. ships in commission have the 50-star jack flown forward and the national ensign aft; when moving the jack is lowered and the flag shifts to the mast. The oldest ship in active commission flies the "rattlesnake" jack of the American Revolution in place of the 50-star jack. (1981, Giorgio Arra)

These were the last diesel-electric combat submarines to be constructed for the U.S. Navy. They are expected to remain in service into the mid-1980s.

Design: SCB No. 150. These submarines have the "tear-drop" or modified-spindle hull tested in the research submarine Albacore (AGSS 569), especially designed for underwater performance. Note the relative surface/submerged speeds of the Barbels compared with those of the previous, conventional-hull Darter.

As built, these submarines had bow-mounted diving planes; they were relocated to the sail structure.

The lines of the diesel submarine Blueback show a strong outer resemblance to the Permit-class SSNs. The tug Cusseta (YTM 405) stands by. (1983, Giorgio Arra)

1 ATTACK SUBMARINE: "DARTER"

Number	Name	FY	Builder	Laid down	Launched	Commissioned	Status
SS 576	DARTER	54	General Dynamics/Electric Boat	10 Nov 1954	28 May 1956	20 Oct 1956	**PA**

Displacement: 1,720 tons standard
2,388 tons submerged
Length: 268⁷/₁₂ feet (81.9 m)
Beam: 27⅛ feet (8.3 m)
Draft: 19 feet (5.8 m)
Propulsion: 3 diesels (Fairbanks Morse); 4,500 bhp
2 electric motors (Elliott); 4,500 shp; 2 shafts
Speed: 19.5 knots surface
14 knots submerged
Manning: 93 (8 officers + 85 enlisted)
Missiles: none
Torpedo tubes: 8 21-inch (533-mm) tubes (6 bow Mk 54 + 2 stern Mk 55)
ASW weapons: Mk 37 torpedoes
Radars: BPS-12
Sonars: BQS-4
BQG-4 PUFFS
Fire control: 1 Mk 106 torpedo FCS

Torpedoes: The two stern tubes were provided for anti-escort torpedoes, i.e., to fire at attacking ASW ships during evasion maneuvers. (In the basic TANG class these tubes were originally to launch only torpedo countermeasure devices.)

The DARTER is the only U.S. submarine still carrying Mk 37 torpedoes. She will not be refitted to fire the Mk 48 now carried by all other U.S. submarines.

The DARTER was built to an improved TANG-class design with the construction of further submarines of this class differing in favor of the more capable BARBEL class. Although scheduled to be stricken in 1978, the DARTER has been retained in service. She is home ported in Sasebo, Japan.

Class: The GRAYBACK and GROWLER were to have been of this class but were completed instead as Regulus guided missile submarines, SSG 574 and SSG 577, respectively.

Design: SCB No. 116. The DARTER and previous TANG class had the hull form, large batteries, streamlined superstructure, snorkel breathing device, and other features of the German Type XXI submarine, a highly advanced undersea craft that went to sea in 1945. The U.S. Navy also incorporated these features into 52 World War II submarines modernized under the GUPPY program (Greater Underwater Propulsive Power).

DARTER (1980, Giorgio Arra)

The DARTER at high speed on the surface in the Far East. She had been scheduled to be stricken in fiscal 1978 but has now been scheduled to remain in service until fiscal 1990. Note her distinctive BQG-4 PUFFS sonar domes, radar mounted on mast, and windows of sheltered navigation bridge atop sail. (1984, Giorgio Arra)

"TANG" CLASS

All six of the TANG-class fast attack submarines, completed in 1952, have been stricken: TANG (SS/AGSS 563) transferred to Turkey 8 February 1980; TRIGGER (SS 564) to Italy 10 July 1973; GUDGEON (SS/SSAG 567) to Turkey 30 September 1983; and HARDER (SS 568) to Italy 15 March 1974.

Three submarines of this class were to have been transferred to Iran, the TANG, WAHOO (SS 565), and TROUT (SS 566). Their transfer was cancelled in 1979 after the fall of the Shah. The WAHOO was decommissioned on 27 June 1980, partially stripped and laid up. The TROUT was technically transferred to Iran on 19 December 1978 but was decommissioned on 6 May 1980 and retained by the U.S. Navy; both ships are laid up at the Philadelphia Naval Shipyard.

1 RESEARCH SUBMARINE: "DOLPHIN"

Number	Name	FY	Builder	Laid down	Launched	Commissioned	Status
AGSS 555	DOLPHIN	61	Portsmouth Naval Shipyard	9 Nov 1962	8 June 1968	17 Aug 1968	**PA**

Displacement: 800 tons standard / 930 tons submerged
Length: 152 feet (46.35 m)
Beam: 19⁵/₁₂ feet (5.9 m)
Draft: 18 feet (5.5 m)
Propulsion: 2 diesels (Detroit) / 1 electric motor (Elliott); 1,650 shp; 1 shaft
Speed: 12+ knots submerged
Manning: 29 (3 officers + 26 enlisted)
Missiles: none
Torpedo tubes: removed
Radars: SPS-53
Sonars: (see notes)
Fire control: none

The DOLPHIN is an experimental, deep-diving submarine. Reportedly, she has reached greater depths than any other operational submarine. The DOLPHIN is assigned to Submarine Development Group 1, providing support to the Naval Ocean Systems Center and several other Navy research activities. Recent research experiments in which the DOLPHIN has participated include aircraft-to-submarine laser communication tests. The DOLPHIN will be modified to serve as an *in situ* test platform for HY-130 steel (see Modification notes).

Design: SCB No. 207. The DOLPHIN has a constant-diameter pressure hull with an outside diameter of approximately 15 feet with hemisphere heads at both ends. An improved rudder design and other features permit maneuvering without conventional submarine diving planes. There are minimal penetrations of the pressure hull (e.g., only one access hatch) and built-in safety systems that automatically surface the submarine in an emergency.

An experimental torpedo tube that was originally fitted was removed in 1970.

Electronics: Various experimental sonar sets have been fitted in the DOLPHIN. Her original bow sonar, which had four arrays that could be extended at 90° angles to the submarine's bow-stern axis, has been removed.

A BQS-15 sonar was installed in 1971.

Engineering: Submerged endurance is approximately 24 hours; her sea endurance is about 14 days.

DOLPHIN (1982, U.S. Navy)

Modification: The DOLPHIN is scheduled to be modified to serve as a test platform for HY-130 steel for possible use in future submarine construction.[2] The modifications will consist of: (1) addition of a new HY-130 pressure hull section of sufficient length to support installation of a second battery for increased submerged endurance; (2) replace-ment of the existing HY-80 non-pressure hull bow and forward end of the pressure hull with HY-130; and (3) addition of a three-foot length to the forward non-pressure hull length for increased ballast tank volume.

The DOLPHIN modifications will alleviate the need for the long-planned Nuclear Hull Test Vehicle (NHTV); see Chapter 27.

The DOLPHIN at high surface speed; note her modified sail structure and absence of bow sonar "pot" compared to earlier configuration. (1980, U.S. Navy)

POST–WORLD WAR II SUBMARINE PROGRAMS

There have been several nuclear-propelled attack submarine designs put forward that have not been constructed. The major programs are listed below:

FLEET ATTACK SUBMARINE

During the later 1970s, the Department of Defense pressed the Navy to develop an SSN *smaller* than the LOS ANGELES. Several preliminary designs were developed, among them:

Type	Reactor	Submerged displacement	Torpedo tubes	Cost*
SSN 688	S6G	6,900 tons	4	1.0
SSNX (Advanced SSN 688)	S6G	>7,200 tons	6	1.01
Re-engineered SSN 688	S6G	~7,000 tons	4	.96
Fleet Attack SSN	S5W	~5,000 tons	6	.74

*Normalized cost average for ten follow-on submarines.

Based on these concepts the Carter Administration (1978–1981) proposed the construction of the Fleet Attack type (nicknamed "Fat Albert" for the initials FA). It would have been about five knots slower than the SSN 688, or about the same speed as the previous STURGEON class.

Strong resistance to the construction of any type other than the LOS ANGELES class was led by Admiral Rickover, and no action was taken to construct a smaller or more capable SSN. In July 1981 the Navy ceased all studies of an alternative to the SSN 688, but the following summer the improved SSN design was initiated.

ADVANCED PERFORMANCE HIGH-SPEED NUCLEAR ATTACK SUBMARINE

In 1970–1971 the Chief of Naval Operations (CNO), Admiral Elmo R. Zumwalt, proposed a series of anti-ship missiles, including an anti-ship missile launched from submarines with a longer range than the then-proposed Harpoon. At about the same time, the Secretary of Defense, Melvin R. Laird, expressed interest in a submarine-launched strategic cruise missile as a backup system in the event of failure of the Strategic Arms Limitation Talks (SALT I).

A CNO-sponsored study was initiated. Available records are unclear as to whether the study arrived independently at the concept of vertical-launch missile tubes in an SSN, or whether this concept originated at the Electric Boat yard. The concept of a Vertical Launch System (VLS) separate from the torpedo tubes would overcome the limited weapons capability of existing SSNs (four torpedo tubes and approximately 25 internally carried weapons). This submarine was designated the Sub-marine Tactical Anti-ship Weapons System (STAWS).

A short time later Admiral Rickover proposed a larger submarine for the anti-ship missile role with a high speed to permit operations against surface warships. A missile compartment was to be provided aft of the sail for 20 vertical-launch cruise missile tubes, while a 60,000-shp re-actor plant was to provide speeds in excess of 30 knots. Rickover had begun work on the reactor plant in 1968, and by 1971 he put forth a plan for a large, specialized SSGN. (See approximate characteristics, below.)

[2] HY-130 indicates High Yield steel capable of withstanding a pressure of 130,000 pounds per square inch.

Admiral Zumwalt strongly opposed a large submarine design, which would be proposed in addition to the new SSN 688-class ASW submarine and, possibly, production of a slower, quieter submarine based on the SSN 685 design. Accordingly, the specialized SSGN was cancelled in 1973. Admiral Rickover subsequently adopted the basic plant design for the OHIO (SSBN 726) class.

Displacement:	approx. 13,700 tons submerged
Length:	472 feet (143.8 m) oa
Beam:	40 feet (12.2 m)
Draft:	
Propulsion:	2 steam turbines; approx. 60,000 shp; 1 shaft
Reactors:	1 pressurized-water (General Electric)
Speed:	30+ knots
Manning:	
Missiles:	20 vertical-launch anti-ship missiles
Torpedo tubes:	4 21-inch (533-mm) amidships
ASW weapons:	torpedoes
Radars:	
Sonars:	

SS 551	BASS (ex-K 2/SSK 2)	comm. 1951	stricken 1 Apr 1965
SS 552	BONITA (ex-K 3/SSK 3)	comm. 1952	stricken 1 Apr 1965
SS 553	(KINN)	Norway OSP	completed 1964
SS 554	(SPRINGEREN)	Denmark OSP	completed 1964
AGSS 555	DOLPHIN		
SS 556–562	not used		
SS 563–568	TANG class		
AGSS 569	ALBACORE	comm. 1953	stricken 1 May 1980
AGSS 570	completed as SST 1		
SSN 571	NAUTILUS	comm. 1954	memorial
SSR 572	SAILFISH (later SS)	comm. 1956	stricken
SSR 573	SALMON (later SS)	comm. 1956	stricken 1 Oct 1977
SSG 574	GRAYBACK (later LPSS/SS)	comm. 1958	stricken 15 Jan 1984
SSN 575	SEAWOLF		
SS 576	DARTER		
SSG 577	GROWLER	comm. 1958	stricken 30 Sep 1980
SSN 578–579	SKATE class		
SS 580–582	BARBEL class		
SSN 583–584	SKATE class		
SSN 585	SKIPJACK		
SSRN 586	TRITON (later SSN)		
SSGN 587	HALIBUT (later SSN)		
SSN 588–592	SKIPJACK class		
SSN 593	THRESHER	comm. 1961	sunk 10 Apr 1963
SSN 594–596	PERMIT class		
SSN 597	TULLIBEE		
SSBN 598–602	GEORGE WASHINGTON class		
SSN 603–607	PERMIT class		
SSBN 608–611	ETHAN ALLEN class		
SSN 612–615	PERMIT class		
SSBN 616–617	LAFAYETTE class		
SSBN 618	ETHAN ALLEN class		
SSBN 619–620	LAFAYETTE class		
SSN 621	PERMIT class		
SSBN 622–636	LAFAYETTE class		
SSN 637–639	STURGEON class		
SSBN 640–645	LAFAYETTE class		
SSN 646–653	STURGEON class		
SSBN 654–659	LAFAYETTE class		
SSN 660–670	STURGEON class		
SSN 671	NARWHAL		

SSN 672–684	STURGEON class
SSN 685	GLENARD P. LIPSCOMB
SSN 686–687	STURGEON class
SSN 688–725	LOS ANGELES class
SSBN 726–749	OHIO class
SSN 750–	LOS ANGELES class

Diesel-Electric Submarines

U.S. submarine programs reached hull number SS 562 during World War II with hulls SS 526–562 being cancelled late in the war. Subsequently, five of these numbers were assigned to postwar submarines, three U.S. submarines and American-financed, foreign-built submarines (Offshore Procurement).

The last war-built submarine on the Naval Register was the transport submarine SEALION (LPSS 315), decommissioned and laid up in 1970 and stricken on 15 March 1977. The last active submarine of World War II construction was the TIGRONE (AGSS 419), decommissioned on 30 June 1975 and stricken on 27 June 1975 (i.e., three days before being formally decommissioned).

All postwar U.S. submarines have been numbered in the same series except for three small, hunter-killer submarines (SSK) and three training submarines (SST), which were in separate series.

The U.S Navy's lone midget submarine, the X-1, completed in 1955, was stricken on 16 February 1973.

HUNTER-KILLER SUBMARINES

SSK 1	BARRACUDA (ex-K 1)	comm. 1951	to SST 3
SSK 2	BASS (ex-K 2)	comm. 1951	to SS 551
SSK 3	BONITA (ex-K 3)	comm. 1952	to SS 552

These were small (1,000-ton, 196-foot) hunter-killer submarines, intended to lie in wait to intercept Soviet submarines off their home ports and in narrow waterways. Several hundred were to have been produced in time of war. They were originally assigned K-number "names" and were given fish names in 1955. The BASS and BONITA were reclassified SS in 1959 for use in the training role; the BARRACUDA was changed to SST in 1959 for training.

TRAINING SUBMARINES

SST 1	MACKEREL (ex-T 1)	comm. 1953	stricken 31 Jan 1973
SST 2	MARLIN (ex-T 2)	comm. 1953	stricken 31 Jan 1973
SST 3	BARRACUDA (ex-K 1/SSK 1)	comm. 1951	stricken 1 Oct 1973

The SST 1 and 2 were small (310-ton, 133-foot) submarines intended for training and target use. The MACKEREL was ordered as AGSS 570 and completed as the SST 1. Originally assigned T-number "names," they were given fish names in 1956.

In addition to three built-for-the-purpose SSKs, the nuclear-powered TULLIBEE was built as an SSKN (although designated SSN 597) and seven GATO (SS 212)-class diesel submarines were converted to SSKs in the 1950s.

13 Aircraft Carriers

The U.S. Navy has 13 aircraft carriers in active commission in late 1984, four nuclear-powered ships (CVN) and nine conventional, oil-fueled ships (CV). Under current operating practice, two carriers are normally forward deployed to the Mediterranean and two to the Western Pacific–Indian Ocean region. The remaining carriers are in transit to or from deployment areas, engaged in fleet exercises or other types of training, or are in overhaul. However, the crises and conflicts of the early 1980s have led to more flexible carrier deployment patterns—called FlexOps—with carriers being withdrawn from some areas and spending more time at sea to provide for multi-carrier exercises or to support special operations, as the continuing crisis in Lebanon and the invasion of Grenada in October 1983. Carrier deployments have thus significantly exceeded the nominal six months' deployment and 12 months in transit/overhaul/local operations.

An additional conventional carrier is in long-term modernization (SLEP) and three nuclear carriers are under construction. The latter ships are the THEODORE ROOSEVELT, that was authorized by Congress during the Carter Administration (1977–1981) after being vetoed by Mr. Carter a year before, and the GEORGE WASHINGTON and ABRAHAM LINCOLN, both authorized as part of the Reagan Administration's buildup of U.S. naval forces. The authorization of the two latter carriers in fiscal 1983 marked the first time since World War II that two aircraft carriers were authorized in one year.

When the ROOSEVELT is commissioned in 1987, the ship should raise the number of operational carriers to 14. The subsequent delivery of the WASHINGTON and LINCOLN will be offset by the retirement from first-line service of the MIDWAY and CORAL SEA of World War II construction. Other factors that will influence carrier force levels include whether the four conventional KITTY HAWK-class carriers will be taken out of service, sequentially, for a two-year-plus SLEP modernization, and the feasibility of continuing the early nuclear carrier ENTERPRISE in service beyond the 1990s. Completed in 1961, the ENTERPRISE has eight outdated nuclear reactors that may prove too difficult to keep in service beyond a 30-year service life. Thus, the U.S. carrier force of the mid-1990s could range from 13 to 15 ships, of which six or seven would be nuclear powered.

Also in service is the former aircraft carrier LEXINGTON, employed as a training ship (AVT) for carrier landings in the Gulf of Mexico. She has no aircraft support capabilities or other features that would permit her to operate in a combat role. The CORAL SEA is scheduled to replace the LEXINGTON in this role about 1991.

Four aircraft carriers are laid up in reserve, all World War II-built ships of the ESSEX/HANCOCK class. In 1981 the Reagan Administration sought to reactivate the ORISKANY or BON HOMME RICHARD to increase the deployable carrier force. The preliminary cost estimate for reactivating one of these ships was $503 million (fiscal 1982 dollars). After extensive consideration, the Congress refused to fund the ships because of their poor material condition, their limited remaining service life, and the problems in obtaining suitable aircraft for them.

There have been several efforts since 1970 to initiate the construction of smaller aircraft carriers—the sea control ship (SCS), VSTOL Support Ship (VSS), and mid-size carrier (CVV). Such programs have been staunchly opposed by proponents of large nuclear carriers within the Navy and Congress, although such ships could supplement and not necessarily replace the larger ships. (See discussion at the end of this chapter.)

Electronic warfare: All active aircraft carriers have the SLQ-17 Deceptive Electronic Countermeasures (DECM) and a variant of the WLR-8 radar intercept set. When installed together these are known as the SLQ-29 EW system. All carriers were scheduled to receive the WLR-8(V)4. That set was installed, however, only in the ENTERPRISE during her 1979–1981 overhaul, and in 1983 the Navy moved to cancel the further installation of that set. Instead all carriers will receive the WLR-1H radar intercept set.

Type	Class/Ship	Comm.	Active	Building	Reserve	Notes
CVN 68	NIMITZ	1975–	3	3	—	nuclear powered
CVN 65	ENTERPRISE	1961	1	—	—	nuclear powered
CV 63	KITTY HAWK	1961–1968	4	—	—	
CV 59	FORRESTAL	1955–1959	3	—	—	plus one ship in yard for SLEP
CV 41	MIDWAY	1945–1947	2	—	—	
CV/CVA	HANCOCK	1944–1950	—	—	2	
CVS	ESSEX	1943–1944	—	—	2	
AVT 16	LEXINGTON	1943	1	—	—	training ship

The aircraft carrier is the centerpiece of the 600-plus ship fleet being developed by the Reagan Administration. Here three carriers—the CORAL SEA (left), MIDWAY, and ENTERPRISE—close for photographs during a fleet exercise in the North Pacific in May 1983. After the exercise the CORAL SEA shifted to the Atlantic Fleet. (U.S. Navy)

The DWIGHT D. EISENHOWER during a port visit to Portsmouth, England. Aircraft carriers are impressive—in appearance as well as in combat capability. (1981, Giorgio Arra)

3 + 3 AIRCRAFT CARRIERS: "NIMITZ" CLASS

Number	Name	FY	Builder	Laid down	Launched	Commissioned	Status
CVN 68	NIMITZ	67	Newport News Shipbuilding	22 June 1968	13 May 1972	3 May 1975	**AA**
CVN 69	DWIGHT D. EISENHOWER	70	Newport News Shipbuilding	14 Aug 1970	11 Oct 1975	18 Oct 1977	**AA**
CVN 70	CARL VINSON	74	Newport News Shipbuilding	11 Oct 1975	15 Mar 1980	13 Mar 1982	**PA**
CVN 71	THEODORE ROOSEVELT	80	Newport News Shipbuilding	31 Oct 1981	Oct 1984	early 1987	Building
CVN 72	ABRAHAM LINCOLN	83	Newport News Shipbuilding	Nov 1984	1987	early 1990	Building
CVN 73	GEORGE WASHINGTON	83	Newport News Shipbuilding	1985	1989	early 1992	Building

Displacement:	81,600 tons standard
	91,400 tons full load
	93,400 tons combat load
Length:	1,040 feet (317.2 m) wl
	1,089 feet (332.1 m) oa
Beam:	134 feet (40.86 m)
Flight deck:	252 feet (76.85 m) max
Draft:	36½ feet (11.1 m)
Propulsion:	4 steam turbines; 260,000 + shp; 4 shafts
Reactors:	2 pressurized-water A2W (Westinghouse)
Speed:	30 + knots

Manning:	Total	Officers	Enlisted
CVN 68	2,998	147	2,851
CVN 69	3,047	148	2,899
CVN 70	3,047	141	2,906

Air wing:	approx. 2,625 (300 officers + 2,325 enlisted)
Aircraft:	approx. 90
Catapults:	4 steam Mk 13-1
Elevators:	4 deck edge (85 × 52 feet │ 25.9 × 15.85 m)
Missiles:	3 8-tube Sea Sparrow launchers Mk 25 in CVN 68, 69
	3 8-tube NATO Sea Sparrow launchers Mk 29 in later ships
Guns:	3 20-mm Phalanx CIWS Mk 16 (3 multibarrel) in CVN 68 and 69;
	4 in later ships
Radars	**SPS-10F surface search**
	SPS-48E 3-D search
	SPS-49 air search
Sonars:	none
Fire control:	3 Mk 115 missile FCS in CVN 68, 69
	3 Mk 91 missile FCS in later ships

These are the largest warships ever built. A program to construct three ships was approved by the Defense Department during the Vietnam War as replacements for the three MIDWAY-class carriers to maintain a force of 12 large carriers. Subsequently, three additional ships have been authorized. The CVN 71 was forced on the Carter Administration by Congress in 1980; the CVN 72 and 73 were the efforts of Secretary of the Navy John Lehman during the Reagan Administration's first year (1982). The CVN 72 and 73 will probably replace the MIDWAY and CORAL SEA, providing the Navy with 14 deployable aircraft carriers in the early 1990s (plus one ship in SLEP overhaul).

The first three ships were delayed during construction by labor strikes and schedule problems at the Newport News yard. The NIMITZ was seven years from keel laying to commissioning compared with less than four years for the more complex (eight-reactor) ENTERPRISE. The Newport News yard plans to deliver the ROOSEVELT in 1986 or 1987, up to 14 months before the contract delivery date of February 1988.

All ships initially operated in the Atlantic, being based on the U.S. East Coast. The VINSON shifted to the Pacific Fleet in 1983 and the NIMITZ is to shift to the Pacific in 1987. The VINSON was replaced in the Atlantic by the CORAL SEA and the NIMITZ will be replaced by the new ROOSEVELT.

Class: A seventh ship, CVN 74, was included in the last year of the five-year (FY 1984–1988) shipbuilding program put forward by the Reagan Administration in January 1983. That ship, however, was included for "planning" purposes only and appeared to be a backup in the event

The NIMITZ at anchor in Naples during a deployment with the Sixth Fleet. Carrier Air Wing 8 is on board. This angle accentuates the amidships location of the island structure. The SPS-43A radar aft of the island has since been replaced by an SPS-49. All three of the starboard deck-edge elevators are lowered to the hangar deck level. (1981, Giorgio Arra)

that Congress declined to authorize one of the two NIMITZ-class ships in the fiscal 1983 program.

Classification: The NIMITZ and EISENHOWER were ordered as attack aircraft carriers (CVAN); they were changed to multi-mission aircraft carriers (CVN) on 30 June 1975. The VINSON and later ships were ordered as CVN.

Cost: By simultaneously awarding a contract for the CVN 72 and 73, construction costs were reduced by a total of $750 million for both ships. Total cost of the two ships was estimated at $6.8 billion at the time of contract award (27 December 1982).

In the fiscal 1984 budget, the CVN 71 and 72 costs were listed as:

	FY 1983	FY 1984
Construction	$6,545.4 million	—
Escalation/cost growth	$ 5.3 million	$88.2 million
Outfitting	$ 3.4 million	$10.0 million

Design: SCB No. 102. The general arrangement of these ships is similar to the previous KITTY HAWK class with respect to flight deck, elevators, and island structure. Full load is the maximum displacement for entering port; combat load is the maximum amount of aviation fuel and ordnance that can be loaded at sea. The hangar deck is 684 feet long, 108 feet wide, and 26½ feet high.

This design has been "in production" longer than any other carrier class in history. The uncertainty of future CVN construction and the general excellence of the NIMITZ design alleviated major changes in the later ships.

Payload includes up to 2,970 tons of aviation ordnance and 2.7 million gallons of aviation fuel (JP-5).

Electronics: To be fitted with SPS-67 in place of the SPS-10F. The SLQ-25 Nixie torpedo countermeasure is planned for installation.

Engineering: These carriers have only two reactors compared with eight in the first nuclear carrier, the ENTERPRISE. The initial fuel cores in these ships are estimated to have a service life of at least 13 years (800,000 to one million n.miles).

Missiles: The NIMITZ and EISENHOWER are scheduled to receive the NATO Sea Sparrow missile system and associated Mk 91 control systems.

Names: The CVN 71–73 have names previously assigned to ballistic missile submarines (SSBN); the GEORGE WASHINGTON (SSBN 598) was still in service when the CVN 72 was named. The CVN 72 and 73 were named prior to their start, in part to preempt congressional pressure for naming one of the ships for Admiral Rickover (with the SSN 709 being named for the admiral).

The NIMITZ in the Indian Ocean with an air wing of more than 70 aircraft arrayed on the flight deck. The Navy has maintained at least one carrier in the Indian Ocean—and at times as many as three—since late 1979. The single portside elevator is lowered to the hangar deck. (1980, U.S. Navy)

The Dwight D. Eisenhower riding at anchor with Carrier Air Wing 7 embarked. When this edition of *Ships and Aircraft* went to press the SPS-43A radar was still mounted; the Independence was the only other carrier with that set. Note the aircraft crane aft of the No. 4 elevator and the ship's boats stacked on that elevator. (1981, Giorgio Arra)

An overhead view of the Eisenhower clearly shows the angled landing deck and how the four deck-edge elevators form part of the flight deck. F-14A fighters with wings swept back are around the after end of the deck. A-6A and A-7E attack planes plus a single EA-6BB electric warfare aircraft and E-2 early warning aircraft are parked forward. (1979, U.S. Navy)

The island of the CARL VINSON is covered with various electronic antennas. The lattice mast at left carries the antenna for SPS-49 long-range search radar; the mast atop the island has an SPN-43A Carrier Controlled Approach (CCA) radar; an SPS-48C 3-D air search radar is mounted atop the bridge. A pair of satellite communication antennas are atop the mast. (1984, Giorgio Arra)

DWIGHT D. EISENHOWER (1981, Giorgio Arra)

The CARL VINSON off San Francisco with a flight deck empty of aircraft belies the massive striking power of a modern aircraft carrier. A Phalanx CIWS and a NATO Sea Sparrow launcher are visible on the starboard bow, just below the flight deck. (1984, Giorgio Arra)

1 NUCLEAR-PROPELLED AIRCRAFT CARRIER: "ENTERPRISE"

Number	Name	FY	Builder	Laid down	Launched	Commissioned	Status
CVN 65	ENTERPRISE	58	Newport News Shipbuilding	4 Feb 1958	24 Sep 1960	25 Nov 1961	**PA**

Displacement:	75,700 tons standard
	89,600 tons full load
Length:	1,040 feet (317.2 m) wl
	1,123 feet (342.5 m) oa
Beam:	133 feet (40.5 m)
Flight deck:	248⅓ feet (75.7 m)
Draft:	35¾ feet (10.9 m)
Propulsion:	4 steam turbines (Westinghouse); approx. 280,000 shp; 4 shafts
Reactors:	8 pressurized-water A2W (Westinghouse)
Speed:	30 + knots
Manning:	3,158 (165 officers + 2,993 enlisted)
Air wing:	approx. 2,625 (300 officers + 2,325 enlisted)
Aircraft:	approx. 90
Catapults:	4 steam C13
Elevators:	4 deck edge (85 × 52 feet | 25.9 × 15.9 m)
Missiles:	3 8-tube NATO Sea Sparrow launchers Mk 29
Guns:	3 20-mm Phalanx CIWS Mk 16 (3 multibarrel)
Radars:	SPS-10 surface search
	SPS-48 3-D search
	SPS-49 air search
	SPS-65 threat warning
Sonars:	none
Fire control:	3 Mk 91 missile FCS

The ENTERPRISE was the world's second nuclear-propelled surface warship and at the time of her construction was the world's largest and most expensive warship. Estimated construction cost was $444 million (contemporary conventional carrier construction cost in same-year dollars was estimated at $265 million).

Class: Congress provided $35 million in the fiscal 1960 budget for long-lead time nuclear components for a second aircraft carrier of this type. The Eisenhower Administration (1953–1961), however, deferred the project. The next nuclear carrier, the NIMITZ, was not ordered until almost ten years after the ENTERPRISE with two oil-burning carriers having been constructed in the interim period.

Classification: Originally classified as an attack aircraft carrier (CVAN), the ENTERPRISE was changed to a multi-mission carrier (CVN) on 30 June 1975.

Design: SCB design No. 160. The ENTERPRISE was built to a modified KITTY HAWK design, but in her original configuration she had a distinctive island structure because of the arrangement of "billboard" radar antennas (see Radar notes). Her hangar deck is 860 feet long, 107 feet wide, and 25 feet high.

Engineering: At the time of her construction, the ENTERPRISE was estimated to have a cruising range of more than 200,000 n.miles without refueling. On her initial fuel cores the ship travelled 207,000 n.miles.

The two-reactor A1W prototype of the ENTERPRISE propulsion plant was constructed at Arco, Idaho.

Missiles: As built the ENTERPRISE had neither defensive missiles nor guns, the planned Terrier system having been deleted from the design because of cost. Late in 1967 she was fitted with two Sea Sparrow Mk 25 launchers. During her 1979–1981 overhaul the NATO Sea Sparrow launchers were installed as were the Phalanx CIWS.

The ENTERPRISE on sea trials after her extensive overhaul which included removal of her fixed-array SPS-32/33 "billboard" radars. She now has an SPS-48 3-D search radar forward of her heavy pole mast and an SPS-49 aft; a SPN-series air control radar is mounted aft, on the starboard side. (1982, U.S. Navy; PHC Ronald Cabral)

Modernization: The ENTERPRISE underwent a 36-month modernization and overhaul from January 1979 to March 1982 at the Puget Sound NSYd. Although not formally considered a SLEP, the work was extensive. Also, the fixed-array SPS-32/33 antennas were removed from the island structure.

Operational: During August–October 1964 the ENTERPRISE, in company with the cruiser LONG BEACH (CGN 9) and frigate BAINBRIDGE (DLGN 25, now CGN 25), formed all-nuclear Task Force 1; the ships steamed around the world without refueling or replenishing, travelling 32,600 n.miles in 64 days, including time for port visits in several countries.

The ENTERPRISE shifted to the Pacific Fleet in 1965 and in November of that year began flying air strikes against North Vietnam, becoming the first nuclear ship to enter combat.

Radar: The ENTERPRISE and cruiser LONG BEACH were the only ships fitted with the Hughes SPS-32 and SPS-33 fixed-array radars. They were difficult to maintain and were replaced during the 1979–1981 modernization with conventional SPS-48 and SPS-49 radars.

ENTERPRISE (1983, Giorgio Arra)

The ENTERPRISE in San Francisco Bay. An SH-3 helicopter sits on the after flight deck. (1983, Giorgio Arra)

4 AIRCRAFT CARRIERS: "KITTY HAWK" AND "JOHN F. KENNEDY" CLASSES

Number	Name	FY	Builder	Laid down	Launched	Commissioned	Status
CV 63	KITTY HAWK	56	New York Shipbuilding, Camden, N.J.	27 Dec 1956	21 May 1960	29 Apr 1961	**PA**
CV 64	CONSTELLATION	57	New York Naval Shipyard, Brooklyn, N.Y.	14 Sep 1957	8 Oct 1960	27 Oct 1961	**PA**
CV 66	AMERICA	61	Newport News Shipbuilding	9 Jan 1961	1 Feb 1964	23 Jan 1965	**AA**
CV 67	JOHN F. KENNEDY	63	Newport News Shipbuilding	22 Oct 1964	27 May 1967	7 Sep 1968	**AA**

Displacement:	60,100 tons standard CV 63, 64			
	60,300 tons standard CV 66			
	61,000 tons standard CV 67			
	80,800 tons full load CV 63, 64, 66			
	82,000 tons full load CV 67			

Manning:

	Total	Officers	Enlisted
CV 63	2,932	148	2,784
CV 64	2,912	148	2,764
CV 66	2,931	144	2,787
CV 67	2,953	142	2,811

Length: 990 feet (301.9 m) wl
1,062½ feet (324.0 m) oa CV 63
1,072½ feet (327.1 m) oa CV 64
1,047½ feet (319.5 m) oa CV 66, 67

Beam: 129½ feet (39.5 m) CV 63, 64
130 feet (39.6 m) CV 66, 67

Flight deck: 250 feet (76.2 m) CV 63, 64
266 feet (81.1 m) CV 66
267½ feet (81.6 m) CV 67

Draft: 36 feet (11.0 m)
Propulsion: 4 steam turbines (Westinghouse); 280,000 shp; 4 shafts
Boilers: 8 1,200 psi (Foster Wheeler)
Speed: 30 + knots
Range: 12,000 n.miles at 20 knots

Air wing: approx. 2,500 (300 officers + 2,200 enlisted)
Aircraft: approx. 85
Catapults: 4 steam C13 in CV 63, 64
3 steam C13 + 1 steam C13-1 in CV 66, 67
Elevators: 4 deck edge (85 × 52 feet | 25.9 × 15.9 m)
Missiles: 3 8-tube NATO Sea Sparrow launchers Mk 29
Guns: 3 20-mm Phalanx CIWS Mk 16 (3 multibarrel) except 1 in CV 67

Radars:

CV 63	CV 64	CV 66	CV 67
SPS-10B	SPS-10B	SPS-10F	SPS-10F
SPS-48C	SPS-48C	SPS-48C	SPS-48C
SPS-49	SPS-49	SPS-49	SPS-49
			SPS-65

Sonars: none (see notes)
Fire control: 3 Mk 91 missile FCS

The CONSTELLATION off the coast of southern California with Carrier Air Wing 9; she now has CVW-14 embarked. Her general arrangement is similar to that of the later (and larger) NIMITZ-class carriers. Nine of her 24 F-14A fighters dominate the after end of the flight deck. The CH-46 Sea Knight at the forward end of her angled deck is not part of the air wing. The twin Terrier missile launchers were removed in her 1982–1984 overhaul. (1981, U.S. Navy)

These ships have a modified FORRESTAL configuration with improved elevator and flight deck arrangements. The KITTY HAWK was delayed because of shipyard problems; the CONSTELLATION was delayed because of a fire on board while under construction; and the KENNEDY because of lengthy debates over whether the ship should have nuclear or conventional propulsion.

Builders: This class includes the last U.S. aircraft carriers to be built by shipyards other than Newport News.

Class: The KENNEDY is officially a separate, one-ship class. All four ships are often grouped with the FORRESTAL class in force level discussions.

Classification: All four ships were originally attack aircraft carriers (CVA). Two ships were changed to multi-mission carriers (CV) when modified to operate ASW aircraft, the KITTY HAWK on 29 April 1973 and the KENNEDY on 1 December 1974; the CONSTELLATION and AMERICA were changed to CV on 30 June 1975, prior to being modified.

Design: SCB No. 127, 127A, 127B, and 127C, respectively. These ships are larger than the FORRESTAL class and have an improved flight deck arrangement with two elevators forward of the island structure and the port-side elevator on the stern quarter rather than at the forward end of the angled flight deck.

The hangar deck in the first three ships is 740 feet long, 101 feet wide, and 25 feet high; in the KENNEDY the hangar deck is 688 feet long, 106 feet wide, and 25 feet high. The KENNEDY has her stack angled out to starboard to help carry exhaust gases away from the approach path to the flight deck.

Guns: All four ships are scheduled to receive three 20-mm Phalanx CIWS.

Missiles: The first three ships were built with Terrier missile launchers (Mk 10 Mod 3 on starboard quarter and Mk 10 Mod 4 on port quarter). The KENNEDY originally had three Sea Sparrow Mk 25 launchers. All four ships are eventually to have four NATO Sea Sparrow Mk 29 launchers and three associated Mk 91 fire control systems.

Sonar: The AMERICA and KENNEDY have bow sonar domes, but only the AMERICA had sonar installed. She was the only U.S. carrier so fitted at the time; the set, an SQS-23, was removed in late 1981.

The KITTY HAWK's island structure is dominated by her antenna mast and the SPS-49 radar; the adjacent lattice mast carries the SPS-48C. A Phalanx CIWS is fitted at the forward end of the island. (1983, Giorgio Arra)

The KENNEDY has a unique, angled stack, designed to help keep hot exhaust gases away from the aircraft approach path. The red E and three stripes indicate four awards for engineering excellence. (1981, Giorgio Arra)

KITTY HAWK with Carrier Air Wing 2 (1983, Giorgia Arra)

The AMERICA was the only active carrier with sonar, having a bow-mounted SQS-23 until 1981. This resulted in her having an anchor fitted into her stem to reduce potential damage to the sonar. A Phalanx CIWS is visible on her port bow sponson. (1983, Giorgio Arra)

With her flight deck clogged with aircraft, Marines exercise at the forward end of the CONSTELLATION's angled flight deck. Carrier Air Wing 9 is embarked, plus a pair of EA-3B Skywarriors from Fleet Air Reconnaissance Squadron 1 (one parked forward of the island structure and one aft). (1980, U.S. Navy)

3 + 1 AIRCRAFT CARRIERS: "FORRESTAL" CLASS

Number	Name	FY	Builder	Laid down	Launched	Commissioned	Status
CV 59	FORRESTAL	52	Newport News Shipbuilding	14 July 1952	11 Dec 1954	1 Oct 1955	Yard
CV 60	SARATOGA	53	New York Naval Shipyard	16 Dec 1952	8 Oct 1955	14 Apr 1956	**AA**
CV 61	RANGER	54	Newport News Shipbuilding	2 Aug 1954	29 Sep 1956	10 Aug 1957	**PA**
CV 62	INDEPENDENCE	55	New York Naval Shipyard	1 July 1955	6 June 1958	10 Jan 1959	**AA**

Displacement: 59,650 tons standard CV 59
60,000 tons standard CV 60–62
78,000 tons full load

Length: 990 feet (301.8 m) wl
1,039 feet (316.7 m) oa CV 59–61
1,046½ feet (319.0 m) oa CV 62

Beam: 129½ feet (39.5 m)

Flight deck: 238 feet (72.5 m) CV 59–61
238½ feet (72.7 m) CV 62

Draft: 37 feet (11.3 m)

Propulsion: 4 steam turbines (Westinghouse); 260,000 shp in CV 59, 280,000 shp in CV 60–62; 4 shafts

Boilers: 8 600 psi (Babcock & Wilcox) CV 59
8 1,200 psi (Babcock & Wilcox) CV 60–62

Speed: 33 knots CV 59
34 knots CV 60–62

Range: 12,000 n.miles at 20 knots

Manning:

	Total	Officers	Enlisted
CV 59	2,965	150	2,815
CV 60	3,036	137	2,899
CV 61	2,938	146	2,792
CV 62	2,833	143	2,690

Air wing: approx. 2,500 (300 officers + 2,200 enlisted)

Aircraft: approx. 90

Catapults: 2 steam C7 + 2 steam C11-1 in CV 59, 60
4 steam C7 in CV 61, 62

Elevators: 4 deck edge (63 × 52 feet | 19.2 × 15.9 m)

Missiles: 2 8-tube Sea Sparrow launchers Mk 25 in CV 59, 60
2 8-tube NATO Sea Sparrow launchers Mk 29 in CV 61, 62

Guns: 3 20-mm Phalanx CIWS Mk 16 (3 multibarrel) in CV 60

Radars: SPS-10 surface search
SPS-43A air search in CV 61
SPS-48 3-D search
SPS-49 air search in CV 59, 60, 62
SPS-58

Sonars: none

Fire control: 2 Mk 91 missile FCS in CV 61, 62
2 Mk 115 missile FCS in CV 59, 60

These were the world's first aircraft carriers to be constructed from the keel up after World War II. They were intended specifically to operate heavy and high-performance turbojet aircraft.

The FORRESTAL is undergoing a major SLEP modernization that began in January 1983 at the Philadelphia Naval Shipyard. The work is expected to be completed in May 1985 and is planned to add 10 to 15 years to the ship's nominal 30-year service life. The SARATOGA has already undergone SLEP (see below).

Classification: The FORRESTAL and SARATOGA were ordered as large aircraft carriers (CVB 59, 60); they were reclassified as attack aircraft carriers (CVA) on 1 October 1952. Two ships were changed to multi-mission aircraft carriers (CV) when modified to operate S-3A Viking

ASW aircraft, the SARATOGA on 30 June 1972, and the INDEPENDENCE on 28 February 1973. The FORRESTAL and RANGER were changed to CV on 30 June 1975, prior to modification.

Design: SCB No. 80. These ships incorporated many design features of the aborted carrier UNITED STATES (CVA 58). They were originally designed as axial (straight) deck ships. The FORRESTAL was modified during construction to incorporate the British-developed angled flight deck. As built the FORRESTAL had a large second mast on her island structure to carry electronic antennas; it has been replaced by a smaller pole mast. Details of these ships differ considerably.

The hangar decks of these ships are 740 feet long, 101 feet wide, and 25 feet high.

Engineering: The SARATOGA was the first U.S. Navy ship to have 1,200-psi boilers. The ship has had major problems with her propulsion plant.

Guns: As built all four ships had eight 5-inch/54 cal DP Mk 42 single guns, mounted in pairs on sponsons, both sides, forward and aft. The forward sponsons were removed early in their service because of damage in heavy seas (except that after deletion of guns, the RANGER retained the forward sponsons—the only ship to be permanently assigned to the Pacific and not have to operate in the rougher seas of the North Atlantic). The after guns were removed as Sea Sparrow launchers became available for these ships.

All ships of this class are to be provided with three Phalanx CIWS.

Missiles: All ships of this class are scheduled to have three Mk 29 NATO Sea Sparrow launchers and three associated Mk 91 missile FCS.

Modernization: The SARATOGA was modernized at the Philadelphia Naval Shipyard from October 1980 to February 1983 under the SLEP (Ship Life Extension Program), intended to extend her service life from a nominal 30 years by approximately 15 additional years.[1] The modernization included rehabilitation of the ship's hull, propulsion, auxiliary machinery, and piping systems, with improved radars, communications equipment, and aircraft launch and recovery systems being provided. The SLEP modernization cost an estimated $550 million; immediately afterwards several problems were found with the yard's work, including improper welding of boiler tubes that cost an additional $8 million to repair.

The FORRESTAL's SLEP modernization is estimated to cost $698.5 million. The INDEPENDENCE will be the third SLEP carrier, entering Philadelphia in April 1985, followed by the KITTY HAWK (mid-1987), CONSTELLATION (mid-1989), and RANGER (mid-1991).

[1]The SLEP could be considered as successor to the Navy's FRAM (Fleet Rehabilitation and Modernization) programs of the early 1960s.

The FORRESTAL swings at anchor in Suda Bay, Crete. Carrier Air Wing 17 shown here shifted to the SARATOGA in 1982 when the FORRESTAL entered the Philadelphia Naval Shipyard for an extensive modernization (SLEP). When this photo was taken the wing still had F-4J Phantoms; it now has F-14As in the two fighter squadrons. Note the dark funnel. (1978, U.S. Navy)

The FORRESTAL underway in the Mediterranean with CVW-17. An S-3A and F-4J are about to be launched from the forward catapults. Other aircraft line up behind them for takeoff while a pair of A-7E attack planes are on the angled-deck catapults. (1980, U.S. Navy; PH2 Paul O'Mara)

The RANGER has had the SPS-43A long-range search radar shown here on the after end of her island structure replaced by the SPS-49. She retains sponsons forward, originally provided to support twin 5-inch/54 cal DP guns. The port-side elevator is located just aft of those sponsons, shown at the flight deck level in this view. (1979, Giorgio Arra)

The RANGER's forward sponsons are clearly visible in this view; they have been deleted from the other ships of this class. The SPS-43A antenna is offset from the island structure. She has Carrier Air Wing 9 on board with tails of S-3A and A-6E aircraft protruding over the bow. (1981, Giorgio Arra)

2 AIRCRAFT CARRIERS: "MIDWAY" CLASS

Number	Name	Builder	Laid down	Launched	Commissioned	Status
CV 41	MIDWAY	Newport News Shipbuilding	27 Oct 1943	20 Mar 1945	10 Sep 1945	**PA**
CV 43	CORAL SEA	Newport News Shipbuilding	10 July 1944	2 Apr 1946	1 Oct 1947	**AA**

Displacement:	51,000 tons standard CV 41
	52,500 tons standard CV 43
	64,000 tons full load
Length:	900 feet (274.3 m) wl
	979 feet (298.4 m) oa
Beam:	121 feet (36.9 m)
Flight deck:	258½ feet (78.8 m) CV 41 (see notes)
	236 feet (71.9 m) CV 43
Draft:	36 feet (11.0 m)
Propulsion:	4 steam turbines (Westinghouse); 212,000 shp; 4 shafts
Boilers:	12 600 psi (Babcock & Wilcox)
Speed:	32 knots
Range:	15,000 n.miles at 15 knots
Manning:	CV 41 2,506 (127 officers + 2,379 enlisted)
	CV 43 2,524 (125 officers + 2,399 enlisted)
Air wing:	approx. 1,950 (225 officers + 1,725 enlisted)
Aircraft:	approx. 75
Catapults:	2 steam C13 in CV 41
	3 steam C11-1 in CV 43
Elevators:	3 deck edge (63 × 52 feet | 19.2 × 15.9 m) in CV 41
	3 deck edge (56 × 44 feet | 17.1 × 13.4 m) in CV 43
Missiles:	2 8-tube Sea Sparrow Mk 25 launchers in CV 41
Guns:	3 20-mm Phalanx CIWS Mk 16 (3 multibarrel) in CV 43 (1983)
Radars:	CV 41 / CV 43
	SPS-10F / SPS-10
	SPS-48C / SPS-30
	SPS-49 / SPS-43A
	SPS-65
Sonars:	none
Fire control:	2 Mk 115 missile FCS in CV 41

These are the only World War II-era warships remaining in commission with the U.S. Navy. The MIDWAY is based in Yokosuka, Japan, the only U.S. carrier ever to be based overseas. (Another U.S. carrier was planned for home porting in Pireaus, Greece, in the early 1970s; that proposal was dropped because of problems with the Greek government.) The CORAL SEA shifted home port from San Francisco (Alameda) to Norfolk in 1983, having been assigned to the Pacific Fleet from 1957 to 1983.

Previous plans to place the MIDWAY and CORAL SEA in reduced commission or decommission them completely have been deferred. The CORAL SEA is scheduled to replace the LEXINGTON as a training carrier about 1991 (with delivery of the CVN 73); the MIDWAY could continue serving as a first-line carrier into the early 1990s.

Aircraft: These ships do not operate F-14 Tomcat fighters or S-3 Viking ASW aircraft. During 1984–1985 these ships were provided with SH-3H Sea King ASW helicopters, replacing the SH-3G utility helicopers previously embarked.

Both ships are scheduled to operate "all" F/A-18 Hornet air wings, i.e., F/A-18s in two fighter and two attack squadrons, plus one squadron of A-6E Intruder attack aircraft. The CORAL SEA was to embark these aircraft in 1985 and the MIDWAY in 1986.

Class: A third ship of this class, the FRANKLIN D. ROOSEVELT (CV 42), was stricken on 1 October 1977 and scrapped. Three additional ships of this class were planned but not constructed, the CVB 44, which was cancelled on 1 November 1943, and the CVB 56 and 57, cancelled on 28 March 1945. None had been laid down.

Classification: These ships were built as large carriers (CVB 41–43), sometimes being referred to as "battle" carriers. They were reclassified as attack aircraft carriers (CVA) on 1 October 1952 and as aircraft carriers (CV) on 30 June 1975.

Design: These were the largest warships designed by the U.S. Navy during World War II, being significantly larger than the previous ESSEX (CV 9) class. They provided a larger aircraft capability and heavier gun battery than their predecessors and were the first U.S. aircraft carriers with an armored flight deck. Their original displacement was 45,000 tons standard and approximately 60,000 tons full load. As built, each ship had two catapults and three elevators (two centerline and one deck edge). Aircraft capacity was rated at 137 at the time completed. They were the first U.S. warships constructed with a beam too great to permit passage through the 110-foot-wide locks of the Panama Canal. Several U.S. battleships damaged at Pearl Harbor on 7 December 1941 were rebuilt with beam blisters that prevented them from passing through the canal.

The MIDWAY-class hangar decks are 692 feet long, 85 feet wide, and 17½ feet high.

Guns: As built, the MIDWAY mounted 18 single 5-inch/54-cal DP Mk 39 guns and the CORAL SEA 14 guns; these were arranged on both sides at the main deck level. Their secondary gun armament consisted of 84 40-mm AA guns and 28 20-mm AA guns at completion. The 40-

MIDWAY (1983, Giorgio Arra)

mm and 20-mm guns were replaced by twin 3-inch/50 AA gun mounts. Their gun armament was reduced until, by the 1970s, each ship had only three 5-inch guns. Subsequently all conventional guns were removed.

The CORAL SEA received three Phalanx CIWS in mid-1980, the first ship to have permanent installation of the system. Three Phalanx are planned for the MIDWAY.

Missiles: Sea Sparrow launchers are not planned for the CORAL SEA.

Modernization: Both ships have been extensively modernized. Their major modernizations, which provided enclosed ("hurricane") bows, angled flight decks, strengthened flight decks and elevators, and steam catapults were:

CV 41 SCB-110*   Puget Sound Naval Shipyard from September
                    1955 to September 1957
       SCB-101**   San Francisco Naval Shipyard from February
                    1966 to January 1970
CV 43 SCB-110A*   Puget Sound Naval Shipyard from April 1957
                    to January 1960

The MIDWAY's 1966–1970 modernization was delayed because of the workload for West Coast shipyards during the Vietnam conflict. A similar modernization for the CORAL SEA was cancelled.

Operational: These ships initially operated in the Atlantic-Mediterranean areas. The MIDWAY transferred to the Pacific Fleet in 1955 and the CORAL SEA in 1957, with the ROOSEVELT having continued to serve in the Atlantic-Mediterranean during the Korean War. All three ships

*Old SCB series.
**New SCB series (101.66).

flew combat strikes in the Vietnam conflict (with the ROOSEVELT based on the East Coast). The CORAL SEA shifted back to the Atlantic in 1983, departing her home port of San Francisco in March and arriving at Norfolk in September 1983.

The CORAL SEA has landed more aircraft than any other carrier afloat except for the LEXINGTON; on 24 December 1981 she recorded her 300,000th aircraft recovery.

MIDWAY (1983, Giorgio Arra)

MIDWAY (1981, Giorgio Arra)

The MIDWAY and RANGER steam together during exercises in the Philippine Sea. The MIDWAY—with Carrier Air Wing 5—is shown in her current configuration. The SPS-30 radar formerly mounted on her forward mast has been replaced by an SPS-49, and the SPS-43A previously fitted outboard of the broad funnel has been deleted with an SPS-48C installed on a new lattice mast aft of the funnel. (1982, U.S. Navy)

The CORAL SEA underway off the California coast before shifting to the Atlantic Fleet and beginning a major overhaul. She had the fleet's last SPS-30 height-finding radar forward and an SPS-43A rigged out from her thick pole mast. A Phalanx CIWS is fitted atop the bridge and another is on the starboard quarter; refueling hoses are rigged out below the island. (1982, U.S. Navy, PH2 Curt Fargo)

2 AIRCRAFT CARRIERS } **"HANCOCK" CLASS**
1 TRAINING CARRIER

Number	Name	Builder	Laid down	Launched	Commissioned	Status
AVT 16	LEXINGTON	Bethlehem Steel, Quincy, Mass.	15 July 1941	26 Sep 1942	17 Feb 1943	**TRA-A**
CVA 31	BON HOMME RICHARD	New York Navy Yard	1 Feb 1943	29 Apr 1944	26 Nov 1944	PR
CV 34	ORISKANY	New York Navy Yard	1 May 1944	13 Oct 1945	25 Sep 1950	PR

Displacement:	approx. 33,000 ton standard except
	33,250 tons standard CV 34
	39,000 tons full load AVT 16
	44,700 tons full load CVA 31
	42,000 tons full load CV 34
Length:	820 feet (250.0 m) wl
	894½ feet (272.8 m) oa except
	890 feet (271.4 m) oa CV 34
Beam:	103 feet (31.4 m) except
	106½ feet (32.5 m) CV 34
Flight deck:	185 feet (56.4 m) (see notes)
Draft:	31 feet (9.5 m)
Propulsion:	4 steam turbines (Westinghouse); 150,000 shp; 4 shafts
Boilers:	8 600 psi (Babcock & Wilcox)
Speed:	30+ knots
Range:	15,000 n.miles at 15 knots
Manning:	approx. 2,090 (110 officers + 1,980 enlisted) in CV/CVA
	1,395 (75 officers + 1,320 enlisted)
Air wing:	approx. 1,200 in CV/CVA
	none in AVT 16
Aircraft:	approx. 70–80
Catapults:	2 steam C11-1
Elevators:	{ centerline 70 × 44 feet | 21.3 × 13.4 m
	3 port deck edge 56 × 44 feet | 17.1 × 13.4 m (see notes)
	starboard deck edge 56 × 44 feet | 17.1 × 13.4 m
Missiles:	none
Guns:	4 5-inch (127-mm) 38 cal DP Mk 24 (4 single) except 2 guns in CV 34; all removed from AVT 16
Radars:	SPS-10 surface search
	SPS-12 air search in AVT 16
	SPS-37 or SPS-43A air search except none in AVT 16
Sonars:	none
Fire control:	1 Mk 37 GFCS with Mk 25 radar in CVA 31; 2 in CV 34; none in AVT 16
	2 Mk 56 GFCS with Mk 35 radar in CVA 31

These three ships and two listed below are the survivors of 23 ESSEX-class aircraft carriers completed from 1942 to 1946, plus the ORISKANY, suspended at the end of World War II and completed to a modified design in 1950. All of these ships have been extensively modernized to operate jet-propelled aircraft and are officially considered as the HANCOCK (CV 19) class.

The LEXINGTON is the only active ship, being employed as a pilot training ship in the Gulf of Mexico (home ported at Pensacola, Fla.). The ship has been assigned to training pilots in landing aboard carriers since December 1962. She was to have been decommissioned in 1979 and replaced in the AVT role by the CORAL SEA. However, under the Reagan Administration program to increase carrier force levels the "Lex" is now scheduled to be replaced in the AVT role by the CORAL SEA about 1991, when she is almost 50 years old. The LEXINGTON recorded

her 435,000th arrested landing in September 1983—significantly more than any other carrier in history. She cannot maintain or support tactical aircraft and her port deck-edge elevator has been deactivated (forms part of the flight deck).

The Reagan Administration in 1981 sought to reactivate the BON HOMME RICHARD or ORISKANY; however, Congress refused to fund the ships, in part because of their poor material condition and lack of suitable fighter aircraft (these ships cannot efficiently operate the F-4 Phantom; during the Vietnam War they flew F-8 Crusader fighters).

The BON HOMME RICHARD was decommissioned on 2 July 1971 and ORISKANY on 30 September 1976. Both are laid up at Bremerton, Wash.

Class: Twenty-four ESSEX-class ships were completed (CV 9–21, 31–34, 36–40, 45, and 47); two started ships were cancelled at the end of World War II (CV 35, 46), while six not-yet-started ships were cancelled on 27 March 1945 (CV 50–55).

One ship has been stricken since the 12th edition of *Ships and Aircraft*, the INTREPID (CV/CVA/CVS 11), stricken on 30 September 1980.

Classification: These ships were designated CV when built. See table for dates of reclassification. In her pilot-training role the LEXINGTON was originally classified as a training aircraft carrier (CVT) but changed to auxiliary aircraft landing training ship (AVT) to avoid confusion with carrier listings.

Design: Original standard displacement was 27,100 tons and full-load displacement 33,000 tons. Construction of the ORISKANY was suspended in 1946; resumed in 1947, she was completed to a modified design. Hangar decks are 644 feet long, 70 feet wide, and 17½ feet high.

Guns: As built, these ships had 12 5-inch/38 cal DP guns plus 68 to 72 40-mm AA guns and 52 20-mm AA guns, except the ORISKANY which was completed with eight 5-inch guns and 28 3-inch/50 cal AA guns. Most ships had their lighter weapons replaced by twin 3-inch mounts during the 1950s. Subsequently, gun armament was reduced to the minimal number of 5-inch guns shown above. The LEXINGTON is unarmed.

Modernization: All of these ships have been extensively modernized, receiving enclosed ("hurricane") bows, strengthened flight decks, improved elevators, etc. (The ORISKANY was completed to an SCB-27A configuration.) Their modernization period were:

AVT 16	SCB-27C	Puget Sound Naval Shipyard 1951–1955
CVA 31	SCB-27C	San Francisco Naval Shipyard 1952–1955
CV 34	SCB-27C	San Francisco Naval Shipyard 1956–1959

Radar: The radars listed above (and in the following class) are those installed at time of decommissioning.

The Bon Homme Richard in the Gulf of Tonkin shortly before her return to the United States and decommissioning. Her starboard deck-edge elevator is in the vertical position to facilitate underway replenishment; on her deck are 41 A-4 Skyhawks, F-8E Crusaders, a pair of KA-3B Skywarriors, a pair of E-1B Tracers, and three helicopters. (1969, U.S. Navy)

The training carrier Lexington operates in the Gulf of Mexico. She is the last of the 24 Essex-class ships in active service. Most of the 24-ship class saw considerable action in World War II. The Lexington can no longer support combat aircraft. The SPS-43A radar shown here has been deleted; the smaller SPS-12 air search radar is barely visible above the SPS-43A antenna. (U.S. Navy)

2 ASW AIRCRAFT CARRIERS: MODERNIZED "ESSEX" CLASS

Number	Name	Builder	Laid down	Launched	Commissioned	Status
CVS 12	HORNET	Newport News Shipbuilding	3 Aug 1942	29 Aug 1943	29 Nov 1943	PR
CVS 20	BENNINGTON	New York Navy Yard	15 Dec 1942	26 Feb 1944	6 Aug 1944	PR

Displacement:	approx. 33,000 tons standard
	40,000 tons full load
Length:	820 feet (250.0 m) wl
	890 feet (271.4 m) oa
Beam:	103 feet (31.4 m)
Flight deck:	approx. 195 feet (59.5 m)
Draft:	31 feet (9.45 m)
Propulsion:	4 steam turbines (Westinghouse); 150,000 shp; 4 shafts
Boilers:	8 600 psi (Babcock & Wilcox)
Speed:	30+ knots
Range:	15,000 n.miles at 15 knots
Manning:	approx. 1,615 (115 officers + 1,500 enlisted)
Air wing:	approx. 800
Aircraft:	approx. 45 as CVS
Catapults:	2 hydraulic H-8
Elevators:	3 (2 deck edge + 1 centerline)
Guns:	4 5-inch (127-mm) 38-cal DP Mk 24 (4 single)
Radars:	SPS-10 surface search
	SPS-30 height finding
	SPS-43A air search
Sonars:	SQS-23 bow-mounted
Fire control:	1 Mk 37 GFCS with Mk 25 radar
	3 Mk 56 GFCS with Mk 35 radar

These ships have not had the degree of modernization of the HAN-COCK-class carriers. The BENNINGTON was decommissioned on 15 January 1970 and the HORNET on 26 June 1970. Both ships are laid up at the Bremerton Naval Shipyard. See HANCOCK class for additional details.

Aircraft: In the CVS role at the time of being laid up, these ships each carried two squadrons of S-2 Tracker fixed-wing ASW aircraft and one squadron of SH-3 Sea King helicopters plus various detachments.

Classification: Built with CV classification; see table for changes.

Modernization: Both ships have been modernized and have enclosed ("hurricane") bows, angled flight decks, strengthened decks, etc.; their elevators have been rearranged and strengthened. Their major modernizations were:

CVS 12 SCB-27A New York Naval Shipyard 1951–1953
         SCB-125 Puget Sound Naval Shipyard 1955–1956
CVS 20 SCB-27A New York Naval Shipyard 1950–1952
         SCB-125 New York Naval Shipyard 1954–1955
Sonar: Both ships have SQS-23 sonar installed.

HORNET (1966, U.S. Navy)

"HANCOCK"/MODERNIZED "ESSEX" CLASSIFICATIONS

Built as	Changed to CVA	Changed to CVS	Changed to CV	Changed to CVT	Changed to AVT
CV 12		27 June 1958	—	—	—
CV 16		1 Oct 1962	—	1 Jan 1969	1 July 1978
CV 20	1 Oct 1952	30 June 1959	—	—	—
CV 31		—	—	—	—
CV 34		—	30 June 1975	—	—

POST-WORLD WAR II AIRCRAFT CARRIER PROGRAMS

World War II aircraft carrier programs reached hull number CVB 57 (a cancelled MIDWAY-class ship). After the war there were several proposals to construct new-design aircraft carriers, but the large number of fleet (CV), light (CVL), and escort (CVE) carriers available precluded any serious consideration of new construction except for "heavy" carriers (CVA) to operate large nuclear-strike aircraft.

The ORISKANY during flight operations in the Gulf of Tonkin. Note the shape of her forward elevator; designed to accommodate longer aircraft than the A-4 Skyhawk seen here. The Vietnam War was apparently the last combat action for the long-serving ESSEX-class carriers. (1968, U.S. Navy)

Underway replenishment was necessary every couple of days for U.S. carriers operating in the Gulf of Tonkin during the Vietnam War. Here the ASW carrier BENNINGTON takes aboard palletized munitions from the ammunition ship MAUNA KEA (AE 22). On her deck are S-2 Trackers, E-1 Tracers, and SH-3 Sea Kings; they flew general patrols, performed search-and-rescue missions, and kept a lookout for Soviet or Chinese submarine activity. (1968, U.S. Navy).

Heavy Aircraft Carriers

One CVA was laid down, the UNITED STATES (CVA 58), and although never completed, she served as the progenitor of the FORRESTAL and later large U.S. aircraft carriers. The UNITED STATES design provided for a flush-deck configuration that could simultaneously launch two heavy attack aircraft and two fighters from a pair of forward catapults and a pair of waist catapults. Three deck-edge elevators and one stern elevator would lift aircraft to the flight deck.

Four ships of this class were apparently contemplated. The UNITED STATES was authorized in fiscal 1948. The ship was laid down at Newport News Shipbuilding on 18 April 1949 but cancelled on 23 April 1949. Her SCB number was 6A. The following are the characteristics of the "final" design.

Displacement:	66,000 tons standard; 83,000 tons full load
Length:	1,030 feet (314.0 m) wl; 1,088 feet (331.7 m) oa
Beam:	125 feet (38.1 m)
Flight deck:	190 feet (57.9 m)
Propulsion:	4 steam turbines; 280,000 shp; 4 shafts
Boilers:	8 600 psi
Speed:	33 knots
Range:	12,000 n.miles at 20 knots
Manning:	4,127 (including air wing)
Guns:	8 5-inch/54 cal DP (8 single)
	16 3-inch/70 cal AA (8 twin)
	20 20-mm AA
Radars:	SPS-6 air search
	SPS-8 height finding
Sonars:	none

Sea Control Ships

The Sea Control Ship (SCS) concept appears to have evolved from proposals of the late 1960s for providing ASW helicopters as the primary armament of convoy escorts (with the designations DH, DDH, and DHK being used). Subsequently, in 1970 the Chief of Naval Operations, Admiral Elmo R. Zumwalt, proposed a class of at least eight sea control ships that would carry several SH-3 Sea King ASW helicopters plus a small number of AV-8 Harriers for self-defense. The SCS concept was evaluated at sea from October 1971 to January 1972 with the helicopter carrier GUAM (LPH 9).

The lead ship was planned for the fiscal 1975 shipbuilding program. However, Congress refused to authorize such ships because of their limited capability and strong opposition by the advocates of large carriers. A modified version of the SCS design was built for the Spanish Navy, the PRINCIPE DE ASTURIAS, launched in 1982.

Displacement:	9,770 tons light; 13,735 tons full load
Length:	585 feet (178.4 m) wl; 610 feet (186.0 m) oa
Beam:	80 feet (24.4 m)
Draft:	21 7/12 feet (6.6 m)
Propulsion:	2 gas turbines (GE LM 2500); 45,000 shp; 1 shaft
Speed:	26 knots
Manning:	approx. 700 (including air wing)
Aircraft:	3 AV-8 Harrier VSTOL aircraft
	17 SH-3 Sea King helicopters
Guns:	2 20-mm Phalanx CIWS Mk 16 (2 multibarrel)
Radars:	SPS-52 3-D
Sonars:	none

VSTOL Support Ships

During the mid-1970s there was increased U.S. Navy interest in VSTOL aircraft, with a major analysis known as the Sea-Based Air Master Study developing a long-term program for several categories of VSTOL aircraft. In 1975 the Chief of Naval Operations, Admiral James L. Holloway, III, proposed a VSTOL aircraft carrier of approximately twice the size of the aborted SCS that would be able to operate a number of improved Harrier combat aircraft in addition to ASW aircraft. About 50 design alternatives were considered, with some having a small number of catapults and arresting wires to permit the use of E-2 Hawkeye AEW aircraft and S-2 Viking aircraft.

The final VSS III design is described below. The Navy did not formally request funding of the ship and none was authorized. However, interest in the concept continued into the 1980s, encouraged in part by development of the AV-8B Advanced Harrier and proposals for an AV-8B + aircraft.

Displacement:	20,115 tons light; 29,130 tons full load
Length:	690 feet (210.4 m) wl; 717 feet (218.6 m) oa
Beam:	
Draft:	25 1/3 feet (7.7 m)
Propulsion:	4 gas turbines (GE LM 2500); 90,000 shp; 2 shafts
Speed:	30 knots
Manning:	1,600 (including air wing)
Aircraft:	approx. 30 VSTOL and helicopters
Missiles:	8 Harpoon SSM
Guns:	2 20-mm Phalanx CIWS Mk 16 (2 multibarrel)
Radars:	SPS-52 3-D
Sonars:	none

Medium Aircraft Carriers

The Ford Administration (1974–1977) and Carter Administration (1977–1981) both proposed the construction of large-deck conventional aircraft carriers of 50-60,000 tons to be constructed in lieu of additional NIMITZ-class ships at a ratio of about 2:1. A variety of designs was considered under this concept, ranging from about 40,000 tons full-load displacement (i.e., about the size of a HANCOCK-class ship) up to a repeat of the KENNEDY design.

The CVV put forth to Congress had the following dimensions; however, the ship was strongly opposed by proponents of the nuclear-powered NIMITZ, especially Admiral Rickover, and none was authorized.

Displacement:	45,200 tons light; 59,800 tons full load
Length:	860 feet (262.2 m) wl; 912 feet (278.0 m) oa
Beam:	126 feet (38.4 m)
Flight deck:	256 1/2 feet (78.2 m)
Draft:	34 7/12 feet (10.5 m)
Propulsion:	2 steam turbines; 140,000 shp; 2 shafts
Boilers:	6 1,200 psi
Speed:	27.8 knots
Manning:	4,025 (including air wing)
Aircraft:	approx. 50
Guns:	3 20-mm Phalanx CIWS Mk 16 (3 multibarrel)
Radars:	SPS-48 3-D
	SPS-49 air search
Sonars:	none

14 Battleships

The four U.S. Iowa-class battleships are the world's only ships of this category remaining in naval service. All four ships are planned for reactivation by the Reagan Administration with a potential remaining service life of 10 to 15 years. The two ships already returned to service are listed separately in this chapter because of their extensive modifications.

The issue of reactivating some or all of the Iowa-class ships to supplement carrier deployments was first raised in the early 1970s, but not until the Reagan Administration took office in January 1981 was their reactivation given a high priority by the Navy's leadership, especially Secretary of the Navy Lehman. The recommissioning of these ships has been Mr. Lehman's highest priority after the construction of the nuclear carriers CVN 72 and 73.

The four ships were in combat in the Pacific theater during World War II with all but the MISSOURI being decommissioned after the war. The MISSOURI, named for the home state of the incumbent president, was the scene of the Japanese surrender ceremonies in Tokyo Bay on 2 September 1945. She remained in service as a training ship until the Korean War (1950–1953), when she was rejoined in active service by all three sister ships. The entire class saw extensive action off Korea as flagships and as gunfire support ships.

All four were decommissioned after the Korean War, the last in 1957. The NEW JERSEY was recommissioned in 1968–1969 for the Vietnam War. (With the NEW JERSEY deactivation, she and the MISSOURI were mothballed at the Bremerton Naval Shipyard and the IOWA and WISCONSIN at the Philadelphia Naval Shipyard.)

In the late 1950s and early 1960s, there were proposals to convert some or all of the Iowa-class ships to strategic "missile monitors," carrying Polaris missiles.

During the 1960s and early 1970s there were several proposals to convert these ships to "commando ships," retaining some or all of their main gun battery with accommodations for several hundred Marines and space for assault helicopters. Other configurations suggested in this period were conversion to cruise missile carriers, with *several hundred* vertical-launch cruise missiles being fitted in place of the after turret, or to a battleship-VSTOL carrier, with the after turret replaced by a flight deck to operate AV-8B Harrier aircraft.

The VLS and Harrier configurations are still being considered for future modification to these ships should they remain in active service beyond the mid-1980s.

NEW JERSEY (1983, Giorgio Arra)

The return of the dreadnought: The NEW JERSEY on sea trials in September 1983, the first time that a battleship of any nation had been under way in 13 years. (1983, U.S. Navy; PH1 H. Gerwien)

2 BATTLESHIPS: MODERNIZED "IOWA" CLASS

Number	Name	Builder	Laid down	Launched	Commissioned	Recommissioned	Status
BB 61	IOWA	New York Navy Yard	27 June 1940	27 Aug 1942	22 Feb 1943	28 Apr 1984	**AA**
BB 62	NEW JERSEY	Philadelphia Navy Yard	16 Sep 1940	7 Dec 1942	23 May 1943	28 Dec 1982	**PA**

Displacement:	48,425 tons standard
	57,500 tons full load
Length:	860 feet (262.3 m) wl
	BB 61 887¼ feet (270.6 m) oa
	BB 62 887⁷⁄₁₂ feet (270.7 m) oa
Beam:	108⅙ feet (33.0 m)
Draft:	38 feet (11.6 m)
Propulsion:	4 steam turbines (General Electric in BB 61; Westinghouse in BB 62); 212,000 shp; 4 shafts
Boilers:	8 600 psi (Babcock & Wilcox)
Speed:	33 knots (see notes)
Range:	15,000 n.miles at 15 kots
Manning:	BB 61 1,510 (65 officers + 1,445 enlisted)
	BB 62 1,518 (65 officers + 1,453 enlisted)
Helicopters:	landing area
Missiles:	32 Tomahawk T-ASM/T-LAMs (4 quad ABL Mk 143)
	16 Harpoon SSMs (4 quad cannisters Mk 141)
Guns:	9 16-inch (406-mm) 50-cal Mk 7 (3 triple)
	12 5-inch (127-mm) 38-cal DP Mk 28 (6 twin)
	4 20-mm Phalanx CIWS Mk 16 (4 multibarrel)
ASW weapons:	none
Radars:	SPS-10F surface search
	SPS-49 air search
Sonars:	none
Fire control:	4 Mk 37 GFCS with Mk 25 radar
	2 Mk 38 gun directors with Mk 13 radar
	1 Mk 40 gun director with Mk 27 radar
	2 Mk 51 gun directors in BB 61
	6 Mk 56 gun directors with Mk 35 radar
	2 Mk 63 GFCS with Mk 34 radar in BB 61

Two IOWA-class battleships have been reactivated under the buildup of the fleet under the Reagan Administration, the NEW JERSEY being recommissioned in December 1982 and the IOWA in April 1984.[1]

The IOWA and NEW JERSEY are listed separately because of their extensive modifications. See subsequent IOWA-class listing for additional notes. The MISSOURI will be the third ship recommissioned; like the NEW JERSEY, she is being reactivated and modified at the Long Beach Naval Shipyard. Reactivation of the WISCONSIN is scheduled for 1985–1986.

Aircraft: In early 1984 the NEW JERSEY was fitted to launch and recover an Israeli-built Mistiff Remotely Piloted Vehicle (RPV) to provide surveillance and gunfire spotting in hostile areas of Beirut. Produced by Tadiran Industries, the RPV has a wing span of approximately 14 feet, length of 11 feet, and gross weight of 250 pounds with a maximum flight endurance of 6 to 9 hours at a 60-knot cruise speed.

Previously the NEW JERSEY had operated QH-50-series DASH unmanned helicopters for gunfire spotting off Vietnam in 1968.

Cost: Congress limited Navy funding for reactivation of the NEW JERSEY at $327 million. The actual costs are listed at $325 million for reactivation plus $7.7 million for outfitting in addition to $4.5 million listed as research and development for the ship; the FY 1983 reactivation of the

IOWA is listed as $297.3 million for reactivation, $9.3 million for outfitting, $9 million for post-delivery costs, plus $6 million for research and development—a total of $337.2 million for the NEW JERSEY and $321.6 million for the IOWA.

Electronics: The NEW JERSEY is fitted with a cruiser (CG/CGN) communications suite. She lacks NTDS (except for Link 11 receiver) and certain other electronic features of a modern surface combatant, including the SLQ-32(V)3 ECM suite. (A full NTDS is planned for later installation, i.e., the fiscal 1987 overhaul of the NEW JERSEY.) The SPS-10 is scheduled for later replacement with the SPS-67.

Engineering: All of these ships are reported to have achieved approximately 35 knots in service.

Guns: Four of the 5-inch/38 twin gun mounts have been removed. Four Phalanx Gatling-type guns have been provided for missile defense.

Manning: The NEW JERSEY was assigned a Marine detachment of 2 officers and 38 enlisted men when she was recommissioned in 1982. That was the first time Marines had served in a U.S. battleship since the Korean War.

Missiles: During the 1970s there was a proposal to provide the IOWAs with the Aegis/SPY-1 AAW weapons system. It was discarded at the time, however, as being too costly and was not considered when the ships were recommissioned in the early 1980s. When reactivation plans were being prepared it was intended to fit the Sea Sparrow PDMS. However, it was determined that the system could not withstand the overpressure when the 16-inch guns were fired.

Modernization: During her reactivation in 1968 the NEW JERSEY was fitted with improved electronic countermeasures. She was reactivated at the Philadelphia Naval Shipyard, where she had been mothballed.

When reactivated in 1982–1983, the NEW JERSEY and IOWA were fitted with Phalanx CIWS, Harpoon and Tomahawk cruise missiles, sewage collection and holding tanks, and improved communications and EW suites.

The NEW JERSEY was reactivated at the Long Beach Naval Shipyard (having been mothballed in 1969 at the Bremerton Naval Shipyard), and the IOWA at the Ingalls Shipyard, Pascagoula, Miss. (having been mothballed at Philadelphia Naval Shipyard). Both ships were towed to their reactivation yards with the IOWA having undergone preliminary reactivation work at Philadelphia and at the Avondale yard in New Orleans prior to reaching the Ingalls yard. She arrived at Avondale on 15 September 1982 and Ingalls on 30 January 1984.

Operational: All ships of the IOWA class saw extensive action in World War II, mainly as AAW support ships in carrier task forces, and in the Korean War as gunfire support ships; they also served as fleet and force flagships in those conflicts. The NEW JERSEY was the only battleship active in any navy between 1958 and 1982.

During her 1968–1969 reactivation the NEW JERSEY made one deployment to the Western Pacific. She was on the "gun line" off South

Vietnam for 120 days during which she fired 5,688 rounds of 16-inch ammunition and 14,891 rounds of 5-inch ammunition. (The NEW JERSEY fired a total of 6,200 main-battery rounds in her 1968–1969 commission, including test and training; she fired 771 rounds from 1943 to 1948, and 6,671 during her participation in the Korean War and midshipmen cruises from1950–1957.)

Following her 1982–1983 reactivation the NEW JERSEY deployed to the Western Pacific in June 1983, but shortly after arrival in the Far East she was ordered off Central America and on 12 September 1983 she transited the Panama Canal into the Caribbean. Later that month she made a hurried trip across the Atlantic and through the Mediterranean to operate off the coast of war-torn Lebanon. (The last time a U S. battleship had been in the Mediterranean was the WISCONSIN, in May 1957.)

The NEW JERSEY fired her 16-inch guns against shore targets near Beirut for the first time on 14 December 1983. She subsequently provided continuous support for the U.S. Marines ashore until the Marines were withdrawn in early 1984. The NEW JERSEY returned to the United States in May 1984, ending an 11-month odyssey that had been planned as a three-month deployment to the Western Pacific.

The NEW JERSEY after her 1981–1982 reactivation. The Phalanx CIWS on the bridge wing is elevated to 90°; her superstructure sports satellite communication antennas, SLQ-32(V)3 electronic warfare antennas, and SPS-10F and SPS-49 radars. (1983, Giorgio Arra)

NEW JERSEY on sea trials (1982, U.S. Navy; PH1 H. Gerwien)

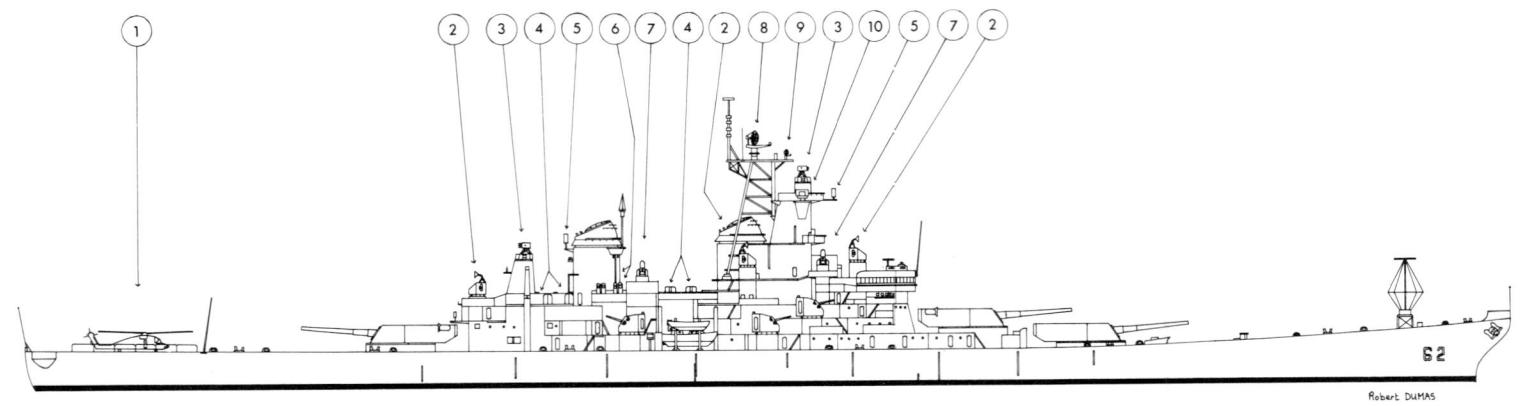

1. helicopter landing area   2. Mk 37 GFCS with Mk 25 radar   3. Mk 38 gun director with Mk 13 radar   4. Tomahawk ABL   5. satellite communications antennas OE-8L   6. Harpoon cannisters   7. Phalanx CIWS   8. SPS-49 radar   9. SPS-10F radar   10. Mk 38 gun director with Mk 13 radar

NEW JERSEY (1983, U.S. Navy; PH1 S. Smith)

This vertical view of the NEW JERSEY shows her revised armament: four 5-inch/38-cal twin gun mounts have been removed; amidships are eight ''coffins'' for Tomahawk cruise missiles; and, alongside the funnel, are four quad Harpoon cannisters. Gone are the scores of World War II-era 40-mm and 20-mm AA guns that helped protect these ships from kamikaze attack. (1983, U.S. Navy; PH1 S. Smith)

The dreadnought Iowa in Chesapeake Bay after being recommissioned. A UH-46 Sea Knight helicopter sits on her fantail. (1984, L. & L. van Ginderen)

The Iowa with her crew manning the rails. The Tomahawk ABLs are located above the boat davits. (1984, U.S. Navy)

2 BATTLESHIPS: "IOWA" CLASS

Number	Name	Builder	Laid down	Launched	Commissioned	Status
BB 63	MISSOURI	New York Navy Yard	6 Jan 1941	29 Jan 1944	11 June 1944	Yard
BB 64	WISCONSIN	Philadelphia Navy Yard	25 Jan 1941	7 Dec 1943	16 Apr 1944	AR

Displacement: 48,425 tons standard
                57,500 tons full load
Length: 860 feet (262.3 m) wl
                887¼ feet (270.6 m) oa
Beam: 108⅙ feet (33.0 m)
Draft: 38 feet (11.6 m)
Propulsion: 4 steam turbines (General Electric in BB 63; Westinghouse in BB 64); 212,000 shp; 4 shafts
Boilers: 8 600 psi (Babcock & Wilcox)
Speed: 33 knots (see notes)
Range: 15,000 n.miles at 15 knots
Manning: (see notes)
Helicopters: landing area
Missiles: none
Guns: 9 16-inch (406-mm) 50-cal Mk 7 (3 triple)
                20 5-inch (127-mm) 38-cal DP Mk 28 (10 twin)
                several 40-mm AA Mk 2 (quad)
ASW weapons: none
Radars: SPG-6 surface search
                SPS-6 air search
                SPS-8A height-finding
Sonars: none

Fire control: 4 Mk 37 GFCS with Mk 25 radar
                2 Mk 38 gun directors with Mk 13 radar
                1 Mk 40 gun director with Mk 27 radar
                20 Mk 51 gun directors
                6 Mk 57 gun FCS with Mk 34 radar in BB 63
                2 Mk 63 gun FCS with Mk 34 radar in BB 63

The MISSOURI began reactivation at the Long Beach Naval Shipyard in 1984 and is scheduled to be recommissioned in 1985.

The IOWAS were the world's last battleships to be constructed, although two ships laid down earlier were completed after the war, the British VANGUARD (completed in 1946) and the French JEAN BART (1952). The U.S. dreadnoughts were exceeded in size and firepower only by the Japanese sister ships YAMATO and MUSASHI (approximately 70,000 tons full load with nine 18.1-inch guns).

Aircraft: These ships were built with two rotating stern catapults and an aircraft crane for handing floatplanes. Three aircraft were normally embarked for scouting and gunfire spotting. The catapults were beached during the Korean War and the ships were assigned utility helicopters.

The MISSOURI floating out of a dry dock at the Long Beach Naval Shipyard during her current rehabilitation and recommissioning. (1985, U.S. Navy, Randy Hayes)

During the Vietnam War the NEW JERSEY also flew QH-50C "snoopy dash" drones for gunfire spotting.

Class: Six ships of this class were ordered; the ILLINOIS (BB 65) was cancelled on 12 August 1945 when 22 percent complete; construction of the KENTUCKY (BB 66) was halted at the end of the war when 73.1 percent complete, and she was cancelled on 22 January 1950.

In the late 1940s it was intended to complete the KENTUCKY as a guided missile ship carrying the Terrier missile system.

Five larger battleships (58,000 tons standard, 903 feet) of the MONTANA class (BB 67–71) were ordered on 9 September 1940, but none was laid down and the program was cancelled on 21 July 1943. They were to each have had four triple 16-inch gun turrets.

Design: Armor protection was intended to protect vital areas of the ship from enemy shells fired by guns up to 16-inches. The Class A steel armor belt tapers vertically from 12.1 inches to 1.62 inches. There is a lower armor belt of 13.5 inches aft of the No. 3 main battery turret to protect the propeller shafts (within hull). Turret faces have 17 inches of armor, turret tops 7.25 inches, turret backs 12 inches, barbettes up to 11.6 inches, second armor deck 6 inches, conning tower sides 17.3 inches, and conning tower top 7.25 inches. As built, these ships were manned by 2,753 to 2,911 officers and enlisted men.

Guns: During World War II, these ships carried up to 80 40-mm AA guns (quad) and almost 60 20-mm AA guns (twin and single). The 20-mm weapons were removed after the war and the number of 40-mm guns successively reduced. Postwar plans to provide twin 3-inch/50-cal AA mounts in place of the quad 40-mm mounts were abandoned.

Operational: The IOWA-class battleships were in commission during the periods indicated below.

"IOWA" CLASS BATTLESHIP COMMISSIONS

	World War II	Korean War	Vietnam War	600-ship Fleet
IOWA	22 Feb 1943–24 Mar 1949	25 Aug 1951–24 Feb 1958	—	28 Apr 1984–
NEW JERSEY	23 May 1943–30 June 1948	21 Nov 1950–21 Aug 1957	6 Apr 1968–17 Dec 1969	28 Dec 1982–
MISSOURI	11 June 1944–	–26 Feb 1955	—	(1985)
WISCONSIN	16 Apr 1944– 1 July 1948	3 Mar 1951– 8 Mar 1958	—	—

The battleships IOWA and MISSOURI load 5-inch ammunition during the Korean War. Both ships have lattice masts against their after funnel to support a radar antenna. Their stern aircraft catapults had been removed, but the cranes were retained to handle ship's boats. (1952, U.S. Navy)

15 Cruisers

The U.S. Navy has 29 guided missile cruisers (CG/CGN) in active commission with the TICONDEROGA-class Aegis cruisers in series production. Nine of the active cruisers are nuclear powered. These ships serve primarily as screening ships for carrier battle groups.

All U.S. cruisers are armed with anti-aircraft missiles, with some ships also fitted with major anti-submarine systems. The new multi-purpose TICONDEROGA-class ships have the most capable ASW suite available in the U.S. Navy (the same as in the SPRUANCE/DD 963 and KIDD/DDG 993 destroyer classes).

The development of the Harpoon anti-ship missile also provides these cruisers with a significant ASUW capability, with each cruiser normally being fitted with eight Harpoons in deck cannisters.

Long-term planning provides for the construction of 27 TICONDEROGA-class ships, to replace all existing missile cruisers except for six of the nuclear cruisers. Despite Congressional legislation passed in 1974 (U.S. Code Title VIII) directing that all future surface combatants for carrier battle groups should be nuclear powered, no nuclear surface combatants have been authorized since 1974 and none is planned. A class of nuclear strike cruisers (CSGN) was proposed in the 1970s as was an improved VIRGINIA-class ship fitted with Aegis (CGN 42), but these ships were not built (see page 136).

The Reagan Administration had included a CGN in the last year of the fiscal 1983–1987 shipbuilding plan, but that ship subsequently "slipped" into oblivion. According to Navy officials, the ship was placed in the long-range program for "planning purposes" and will not be pursued in the near future. This lack of support for resuming nuclear cruiser construction means that the increasing number of nuclear carriers will have mostly conventional escorts. In 1984 there were nine nuclear escorts for four nuclear carriers, essentially a 2-to-1 ratio, but after the mid-1990s there will probably be only six or seven nuclear escorts (CGN 35–41) for screening six or seven nuclear carriers.

While the nuclear cruisers have a high-speed endurance far superior to that of the fossil-fuel ships, the debut of the TICONDEROGA-class Aegis ships means that the few nuclear cruisers available are also inferior in firepower. There were proposals in the 1970s to provide the large cruiser LONG BEACH with Aegis during her "mid-life" modernization and even to complete the then-building ARKANSAS with an Aegis system. But those efforts were halted, in large part through the efforts of Admiral Rickover, then head of naval nuclear propulsion, who feared that making those

ships more capable would reduce the chances of additional cruiser construction. In the event, the Navy lost both ways: Neither the LONG BEACH nor ARKANSAS have Aegis, and no further nuclear cruisers have been built.

Thus, the cruiser force level objective for the mid-1990s is six nuclear cruisers and 27 ships of the TICONDEROGA class. The following table shows the Navy's force level goals for cruisers and destroyers. The similarity between the two ship types makes it necessary to address them together.

Surface Combat Force Level Objectives

	CGN	CG 47	DDG 51	DDG 993	DD 963
7 Carrier Battle Groups (CVBG) with 2 carriers	6	21	29		28
1 Carrier Battle Group with 1 carrier		2	2		2
4 Surface Action Groups (SAG) with 1 battleship		4	12		
Amphibious Forces			10	4	
7 Military Convoys					7
10 Underway Replenishment Groups			10		
Totals	6	27	63	4	37

Note that these force level objectives are based on 15 carrier battle groups and four battleship groups.

No "gun ships" remain in active commission. The largest guns in active U.S. cruisers are 5-inch weapons with ten cruisers having no guns except for the Phalanx CIWS. Two heavy cruisers (CA) with 8-inch guns are in reserve while the stricken NEWPORT NEWS also remained in tack when this edition went to press. At the time of the NEW JERSEY (BB 62) recommissioning in 1982 there were proposals to reactivate the two surviving heavy cruisers instead of or in addition to the battleships. The Navy rejected these proposals, preferring the larger guns of the more impressive dreadnoughts.

Electronic warfare: All active cruisers are being fitted with the SLQ-32(V)3 ECM suite; most also carry towed torpedo countermeasures, either the T-Mk-6 Fanfare or, in the newer ships, the SLQ-25 Nixie. See Chapter 31.

The nuclear-propelled missile cruiser CALIFORNIA leads the nuclear-powered carrier NIMITZ (CVN 68) into their home port of Norfolk after a lengthy deployment to the Mediterranean Sea and Indian Ocean. All U.S. cruisers now in active service are designed to provide AAW/ASW defense for aircraft carriers and battleships, a role that they share with destroyers. (1980, U.S. Navy)

Type	Class/Ship	Comm.	Active	Building	Reserve	Notes
CG 47	TICONDEROGA	1983–	2	11	—	Aegis weapons system; in production
CGN 38	VIRGINIA	1976–1980	4	—	—	nuclear powered
CGN 36	CALIFORNIA	1974–1975	2	—	—	nuclear powered
CGN 35	TRUXTUN	1967	1	—	—	nuclear powered
CG 26	BELKNAP	1964–1967	9	—	—	
CGN 25	BAINBRIDGE	1962	1	—	—	nuclear powered
CG 16	LEAHY	1962–1964	9	—	—	
CG 10	ALBANY	1946	—	—	1	converted heavy cruiser
CGN 9	LONG BEACH	1961	1	—	—	nuclear powered
CA 134	DES MOINES	1948–1949	—	—	2	armed with 8-inch guns

2 + 25 GUIDED MISSILE CRUISERS: "TICONDEROGA" CLASS

Number	Name	FY	Builder	Laid down	Launched	Commissioned	Status
CG 47	TICONDEROGA	78	Litton/Ingalls Shipbuilding	21 Jan 1980	25 Apr 1981	22 Jan 1983	**AA**
CG 48	YORKTOWN	80	Litton/Ingalls Shipbuilding	19 Oct 1981	17 Jan 1983	4 July 1984	**AA**
CG 49	VINCENNES	81	Litton/Ingalls Shipbuilding	19 Oct 1982	14 Jan 1984	1985	Building
CG 50	VALLEY FORGE	81	Litton/Ingalls Shipbuilding	14 Apr 1983	Sep 1984	1986	Building
CG 51	THOMAS S. GATES	82	Bath Iron Works, Maine	Sep 1984	1985	1986	Building
CG 52	. . . . . .	82	Litton/Ingalls Shipbuilding		1985	1986	Building
CG 53	. . . . . .	82	Litton/Ingalls Shipbuilding		1985	1986	Building
CG 54	. . . . . .	83	Litton/Ingalls Shipbuilding		1986	1987	Building
CG 55	. . . . . .	83	Litton/Ingalls Shipbuilding		1986	1987	Building
CG 56	. . . . . .	83	Litton/Ingalls Shipbuilding		1986	1987	Building
CG 57	. . . . . .	84				1988	Building
CG 58	. . . . . .	84				1988	Building
CG 59	. . . . . .	84				1988	Building
CG	(3 ships)	85					Planned
CG	(3 ships)	86					Planned
CG	(3 ships)	87					Planned
CG	(2 ships)	88					Planned
CG	(2 ships)	89					Planned
CG	(1 ship)	90					Planned

Displacement:	9,530 tons full load
Length:	529 feet (161.3 m) wl
	563⅓ feet (171.8 m) oa
Beam:	55 feet (16.8 m)
Draft:	31 feet (9.5 m)
Propulsion:	4 gas turbines (General Electric LM 2500); 80,000 shp; 2 shafts
Speed:	30 + knots
Range:	approx. 6,000 n.miles at 20 knots
Manning:	353 (22 officers + 331 enlisted)
Helicopters:	2 SH-2F LAMPS I in CG 47, 48
	2 SH-60B Seahawk LAMPS III in CG 49 and later ships
Missiles:	2 twin Mk 26 Mod 1 launchers for Standard-MR (88) in CG 47–51
	2 61-cell Mk-41 VLS for Standard-MR and other weapons in CG 52 and later ships
	8 Harpoon SSMs (2 quad cannisters Mk 141)
Guns:	2 5-inch (127-mm) 54-cal DP Mk 45 (2 single)
	2 20-mm Phalanx CIWS Mk 16 (2 multibarrel)
ASW weapons:	ASROC fired from Mk 26 launcher in CG 47–51
	VLA fired from VLS in CG 52 and later ships
	6 12.75-inch (324-mm) torpedo tubes Mk 32 (2 triple)
Radars:	SPS-49 air search
	SPS-55 surface search in CG 47, 48; SPS-64 in later ships
	(4) SPY-1A multi-function in CG 47–58; SPY-1B in later ships
Sonars:	SQS-53A bow mounted in CG 47–55; SQS-53B in later ships
	SQR-19 TACTAS in CG 54 and later ships
Fire control:	1 Mk 7 Aegis weapon system
	1 Mk 86 GFCS with SPQ-9A radar
	4 Mk 99 missile directors
	1 Mk 116 ASW FCS

These are the U.S. Navy's most capable AAW ships, developed to provide carrier battle group defense against aircraft and anti-ship missiles. These ships additionally have the full anti-submarine capabilities of a SPRUANCE (DD 963)-class destroyer, the Navy's most capable ASW surface ship. Incremental improvements are being made to this class, as indicated in the data table.

Class: The Navy plans to construct 27 of these ships to provide air and missile defense for 15 aircraft carriers and 4 battleships. Navy analysis has determined that each carrier requires 1.5 Aegis ships in high-threat areas, i.e., three TICONDEROGA-class ships for each two-carrier battle group.

Initially these ships were intended to complement the so-called strike cruiser (CSGN), which was to be fitted with the Aegis AAW system. Congress refused to fund the strike cruiser, however, and only the

The superstructure of the TICONDEROGA, looking foward. The after SPY-1A radar antennas are visible as are the two after Mk 99 directors. The SLQ-32(V)3 ECM suite is located just below the Phalanx CIWS mount. (1983, Giorgio Arra)

conventionally propelled CG 47 class is being built. (A variation of the Aegis system will be fitted in the DDG 51 class.) The CG 47 carries the same (or more) weapons intended for the CSGN except that the nuclear cruiser was to have Tomahawk missiles in Armored Box Launchers (ABL) as well as the Harpoon cannisters and Mk 26 launching systems of the early TICONDEROGA-class ships. The VLS will provide the later TICONDEROGA class with a Tomahawk capability.

Bath Iron Works was selected as a second shipyard for the CG 47 program. Beginning with fiscal 1984 the Navy plans to award one ship each to the Ingalls and Bath yards, with the third ship of the program being awarded on a competitive basis to one of the yards.

Cost: The three ships in the fiscal 1985 program had an average construction cost of $1,050 million plus $10 million for outfitting and $4.76 million for post delivery, a total of $1.065 *billion* per ship.

Classification: These ships were changed from guided missile destroyers (DDG with same hull numbers) to guided missile cruisers on 1 January 1980 to better reflect their capabilities and costs.

Design: SCB No. 226. These ships are based on the SPRUANCE design, employing the same hull and propulsion plant. The superstructure has been enlarged to accommodate the Aegis/SPY-1 equipment, with two fixed-array radar antennas on the forward deckhouse facing forward and to starboard, and two on the after deckhouse, facing aft and to port. Internal changes include limited armor plating for the magazine and critical electronic spaces, increases in the ship's service generators from three 2,000 kw to three 2,500 kw, additional accommodations, and additional fuel tanks. The LAMPS III ships will have the RAST helicopter-hauldown system (see OLIVER HAZARD PERRY/FFG 7 class).

During construction the design was changed to provide higher exhaust stacks and a bow bulwark, the latter required to reduce the water taken over the bow because of the greater draft compared with the SPRUANCE class.

The VINCENNES and later ships have a tripod (vice quadrapod) lattice mast amidships, providing a reduction of some nine tons in topside weight.

The first Aegis missile cruiser, the TICONDEROGA, on sea trials displays the similarity in design to the DDG 993/DD 963 designs. The SPY-1A radar "faces" visible on the forward and starboard sides of the superstructure belie the long-range, multi-function capability of the system. The Mk 99 missile directors are side by side on the forward structure and tandem amidships. (1982, Litton/Ingalls Shipbuilding)

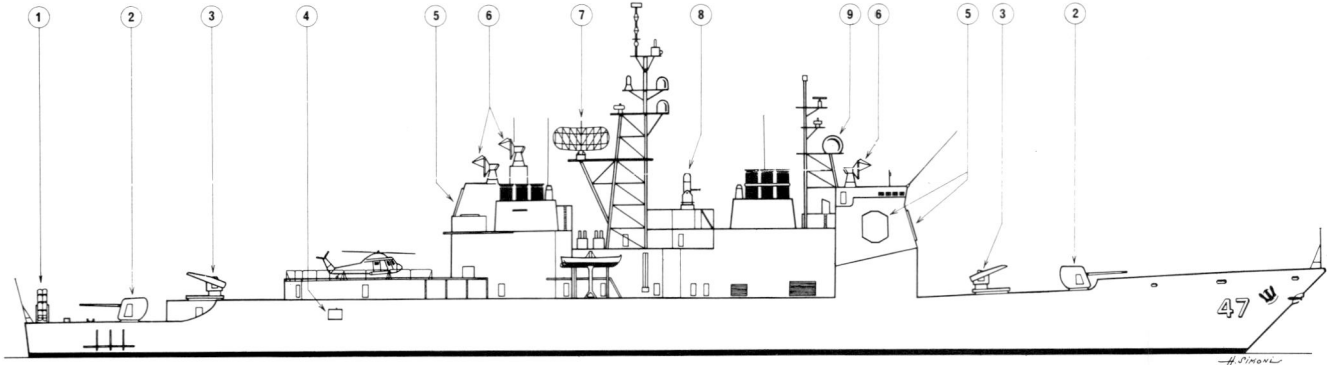

1. quad Harpoon cannisters   2. 5-inch/54-cal Mk 45 gun   3. Mk 26 missile launcher   4. Mk 32 torpedo tubes   5. SPY-1A antenna
6. Mk 99 directors   7. SPS-49 radar   8. Phalanx CIWS   9. Mk 86 GFCS with SPQ-9A radar

The large helicopter landing area dominates this view of the TICONDEROGA. The CG 47 design provides for a full, two-helicopter LAMPS system in addition to the Aegis system with two Mk 26 or 61-cell vertical missile launchers. This class is thus superior in AAW/ASW capability to any Western surface combatant, including the U.S. nuclear cruisers. (1982, Litton/Ingalls Shipbuilding)

The Aegis cruiser Vincennes firing an RUR-5A ASROC antisubmarine weapon from her forward Mk 26 missile launcher. The launcher is clearly seen, already rotating and elevating to the reload position. (1985, Litton/Ingalls Shipbuilding)

An artist's concept of the Bunker Hill, the first Aegis cruiser to be fitted with the Mk 41 vertical-launch missile system. The Harpoon will not be capable of vertical launch, hence eight tubes are provided on the fantail. (RCA)

The stern of the TICONDEROGA shows the twin openings for the SLQ-25 Nixie torpedo countermeasures and the cross-mounted quad Harpoon cannisters. The deck structure housing the after SPY-1A antennas is offset to port with the after exhaust stack to starboard. (1983, Giorgio Arra)

The TICONDEROGA on sea trials (1982, Litton/Ingalls Shipbuilding)

4 NUCLEAR-PROPELLED GUIDED MISSILE CRUISERS: "VIRGINIA" CLASS

Number	Name	FY	Builder	Laid down	Launched	Commissioned	Status
CGN 38	VIRGINIA	70	Newport News Shipbuilding	19 Aug 1972	14 Dec 1974	11 Sep 1976	**AA**
CGN 39	TEXAS	71	Newport News Shipbuilding	18 Aug 1973	9 Aug 1975	10 Sep 1977	**PA**
CGN 40	MISSISSIPPI	72	Newport News Shipbuilding	22 Feb 1975	31 July 1976	5 Aug 1978	**AA**
CGN 41	ARKANSAS	75	Newport News Shipbuilding	21 Jan 1977	21 Oct 1978	18 Oct 1980	**PA**

Displacement:	11,000 tons full load
Length:	585 feet (178.4 m) oa
Beam:	63 feet (19.2 m)
Draft:	29½ feet (9.0 m)
Propulsion:	2 steam turbines; approx. 60,000 shp; 2 shafts
Reactors:	2 pressurized-water D2G (General Electric)
Speed:	30+ knots
Manning:	530 to 532 (28 to 30 officers + 502 enlisted)
Helicopters:	VERTREP area only (see notes)
Missiles:	2 twin Mk 26 Mod 0/1 launchers for Tartar/Standard-MR SAM and Harpoon SSM (68)
	8 Harpoon SSMs (2 quad cannisters Mk 141)
Guns:	2 5-inch (127-mm) 54 cal DP Mk 45 (2 single)
ASW weapons:	ASROC fired from forward Mk 26 launcher
	6 12.75-inch (324-mm) torpedo tubes Mk 32 (2 triple)
Radars:	SPS-40B air search
	SPS-48C 3-D search
	SPS-55 surface search
Sonars:	SQS-53A bow mounted
Fire control:	1 Mk 13 weapon direction system
	1 Mk 86 GFCS with SPG-60 and SPQ-9A radars
	1 Mk 74 missile FCS
	1 Mk 116 ASW FCS
	2 SPG-51D radar

These are the last nuclear surface combatants to be built for the U.S. Navy. The ARKANSAS and TEXAS were reassigned from the Atlantic to the Pacific Fleet in 1983, accompanying the shift of the nuclear carrier VINSON (CVN 70) to the Pacific Fleet.

Class: The number of nuclear fleet escorts proposed for the fleet has varied considerably, apparently reaching a peak of 28 ships in 1970 in Navy program proposals—the cruiser LONG BEACH, the 4 then-DLGN ships already built and under construction, and 23 of the DXGN design, which evolved into the VIRGINIA class. This ambitious program was soon reduced to more fiscally possible numbers, and in May 1971 the Department of Defense decided to hold this class at 3 ships (then DLGN 38–40), i.e., a total of 8 ships that would be sufficient escorts for 2 all-nuclear carrier groups. Subsequent Navy efforts to garner support for nuclear ships led to congressional funding of a fourth ship (DLGN 41) and for long-lead components of a fifth ship (DLGN 42) that would be authorized in fiscal 1975. However, Congress then declined to fund the later ship when the Navy proposed the strike cruiser (CSGN) for later construction and the DLGN/CGN 42 was never built.

Classification: CGN 38–40 were originally classified as frigates (DLGN 38–40); they were changed to cruisers on 30 June 1975. The ARKANSAS was ordered as CGN 41.

Design: These ships are of an improved design, superior to the previous CALIFORNIA class with Mk 26 missile launchers and provision for a helicopter hangar and elevator in their sterns. These were the first U.S. ships built since World War II to have the latter feature. (See Helicopters note.)

Engineering: The Mk 14 weapon direction system is planned to replace the currently provided Mk 13 system.

Helicopters: As built the ships had a stern hangar with a folding hatch cover and elevator arrangement to accommodate a single SH-2F LAMPS. The hangar was 42 feet long, 14 feet wide, and 14¼ feet high. The ships encountered problems in keeping the hangars watertight and with the elevators. Accordingly, in the early 1980s the decision was made to delete the hangars and provide 3 Tomahawk Armored Box Launchers (ABL) in their place with 12 missiles. These installations will be completed in 1984–1988.

Guns: Two Phalanx CIWS are being installed in each of these ships.

This view of the TEXAS shows the distinctive "pyramid" towers of the Navy's last two nuclear cruiser classes. The TEXAS has quad Harpoon cannisters immediately forward of the bridge; a satellite communications antenna above the bridge; and a second SATCOM antenna amidships, between the after SPG-51D radar antennas and the after 5-inch gun. The starboard boat davits are empty. (1981, Giorgio Arra)

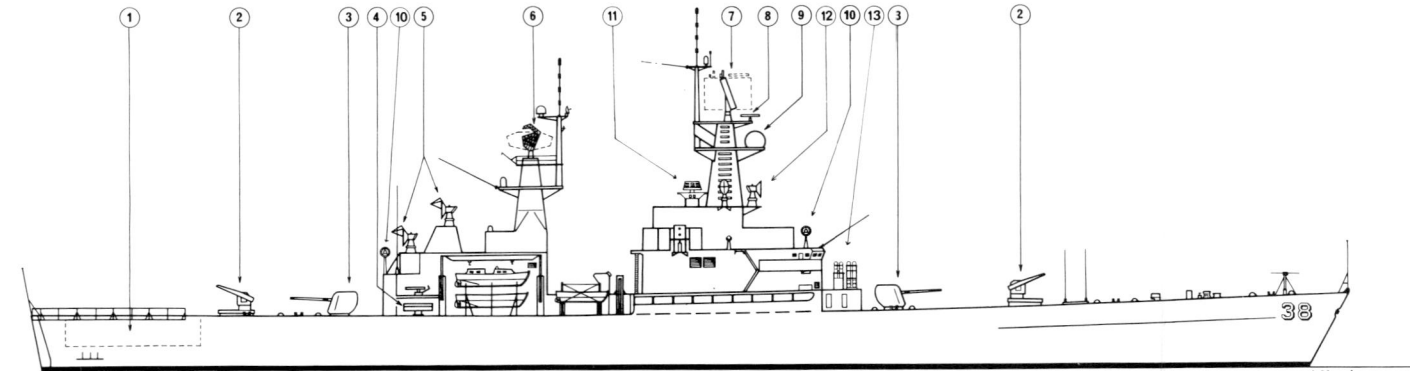

1. helicopter hangar/Tomahawk missiles   2. Mk 26 missile launcher   3. 5-inch/54-cal Mk 45 gun   4. Mk 32 torpedo tubes   5. SPG-51D radar   6. SPS-40B radar   7. SPS-48C radar   8. SPS-55 radar   9. SPQ-9A radar   10. satellite communications antenna OE-82   11. SLQ-32(V)3 ECM antenna   12. SPG-60 radar   13. quad Harpoon cannisters

The MISSISSIPPI at anchor in Piraeus, Greece. Quad cannisters for Harpoon missiles have been installed immediately forward of the bridge. (1981, Giorgio Arra)

The ARKANSAS was the last nuclear-propelled cruiser to be built for the U.S. Navy. No additional ships are planned because of their high cost and manning requirements compared to the TICONDEROGA class, which carries the same armament (actually increased in ships with the vertical launch system). The VERTREP position is marked on the deck forward of the Mk 26 launcher. (1980, U.S. Navy)

The ARKANSAS and her three sister ships plus the TRUXTUN were built with a helicopter capability. The four other U.S. nuclear cruisers have landing areas only. The hangar arrangement on the four VIRGINIA-class ships has not been successful and is being deleted, with the space being used for Tomahawk missiles. (1980, U.S. Navy)

2 NUCLEAR-PROPELLED GUIDED MISSILE CRUISERS: "CALIFORNIA" CLASS

Number	Name	FY	Builder	Laid down	Launched	Commissioned	Status
CGN 36	CALIFORNIA	67	Newport News Shipbuilding	23 Jan 1970	22 Sep 1971	16 Feb 1974	**PA**
CGN 37	SOUTH CAROLINA	68	Newport News Shipbuilding	1 Dec 1970	1 July 1972	25 Jan 1975	**AA**

Displacement:	10,105 tons full load
Length:	596 feet (181.8 m) oa
Beam:	61 feet (18.6 m)
Draft:	31½ feet (9.6 m)
Propulsion:	2 steam turbines; approx. 60,000 shp; 2 shafts
Reactors:	2 pressurized-water D2G (General Electric)
Speed:	30+ knots
Manning:	CGN 36 549 (30 officers + 519 enlisted)
	CGN 37 550 (31 officers + 519 enlisted)
Helicopters:	VERTREP area only
Missiles:	2 single Mk 13 Mod 3 launchers for Tartar/Standard-MR SAM (80)
	8 Harpoon SSMs (2 quad cannisters Mk 141)
Guns:	2 5-inch (127-mm) 54-cal DP Mk 45 (2 single)
ASW weapons:	1 8-tube ASROC launcher Mk 16
	4 12.75-inch (324-mm) torpedo tubes Mk 32 (4 fixed single)
Radars:	SPS-40B air search
	SPS-48C 3-D search
	SPS-55 surface search
Sonars:	SQS-26CX bow-mounted
Fire control:	1 Mk 11 weapon direction system
	2 Mk 74 missile FCS
	1 Mk 86 GFCS with SPG-60 and SPQ-9A radars
	1 Mk 114 ASW FCS
	4 SPG-51D radar

These two ships are essentially nuclear-propelled versions of guided missile designs proposed in the early 1960s, with the so-called Tartar-D missile system vice the Terrier-type missile systems of other U.S. cruisers and some destroyer classes. Their construction was delayed because of opposition to nuclear ship construction by Secretary of Defense Robert McNamara and the fiscal demands of the Vietnam War. Funds for their construction were released only after strong Congressional efforts. The ships were ordered in June 1968 and did not enter service until 1974–1975.

This was the first class of nuclear-propelled surface warships intended for series production. The construction of additional units was deferred in favor of the VIRGINIA class.

Class: A third ship of this design was authorized in fiscal 1968 but was not built because of rising costs and the development of the VIRGINIA design.

Classification: Both ships originally were classified as guided missile frigates (DLGN); they were changed to cruisers on 30 June 1975.

Design: SCB No. 241. These ships have a large helicopter landing area aft, but no hangar or maintenance facilities. They have a separate ASROC "box" launcher because of the Mk 13 launchers that cannot accommodate the anti-submarine rockets.

Their SCB number is part of the new SCB series (241.65).

Electronics: The Mk 13 weapon direction system is scheduled to be fitted in place of the Mk 11.

Guns: These ships are scheduled to be fitted with two Phalanx CIWS.

Missiles: Tomahawk cruise missiles are scheduled for installation in these ships.

The SOUTH CAROLINA at high speed off Norfolk. Note the single-arm Mk 13 missile launchers; after 5-inch gun on 01 level; and ASROC launcher behind forward 5-inch gun. (1981, Giorgio Arra)

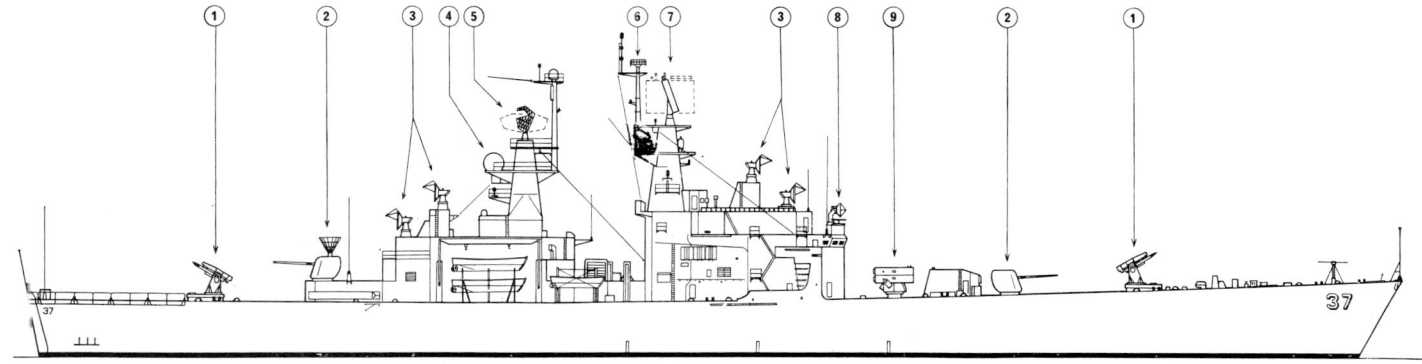

1. MK 13 missile launcher   2. 5-inch/54-cal Mk 45 gun   3. SPG-51D radars   4. SPQ-9A radars   5. SPS-40B radar   6. SPS-55 radar   7. SPS-48C radar   8. SPG-60 radar   9. ASROC launcher

CALIFORNIA (1984, Giorgio Arra)

CALIFORNIA superstructure, as fitted with SLQ-32(V)3 and Phalanx CIWS. (1984, Giorgio Arra)

1 NUCLEAR-PROPELLED GUIDED MISSILE CRUISER: "TRUXTUN"

Number	Name	FY	Builder	Laid down	Launched	Commissioned	Status
CGN 35	TRUXTUN	62	New York Shipbuilding, Camden, N.J.	17 June 1963	19 Dec 1964	27 May 1967	**PA**

Displacement:	8,200 tons standard
	9,200 tons full load
Length:	564 feet (172.0 m) oa
Beam:	58 feet (17.7 m)
Draft:	31 feet (9.5 m)
Propulsion:	2 steam turbines; approx. 60,000 shp; 2 shafts
Reactors:	2 pressurized water D2G (General Electric)
Speed:	30+ knots
Manning:	534 (31 officers + 503 enlisted)
Helicopters:	1 SH-2F LAMPS I
Missiles:	1 twin Mk 10 Mod 8 launcher for Terrier/Standard-ER SAM (60)
	8 Harpoon SSMs (2 quad cannisters Mk 141)
Guns:	1 5-inch (127-mm) 54-cal DP Mk 42
ASW weapons:	ASROC fired from Mk 10 missile launcher
	4 12.75-inch (324-mm) torpedo tubes Mk 32 (4 fixed single)
Radars:	SPS-10 surface search
	SPS-40 air search
	SPS-48 3-D search
Sonars:	SQS-26 bow mounted
Fire control:	1 Mk 11 weapon direction system
	1 Mk 68 GFCS with SPG-53F radar
	2 Mk 76 missile FCS
	1 Mk 114 ASW FCS
	2 SPG-55B radars

The TRUXTUN was the U.S. Navy's fourth nuclear-propelled surface warship. The ship was requested by the Navy as one of seven oil-burning frigates in the fiscal 1962 program; however, Congress directed that one of the ships have nuclear propulsion.

Classification: Originally classified as a guided missile frigate (DLGN); changed to cruiser (CGN) on 30 June 1975.

Design: SCB No. 222. The TRUXTUN was built to a modified BELKNAP-class design with the gun and missile-launcher positions reversed. The ship has a distinctive appearance with four-legged lattice masts replacing the "macks" of the oil-burning ships.

Guns: As built the TRUXTUN additionally carried two 3-inch 50-cal AA single gun mounts amidships. They were deleted and the positions are now used for Harpoon missile cannisters.

The ship is scheduled to receive two Phalanx CIWS.

Helicopters: The TRUXTUN's hangar is 40⅓-feet long and 16¾-feet wide.

Torpedoes: As built the ship had two Mk 25 torpedo tubes built into the stern counter with ten torpedo reloads provided; subsequently removed. The Mk 32 tubes are built into the after deckhouse.

The one-of-a kind TRUXTUN at Pearl Harbor. The large Mk 10 missile launcher is aft, behind the two large, SPG-55B fire control radars. There are quad Harpoon missile launchers amidships, in the "tubs" previously occupied by twin 3-inch AA guns. The TRUXTUN has the same weapons and sensors as the oil-burning BELKNAP class, but with the arrangement of the 5-inch gun and Mk 10 launcher reversed. (1980, Giorgio Arra)

TRUXTUN at San Diego (1977, Giorgio Arra)

TRUXTUN with 3-inch guns amidships (1978, Giorgio Arra)

9 GUIDED MISSILE CRUISERS: "BELKNAP" CLASS

Number	Name	FY	Builder	Laid down	Launched	Commissioned	Status
CG 26	BELKNAP	61	Bath Iron Works, Maine	5 Feb 1962	20 July 1963	7 Nov 1964	**AA**
CG 27	JOSEPHUS DANIELS	61	Bath Iron Works, Maine	23 Apr 1962	2 Dec 1963	8 May 1965	**AA**
CG 28	WAINWRIGHT	61	Bath Iron Works, Maine	2 July 1962	25 Apr 1964	8 Jan 1966	**AA**
CG 29	JOUETT	62	Puget Sound Naval Shipyard	25 Sep 1962	30 June 1964	3 Dec 1966	**PA**
CG 30	HORNE	62	San Francisco Naval Shipyard	12 Dec 1962	30 Oct 1964	15 Apr 1967	**PA**
CG 31	STERETT	62	Puget Sound Naval Shipyard	25 Sep 1962	30 June 1964	8 Apr 1967	**PA**
CG 32	WILLIAM H. STANDLEY	62	Bath Iron Works, Maine	29 July 1963	19 Dec 1964	9 July 1966	**PA**
CG 33	FOX	62	Todd Shipyards, San Pedro, Calif.	15 Jan 1963	21 Nov 1964	28 May 1966	**PA**
CG 34	BIDDLE	62	Bath Iron Works, Maine	9 Dec 1963	2 July 1965	21 Jan 1967	**AA**

Stern of the JOUETT with the port-side Gatling gun and Harpoon cannisters on starboard side visible. There is another Gatling gun to starboard, forward of the Harpoons. SLQ-32(V)3 antennas are also visible, outboard of the forward mack. (1982, Giorgio Arra)

Displacement:	6,570 tons standard
	7,930 tons full load
Length:	547 feet (166.8 m) oa
Beam:	54¾ feet (16.7 m)
Draft:	28¾ feet (8.8 m)
Propulsion:	2 steam turbines (General Electric in CG 26-28, 32, 34; De Laval in CG 29-31, 33); 85,000 shp; 2 shafts
Boilers:	4 1,200 psi (Babcock & Wilcox in CG 26-28, 32, 34; Combustion Engineering in CG 29-31, 33)
Speed:	33 knots
Range:	7,100 n.miles at 20 knots
Manning:	461 to 480 (24 to 28 officers + 435 to 453 enlisted)
Helicopters:	1 SH-2F LAMPS I
Missiles:	1 twin Mk 10 Mod 7 launcher for Terrier/Standard-ER SAM (60)
	8 Harpoon SSMs (2 quad cannisters Mk 141)
Guns:	1 5-inch (127-mm) 54-cal DP Mk 42
	2 20-mm Phalanx CIWS Mk 16 (2 multibarrel) in CG 26–30, 32, 34
ASW weapons:	ASROC fired from Mk 10 missile launcher
	6 12.75-inch (324-mm) torpedo tubes Mk 32 (2 triple)
Radars:	SPS-10F surface search
	SPS-40 air search in CG 31-34; being replaced by SPS-49
	SPS-43 air search in CG 28; to be replaced by SPS-49
	SPS-48C 3-D search
	SPS-49 air search in CG 26, 27, 29, 30
Sonars:	SQS-26BX bow mounted except SQS-53A in CG 26
Fire control:	1 Mk 7 weapon direction system in CG 27
	1 Mk 11 weapon direction system in CG 31-34
	1 Mk 14 weapon direction system in CG 26, 29, 30
	1 Mk 68 GFCS with SPG-53F radar
	1 Mk 114 ASW FCS except Mk 116 in CG 26
	2 SPG-55B radar

These are "single-end" guided missile cruisers built to screen aircraft carriers. The nuclear-propelled TRUXTUN is similar. The STERETT of this class is home ported in Subic Bay, Philippines.

The BELKNAP was severely damaged in a collision with the carrier JOHN F. KENNEDY (CV 67) in the Ionian Sea on the night of 22 November 1975. The cruiser was rebuilt at the Philadelphia Naval Shipyard, arriving at the yard on 30 January 1976 and returning to sea in April 1980. (Recommissioned on 10 May 1980.)

Classification: These ships were originally classified as guided missile frigates (DLG 26–34); they were changed to CG on 30 June 1975.

Design: SCB No. 212. These ships were built to an improved LEAHY-class design with a 5-inch gun substituted for one (after) missile launcher.

The Mk 10 Mod 7 launcher has three 20-round magazine "rings" compared with two 20-missile rings in the previous class, thus partially compensating for the reduction in launchers.

Electronics: All of these ships are to receive the Mk 14 weapon direction system.

Guns: Two 3-inch/50-cal AA single gun mounts that were originally mounted amidships have been removed with quad Harpoon missile cannisters fitted in their place. Two Phalanx CIWS are to be installed in these ships.

Helicopters: The helicopter hangar in these ships varies in size; most

are approximately 43 feet long and 14 feet wide; the JOUETT and STANDLEY have hangars approximately 55 feet long.

Missiles: The WAINWRIGHT was the first ship to be fitted with the SM-2 version of the Standard missile, conducting evaluation of that missile in 1977.

Radar: All ships originally carried SPS-40 or SPS-43 air search radars, being replaced by SPS-49.

Torpedoes: As built, these ships had two Mk 25 torpedo tubes in their after superstructure, angled out one to starboard and one to port. They have been removed.

The BIDDLE underway, showing the forward Mk 10 launcher and after 5-inch gun of these "single-end" missile cruisers. The 5-inch gun is a Mk 42 Mod 10, with two "frog-eye" projections; that of the STERETT, below, is a Mk 42 Mod 7. The rebuilt BELKNAP is similar but has stern openings for SLQ-25 Nixie torpedo countermeasures. (1983, Giorgio Arra)

The STERETT, prior to installation of Gatling guns. Her hangar door is partially open while a division musters on the flight deck. These ships will continue to operate the SH-2F LAMPS. The starboard Harpoon cannisters are alongside the hangar; the port-side Harpoons are approximately between the macks, facing forward. (1983, Giorgio Arra)

1 NUCLEAR-PROPELLED GUIDED MISSILE CRUISER: "BAINBRIDGE"

Number	Name	FY	Builder	Laid down	Launched	Commissioned	Status
CGN 25	BAINBRIDGE	59	Bethlehem Steel, Quincy, Mass.	15 May 1959	15 Apr 1961	6 Oct 1962	**PA**

Displacement:	7,700 tons standard
	8,580 tons full load
Length:	550 feet (167.7 m) wl
	565 feet (172.3 m) oa
Beam:	58 feet (17.7 m)
Draft:	29 feet (8.8 m)
Propulsion:	2 steam turbines; 60,000 shp; 2 shafts
Reactors:	2 pressurized-water D2G (General Electric)
Speed:	30 knots
Range:	90,000 n.miles at 20 knots
Manning:	541 (32 officers + 509 enlisted)
Helicopters:	VERTREP area only
Missiles:	2 twin Mk 10 Mod 5/6 launchers for Terrier/Standard-ER SAM (80)
	8 Harpoon SSMs (2 quad cannisters Mk 141)
Guns:	none
ASW weapons:	1 8-tube ASROC launcher Mk16
Torpedoes:	6 12.75-inch (324-mm) torpedo tubes Mk 32 (2 triple)
Radars:	SPS-10D surface search
	SPS-37 air search
	SPS-39 3-D search
Sonars:	SQQ-23A PAIR bow mounted
Fire control:	1 Mk 11 weapon direction system
	4 Mk 76 missile FCS
	1 Mk 111 ASW FCS
	4 SPG-55B radars

The BAINBRIDGE was the U.S. Navy's third nuclear-propelled surface warship. She differs from the later TRUXTUN in being a "double-end" missile ship and in not having a 5-inch gun and helicopter-support capability.

Classification: Originally classified as a guided missile frigate (DLGN 25); changed to cruiser on 30 June 1975.

Design: SCB No. 189. No ASROC reloads are provided.

Electronics: The Mk 14 weapon direction system is planned to replace the Mk 11.

Guns: The two 3-inch/50 cal AA twin mounts previously fitted amidships have been removed. Two single-barrel 20-mm guns can be mounted on pedestals alongside the after missile directors. Two Phalanx CIWS are planned for installation.

Sonar: The original SQS-23 sonar has been upgraded to the SQQ-23A PAIR.

BAINBRIDGE with lattice foremast hidden by radar, EW, and radio antennas. (1982, Giorgio Arra)

The BAINBRIDGE at Hong Kong; note the built up amidships structure; the Harpoons are alongside the after SPG-55B radars—the starboard quad mount facing aft and the port quad facing forward. (1981, Giorgio Arra)

BAINBRIDGE (1981, Giorgio Arra)

9 GUIDED MISSILE CRUISERS: "LEAHY" CLASS

Number	Name	FY	Builder	Laid down	Launched	Commissioned	Status
CG 16	Leahy	58	Bath Iron Works, Maine	3 Dec 1959	1 July 1961	4 Aug 1962	**PA**
CG 17	Harry E. Yarnell	58	Bath Iron Works, Maine	31 May 1960	9 Dec 1961	2 Feb 1963	**AA**
CG 18	Worden	58	Bath Iron Works, Maine	19 Sep 1960	2 June 1962	3 Aug 1963	**PA**
CG 19	Dale	59	New York Shipbuilding, Camden, N.J.	6 Sep 1960	28 July 1962	23 Nov 1962	**AA**
CG 20	Richmond K. Turner	59	New York Shipbuilding, Camden, N.J.	9 Jan 1961	6 Apr 1963	13 June 1964	**AA**
CG 21	Gridley	59	Puget Sound Bridge & Dry Dock, Wash.	15 July 1960	31 July 1961	25 May 1963	**PA**
CG 22	England	59	Todd Shipyards, San Pedro, Calif.	4 Oct 1960	6 Mar 1962	7 Dec 1962	**PA**
CG 23	Halsey	59	San Francisco Naval Shipyard	26 Aug 1960	15 Jan 1962	20 July 1963	**PA**
CG 24	Reeves	59	Puget Sound Naval Shipyard	1 July 1960	12 May 1962	15 May 1964	**PA**

Displacement:	5,670 tons standard	Fire control:	1 Mk 11 weapon direction system
	7,800 tons full load		4 Mk 76 missile FCS
Length:	533 feet (162.5 m) oa		1 Mk 114 ASW FCS
Beam:	55 feet (16.8 m)		4 SPG-55B radars
Draft:	25 feet (7.6 m)		

Propulsion: 2 steam turbines (General Electric in CG 16-18, De Laval in CG 19-22, Allis-Chalmers in CG 23-24; 85,000 shp; 2 shafts
Boilers: 4 1,200 psi (Babcock & Wilcox in CG 16-18, Foster Wheeler in CG 19-24)
Speed: 32 knots
Range: 8,000 n.miles at 20 knots
Manning: 423 or 424 (26 or 27 officers + 397 enlisted)
Helicopters: VERTREP area only
Missiles: 2 twin Mk 10 Mod 5/6 launchers for Terrier/Standard-ER SAM (80)
8 Harpoon SSMs (2 quad cannisters Mk 141)
Guns: 4 3-inch (76-mm) 50 cal AA Mk 33 (2 twin) in CG 16, 18, 19, 22 (see notes)
ASW weapons: 1 8-tube ASROC launcher Mk 16
6 12.75-inch (324-mm) torpedo tubes Mk 32 (2 triple)
Radars: SPS-10D surface search
SPS-43 air search; being replaced by SPS-49
SPS-48C 3-D search
Sonars: SQS-23 or SQQ-23B PAIR bow mounted

These are "double-end" missile cruisers, the smallest U.S. Navy ships currently classified as cruisers. The Reeves is home ported in Yokosuka, Japan.

Classification: These ships were built as guided missile frigates (DLG 16-24); they were changed to cruisers on 30 June 1975.

Design: SCB No. 172. This class introduced the "mack" superstructure (combination masts and exhaust stacks) to U.S. warships. There are no ASROC reloads provided.

Electronics: The Mk 14 weapon direction system is scheduled for installation in all ships of this class. The SQQ-23B PAIR sonar is being substituted for the original SQS-23 sonar.

Guns: As built, all ships of this class had two 3-inch/50-cal AA twin mounts amidships. They have been removed, with Harpoon missile cannisters fitted in their place.

These ships are scheduled to receive two Phalanx CIWS.

The Harry E. Yarnell at Messina with crew manning the rail. (1982, L. & L. van Ginderen)

Leahy superstructure; there is a red E and chevron on the after mack, indicating two awards for engineering excellence. (1983, Giorgio Arra)

The LEAHY getting underway. Compared with the similar view of the STERETT, the differences in configuration between that "single-ender" and this "double-ender" are readily evident. (1983, Giorgio Arra)

HARRY E. YARNELL (1983, Giorgio Arra)

1 GUIDED MISSILE CRUISER: "ALBANY" CLASS

Number	Name	Builder	Laid down	Launched	CA Comm.	CG Comm.	Status
CG 10 (ex-CA 123)	ALBANY	Bethlehem Steel, Quincy, Mass.	6 Mar 1944	30 June 1945	15 June 1946	3 Nov 1962	AR

Displacement:	13,700 tons standard
	17,500 tons full load
Length:	664 feet (202.5 m) wl
	673 feet (205.2 m) oa
Beam:	70 feet (21.3 m)
Draft:	27 feet (8.2 m)
Propulsion:	4 steam turbines (General Electric); 120,000 shp; 4 shafts
Boilers:	4 600 psi (Babcock & Wilcox)
Speed:	32.5 knots
Range:	7,300 n.miles at 15 knots
Manning:	835 (50 officers + 785 enlisted)
Helicopters:	none
Missiles:	2 twin Mk 12 Mod 1 launchers for Talos SAM (92)
	2 twin Mk 11 Mod 1/2 launchers for Tartar SAM (80)
Guns:	2 5-inch (127-mm) 38-cal DP Mk 24 (2 single)
ASW weapons:	1 8-tube ASROC launcher Mk 16
	6 12.75-inch (324-mm) torpedo tubes Mk 32 (2 triple)
Radars:	SPS-10C surface search
	SPS-43A air search
	SPS-48 3-D search
Sonars:	SQS-23 keel mounted
Fire control:	1 Mk 6 weapon direction system
	2 Mk 56 GFCS with Mk 35 radars
	4 Mk 74 missile FCS
	2 Mk 77 missile FCS
	1 Mk 111 ASW FCS
	4 SPG-49B radars

The ALBANY was one of three ships fully converted from conventional heavy (8-inch gun) cruisers to "double-end" missile ships. The ALBANY was originally of the OREGON CITY (CA 122) class. She was decommissioned on 1 February 1980 and laid up in reserve.

Aircraft: The ALBANY's stern aircraft hangar was removed during her conversion to a missile ship.

Class: The CHICAGO (CG 11, ex-CA 136) was laid up in reserve in 1980 and stricken on 31 January 1984 (to become a museum in Chicago); the COLUMBUS (CG 12, ex-CA 74) was laid up in reserve in 1975 and stricken on 9 August 1976. The CHICAGO was the U.S. Navy's last cruiser of World War II construction in active service.

Conversion: During her missile conversion the ALBANY was stripped down to the main deck, with all guns and existing superstructure removed. The new superstructure is largely aluminum, with a large "mack" structure combining masts and exhaust stacks. The macks rise 104 5/12 feet above the main deck. No ASROC reloads are provided. The missile ship conversion was SCB-173.

Electronics: As converted the ship had distinctive SPS-30 radars mounted atop the bridge and on a short lattice mast after of the second "mack."

Guns: No guns were fitted as converted to a missile cruiser; subsequently fitted with single, open-mount 5-inch guns to provide minimal defense against attacks from low-flying subsonic aircraft or small boats.

Missiles: The original missile cruiser conversion provided for these ships to carry the Regulus II strategic cruise missile. After cancellation of that program in 1958, plans were developed to arm these ships with eight Polaris SLBMs; however, those weapons were not installed.

Photographed with the after SPS-30 replaced by a SATCOM antenna, the ALBANY seems to show her age here. All vestiges of her original 8-inch gun configuration are gone. (1976, Stefan Terzibaschitsch)

The ALBANY in essentially her final configuration. The after SATCOM antenna is mounted on a light lattice mast aft of the second mack. (1975, L. & L. van Ginderen)

The ALBANY at sea off Genoa. She still carries an SPS-30 radar on the after lattice mast, later replaced by the SATCOM mast. The ship's ASROC box launcher is fitted between the macks. (1972, Giorgio Arra)

The LONG BEACH retains her graceful lines following her 1980–1983 rebuilding. Despite her large size and nuclear propulsion, however, the LONG BEACH has essentially the same weapons and electronics as the smaller LEAHY-class cruisers. Proposals to provide the Aegis system were defeated by those who wanted additional nuclear cruisers instead. (1983, Giorgio Arra)

1 NUCLEAR-PROPELLED GUIDED MISSILE CRUISER: "LONG BEACH"

Number	Name	FY	Builder	Laid down	Launched	Commissioned	Status
CGN 9 (ex-CLGN/CGN 160)	LONG BEACH	57	Bethlehem Steel, Quincy, Mass.	2 Dec 1957	14 July 1959	9 Sep 1961	**PA**

Displacement:	14,200 tons standard
	17,350 tons full load
Length:	721¼ feet (220.0 m) oa
Beam:	73¼ feet (22.3 m)
Draft:	29 feet (8.8 m)
Propulsion:	4 steam turbines (General Electric); approx. 80,000 shp; 2 shafts
Reactors:	2 pressurized-water C1W (Westinghouse)
Speed:	30+ knots
Range:	approx. 90,000 n.miles at 30 knots
	approx. 360,000 n.miles at 20 knots
Manning:	921 (64 officers + 857 enlisted)
Helicopters:	landing area only
Missiles:	2 twin Mk 10 Mod 1/2 launchers for Terrier/Standard-ER SAM (120)
	8 Harpoon SSMs (2 quad cannisters Mk 141)
Guns:	2 5-inch (127-mm) 38-cal DP Mk 30 (2 single)
ASW weapons:	1 8-tube ASROC launcher Mk 16
	6 12.75-inch (324-mm) torpedo tubes Mk 32 (2 triple)
Radars:	SPS-48C 3-D search
	SPS-49 air search
	SPS-65 threat warning
Sonars:	SQQ-23B PAIR bow mounted
Fire control:	1 Mk 14 weapon direction system
	2 Mk 56 GFCS with Mk 35 radar
	4 Mk 76 missile FCS
	1 Mk 111 ASW FCS
	2 SPG-49B radars
	4 SPG-55B radars

The LONG BEACH was extensively modernized at the Bremerton Naval Shipyard from October 1980 through March 1983. The ship's two Mk 10 Terrier/Standard systems were upgraded as was the ship's other combat systems. The SPS-32/33 3-D "billboard" radars were removed and the ship was fitted with conventional radars (as was the carrier ENTERPRISE/CVN 65, the only other ship fitted with SPS-32/33 radars).

Class: The LONG BEACH was the first U.S. cruiser to be constructed after World War II, the first nuclear-propelled surface warship, and the world's first warship to be built with guided missiles as the main battery.

Classification: The LONG BEACH was ordered as a guided missile light cruiser (CLGN 160) on 15 October 1956, reclassified as a guided missile cruiser (CGN 160) on 6 December 1956, and renumbered CGN 9 on 1 July 1957.

Design: SCB No. 169. The LONG BEACH was initially proposed as a large destroyer or "frigate" of some 7,800 tons (standard displacement); her design subsequently was enlarged to accommodate additional missile systems to take maximum advantage of the benefits of nuclear propulsion.

Twenty ASROC missiles are provided.

Electronics: The ship was built with the fixed-array SPS-32 and SPS-33 radars mounted on the forward, square superstructure. The radars were difficult to maintain; see Chapter 31.

The after section of the LONG BEACH, which previously carried a two-rail Talos missile launcher, seems bare despite the presence of quad Harpoon cannisters, one quad angles to port and one to starboard. A pair of Gatling guns are stepped on the after superstructure. (1983, Giorgio Arra)

In the late 1970s it was proposed that the LONG BEACH be fitted with the Aegis weapon system. The fiscal 1978 budget provided $371 million to begin Aegis conversion. The Aegis AAW system would have included the fixed-array SPY-1A radars in place of the existing SPS-32/33 radars (plus two Mk 26 missile launchers). The conversion was cancelled, however, because of concern that new cruiser construction programs would be reduced.

Instead, during the 1980 modernization the LONG BEACH received SFS-48C and SPS-49 radars in place of her SPS-32/33 radars. (The square island structure is retained with 1¾-inch armor being fitted from the 05 to 08 levels.)

Engineering: The C1W reactors in the LONG BEACH are essentially the same as the A2Ws in the aircraft carrier ENTERPRISE.

Guns: As built, the LONG BEACH had no guns; subsequently she was fitted with two 5-inch guns to provide minimal defense against attacks by subsonic aircraft or small craft.

The ship has had two Phalanx CIWS installed.

Missiles: The LONG BEACH was built with a twin Talos Mk 12 launcher aft. It was removed in 1979 along with the associated Mk 77 missile FCS, SPG-49B and SPW-2B radars. Harpoon SSM tubes were installed aft of the superstucture on the main deck.

Mk 26 Standard missile launchers were to have been installed in place of the Mk 10 launchers during the planned Aegis conversion (See Electronics).

The original LONG BEACH design provided for the ship to carry the Regulus II strategic cruise missile and, after cancellation of that program in 1958, the Polaris SLBM. Neither weapon was installed.

Sonar: Built with SQS-23 bow-mounted sonar; upgraded to SQQ-23B PAIR configuration.

LONG BEACH (1983, Giorgio Arra)

LONG BEACH (1983, Giorgio Arra)

2 HEAVY CRUISERS: "DES MOINES" CLASS

Number	Name	Builder	Laid down	Launched	Commissioned	Status
CA 134	DES MOINES	Bethlehem Steel, Quincy, Mass.	28 May 1945	27 Sep 1946	16 Nov 1948	AR
CA 139	SALEM	Bethlehem Steel, Quincy, Mass.	4 June 1945	25 Mar 1947	14 May 1949	AR

Displacement:	17,000 tons standard
	21,500 tons full load
Length:	700 feet (213.5 m) wl
	716½ feet (218.5 m) oa
Beam:	76⅓ feet (23.3 m)
Draft:	26 feet (7.9 m)
Propulsion:	4 steam turbines (General Electric); 120,000 shp; 4 shafts
Boilers:	4 600 psi (Babcock & Wilcox)
Speed:	32 knots
Range:	10,500 n.miles at 15 knots
Manning:	1,800 (115 officers + 1,685 enlisted)
Helicopters:	utility helicopter embarked (no hangar)
Guns:	9 8-inch (203-mm) 55-cal Mk 16 (3 triple)
	12 5-inch (127-mm) 38-cal DP Mk 32 (6 twin)
	16 3-inch (76-mm) 50-cal AA Mk 27 (8 twin)
	4 3-inch (76-mm) 50-cal AA Mk 33 (2 twin) except 6 guns in CA 139 (3 twin)
ASW weapons:	none
Radars:	SG-6 air search
	SPS-8A height-finding
	SPS-12 air search in CA 139
Sonars:	none
Fire control:	4 Mk 37 GFCS with Mk 25 radar
	2 Mk 54 gun director with Mk 13 radar
	4 Mk 56 GFCS with Mk 35 radar
	2 Mk 63 GFCS (with Mk 34 radar in CA 139)
	2 SPG-50 radar in CA 134

The DES MOINES class represents the final heavy cruiser (8-inch gun) design to be constructed by any navy and the ships are the only heavy cruisers in existence, as well as the largest non-missile cruisers afloat. They were completed too late for service in World War II but were employed extensively as fleet flagships during their active careers. The SALEM was decommissioned on 30 January 1959 and the DES MOINES on 14 July 1961.

Aircraft: The DES MOINES was completed with two stern catapults and embarked four floatplanes. The catapults were subsequently removed and all ships of the class operated utility helicopters.

Class: Twelve ships of this class were planned, the CA 134, 139–143, and 148–153. Only three ships were completed, the two above units and the NEWPORT NEWS (CA 148), decommissioned in 1975 and stricken on 31 July 1978 after extensive service in the Vietnam War. The NEWPORT NEWS was the world's last active heavy cruiser.

These ships are often referred to as the SALEM class, since the CA 134 was originally planned as a BALTIMORE-class ship but was changed to the revised new design in October 1943.

Design: The class was designed specifically to carry the 8-inch gun Mk 16; they thus needed a larger hull than previous heavy cruisers. The design is an improved version of the previous OREGON CITY (CA 122) class which, in turn, was a modification of the BALTIMORE (CA 68) class.

The DES MOINES steams through the Mediterranean during her 1958–1961 tour as flagship of the U.S. Sixth Fleet in the Mediterranean. These are the only heavy cruisers still afloat; their Mk 54 gun directors are fitted in distinctive towers forward and aft; they were among the relatively few single-funnel cruisers built. (1960, U.S. Navy)

Guns: The principal innovation of this class was the rapid-firing 8-inch gun Mk 16, which uses metal cartridge cases in place of the bagged powder charges used in all other 8-inch gun cruisers.

As built, these ships had a secondary battery of 12 5-inch DP guns, up to 24 3-inch AA guns, and 12 20-mm AA guns. The 20-mm weapons were quickly removed and the 3-inch guns reduced.

Moored in the reserve fleet group at Philadelphia are the stricken NEWPORT NEWS (foreground), the SALEM, and the DES MOINES. The latter ships remain on the Naval Vessel register. In mothballs the NEWPORT NEWS had an SPS-37 radar antenna on the forward mast; an SPS-8A height-finding radar and an SG-6 on the after mast. (1982, Giorgio Arra)

POST-WORLD WAR II CRUISER PROGRAMS

World War II cruiser programs reached hull number CL 159 (with hulls 154–159 being cancelled in 1945). All heavy (CA), light (CL), and anti-aircraft (CLAA) cruisers were numbered in the same series. Only one ship was added to this series in the postwar period, the LONG BEACH, ordered as CLGN 160, changed to CGN 160, and completed as CGN 9. Further "cruiser" construction was halted in favor of the smaller and less expensive "frigates" which could carry most of a cruiser's armament.

One cruiser hull was completed as a command ship after the war, the NORTHAMPTON. Begun as a heavy cruiser (CA 125), she was cancelled in 1945 when partially complete, reordered in 1948 and completed as a tactical command ship in 1953 (CLC 1) and later changed to a national command ship (CC 1). She was stricken in 1977.

HUNTER-KILLER CRUISERS

| CLK 1 | NORFOLK | completed as DL 1 |
| CLK 2 | NEW HAVEN | deferred 1949; cancelled 1951 |

After World War II the U.S. Navy established the classification of hunter-killer cruiser (CLK) for a planned series of small cruisers intended for ASW operations against high-speed submarines. Only the lead ship, the NORFOLK, was completed; she was reclassified as a frigate (DL) while under construction. She was employed mainly in ASW test and evaluation until stricken in 1973.

GUIDED MISSILE CRUISERS

CAG 1	BOSTON (ex-CA 69)	reverted to CA; stricken 1973
CAG 2	CANBERRA (ex-CA 70)	reverted to CA; stricken 1978
CLG 3	GALVESTON (ex-CL 93)	stricken 1973
CLG 4	LITTLE ROCK (ex-CL 92)	changed to CG; stricken 1977
CLG 5	OKLAHOMA CITY (ex-CL 91)	changed to CG; stricken 1979
CLG 6	PROVIDENCE (ex-CL 82)	changed to CG; stricken 1978
CLG 7	SPRINGFIELD (ex-CL 66)	changed to CG; stricken 1978
CLG 8	TOPEKA (ex-CL 67)	stricken 1973
CGN 9	LONG BEACH (ex-CLGN/CGN 160)	
CG 10-12	Converted heavy cruisers (CA)	
CG 13-14	BALTIMORE class; conversion cancelled	
CG 15	not used	

CG 16-24	LEAHY class (ex-DLG 16-24)
CGN 25	BAINBRIDGE (ex-DLGN 25)
CG 26-34	BELKNAP (ex-DLG 26-34)
CGN 35	TRUXTUN (ex-DLGN 35)
CGN 36-37	CALIFORNIA class (ex-DLGN 36-37)
CGN 38-40	VIRGINIA class (ex-DLGN 38-40)
CGN 41	VIRGINIA class
CG 42-46	not used
CG 47	TICONDEROGA (ex-DDG 47)

The guided missile cruiser classifications were established in 1952 to reflect the specialized weapons and AAW roles of these ships. In 1975, 25 guided missile frigates (DLG/DLGN) were changed to cruisers, and in 1980 the Aegis-equipped destroyers were reclassified as cruisers.

Two BALTIMORE (CA 69)-class 8-inch gun cruisers and 6 CLEVELAND (CL 55)-class 6-inch gun cruisers converted to a missile configuration (CAG and CLG, respectively) have all been stricken. The CAGs had Terrier launchers aft; the CLGs were fitted with either Talos or Terrier. The two CAGs lost their missile systems and reverted to CA designations during the Vietnam War; 4 of the CLGs were changed to CG in 1975 although all retained 6-inch guns forward.

Strike Cruisers

The strike cruiser (CSGN) was an outgrowth of the DLGN concept, developed in 1973–1974 as an enlarged DLGN intended specifically to carry the Aegis weapon system. As more weapons were added, the Harpoon and Tomahawk cruise missiles, the ship was enlarged and the twin-reactor D2G propulsion plant was upgraded.

The basic CSGN design was an improved CGN 38-class hull with several thousand tons of armor added. She would have been the first armored ship built by the U.S. Navy since the LONG BEACH. The additional displacement would have reduced speed to 28 or 28½ knots; accordingly, the design was lengthened until at least 30 knots could be achieved, resulting in a very shallow draft.

Initially the ship was to carry only Phalanx CIWS; however, in an effort to make the ship more competitive with the proposed Aegis-armed destroyer (DG/Aegis and later DDG/CG 47), an 8-inch Mk 71 lightweight gun was fitted forward.

The ship was proposed as a carrier escort, with up to four CSGNs being considered to screen each carrier. The cost of the lead strike cruiser in fiscal 1976 was estimated at $1.371 *billion* and she was to have been completed in December 1983.

The following characteristics are those of the basic CSGN. After the ship was ignored by Congress, the Naval Sea Systems Command hurriedly developed a strike cruiser Mark II design retaining the same armament but with a flight deck added, presenting a superficial similarity to the Soviet KIEV-class VTOL carriers. However, the U.S. ship, with two Mk 26 launchers and two 8-inch lightweight guns, would have an enlarged island structure with hangars for six Harrier VSTOL aircraft and three LAMPS III helicopters (far fewer than the KIEV carriers). A further modification of the Mk II design considered a hangar below the flight deck, resulting in a design somewhat similar to the Navy's small or light carrier of World War II (CVL 22-30). That ship would have carried about 18 Harriers on a displacement of some 18,000 tons.

Displacement:	15,900 tons standard; 17,210 tons full load
Length:	666 feet (203.1 m) wl; 709 7/12 feet (216.5 m) oa
Beam:	76 7/12 feet (23.4 m)
Draft:	22 1/4 feet (6.8 m)
Propulsion:	2 steam turbines; 2 shafts
Reactors:	2 pressurized-water D2G (General Electric)
Speed:	approx. 30 knots
Manning:	
Helicopters:	2 LAMPS III
Missiles:	2 twin Mk 26 Mod 2 launchers for Standard-MR SAMs (128)
	8 Tomahawk T-ASMs (2 quad cannisters)
	8-16 Harpoon SSMs (2-4 quad cannisters)
Guns:	1 8-inch (203-m) 55-cal Mk 71 lightweight
	2 20-mm Phalanx CIWS Mk 16 (2 multibarrel)
ASW weapons:	ASROC fired from Mk 26 launcher
	6 12.75-inch (324-mm) torpedo tubes Mk 32 (2 triple)
Radars:	SPS-49 air search
	(4) SPY-1 fixed-array multi-purpose
Sonars:	SQS-53 bow mounted
	TACTAS

FRIGATES

The frigate classifications (DL/DLG/DLGN) were established after 1951 for large destroyer-type ships that were designed to operate with fast carrier forces. In general, the emphasis has been on AAW systems, although some ships additionally had the most capable ASW systems available (i.e., large sonar, helicopters, ASROC). The hunter-killer cruiser NORFOLK was completed as the DL 1, while four MITSCHER-class ships ordered as destroyers were completed as DL 2-5. Note that the missile-armed frigates and all-gun frigates are numbered in the same series; in the cruiser, destroyer, and frigate/destroyer escort categories the missile and non-missile ships were in separate series.

The frigate classification was abolished on 30 June 1975, and frigate (FF/FFG) was established to indicate smaller escort ships (formerly DE/DEG).

DL 1	NORFOLK (ex-CLK 1)	comm. 1953; stricken 1973
DL 2	MITSCHER (ex-DD 927)	converted to DDG 35
DL 3	JOHN S. McCAIN (DD 928)	converted to DDG 36
DL 4	WILLIS A. LEE (ex-DD 930)	comm. 1954; stricken 1972
DL 5	WILKINSON (ex-DD 930)	comm. 1954; stricken 1974
DLG 6-15	FARRAGUT class	to DDG 37-46
DLG 16-24	LEAHY class	to CG 16-24
DLGN 25	BAINBRIDGE	to CGN 25
DLG 26-34	BELKNAP class	to CG 26-34
DLGN 35	TRUXTUN	to CGN 35
DLGN 36-37	CALIFORNIA class	to CGN 36-37
DLGN 38-40	VIRGINIA class	to CGN 38-40

Typhon-class Frigates

In the early 1960s, the Navy planned to construct a class of at least seven DLGNs fitted with the Typhon AAW system. The Typhon consisted of an advanced radar/fire control system plus a medium-range missile to replace the Terrier and a long-range missile to replace the Talos then being fitted to U.S. ships. Construction of the lead ship was to begin in 1963–1964.

The high costs of the Typhon DLGN led Secretary of Defense McNamara to cancel the program late in 1963. The system's SPG-59 fixed-array search/tracking radar was tested in the guided missile ship NORTON SOUND (AVM 1). Several Typhon concepts and features were incorporated in the subsequent Aegis system.

Several variations of the Typhon DLGN were put forward. The Typhon was assigned SCB No. 227. (Later DLGN designs that were not built included two that reached sufficient maturity to be assigned SCB numbers, 243/240.65 and 241.66.)

Displacement:	9,750 tons standard; approx. 12,000 tons full load
Length:	650 feet (198.2 m) wl
Beam:	64 feet (19.5 m)
Draft:	21 feet (6.4 m)
Propulsion:	2 steam turbines; 2 shafts
Reactors:	2 pressurized-water D2G (General Electric)
Speed:	30+ knots
Manning:	approx. 500
Helicopters:	no facilities
Missiles:	1 twin Typhon long-range launcher (60)
	2 single Typhon medium-range launcher (160)
Guns:	2 5-inch (127-mm) 54-cal DP guns Mk 42 (2 single)
ASW weapons:	ASROC fired from Typhon long-range launcher
	6 12.75-inch (324-mm) torpedo tubes Mk 32 (2 triple)
Radars:	SPS-49 air search
Sonars:	SQS-26 bow mounted
	possible variable depth sonar
Fire control:	SPG-59

The so-called Strike Cruiser Mark II was heavily influenced by the Soviet KIEV VTOL carrier design but retained the basic strike cruiser (CSGN) hull, with all aviation support facilities on the main deck. Note the Harrier and LAMPS hangars in the island structure; Mk 26 missile launchers and 8-inch lightweight guns. A later version had vertical-launch systems. (Courtesy M. Rosenblatt and Son)

16 Destroyers

The U.S. Navy has 68 destroyers (DD/DDG) in active commission plus one ship used for both Naval Reserve and officer candidate training.

Destroyers provide AAW and ASW defense for other surface forces (see page 137 for assignments under planned force levels), and the Harpoon missile now being fitted to most destroyers also provides an anti-ship capability. Further, the longer-range Tomahawk missile is planned for the 31 larger destroyers of the SPRUANCE class, to be carried in either Armored Box Launchers (ABL) or Vertical Launch Systems (VLS).

Thirty-seven destroyers have surface-to-air missile launchers (DDG type) and all carry 5-inch guns as well as ASROC and other ASW weapons. Only 35 destroyers, however, carry helicopters, a key factor in ASW operations.

A new series of destroyers is planned, the ARLEIGH BURKE class. Originally up to 49 of these ships were scheduled to replace that number of older destroyers and cruisers that would be retired in the 1980s and 1990s of the CG 16, CG 26, DDG 2, and DDG 37 classes. The number was increased to 63 by the Reagan Administration to provide for the larger number of carrier and battleship groups being planned. But by 1984 the number of BURKE-class destroyers being requested was down to 29 because of budgetary and political realities.

The lead BURKE-class ship is planned for authorization in the fiscal 1985 shipbuilding program with completion in 1989–1990. There has been significant Congressional opposition to these ships, however, with some critics saying they have too many "frills" while others consider them too limited in capability, with both opponents attacking their cost.

The older, World War II-era destroyers that had been assigned to the Naval Reserve Force with composite active-reserve crews have all been discarded. The postwar EDSON is an NRF/OCS training ship at Newport, R.I. Plans to assign the other FORREST SHERMAN-class destroyers to NRF were discarded because of their operating costs and limited capabilities. Instead, frigates are being transferred to NRF status.

Electronic Warfare: All active destroyers are being fitted with the SLQ-32(V)3 or (V)2 ECM suite. The DDG 993 and DD 963 classes have the SLQ-25 Nixie towed torpedo countermeasures.

Type	Class/Ship	Comm.	Active	NRF	Building	Reserve	Notes
DDG 993	KIDD	1980–1981	4	—	—	—	modified SPRUANCE design
DDG 37	FARRAGUT	1960–1961	10	—	—	—	former frigates (DLG)
DDG 31	Converted SHERMAN	1956–1959	—	—	—	4	
DDG 2	CHARLES F. ADAMS	1960–1964	23	—	—	—	
DD 963	SPRUANCE	1975–1983	31	—	—	—	
DD 931	FORREST SHERMAN	1955–1956	—	1	—	13	

The old and the new: The KING and ARTHUR W. RADFORD represent the oldest and newest destroyer classes in active U.S. service. The KING was one of almost two score ships built as missile frigates (DLG/DLGN) that survive with the classification of cruiser or destroyer. The RADFORD represents the highly successful SPRUANCE class, which also served as the basis for the KIDD-class missile destroyers and TICONDEROGA (CG 47)-class cruisers. (U.S. Navy)

Naval Reserve Force: As indicated only one destroyer, the EDSON, is assigned to the Naval Reserve Force. There had been proposals to assign some or all of the other 17 ships of the FORREST SHERMAN class to NRF (13 DD + 4 DDG); however, the frigates being provided to the NRF have more capability in all respects except for that of naval gunfire support.

(29) GUIDED MISSILE DESTROYERS: "ARLEIGH BURKE" CLASS

Number	Name	FY	Builder	Laid down	Launch	Commission	Status
DDG 51	ARLEIGH BURKE	85				1990	Authorized
DDG	(3 ships)	87					Planned
DDG	(5 ships)	88					Planned
DDG	(20 ships)	89–92					Planned

Displacement:	8,300 tons full load
Length:	466 feet (142.1 m) oa
Beam:	59 feet (18.0 m)
Draft:	30$^{7}/_{12}$ feet (9.3 m)
Propulsion:	4 gas turbines (General Electric LM 2500); 80,000 shp; 2 shafts
Speed:	30 + knots
Range:	4,400 n.miles at 20 knots
Manning:	303 (22 officers + 289 enlisted)
Helicopters:	landing deck only
Missiles:	90-cell VLS for Standard SM-2/Tomahawk/VLA (ASROC) (29 cells forward + 61 cells aft)
	8 Harpoon SSMs (2 quad cannisters Mk 141)
Guns:	1 5-inch (127-mm) 54-cal DP Mk 45
	2 20-mm Phalanx CIWS Mk 16 (2 multibarrel)
ASW weapons:	VLA (ASROC)
	6 12.75-inch (324-mm) torpedo tubes Mk 32 (2 triple)
Radars:	1 SPS-67 surface search/navigation
	(4) SPY-1D multi-function
Sonars:	SQS-53C bow mounted
	SQR-19 towed array
Fire control:	3 Mk 99 illuminators
	1 Mk 116 ASW control system
	1 GFCS

These destroyers emphasize AAW capabilities and are intended to support Aegis cruisers (CG 47) in the air/missile defense of carrier battle groups. Initial plans for a more advanced radar and propulsion plant for these ships have been dropped in favor of the propulsion plant in the CG 47/DDG 993/DD 963 classes and a derivative of the CG 47 Aegis radar.

The production DDG 51 units are planned to cost approximately 75 percent of a CG 47-class cruiser. The significant differences in the weapon and sensor systems of the two classes will be the DDG 51 having:

- three vice four missile illuminators
- 75 percent missile loadout
- no helicopter hangars
- no AAW commander/coordination facilities

Class: The Carter Administration (1977–1980) proposed the construction of 49 ships of this class, while the Reagan Administration (from January 1981) initially proposed a program of 63 ships. .

In March 1983, however, the Deputy CNO (Surface Warfare), Vice Admiral R. C. Walters, told Congress, "If you examine the full requirements for surface combatants to fill our total objective to support 15-carrier battle groups, 600-ship Navy, we need 60 new ships.

"We feel that the 29 ships that we [now] have planned in this class will take us through a building period to about 1994 or 1995, by which time we will want to build another 30 or something else."

When asked, "What about something else?" the Admiral responded, "We don't know yet . . . but generally we feel that by the time this class

is well under construction we will be a lot smarter about what the threat is, what we need, and that sort of thing."

"We are not planning more than about 30 ships in this class."

The DDG 51 class is planned for construction at a maximum rate of 5 ships per year in 2 or 3 shipyards.

Classification: The initial study leading to the preliminary design of this ship conducted in 1979 used the designation DDX and subsequently DDGX. (Of the various design/capability options developed in the study, number 3A was selected for development as the DDG 51.)

Cost: The lead ship cost is $79 million in fiscal 1984 plus $1.173 billion in fiscal 1985.

Design: From the outset these ships were directed by the Chief of Naval Operations to be smaller and less expensive than the DDG/CG 47 design. Early design concepts envisioned a ship as small as 6,000 tons full load displacement.

These will be the first U.S. destroyers of post-World War II construction with steel superstructures; that decision was made as a result of the cruiser BELKNAP (CG 26) colliding with an aircraft carrier in 1975 and not a result of the 1982 conflict in the Falklands. The steel construction provides increased resistance to blast over pressure, fragment and fire damage plus Electromagnetic Pulse (EMP) protection.

The DDG 51 has steel armor plating to protect vital spaces and for the first time in a U.S. warship an enhanced partial CBR protective system will be fitted from the outset.

Early designs provided for a 61-foot beam; subsequently reduced to 59 feet.

Electronics: A derivative of the CG 47 Aegis system is provided, with all four SPY-1D radar "faces" on a single, forward deck house.

Engineering: Essentially the same propulsion plant as CG 47/DD 963/DDG 997 classes will be fitted in this class.

This ship was originally intended to have the Rankine Cycle Energy Recovery (RACER) system that improves the efficiency of the gas turbine propulsion plant through using waste heat to produce steam that, through a turbine and reduction gear, provides additional power. The system could not be developed in time to meet the lead ship. The design will be compatible with RACER. The RACER is being tested in the gas turbine cargo ship ADM WM. M. CALLAGHAN and may be installed in later ships of the DDG 51 class.

Guns: The original DDGX proposal called for a gun armament of only two Phalanx CIWS. Subsequently, a single 76-mm OTO Malera Mk 75 was provided in the design and later the single 5-inch/54-cal Mk 45, in addition to the two CIWS.

Helicopter: A landing deck and limited support capability is provided, but no hangar. Lamps III electronics will be fitted although a helicopter will not normally be embarked.

An artist's concept of the Aʀʟᴇɪɢʜ Bᴜʀᴋᴇ, the lead ship of a class of Aegis destroyers. All four "faces" of the SPY-1D multi-function radar are mounted on the forward deckhouse. No helicopter hangar is provided, an omission considered to be a major shortfall by some naval officers and naval analysts. (RCA)

An overhead view of the Aʀʟᴇɪɢʜ Bᴜʀᴋᴇ showing the unusual superstructure configuration; in earlier designs the 5-inch gun was mounted aft. (RCA)

4 GUIDED MISSILE DESTROYERS: "KIDD" CLASS (FORMER IRANIAN SHIPS)

Number	Name	FY	Builder	Laid down	Launched	Commissioned	Status
DDG 993	KIDD	79S	Litton/Ingalls Shipbuilding, Pascagoula, Miss.	26 June 1978	13 Oct 1979	27 July 1981	**AA**
DDG 994	CALLAGHAN	79S	Litton/Ingalls Shipbuilding, Pascagoula, Miss.	23 Oct 1978	19 Jan 1980	29 Aug 1981	**PA**
DDG 995	SCOTT	79S	Litton/Ingalls Shipbuilding, Pascagoula, Miss.	12 Feb 1979	29 Mar 1980	24 Oct 1981	**AA**
DDG 996	CHANDLER	79S	Litton/Ingalls Shipbuilding, Pascagoula, Miss.	12 May 1979	24 May 1980	13 Mar 1982	**PA**

Displacement: 8,140 tons full load
Length: 529 feet (161.3 m) wl
563⅓ feet (171.8 m) oa
Beam: 55 feet (16.8)
Draft: 30 feet (9.1 m)
Propulsion: 4 gas turbines (General Electric LM 2500); 80,000 shp; 2 shafts
Speed: 30+ knots
Manning: DDG 993, 994 339 (19 officers + 320 enlisted)
DDG 995, 996 340 (20 officers + 320 enlisted)
Helicopters: 2 SH-60B Seahawk LAMPS III (planned)
Missiles: 2 twin Mk 26 Mod 0/1 launchers for Standard-ER SAM (68)
8 Harpoon SSMs (2 quad cannisters Mk 141)
Guns: 2 5-inch (127-mm) 54-cal DP Mk 45 (2 single)
2 20-mm Phalanx CIWS Mk 16 (2 multibarrel)
ASW weapons: ASROC fired from forward Mk 26 launcher
6 12.75-inch (324-mm) torpedo tubes Mk 32 (2 triple)
Radars: SPS-48C 3-D search
SPS-55 surface search
Sonars: SQS-53 bow mounted

Fire control: 2 Mk 74 missile FCS
1 Mk 86 GFCS with SPG-60 and SPQ-9A radars
1 Mk 116 ASW FCS
2 SPG-51D radars

These are the most capable destroyers currently in U.S. service with excellent AAW and ASW capabilities. The four ships were ordered by the government of the Shah of Iran, which fell in 1979. Subsequently, the U.S. Navy sought to acquire the ships which were then under construction. The FY 1979 supplemental budget provided $1.353 *billion* for the purchase of the ships, and they were formally acquired on 24 July 1979.

The ships differ from the contemporary CG 47 Aegis cruisers primarily in not having the Aegis/SPY-1A AAW system.

Class: The Iranian government announced plans to order two AAW ships based on the SPRUANCE design on 15 December 1973, with an

The CALLAGHAN underway in the Sea of Okhotsk has an ominous appearance. This missile-armed version of the SPRUANCE represents the DXG variant of the class, a type planned but not ordered for the U.S. Navy. These ships are quickly distinguished from the SPRUANCES by the Mk 26 missile launchers forward and aft and the SPS-48 three-dimensional radar antenna. (1983, U.S. Navy)

announcement for four additional ships on 27 August 1974. Four ships were ordered on 23 March 1978 under the U.S. foreign military sales program. The fifth and sixth ships were not ordered.

Classification: These ships were originally ordered as DD 993-996, indicating that they were variations of the SPRUANCE-class ships. They were changed to DDG with the same non-missile hull numbers on 8 August 1979.

Design: The original SPRUANCE destroyer concept consisted of a missile-armed variant (designated DXG) as well as the basic ASW ship (CX). These are the only ships that were built to the DXG design, none having been ordered for the U.S. Navy.

The Iranian government required that these ships be provided with increased air-conditioning capacity and dust separators for their engine air intakes. See SPRUANCE class for additional notes.

Guns: The Mk 26 Mod 0 missile launcher installed forward has a smaller (24-missile) magazine than the after Mk 26 Mod 1 launcher to provide space for possible installation of the 8-inch Mk 71 gun.

These ships are the only DDGs being fitted with the Phalanx CIWS.

The CHANDLER does not have Harpoon missiles fitted in this view; they are normally installed in two quad mountings aft of the first funnel, as in the SPRUANCE class. The funnels are offset to port and starboard. (1983, Giorgio Arra)

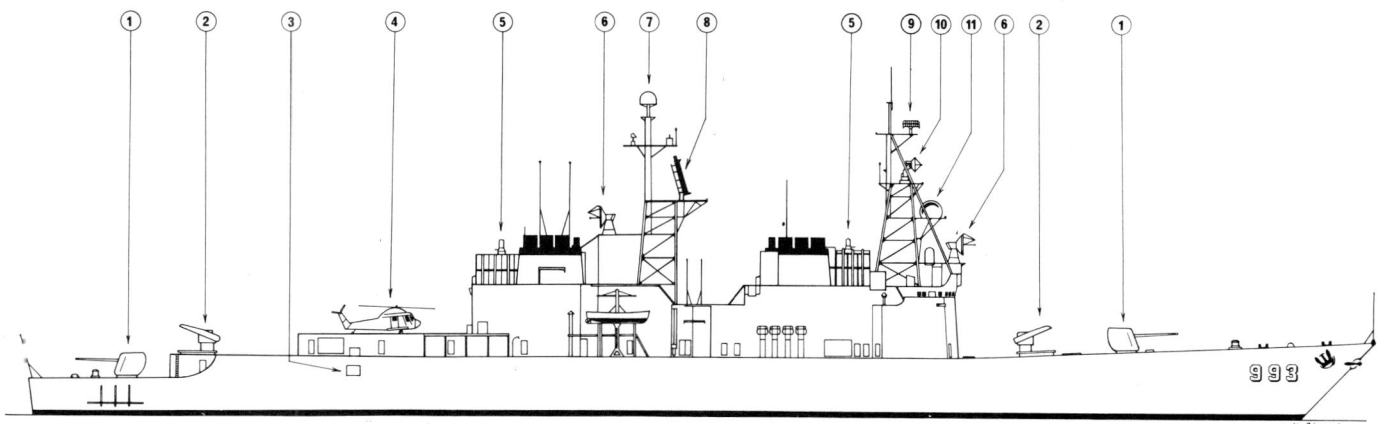

1. 5-inch/54-cal Mk 45 gun   2. Mk 26 missile launcher   3. Mk 32 torpedo tubes   4. helicopter deck   5. Phalanx CIWS   6. SPG-51D   7. TACAN   8. SPS-48C radar   9. SPS-55 radar   10. SPG-60 radar   11. SPQ-9A radar

The CHANDLER underway, showing the large helicopter deck and hangar intended to accommodate two SH-60B LAMPS III helicopters. (1983, Giorgio Arra)

10 GUIDED MISSILE DESTROYERS: "FARRAGUT" CLASS

Number	Name	FY	Builder	Laid down	Launched	Commissioned	Status
DDG 37 (ex-DLG 6)	FARRAGUT	56	Bethlehem Steel, Quincy, Mass.	3 June 1957	18 July 1958	10 Dec 1960	**AA**
DDG 38 (ex-DLG 7)	LUCE	56	Bethlehem Steel, Quincy, Mass.	1 Oct 1957	11 Dec 1958	20 May 1961	**AA**
DDG 39 (ex-DLG 8)	MACDONOUGH	56	Bethlehem Steel, Quincy, Mass.	15 Apr 1958	9 July 1959	4 Nov 1961	**AA**
DDG 40 (ex-DLG 9)	COONTZ	56	Puget Sound Naval Shipyard	1 Mar 1957	6 Dec 1958	15 July 1960	**AA**
DDG 41 (ex-DLG 10)	KING	56	Puget Sound Naval Shipyard	1 Mar 1957	6 Dec 1958	17 Nov 1960	**AA**
DDG 42 (ex-DLG 11)	MAHAN	56	San Francisco Naval Shipyard	31 July 1957	7 Oct 1959	25 Aug 1960	**AA**
DDG 43 (ex-DLG 12)	DAHLGREN	57	Philadelphia Naval Shipyard	1 Mar 1958	16 Mar 1960	8 Apr 1961	**AA**
DDG 44 (ex-DLG 13)	WM. V. PRATT	57	Philadelphia Naval Shipyard	1 Mar 1958	16 Mar 1960	4 Nov 1961	**AA**
DDG 45 (ex-DLG 14)	DEWEY	57	Bath Iron Works, Maine	10 Aug 1957	30 Nov 1958	7 Dec 1959	**AA**
DDG 46 (ex-DLG 15)	PREBLE	57	Bath Iron Works, Maine	16 Dec 1957	23 May 1959	9 May 1960	**PA**

Displacement:	4,700 tons standard
	5,800 tons full load
Length:	512½ feet (156.3 m) oa
Beam:	52½ feet (16.0 m)
Draft:	25 feet (7.6 m)
Propulsion:	2 steam turbines (De Laval in DDG 37–39, 45–46; Allis-Chalmers in DDG 40–44); 85,000 shp; 2 shafts
Boilers:	4 1,200 psi (Foster Wheeler in DDG 37–39; Babcock & Wilcox in DDG 40–46)
Speed:	33 knots
Range:	4,500 n.miles at 20 knots
Manning:	403 (25 officers + 378 enlisted)
Helicopters:	VERTREP area only
Missiles:	1 twin Mk 10 Mod 0 launcher for Terrier/Standard-ER SAM (40)
	8 Harpoon SSMs (2 quad cannisters Mk 141)
Guns:	1 5-inch (127-mm) 54-cal DP Mk 42
ASW weapons:	1 8-tube ASROC launcher Mk 16
	6 12.75-inch (324-mm) torpedo tubes Mk 32 (2 triple)
Radars:	SPS-10B search radar
	SPS-29E air search in DDG 37, 38
	SPS-49 in all except DDG 37, 38
	SPS-48 3-D search
Sonars:	SQS-23 hull mounted
Fire control:	1 Mk 11 weapon direction system except Mk 14 in DDG 42
	1 Mk 68 GFCS with SPG-53A radar
	2 Mk 76 missile FCS
	1 Mk 111 ASW FCS
	2 SPG-55B radar

These ships originally were classified as "frigates" (DLG). While classified as destroyers, they have the Terrier/Standard-ER missile system and Naval Tactical Data System (NTDS) of U.S. cruiser classes.

Class: These ships are also referred to as the COONTZ class, that ship being the first ordered with a DLG designation.

Classification: The first three ships of this class were ordered on 27 January 1956 as all-gun frigates (DL 6-8); they were changed to guided missile frigates (DLG 6-8) on 14 November 1956. All 10 ships were classified as DLG from the time of their commissioning until 30 June 1975 when they were changed to guided missile destroyers.

Design: SCB No. 142. At the time they were ordered these ships had a second 5-inch gun mount in the "B" position; however, they were fitted with an ASROC launcher in that position before completion. At the same time, the planned SQS-4 sonar was changed to the much improved SQS-23 (keel mounted). As built, no ASROC reloads were provided, with only the FARRAGUT being subsequently provided with a reload capability.

Electronics: The KING and MAHAN were test ships for the Naval Tactical Data System (NTDS) in 1961–1962. In 1982 the MAHAN was fitted with the New Threat Upgrade modification to reduce reaction time to anti-ship missile attack; she was fitted with the SPS-48E and SPS-49(V)5 radars, the Standard SM-2(ER) Block II missile, and other features.

Guns: As built, each ship had two 3-inch/50-cal Mk 33 AA twin gun mounts aft of the second funnel; these have been removed from all ships. The KING was fitted with the Phalanx CIWS from August 1973 until March 1974 for at-sea evaluation; installed on fantail. These ships are not scheduled to receive the Phalanx CIWS.

The Mk 14 GFCS is planned for installation in all of these ships.

Missiles: The MAHAN was the first ship of the class to be fitted with the improved Standard-ER SM-2 missile (1979). (The cruiser WAINWRIGHT was the first ship fitted with the SM-2, in 1978.) The Mk 76 missile FCS was installed in the ships with the SM-2 refit (previously Mk 74 provided).

Modernization: All ships underwent AAW modernization between 1968 and 1977 (SCB-243). Radars and fire control systems were updated and NTDS installed (updated in KING and MAHAN) and 3-inch guns removed.

Names: The LUCE was to have been named DEWEY; changed in 1957.

Sonars: These ships will be refitted with the SQQ-23 PAIR sonar.

The DEWEY in the latest class configuration with SLQ-32(V)2 EW antenna outboard of forward mast; SPS-49 on after mast; and quad Harpoon cannisters amidships. (1983, Giorgio Arra)

The lines of the destroyers of the FARRAGUT or COONTZ class reveal their 1950s vintage. In some respects an enlargement of the CHARLES F. ADAMS class, they were intended to mount a second 5-inch gun in the B position; instead an ASROC box launcher was provided. The larger Terrier missile launcher in the FARRAGUT class prevented installation of an after 5-inch gun. (1983, Giorgio Arra)

The MAHAN with crew lining the starboard rail. The KING, above, has an SPS-29/37 antenna aft; the MAHAN the SPS-49 that is going into the entire class. These ships will not receive Gatling guns. (1983, Giorgio Arra)

4 GUIDED MISSILE DESTROYERS: CONVERTED "FORREST SHERMAN" CLASS

Number	Name	FY	Builder	Laid down	Launched	DD Comm.	DDG Comm.	Status
DDG 31 (ex-DD 936)	DECATUR	54	Bethlehem Steel, Quincy, Mass.	13 Sep 1954	15 Dec 1955	7 Dec 1956	29 Apr 1967	PR
DDG 32 (ex-DD 932)	JOHN PAUL JONES	53	Bath Iron Works, Maine	18 Jan 1954	7 May 1955	5 Apr 1956	23 Sep 1967	PR
DDG 33 (ex-DD 949)	PARSONS	56	Ingalls Shipbuilding, Pascagoula	17 June 1957	19 Aug 1958	29 Oct 1959	3 Nov 1967	PR
DDG 34 (ex-DD 947)	SOMERS	56	Bath Iron Works, Maine	4 Mar 1957	30 May 1958	3 Apr 1959	10 Feb 1968	PR

Displacement:	4,150 tons full load	Missiles:	1 single Mk 13 Mod 1 launcher for Tartar/Standard-MR SAM (40)
Length:	407 feet (124.1 m) wl	Guns:	1 5-inch (127 mm) 54-cal DP Mk 42
	DDG 31–32 418 feet (127.5 m) oa	ASW weapons:	1 8-tube ASROC launcher Mk 16
	DDG 33–34 418⁵⁄₁₂ feet (127.6 m) oa		6 12.75-inch (324-mm) torpedo tubes Mk 32 (2 triple)
Beam:	45 feet (13.7 m)	Radars:	SPS-10B surface search
Draft:	20 feet (6.1 m)		SPS-29E air search except SPS-40 in DDG 34
Propulsion:	2 steam turbines (General Electric, except Westinghouse in DDG		SPS-48 3-D search
	32); 70,000 shp; 2 shafts	Sonars:	SQS-23 keel mounted
Boilers:	4 1,200 psi (Foster Wheeler in DDG 31, 33; Babcock & Wilcox in	Fire control:	1 Mk 4 weapon direction system
	DDG 32, 34)		1 Mk 68 GFCS with SPG-53B radar
Speed:	32.5 knots		1 Mk 74 missile FCS
Range:	3,800 + n.miles at 20 knots		1 Mk 114 ASW FCS
Manning:	333 to 344 (20 officers + 313–324 enlisted)		1 SPG-51C radar
Helicopters:	VERTREP area only		

The DECATUR riding at anchor in Hong Kong. (1981, Giorgio Arra)

These ships were converted from FORREST SHERMAN-class destroyers. They have a limited ASW capability and retain only one 5-inch gun; along with the larger COONTZ-class ships, they were the U.S. Navy's only one-gun destroyers pending completion of the BURKE class. See FORREST SHERMAN class for additional details.

All four ships have been decommissioned, the PARSONS and SOMERS on 19 November 1982, JOHN PAUL JONES on 15 December 1982, and DECATUR on 30 June 1983.

Class: One other SHERMAN-class destroyer (DD) remains in NRF service and 13 are laid up in reserve (DD)

Classification: The DECATUR was changed from DD to DDG 31 on 15 September 1966; the three other ships were changed to DDG on 15 March 1967.

Conversion: Converted to Tartar missile configuration beginning in 1965–1966. The original tripod masts were replaced with lattice masts to support additional radars; ASROC and deckhouse were added aft of second funnel; two after 5-inch gun mounts were removed, and a single-arm missile launcher was installed. The original DDG conversion plan (SCB No. 240) provided for a Drone Anti-Submarine Helicopter (DASH) facility; however, it was deleted in favor of ASROC.

Design: DDG 31 and 32 built as SCB No. 85; DDG 33 and 34 as No. 85A.

Missiles: These ships have been fitted with the Mk 13 lightweight launcher, which is capable of a high rate of fire (eight rounds per minute). They are limited in firepower by having only one director compared with two directors per launcher in other U.S. missile destroyers.

The DECATUR has the rounded bow of the first six SHERMAN-class destroyers; bow configurations were changed to improve seakeeping. (1981, Giorgio Arra)

The PARSONS and sister ships were converted to a missile configuration from FORREST SHERMAN-class destroyers. The ship's single-arm Tartar/Standard-MR launcher is in the vertical (loading) position. Plans for more conversions were dropped because of funding constraints. (1980, Giorgio Arra)

23 GUIDED MISSILE DESTROYERS: "CHARLES F. ADAMS" CLASS

Number	Name	FY	Builder	Laid down	Launched	Commissioned	Status
DDG 2	CHARLES F. ADAMS	57	Bath Iron Works, Maine	16 June 1958	8 Sep 1959	10 Sep 1960	AA
DDG 3	JOHN KING	57	Bath Iron Works, Maine	25 Aug 1958	30 Jan 1960	4 Feb 1961	AA
DDG 4	LAWRENCE	57	New York Shipbuilding	27 Oct 1958	27 Feb 1960	6 Jan 1962	AA
DDG 5	CLAUDE V. RICKETTS	57	New York Shipbuilding	18 May 1959	4 June 1960	5 May 1962	AA
DDG 6	BARNEY	57	New York Shipbuilding	18 May 1959	10 Dec 1960	11 Aug 1962	AA
DDG 7	HENRY B. WILSON	57	Defoe Shipbuilding	28 Feb 1958	23 Apr 1959	17 Dec 1960	PA
DDG 8	LYNDE MCCORMICK	57	Defoe Shipbuilding	4 Apr 1958	9 Sep 1960	3 June 1961	PA
DDG 9	TOWERS	57	Todd Shipyards, Seattle, Wash.	1 Apr 1958	23 Apr 1959	6 June 1961	PA
DDG 10	SAMPSON	58	Bath Iron Works, Maine	2 Mar 1959	9 Sep 1960	24 June 1961	AA
DDG 11	SELLERS	58	Bath Iron Works, Maine	3 Aug 1959	9 Sep 1960	28 Oct 1961	AA
DDG 12	ROBISON	58	Defoe Shipbuilding	23 Apr 1959	27 Apr 1960	9 Dec 1961	PA
DDG 13	HOEL	58	Defoe Shipbuilding	1 June 1960	4 Aug 1960	16 June 1962	PA
DDG 14	BUCHANAN	58	Todd Shipyards, Seattle, Wash.	23 Apr 1959	11 May 1960	7 Feb 1962	PA
DDG 15	BERKELEY	59	New York Shipbuilding	1 June 1960	29 July 1961	15 Dec 1962	PA
DDG 16	JOSEPH STRAUSS	59	New York Shipbuilding	27 Dec 1960	9 Dec 1961	20 Apr 1963	PA
DDG 17	CONYNGHAM	59	New York Shipbuilding	1 May 1961	19 May 1962	13 July 1963	AA
DDG 18	SEMMES	59	Avondale Marine Ways, New Orleans, La.	18 Aug 1960	20 May 1961	10 Dec 1962	AA
DDG 19	TATTNALL	59	Avondale Marine Ways, New Orleans, La.	14 Nov 1960	26 Aug 1961	13 Apr 1963	AA
DDG 20	GOLDSBOROUGH	60	Puget Sound Bridge & Dry Dock, Seattle	3 Jan 1961	15 Dec 1961	9 Nov 1963	PA
DDG 21	COCHRANE	60	Puget Sound Bridge & Dry Dock, Seattle	31 July 1961	18 July 1962	21 Mar 1964	PA
DDG 22	BENJAMIN STODDERT	60	Puget Sound Bridge & Dry Dock, Seattle	11 June 1962	8 Jan 1963	12 Sep 1964	PA
DDG 23	RICHARD E. BYRD	61	Todd Shipyards, Seattle, Wash.	12 Apr 1961	6 Feb 1962	7 Mar 1964	AA
DDG 24	WADDELL	61	Todd Shipyards, Seattle, Wash.	6 Feb 1962	26 Feb 1963	28 Aug 1964	PA

Displacement:	3,380 tons standard
	4,500 tons full load
Length:	420 feet (128.1 m) wl
	437 feet (133.3 m) oa
Beam:	47 feet (14.3 m)
Draft:	22 feet (6.7 m)
Propulsion:	2 steam turbines (General Electric in DDG 2–3, 7–8, 10–13, 15–22; Westinghouse in DDG 4–6, 9, 14, 23–24); 70,000 shp; 2 shafts
Boilers:	4 1,200 psi (Babcock & Wilcox in DDG 2–3, 7–8, 10–13, 20–22; Foster Wheeler in DDG 4–6, 9, 14; Combustion Engineering in DDG 15–19)
Speed:	31.5 knots
Range:	4,500 n.miles at 20 knots
Manning:	361 (21 officers + 340 enlisted)
Helicopters:	VERTREP area only
Missiles:	1 twin Mk 11 Mod 0 launcher for Tartar/Standard-MR SAM and Harpoon SSM (42) in DDG 2–14
	1 twin Mk 13 Mod 0 launcher for Tartar/Standard-MR SAM and Harpoon SSM (40) in DDG 15–24
Guns:	2 5-inch (127-mm) 54-cal DP Mk 42 (2 single)
ASW weapons:	1 8-tube ASROC launcher Mk 16
Torpedoes:	6 12.75-inch (324-mm) torpedo tubes Mk 32 (2 triple)
Radars:	SPS-10F surface search
	SPS-37 air search in DDG 2–14
	SPS-40B/D air search in DDG 15–24
	SPS-39A or SPS-52 3-D search
	SPS-65 in DDG 19, 20, 22
Sonars:	SQS-23 keel mounted except bow mounted in DDG 20–24
	SQQ-23A PAIR fitted in several ships
Fire control:	1 Mk 4 weapon direction system except Mk 13 weapon direction system in DDG 9, 12, 15, 19–22
	1 Mk 68 GFCS with SPG-53A/F radar except Mk 86 with SPG-60 and SPQ-9A radar in DDG 19, 20, 22
	2 Mk 74 missile FCS
	1 Mk 111 ASW FCS in DDG 2–15; Mk 114 ASW FCS in DDG 16–24
	2 SPG-51C radar

These are highly capable destroyers for their relatively small size, although they lack helicopter facilities. This was the largest class of missile-armed surface warships to be constructed for the U.S. Navy prior to the FFG 7 class.

The TOWERS and COCHRANE are based in Yokosuka, Japan.

Class: Three additional ships of this class were built for Australia (assigned U.S. hull numbers DDG 25-27) and three for West Germany (DDG 28-30).

Classification: The first eight ships of this class were authorized as all-gun/ASW destroyers (DD 952-959), then changed to guided missile ships and reclassified DDG 952-959 on 16 August 1956; they were changed to DDG 2-9 on 26 June 1957.

Design: SCB No. 155. The ADAMS design is based on an improved FORREST SHERMAN arrangement, with a Tartar missile launching system in place of the SHERMAN's aftermost 5-inch gun. The last five ships have their sonar in the improved, bow position.

No ASROC reloads are provided.

Missiles: These ships can fire the Harpoon anti-ship missile from their Mk 11 or Mk 13 launcher.

Modernization: The Navy had planned to modernize all 23 ships of this class, extending their useful service life for 15 years beyond the nominal 30 years. The modernizations were to be funded in fiscal 1980–1983. However, increasing costs and congressional interest in constructing new destroyer-type ships rather than upgrading older units has led to a cutback in the modernization program. Now only three ships, the DDG 19, 20, and 22, are receiving the AAW/radar update. All ships will receive ASW/sonar improvements, including SQQ-23 configuration of original SQS-23 sonar.

Names: DDG 5 was originally named BIDDLE; was renamed CLAUDE V. RICKETTS on 28 July 1964 (with DLG/CG 34 subsequently named BIDDLE).

The BERKELEY, a later ship of the CHARLES F. ADAMS class, has the single-arm Mk 13 launcher for Tartar/Standard-MR m ssiles. Two vertical replenishment spots are marked aft, one on the fantail and one on the 01 level, between the after gun and missile launcher. (1983, Giorgio Arra)

The ROBISON underway. These ships are too tight to accommodate Harpoon missile cannisters or the Phalanx CIWS. Prior to the deployment of those weapons, the ADAMS were considered highly capable destroyers. Ships of this class were also constructed for Australia and West Germany. (1983, Giorgio Arra)

The HENRY B. WILSON entering San Diego harbor. The SATCOM antennas are just visible, mounted on the starboard side of the bridge and port side amidships (just above the motor launch). (1983, Giorgio Arra)

The ROBISON shows the manner in which the superstructure of this class has been built up, mainly to accommodate new electronic equipment. These ships are too tight to fit the Phalanx CIWS; but the ROBISON does have SLQ-32 ECM gear mounted atop the bridge, adjacent to the Mk 68 GFCS and above the Super RBOC launching system. (1982, Giorgio Arra)

This view of the ROBISON clearly shows the twin-arm Mk 11 missile launcher, which sits atop the circular magazine at the ship's 01 level. Also visible are the SLQ-32(V)2 antennas atop the bridge. (1983, Giorgio Arra)

31 DESTROYERS: "SPRUANCE" CLASS

Number	Name	FY	Builder	Laid down	Launched	Commissioned	Status
DD 963	SPRUANCE	70	Litton/Ingalls, Pascagoula, Miss.	1 Nov 1972	10 Nov 1973	20 Sep 1975	**AA**
DD 964	PAUL F. FOSTER	70	Litton/Ingalls, Pascagoula, Miss.	6 Feb 1973	23 Feb 1974	21 Feb 1976	**PA**
DD 965	KINKAID	70	Litton/Ingalls, Pascagoula, Miss.	19 Apr 1973	25 May 1974	10 July 1976	**PA**
DD 966	HEWITT	71	Litton/Ingalls, Pascagoula, Miss.	23 July 1973	24 Aug 1974	25 Sep 1976	**PA**
DD 967	ELLIOTT	71	Litton/Ingalls, Pascagoula, Miss.	15 Oct 1973	19 Dec 1974	22 Jan 1977	**PA**
DD 968	ARTHUR W. RADFORD	71	Litton/Ingalls, Pascagoula, Miss.	14 Jan 1974	1 Mar 1975	9 Apr 1977	**AA**
DD 969	PETERSON	71	Litton/Ingalls, Pascagoula, Miss.	29 Apr 1974	21 June 1975	9 July 1977	**AA**
DD 970	CARON	71	Litton/Ingalls, Pascagoula, Miss.	1 July 1974	24 June 1975	1 Oct 1977	**AA**
DD 971	DAVID R. RAY	71	Litton/Ingalls, Pascagoula, Miss.	23 Sep 1974	23 Aug 1975	19 Nov 1977	**PA**
DD 972	OLENDORF	72	Litton/Ingalls, Pascagoula, Miss.	27 Dec 1974	21 Oct 1975	4 Mar 1978	**PA**
DD 973	JOHN YOUNG	72	Litton/Ingalls, Pascagoula, Miss.	17 Feb 1975	7 Feb 1976	20 May 1978	**PA**
DD 974	COMTE DE GRASSE	72	Litton/Ingalls, Pascagoula, Miss.	4 Apr 1975	26 Mar 1976	5 Aug 1978	**AA**
DD 975	O'BRIEN	72	Litton/Ingalls, Pascagoula, Miss.	9 May 1975	8 July 1976	3 Dec 1977	**PA**
DD 976	MERRILL	72	Litton/Ingalls, Pascagoula, Miss.	16 June 1975	1 Sep 1976	11 Mar 1978	**PA**
DD 977	BRISCOE	72	Litton/Ingalls, Pascagoula, Miss.	21 July 1975	8 Jan 1977	3 June 1978	**AA**
DD 978	STUMP	72	Litton/Ingalls, Pascagoula, Miss.	22 Aug 1975	30 Apr 1977	19 Aug 1978	**AA**
DD 979	CONOLLY	74	Litton/Ingalls, Pascagoula, Miss.	29 Sep 1975	25 June 1977	14 Oct 1978	**AA**
DD 980	MOOSBRUGGER	74	Litton/Ingalls, Pascagoula, Miss.	3 Nov 1975	20 Aug 1977	16 Dec 1978	**AA**
DD 981	JOHN HANCOCK	74	Litton/Ingalls, Pascagoula, Miss.	16 Jan 1976	29 Oct 1977	10 Mar 1979	**AA**
DD 982	NICHOLSON	74	Litton/Ingalls, Pascagoula, Miss.	20 Feb 1976	28 Jan 1978	12 May 1979	**AA**
DD 983	JOHN RODGERS	74	Litton/Ingalls, Pascagoula, Miss.	12 Aug 1976	25 Feb 1978	14 July 1979	**AA**
DD 984	LEFTWICH	74	Litton/Ingalls, Pascagoula, Miss.	12 Nov 1976	8 Apr 1978	25 Aug 1979	**PA**
DD 985	CUSHING	74	Litton/Ingalls, Pascagoula, Miss.	2 Feb 1977	17 June 1978	20 Oct 1979	**PA**
DD 986	HARRY W. HILL	75	Litton/Ingalls, Pascagoula, Miss.	1 Apr 1977	10 Aug 1978	17 Nov 1979	**PA**
DD 987	O'BANNON	75	Litton/Ingalls, Pascagoula, Miss.	24 June 1977	25 Sep 1978	15 Dec 1979	**AA**
DD 988	THORN	75	Litton/Ingalls, Pascagoula, Miss.	29 Aug 1977	14 Nov 1978	16 Feb 1980	**AA**
DD 989	DEYO	75	Litton/Ingalls, Pascagoula, Miss.	14 Oct 1977	20 Jan 1979	22 Mar 1980	**AA**
DD 990	INGERSOLL	75	Litton/Ingalls, Pascagoula, Miss.	16 Dec 1977	10 Mar 1979	12 Apr 1980	**PA**
DD 991	FIFE	75	Litton/Ingalls, Pascagoula, Miss.	6 Mar 1978	1 May 1979	31 May 1980	**PA**
DD 992	FLETCHER	75	Litton/Ingalls, Pascagoula, Miss.	24 Apr 1978	16 June 1979	12 July 1980	**PA**
DD 997	HAYLER	78	Litton/Ingalls, Pascagoula, Miss.	20 Oct 1980	27 Mar 1982	5 Mar 1983	**AA**

Displacement:	7,800 tons full load
Length:	529 feet (161.3 m) wl
	563⅓ feet (171.8 m) oa
Beam:	55 feet (16.8 m)
Draft:	29 feet (8.8 m)
Propulsion:	4 gas turbines (General Electric LM 2500); 80,000 shp; 2 shafts
Speed:	30 + knots
Range:	6,000 + n.miles at 20 knots
Manning:	324 (18 officers + 306 enlisted) in most ships
Helicopters:	2 SH-60B Seahawk LAMPS III (planned)
Missiles:	1 8-tube NATO Sea Sparrow launcher Mk 29
	8 Harpoon SSMs (2 quad cannisters Mk 141)
Guns:	2 5-inch (127-mm) 54-cal DP Mk 45 (2 single)
	2 20-mm Phalanx CIWS Mk 16 (2 multibarrel) in DD 965, 967–971, 997
ASW weapons:	1 8-tube ASROC launcher Mk 16
	6 12.75-inch (324-mm) torpedo tubes Mk 32 (2 triple)
Radars:	SPS-40B air search
	SPS-55 surface search
Sonars:	SQS-53 bow mounted
Fire control:	1 Mk 86 GFCS with SPG-60 and SPQ-9A radars
	1 Mk 91 missile FCS
	1 Mk 116 ASW FCS

The SPRUANCE-class destroyers were developed as replacements for the large number of World War II-built general purpose destroyers of the ALLEN M. SUMNER (DD 692) and GEARING (DD 710) classes that reached the end of their service lives in the mid-1970s. The SPRUANCES are specialized ASW ships, built with only point-defense missiles. They are now scheduled, however, for Vertical Launch Systems (VLS) or Armored Box Launchers (ABL) for Tomahawk missiles.

The four KIDD-class missile destroyers and TICONDEROGA (CG 47)-class missile cruisers have the same hull, propulsion, and auxiliary systems. The SPRUANCE class represents the largest destroyer class built by any Western navy since World War II.

Builders: The entire SPRUANCE class was contracted with a single shipyard to facilitate design and mass production. A contract for the development and production of 30 ships was awarded on 23 June 1970 to a new yard established by the Ingalls Shipbuilding Division of Litton Industries at Pascagoula, Miss. Labor and technical problems delayed the construction of these ships. One additional ship was placed under contract in September 1979.

Class: In addition to these 31 ships, four similar ships were ordered with the Mk 26/Standard AAW missile system for the Iranian Navy, but were completed as the KIDD class, accounting for hull numbers DD 993-996.

One additional ship of this class was ordered on 29 September 1979 (DD 997). This ship was one of two authorized (one funded) by Congress with the proviso that, in the wording of the Senate Committee on Armed Services, "the committee does not intend for these funds to be used for acquisition of two standard DD 963-class destroyers; rather, it is the committee's intention that these ships be the first element in a new technology approach to the problems of designing surface escorts. The standard 963 class design should be modified to substantially increase the number of helicopter aircraft carried." This feature could permit the eventual modification of the ships to operate VSTOL aircraft as well. The Navy, however, chose to build the ship as a standard SPRUANCE, and no additional ships were funded by Congress. (The ship was initially listed as DDH 997 in Navy working papers.)

Design: SCB No. 224. The original concept for this class provided for an AAW missile version (DXG) as well as the ASW version (DX); these designs became the KIDD and SPRUANCE classes, respectively.

The SPRUANCE design provides for the subsequent installation of additional weapon systems, specifically the Mk 26 missile launcher (and subsequently the Mk 41 VLS) forward with removal of the ASROC launcher and aft with removal of the Sea Sparrow launcher. In addition, the forward 5-inch gun could be replaced by the now-cancelled 8-inch Mk 71 Major Caliber Lightweight Gun.

Engineering: These are the first U.S. Navy surface combatants to have gas-turbine propulsion. Gas turbines previously were installed in several Navy patrol combatants (PGM/PG 84 class) and in the Coast Guard HAMILTON (WHEC 715) class as well as some RELIANCE (WMEC 615)-class cutters.

The SPRUANCE-class ships have four LM 2500 gas turbines, which are modified TF39 aircraft turbofan engines. One engine can propel the ships at about 19 knots, two engines at about 27 knots, and three and four engines can provide speeds in excess of 30 knots.

Guns: These ships are each scheduled to receive two Phalanx CIWS.

The 8-inch Major Caliber Lightweight Gun (MCLWG), at one time proposed for the entire SPRUANCE class, has been terminated. The gun was successfully evaluated at sea in the older destroyer HULL in 1975–1979.

Helicopters: The hangar sizes in these ships vary; they are 49 to 54 feet long and 21 to 23½ feet wide.

Missiles: The MERRILL was fitted with twin ABLs for four Tomahawk anti-ship cruise missiles in October 1982, the first U.S. ship to have that weapon.

Sonars: Original plans provided for these ships to have the SQS-35 Independent Variable Depth Sonar (IVDS) in addition to their bow mounted SQS-53. The IVDS was deleted because of the effectiveness of the SQS-53. The decision has subsequently been made to fit these ships with the SQR-19 TACTAS when that sonar becomes available.

The MERRILL firing a Tomahawk from her box launcher. Most SPRUANCES will be fitted with vertical launch systems for Tomahawks and, when developed, Vertical-Launch ASROC (VLA). (1980, U.S. Navy)

The HARRY W. HILL steaming off Hong Kong shows the boxy lines of the SPRUANCE class, with the attractive bow rake caused by the large SQS-53 sonar dome. The ships are quite roomy, having been built with space and weight to accommodate the weapon-sensor systems and additional manning of the KIDD-class missile destroyers. (1981, Giorgio Arra)

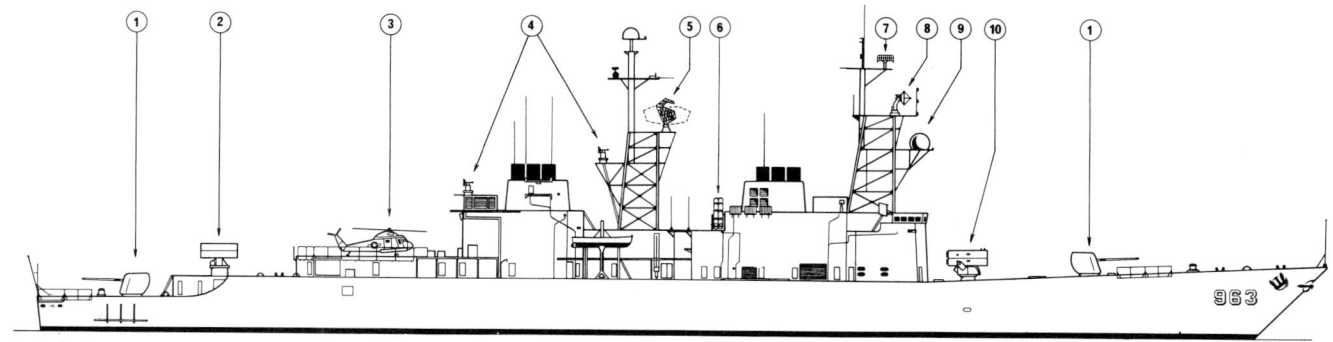

1. 5-inch/54-cal Mk 45 gun   2. Sea Sparrow missile launcher   3. helicopter deck (Mk 32 tubes are fitted below helicopter deck)   4. Sea Sparrow guidance   5. SPS-40 radar   6. Harpoon cannisters   7. SPS-55 radar   8. SPG-60 radar   9.SPQ-9 radar   10. ASROC launcher

The DEYO with ASROC launched rotated 180° and exhaust panels visible behind the forward 5-inch gun. A SATCOM antenna is fitted above the bridge, port side. (1982, Giorgio Arra)

The HARRY W. HILL prior to installation of Phalanx CIWS. The port-side Harpoon cannsters are visible (aimed to starboard, firing across the ship); the funnels are offset to port and starboard. The stern openings are for the SLQ-25 Nixie torpedo countermeasures. The WADDELL is moored nearby. (1981, Giorgio Arra)

The O'Brien has Gatling guns mounted forward, atop the bridge, and amidships, on the port side next to the second funnel; an SH-2F LAMPS helicopter sits on the flight deck. The twin hangars are separated, sized for the larger SH-60B LAMPS III helicopter. (1983, Giorgio Arra)

The Comte De Grasse riding at anchor with the port-side hangar open and an SH-2F LAMPS with rotor blades folded back for stowage. (1982, Giorgio Arra)

14 DESTROYERS: "FORREST SHERMAN" CLASS

Number	Name	FY	Builder	Laid down	Launched	Commissioned	Decommissioned	Status
DD 931	FORREST SHERMAN	53	Bath Iron Works, Maine	27 Oct 1953	5 Oct 1955	9 Nov 1955	5 Nov 1982	AR
*DD 933	BARRY	53	Bath Iron Works, Maine	15 Mar 1954	1 Oct 1955	31 Aug 1956	5 Nov 1982	AR
*DD 937	DAVIS	54	Bethlehem Steel, Quincy, Mass.	1 Feb 1955	28 Mar 956	28 Feb 1957	20 Dec 1982	AR
*DD 938	JONAS INGRAM	54	Bethlehem Steel, Quincy, Mass.	15 June 1955	8 July 1956	19 July 1957	4 Mar 1983	AR
*DD 940	MANLEY	55	Bath Iron Works, Maine	10 Feb 1955	12 Apr 1956	1 Feb 1957	4 Mar 1983	AR
*DD 941	DU PONT	55	Bath Iron Works, Maine	11 May 1955	8 Sep 1956	1 July 1957	4 Mar 1983	AR
DD 942	BIGELOW	55	Bath Iron Works, Maine	6 July 1955	2 Feb 1957	8 Nov 1957	5 Nov 1982	AR
*DD 943	BLANDY	55	Bethlehem Steel, Quincy, Mass.	29 Dec 1955	19 Dec 1956	26 Nov 1957	5 Nov 1982	AR
DD 944	MULLINNIX	55	Bethlehem Steel, Quincy, Mass.	5 Apr 1956	18 Mar 1957	7 Mar 1958	11 Aug 1983	AR
DD 945	HULL	56	Bath Iron Works, Maine	12 Sep 1956	10 Aug 1957	3 July 1958	11 July 1983	PR
DD 946	EDSON	56	Bath Iron Works, Maine	3 Dec 1956	1 Jan 1958	7 Nov 1958	—	NRF-A
*DD 948	MORTON	56	Ingalls Shipbuilding, Pascagoula	4 Mar 1957	23 May 1958	26 May 1959	22 Nov 1982	PR
*DD 950	RICHARD S. EDWARDS	56	Puget Sound Bridge & DD, Wash.	20 Dec 1956	24 Sep 1956	5 Feb 1959	15 Dec 1982	PR
DD 951	TURNER JOY	56	Puget Sound Bridge & DD, Wash.	30 Sep 1957	5 May 1958	3 Aug 1959	22 Nov 1982	PR

*ASW-modified ships

Displacement:	approx. 2,800 tons standard
	approx. 4,050 tons full load
Length:	407 feet (124.1 m) wl
	DD 931–938 series 418 feet (127.5 m) oa except
	DD 933 425 feet (129.6 m) oa
	DD 940–951 series 418 5/12 feet (127.6 m) oa
Beam:	45 feet (13.7 m)
Draft:	22 feet (6.7 m)
Propulsion:	steam turbines (General Electric, except Westinghouse in DD 931, 933); 70,000 shp; 2 shafts
Boilers:	4 1,200 psi (Foster Wheeler except Babcock & Wilcox in DD 937, 938, 943, 944, 948)
Speed:	32.5 knots
Range:	4,500 n.miles at 20 knots
Manning:	226 (15 officers + 211 enlisted) active + 125 (6 officers + 119 enlisted) in DD 946
	319–332 (19 officers + 300–313 enlisted) except
	309 (17 officers + 292 enlisted) in ASW-modified ships(*)
Helicopters:	VERTREP area only
Missiles:	none
Guns	3 5-inch (127-mm) 54-cal DP Mk 42 (3 single) except 2 guns in ASW modified ships(*)
ASW weapons:	1 8-tube ASROC launcher Mk 16 in ASW-modified ships(*)
	6 12.75-inch (324-mm) torpedo tubes Mk 32 (2 triple)
Radars:	SPS-10 surface search
	SPS-37 air search in DD 933, 940, 942, 946, 951
	SPS-40 air search in DD 931, 937, 938, 941, 943–945, 948, 950
Sonars:	SQS-23 keel mounted except bow mounted in DD 933
	SQS-35 IVDS in ASW-modified ships(*)
Fire control:	1 Mk 5 target designation system
	1 Mk 56 GFCS with Mk 35 radar
	1 Mk 68 GFCS with SPG-53 radar except SPG-53A in DD 945–951
	1 Mk 114 ASW FCS in ASW-modified ships(*)

Originally numbering 18 ships, the FORREST SHERMAN class was the first U.S. post-World War II design after the larger DD 927-930, which were completed as "frigates" (DL 2-5). Only one ship remains in service, the EDSON as an NRF/OCS training ship at Newport, R.I., with a composite active-reserve crew; she was assigned to the Naval Reserve Force on 1 April 1977. The decommissioned BARRY was shifted to the Navy Yard in Washington, D.C., in 1983 for use in ceremonies.

Thirteen ships have been decommissioned and laid up in reserve. Four other ships were converted to a guided missile configuration (DDG 31-34).

ASW weapons: The ASW-modified ships carry 20 ASROCs.

Conversion: All 18 ships of the class were scheduled for Tartar-DDG conversion. After that program was limited to 4 ships, all were scheduled for ASW modification. Both programs were curtailed because of relatively high costs.

Design: SCB No. 85 except DD 945-951 are 85A. These were the first major U.S. combatants with more firepower aft than forward. The DECATUR and later ships have higher bows to improve seakeeping; the HULL and later ships have a slightly different bow configuration.

Their original ASW armament consisted of two Mk 10/11 hedgehogs, over-the-side torpedo launchers (replaced by Mk 32 tubes), and depth charges. Four 21-inch fixed torpedo tubes were planned, but only the first two ships were completed with these tubes. The SPS-6 radar and SQS-4 sonar were originally provided.

Guns: As built, the SHERMANS each had three 5-inch Mk 42 guns plus four 3-inch/50-cal Mk 33 AA guns in twin mounts, forward of the bridge and between the second funnel and the No. 2 5-inch mount. The 3-inch guns were removed during the 1960s and 1970s. In addition, the No. 2 5-inch gun was deleted from the eight ASW modified destroyers to accommodate the ASROC launcher.

The HULL was test ship for the Mk 71 8-inch MCLWG. The gun, installed from 1975 to 1979, replaced the ship's forward 5-inch mount.

The BIGELOW conducted at-sea evaluation of the Phalanx CIWS in the late 1970s.

Modernization: Eight SHERMANS were modernized to improve their ASW capabilities. An ASROC launcher and variable-depth sonar were installed; the BARRY was additionally fitted with bow-mounted SQS-23 sonar. The BARRY modernization was SCB-251; the others were SCB-221. Plans to modernize the six remaining ships were dropped because of increasing costs.

TURNER JOY (1980, Giorgio Arra)

The TURNER JOY, a three-gun FORREST SHERMAN off Pearl Harbor. The open space behind of the No. 1 5-inch gun and between the No. 2 gun and the after funnel originally mounted twin 3-inch gun mounts. These ships were being considered for transfer to the NRF but were retired to provide more effective FF/FFGs to the reserves. (1980, Giorgio Arra)

The Du Pont with an ASW refit; an ASROC launcher and VERTREP spot replace the second 5-inch gun; a VDS is installed on her fantail. (1981, U.S. Navy, PH1 Greg Toon)

Stern view of the Du Pont with fenders over the starboard side. The front panels of the ASROC launcher have been painted in checkerboard style. (1982, Giorgio Arra)

The Hull shows the traditional destroyer lines from this stern aspect. The ship previously carried a Mk 71 8-inch gun forward, demonstrating the feasibility of that weapon for destroyer-type ships. (1983, Giorgio Arra)

"GEARING" AND "CARPENTER" CLASSES

The 16 destroyers of the GEARING (DD 710) and CARPENTER (DD 825) classes that were in NRF service in 1980 have been stricken and/or transferred to other navies. (In addition, the DYESS/DD 880 was stricken on 1 October 1979 and transferred to Greece in July 1981.) See the 12th edition of *Ships and Aircraft* for details of these ships.

DD 743	SOUTHERLAND	stricken 23 Feb 1981
DD 763	WILLIAM C. LAWE	leased to Mexico
DD 784	MCKEAN	stricken 1 Oct 1981; to Turkey 2 Nov 1982
DD 817	CORRY	stricken 27 Feb 1981; to Greece Feb 1981
DD 821	JOHNSTON	stricken 1 Oct 1980; to Taiwan Feb 1981
DD 822	ROBERT H. MCCARD	leased to Turkey 5 June 1980
DD 825	CARPENTER	stricken 20 Feb 1981; to Turkey Feb 1981
DD 827	ROBERT A. OWENS	leased to Turkey 16 Feb 1982
DD 842	FISKE	leased to Turkey 5 June 1980
DD 862	VOGELGESANG	stricken 23 Feb 1982; to Mexico Feb 1982
DD 863	STEINAKER	stricken 24 Feb 1982; to Mexico Feb 1982;
DD 864	HAROLD J. ELLISON	to Pakistan 31 Sep 1983
DD 866	CONE	stricken 1 Oct 1982; to Pakistan 1 Oct 1982
DD 876	ROGERS	stricken 1 Oct 1980; to South Korea 25 July 1981
DD 883	NEWMAN K. PERRY	stricken 27 Feb 1981; to South Korea Feb 1981
DD 886	ORLECK	leased to Turkey 1 Oct 1982

POST-WORLD WAR II DESTROYERS

U.S. World War II destroyer programs reached hull number DD 926 (with hulls DD 891–926 being cancelled in 1945). Many ships built during the war were subsequently reclassified as escort destroyers (DDE), hunter-killer destroyers (DDK), radar picket destroyers (DDR), and experimental destroyers (EDD). One GEARING-class ship was converted to a missile configuration (DDG 1) to evaluate the Terrier system in a destroyer-size ship. All except the DDG retained their DD hull numbers in their new roles.

All surviving destroyers reverted to "straight" DD classification during the early 1960s, except for six DDRs. Most ships were updated under the FRAM (Fleet Rehabilitation and Modernization) program of the early 1960s.

As indicated below, several war prizes and foreign-built ships (offshore procurement) had DD-series hull numbers, as did one British destroyer acquired for transfer to Pakistan with U.S. funds.[1]

Six missile-armed ships of the SPRUANCE class ordered by Iran were assigned DD hull numbers by the U.S. Navy. The four ships actually begun went to the U.S. Navy, not with DDG designations but with their original (DD) hull numbers. The two other ships were cancelled, with one number being subsequently assigned to the thirty-first SPRUANCE-class ship.

---

[1]While three axis destroyers were given DD numbers, the Japanese battleship NAGATO, the German heavy cruiser PRINZ EUGEN, and several German and Japanese submarines acquired in 1945 were not given warship numbers; the German cruiser was assigned the designation IX 300 (sunk in the Bikini atomic bomb tests of 1946 along with the NAGATO); the German supply ship CONECUH became IX 301 and subsequently saw U.S. Navy service as the AO 110.

DD 927-930	MITSCHER class	completed as DL 2-5
DD 931-933	FORREST SHERMAN class	
DD 934	ex-Japanese HANAZUKI	
DD 935	ex-German T-35	
DD 936-938	FORREST SHERMAN class	
DD 939	ex-German Z-39	
DD 940-951	FORREST SHERMAN class	
DD 952-959	CHARLES F. ADAMS class	completed as DDG 2-9
DD 960	(AKIZUKI)	Japan OSP 1960
DD 961	(TERUZUKI)	Japan OSP 1960
DD 962	(ex-British CHARITY)	to Pakistan 1958 (SHAH JAHAN)
DD 963-992	SPRUANCE class	
DD 993	(ex-Iranian KOUROSH)	completed as U.S. DDG 993
DD 994	(ex-Iranian DARYUSH)	completed as U.S. DDG 994
DD 995	(ex-Iranian ARDESHIR)	completed as U.S. DDG 995
DD 996	(ex-Iranian NADER)	completed as U.S. DDG 996
DD 997	(Iranian SHAPOUR)	cancelled 1976; reassigned to SPRUANCE class
DD 998	(Iranian ANOUSHIRVAN)	cancelled 1976

GUIDED MISSILE DESTROYERS

DDG 1	GYATT (ex-DD 712)	comm. 1956; stricken (as DD 712)
DDG 2-24	CHARLES F. ADAMS class	
DDG 25	(Australian PERTH)	comm. 1965
DDG 26	(Australian HOBART)	comm. 1965
DDG 27	(Australian BRISBANE)	comm. 1967
DDG 28	(German LUTJENS)	comm. 1969
DDG 29	(German MOLDERS)	comm. 1969
DDG 30	(German ROMMEL)	comm. 1970
DDG 31-34	Conv. FORREST SHERMAN class	(ex-DD 936, 932, 949, 947)
DDG 35	MITSCHER (ex-DL 2)	comm. 1968; stricken 1978
DDG 36	JOHN S. MCCAIN (ex-DL 3)	comm. 1969; stricken 1978
DDG 37-46	FARRAGUT class (ex-DLG 6-15)	
DDG 47-50	TICONDEROGA class	changed to CG 47-50
DDG 51	ARLEIGH BURKE class	

The guided missile destroyer classification (DDG) was established in 1956. The first DDG was the GEARING-class destroyer GYATT (DD 712), fitted with a twin Terrier SAM launcher aft, replacing the after 5-inch twin gun mount. The GYATT became DDG 712 on 3 December 1956 and DDG 1 on 23 April 1957. Subsequent DDGs had the smaller Tartar (later Standard-MR) missile system, until the FARRAGUT-class frigates were reclassified as destroyers in 1975. Six ADAMS-class DDGs built for Australia and Germany in the United States were built as the DDG 25-30.

DG (AEGIS)

A large number of destroyer designs were developed by the U.S. Navy from the 1950s onward. The current Aegis program (manifested in the CG 47/DDG 51 designs) originated in 1963 with the Advanced Surface Missile System (ASMS). As the development of the large Typhon missile frigate (DLGN) began to encounter difficulties, the ASMS effort was undertaken, partially based on the expectations of new solid-state electronics.

The development was protracted and in 1971 the Chief of Naval Operations, Admiral Zumwalt, directed a design effort to provide the smallest possible ship that could carry the new air-defense weapons/electronics system. The initial goal was a displacement of 5,000 tons, but that was soon raised to 6,000 tons. Several designs were put forward, with the more austere versions having a single Mk 26 Mod 1 missile launcher for surface-to-air missiles as well as ASROC, a small sonar, and a helicopter landing deck but no hangar. By early 1973 the design had been recast, with two Mk 13 launchers (a total of 80 missiles but no ASROC capability) plus a full LAMPS facility for one helicopter. The desire for longer-range as well as nuclear SAMs led to still another recasting, this time to provide the Mk 26 Mod 2 launcher (64 missiles).

However, congressional confusion, the change of CNO in mid-1974,

and advocacy of an all-nuclear Aegis force by Admiral Rickover led to the demise of the DG(Aegis) in favor of various DLGN-type designs as well as the CSGN strike cruiser (see Chapter 15).

The ARLEIGH BURKE class represents a return to the DG Aegis concept. The availability of the vertical-launch missile system (90 weapons) and improvements in the SPY-1 radar coupled with the deletion of the LAMPS helicopter facilities as well as one 5-inch gun permit the construction of a smaller Aegis ship—as envisioned in the early 1970s. Should the proposed Sperry Corporation's phased-array radar derivative of the Mk 92 weapon system come into being, there is the potential for a smaller radar/fire control suite suitable for a DG Aegis-type ship.

The Tomahawk test ship MERRILL of the SPRUANCE class has a box launcher—referred to as "coffin"—fitted on the main deck, forward of the bridge. (1980, U.S. Navy, PH1 Lawrence B. Foster)

17 Frigates

At the end of 1984, the Navy has 95 frigates (FF/FFG) in active commission plus nine ships assigned to the Naval Reserve Force (NRF) with composite active-reserve crews. Twelve additional frigates are under construction. Beyond those ships no additional frigates are planned for construction in the remainder of this decade.

Frigates are primarily ASW ships with the large OLIVER HAZARD PERRY class additionally intended to provide limited AAW defense to amphibious groups, military convoys, and replenishment groups. Despite the higher speed and missile capabilities of the PERRY class, these ships are still not capable of serving as effective escorts for carrier battle groups in wartime. All frigates except for the small BROOKE, GLOVER, and BRONSTEIN classes can additionally fire Harpoon anti-ship missiles from their Mk 13 launcher (FFG) or ASROC launcher (FF).

The large PERRY class has been quite controversial, having been initiated in the early 1970s together with the planned Sea Control Ship (SCS) to provide a viable capability for defending Sea Lines of Communications (SLOC) against Soviet air and submarine attacks. Subsequent Navy planning has emphasized other missions and frigates, and while there are inadequate numbers of frigates to provide SLOC defense in the face of a Soviet attack, frigates are the only U.S. warship category in which the planned forces will exceed the force level goals. The following table indicates the planned assignment of frigates to derive the frigate force level goals under the Reagan Administration's planned 600+ ship fleet; the previous 92-frigate force level objective is shown in parentheses.

Amphibious Forces	8 frigates (5)
7 Military Convoys	63 frigates (63)
10 Underway Replenishment	
Groups (URG)	30 frigates (24)
Totals	101 frigates (92)

As noted under the PERRY-class listing, approximately 25 additional ships were originally planned. A smaller frigate (FFX) intended for NRF service was planned by the Carter Administration but was not built nor will the long-gestation surface effect ship frigate (FFGS) be built. See pages 176–177 for details of these programs.

Several frigates of the PERRY and KNOX classes have been transferred to the NRF with a total of 26 ships scheduled for assignment by 1988. These frigates are replacing outdated World War II-era destroyers. Transfer of the PERRY-class mark the first time that new ships have been provided to the reserves since World War II. (See Chapter 7.)

Classification: This type of warship was classified as destroyer escort (DE) from its inception in the U.S. Navy in 1941 until the early 1950s when DE was changed to "ocean escort." (At that time the term *frigate* was applied to large destroyer-type ships—DL/DLG.)

Subsequently, missile-armed escort ships were designated DEG and the escort research ship GLOVER became AGDE. All escort ships were changed to "frigate" (FF/FFG/AGFF) on 30 June 1975.

Electronic warfare: the PERRY-class ships will have SLQ-32(V)2 and the earlier classes have lesser ECM suites. The PERRY class also has the SLQ-25 Nixie torpedo countermeasures; some of the older classes have the T-Mk-6 Fanfare.

New design: The Navy has begun conceptual studies of an advanced frigate (see page 162). When this edition of *Ships and Aircraft* went to press, the Navy was still examining potential mission requirements and related combat systems for the ship.

The most significant combat system development being proposed for the new ship at this time is a phased-array derivative of the Mk 92 weapon system under development by the Sperry Corporation. This system—if successful—would probably compete with a derivative of the RCA Corporation's SPY-1 Aegis radar now used in the CG 47/DDG 51 classes. Sperry has sought to have a prototype of their phased-array radar fitted in the OLIVER HAZARD PERRY-class ship proposed for fiscal 1985. Fitting the ship with the radar would probably cause a significant delay in that ship.

Type	Class/Ship	Comm.	Active	NRF	Building	Notes
FFG 7	OLIVER HAZARD PERRY	1977–	37	2	12	class in production
FFG 1	BROOKE	1966–1968	6	—	—	
FF 1098	GLOVER	1965	1	—	—	formerly AGFF/AGDE
FF 1052	KNOX	1969–1974	38	8	—	
FF 1040	GARCIA	1964–1968	10	—	—	
FF 1037	BRONSTEIN	1963	2	—	—	

A trio of OLIVER HAZARD PERRY-class frigates: This is the largest class of surface combatants built in the West since World War II with 51 ships being built for the U.S. Navy, plus 4 in a U.S. shipyard for the Australian Navy. Australia and Spain will build additional ships in their own yards.

ADVANCED FRIGATE DESIGN

The Navy is in the conceptual development stage of a new frigate design intended to replace the GARCIA, BROOKE, and KNOX classes, and the GLOVER, from the late 1990s onward. The ship is expected to be oriented primarily toward the AAW/ASW missions.

39 + 12 GUIDED MISSILE FRIGATES: "OLIVER HAZARD PERRY" CLASS

Number	Name	FY	Builder	Laid down	Launched	Commissioned	Status
FFG 7	OLIVER HAZARD PERRY	73	Bath Iron Works, Maine	12 June 1976	25 Sep 1978	17 Dec 1977	**NRF-A**
FFG 8	MCINERNEY	75	Bath Iron Works, Maine	16 Jan 1978	4 Nov 1978	15 Dec 1979	**AA**
FFG 9	WADSWORTH	75	Todd Shipyards, San Pedro, Calif.	13 July 1977	29 July 1978	2 Apr 1980	**PA**
FFG 10	DUNCAN	75	Todd Shipyards, Seattle, Wash.	29 Apr 1977	1 Mar 1978	24 May 1980	**NRF-P**
FFG 11	CLARK	76	Bath Iron Works, Maine	17 July 1978	24 Mar 1979	17 May 1980	**AA**
FFG 12	GEORGE PHILIP	76	Todd Shipyards, San Pedro, Calif.	14 Dec 1977	16 Dec 1978	15 Nov 1980	**PA**
FFG 13	SAMUEL ELIOT MORISON	76	Bath Iron Works, Maine	4 Dec 1978	14 July 1979	11 Oct 1980	**AA**
FFG 14	JOHN H. SIDES	76	Todd Shipyards, San Pedro, Calif.	7 Aug 1978	19 May 1979	30 May 1981	**PA**
FFG 15	ESTOCIN	76	Bath Iron Works, Maine	2 Apr 1979	3 Nov 1979	10 Jan 1981	**AA**
FFG 16	CLIFTON SPRAGUE	76	Bath Iron Works, Maine	30 July 1979	16 Feb 1980	21 Mar 1981	**AA**
FFG 19	JOHN A. MOORE	77	Todd Shipyards, San Pedro, Calif.	19 Dec 1978	20 Oct 1979	14 Nov 1981	**PA**
FFG 20	ANTRIM	77	Todd Shipyards, Seattle, Wash.	21 June 1978	27 Mar 1979	26 Sep 1981	**AA**
FFG 21	FLATLEY	77	Bath Iron Works, Maine	13 Nov 1979	15 May 1980	20 June 1981	**AA**
FFG 22	FAHRION	77	Todd Shipyards, Seattle, Wash.	1 Dec 1978	24 Aug 1979	16 Jan 1982	**AA**
FFG 23	LEWIS B. PULLER	77	Todd Shipyards, San Pedro, Calif.	23 May 1979	15 Mar 1980	17 Apr 1982	**PA**
FFG 24	JACK WILLIAMS.	77	Bath Iron Works, Maine	25 Feb 1980	30 Aug 1980	19 Sep 1981	**AA**
FFG 25	COPELAND	77	Todd Shipyards, San Pedro, Calif.	24 Oct 1979	26 July 1980	7 Aug 1982	**PA**
FFG 26	GALLERY	77	Bath Iron Works, Maine	17 May 1980	20 Dec 1980	5 Dec 1981	**AA**
FFG 27	MAHLON S. TISDALE	78	Todd Shipyards, San Pedro, Calif.	19 Mar 1980	7 Feb 1981	13 Nov 1982	**PA**
FFG 28	BOONE	78	Todd Shipyards, Seattle, Wash.	27 Mar 1979	16 Jan 1980	13 Nov 1982	**AA**
FFG 29	STEPHEN W. GROVES	78	Bath Iron Works, Maine	16 Sep 1980	4 Apr 1981	17 Apr 1982	**AA**
FFG 30	REID	78	Todd Shipyards, San Pedro, Calif.	8 Oct 1980	27 June 1981	19 Feb 1983	**PA**
FFG 31	STARK	78	Todd Shipyards, Seattle, Wash.	24 Aug 1979	30 May 1980	23 Oct 1982	**AA**
FFG 32	JOHN L. HALL	78	Bath Iron Works, Maine	5 Jan 1981	24 July 1981	26 June 1982	**AA**
FFG 33	JARRETT	78	Todd Shipyards, San Pedro, Calif.	11 Feb 1981	17 Oct 1981	2 July 1983	**PA**
FFG 34	AUBREY FITCH	78	Bath Iron Works, Maine	10 Apr 1981	17 Oct 1981	9 Oct 1982	**AA**
FFG 36	UNDERWOOD	79	Bath Iron Works, Maine	3 Aug 1981	6 Feb 1982	29 Jan 1983	**AA**
FFG 37	CROMMELIN	79	Todd Shipyards, Seattle, Wash.	30 May 1980	2 July 1981	1983	**PA**
FFG 38	CURTS	79	Todd Shipyards, San Pedro, Calif.	1 July 1981	6 Mar 1982	8 Oct 1983	**PA**
FFG 39	DOYLE	79	Bath Iron Works, Maine	23 Oct 1981	22 May 1982	21 May 1983	**AA**
FFG 40	HALYBURTON	79	Todd Shipyards, Seattle, Wash.	26 Sep 1980	13 Oct 1981	7 Jan 1984	**AA**
FFG 41	MCCLUSKY	79	Todd Shipyards, San Pedro, Calif.	21 Oct 1981	18 Sep 1982	10 Dec 1983	**PA**
FFG 42	KLAKRING	79	Bath Iron Works, Maine	19 Feb 1982	18 Sep 1982	20 Aug 1983	**AA**
FFG 43	THACH	79	Todd Shipyards, San Pedro, Calif.	6 Mar 1982	18 Dec 1982	17 Mar 1984	**PA**
FFG 45	DE WERT	80	Bath Iron Works, Maine	14 June 1982	18 Dec 1982	19 Nov 1983	**AA**
FFG 46	RENTZ	80	Todd Shipyards, San Pedro, Calif.	18 Sep 1982	16 July 1983	30 June 1984	**PA**
FFG 47	NICHOLAS	80	Bath Iron Works, Maine	27 Sep 1982	23 Apr 1983	10 Mar 1984	**AA**
FFG 48	VANDEGRIFT	80	Todd Shipyards, Seattle, Wash.	13 Oct 1981	15 Oct 1982	1984	**AA**
FFG 49	ROBERT G. BRADLEY	80	Bath Iron Works, Maine	28 Dec 1982	13 Aug 1983	1984	**PA**
FFG 50	JESSE L. TAYLOR	81	Bath Iron Works, Maine	5 Feb 1983	5 Nov 1983	1985	Building
FFG 51	GARY	81	Todd Shipyards, San Pedro, Calif.	18 Dec 1982	19 Nov 1983	1985	Building
FFG 52	CARR	81	Todd Shipyards, Seattle, Wash.	26 Mar 1982	26 Feb 1983	1985	Building
FFG 53	HAWES	81	Bath Iron Works, Maine	22 Aug 1983	18 Feb 1984	1985	Building
FFG 54	FORD	81	Todd Shipyards, San Pedro, Calif.	16 July 1983	18 Feb 1984	1985	Building
FFG 55	ELROD	81	Bath Iron Works, Maine		1984	1985	Building
FFG 56	SIMPSON	82	Bath Iron Works, Maine		1984	1985	Building
FFG 57	REUBEN JAMES	82	Todd Shipyards, San Pedro, Calif.		1984	1986	Building
FFG 58	SAMUEL B. ROBERTS	82	Bath Iron Works, Maine	21 May 1984	1984	1986	Building
FFG 59	. . . . . .	83	Bath Iron Works, Maine		1986	1987	Building
FFG 60	RODNEY M. DAVIS	83	Todd Shipyards, San Pedro, Calif.		1985	1987	Building
FFG 61	. . . . . .	84	Todd Shipyards, San Pedro, Calif.		1986	1988	Building

Displacement:	3,650 tons full load
	408 feet (124.4 m) wl
Length:	445 feet (135.6 m) oa except
	453 feet (138.2 m) oa for ships with LAMPS III modification
Beam:	45 feet (13.7 m)
Draft:	24 feet 6 in (7.5 m)
Propulsion:	2 gas turbines (General Electric LM2500); 40,000 shp; 1 shaft
Speed:	28 + knots (sustained)
Range:	4,500 n.miles at 20 knots
Manning:	active ships 193 (13 officers + 180 enlisted)
	NRF ships 193 (9 officers + 113 enlisted) active + 76 (4 officers + 72 enlisted) reserve
Helicopters:	2 SH-60B Seahawk ASW helicopters in active ships (planned)
	1 or 2 SH-2F ASW helicopters in NRF ships
Missiles:	1 single Mk 13 Mod 4 launcher for Standard-MR SAM and Harpoon SSM (40)
Guns:	1 76-mm/62-cal AA Mk 75
	1 20-mm Phalanx CIWS Mk 16 (multibarrel)
ASW weapons:	6 12.75-in (324-mm) torpedo tubes Mk 32 (2 × triple)
Radars:	SPS-49 air search
	SPS-55 surface search
Sonars:	SQR-18A towed array being fitted in NRF ships
	SQR-19 towed array being fitted in active ships
	SQS-56 keel mounted
Fire control:	1 Mk 13 weapon direction system
	1 Mk 92 weapons FCS
	1 STIR radar

This is the largest class of major surface warships built in the West since World War II; only the Soviet SKORYY destroyer class was larger with 72 ships completed between 1950 and 1954. Several of the PERRY-class frigates are shifting to the Naval Reserve (NRF), the first "new" ships to be assigned to the reserves since World War II. After the cutback of the DX/DXG program (i.e., SPRUANCE/DD 963 class), the FFG 7 class was additionally looked upon as a replacement for the surviving GEARING (DD 710)-class destroyers.

Eighteen of these ships are scheduled to be assigned to the NRF by 1988.

The PERRY's gun, fire control, and sonar systems were evaluated in the frigate TALBOT.

ASW weapons: The only ship-mounted ASW weapons are torpedo tubes, with the SH-60B helicopters being their primary ASW weapon. These are the first U.S. surface combatants built without ASROC since that weapon became available in the early 1960s.

Class: Early U.S. Navy planning provided for approximately 75 ships of this class. Shipbuilding programs of the early 1970s reduced the number of ships to be built in "later" years, in part because of the planned FFX, a smaller frigate intended specifically for NRF operation (see page 176).

The last Carter Administration five-year plan, for FY 1982–1986, deleted all FFG 7 construction after one ship in the 1983 program. However, the Reagan Administration's shipbuilding program put forward in January 1982 for FY 1983–1987 provided for 12 additional FFGs:

FY 1983	2 ships
FY 1984	2 ships
FY 1985	2 ships
FY 1986	3 ships
FY 1987	3 ships

Congress voted the 2 ships in the FY 1983 budget, but the Reagan Administration's subsequent five-year plan (FY 1984–1988) deleted all further frigate construction, thus halting the FFG 7 program at 50 ships. However, Congress subsequently voted one additional ship in the FY 1984 budget for construction at the Todd San Pedro yard (FFG 61).

The Todd-Seattle yard built 4 ships of this class for the Australian Navy: HMAS ADELAIDE (FFG 17), CANBERRA (FFG 18), SYDNEY (FFG 35), and DARWIN (FFG 44), delivered from 1980 to 1984.

Additional ships of this design will be constructed in Australia and in Spain for their respective navies. Note that the latter ships will have the same propulsion plant and some of the same combat systems as the new Spanish VSTOL carrier PRINCIPE DE ASTURIAS.

The FLATLEY steaming off Messina shows the boxy lines of the OLIVER HAZARD PERRY class. Although these ships have a keel-mounted SQS-56 sonar, they have a rakish stem and have exceeded 30 knots on sea trials, with some ships reported to have attained 36 knots. (1983, L. & L. van Ginderen)

Classification: When conceived these ships were classified as "patrol frigates" (PF), a designation previously applied to a series of smaller, World War II-era ships (PF 1–102) and postwar coastal escorts that were constructed specifically for foreign transfer (PF 103–108). The PERRY was designated PF 109 until changed to "frigate" FFG 7 on 30 June 1975.

Cost: The last multi-ship buy was in FY 1983 with the costs being higher per unit than in previous years because of the small number procured. The FY 1984 ship costs per ship were: $300 million for construction, $63.8 million for outfitting, and $35.1 million for post delivery, a total of $398.9 million for the ship.

Design: SCB design No. 261. These ships were designed specifically for modular assembly and mass production. All major components were tested at sea or in land facilities before completion of the lead ship. Space and weight were reserved for fin stabilizers. Early designs provided a single hangar aft with twin funnels ("split" by the hangar). The design was revised to provide side-by-side hangars to accommodate two SH-60B helicopters.

The original complement was to be 179 (12 officers + 167 enlisted).

Electronics: The STIR (Separate Target Illumination Radar) is a modified SPG-60 radar. Fitted with SLQ-32(V)2.

Engineering: These ships have two LM 2500 gas turbine main propulsion engines and can attain 25 knots on one engine. On trials some ships reportedly have reached 36 knots.

The ships have two 350-hp electric-drive, retractable auxiliary propulsion pods for precise maneuvering; they also provide a "come-home" capability at 6 knots in the event of main propulsion failure. They are fitted with four 1,000-kilowatt diesel ship's service generators, thus lacking the elaborate silencing of the SPRUANCE-class destroyers which have gas turbine generators.

Guns: Early designs addressed a variety of guns for these ships, among them a twin 35-mm rapid-fire gun in place of the later 76-mm gun and CIWS. These are the first U.S. major surface combatants built without a 5-inch gun since the early 1960s.

Helicopters: These are the first U.S. ships fitted with a helicopter hauldown system, designated RAST for Recovery Assist Secure and Traversing. The system winches down the helicopters and can move them along tracks into either hangar. This provides a significant capability to operate helicopters in rough seas. The RAST system is planned only for this class and not for larger cruisers and destroyers that are provided with the LAMPS III/SH-60 helicopter.

The MCINERNEY tested the hauldown system and conducted FFG sea trials with the SH-60B in 1980. Modification for RAST requires extensive modification of stern, lengthening the original ship by 8 feet.

The NRF-assigned ships will not be provided with SH-60B facilities but will operate the SH-2F ASW helicopter.

A SH-60B LAMPS III landing aboard the frigate CROMMELIN. (1983, R. Lawson)

LEWIS B. PULLER (1983, Giorgio Arra)

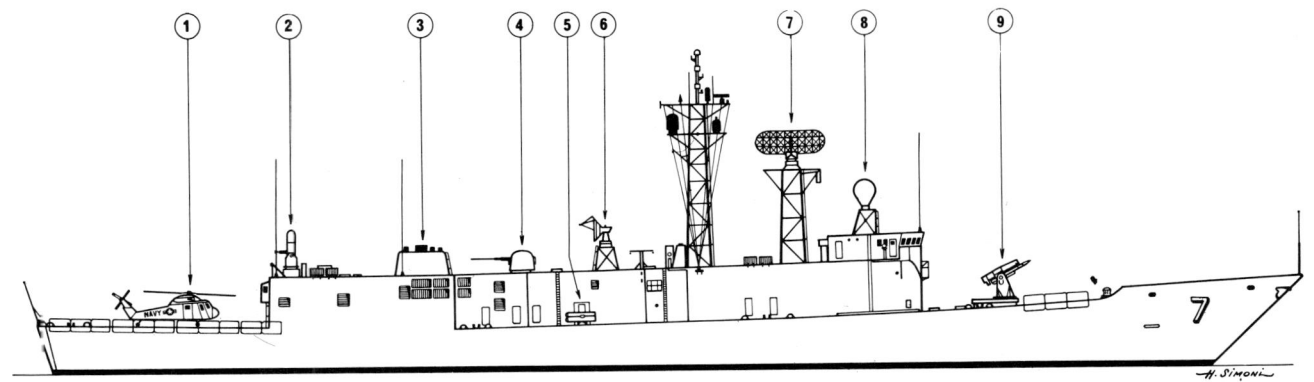

1. helicopter deck 2. Phalanx CIWS 3. exhaust funnel 4. 76-mm/62-cal Mk 75 (OTO Melara) gun 5. Mk 32 torpedo tubes 6. STIR radar
7. SPS-49 radar 8. Mk 92 fire control system. 9. Mk 13 missile launcher

The COPELAND with the Mk 13 missile launcher is the vertical (loading) position. Note the restricted arc of fire for the 76-mm gun atop the superstructure. A Phalanx CIWS will be fitted to all ships of the class, at the after end of the twin-hangar structure. (1983, Giorgio Arra)

The McCLUSKY, with her stern fitted for the LAMPS III/RAST helicopter system. Note that Gatling gun atop the hangar structure has a better field of fire than the 76-mm gun forward of the funnel. A Standard missile is on the Mk 13 launcher. (1984, Giorgio Arra)

The GALLERY's superstructure with the 76-mm gun (right) at full elevation. The SLQ-32(V)2 antennas are visible just aft of the bridge, between the Mk 92 and the SPS-49 antennas. Other frigates are receiving the SLQ-32(V)1 or (V)2. (1983, Giorgio Arra)

Sailors aboard the frigate McINERY work the RAST helicopter recovery system. The system is intended to permit the large SH-60B helicopters to operate from the PERRY-class ships in rough seas. (U.S. Navy)

LEWIS B. PULLER (1983, Giorgio Arra)

6 GUIDED MISSILE FRIGATES: "BROOKE" CLASS

Number	Name	FY	Builder	Laid down	Launched	Commissioned	Status
FFG 1	BROOKE	62	Lockheed SB & Constn, Seattle, Wash.	10 Dec 1962	19 July 1963	12 Mar 1966	**PA**
FFG 2	RAMSEY	62	Lockheed SB & Constn, Seattle, Wash.	4 Feb 1963	15 Oct 1963	3 June 1967	**PA**
FFG 3	SCHOFIELD	62	Lockheed SB & Constn, Seattle, Wash.	15 Apr 1963	7 Dec 1963	11 May 1968	**PA**
FFG 4	TALBOT	63	Bath Iron Works, Maine	4 May 1964	6 Jan 1966	22 Apr 1967	**AA**
FFG 5	RICHARD L. PAGE	63	Bath Iron Works, Maine	4 Jan 1965	4 Apr 1966	5 Aug 1967	**AA**
FFG 6	JULIUS A. FURER	63	Bath Iron Works, Maine	12 July 1965	22 July 1966	11 Nov 1967	**AA**

Displacement:	2,640 tons standard
	3,245 tons full load
Length:	390 feet (118.9 m) wl
	414½ feet (126.4 m) oa
Beam:	44⅙ feet (13.5 m)
Draft:	24 feet (7.3 m)
Propulsion:	2 steam turbines (Westinghouse); 35,000 shp; 1 shaft
Boilers:	2 1,200 psi (Foster Wheeler)
Speed:	27 knots
Range:	4,000 n.miles at 20 knots
Manning:	277 (17 officers + 260 enlisted)
Helicopters:	1 SH-2F LAMPS I
Missiles:	1 single Mk 22 Mod 0 launcher for Tartar/Standard SAM (16)
Guns:	1 5-inch (127-mm) 38-cal DP Mk 30
ASW weapons:	1 8-tube ASROC launcher Mk 16
	6 12.75-inch (324-mm) torpedo tubes Mk 32 (2 triple)
Radars:	SPS-10F surface search
	SPS-52A/D 3-D search
Sonars:	SQS-26AX/BX bow mounted
Fire control:	1 Mk 4 weapon direction system
	1 Mk 56 GFCS with Mk 35 radar
	1 Mk 74 missile FCS
	1 Mk 114 ASW FCS
	1 SPG-51C radar

This class is essentially the same as the GARCIA class but fitted with a SAM launcher in place of the second 5-inch gun. The TALBOT was used as test ship for the gun, missile, fire control, and sonar system of the PERRY class.

Class: Ten additional ships were planned for the FY 1964 shipbuilding program and three later units were not built because of the significantly higher costs for the missile and fire control systems compared with all-gun ships. (Note also the small missile magazine size.)

Classification: As built, these ships were classified as guided missile escort ships (DEG); changed to frigates (FFG) on 30 June 1975.

Design: SCB No. 199B. Sixteen ASROC rockets are carried, with a reload facility built into the face of the superstructure, aft of the ASROC launcher.

The original hangar, designed for the Drone Anti-Submarine Helicopter (DASH), has been enlarged to accommodate the SH-2F helicopter. The basic hangars now vary in size, from approximately 39½ to 52 feet in length and 14½ to 16⅚ feet in width. Flexible extensions are fitted to the hangars.

Torpedoes: Two Mk 25 torpedo tubes with 12 torpedoes were originally fitted into the stern (in addition to the Mk 32 tubes). They were subsequently removed.

SCHOFIELD (1983, Giorgio Arra)

BROOKE (1983, Giorgio Arra)

The TALBOT at Toulon; an electronics van is fitted on the helicopter deck. Note the expandable hangar configuration. (1981, Giorgio Arra)

The SCHOFIELD at sea with her hangar, built for the DSN/QH-50 Drone Anti-Submarine Helicopter (DASH), enlarged to accommodate an SH-2F LAMPS helicopter. These ships have smaller missile magazines, less helicopter capability, and less speed than the PERRY class. The older frigates, however, have 5-inch guns, more capable hull-mounted sonars, and ASROC. (1983, Giorgio Arra)

1 FRIGATE: "GLOVER"

Number	Name	FY	Builder	Laid down	Launched	Commissioned	Status
FF 1098 (ex-AGFF 1)	GLOVER	61	Bath Iron Works, Maine	29 July 1963	17 Apr 1965	13 Nov 1965	**AA**

Displacement:	2,643 tons standard
	3,426 tons full load
Length:	390 feet (118.9 m) wl
	414½ feet (126.4 m) oa
Beam:	44⅙ feet (13.5 m)
Draft:	24 feet (7.3 m)
Propulsion:	2 steam turbines (Westinghouse); 35,000 shp; 1 shaft
Boilers:	2 1,200 psi (Foster Wheeler)
Speed:	27 knots
Range:	4,000 n.miles at 20 knots
Manning:	270 (18 officers + 252 enlisted)
Helicopters:	no facilities
Missiles:	none
Guns:	1 5-inch (127-mm) 38-cal DP Mk 30
ASW weapons:	1 8-tube ASROC launcher Mk 16
	6 12.75-inch (324-mm) torpedo tubes Mk 32 (2 triple)
Radars:	SPS-10 surface search
	SPS-40 air search
Sonars:	SQS-26AXR bow mounted
	SQS-35 VDS
Fire control:	1 Mk 1 target designation system
	1 Mk 56 GFCS with Mk 35 radar
	1 Mk 114 ASW FCS

The GLOVER was built as an experimental frigate with a modified propeller configuration. The ship was originally authorized in the fiscal 1960 program but was postponed until fiscal 1961. The ship was used primarily for research into the 1970s, after which the ship served as an operational frigate.

Classification: The GLOVER was authorized as a miscellaneous auxiliary (AG 163); completed as an escort research ship (AGDE 1); and changed to a frigate research ship (AGFF 1) on 30 June 1975. The ship was redesignated as a frigate (FF 1098) on 1 October 1979, being assigned the hull number of a cancelled KNOX-class frigate.

Design: SCB No. 198. The ship is similar to the BROOKE and GARCIA classes, but with a modified hull and propulsor. The ship has no after weapon (i.e., 5-inch gun or Mk 22 missile launcher); there is a raised platform aft 2 feet 8 inches above the main deck. A DASH hangar was provided, but the ship has not been modified to operate LAMPS.

No ASROC reloads are carried.

Engineering: The ship's propeller is fitted in a shroud.

Torpedoes: Two Mk 25 torpedo tubes with 12 torpedoes were originally fitted into the stern (in addition to the Mk 32 tubes). They have been subsequently removed.

The GLOVER with the small DASH hangar originally fitted to frigates built in the 1960s and early 1970s. (1982, Giorgio Arra)

46 FRIGATES: "KNOX" CLASS

Number	Name	FY	Builder	Laid down	Launched	Commissioned	Status
FF 1052	KNOX	64	Todd Shipyards, Seattle. Wash.	5 Oct 1965	19 Nov 1966	12 Apr 1969	**PA**
FF 1053	ROARK	64	Todd Shipyards, Seattle. Wash.	2 Feb 1966	24 Apr 1967	22 Nov 1969	**PA**
FF 1054	GRAY	64	Todd Shipyards, Seattle. Wash.	19 Nov 1966	3 Nov 1967	4 Apr 1970	**NRF-P**
FF 1055	HEPBURN	64	Todd Shipyards, Seattle. Calif.	1 June 1966	25 Mar 1967	3 July 1969	**PA**
FF 1056	CONNOLE	64	Avondale Shipyards, New Orleans	23 Mar 1967	20 July 1968	30 Aug 1969	**AA**
FF 1057	RATHBURNE	64	Lockheed SB & Constn. Seattle	8 Jan 1968	2 May 1969	16 May 1970	**PA**
FF 1058	MEYERKORD	64	Todd Shipyards, San Pedro, Calif.	1 Sep 1966	15 July 1967	28 Nov 1969	**PA**
FF 1059	W. S. SIMS	64	Avondale Shipyards, New Orleans	10 Apr 1967	4 Jan 1969	3 Jan 1970	**AA**
FF 1060	LANG	64	Todd Shipyards, San Pedro, Calif.	25 Mar 1967	17 Feb 1968	28 Mar 1970	**NRF-P**
FF 1061	PATTERSON	64	Avondale Shipyards, New Orleans	12 Oct 1967	3 May 1969	14 Mar 1970	**AA**
FF 1062	WHIPPLE	65	Todd Shipyards, Seattle, Wash.	24 Apr 1967	12 Apr 1968	22 Aug 1970	**PA**
FF 1063	REASONER	65	Lockheed SB & Constn. Seattle	6 Jan 1969	1 Aug 1970	31 July 1971	**PA**
FF 1064	LOCKWOOD	65	Todd Shipyards, Seattle. Wash.	3 Nov 1967	5 Sep 1964	5 Dec 1970	**PA**
FF 1065	STEIN	65	Lockheed SB & Constn. Seattle	1 June 1970	19 Dec 1970	8 Jan 1972	**PA**
FF 1066	MARVIN SHIELDS	65	Todd Shipyards, Seattle. Wash.	12 Apr 1968	23 Oct 1969	10 Apr 1971	**PA**
FF 1067	FRANCIS HAMMOND	65	Todd Shipyards, San Pedro, Calif.	15 July 1967	11 May 1968	25 July 1970	**PA**
FF 1068	VREELAND	65	Avondale Shipyards, New Orleans	20 Mar 1968	14 June 1969	13 June 1970	**AA**
FF 1069	BAGLEY	65	Lockheed SB & Constn. Seattle	22 Sep 1970	24 Apr 1971	9 May 1972	**PA**
FF 1070	DOWNES	65	Todd Shipyards, Seattle. Wash.	5 Sep 1968	13 Dec 1969	28 Aug 1971	**PA**
FF 1071	BADGER	65	Todd Shipyards, Seattle. Wash.	17 Feb 1968	7 Dec 1968	1 Dec 1970	**PA**
FF 1072	BLAKELY	65	Avondale Shipyards, New Orleans	3 June 1968	23 Aug 1969	18 July 1970	**AA**
FF 1073	ROBERT E. PEARY	65	Lockheed SB & Constn, Seattle	20 Dec 1970	23 June 1971	23 Sep 1972	**PA**
FF 1074	HAROLD E. HOLT	65	Todd Shipyards, San Pedro, Calif.	11 May 1968	3 May 1969	26 Mar 1971	**PA**
FF 1075	TRIPPE	65	Avondale Shipyards, New Orleans	29 July 1968	1 Nov 1969	19 Sep 1970	**AA**
FF 1076	FANNING	65	Todd Shipyards, San Pedro, Calif.	7 Dec 1968	24 Jan 1970	23 July 1971	**PA**
FF 1077	OUELLET	65	Avondale Shipyards, New Orleans	15 Jan 1969	17 Jan 1970	12 Dec 1970	**PA**
FF 1078	JOSEPH HEWES	66	Avondale Shipyards, New Orleans	15 May 1969	7 Mar 1970	27 Feb 1971	**AA**
FF 1079	BOWEN	66	Avondale Shipyards, New Orleans	11 July 1969	2 May 1970	22 May 1971	**AA**
FF 1080	PAUL	66	Avondale Shipyards, New Orleans	12 Sep 1969	20 June 1970	14 Aug 1971	**AA**
FF 1081	AYLWIN	66	Avondale Shipyards, New Orleans	13 Nov 1969	29 Aug 1970	18 Sep 1971	**AA**
FF 1082	ELMER MONTGOMERY	66	Avondale Shipyards, New Orleans	23 Jan 1970	21 Nov 1970	30 Oct 1971	**AA**
FF 1083	COOK	66	Avondale Shipyards, New Orleans	20 Mar 1970	23 Jan 1971	18 Dec 1971	**PA**
FF 1084	MCCANDLESS	66	Avondale Shipyards, New Orleans	4 June 1970	20 Mar 1971	18 Mar 1972	**AA**
FF 1085	DONALD B. BEARY	66	Avondale Shipyards, New Orleans	24 July 1970	22 May 1971	22 July 1972	**AA**
FF 1086	BREWTON	66	Avondale Shipyards, New Orleans	2 Oct 1970	24 July 1971	8 July 1972	**PA**
FF 1087	KIRK	66	Avondale Shipyards, New Orleans	4 Dec 1970	25 Sep 1971	9 Sep 1972	**PA**
FF 1088	BARBEY	67	Avondale Shipyards, New Orleans	5 Feb 1971	4 Dec 1971	11 Nov 1972	**PA**
FF 1089	JESSE L. BROWN	67	Avondale Shipyards, New Orleans	8 Apr 1971	18 Mar 1972	17 Feb 1973	**AA**
FF 1090	AINSWORTH	67	Avondale Shipyards, New Orleans	11 June 1971	15 Apr 1972	31 Mar 1973	**AA**
FF 1091	MILLER	67	Avondale Shipyards, New Orleans	6 Aug 1971	3 June 1972	30 June 1973	**NRF-A**
FF 1092	THOMAS C. HART	67	Avondale Shipyards, New Orleans	8 Oct 1971	12 Aug 1972	28 July 1973	**AA**
FF 1093	CAPODANNO	67	Avondale Shipyards, New Orleans	12 Oct 1971	21 Oct 1972	17 Nov 1973	**AA**
FF 1094	PHARRIS	67	Avondale Shipyards, New Orleans	11 Feb 1972	16 Dec 1972	26 Jan 1974	**AA**
FF 1095	TRUETT	67	Avondale Shipyards, New Orleans	27 Apr 1972	3 Feb 1973	1 June 1974	**AA**
FF 1096	VALDEZ	67	Avondale Shipyards, New Orleans	30 June 1972	24 Mar 1973	27 July 1974	**NRF-A**
FF 1097	MOINESTER	67	Avondale Shipyards, New Orleans	25 Aug 1972	24 Mar 1973	2 Nov 1974	**AA**

Displacement:	3,011 tons standard	Guns:	1 5-inch (127-mm) 54-cal DP Mk 42
	4,100 tons full load		1 20-mm Phalanx CIWS Mk 16 (multibarrel) in FF 1070, 1073,
Length:	415 feet (126.6 m) wl		1087
	438 feet (133.6 m) oa	ASW weapons:	1 8-tube ASROC launcher Mk 16
Beam:	46¾ feet (14.25 m)		4 12.75-inch (324-mm) torpedo tubes Mk 32 (4 single)
Draft:	24¾ feet (7.5 m)	Radars:	1 SPS-10 surface search
Propulsion:	2 steam turbines (Westinghouse); 35,000 shp; 1 shaft		1 SPS-40 air search
Boilers:	2 1,200 psi (Combustion Engineering)		1 SPS-58 threat warning in some ships
Speed:	27 + knots	Sonars:	SQS-26CX bow mounted
Range:	4,500 n.miles at 20 knots		SQS-35 IVDS in FF 1052, 1056, 1063–1071, 1073–1076, 1078–
Manning:	active ships 287 (17 officers + 270 enlisted) in most ships		1097
	NRF ships 168–169 (8 officers + 159–160 enlisted) active +		SQR-18 towed array being fitted in all ships
	136–164 (9 officers + 127–155 enlisted) reserve	Fire control:	1 Mk 1 target designation system
Helicopters:	1 SH-2F LAMPS I		1 Mk 68 GFCS with SPG-53A/D/F radar
Missiles:	1 8-tube Sea Sparrow BPDMS launcher Mk 25 in FF 1052–1069,		1 Mk 114 ASW FCS
	1071–1083		1 Mk 115 missile FCS in ships with Sea Sparrow
	Harpoon SSM fired from ASROC launcher		

This was the largest class of surface combatants to be constructed in the West since World War II prior to the OLIVER HAZARD PERRY class. The ships have been highly criticized for their large size (comparable to World War II-era destroyers) with a single propeller shaft and limited AAW/ASUW capabilities. The latter limitation has been partially corrected with the Harpoon missile fired from the ASROC launcher.

Eight of these ships are to be assigned to the NRF (see Chapter 7). The KNOX, LOCKWOOD, FRANCIS HAMMOND, and KIRK are home ported in Yokosuka, Japan.

Class: Ten additional ships were authorized in the fiscal 1968 budget (DE 1098–1107); the construction of the last six ships (DE 1102–1107) was deferred in 1968 in favor of the more capable SPRUANCE (DD 963)-class destroyers, and three other ships (DE 1099–1101) were deferred later that year to help pay for cost overruns of nuclear submarines; one ship (DE 1098) was deferred in 1969. Note that hull number 1098 was reassigned to the earlier GLOVER (formerly AGDE/AGFF 1).

Five similar ships were built in Spain with a SAM launcher amidships; they were designated DEG 7–11 by the U.S. Navy for record purposes.

Classification: These ships were built as ocean escorts (DE); changed to frigates on 30 June 1975.

Design: FF 1052–1061 were assigned SCB No. 199C; the later ships were given SCB No. 200.65 in the new series.

These ships are considerably larger than the previous BROOKE and GARCIA classes because of the use of non-pressure-fired boilers. The superstructure is topped by a distinctive cylindrical "mack" that combines mast and stacks. The "mack" was to mount an advanced electronic warfare suite, but that was not developed. A port-side anchor is fitted at the bow, and a larger anchor retracts into the after end of the bow sonar dome fairing.

The original DASH hangar has been enlarged to accommodate the LAMPS I helicopter. Hangars vary in size from 41½ feet to 47⅙ feet in length and 14½ to 18¼ feet in width.

As built the ships took water over their bows in rough seas. Beginning in 1980 they have had raised bulwarks fitted forward.

An ASROC reload capability is provided with 16 rockets and Harpoon missiles being carried.

Engineering: The cancelled DE 1101 was to have had gas turbine propulsion to evaluate that plant for future use in surface combatants. The BARBEY was test ship for the controllable-pitch propeller.

Guns: The design originally provided for a single 5-inch/38-cal gun forward, but the improved 54-cal Mk 42 became available and was installed in all ships.

These ships are all to be fitted with a single Phalanx CIWS.

Missiles: Thirty-one ships were fitted after completion with Sea Sparrow point-defense systems. Installation of the Sea Chapparal, adopted from an Army SAM system, was planned for 14 other ships but was not undertaken. Those ships with Sea Sparrow are being refitted with the Phalanx CIWS beginning in 1983.

The DOWNES served as evaluation ship for the NATO Sea Sparrow missile; replaced by Phalanx CIWS.

Torpedoes: The original design called for two Mk 25 torpedo tubes to be fitted in the stern counter (with 12 torpedoes carried); they were not installed. The Mk 32 tubes are fitted into the after superstructure.

The JOSEPH HEWES with SLQ-32(V)1 antennas fitted. (1982, Giorgio Arra)

The AYLWIN with SLQ-32(V)1; note the stern hatch covering the VDS installation. (1983, Giorgio Arra)

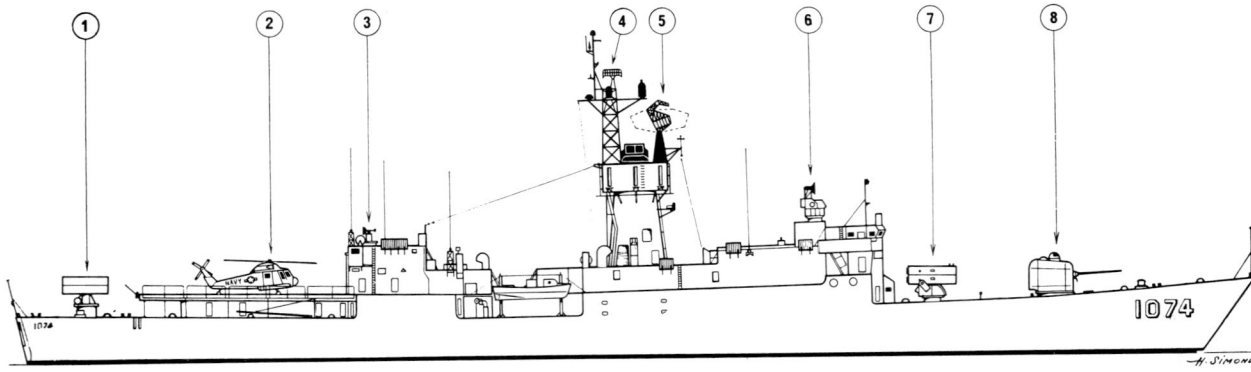

1. Sea Sparrow missile launcher   2. helicopter deck   3. Sea Sparrow guidance   4. SPS-10 radar   5. SPS-40 radar   6. Mk 68 gun fire control system.   7. ASROC launcher   8. 5-inch/54-cal Mk 42 gun

The DOWNES with original bow configuration and Phalanx CIWS mounted aft in place of NATO Sea Sparrow. (1984, Giorgio Arra)

The OUELLET with the modified bow installed from the late 1970s to improve seakeeping. Note the expandable hangar; the SLQ-32 antenna is being installed between the bridge and mack in these ships (1980, Giorgio Arra)

10 FRIGATES: "GARCIA" CLASS

Number	Name	FY	Builder	Laid down	Launched	Commissioned	Status
FF 1040	GARCIA	61	Bethlehem Steel, San Francisco	16 Oct 1962	31 Oct 1963	21 Dec 1964	**AA**
FF 1041	BRADLEY	61	Bethlehem Steel, San Francisco	17 Jan 1963	26 Mar 1964	15 May 1965	**PA**
FF 1043	EDWARD MCDONNELL	62	Avondale Shipyards, New Orleans	1 Apr 1963	15 Feb 1964	15 Feb 1965	**AA**
FF 1044	BRUMBY	62	Avondale Shipyards, New Orleans	1 Aug 1963	6 June 1964	5 Aug 1965	**AA**
FF 1045	DAVIDSON	62	Avondale Shipyards, New Orleans	20 Sep 1963	2 Oct 1964	7 Dec 1965	**PA**
FF 1047	VOGE	63	Defoe Shipbuilding, Bay City, Mich.	21 Nov 1963	4 Feb 1965	25 Nov 1966	**AA**
FF 1048	SAMPLE	63	Lockheed SB & Constn, Seattle	19 July 1963	28 Apr 1964	23 Mar 1968	**PA**
FF 1049	KOELSCH	63	Defoe Shipbuilding, Bay City, Mich.	19 Feb 1964	8 June 1965	10 June 1967	**AA**
FF 1050	ALBERT DAVID	63	Lockheed SB & Constn, Seattle	29 Apr 1964	19 Dec 1964	19 Oct 1968	**PA**
FF 1051	O'CALLAHAN	63	Defoe Shipbuilding, Bay City, Mich.	19 Feb 1964	20 Oct 1965	13 July 1968	**PA**

Displacement:	2,620 tons standard
	3,400 tons full load
Length:	390 feet (118.9 m) wl
	414½ feet (126.4 m) oa
Beam:	44⅙ feet (13.5 m)
Draft:	24 feet (7.3 m)
Propulsion:	2 steam turbines (Westinghouse); 35,000 shp; 1 shaft
Boilers:	2 1,200 psi (Foster Wheeler)
Speed:	27 knots
Range:	4,000 n.miles at 20 knots
Manning:	280 (18 officers + 262 enlisted) in FF 1040, 1043
	270 (18 officers + 252 enlisted) in FF 1041, 1044, 1045, 1050, 1051
	286 (19 officers + 267 enlisted) in FF 1047, 1049
	269 (17 officers + 252 enlisted) in FF 1048
Helicopters:	1 SH-2F LAMPS I except none in FF 1040, 1043, 1048, 1050
Missiles:	none
Guns:	2 5-inch (127-mm) 38-cal DP Mk 30 (2 single)
ASW weapons:	1 8-tube ASROC launcher Mk 16
	6 12.75-inch (324-mm) torpedo tubes Mk 32 (2 triple)
Radars:	SPS-10 surface search
	SPS-40 air search
Sonars:	SQS-26AXR bow mounted in FF 1040–1045
	SQS-26BX bow mounted in FF 1047–1051
	SQR-15 towed array in FF 1040, 1043, 1048, 1050
Fire control:	1 Mk 1 target designation system
	1 Mk 56 GFCS with Mk 35 radar
	1 Mk 114 ASW FCS

These ships are similar to the contemporary BROOKE-class frigates but with a second 5-inch gun in place of the missile ships' Mk 22 launcher.

Classification: As built, these ships were classified as ocean escorts (DE); changed to frigates on 30 June 1975.

Design: SCB No. 199A. The ships were originally fitted with DASH hangars; they were modified to accommodate the LAMPS I helicopter. The enlarged hangars are 41⅓ feet to 47⅚ feet in length and 14⁵⁄₁₂ feet to 17⁷⁄₁₂ feet in width. The already limited field of fire of the after 5-inch gun was further inhibited by the enlarging of the hangar to accommodate the SH-2F helicopter.

Sixteen ASROC rockets are carried or 12 ASROC and 4 Harpoons.

Engineering: This class introduced pressure-fired boilers, also used in the BROOKE and GLOVER designs.

Missiles: The BRADLEY evaluated the Sea Sparrow BPDMS launcher Mk 25 in 1967–1968. The launcher was fitted between the funnel and the after 5-inch gun mount.

Radar: SPS-67 will replace the SPS-10.

Sonar: Four ships have been fitted with towed sonar arrays.

Torpedoes: Several ships were built with two Mk 25 tubes in their stern (eight torpedoes carried); they were removed from the earlier ships and not fitted in the later units.

DAVIDSON (1983, Giorgio Arra)

The ALBERT DAVID retains the original DASH hangar of these ships. The BROOKE and GARCIA classes are virtually identical except that the former have an Mk 22 missile launcher and associated fire control equipment in place of the second 5-inch gun. (1983, Giorgio Arra)

The DAVIDSON with an enlarged, expanding helicopter hangar for SH-2F LAMPS. (1983, Giorgio Arra)

2 FRIGATES: "BRONSTEIN" CLASS

Number	Name	FY	Builder	Laid down	Launched	Commissioned	Status
FF 1037	BRONSTEIN	60	Avondale Shipyards, New Orleans, La.	16 May 1961	31 Mar 1962	15 June 1963	**PA**
FF 1038	McCLOY	60	Avondale Shipyards, New Orleans, La.	15 Sep 1961	9 June 1962	21 Oct 1963	**AA**

Displacement:	2,360 tons standard
	2,650 tons full load
Length:	350 feet (106.7 m) wl
	371½ feet (113.3 m) oa
Beam:	40½ feet (12.3 m)
Draft:	23 feet (7.0 m)
Propulsion:	2 steam turbines (De Laval); 20,000 shp; 1 shaft
Boilers:	2 600 psi (Foster Wheeler)
Speed:	24 knots
Range:	3,200 n.miles at 20 knots
	4,000 n.miles at 15 knots
Manning:	216 (14 officers + 202 enlisted) in FF 1037
	217 (15 officers + 202 enlisted) in FF 1038
Helicopters:	VERTREP area only
Missiles:	none
Guns:	2 3-inch (76-mm) 50-cal AA Mk 33 (1 twin)
ASW weapons:	1 8-tube ASROC launcher Mk 16
	6 12.75-inch (324-mm) torpedo tubes Mk 32 (2 triple)
Radars:	SPS-10 surface search
	SPS-40 air search
Sonars:	SQS-26 bow mounted
	SQR-15 towed array
Fire control:	1 Mk 1 target designation system
	1 Mk 56 GFCS with Mk 35 radar
	1 Mk 114 ASW FCS

These ships were the prototype for a new generation of ASW ocean escorts, featuring large bow-mounted sonar, ASROC, and a DASH capability. These features were provided in the next 63 escort ships built by the U.S. Navy as well as in several foreign ships. However, the BRONSTEIN class was too slow and lacked the seakeeping and range necessary to counter contemporary Soviet submarines. These ships were the last U.S. escort ships to be built with 3-inch guns until the PERRY class 15 years later.

The McCLOY lost part of a towed array when it fouled a Soviet Victor III-class submarine off the U.S. Atlantic coast in late 1983.

Classification: Both ships were built as ocean escorts (DE); changed to frigates on 30 June 1975.

Design: SCB No. 199. These ships introduced the raked stem configuration found in subsequent ships with bow-mounted sonar, and the stem anchor location. The ships were provided with a DASH hangar and landing area but cannot accommodate larger, manned helicopters.

No ASROC reloads are provided.

Guns: As built, a single 3-inch gun mount was fitted aft; subsequently removed with installation of towed-array sonar.

Sonars: A Towed Array Surveillance System (TASS) was fitted to both ships in the mid-1970s.

The McCLOY at Messina. The flat bridge face reveals that the ships do not have ASROC reloads. (1982, L. & L. van Ginderen)

The BRONSTEIN and McCLOY lost their after, single 3-inch gun mount and have been employed lately in the development of towed array sonars. Their former DASH helicopter deck is suitable only for VERTREP. (1983, Giorgio Arra)

POST-WORLD WAR II ESCORT/FRIGATE PROGRAMS

U.S. World War II destroyer escort programs reached hull number DE 1005 (with DE 801–1005 being cancelled). After the war several destroyer escorts were converted to radar picket escorts (DER), a few for the tactical fleet role, but most for strategic early warning of bomber attack against the continental United States. A few also were modified to an escort control (DEC) configuration to support amphibious landings.

The first postwar DEs were actually envisioned as successors to the war-built, steel-hulled submarine chasers (PC). With the start of the postwar programs in the early 1950s, these ships were reclassified as ocean escorts (DE), partly to avoid confusion with escort destroyers (DDE).

U.S. hull numbers were assigned to 17 ships built in Europe with American funding (Offshore Procurement or OSP). Thirteen U.S. ships were completed between 1954 and 1957, built to the similar DEALEY and COURTNEY designs, and four ships to the CLAUD JONES design. These classes were intended for mass production in wartime.

FFX DESIGN

During the late 1970s the Navy proposed the construction of a class of small frigates (design designation FFX) for use by the Naval Reserve Force. These ships were intended to augment the FFG 7 class in the ASW role in low-threat areas. A class of approximately 12 ships was planned with the lead ship intended for authorization in FY 1984. For reasons not fully clear, although such ships would have had marginally effective ASW capabilities, the FFX class was not started. Subsequently, the Naval Reserve Force has been provided with frigates of the KNOX and PERRY classes to replace the aging GEARING (DD 710)-class ships previously assigned to the NRF.

The following are the tentative characteristics of the proposed FFX:

Displacement:	2,000–2,400 tons full load
Length:	
Beam:	
Draft:	
Propulsion:	
Speed:	25 knots
Range:	5,000 n.miles at 16–18 knots
Manning:	120 officers + enlisted
Helicopters:	1 SH-2F LAMPS I
Missiles:	
Guns:	
ASW weapons:	6 12.75-inch (324-mm) torpedo tubes Mk 32 (2 triple)
Torpedoes:	
Radars:	
Sonars:	towed array
Fire control:	

SES FRIGATE DESIGN

During the late 1970s the Navy planned to construct a class of Surface Effect Ship (SES) frigates in the mid-1980s. These ships were to be based on a 3,000-ton SES prototype that was to be constructed in 1980–1984. This ship was to have been capable of speeds as high as 80 to 100 knots with a trans-ocean range and to have carried frigate-type weapons, including two LAMPS helicopters.

The Secretary of Defense decided in May 1976 to proceed with the design and construction of a 3,000-ton, "weaponized" prototype SES. This followed 10 years of extensive conceptual and technical development. A contract for design with an option to construct was awarded in December 1976 to Rohr Marine, Inc. of San Diego. The ship was to be completed during fiscal 1983. Subsequently, the Carter Administration cancelled the SES program in its entirety.

n addition to high speed, the SES design offered a large amount of usable space which would have provided flexibility in the installation of weapons and sensors, with ample space to hangar and operate two helicopters. Also, the design provided considerable stability in heavy seas.

Below are the tentative characteristics of the planned 3,000-ton SES prototype:

Displacement:	3,000 tons full load
Length:	270 feet (82.3 m) oa
Beam:	108 feet (32.9 m)
Draft:	14 feet (4.3 m) on cushion
	31 feet (9.5 m) off cushion
Propulsion:	4 gas turbines (Pratt & Whitney FT9); 4 waterjet propulsion units
	2 gas turbines (General Electric LM 2500); 6 lift fans
Speed:	80 + knots on cushion
Range:	
Manning:	approx. 125
Helicopters:	2 LAMPS III
Missiles:	
Guns:	
ASW weapons:	FF/FFG weapons suite
Torpedoes:	
Radars:	
Sonars:	VDS

The AUBREY FITCH with Phalanx CIWS installed atop the twin LAMPS III helicopter hangar. (1983, Giorgio Arra)

DE 1006	DEALEY	Comm. 1954; to Uruguay 1972
DE 1007	(French LE NORMAND)	OSP 1956
DE 1008	(French LE LORRAIN)	OSP 1956
DE 1009	(French LE PICARD)	OSP 1956
DE 1010	(French LE GASCON)	OSP 1957
DE 1011	(French LE CHAMPENOIS)	OSP 1957
DE 1012	(French LE SAVOYARD)	OSP 1957
DE 1013	(French LE BOURGUIGNON)	OSP 1957
DE 1014	CROMWELL	Comm. 1954; stricken 1972
DE 1015	HAMMERBERG	Comm. 1955; stricken 1973
DE 1016	(French LE CORSE)	OSP 1952
DE 1017	(French LE BRESTOIS)	OSP 1952
DE 1018	(French LE BOULONNAIS)	OSP 1953
DE 1019	(French LE BORDELAIS)	OSP 1953
DE 1020	(Italian CIGNO)	OSP 1957
DE 1021	COURTNEY	Comm. 1956; stricken 1973
DE 1022	LESTER	Comm. 1957; stricken 1973
DE 1023	EVANS	Comm. 1957; stricken 1973
DE 1024	BRIDGET	Comm. 1957; stricken 1973
DE 1025	BAUER	Comm. 1957; stricken 1973
DE 1026	HOOPER	Comm. 1958; stricken 1973
DE 1027	JOHN WILLIS	Comm. 1957; stricken 1972
DE 1028	VAN VOORHIS	Comm. 1957; stricken 1972
DE 1029	HARTLEY	Comm. 1957; to Colombia 1972
DE 1030	JOSEPH K. TAUSSIG	Comm. 1957; stricken 1972
DE 1031	(Italian CASTORE)	OSP 1957
DE 1032	(Portuguese PERO ESCOBAR)	OSP 1957
DE 1033	CLAUD JONES	Comm. 1959; to Indonesia 1974
DE 1034	JOHN R. PERRY	Comm. 1959; to Indonesia 1973
DE 1035	CHARLES BERRY	Comm. 1959; to Indonesia 1974
DE 1036	MCMORRISS	Comm. 1960; to Indonesia 1974
DE 1037–1038	BRONSTEIN class	
DE 1039	(Portuguese ALMIRANTE PEREIRA DA SILVA)	OSP 1966
DE 1040–1041	GARCIA class	
DE 1042	(Portuguese ALMIRANTE GAGO COUTINHO)	OSP 1967
DE 1043–1045	GARCIA class	
DE 1046	(Portuguese ALMIRANTE MAGALHAES CORREA)	OSP 1967
DE 1047–1051	GARCIA class	
DE 1052–1107[a]	KNOX class	

[a] FF 1098 subsequently reassigned to GLOVER (formerly AGFF/AGDE 1).

18 Command Ships

The U.S. Navy has four specialized command ships in service: The former amphibious command ships BLUE RIDGE, flagship of Commander, Seventh Fleet in the Western Pacific, and MOUNT WHITNEY, flagship of Commander, Second Fleet in the Atlantic; and the former amphibious transport docks LA SALLE, flagship of the Commander, U.S. Middle East Force,[1] and CORONADO, to become flagship of Commander, Sixth Fleet in the Mediterranean.

The numbered fleets had cruiser flagships until the 1970s. The cruisers now in service do not have flag facilities and accommodations, nor are the reactivated IOWA (BB 61)-class battleships fitted as flagships. The destroyer tender PUGET SOUND (AD 38) has served as flagship of the Sixth Fleet. She is to be relieved by the CORONADO during 1985. The CORONADO had originally been modified from an amphibious ship to a command ship to serve in the Persian Gulf–Indian Ocean while the LA SALLE was being overhauled.

Prior to the conversion of the LA SALLE, the flagship of the Commander, Middle East Force had been a small seaplane tender (AVP) from the time that command was established in the late 1940s.

[1] The ship operates in the Persian Gulf–Indian Ocean area.

The BLUE RIDGE, flagship of the U.S. Seventh Fleet, enters Hong Kong harbor. Although not as impressive as the previous cruisers employed as flagships for the forward-deployed fleets in the Western Pacific and Mediterranean, the BLUE RIDGE and MOUNT WHITNEY provide effective command facilities and accommodations for fleet commanders. (1980, Giorgio Arra)

2 AMPHIBIOUS COMMAND SHIPS: "BLUE RIDGE" CLASS

Number	Name	FY	Builder	Laid down	Launched	Commissioned	Status
LCC 19	BLUE RIDGE	65	Philadelphia Naval Shipyard	27 Feb 1967	4 Jan 1969	14 Nov 1970	**PA**
LCC 20	MOUNT WHITNEY	66	Newport News Shipbuilding, Va.	8 Jan 1969	8 Jan 1970	16 Jan 1971	**AA**

Displacement:	19,290 tons full load
Length:	596 feet (181.8 m) wl
	620 feet (189.1 m) oa
Beam:	82 feet (25.0 m)
Extreme width:	108 feet (32.9 m)
Draft:	27 feet (8.2 m)
Propulsion:	1 steam turbine (General Electric); 22,000 shp; 1 shaft
Boilers:	2 600 psi (Foster Wheeler)
Speed:	23 knots
Range:	13,500 n.miles at 16 knots
Manning:	LCC 19 825 (52 officers + 773 enlisted)
	LCC 20 816 (44 officers + 772 enlisted)
Flag:	LCC 19 241 (46 officers + 195 enlisted)
	LCC 20 188 (65 officers + 123 enlisted)
Helicopters:	helicopter landing area
Missiles:	2 8-tube Sea Sparrow BPDMS launchers Mk 25
Guns:	4 3-inch (76-mm) 50-cal AA Mk 33 (2 twin)
Radars:	SPS-10 surface search
	SPS-40 air search
	SPS-48 3-D search
	SPS-62 threat warning
Fire control:	2 Mk 115 missile FCS

These are large command ships, the only ships to be designed from the outset specifically for the amphibious command ship role. The Navy's earlier command ships could not operate with the 20-knot amphibious ships built from the 1960s onward. Both ships are now employed as fleet flagships.

The BLUE RIDGE is home ported in Yokosuka, Japan, having relieved the cruiser OKLAHOMA CITY (CG 5) in October 1979 as flagship of the

MOUNT WHITNEY (1983, Giorgio Arra)

The MOUNT WHITNEY showing her clear "flight deck," designed specifically for optimum placement of communication antennas. A Sea Knight from Helicopter Combat Support Squadron 1 rests on the helicopter deck aft. No hangar is provided. (1983, Giorgio Arra)

Seventh Fleet; the MOUNT WHITNEY is based at Norfolk, having relieved the ALBANY (CG 10) as flagship of the Second Fleet in January 1981.

Class: A third ship of this class (AGC 21) was planned; she was to have been configured for service as both an amphibious flagship and fleet flagship.

Classification: These ships were originally classified as amphibious force flagships (AGC); they were changed to amphibious command ships (LCC) on 1 January 1969.

Design: SCB No. 400. The hull and propulsion machinery are similar to that of the Iwo JIMA (LPH 2)-class helicopter carriers. The command ship facilities originally provided in this class were for a Navy amphibious task force ccommander and a Marine assault force commander and their staffs. Their designed flag/staff accommodations were for 200 officers and 500 enlisted men; see Operational notes for currently embarked staffs.

They have large open deck areas to provide for optimum antenna placement. There is a helicopter landing area aft, but no hangar. (A small vehicle hangar is serviced by an elevator.)

Engineering: Maximum sustained speed is 20 knots.

Guns: The early designs for this ship provided for an additional pair of twin 3-inch AA mounts forward, on the forecastle; they were not installed.

Two Phalanx CIWS are scheduled for installation in these ships.

Missiles: The Sea Sparrow BPDMS launchers were fitted in 1974.

Operational: The flag-staff personnel embarked in the MOUNT WHITNEY in 1984 consisted of the Commander Second Fleet (40 officers + 71 enlisted), Commanding General 4th Marine Amphibious Brigade (24 officers + 41 enlisted), and a Marine communications detachment (1 officer + 11 enlisted).

The MOUNT WHITNEY during NATO exercises off Norway. Note the rows of liferaft cannisters forward; the boat stowage along the sides; 3-inch gun mounts and Sea Sparrow launchers amidships; and helicopter deck aft. A Sea Knight is hovering over a Huey. Each ship is scheduled to receive 2 Phalanx CIWS while retaining the 3-inch guns. (1980, U.S. Navy)

1 MISCELLANEOUS FLAGSHIP: CONVERTED "AUSTIN" CLASS

Number	Name	FY	Builder	Laid down	Launched	Commissioned	Status
AGF 11 (ex-LPD 11)	CORONADO	64	Lockheed Shipbuilding & Construction, Seattle	3 May 1965	30 July 1966	23 May 1970	**AA**

Displacement:	10,000 tons light
	16,900 tons full load
Length:	570 feet (173.8 m) oa
Beam:	84 feet (25.6 m)
Draft:	23 feet (7.0 m)
Propulsion:	2 steam turbines (De Laval); 24,000 shp; 2 shafts
Boilers:	2 600 psi (Babcock & Wilcox)
Speed:	20 knots
Range:	7,700 n.miles at 20 knots
Manning:	438 (26 officers + 412 enlisted)
Flag:	
Helicopters:	1 SH-3G Sea King
Missiles:	none
Guns:	4 3-inch (76-mm) 50-cal AA Mk 33 (2 twin)
Radars:	SPS-10 surface search
	SPS-40 air search
Fire control:	local control only

The CORONADO was built and served as a dock landing ship until 1980 when she was modified to serve as a flagship to permit the Middle East flagship LA SALLE to undergo a lengthy overhaul at the Philadelphia Naval Shipyard. Subsequently, after overhaul in 1983–1984 she was to become flagship of the Sixth Fleet and home ported in Gaeta, Italy.

Classification: Changed from LPD 11 to AGF on 1 October 1980.

Conversion: See LA SALLE for description of conversion to flagship. The CORONADO's hangar is 57¾ feet long and 20⅔ feet wide.

Design: SCB No. 187C. See AUSTIN (LPD 4) listing for additional details. The ship is similar to but larger than the LA SALLE.

Guns: The CORONADO is to have two Phalanx CIWS installed.

The CORONADO during her overhaul at the Philadelphia Naval Shipyard in 1983. Note the expandable hangar; flight control station next to the port funnel. (1983, U.S. Navy)

The flagship née amphibious ship CORONADO anchored off Messina. (1983, L. & L. van Ginderen)

1 MISCELLANEOUS FLAGSHIP: CONVERTED "RALEIGH" CLASS

Number	Name	FY	Builder	Laid down	Launched	Commissioned	Status
AGF 3 (ex-LPD 3)	LA SALLE	61	New York Naval Shipyard	2 Apr 1962	3 Aug 1963	22 Feb 1964	**Indian Ocean**

Displacement:	8,040 tons light
	13,900 tons full load
Length:	500 feet (152.5 m) wl
	521¾ feet (159.1 m) oa
Beam:	84 feet (25.6 m)
Draft:	21 feet (6.4 m)
Propulsion:	2 steam turbines (De Laval); 24,000 shp; 2 shafts
Boilers:	2 600 psi (Babcock & Wilcox)
Speed:	21.6 knots (20 knots sustained)
Range:	9,600 n.miles at 16 knots
	16,500 n.miles at 10 knots
Manning:	512 (29 officers + 483 enlisted)
Flag:	66 (14 officers + 52 enlisted)
Helicopters:	1 SH-3G Sea King
Missiles:	none
Guns:	4 3-inch (76-mm) 50-cal AA Mk 33 (2 twin)
	2 20-mm Phalanx CIWS Mk 16 (2 multibarrel)
Radars:	SPS-10 surface search
	SPS-40 air search
Fire control:	local control only

The LA SALLE was converted from an amphibious transport dock specifically to serve as flagship for the U.S. Middle East Force. The LA SALLE initially served as an amphibious ship. She operated in the Persian Gulf–Indian Ocean area from 1972 to 1980, when she was relieved by the CORONADO. She underwent an extensive overhaul at the Philadelphia Naval Shipyard from December 1980 to September 1982. After that overhaul she in turn relieved the CORONADO as flagship of the U.S. Middle East Force on 16 June 1983 at Mina Silman, Bahrain.

Class: The LA SALLE is one of three RALEIGH (LPD 1)-class amphibious transport docks.

Classification: Built as LPD 3 and served as an amphibious ship until 1 July 1972 when changed to AGF 3.

Conversion: The ship was converted to a flagship in 1972, being fitted with command and communication facilities, a helicopter hangar, and additional air conditioning. The amidships hangar is 47⁵⁄₁₂ feet long and 19⅓ feet wide.

Design: SCB No. 187A

Guns: Two 3-inch twin mounts have been removed and two Phalanx CIWS have been installed in their place.

The LA SALLE, still carrying four 3-inch twin gun mounts. Two mounts have since been replaced by Gatling guns. There is a SATCOM antenna atop the lattice mast amidships; a helicopter hangar is provided as well as a covered deck area for VIP receptions. (1983, U.S. Navy)

La Salle (1983, Giorgio Arra)

COMMAND SHIPS

The Navy built one ship and converted another specifically for use as major command ships, while a third such ship was planned for conversion.

The heavy cruiser Northampton (CA 125), cancelled in 1945 while under construction, was subsequently reordered in 1948 as a tactical light command ship (CLC 1) and completed in that configuration in 1953. After operating as a fleet flagship, she was reconfigured to serve as a National Emergency Command Post Afloat (NECPA) in 1961 and reclassified as CC 1. She was decommissioned in 1970 and laid up in reserve until stricken in 1977.

The light carriers Wright (originally CVL 49) and Saipan (CVL 48) were similarly designated for conversion to the NECPA role. The Wright, also designated AVT 7 while in reserve, was converted in 1962–1963 and became CC 2; she operated in the NECPA role until 1970 when she was laid up in reserve. She was stricken in 1977.

The Saipan, also AVT 6 while in reserve after World War II, began conversion to the CC 3 in 1964, but was instead completed as a major communications relay ship in 1966 (renamed Arlington and classified AGMR 2).

In the NECPA role these ships were to provide afloat facilities for the President in the event of a national emergency or war.

MISCELLANEOUS FLAGSHIPS

From the late 1940s until 1972 the Navy employed small seaplane tenders (AVP) as flagships for U.S. forces in the Persian Gulf area. Subsequently, one of those ships, the Valcour (AVP 55), was reclassified as a miscellaneous flagship (AGF 1) on December 1965 specifically for that role and home ported in Bahrain. She was replaced in that role by the La Salle in 1972.

Note that the La Salle and Coronado have retained their LPD hull numbers in the AGF role.

19 Amphibious Ships

The U.S. Navy has 58 amphibious ships in active commission plus 2 tank landing ships operated by the Naval Reserve Force (NRF). These 60 ships have a theoretical lift capability of the assault echelon of one Marine Amphibious Force.[1] In addition, 2 amphibious command ships (LCC) are employed as flagships for numbered fleets as is one amphibious transport dock (LPD), while another modified LPD serves as U.S. flagship in the Persian Gulf–Indian Ocean area (see Chapter 18).

Amphibious lift goals for large forces, as a MAF, are theoretical because the Navy's amphibious ships are divided about equally between the Atlantic–Mediterranean and Pacific–Indian Ocean areas. Further, 15 to 20 percent of the ships are in various stages of overhaul at any given time.

One of the Navy's seven amphibious squadrons is normally deployed to the Mediterranean, serving as an Amphibious Readiness Group with a Marine Assault Unit (MAU) embarked, and a second squadron is deployed to the Western Pacific–Indian Ocean. Periodically, a third amphibious squadron operates in the Caribbean area and a fourth in the Western Pacific. Including squadrons that are en route to and from deployments, or on special exercises, a significant fraction of the Navy's amphibious lift capability is at sea in widely separated areas at any given time. This peacetime deployment pattern could inhibit the rapid assembly of a large number of "amphibs" in one place in a crisis or war.

A final factor in amphibious ship availability is the assignment of two tank landing ships (LST) to the Naval Reserve Force. While NRF ships have demonstrated a high degree of readiness, they do not rotate on forward deployments to forward areas and their availability in time of crisis without a major reserve mobilization is questionable. Thus, four amphibious cargo ships (LKA) that had been assigned to NRF have been returned to the active fleet.

Under the Reagan Administration's goal of 600+ ships, the Navy is constructing additional amphibious shipping to provide lift for a Marine Amphibious Force plus a Marine Amphibious Brigade (MAB) by 1994. Approximately 50 to 60 ships will be required for the MAF lift and another 20 ships for the MAB lift.

The Navy is now building a new class of dock landing ships (LSD), a new class of amphibious assault ships (LHD), and a new class of amphibious transport docks (LPD). A total of 13 ships in these three classes are scheduled for construction in the fiscal 1984–1988 shipbuilding programs. At the same time, 20 amphibious ships that were constructed during the 1960s will reach the end of their nominal 30-year service life in the 1990s. A Service Life Extension Program (SLEP) is being initiated for some of these ships that, with the planned construction rate, can provide the MAF + MAB lift by the mid-1990s.

The Reagan Administration's buildup of amphibious shipping is the third major "spurt" of amphibious ship construction since World War II. The first, during the Korean War, produced the LSD 28 and LST 1156 classes (23 ships); the second, in the Kennedy–Johnson Administration of the early 1960s, produced the LCC 19, LHA 1, LKA 112, LPD 12, LSD 36, and LST 1179 classes (49 ships).

The third and current postwar buildup in this category began with the LSD 41, the first amphibious ship authorized in a decade. That ship was funded by the Congress in fiscal 1981 over the objections of the Carter Administration.

The new classes of amphibious ships, like all of those currently in service, will have a 20-knot sustained speed and a significant helicopter capability. The new ships will additionally have an increased capability for carrying the Landing Craft Air Cushion (LCAC).

Electronics: The LHA, LHD, and LPH classes are being fitted with the SLQ-32(V)3 electronic warfare suite; the LKA, LPD, LSD, and LST classes are receiving the SLQ-32(V)1. The SLQ-25 Nixie will be fitted to the LHD 1 class.

---

[1] The Marine Amphibious Force (MAF) consists of a Marine division plus an aircraft wing and supporting units; see Chapter 4.

The amphibious assault ship GUADALCANAL steams off the coast of Beirut while a U.S. Marine battalion was ashore as part of the ill-fated international peacekeeping force in 1983–1984. Putting the Marines ashore in Beirut was an administrative landing. The Navy-Marine team has not made a major opposed amphibious assault since the brilliant Inchon landing of September 1950. (1983, U.S. Navy, PH2 T. Lally/PH3 J. Donnelly)

Type	Class/Ship	Comm.	Active	NRF	Building	Reserve	Notes
LHD 1	. . . . . .	1989–	—	—	1	—	helicopter carrier + docking well
LHA 1	TARAWA	1976–1980	5	—	—	—	helicopter carrier + docking well
LPH 2	IWO JIMA	1961–1970	7	—	—	—	helicopter carrier
LKA 113	CHARLESTON	1968–1970	5	—	—	—	
LPD 12	AUSTIN	1965–1971	11	—	—	—	docking well
LPD 1	RALEIGH	1962–1963	2	—	—	—	docking well
LSD 41	WHIDBEY ISLAND	1984	1	—	4	—	docking well
LSD 36	ANCHORAGE	1969–1972	5	—	—	—	docking well
LSD 28	THOMASTON	1954–1957	4	—	—	4	docking well
LST 1179	NEWPORT	1969–1972	18	2	—	—	
LST 1171	DE SOTO COUNTY	1957–1959	—	—	—	3	
LST 1156	TERREBONNE PARISH	1953	—	—	—	6	

(5) AMPHIBIOUS ASSAULT SHIPS: "WASP" CLASS

Number	Name	FY	Builder	Comm.	Status
LHD 1	WASP	84	Litton/Ingalls, Pascagoula, Miss.	1989	Building
LHD 2	. . . . . .	86			Planned
LHD 3	. . . . . .	88			Planned
LHD 4	. . . . . .	90			Planned
LHD 5	. . . . . .	92			Planned

Displacement:	40,500 tons full load
Length:	844 feet (257.4 m) oa
Beam:	106 feet (32.3 m)
Draft:	26 1/12 feet (8.0 m)
Propulsion:	steam turbine; 70,000 shp; 2 shafts
Boilers:	2 600 psi
Speed:	22 + knots
Range:	
Manning:	1,081 (98 officers + 983 enlisted)
Troops:	1,875
Helicopters:	30 +
Elevators:	2
Missiles:	2 8-tube NATO Sea Sparrow missile launchers Mk 29
Guns:	3 20-mm Phalanx CIWS Mk 16 (3 multibarrel)
	8 .50-cal MG
Radars:	SPS-49 air search
	SPS-52C 3-D search
Fire control:	2 Mk 91 missile FCS

These ships were conceived as helicopter-carrying amphibious ships smaller and less costly than the TARAWA class. In the event, however, the basic LHA 1 design was adopted with the following principal differences: (1) increased Harrier VSTOL aircraft support capability; (2) movement of the stern elevator to the starboard side of the flight deck; (3) redesign of the docking well to accommodate three LCAC; and (4) modification of the self-defense armament.

The lead ship was laid down in 1984. A class of five LHDs is tentatively planned, in part as replacements for the IWO JIMA-class LPHs.

Classification: During the preliminary design stage these ships were designated LHDX. It is anticipated that they will be redesignated in the LHA series.

Cost: The fiscal 1984 budget provides $1.3657 *billion* for construction of the lead ship; previous funding in fiscal 1983 for long-lead procurement was $55 million.

Design: The basic configuration of these ships will be similar to the LHA 1 class. They will have less vehicle storage space, only 22,000 square feet, but will be superior in most other capabilities. Although intended to operate Harriers as well as helicopters, these ships will not have ski-jump ramps to assist VSTOL operations because the size of the flight deck will permit STOL takeoff runs.

These ships will have a collective CBR protective system with "citadels" fitted with an overpressure capacity to keep out contaminants. These and the ARLEIGH BURKE (DDG 51)-class destroyers will be the first U.S. ships so fitted.

Medical: Medical facilities will be double those of the LHA 1 class, i.e., six operating rooms and facilities for 600 bed patients.

5 AMPHIBIOUS ASSAULT SHIPS: "TARAWA" CLASS

Number	Name	FY	Builder	Laid down	Launched	Commissioned	Status
LHA 1	TARAWA	69	Litton/Ingalls Shipbuilding, Pascagoula, Miss.	15 Nov 1971	1 Dec 1973	29 May 1976	FA
LHA 2	SAIPAN	70	Litton/Ingalls Shipbuilding, Pascagoula, Miss.	21 July 1972	18 July 1974	15 Oct 1977	AA
LHA 3	BELLEAU WOOD	70	Litton/Ingalls Shipbuilding, Pascagoula, Miss.	5 Mar 1973	11 Apr 1977	23 Sep 1978	PA
LHA 4	NASSAU	71	Litton/Ingalls Shipbuilding, Pascagoula, Miss.	13 Aug 1973	28 Jan 1978	28 July 1979	AA
LHA 5	PELELIU	71	Litton/Ingalls Shipbuilding, Pascagoula, Miss.	12 Nov 1976	6 Jan 1979	3 May 1980	PA

Displacement:	39,300 tons full load
Length:	778 feet (237.3 m) wl
	820 feet (250.1 m) oa
Beam:	106 2/3 feet (32.5 m)
Extreme width:	126 feet (38.4 m)
Draft:	26 feet (7.9 m)
Propulsion:	steam turbine (Westinghouse); 70,000 shp; 2 shafts
Boilers:	2 600 psi (Combustion Engineering)
Speed:	24 knots (22 knots sustained)
Range:	10,000 n.miles at 20 knots
Manning:	LHA 1 937 (58 officers + 879 enlisted)
	LHA 2 930 (57 officers + 873 enlisted)
	LHA 3, 5 936 (57 officers + 879 enlisted)
	LHA 4 935 (57 officers + 878 enlisted)
Troops:	1,900 +
Helicopters:	approx. 30
Elevators:	1 deck edge (50 × 34 feet | 15.2 × 10.3 m)
	1 stern (59¾ × 34¾ feet | 18.2 × 10.6 m)
Missiles:	2 8-tube Sea Sparrow BPDMS launchers Mk 25

Guns:	3 5-inch (127-mm) 54-cal DP Mk 45 (3 single)
	6 20-mm AA Mk 67 (6 single)
Radars:	SPS-10F surface search
	SPS-40B air search
	SPS-52B 3-D search
Fire control:	1 Mk 86 GFCS with SPG-60 and SPQ-9A radars
	2 Mk 115 missile FCS

These are the largest amphibious ships ever built (some ESSEX-class aircraft carriers were converted to that role; see page 190). They were intended to combine the capabilities of several types of amphibious ships in a single hull. In addition, these ships periodically have operated AV-8 Harrier VSTOL aircraft and OV-10 Bronco STOL aircraft.

Class: Nine ships of this class were originally planned. The Navy announced on 20 January 1971 that LHA 6–9 would not be constructed.

Design: SCB No. 410. Special features of this class include an 18-foot section of the mast that is hinged to permit passage under bridges;

a 5,000-square-foot training and acclimatization room to permit troops to exercise in a controlled environment; over 30,000 square feet of vehicle storage decks connected by ramps to the flight deck and docking well; five cargo elevators that move equipment between the holds and flight deck; and extensive command and communications facilities are provided for an amphibious force commander.

The hangar deck is 820 feet long and 78 feet wide with a 20-foot overhead.

The stern docking well is 268 feet long and 78 feet wide and can accommodate 4 LCU-1610 landing craft or 2 LCUs and 3 LCM-8s or 17 LCM-6s or 45 LVTP-7 amphibian tractors. Because of the arrangement of the docking well, only one LCAC can be carried. In addition, 35 amphibious tractors can be carried on the third deck of an LHA.

Engineering: A 900-hp through-tunnel thruster is fitted in the forward part of the hull to assist in maneuvering while launching landing craft.

The ships' boilers are the largest ever manufactured in the United States.

Guns: These are the only U.S. amphibious ships armed with 5-inch guns. The 20-mm Mk 67 weapons are manually operated and intended for defense against swimmers and small craft. Each ship is scheduled to have two Phalanx CIWS installed.

Helicopters: These ships were designed to simultaneously operate 12 CH-46 Sea Knight or 9 CH-53 Sea Stallion helicopters from the flight deck. The hangar deck can accommodate 30 Sea Knights or 19 Sea Stallions or various combinations of aircraft. A normal LHA "air wing" consists of a composite squadron of 18 Sea Knights, 4 Sea Stallions, and 4 AH-1 SeaCobra helicopters.

During a 1983 exercise the NASSAU operated 19 AV-8A Harriers without difficulties.

Medical: Extensive medical facilities are provided including three operating rooms and bed space for 300 patients.

Names: The PELELIU was originally named DA NANG; the ship was renamed on 15 February 1978 after the fall of the Republic of (South) Vietnam to communist forces.

SAIPAN (1982, Giorgio Arra)

The BELLEAU WOOD with 3 Marine OV-10 Broncos parked forward. The ships have massive island superstructures; the hangar deck opening for the port-side elevator is visible. These ships displace more than the Soviet KIEV-class VTOL carriers, although the Soviet ships are longer (approximately 38,000 tons full load, 901 feet overall length). (1982, Giorgio Arra)

The BELLEAU WOOD at sea with her normal brood of Marine helicopters. CH-46 Sea Knight and CH-53 Sea Stallion helicopters are parked forward and aft. The stern elevator is lowered to the hangar deck in this view. (1983, Giorgio Arra)

NASSAU (1983, Giorgio Arra)

The BELLEAU WOOD with stern gate open. The LHDs will be similar, but without the buffer within the docking well that prevents the LHAs from carrying more than one air cushion landing craft. Amphibian tractors (LVTs) can be launched from all current docking well ships while the ships are underway, with ship speeds in excess of 20 knots being possible. (1982, Giorgio Arra)

7 AMPHIBIOUS ASSAULT SHIPS: "IWO JIMA" CLASS

Number	Name	FY	Builder	Laid down	Launched	Commissioned	Status
LPH 2	Iwo Jima	58	Puget Sound Naval Shipyard	2 Apr 1959	17 Sep 1960	26 Aug 1961	**AA**
LPH 3	Okinawa	59	Philadelphia Naval Shipyard	1 Apr 1960	14 Aug 1961	14 Apr 1962	**PA**
LPH 7	Guadalcanal	60	Philadelphia Naval Shipyard	1 Sep 1961	16 Mar 1963	20 July 1963	**AA**
LPH 9	Guam	62	Philadelphia Naval Shipyard	15 Nov 1962	22 Aug 1964	16 Jan 1965	**AA**
LPH 10	Tripoli	63	Ingalls Shipbuilding, Pascagoula	15 June 1964	31 July 1965	6 Aug 1966	**PA**
LPH 11	New Orleans	65	Philadelphia Naval Shipyard	1 Mar 1966	3 Feb 1968	16 Nov 1968	**PA**
LPH 12	Inchon	66	Ingalls Shipbuilding, Pascagoula	8 Apr 1968	24 May 1969	20 June 1970	**AA**

Displacement:	17,000 tons light
	18,300 tons full load
Length:	556 feet (169.6 m) wl
	592 feet (180.5 m) oa
Beam:	84 feet (25.6 m)
Extreme width:	112 feet (34.2 m)
Draft:	26 feet (7.9 m)
Propulsion:	steam turbine (Westinghouse); 22,000 shp; 1 shaft
Boilers:	2 600 psi (Combustion Engineering)
Speed:	22 knots (21 knots sustained)
Range:	10,000 n.miles at 20 knots
	16,600 n.miles at 11.5 knots
Manning:	LPH 2 683 (47 officers + 636 enlisted)
	LPH 3 673 (46 officers + 627 enlisted)
	LPH 7, 12 684 (46 officers + 638 enlisted)
	LPH 9 685 (47 officers + 638 enlisted)
	LPH 10, 11 674 (46 officers + 628 enlisted)
Troops:	approx. 2,000+
Helicopters:	approx. 20
Elevators:	2 deck edge (50 × 34 feet | 15.2 × 10.4 m)
Missiles:	2 8-tube Sea Sparrow BPDMS launchers Mk 25 (being deleted for CIWS)
Guns:	4 3-inch (76-mm) 50-cal AA Mk 33 (2 twin)
Radars:	2 20-mm Phalanx CIWS Mk 16 (2 multibarrel) in LPH 3 (see notes)
	SPS-10 surface search
	SPS-40 air search
Fire control:	2 Mk 115 missile FCS
	local control only for guns

These ships were the first of any navy constructed specifically to operate helicopters. Unlike the Royal Navy's commando carriers of the 1960s and 1970s, and the later Tarawa class, these ships do not carry landing craft (except for the LCVP davits in the Inchon).

Design: SCB No. 157. These ships represent an improved World War II-type escort carrier design with accommodations for a Marine battalion and supporting helicopter squadron. The Inchon has davits for two LCVPs.

No catapults or arresting gear are fitted.

Guns: As built, these ships had four 3-inch twin gun mounts, two forward of the island structure and two on the after corners of the flight deck. Between 1970 and 1974 all ships had two gun mounts replaced by Sea Sparrow launchers (one forward of the island and one on the port quarter).

From 1982 onward, these ships are additionally being fitted with two Phalanx CIWS in place of the Sea Sparrow launchers.

All gun FCS have been removed and only local control is now available.

Helicopters: The ships have the capability of handling up to seven CH-46 Sea Knight or four CH-53 Sea Stallion helicopters on their flight decks. The hangar deck can accommodate 19 Sea Knights or 11 Sea Stallions or various mixes of these and other aircraft.

The Guadalcanal off Lebanon with CH-46 Sea Knights forward; a UH-1 Huey, CH-53 Sea Stallion, and trio of Sea Knights aft. (U.S. Navy, 1983, PH2 T. Lally/PH3 J. Donnelly)

Medical: These ships have extensive medical facilities with a 300-bed sick bay.

Operational: The GUAM operated as an interim Sea Control Ship (SCS) from 1972 to 1974 to evaluate the concept of flying VSTOL aircraft and ASW helicopters from a ship of about this size in the convoy defense role. She operated AV-8A Harriers and SH-3 Sea Kings. The ship subsequently reverted to an amphibious assault role.

These ships have also operated CH-53 helicopters in the mine countermeasures role off North Vietnam and in the Suez Canal.

The OKINAWA at San Diego with a Phalanx CIWS installed forward of the island. (1982, Giorgio Arra)

GUAM (1982, U.S. Navy, PH3 R. P. Fitzgerald)

AMPHIBIOUS ASSAULT SHIP PROGRAMS

The LPH classification was established in 1955. The World War II-era escort carrier BLOCK ISLAND was to have been LPH 1, but her conversion was cancelled. Three ESSEX-class carriers were subsequently modified to LPHs, as was the escort carrier THETIS BAY. The smaller ship had been designated a helicopter assault carrier (CVHA 1) upon her conversion in 1955–1956. She was changed to LPH to avoid confusion and budget competition with CV-type aircraft carriers.

LPH 1	BLOCK ISLAND (ex-CVE 106)	conversion cancelled
LPH 2–3	IWO JIMA class	
LPH 4	BOXER (ex-CV/CVA/CVS 21)	to LPH 1959; stricken 1969
LPH 5	PRINCETON (ex-CV/CVA/CVS 37)	to LPH 1959; stricken 1970
LPH 6	THETIS BAY (ex-CVE 90)	to CVHA 1/LPH 1956; stricken 1966
LPH 7	IWO JIMA class	
LPH 8	VALLEY FORGE (ex-CV/CVA/CVS 45)	to LPH 1961; stricken 1970
LPH 9–12	IWO JIMA class	

5 AMPHIBIOUS CARGO SHIPS: "CHARLESTON" CLASS

Number	Name	FY	Builder	Laid down	Launched	Commissioned	Status
LKA 113	CHARLESTON	65	Newport News Shipbuilding	5 Dec 1966	2 Dec 1967	14 Dec 1968	**AA**
LKA 114	DURHAM	65	Newport News Shipbuilding	10 July 1967	29 Mar 1968	24 May 1969	**PA**
LKA 115	MOBILE	65	Newport News Shipbuilding	15 Jan 1968	19 Oct 1968	20 Sep 1969	**PA**
LKA 116	ST. LOUIS	65	Newport News Shipbuilding	3 Apr 1968	4 Jan 1969	22 Nov 1969	**PA**
LKA 117	EL PASO	66	Newport News Shipbuilding	22 Oct 1968	17 May 1969	17 Jan 1970	**AA**

Displacement:	20,700 tons full load
Length:	575½ feet (175.5 m) oa
Beam:	82 feet (25.0 m)
Draft:	25½ feet (7.8 m)
Propulsion:	steam turbine (Westinghouse); 22,000 shp; 1 shaft
Boilers:	2 600 psi (Combustion Engineering)
Speed:	20+ knots
Range:	
Manning:	930 to 937 (57 or 58 officers + 873 to 879 enlisted)
Troops:	225
Helicopters:	landing area only
Missiles:	none
Guns:	6 3-inch (76-mm) 50-cal AA Mk 33 (3 twin)
Radars:	SPS-10 surface search
Fire control:	local control only

Ship	to NRF	return to Active
LKA 113	21 Nov 1979	13 Feb 1983
LKA 114	1 Oct 1979	1 Oct 1982
LKA 115	1 Sep 1980	1 July 1983
LKA 117	1 Mar 1981	1 Oct 1982

These ships carry heavy equipment and supplies for amphibious assaults. They are configured for rapid unloading of equipment into landing craft and onto helicopters in a combat environment.

During 1979–1981 four of the ships were shifted to the NRF; they were returned to active Navy service in the early 1980s to improve amphibious readiness in response to the crises in the Persian Gulf, Lebanon, and Caribbean areas:

Classification: These ships were ordered as attack cargo ships (AKA). The CHARLESTON was changed to LKA on 14 December 1968 and the others were changed to LKA on 1 January 1969.

Design: SCB No. 403. This is the first class of ships designed specifically for this role; all previous ships of the LKA/AKA type were converted from or built to merchant designs.

These ships have a helicopter landing area aft, but no hangar or maintenance facilities. They have 38,000 square feet of vehicle storage space. There are two 78-ton-capacity cranes, two 40-ton-capacity booms, and eight 15-ton-capacity booms.

Guns: As built, four 3-inch twin gun mounts were provided. One mount has been removed from each ship as well as the Mk 56 GFCS. Two Phalanx CIWS are planned for installation in these ships.

The lead ship of the CHARLESTON class, with LCMs stowed forward and aft over her cargo hatches. There is a helicopter deck but no hangar. These ships carry equipment and bulk supplies needed for amphibious operations. (1983, Giorgio Arra)

El Paso (1980, L. & L. van Ginderen)

MARINER CLASS

The Navy's only other post-World War II amphibious cargo ship, the Tulare (AKA/LKA 112), was stricken on 1 August 1981. She is employed as a training ship by the Massachusetts Maritime Academy (renamed Bay State).

AMPHIBIOUS TRANSPORTS

The Navy had two postwar-built amphibious transports, the Paul Revere (APA/LPA 248) and Francis Marion (APA/LPA 249); both ships were stricken on 1 January 1980 and sold to Spain in January 1980 and July 1980, respectively.

The LKA 112, LPA 248, and LPA 249 were built as Mariner-class merchant ships. Other ships of this class remain on the Navy List as miscellaneous auxiliaries (AG); see Chapter 24.

Juneau (1983, Giorgio Arra)

(1 +) AMPHIBIOUS TRANSPORT DOCKS: NEW CONSTRUCTION

Number	Name	FY	Comm.	Status
LPD	......	88		Planned

Displacement:	17,303 tons full load
Length:	609 feet (185.7 m) oa
Beam:	84 feet (25.6 m)
Draft:	20½ feet (6.25 m)
Propulsion:	diesels; 33,600 bhp; 2 shafts
Speed:	20 + knots
Range:	
Manning:	445
Troops:	860

11 AMPHIBIOUS TRANSPORT DOCKS: "AUSTIN" CLASS

Number	Name	FY	Builder	Laid down	Launched	Commissioned	Status
LPD 4	AUSTIN	62	New York Naval Shipyard	4 Feb 1963	27 June 1964	6 Feb 1965	**AA**
LPD 5	OGDEN	62	New York Naval Shipyard	4 Feb 1963	27 June 1964	19 June 1965	**PA**
LPD 6	DULUTH	62	New York Naval Shipyard	18 Dec 1963	14 Aug 1965	18 Dec 1965	**PA**
LPD 7	CLEVELAND	63	Ingalls Shipbuilding, Pascagoula	30 Nov 1964	7 May 1966	21 Apr 1967	**PA**
LPD 8	DUBUQUE	63	Ingalls Shipbuilding, Pascagoula	25 Jan 1965	6 Aug 1966	1 Sep 1967	**PA**
LPD 9	DENVER	63	Lockheed SB & Constn, Seattle	7 Feb 1964	23 Jan 1965	26 Oct 1968	**PA**
LPD 10	JUNEAU	63	Lockheed SB & Constn, Seattle	23 Jan 1965	12 Feb 1966	12 July 1969	**PA**
LPD 12	SHREVEPORT	64	Lockheed SB & Constn, Seattle	27 Dec 1965	25 Oct 1966	12 Dec 1970	**AA**
LPD 13	NASHVILLE	64	Lockheed SB & Constn, Seattle	14 Mar 1966	7 Oct 1967	14 Feb 1970	**AA**
LPD 14	TRENTON	65	Lockheed SB & Constn, Seattle	8 Aug 1966	3 Aug 1968	6 Mar 1971	**AA**
LPD 15	PONCE	65	Lockheed SB & Constn, Seattle	31 Oct 1966	30 May 1970	10 July 1971	**AA**

Displacement:	10,000 tons light
	16,900 tons full load
Length:	570 feet (173.8 m) oa
Beam:	84 feet (25.6 m)
Draft:	23 feet (7.0 m)
Propulsion:	2 steam turbines (De Laval); 24,000 shp; 2 shafts
Boilers:	2 600 psi (Babcock & Wilcox)
Speed:	20 knots
Range:	7,700 n.miles at 20 knots
Manning:	409 to 452 (26 officers + 383 to 426 enlisted)
Troops:	930 in LPD 4–6, 14, 15
	840 in LPD 7–10, 12, 13
Flag:	90 in LPD 7–10, 12, 13
Helicopters:	landing area and hangar
Missiles:	none
Guns	4 3-inch (76-mm) 50-cal AA Mk 33 (2 twin)
Radars:	SPS-10F surface search
	SPS-40C air search
Fire control:	local control only

These ships are enlarged versions of the previous RALEIGH-class LPDs. They are intended to carry Marines into forward areas and unload them by using landing craft and vehicles carried in their docking well and by using helicopters provided mainly from amphibious assault ships. The general configuration of these ships is similar to dock landing ships, but with a relatively smaller docking well and additional space for troop berthing and vehicle parks.

Builders: The DULUTH was completed at the Philadelphia Naval Shipyard after the closing of the New York Naval Shipyard; she was reassigned to Philadelphia on 24 November 1965.

Class: An additional ship of this class (LPD 16) was provided in the

Helicopters:	6 CH-46 Sea Knight
Missiles:	none
Guns:	2 20-mm Phalanx CIWS Mk 16 (2 multibarrel)
Radars:	
Fire control:	

This ship will be similar to the WHIDBEY ISLAND-class LSDs, but will have a smaller docking well to provide for increased troop, vehicle, cargo, and helicopter capacity.

During the design stage the ship was designated LPDX.

Design: The ship's docking well will accommodate 2 LCACs or 10 LCM-6 landing craft and will have more than 17,000 square feet of vehicle storage space.

fiscal 1966 shipbuilding program, but construction was deferred in favor of the LHA program and officially cancelled in February 1969.

The CORONADO (LPD 11) of this class was modified for use as a flagship in late 1980 and reclassified AGF 11; see Chapter 18.

Design: LPD 4–10 are SCB No. 187B and LPD 11–13 are No. 187C; changed to No. 402 for LPD 14 and 15 under the new SCB numbering scheme.

The LPD 7–13 are configured as amphibious squadron flagships and have an additional bridge level. The docking well in these ships is 168 feet long and 50 feet wide; see RALEIGH class for well capacity. The ships have 15,700 square feet of vehicle storage space.

These ships have a fixed flight deck above the docking well with two landing spots. All except the AUSTIN are fitted with a hangar varying from 58 to 64 feet in length and 18½ to 24 feet in width; the hangars have an extension that can extend to provide a length of approximately 80 feet.

Guns: As built, these ships had eight 3-inch guns in twin mounts. The number was reduced in the late 1970s and the associated Mk 56 and Mk 63 GFCS were removed. The ships are to receive two Phalanx CIWS.

Modernization: A Service Life Extension Program (SLEP) has been developed for these ships to permit them to operate beyond a nominal 30-year service life by 10 to 15 years. In addition to general improvements, they will be modified to carry two LCACs and their aviation capabilities will be improved. The first SLEP is scheduled to begin in fiscal 1986.

Operational: These ships have deployed with up to six CH-46 Sea Knights embarked.

The CLEVELAND, showing the traditional LPD/LSD lines. The two types differ, in part, by the helicopter deck in the LPDs being faired into the after hull while the LSDs have a separate deck, above the hull. There are life rafts in cannisters along the side of the superstructure. A foreign A-4 Skyhawk being returned to the United States is on the helicopter deck. (1983, Giorgio Arra)

Two LCMs enter the docking well of the CLEVELAND while the ship's crane lifts aboard an LCVP. Note the two-spot helicopter deck; partially opened hangar door with screen attached in preparation for the nightly movie. (U.S. Navy)

JUNEAU (1983, Giorgio Arra)

2 AMPHIBIOUS TRANSPORT DOCKS: "RALEIGH" CLASS

Number	Name	FY	Builder	Laid down	Launched	Commissioned	Status
LPD 1	RALEIGH	59	New York Naval Shipyard	23 June 1960	17 Mar 1962	8 Sep 1962	**AA**
LPD 2	VANCOUVER	60	New York Naval Shipyard	19 Nov 1960	15 Sep 1962	11 May 1963	**PA**

Displacement:	8,040 tons light
	13,900 tons full load
Length:	500 feet (152.5 m) wl
	521¾ feet (159.0 m) oa
Beam:	84 feet (25.6 m)
Draft:	21⁷/₁₂ feet (6.6 m)
Propulsion:	2 steam turbines (De Laval); 24,000 shp; 2 shafts
Boilers:	2 600 psi (Babcock & Wilcox)
Speed:	21.6 knots (20 knots sustained)
Range:	9,600 n.miles at 16 knots
	16,500 n.miles at 10 knots
Manning:	LPD 1 419 (26 officers + 393 enlisted)
	LPD 2 426 (26 officers + 400 enlisted)
Troops:	930
Helicopters:	landing area only
Missiles:	none
Guns:	6 3-inch (76-mm) 50-cal AA Mk 33 (3 twin)
Radars:	SPS-10 surface search
	SPS-40 air search
Fire control:	local control only

The LPD is a development of the dock landing ship (LSD) concept with increased troop and vehicle capacity and a relatively small docking well.

Class: The third ship of this class, the LA SALLE (LPD 3) was converted to a flagship and reclassified as AGF 3; see Chapter 18.

Design: SCB No. 187. There is a fixed helicopter deck fitted over the docking well in these ships. The well is 168 feet long and 50 feet wide and can accommodate 2 LCACs or 1 LCU and 3 LCM-6s or 4 LCM-8 or 24 LVTP-7 amphibian tractors. In addition, 2 LCM-6s or 4 LCVP/LCPLs are normally carried on the helicopter deck; up to 16 amphibian tractors can be parked on the main deck (slightly more in the LPD 4 class). The ships have 12,500 square feet of vehicle storage space.

No helicopter hangar or support facilities are provided.

Guns: All guns originally installed have been retained. However, the Mk 56 and Mk 51 GFCS have been removed from both ships. Two Phalanx CIWS are scheduled for installation in these ships.

The RALEIGH anchored off Beirut. (1983, U.S. Navy, PH2 T. Lally/PH3 J. Donnelly)

1 + 13 DOCK LANDING SHIPS: "WHIDBEY ISLAND" CLASS

Number	Name	FY	Builder	Laid down	Launched	Commissioned	Status
LSD 41	WHIDBEY ISLAND	81	Lockheed Shipbuilding, Seattle, Wash.	4 Aug 1981	10 June 1983	late 1984	**AA**
LSD 42	GERMANTOWN	82	Lockheed Shipbuilding, Seattle, Wash.	5 Aug 1982	29 June 1984	1985	Building
LSD 43	. . . . . .	83	Lockheed Shipbuilding, Seattle, Wash.	10 June 1983	1985	1987	Building
LSD 44	. . . . . .	84	Avondale Shipyards, New Orleans, La.		1987	1988	Building
LSD	(2 ships)	85					Planned
LSD	(2 ships)	86					Planned
LSD	(2 ships)	87					Planned
LSD	(2 ships)	88					Planned
LSD	(2 ships)	89					Planned

Displacement:	11,125 tons standard
	15,745 tons full load
Length:	580 feet (176.9 m) wl
	609⁷⁄₁₂ feet (185.9 m) oa
Beam:	84 feet (25.6 m)
Draft:	20 feet (6.1 m)
Propulsion:	4 diesels (SEMT-Pielsticks); 34,000 bhp; 2 shafts
Speed:	20+ knots
Range:	
Manning:	356 (19 officers + 337 enlisted)
Troops:	340
Helicopters:	landing area only
Missiles:	none
Guns:	2 20-mm Phalanx CIWS Mk 16 (2 multibarrel)
Radars:	SPS-40B air search
	SPS-67 surface search
Fire control:	none

These ships are being constructed to replace the THOMASTON class and to provide lift for air cushion landing craft.

Class: Navy planning in the early 1980s called for 9 or 10 ships of this class to replace the LSD 28 class; the number was subsequently increased to 12 ships through the fiscal 1988 shipbuilding program.

Cost: The FY 1984 ship had a budget cost of $509 million for construction, $1 million for escalation/cost growth, and $15.1 million for outfitting plus a small amount for research and development, a total $525.4 million.

Design: The docking well is 440 feet long and 50 feet wide and can accommodate 4 LCACs or 21 LCM-6 landing craft. There is 12,300 square feet of vehicle storage space. Fitted with one 60-ton capacity and one 20-ton crane.

Engineering: These will be the first U.S. ships powered by medium speed diesel engines. Of French design, the diesels are produced under license by the Fairbanks Morse Division of Colt Industries.

The WHIDBEY ISLAND. Note the asymmetrical arrangement of twin funnels and twin cranes; two landing spots marked on the helicopter deck; and flight deck control station on the after funnel. (1984, Lockheed Shipbuilding)

The WHIDBEY ISLAND under way. Note the two Gatling guns atop the superstructure. (1984, Lockheed Shipbuilding)

5 DOCK LANDING SHIPS: "ANCHORAGE" CLASS

Number	Name	FY	Builder	Laid down	Launched	Commissioned	Status
LSD 36	ANCHORAGE	65	Ingalls Shipbuilding, Pascagoula, Miss.	13 Mar 1967	5 May 1968	15 Mar 1969	**PA**
LSD 37	PORTLAND	66	General Dynamics, Quincy, Mass.	21 Sep 1967	20 Dec 1969	3 Oct 1970	**AA**
LSD 38	PENSACOLA	66	General Dynamics, Quincy, Mass.	12 Mar 1969	11 July 1970	27 Mar 1971	**AA**
LSD 39	MOUNT VERNON	66	General Dynamics, Quincy, Mass.	29 Jan 1970	17 Apr 1971	13 May 1972	**PA**
LSD 40	FORT FISHER	67	General Dynamics, Quincy, Mass.	15 July 1970	22 Apr 1972	9 Dec 1972	**PA**

Displacement:	8,600 tons light
	13,700 tons full load
Length:	553⅓ feet (168.75 m) oa
Beam:	84 feet (25.6 m)
Draft:	18½ feet (5.6 m)
Propulsion:	2 steam turbines (De Laval); 24,000 shp; 2 shafts
Boilers:	2 600 psi (Foster Wheeler except Combustion Engineering in LSD 36)
Speed:	20 knots
Range:	
Manning:	349 to 355 (18 officers + 331 to 337 enlisted)
Troops:	375
Helicopters:	landing area only
Missiles:	none
Guns	6 3-inch (76-mm) 50-cal AA Mk 33 (3 twin)
Radars:	SPS-10 surface search
	SPS-40 air search
Fire control:	local control only

These LSDs were part of the large amphibious ship construction program of the early 1960s and were to supplement the LPDs (and later LHAs) by carrying additional landing craft to the assault area.

Design: SCB No. 404. The docking well is 430 feet long and 50 feet wide; it can accommodate 4 LCACs or 3 LCUs or 9 LCM-8s or 52 LVTP-7 amphibian tractors. Another 15 tractors can be stowed on a "mezzanine" deck. A removable helicopter deck is fitted over the docking well. Total vehicle storage space is 15,800 square feet. No hangar or maintenance facilities are provided.

Guns: As built, these ships had eight 3-inch guns in twin mounts; one amidships mount and the GFCS were removed in the late 1970s. Two Phalanx CIWS are scheduled for each of these ships.

The ANCHORAGE was one of five LSDs constructed during the rejuvenation of the amphibious force in the 1960s. These ships are similar in design to the previous THOMASTON class. One of the two forward 3-inch twin gun mounts has been removed. (1980, Giorgio Arra)

ANCHORAGE (1980, Giorgio Arra)

8 DOCK LANDING SHIPS: "THOMASTON" CLASS

Number	Name	FY	Builder	Laid down	Launched	Commissioned	Status
LSD 28	THOMASTON	52	Ingalls Shipbuilding, Pascagoula	3 Mar 1953	9 Feb 1954	17 Sep 1954	PR
LSD 29	PLYMOUTH ROCK	52	Ingalls Shipbuilding, Pascagoula	5 May 1953	7 May 1954	29 Nov 1954	AR
LSD 30	FORT SNELLING	52	Ingalls Shipbuilding, Pascagoula	17 Aug 1953	16 July 1954	24 Jan 1955	AR
LSD 31	POINT DEFIANCE	52	Ingalls Shipbuilding, Pascagoula	23 Nov 1953	28 Sep 1954	31 Mar 1955	PR
LSD 32	SPIEGEL GROVE	54	Ingalls Shipbuilding, Pascagoula	7 Sep 1954	10 Nov 1955	8 June 1956	**AA**
LSD 33	ALAMO	54	Ingalls Shipbuilding, Pascagoula	11 Oct 1954	20 Jan 1956	24 Aug 1956	**PA**
LSD 34	HERMITAGE	55	Ingalls Shipbuilding, Pascagoula	11 Apr 1955	12 June 1956	14 Dec 1956	**AA**
LSD 35	MONTICELLO	55	Ingalls Shipbuilding, Pascagoula	6 June 1955	10 Aug 1956	29 Mar 1957	**PA**

The PLYMOUTH ROCK at Portsmouth, England, with stern gate lowered; note height of helicopter deck above the docking well. (1982, L. & L. van Ginderen)

Displacement:	6,880 tons light
	11,270 tons full load except LSD 32–34 12,150 tons
Length:	510 feet (155.5 m) oa
Beam:	84 feet (25.6 m)
Draft:	19 feet (5.8 m)
Propulsion:	2 steam turbines (General Electric); 24,000 shp; 2 shafts
Boilers:	2 600 psi (Babcock & Wilcox)
Speed:	22.5 knots
Range:	5,300 n.miles at 22.5 knots
	13,000 n.miles at 10 knots
Manning:	311 to 350 (18 officers + 293 to 332 enlisted)
Troops:	340
Helicopters:	landing area only
Missiles:	none
Guns:	6 3-inch (76-mm) 50-cal AA Mk 33 (3 twin)
Radars:	SPS-6 air search
	SPS-10B surface search
Fire control:	local control only

These ships were built as a result of the renewed interest in amphibious operations during the Korean War. They are the only amphibious ships of that era that remain in active Navy service. They were to

The THOMASTON class resulted from renewed U.S. interest in amphibious warfare during the Korean War. (1983, Giorgio Arra)

have been retired in the late 1980s, but are being decommissioned earlier because of funding shortages.

The PLYMOUTH ROCK and POINT DEFIANCE were decommissioned on 30 September 1983; the THOMASTON and FORT SNELLING in September 1984.

Design: SCB No. 75. The docking well in these ships is 391 feet long and 48 feet wide and can transport 3 LCACs or 3 LCUs or 9 LCM-8s or about 50 LVTP-7 amphibian tractors. There are 10,200 feet of vehicle storage space. A removable helicopter deck is fitted above the well, but there are no hangar or support facilities.

Guns: These ships were built with an armament of 16 3-inch guns in twin mounts plus 12 20-mm AA guns. Their armament was reduced to 12 3-inch guns during the 1960s and to the above armament during the late 1970s. Their fire control systems were also removed, leaving them with local control only.

THOMASTON (1983, Giorgio Arra)

The FRESNO with pontoon causeways mounted aft; Marine vehicles crowd her after deck; the "3" and "1" mark unloading stations for small craft coming alongside. A pair of SATCOM antennas are visible atop the bridge while the twin 3-inch gun mounts are barely visible. (1980, Giorgio Arra)

20 TANK LANDING SHIPS: "NEWPORT" CLASS

Number	Name	FY	Builder	Laid down	Launched	Commissioned	Status
LST 1179	Newport	65	Philadelphia Naval Shipyard	1 Nov 1966	3 Feb 1968	7 June 1969	**AA**
LST 1180	Manitowoc	66	Philadelphia Naval Shipyard	1 Feb 1967	4 June 1969	24 Jan 1970	**AA**
LST 1181	Sumter	66	Philadelphia Naval Shipyard	14 Nov 1967	13 Dec 1969	20 June 1970	**AA**
LST 1182	Fresno	66	National Steel & SB, San Diego	16 Dec 1967	20 Sep 1968	22 Nov 1969	**PA**
LST 1183	Peoria	66	National Steel & SB, San Diego	22 Feb 1968	23 Nov 1968	21 Feb 1970	**PA**
LST 1184	Frederick	66	National Steel & SB, San Diego	13 Apr 1968	8 Mar 1969	11 Apr 1970	**PA**
LST 1185	Schenectady	66	National Steel & SB, San Diego	2 Aug 1968	24 May 1969	13 June 1970	**PA**
LST 1186	Cayuga	66	National Steel & SB, San Diego	28 Sep 1968	12 July 1969	8 Aug 1970	**PA**
LST 1187	Tuscaloosa	66	National Steel & SB, San Diego	23 Nov 1968	6 Sep 1969	24 Oct 1970	**PA**
LST 1188	Saginaw	67	National Steel & SB, San Diego	24 May 1969	7 Feb 1970	23 Jan 1971	**AA**
LST 1189	San Bernardino	67	National Steel & SB, San Diego	12 July 1969	28 Mar 1970	27 Mar 1971	**PA**
LST 1190	Boulder	67	National Steel & SB, San Diego	6 Sep 1969	22 May 1970	4 June 1971	**NRF-A**
LST 1191	Racine	67	National Steel & SB, San Diego	13 Dec 1969	15 Aug 1970	9 July 1971	**NRF-P**
LST 1192	Spartanburg County	67	National Steel & SB, San Diego	7 Feb 1970	11 Nov 1970	1 Sep 1971	**AA**
LST 1193	Fairfax County	67	National Steel & SB, San Diego	28 Mar 1970	19 Dec 1970	16 Oct 1971	**AA**
LST 1194	La Moure County	67	National Steel & SB, San Diego	22 May 1970	13 Feb 1971	18 Dec 1971	**AA**
LST 1195	Barbour County	67	National Steel & SB, San Diego	15 Aug 1970	15 May 1971	12 Feb 1972	**PA**
LST 1196	Harlan County	67	National Steel & SB, San Diego	7 Nov 1970	24 July 1971	8 Apr 1972	**AA**
LST 1197	Barnstable County	67	National Steel & SB, San Diego	19 Dec 1970	2 Oct 1971	27 May 1972	**AA**
LST 1198	Bristol County	67	National Steel & SB, San Diego	13 Feb 1971	4 Dec 1971	5 Aug 1972	**PA**

Displacement:	8,342 tons full load	Manning:	active ships 223 (13 officers + 210 enlisted) except 257
Length:	522⅓ feet (159.3 m) oa		(13 officers + 244 enlisted) in LST 1180, 1182, 1193
	562 feet (171.4 m) over derrick arms		NRF ships 169 (9 officers + 160 enlisted) active + 92 (6 officers
Beam:	69½ feet (21.2 m)		+ 86 enlisted) reserved
Draft:	17½ feet (5.3 m)	Troops:	385
Propulsion:	diesels (Arco); 16,500 bhp; 2 shafts	Helicopters:	landing area only
Speed:	20 knots	Guns:	4 3-inch (76-mm) 50-cal AA Mk 32 (2 twin)
Range:		Radars:	SPS-10F surface search
		Fire control:	local control only

The Manitowoc at near-maximum speed. The opening in the superstructure permits vehicles to shift between the forward ramp to the tank deck and the after helicopter deck/parking area. The funnels are asymmetrical and differ in size. (1983, Giorgio Arra)

These ships represent the "ultimate" design in landing ships that can be "beached." However, they generally unload onto pontoon causeways. They depart from the traditional LST bow-door design to obtain a hull design for a sustained speed of 20 knots.

The BOULDER and RACINE were assigned to the Naval Reserve Force on 1 December 1980 and 15 January 1981, respectively.

Design: SCB No. 405. The design has bow and stern ramps for unloading tanks and other vehicles. The bow ramp is 112 feet long and is handled over the bow by twin, fixed derrick arms. Vehicles can be driven between the main deck forward and aft through a passage in the superstructure. The stern ramp permits unloading amphibious vehicles into the water while the ships are underway or "mating" the LST to landing craft or a pier. The ships have 17,300 square feet of vehicle storage space. Four LCVPs are carried in amidship davits.

The cargo capacity of these ships is 500 tons of vehicles with 19,000 square feet of parking area (not including helicopter landing area). The draft listed is maximum aft; the full-load draft forward is 11½ feet.

Guns: The twin 3-inch gun mounts, installed atop the superstructure, are scheduled to be replaced by two 20-mm Phalanx CIWS in all ships except the LST 1190 and 1191.

Names: The first 13 ships do not have "county" or "parish" name suffixes as had all previously named LSTs.

The BOULDER at Portsmouth, England, showing the ship's stern gate and stern anchor, the latter for helping to retract the ship off beach areas. (1982, L. & L. van Ginderen)

The SPARTANBURG COUNTY with the FAIRFAX COUNTY in background while off Beirut. The SPARTANBURG's bow "doors" are open and her stern ramp is partially down. These are "drive-through" ships, which can load or unload amphibian tractors and other vehicles at either end. (1983, U.S. Navy, PH2 T. Lally/PH3 J. Donnelly)

The SCHENECTADY (left) and TUSCALOOSA at Subic Bay; note the manner in which the bow ramp is lowered from the derrick through the open bow doors. (1977, Giorgio Arra)

The SAGINAW with four pontoon causeways lashed amidships, necessary for unloading in shallow beach areas, with her after deck being used as an exercise area by embarked Marines. The twin 3-inch gun mounts are lost in the clutter atop the ship's superstructure. (1980, U.S. Navy, PH1 Thomas Beauchesne)

3 TANK LANDING SHIPS: "DE SOTO COUNTY" CLASS

Number	Name	FY	Builder	Laid down	Launched	Commissioned	Status
LST 1173	SUFFOLK COUNTY	55	Boston Naval Shipyard	17 July 1956	5 Sep 1956	15 Aug 1957	NDRF
LST 1177	LORAIN COUNTY	55	American Shipbuilding, Lorain, Ohio	9 Aug 1956	22 June 1957	3 Oct 1958	NDRF
LST 1178	WOOD COUNTY	55	American Shipbuilding, Lorain, Ohio	1 Oct 1956	14 Dec 1957	5 Aug 1959	NDRF

Displacement:	4,164 tons light
	8,000 tons full load
Length:	426 feet (129.9 m) wl
	445 feet (135.7 m) oa
Beam:	62 feet (18.9 m)
Draft:	16⅔ feet (5.1 m)
Propulsion:	6 diesels; 13,700 bhp; 2 shafts
Speed:	17.5 knots
Range:	9,000 n.miles at 15 knots
Manning:	184 (10 officers + 174 enlisted)
Troops:	approx. 575
Helicopters:	landing area only
Guns:	6 3-inch (76-mm) 50-cal AA Mk 33 (3 twin)
Radars:	SPS-10 surface search
Fire control:	2 Mk 63 GFCS with SPG-34 radar

These were the last U.S. Navy LSTs to be built with the traditional bow doors and ramp, and superstructure aft. Seven ships of this class were built. The three surviving ships were laid up in reserve in 1972.

Class: The LST 1171 and 1173–1178 of this class were completed in 1957–1959. The GRAHAM COUNTY (LST 1176) was converted to a gunboat support ship (AGP 1176) to support ASHEVILLE (PG 84)-class units in the Mediterranean before being stricken; the WOOD COUNTY was to have been converted to support the PEGASUS (PHM 1)-class hydrofoil missile craft; that conversion was deferred in 1977 (to have been redesignated AGHS).

These ships are sometimes referred to as the SUFFOLK COUNTY class for the first ship of this type to be completed.

Design: SCB No. 119. This class is more habitable than previous LSTs with air-conditioned crew and troops spaces. Up to 20 amphibian tractors or 23 medium tanks could be carried on the 288-foot-long tank deck. Four LCVPs were carried in davits.

Engineering: All built with Nordburg diesel engines; the SUFFOLK COUNTY was refitted with Fairbanks Morse diesels and the two other surviving ships with Cooper Bessemer diesels.

The WOOD COUNTY during a highline operation with the hydrofoil gunboat TUCUMCARI (PGH 2) off Cape Henry, Va. These were the last American LSTs with conventional bow doors of World War II-era ships. (1971, U.S. Navy)

6 TANK LANDING SHIPS: "TERREBONNE PARISH" CLASS

Number	Name	FY	Builder	Laid down	Launched	Commissioned	Status
LST 1158	TIOGA COUNTY	53	Bath Iron Works, Maine	16 June 1952	11 Apr 1953	20 June 1953	NDRF
LST 1160	TRAVERSE COUNTY	53	Bath Iron Works, Maine	18 Dec 1962	3 Oct 1953	19 Dec 1953	NDRF
LST 1162	WAHKIAKUM COUNTY	53	Ingalls Shipbuilding, Pascagoula	21 July 1952	23 Jan 1953	13 Aug 1953	NDRF
LST 1163	WALDO COUNTY	53	Ingalls Shipbuilding, Pascagoula	Aug 1952	17 Mar 1953	17 Sep 1953	NDRF
LST 1164	WALWORTH COUNTY	53	Ingalls Shipbuilding, Pascagoula	22 Sep 1952	15 May 1953	26 Oct 1953	NDRF
LST 1165	WASHOE COUNTY	53	Ingalls Shipbuilding, Pascagoula	1 Dec 1952	14 July 1953	30 Nov 1953	NDRF

Displacement:	2,590 tons light
	5,800 tons full load
Length:	370 feet (112.8 m) wl
	384 feet (117.1 m) oa
Beam:	55 feet (16.8 m)
Draft	17 feet (5.2 m)
Propulsion:	diesels (General Motors); 6,000 bhp; 2 shafts
Speed:	14 knots
Range:	10,000 n.miles at 10 knots
Manning:	116
Troops:	approx. 400
Helicopters:	landing area only
Missiles:	none
Guns:	6 3-inch (76-mm) 50-cal AA Mk 33 (3 twin)
Radars:	SPS-10 surface search
Fire control:	2 Mk 63 GFCS with SPG-34 radar

These LSTs are the survivors of a class of 15 ships built during the Korean War. They were the Navy's first post-World War II design.

All were in Navy service until decommissioned in 1970, except WALWORTH COUNTY in 1971; all then served with the Military Sealift Command in 1972–1973 (designated T-LST). The WAHKIAKUM COUNTY was stricken on 11 January 1973 and the others on 1 November 1973. However, the ships are retained in the National Defense Reserve Fleet, reserved for possible MSC use. They are in Suisun Bay, Calif.

Class: This class originally included hull numbers LST 1156–1170. The WASHTENAW COUNTY (LST 1166) was reclassified as a minesweeper support ship (MSS 2) before being stricken.

Design: SCB No. 9. These ships had a conventional design, with bow doors and ramp, and superstructure aft. Up to 17 LVTs were carried on their tank deck. They stow four LCVPs in davits.

Names: These ships were assigned names on 1 July 1955. Previously LSTs were not named.

POST-WORLD WAR II TANK LANDING SHIP PROGRAMS

Through June 1945 a total of 1,052 LSTs were completed for the U.S. Navy (numbered LST 1–1152, with 100 ships cancelled). All were of the same basic design, with the latter 611 ships (LST 542 onward) having minor improvements over the earlier series. Three larger, improved LSTs with steam-turbine propulsion were ordered during the war with two being completed, the LST 1153 and LST 1154. (All other U.S. LSTs have had diesel propulsion.) LST 1155 was cancelled in 1946 and LST 1172 was cancelled in 1955.

LST 1153	TALBOT COUNTY	Comm. 1947; stricken 1973
LST 1154	TALLAHATCHEE COUNTY	Comm. 1949; conv. to AVB 2
LST 1155	cancelled 1946	
LST 1156–1170	TERREBONNE PARISH class	
LST 1171–1178	SUFFOLK COUNTY class	
LST 1179–1198	NEWPORT class	

TRAVERSE COUNTY (1970, U.S. Navy)

20 Landing Craft

The U.S. Navy operates several hundred landing craft. The larger Landing Craft Air Cushion (LCAC) and utility landing craft (LCU) are usually identified by "hull" numbers. The smaller landing craft are identified by the ships, units, or stations to which they are assigned. All landing craft are operated by Navy personnel. The amphibian tractors, operated by the Marine Corps, are listed separately (Chapter 21).

The large-scale production of LCACs will provide the amphibious forces with increased speed and flexibility in assaults. However, the tactical doctrine for integrating LCACs' speed and radius with helicopters, amphibious tractors, and the movement of the amphibious ships themselves has not yet been developed.

U.S. and Australian landing craft participate in a joint Kangaroo-series exercise off Queensland, Australia. Such conventional landing craft are no longer suitable for opposed landings. From left are an American LCM, in the background the DENVER (LPD 9) with a CH-46 Sea Knight overhead, the Australian heavy landing craft BETANO, and a control boat from the ALAMO (LSD 33). (1981, U.S. Navy, PH1 Bob Wessleder)

(90 +) LANDING CRAFT AIR CUSHION: LCAC TYPE

Number	FY	Status
LCAC (2 units)	82	**Trials**
LCAC (1 unit)	82	Building
LCAC (3 units)	83	Building
LCAC (6 units)	84	Building
LCAC (9 units)	85	Planned
LCAC (69 units)	86–91	Planned

Builders:	Bell Aerospace Textron/Halter Marine, New Orleans, La.
Weight:	88 tons light
	200 tons loaded
Length:	87^{11}/$_{12}$ feet (26.8 m) oa
Beam:	47 feet (14.3 m)
Draft:	
Propulsion:	2 gas turbines (AVCO TF-40B) } 12,44 shp
Lift:	2 gas turbines (AVCO TF-40B) }
Speed:	50 knots maximum
	40 knots with payload
Range:	200 n.miles at 50 knots with payload
Manning:	5
Guns:	none

The LACAC-2 under way at high speed during trials. Note the navigation radar atop the control cockpit on the starboard side and the drive-through configuration of the cargo deck. (1985, Bell Aerospace Textron)

These landing craft are the first advanced-technology surface ships to be produced in series by the U.S. Navy. They are designed to carry 60 tons of cargo, including one M60 medium tank (48 tons) or six towed howitzers and trucks. The cargo deck area is 1,809 square feet; maximum cargo overload is 75 tons.

The first two LCACs are scheduled to complete in 1984 with an IOC of mid-1986. The craft will be based at the Naval Amphibious Base Little Creek, Va., and at the Marine Corps Base Camp Pendleton, Calif. (just north of San Diego). The original Navy-Marine plan was for 107 LCACs to support one MAF plus one MAB; however, in early 1984 the Department of Defense announced a plan for "at least 90" units.

Current doctrine calls for deploying the LCACs with amphibious squadrons in six-craft units. The first LCAC unit is Assault Craft Unit 5 established at Panama City, Fla., on 1 October 1983.

Cost: The 6 LCACs in the fiscal 1984 program are expected to cost an average of $26.46 million each; the 9 in fiscal 1985, $27.3 million; and the 12 in fiscal 1986, $27.15 million.

Design: The Navy began development of air cushion craft in 1960 (see Appendix C). The production LCACs are based on the JEFF(B), one of two competitive prototypes delivered in 1977.

The craft are fully "skirted"; they are amphibious and can clear land obstacles up to 4 feet high. Bow and stern ramps are fitted. The LCAC can be carried in LHA, LHD, LPD, and LSD amphibious ships.

The LCAC-1 is shown in this artist's concept bringing ashore a Marine M60 tank and five jeeps carrying anti-tank weapons. The LCAC has both bow and stern ramps. (Bell Aerospace Textron)

LCAC-1 under construction (Bell Aerospace Textron)

1 AMPHIBIOUS ASSAULT LANDING CRAFT: "JEFF(B)"

Number	Name	Status
(AALC)	JEFF(B)	**Test**

Weight:	162.5 tons gross
Length:	80 feet (24.4 m) hullborne
	86¾ feet (26.4 m) on air cushion
Beam:	43 feet (13.1 m) hullborne
	47 feet (14.3 m) on air cushion
Propulsion:	6 gas turbines (Avco Lycoming); 16,800 shp; 2 aircraft-type propellers in shrouds
Lift:	4 horizontal fans (interconnected to propulsion engines)
Speed:	approx. 50 knots
Manning:	6 (enlisted)
Guns:	none

The JEFF(B) is a competitive prototype with the JEFF(A) landing craft. This craft was developed and built by Bell Aerosystems at the former National Aeronautics and Space Administration's facility in Michoud, La., and delivered in 1977.

Design: The craft has bow and stern ramps, 1,738 square feet of open cargo area, and a cargo capacity of about 120,000 pounds. The JEFF(B) is all-aluminum construction. Unlike the JEFF(A), this craft does not have separate lift engines. No SCB number is assigned to this craft.

Operational: The JEFF(A) and JEFF(B) are based at Panama City, Fla.

JEFF(B) unloading an M60 tank (1979, Bell Aerospace Textron)

JEFF(A) on shore (1979, U.S. Navy)

The JEFF(B), in foreground, and JEFF(A) prototype air cushion landing craft during trials off Panama City, Florida. There is an M60 tank in the JEFF(B), which was selected as the design for the production LCAC series. (1979, Bell Aerospace Textron)

1 AMPHIBIOUS ASSAULT LANDING CRAFT: "JEFF(A)"

Number	Name	Status
(AALC)	JEFF(A)	**Test**

Weight:	85.8 tons empty
	186.4 tons gross
Length:	97 feet (29.6 m) hullborne
	99⅙ feet (30.2 m) on air cushion
Beam:	44 feet (13.4 m) hullborne
	48 feet (14.6 m) on air cushion
Propulsion:	4 gas turbines (Avco Lycoming); 11,200 shp; 4 aircraft-type propellers in shrouds
Lift:	2 gas turbines (Avco Lycoming); 5,600 shp; 8 horizontal fans
Speed:	approx. 50 knots
Manning:	6 (enlisted)
Guns	none

The JEFF(A) is one of two competitive prototypes of Amphibious Assault Landing Craft (AALC) constructed for Navy-Marine Corps evaluation. The JEFF(A) design was developed by the Aerojet-General Corporation, built by Todd Shipyards, Seattle, Wash., and delivered in 1977.

Design: The all-aluminum craft has bow and stern ramps, 1,850 square feet of open cargo area, and can carry 120,000 pounds of cargo or vehicles. No SCB number is assigned.

52 UTILITY LANDING CRAFT: "LCU 1610" CLASS

Number	Number	Number	Number
LCU 1616	LCU 1634	LCU 1654	LCU 1667
LCU 1617	LCU 1635	LCU 1655	LCU 1668
LCU 1619	LCU 1641	LCU 1656	LCU 1669
LCU 1621	LCU 1643	LCU 1657	LCU 1670
LCU 1623	LCU 1644	LCU 1658	LCU 1671
LCU 1624	LCU 1645	LCU 1659	LCU 1672
LCU 1627	LCU 1646	LCU 1660	LCU 1673
LCU 1628	LCU 1648	LCU 1661	LCU 1674
LCU 1629	LCU 1649	LCU 1662	LCU 1675
LCU 1630	LCU 1650	LCU 1663	LCU 1676
LCU 1631	LCU 1651	LCU 1664	LCU 1677
LCU 1632	LCU 1652	LCU 1665	LCU 1678
LCU 1633	LCU 1653	LCU 1666	LCU 1679

Displacement:	170 tons light
	390 tons full load
Length:	134¾ feet (41.1 m) oa
Beam:	29¾ feet (9.1 m)
Draft:	6 feet (1.8 m)
Propulsion:	geared diesels (Detroit); 2,000 bhp; 2 shafts, except LCU 1621— see notes
Speed:	11 knots
Range:	1,200 n.miles at 8 knots with payload
Manning:	6 (enlisted)
Troops:	8
Guns:	2 20-mm AA or 2 .50-cal MG (2 single)

The LCU 1645 in combat configuration during an amphibious exercise. The craft is carrying two M60 tanks and other gear; her mast is lowered (for entering ship docking wells); a navigation radar pod is mounted above the bridge. (1982, U.S. Navy)

ASDV 2 with built up structure amidships (1983, Giorgio Arra)

The LCU 1641 (1984, Giorgio Arra)

The LCU 1652 off Coronado, Calif., with awning spread over her bridge and mast raised. Note the stern gate. (1982, U.S. Navy)

ASDV 3 (1983, Giorgio Arra)

These are improved LCUs with 15 units (LCU 1610–1624) completed in 1960 and the remainder from 1967 to 1976. Several small shipyards constructed these craft.

The LCU 1641 serves as a training minelayer for Mine Division 125 at Charleston.

Class: This class originally consisted of hull numbers LCU 1610–1624 and 1627–1680. The LCU 1637 was a prototype all-aluminum craft, otherwise identical to the LCU 1610 class; no additional aluminum units were built.

Four additional LCUs of this class have been converted to Auxiliary Swimmer Delivery Vehicles (ASDV) and are operated by Small Boat Units to support diving operations. The craft are fitted with decompression chambers and have 13-man crews.

Several units have been transferred to other navies, reclassified, or stricken; others serve as a test support craft (IX), ferry boats (YFB), and harbor utility craft (YFU) and are described in Chapter 25.

Design: The LCU 1610–1624 were SCB No. 149; the LCU 1627 and later units were SCB No. 149B (new series SCB No. 406).

These LCUs have a "drive-through" configuration with bow and stern ramps, and a small, starboard-side island structure housing controls and accommodations. Previous LCU/LCT-type landing craft had a small deck structure aft. They are welded-steel construction; the mast folds down for entering well decks of amphibious ships.

Cargo capacity is two medium tanks or up to about 190 tons of cargo or, for short distances, 350 troops.

Engineering: The LCU 1621 has vertical shafts fitted with vertical axis, cyclodial six-bladed propellers. All other units have Kort-nozzle propellers.

Guns: Weapons are not normally fitted in these craft.

LCM-8 approaching beach (1982, U.S. Navy)

LCM-8 assigned to Assault Craft Unit 2 (1982, Giorgio Arra)

MECHANIZED LANDING CRAFT: LCM-8 MOD 1 TYPE

Weight:	62.65 tons light
	130.25 tons full load
Length:	73⁷/₁₂ feet (22.4 m) oa
Beam:	21¹/₁₂ feet (6.4 m)
Draft	5⅙ feet (1.6 m)
Propulsion:	diesels (Detroit); 1,300 bhp; 2 shafts
Speed:	9 knots
Range:	190 n.miles at 9 knots
Manning:	5 (enlisted)
Guns	none

Design: These are welded-steel landing craft, capable of carrying one M60 tank or 60 tons of cargo or, for short distances, 200 troops.
Engineering: Some units have been fitted with Kort nozzles.

MECHANIZED LANDING CRAFT: LCM-8 MOD 2 TYPE

Weight:	36.5 tons light
	106.75 tons full load
Length:	74¹/₁₂ feet (22.6 m) oa
Beam:	21¹/₁₂ feet (6.4 m)
Draft:	4½ feet (1.4 m)
Propulsion:	diesels (Detroit); 1,300 bhp; 2 shafts
Speed:	12 knots
Range:	
Manning:	5 (enlisted)
Guns:	none

The LCM-8 Mod 2 is an aluminum version of the steel-hulled LCM-8 developed for use with the CHARLESTON (LKA 113)-class amphibious cargo ships.
Design: These craft are constructed of welded aluminum. They can carry one M60 tank or 65 tons of cargo.
Engineering: Some units have been refitted with Kort nozzles.

MECHANIZED LANDING CRAFT: LCM-6 MOD 2 TYPE

Weight:	26.7 tons light
	62.35 tons full load
Length:	56 feet (17.1 m) oa
Beam:	14⅓ feet (4.4 m)
Draft:	3⅚ feet (1.2 m)
Propulsion:	diesels (Gray Marine); 450 bhp; 2 shafts
Speed:	10 knots
Range:	130 n.miles at 9 knots
Manning:	5 (enlisted)
Guns:	none

Numerous craft of this type were converted to riverine combat craft during the Vietnam War.
Design: Welded steel construction. They can carry 34 tons of cargo or, for short distances, 120 troops.

LANDING CRAFT VEHICLE AND PERSONNEL (LCVP)

Weight	13.5 tons full load
Length:	35¾ feet (12.1 m) oa
Beam:	10½ feet (3.2 m)
Draft:	3½ feet (1.1 m)
Propulsion:	diesel; 325 bhp; 1 shaft
Speed:	9 knots
Range:	110 n.miles at 8 knots
Manning:	2 or 3 (enlisted)
Guns:	none

These small landing craft can be carried by all U.S. amphibious ships.
Design: These craft are built of wood or fiberglass-reinforced plastic. They can carry light vehicles or four tons of cargo or 36 troops.

LCM-6 from the PENSACOLA (LSD 38) (1983, Giorgio Arra)

LCM-6 (1983, Giorgio Arra)

LCVP from BLUE RIDGE (LCC 19) (1977, Giorgio Arra)

21 Landing Vehicles

Tracked landing vehicles are used by the Marine Corps for assault landings and for subsequent operations ashore. The Marines currently operate some 985 amphibian tractors or "amtracs" of the LVT-7 series—the LVTP-7 troop carrier, the LVTC-7 command and control vehicle, and the LVTR-7 recovery vehicle. Although these vehicles can be used on land, they lack the heavier armor common to most Armored Personnel Carriers (APC).

The Marine Corps has three active amphibian tractor battalions: the 3rd Amphibian Tractor Battalion at Camp Pendleton, Calif., to support the 1st Marine Division; the 2nd Amphibian Tractor Battalion at Camp Lejeune, N.C., to support the 2nd Marine Division; and the 1st Tracked Vehicle Battalion on Okinawa, to support the 3rd Marine Division.

The 2nd and 3rd battalions are each assigned 187 LVTP-7s, 15 LVTC-7s, and 6 LVTR-7s, with the capability of simultaneously lifting the assault elements of a reinforced regiment. The 1st Tracked Vehicle Battalion is assigned 96 LVTP-7s, 8 LVTC-7s, and 3 LVTR-7s. (The last unit also has 34 M60 tanks and 3 tank recovery vehicles; other Marine tanks are in separate battalions.)

In addition, 327 LVTP-7A1 vehicles are also required for forward deployment aboard maritime prepositioning ships to support the Rapid Deployment Force. There will be 109 amphibian tractors for each of three sets of weapons and equipment forward deployed for Marine brigades plus several specialized vehicles.

The service life of the present LVT-7 "family" of vehicles is expected to end in the mid-1980s. The Marines have embarked on a Service Life Extension Program (SLEP) for existing vehicles pending the introduction of a follow-on amtrac in the mid-1990s. Because of the delays in developing the follow-on LVT(X), the fiscal 1982 budget provided 73 new LVTP-7A1 vehicles at a cost of $68.7 million.

The LVT(X) will provide only marginal capability improvements over the existing LVT-7 series while carrying fewer troops.

The Marine Corps initially planned to replace the LVT-7A1 vehicles with a higher-speed Landing Vehicle Assault (LVA). The LVA was to have had a water speed of 25 to 40 mph and was to have carried 18 troops. The LVA program was cancelled in January 1979 because the vehicle was judged to be too large, too difficult to maintain, and too expensive to procure.

Armament: Tests have been conducted of the LVTP-7 series fitted with the .50-cal M2 heavy machine gun, 40-mm cannon, and the 40-mm Mk 19 machine gun. An adapter for firing the TOW and Dragon anti-tank missiles from amtracs is being developed.

ADVANCED TRACKED LANDING VEHICLE: LVT(X) TYPE

The Marine Corps is planning a follow-on tracked landing vehicle as successor to the LVT-7 series. Currently designated LVT(X), the new amphibious tractor has a planned IOC of 1994. It will be used for combat ashore as well as for ship-to-shore movement. A troop capacity of 17 is used for planning purposes. The water speed of the LVT(X) is envisioned to be between 9 and 12 mph. Armament for the LVT(X) will probably include a 25-mm rapid-fire cannon.

In service the LVT(X) will probably be designated LVT-8. In addition to the personnel vehicle (LVTP), command and control (LVTC), assault gun (LVTAG), engineer (LVTE), and recovery (LVTR) variants are also being developed.

The current plan is to procure 1,698 vehicles for active and reserve units.

LVTP-7 amphibian tractors come ashore on San Clemente Island, Calif., during exercise Kernel Egress. Tank landing ships stand offshore—much closer than they could be during an opposed landing. (1982, U.S. Navy, James Wallace)

TRACKED LANDING VEHICLES, PERSONNEL: LVTP-7 SERIES

Weight:	38,450 pounds empty
	50,350 pounds loaded
Length:	26 feet (7.9 m) oa
Width:	10¾ feet (3.3 m)
Height	10¼ feet (3.1 m)
Draft:	5⅔ feet (1.7 m)
Propulsion:	turbo-supercharged diesel (Detroit); 400 hp;
	tracked running gear on land
	2 waterjets in water (3,025 lbst each)
Speed	40 mph maximum, 20-30 mph cruise on land
	8.4 mph maximum, 8 mph cruise in water
Range	300 miles at 25 mph on land
	approx. 55 miles at 8 mph in water
Crew:	3
Troops:	25
Guns:	1 .50-cal MG M85

The LVTP-7 is a full-tracked, amphibious vehicle, providing an over-the-beach capability for landing troops and material through heavy surf. It is the world's only vehicle capable of operating in rough seas and plunging surf (up to ten feet high).

These vehicles were designed and manufactured by the Ordnance Division of FMC Corporation, San Jose, Calif. The LVTP-7 is also used by the marine forces of Italy, Spain, and Venezuela.

An LVTP-7 in Arctic camouflage ashore in Norway during NATO exercise Alloy Express. Snowshoes, camouflage nets, and other gear is tied atop the vehicle. (1982, U.S. Marine Corps, SGT B. Walsh)

Armament: The LVTP-7 was designed to mount a 20-mm cannon coaxially with a 7.62-mm machine gun; because of development problems, however, the cannon was deleted. The .50-cal MG is in a 360°-powered turret and has 1,000 rounds of ammunition.

A mine clearance kit can be fitted for clearing beach obstacles. This consists of a rack launcher firing three 350-foot-long explosive line charges. Detonation is controlled by wire from within the vehicle.

Class: The prototypes for the LVTP-7 design were 15 LVTPX-12 vehicles delivered to the Marines in 1967–1968. These were followed by a production run of 965 LVTP-7s delivered from 1970 to 1974 plus the specialized LVTC and LVTR vehicles described below. In addition, one LVTE-7 prototype of an assault engineer/mine clearance vehicle was delivered in 1970, but none were series produced.

The RDF/MPS program calls for procurement of 294 new LVTP-7A1 vehicles plus 29 of the LVTC-7A1 and 10 LVTR-7A1 vehicles. These will be added to existing vehicles to provide the required number for forward deployment.

Design: The LVTP-7 was designed to replace the LVTP-5 series amtracs and offered increased land and water speeds, more range, with less vehicle weight. In lieu of troops, an LVTP-7 can carry 10,000 pounds of cargo. The LVTP-7 has a rear door and ramp for loading/unloading troops and cargo; it can turn 360° within its own length on land or in water.

Modernization: The SLEP modernization program will provide a Cummins VT400 engine in place of the original liquid-cooled Detroit diesel 8V53T (same horsepower), providing an improved power train; automatic fire detection and suppression system; night-vision driving device; position locating and reporting system; secure voice radio system; smoke generator; improved ventilation; and maintenance diagnostics system.

Proposals to provide a more capable gun were discarded.

The modernized vehicles are designated LVTP-7A1; the first updated vehicles were delivered to the Marine Corps on 24 October 1983. A total of 853 LVTPs, 77 LVTCs, and 54 LVTRs are to be modernized.

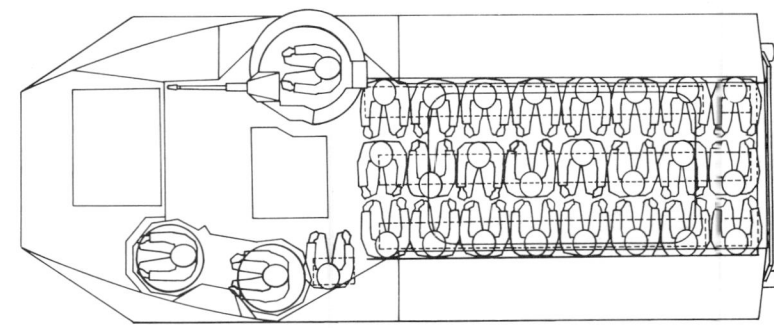

LVTP-7 Configuration (FMC)

LVTP-7 (1980, U.S. Marine Corps)

LVTP-7 (U.S. Marine Corps)

LVTR-7 (U.S. Marine Corps)

An LVTP-7A1 climbs out of the surf. (FMC)

An LVTR-7A1 with crane raised; note towing winch above rear door. (FMC)

TRACKED LANDING VEHICLES, COMMAND: LVTC-7 SERIES

Weight:	40,187 pounds empty
	44,111 pounds loaded
Crew:	12 (3 vehicle crew, 5 radiomen, 4 unit commander and staff)
Troops:	none
Guns:	1 7.62-mm MG M60D

Except as indicated above, the LVTC-7 characteristics are similar to those of the LVTP-7 series. Eighty-five of these vehicles were originally procured for use as command vehicles in amphibious landings.

These vehicles are fitted with radios, crypto equipment, and telephones. Seventy-seven of the original vehicles are being modernized to the LVTC-7A1 configuration.

TRACKED LANDING VEHICLES, RECOVERY: LVTR-7 SERIES

Weight:	47,304 pounds empty
	49,853 pounds loaded
Crew:	5 (3 vehicle crew, 2 mechanics)
Troops:	none
Guns:	1 7.62-mm MG M60D

Except as indicated above, the LVTR-7 characteristics are similar to the LVTP-7 series. Sixty of these vehicles were procured for the recovery of damaged amtracs during amphibious landings.

They are fitted with a 6,000-pound-capacity telescoping boom-type crane and 30,000-pound pull winch, plus maintenance equipment. Fifty-four vehicles are being modernized; they are redesignated LVTR-7A1.

POST-WORLD WAR II AMPHIBIOUS TRACTORS

The U.S. Marine Corps procured 18,620 "amtracs" of various LVT/LVTA models during World War II. The first postwar LVT design produced for the Marine Corps was the LVTP-5 troop carrier and LVTH-6 mounting a 105-mm howitzer; a total of 1,332 of these vehicles were manufactured between 1951 and 1957.

During the late 1970s, the term *amphibian* tractors was substituted for the previous amphibious tractors.

22   Patrol Ships and Craft

The U.S. Navy currently has six hydrofoil missile craft plus a large number of inshore and special warfare craft, with many of the latter operated by the Naval Reserve Force. The U.S. Navy has historically shown little interest in small combatants in peacetime, in part because of the emphasis on long-range, blue water operations that support the Navy's primary missions, and because of the belief that the tactics and craft needed for coastal and inshore operations can be rapidly developed in wartime.

The six hydrofoil missile craft are the survivors of a program of at least 30 units envisioned in the early 1970s by the Chief of Naval Operations, Admiral Zumwalt. As noted below, even these six units were built as a result of congressional pressure.

The Navy has evaluated several advanced-technology combat craft, with several being used in the Vietnam War. These craft have been discarded or reclassified as service craft (see Appendix C). All of the Asheville-class patrol gunboats and most of the various fast patrol boats produced in the 1960s have been discarded.

During the Vietnam War the lack of a capability in small combatant craft forced the Navy to procure Norwegian-built fast patrol boats and to adopt commercial designs for naval use. Subsequently, the Navy has sought to keep abreast of small craft design and during 1980–1982 U.S. yards delivered a series of missile craft (PCG/PGG types) to Saudi Arabia as well as smaller patrol/combat craft to several other navies.

The six PHMs form Patrol Combat Missile Hydrofoil Squadron 2, based at NAS Key West, Fla. The last of the six craft arrived at Key West in mid-1983. Most of the smaller combat craft are assigned to Special Boat Units (SBU) under Special Boat Squadron 1 at Naval Amphibious Base Coronado (San Diego), Calif., and Special Boat Squadron 2 at Naval Amphibious Base Little Creek (Norfolk), Va. Under these squadrons are two active and four NRF boat units.

The active SBU-12 at Coronado and SBU-20 at Little Creek are oriented toward coastal operations. SBU-12 has four PB Mk III, 12 Seafox, two converted LCUs, and several lesser craft; a detachment at Subic Bay in the Philippines has another pair of PB Mk IIIs and a pair of Seafox craft. SBU-20 has nine PB Mk IIIs and 12 Seafox craft in addition to smaller craft, with a PB Mk III and Seafox at Roosevelt Roads, Puerto Rico. These SBUs regularly deploy detachments overseas.

The reserve SBU-11, 13, 22, and 24 operate mostly riverine craft— PCF Swift boats, PBRs, and mini-ATCs as well as the Seafox craft.

The SBUs provide a coastal and inshore warfare capability, including the support of clandestine operations, delivery and recovery of SEAL teams,[1] and gunfire and spotter support.

Classification: The smaller, unnamed patrol boats and craft are individually designated by their hull length, hull type, calendar year of construction, and consecutive hull of that type built during the year. Thus, 65PB776 indicates the sixth 65-foot PB-type craft built in 1977. The first two letters in this scheme are generally used in the designation except RP is used for PBRs and NS for PCFs.

---

[1] Sea Air Land (SEAL) teams are the Navy's equivalent of the Army's Special Forces (Green Berets).

The U.S. Navy's 6 PEGASUS-class hydrofoil missile craft maneuver off their base at Key West, Fla. The U.S. Navy has historically shown little interest in small combatants in peacetime, and most of the U.S. Navy's capability in this area is in the Naval Reserve Force. (1983, U.S. Navy, Lt. R. W. Coldiron)

6 PATROL COMBATANTS—MISSILE (HYDROFOIL): "PEGASUS" CLASS

Number	Name	FY	Builder	Laid down	Launched	Commissioned	Status
PHM 1	PEGASUS	73	Boeing Marine Systems, Seattle, Wash.	10 May 1973	9 Nov 1974	9 July 1977	AA
PHM 2	HERCULES	76	Boeing Marine Systems, Seattle, Wash.	12 Sep 1980	13 Apr 1982	15 Jan 1983	AA
PHM 3	TAURUS	75	Boeing Marine Systems, Seattle, Wash.	30 Jan 1979	8 May 1981	10 Oct 1981	AA
PHM 4	AQUILA	75	Boeing Marine Systems, Seattle, Wash.	10 July 1979	16 Sep 1981	19 Dec 1981	AA
PHM 5	ARIES	75	Boeing Marine Systems, Seattle, Wash.	7 Jan 1980	5 Nov 1981	11 Sep 1982	AA
PHM 6	GEMINI	75	Boeing Marine Systems, Seattle, Wash.	13 May 1980	17 Feb 1982	13 Nov 1982	AA

Displacement:	198 tons light
	242 tons full load
Length:	147⅙ feet (44.9 m) oa foils retracted
	131½ feet (40.1 m) oa foils extended
Beam:	28⅙ feet (8.6 m)
Draft:	6⅙ feet (1.9 m) foils retracted
	23⅙ feet (7.1 m) foils extended
Propulsion:	2 diesels (Mercedes-Benz); 1,636 bhp; 2 waterjets hullborne
	1 gas turbine (General Electric); 16,767 shp; 1 waterjet foilborne
Speed:	12 knots hullborne
	40+ knots foilborne
Range:	600+ n.miles at 40+ knots foilborne
	1,225 n.miles at 38 knots foilborne
Manning:	23 (4 officers + 19 enlisted)
Missiles:	8 Harpoon SSM (2 quad cannisters Mk 141)
Guns:	1 76-mm 62-cal AA Mk 75
ASW weapons:	none
Radars:	(see Fire Control)
Sonars:	none
Fire control:	1 Mk 92 weapon FCS except Mk 94 in PHM 1

These are high speed, heavily armed missile craft, intended to conduct sea control operations in restricted seas. All are based at Key West, Fla. Earlier plans to deploy the PHMs to the Mediterranean, supported by a specially configured LST, have been discarded.

At one time the HERCULES was to have been completed without armament because of fiscal problems; subsequently, Congress funded a full weapons suite for the craft.

The HERCULES was originally authorized in fiscal 1973 and laid down on 30 May 1974; however, all work on her halted later that year to fund cost increases of the PEGASUS. The ship was reauthorized in fiscal 1976 and begun a second time in 1980. She was originally placed in commission on 15 January 1983 upon completion in Seattle; she was formally commissioned a second time in ceremonies upon her arrival at Key West on 12 March 1983.

Class: This design was one of the new warship types initiated by Admiral Zumwalt when Chief of Naval Operations (1970–1974). A class of at least 30 missile craft of this type were planned. When Zumwalt left office the Navy reduced the program to only the prototype; however, congressional pressure led to the first "flight" of six ships, already funded, being completed.

Design: SCB No. 602. In November 1972 the governments of West Germany, Italy, and the United States signed a memorandum of understanding in which the three nations agreed to share the development costs of the PHM with procurement planned for all three navies. After the reduction of the planned U.S. procurement to one (later six) craft, the other nations withdrew from the program. The foreign units were to be similar, with the addition of light guns on the bridge structure.

The PHM design provides for fully submerged canard foils, with approximately 32 percent of the dynamic lift provided by the single bow foil and 68 percent by the double-strut after foil. The foils retract forward (into a bow recess) and rearward, respectively. Steep flaps are fitted to the training edges of the bow and after foils to provide control and lift augmentation.

The superstructure is all aluminum.

Engineering: Foilborne propulsion consists of a single waterjet driven through reduction gears from an LM 2500 gas turbine engine. The foil-mounted propulsor is capable of pumping 141,000 gallons per minute. Foilborne speeds exceeding 40 knots are possible in 8- to 13-foot seas. When hullborne the PHM is propelled by twin waterjets powered by two MTU V-8 diesel engines. Each of these waterjets can pump 30,000 gallons per minute.

A through-bow thruster is provided for low-speed maneuvering.

Guns: No secondary gun battery is provided. The PHM design provides for two 20-mm Mk 20 single gun mounts to be fitted abaft the mast.

Manning: These craft are normally commanded by lieutenant commanders. The other officers are the executive, combat systems, and engineer.

Missiles: The original PHM design provided for two single Harpoon tubes fitted aft; the design was revised to provide two quad cannisters on the fantail.

Names: The PHM 1 was originally named DELPHINUS; she was renamed PEGASUS on 26 April 1974.

TAURUS at high speed on trials (1981, Boeing Marine Systems)

The ⁻AURUS and AQUILA (background) and their four sister ships are the Navy's most potent warships on the basis of firepower per displacement ton. Although they lack the range, endurance, and versatility of larger warships, they can be highly effective in certain situations. (U.S. Navy)

PEGASUS with foils retracted (1979, Giorgio Arra)

PEGASUS with foils retracted (1979, Giorgio Arra)

1 SUBMARINE CHASER (HYDROFOIL): "HIGH POINT"

Number	Name	FY	Builder	Laid down	Launched	Commissioned	Status
PCH 1	HIGH POINT	60	Boeing/J.M. Martinac Shipbuilding, Seattle, Wash.	27 Feb 1961	17 Aug 1962	15 Aug 1963	**Test**

Displacement:	110 tons full load
Length:	115 feet (35.07 m) oa
Beam:	31 feet (9.45 m)
Draft:	6 feet (1.8 m) foils retracted
	17 feet (5.2 m) foils extended
Propulsion:	1 diesel (Packard); 600 bhp; 1 shaft hullborne
	2 gas turbines (Bristol Siddeley Marine Proteus); 6,200 shp; 2 shafts foilborne
Speed:	12 knots hullborne
	48 knots foilborne
Range:	2,000 n.miles at 12 knots
	500 n.miles at 45 knots
Manning:	13 (1 officer + 12 enlisted)
Missiles:	none
Guns:	removed
ASW weapons:	removed
Radars:	
Sonars:	VDS
Fire control:	none

The HIGH POINT was the U.S. Navy's first operational hydrofoil. She was built to evaluate structural and hydrodynamic features of hydrofoils, as well as to develop ASW concepts for hydrofoils.

The craft was transferred to the Coast Guard in 1975 for evaluation by that service (designated WMEH 1); subsequently returned to the Navy for continued test and evaluation work. She was not stricken in September 1978 as planned because Congress provided funds for her continued use. The craft is now engaged in a joint U.S.-Canadian project of high-speed towed arrays (HYTOW).

Builders: The HIGH POINT was designed and built by the Boeing Airplane Company and the Martinac firm.

Design: SCB No. 202. The craft has an all-welded aluminum hull and superstructure. She was the first large craft to have fully submerged foils. The canard foil arrangement provides for most of the ship's weight to be carried by the large after foil, which is supported by two 18⅝-foot struts that can partially retract into the after deck housings. The forward foil is used to steer the craft. An autopilot activated by an electronic wave height sensor controls rolls and pitch.

Guns: The single 40-mm gun previously mounted forward has been removed. Her original design had provided for a twin .50-cal MG forward.

Missiles: During 1973–1974 the HIGH POINT was employed in tests of the Harpoon SSM in support of the PHM program.

Propulsion: Power from the gas turbines is transmitted via right-angle drive mechanisms down the after foil struts to twin propeller pods. Each pod is fitted with two propellers, one forward and one aft.

Sonar: The HIGH POINT has been used extensively for testing Variable Depth Sonars (VDS) from high-speed craft.

Torpedoes: As built, four 12.75-inch ASW torpedo tubes were installed for firing Mk 44 torpedoes.

The hydrofoil patrol craft HIGH POINT undergoing overhaul at the Puget Sound Naval Shipyard. (1983, W. Donko)

HIGH POINT (1983, W. Donko)

The HIGH POINT while serving as test ship for high-speed launching of Harpoon missiles. (1973, McDonnell Douglas)

PATROL GUNBOATS: "ASHEVILLE" CLASS

Fourteen of the 17 ASHEVILLE-class patrol gunboats have been stricken, loaned to other U.S. government or state agencies, or transferred to other nations; three other ships, the CHEHALIS (PG 94), GRAND RAPIDS (PG 98), and DOUGLAS (PG 100), have been stripped of armament and are employed as research craft (see Chapter 25).

These ships were originally classified as motor gunboats (PGM); changed to patrol combatants (PG) on 1 April 1967. (The post–World-War-II-built PGM 33–83, 91, and 102–124 were gunboats built in the United States or overseas from 1955 onwards specifically for transfer to foreign navies; none served in the U.S. Navy.)

The last two U.S. Navy units in service as combat craft, the TACOMA and WELCH, were used in the late 1970s to train Saudi Arabian naval personnel at Norfolk, Va.; both were decommissioned and laid up in reserve on 30 September 1981 pending transfer to Colombia. See the 12th edition of *Ships and Aircraft* for details and characteristics.

PG 84	ASHEVILLE	to Massachusetts Maritime Academy 15 Dec 1976
PG 85	GALLUP	laid up/to be stricken
PG 86	ANTELOPE	to Environmental Protection Agency Jan 1978
PG 87	READY	to Maritime Academy Mar 1978
PG 88	CROCKETT	to Environmental Protection Agency Apr 1977
PG 89	MARATHON	to Massachusetts Maritime Academy Apr 1977
PG 90	CANON	laid up/to be stricken
PG 92	TACOMA	transferred to Colombia 6 May 1983
PG 93	WELCH	transferred to Colombia 6 May 1983
PG 95	DEFIANCE	transferred to Turkey June 1973
PG 96	BENICA	transferred to South Korea Oct 1971
PG 97	SURPRISE	transferred to Turkey Feb 1973
PG 99	BEACON	stricken 1 Apr 1977—laid up
PG 101	GREEN BAY	stricken 1 Apr 1977—laid up

TRANSPORTABLE FAST ATTACK CRAFT

The transportable fast attack craft (TFAC) effort is developing a small combat craft that can be easily transported by amphibious ships or maritime pre-positioning ships.

(19) SPECIAL WARFARE CRAFT—MEDIUM: SEA VIKING CLASS

Number	FY
PBM 1	84
(3 ships)	86
(6 ships)	87
(6 ships)	88
(3 ships)	89

Builders:	RMI, San Diego, Calif.
Displacement:	
Length:	approx. 36 feet (11.0 m) oa
Beam:	
Draft:	
Propulsion:	
Speed:	40 + knots
Range:	
Manning:	
Missiles:	Stinger surface-to-air launcher
Guns:	2 25-mm Bushmaster (2 single)
	2 40-mm machine guns Mk 19 (2 single)
ASW weapons:	none
Radar:	SPS-64(V)9 surface search

These ships are designated as both special warfare craft—medium (SWCM) and multi-mission patrol boats (PBM), with the commercial name Sea Viking also being used. The craft are intended for both swimmer delivery and offshore patrol. The former role, however, requires a high degree of stealth and the Sea Viking design is limited in this regard.

The lead craft was provided in the fiscal 1984 shipbuilding program with $15 million allocated for construction; estimated cost of 19 units was $248 million. The status of future units was uncertain when this edition went to press. Lead ship IOC is planned for 1986.

Design: These ships have a Surface Effects Ship (SES) design and are intended to be carried to forward areas in the docking wells of amphibious ships. A single Swimmer Delivery Vehicle (SDV) or several rubber raiding craft can be carried.

17 PATROL BOATS: PB MK III TYPE

Builders:	Marinette Marine, Wisc.
	Peterson Builders, Sturgeon Bay, Wisc.
Displacement:	28.6 tons light
	37.5 tons full load
Length:	64¹¹/₁₂ feet (19.8 m) oa
Beam:	18¹/₁₂ feet (5.5 m)
Draft:	5⅚ feet (1.8 m)
Propulsion:	3 diesels (General Motors); 1,800 bhp; 3 shafts
Speed:	26 knots
Range:	450 n.miles at full speed
	2,000 n.miles at slow speeds
Manning:	5 (1 officer + 4 enlisted) minimum
Missiles:	(see notes)
Guns:	1 40-mm AA Mk 3
	4 .50-cal MG (4 single)
ASW weapons:	(see notes)
Radars:	navigation

The PB Mk III was developed as a multi-mission inshore warfare craft for U.S. and foreign naval service. The U.S. craft are operated by the active SBUs.

Classification: These craft are also designated as Special Warfare Craft, Medium (SWCM). The Naval Sea Systems Command designates these craft as PB Mk 3; however, they are listed as Mk III in the Fleet.

Design: The Mk III is a modified commercial craft used to support offshore drilling platforms in the Gulf of Mexico. These craft are of all-aluminum construction with their pilot house offset to starboard to provide maximum deck space for weapons and equipment. The craft has a low radar cross-section and quiet engines for clandestine operations. Mission duration is up to five days.

Guns: These craft generally are fitted with an automatic 40-mm gun forward and up to four .50-cal machine guns on pintle mountings. There are also hard points on the deck for fitting larger guns as well as missiles. They can also be rigged to carry mines, torpedoes, or minesweeping gear.

One unit was used to evaluate the 25-mm Bushmaster cannon.

Missiles: The PB III was used to evaluate the Norwegian-developed Penguin SSM with four stowage/launcher containers being fitted on the after portion of the deck. See Chapter 30 for missile data.

2 PATROL BOATS: PB MK I TYPE

Builders:	Sewart Seacraft, Berwick, La.
Displacement:	26.9 tons light
	36.3 tons full load
Length:	65 feet (19.8 m) oa
Beam:	16 feet (4.9 m)
Draft:	4⅚ feet (1.5 m)
Propulsion:	diesels (Detroit); 1,635 bhp; 3 shafts
Speed:	26 knots
Range:	
Manning:	
Missiles:	none
Guns:	6 20-mm or .50-cal MG (1 twin; 4 single)
ASW weapons:	none
Radars:	navigation

These are prototype patrol boats developed as replacements for the "Swift" PCFs. They were completed in 1972 and delivered to the Navy in 1973 for evaluation. They were subsequently transferred to the NRF and are operated by SBU-24 at Little Creek.

Design: These craft are based on a commercial offshore support craft. They differ from the Mk III in size and in having a center-line superstructure.

APPROX. 40 SPECIAL WARFARE CRAFT—LIGHT: SEAFOX TYPE

Displacement:	9.6 tons light
	11.8 tons full load
Length:	36 feet (10.8 m) oa
Beam:	9⅚ feet (3.0 m)
Draft:	2¾ feet (0.84 m)
Propulsion:	2 diesels; 900 bhp; 2 shafts
Speed:	32 knots
Range:	
Manning:	3
Missiles:	none
Guns:	(see notes)
ASW weapons:	none
Radars:	navigation

These are small, high-speed craft intended primarily to support SEAL operations. They were delivered from 1981 onward by Uniflite Inc., Bellingham, Wash. They are formally designated Special Warfare Craft, Light (SWCL). Four weapon stations are provided.

PB Mk III armed with machine guns and 40-mm grenade launcher. Note lifting padeyes forward and aft; bridge structure offset to starboard. (1982, Giorgio Arra)

PB Mk III fitted with 40-mm automatic cannon forward and machine guns. (1983, Giorgio Arra)

PB Mk III with machine guns forward, 40-mm grenade launcher amidships, and Norwegian-produced Penguin SSM cannister aft. (1982, Giorgio Arra)

PB Mk I armed with machine guns; a two-MG mounting is installed above the bridge. (U.S. Navy)

PB Mk I without armament installed. (1983, Giorgio Arra)

A Seafox at high speed. The twin-engine, fiberglass-hull craft was developed specifically for use by the Navy's Special Warfare Forces. A navigation radar and other electronics are fitted. (1980, U.S. Navy)

2 PATROL CRAFT—FAST: SWIFT TYPE

Displacement:	17.5 tons light
	22.2 tons full load
Length:	51$^{5}/_{12}$ feet (15.7 m)
Beam:	14$^{11}/_{12}$ feet (4.6 m)
Draft:	3½ feet (1.1 m)
Propulsion:	2 diesels (General Motors); 960 bhp; 2 shafts
Speed:	28 knots
Range:	350 n.miles at 28 knots
Manning:	6 (1 officer + 5 enlisted)
Missiles:	none
Guns:	1 81-mm mortar Mk 2/1 .50-cal MG M2
	2 .50-cal MG (1 twin)
ASW weapons:	none
Radars:	navigation

These are PCFs, the survivors of a well-known series of inshore patrol craft. Both are assigned to SBU-11.

Class: Approximately 125 of these craft were built from 1965 onward. Most were used by the U.S. Navy in Vietnam with 104 having been transferred to South Vietnam in 1968–1970. Others were built for South Korea, the Philippines, and Thailand. Variations used by the U.S. Navy were a torpedo weapons recovery (TWR) craft and utility/rescue craft.

Design: These are all-metal craft adopted from an oil rig crew boat used to support offshore drilling rigs in the Gulf of Mexico. Mission endurance is up to five days.

Guns: A twin machine gun mount is fitted atop the bridge structure and an over/under mounting is fitted aft.

PCF Mk II with canvas cover over the after machine gun/81-mm mortar; the PCF Mk I had larger windows on the after section of the deckhouse. (1968, U.S. Navy)

APPROX. 25 RIVER PATROL BOATS: PBR MK 2 TYPE

Displacement:	6.8 tons light
	8.1 tons full load
Length:	32 feet (9.75 m) oa
Beam:	11⅔ feet (3.6 m)
Draft:	2⁷/₁₂ feet (0.8 m)
Propulsion:	2 diesels (General Motors); 430 bhp; waterjets
Speed:	25+ knots
Range:	
Manning:	4 or 5 (enlisted)
Missiles:	none
Guns:	1 60-mm mortar Mk 4 in some units
	1 40-mm machine gun Mk 19
	3 .50-cal MG (1 twin, 1 single)
ASW weapons:	none
Radars:	navigation

These heavily armed craft were developed for riverine warfare in Vietnam. All U.S. survivors are operated by the NRF.

Class: More than 500 PBRs were built in 1965–1973, with most transferred to South Vietnam after being used by the U.S. Navy.

Design: These craft have fiberglass-reinforced plastic hulls and ceramic armor.

Engineering: The pump-jet propulsion enables the boats to operate in shallow and debris-filled water with a very high degree of maneuverability.

APPROX. 20 ARMORED TROOP CARRIERS: MINI-ATC TYPE

Displacement:	10 tons light
	13.4 tons full load
Length:	36 feet (11.0 m) oa
Beam:	12¾ feet (3.9 m)
Draft:	3½ feet (1.0 m)
Propulsion:	2 diesels (General Motors); 566 bhp; waterjets
Speed:	28 knots
Range:	
Manning:	2 (enlisted)
Troops:	15
Missiles:	none
Guns:	(see notes)
ASW weapons:	none
Radars:	navigation

These craft were developed from lessons learned in the Vietnam War and are intended for clandestine operations during riverine campaigns. They have low radar signatures and quiet engines.

Design: The mini-ATCs have aluminum hulls and ceramic armor. At high speed they have a one-foot draft. They can carry two tons of cargo.

3 FAST PATROL BOATS: OSPREY TYPE

Number	FY	In service
PTF 23	67	13 Mar 1968
PTF 24	67	13 Mar 1968
PTF 26	67	8 Apr 1968

Builders:	Sewart Seacraft, Berwick, La.
Displacement:	72.7 tons light
	111.6 tons full load
Length:	94¾ feet (28.9 m) oa
Beam:	23⅙ feet (7.1 m)
Draft:	7 feet (2.1 m)
Propulsion:	2 diesels (Napier-Deltic); 6,200 bhp; 2 shafts
Speed:	approx. 40 knots
Range:	
Manning:	19 (1 officer + 18 enlisted)
Missiles:	none
Guns:	1 81-mm mortar Mk 2/1 .50-cal MG M2
	1 40-mm AA Mk 3
	2 20-mm AA Mk 67 (2 single)
ASW weapons:	none
Radars:	navigation

These boats are the survivors of 26 fast patrol boats acquired during the Vietnam War, two of which were former PT-boats constructed in the late 1940s to evaluate new motor torpedo boat designs (see below).

After Vietnam these boats were operated by the Naval Reserve Force. The remaining craft are believed to be laid up.

Class: Four boats of this design were built, PT 23–26. The PTF 25 was experimentally fitted with gas turbine engines in 1978; stricken in 1980. The remaining boats are classified as service craft.

Design: These are aluminum-hulled boats, being larger than the previous Norwegian-designed, wooden-hulled Nasty class; they also have improved habitability, including air conditioning. Osprey is the commercial name for this design.

Engineering: The PTF 25 had her two Napier Deltic T18-37 diesels replaced in 1979 with two Garrett PF 990 gas turbines providing propulsion through two water jets generating some 6,000 hp.

These boat can be configured as torpedo boats, minelayers, or submarine chasers.

PBR Mk II (1968, U.S. Navy)

Mini-ATC (U.S. Navy)

PTF 23 (1975, Giorgio Arra)

The PTF 23 while assigned to Coastal River Squadron 2. There is an 81-mm mortar under canvas forward, a light gun on the port side of the bridge, and a 40-mm gun aft. The PTFs came into service during the Vietnam War to conduct clandestine missions. (1973, U.S. Navy)

1 COASTAL PATROL AND INTERDICTION CRAFT

Builders:	Tacoma Boatbuilding, Wash.
Displacement:	52.4 tons light
	75.1 tons full load
Length:	99¹¹/₁₂ feet (30.5 m) oa
Beam:	18½ feet (5.6 m)
Draft:	6 feet (1.8 m)
Propulsion:	3 gas turbines (Avco Lycoming), 6,050 shp, 3 shafts; auxiliary propulsion = 2 diesels (Volvo-Penta), 440 bhp; 2 outboard drive units
Speed:	40 + knots
Range:	
Manning:	approx. 11 (1 officer + 10 enlisted)
Missiles:	(see notes)
Guns:	(see notes)
ASW weapons:	(see notes)
Radars:	navigation

The CPIC was developed by the U.S. Navy as a successor to the PT/PTF-type small combatants in U.S. service and for foreign sales. The prototype CPIC was built in the United States; she was launched in 1974 and, after exhaustive trials, was transferred to South Korea on 1 August 1975.

The prototype was designated PKM 123 and named GIREOGI in Korean service. She was returned to the United States in 1980 for use as a research craft. She has now been laid up and is expected to be disposed of in the near future.

Additional craft of this type were constructed in South Korea.

Design: The CPIC was designed for maximum mission and weapons flexibility, with provisions for up to 20,000 pounds of weapons. There is a provision for a major weapon installation.

Engineering: Two independent propulsion systems are provided: three TF-25 gas turbines with propellers are fitted for high-speed operations; two TAMD-70 diesels with outboard drive are installed for low-speed cruising. The primary machinery cooling systems have external, hull-mounted heat exchangers without seawater intakes to permit operation in shallow and debris-filled water. The gas turbines are of a modular design to facilitate maintenance and replacement.

Guns: There is a gun position forward and one on the 01 level aft of the mast. During initial U.S. Navy trials in 1974–1975 the CPIC was fitted with a twin 30-mm Mk 74 mount forward. The gun has a firing rate of 600 rounds-per-minute per barrel with 2,000 rounds of ammunition stored in the mount. A second Mk 74 mount or a twin 20-mm mount could be fitted amidships.

CPIC on sea trials (1974, U.S. Navy)

The CPIC before being turned over to South Korea. A twin 30-mm Mk 74 mount is fitted forward; a second gun mount could be installed on the 01 level behind the bridge. Only Korea has produced craft of this type and the prototype has been returned to the United States. (1974, U.S. Navy)

POST-WORLD WAR II MOTOR TORPEDO BOATS

U.S. World War II motor torpedo boat construction programs reach hull number PT 809 with 774 units having been completed through 1945 (another 34 were cancelled before completion). Many survivors served with allied fleets after the war.

Four competitive prototypes PT-boats of advanced designs were completed in 1950–1951: the PT 809 by Electric Boat, PT 810 by Bath Iron Works, PT 811 by John Trumpy (Annapolis, Md.), and PT 812 by the Philadelphia Naval Shipyard. They were reclassified (as PTs) from patrol vessels to service craft on 13 April 1951. All were stricken, but the PT 810 and 811 were reinstated in service (vice in commission) as the PTF 1 and PTF 2 on 21 December 1962 for Vietnam service. The PT 809 was reinstated in service for use by the Secret Service and subsequently by the Navy and survives as the drone recovery craft RETRIEVER (DR-1); see Chapter 25.

FAST PATROL BOATS

The classification fast patrol boat (PTF) was established in 1963 for a fast seagoing craft to support clandestine operations off the coast of Vietnam. The PTFs 3 through 16 were Norwegian-built Nasty-class boats, taken over by the U.S. Navy upon completion in 1962–1965. The first four units had been assigned Norwegian names in preparation for service in that Navy. The subsequent PTFs 17–22 were built by Trumpy to the Nasty design and the PTFs 23–26, built by Sewart Seacraft, were of a different design.

Most saw combat service in Vietnam; all except three Ospreys have been stricken, some expended as targets.

PTF 1	ex-PT 810	
PTF 2	ex-PT 811	
PTF 3, 4	Norwegian-built Nasty class	completed 1962
PTF 5	Nasty (ex-KNURR)	completed 1963
PTF 6	Nasty (ex-LYR)	completed 1963
PTF 7	Nasty (ex-SKREI)	completed 1963
PTF 8	Nasty (ex-DELFIN)	completed 1963
PTF 9–16	Norwegian-built Nasty class	completed 1965
PTF 17–22	U.S.-built Nasty class	completed 1967–1968
PTF 23–26	U.S.-built Osprey class	completed 1967–1968

RIVERINE AND INSHORE COMBAT CRAFT

During the Vietnam War (1963–1972) the U.S. Navy operated several hundred riverine and inshore combat craft built for the purpose or converted from landing craft. These were used mainly for Operation Market Time (coastal surveillance), Game Warden (river patrol), and operations with U.S. Army troops in the Rung Sat special zone. About 650 river and coastal craft were turned over to South Vietnamese forces in 1970–1971 as the United States withdrew from the conflict.

In addition to the PCF and PBR types listed above, the principal Vietnam-era small craft were:

ASPB	assault support patrol boat
ATC	armored troop carrier
CCB	command and control boat (converted LCM)
MON	monitor (converted LCM)
PACV	patrol air cushion vehicles (see Appendix C)

All of the above craft were produced in large numbers. Several other craft were also developed and evaluated.

The HERCULES during a high-speed run in Puget Sound. (1983)

23 Mine Countermeasures Ships and Craft

The U.S. Navy is embarked on a belated program of constructing mine countermeasures craft to keep U.S. naval and commercial ports open in the event of a conventional conflict with the Soviet Union. According to the Deputy Chief of Naval Operations (Surface Warfare), Vice Admiral R. L. Walters, speaking in 1983, "No segment of Naval Warfare has been underfunded for so many years as has the Mine Warfare community. Despite the large stockpiles of sophisticated modern mines possessed by the Soviets, we have only recently begun to respond to the threat."

Two new classes are under construction, the mine countermeasure ship (MCM) and mine hunter (MSH). These will be the first new mine-sweeping craft built for the U.S. Navy in almost three decades. Pending the delivery of these craft, beginning in late 1985, the Navy operates a small number of ocean minesweepers (MSO) of Korean War vintage, most operated by the NRF. These craft, originally intended for overseas operation, lack modern mine countermeasure systems as well as the transit speeds necessary for long-range operations or to accompany modern, 20-knot amphibious forces.

Type	Ship/Class	Comm.	Active	NRF	Building
MCM 1	AVENGER	1985–	—	—	2
MSO 508	ACME	1957–1958	—	2	—
MSO 421	AGILE/AGGRESSIVE	1954–1956	3	16	—
MSB	(unnamed)		7	—	—

Instead, since 1971 the U.S. Navy has relied primarily on helicopters for Airborne Mine Countermeasures (AMCM). Three AMCM squadrons are in service, providing a limited minesweeping capability (see Chapter 28).

A total of 14 of the MCM and 17 of the MSH craft are planned. All will initially be operated by the active Navy and transferred to NRF after "shakedown" operations of 9 to 12 months.

The MCM and MSH classes will use hull-mounted Variable Depth Sonar (VDS) as the primary means of mine detection and cable-controlled Mine Neutralization Vehicles (MNV) for examination and destruction of the mines. The MNVs will use closed-circuit television and be capable of severing cables of moored mines or placing an explosive charge near a bottom mine. The MNVs will weigh about 2,200 pounds.

The Navy is considering the use of an Air Cushion Vehicle (ACV) configuration for the MSH. The Royal Navy has extensively tested ACVs in the mine countermeasure role.

The MCM concept has undergone several changes in the past few years, originally being proposed in the late 1970s as an ocean-going ship to protect U.S. strategic missile submarines against Soviet deep-ocean mines. A Small Waterplane Area Twin Hull (SWATH) design was considered for that concept to provide improved seakeeping in northern waters. Under that concept the MCMs would have operated in pairs, towing a sweep gear between them. Nineteen of these ships were proposed, to have displaced 1,640 tons and with a length of 265 feet.

Operational: The new mine countermeasure ships and mine hunters are scheduled to be assigned to the following ports:

Port	MCM	MSH
Newport, R.I./Groton, Conn.	3	3
Norfolk, Va.	2	5
Charleston, S.C.	2	6
Mayport, Fla.	1	3
Seattle/Tacoma, Wash.	1	—
San Francisco, Calif.	2	—
San Diego, Calif.	2	—
Pearl Harbor, Hawaii	1	—

The current U.S. mine countermeasures force consists primarily of outdated, MSO-type ocean minesweepers, most manned by the Naval Reserve Force, and a small number of RH-53D Sea Stallion helicopters. Here an RH-53D from Mine Countermeasures Squadron 14 prepares to transfer a towed minesweeping device to the minesweeper ILLUSIVE. (1981, U.S. Navy, JO1 Peter Sundberg)

(17) MINESWEEPER HUNTERS: MSH TYPE

Number	Name	FY	Commission	Status
MSH 1	CARDINAL	84	1987	Building
MSH	(4 ships)	86	1989	Planned
MSH	(4 ships)	87		Planned
MSH	(4 ships)	88		Planned
MSH	(4 ships)	89		Planned

Builders:	Bell Halter
Displacement:	approx. 450—500 tons full load
Length:	189 feet (57.6 m) oa
Beam:	
Draft:	
Propulsion:	2 diesels; approx. 1,200 bhp; 2 shafts
Speed:	
Range:	
Manning:	40–45
Guns:	none
Radars:	SPS-64(V)9 surface search
Sonars:	SQQ-32 variable depth

These are small mine hunters, intended to complement the larger MCM class in coordinated mine countermeasure operations. Seventeen ships of this design are planned for the five-year defense plan with up to 35 being considered. The MSHs will be operated by the NRF with composite active-reserve crews.

Bell Aerospace Textron received a contract in April 1983 for the development of an MSH employing an air cushion (ACV) concept. This design was selected over a conventional hull design, using glass-reinforced plastic, developed by Marinette Marine. (The Marinette design is based on an association with Intermarine, Italy.)

Cost: Series construction of this ship is planned at $65 million per ship (fiscal 1984 estimate).

Design: The MSH will be wooden-hulled; the craft is to be capable of five-day sweep missions. One MNV will be carried.

Electronics: These craft will have AN/SSN-2 Precise Integrated Navigation Systems (PINS) with a command and control suite for displaying data on mine location and channel conditions, and exchanging data with other ships. The system is fitted in the Navy's cable ships (T-ARC type).

The Bell Halter design for an MSH which is a hybrid design of a surface effect ship and a conventional hull. The craft will employ the Mine Neutralization Vehicle (MNV) that is being fitted to the larger MCM. The MSH is intended to clear U.S. ports and harbors of Soviet submarine-laid mines. (Bell Halter)

The Martinette Marine design for the MSH showed a more conventional configuration. A VDS is fitted forward of the bridge with sweep gear and MNVs carried aft. (Martinette Marine)

(14) MINE COUNTERMEASURE SHIPS: "AVENGER" CLASS

Number	Name	FY	Launch	Commission	Status
MCM 1	AVENGER	82	15 June 1985	1986	Building
MCM 2	DEFENDER	83		1986	Building
MCM 3	SENTRY	84		1987	Building
MCM 4	CHAMPION	84		1987	Building
MCM 5	GUARDIAN	84		1987	Building
MCM	(4 ships)	85			Planned
MCM	(4 ships)	86			Planned
MCM	(1 ship)	87			Planned

Builders: MCM 1, 3, 5 Peterson Builders, Sturgeon Bay, Wisc.
MCM 2, 4   Marinette Marine, Wisc.
Displacement: 1,312 tons full load
Length: 224 feet (68.3 m) oa
Beam: 39 feet (11.9 m)
Draft: 11½ feet (3.5 m)
Propulsion: 4 diesels; 2,280 bhp; 2 shafts
Speed: 16 knots
Range:
Manning: 82 (6 officers + 76 enlisted)
Guns: possible 20-mm Phalanx CIWS
Radars: SPS-64(V)9 surface search
Sonars: SQQ-30 variable depth in early ships
SQQ-32 variable depth in later ships

Fourteen ships of this class are planned for harbor clearance in conjunction with MSH-type mine hunters. The Navy originally planned a one-year "program gap" between the fiscal 1982 lead ship and four ships in fiscal 1984. Subsequently, the Navy sought to accelerate the program with four ships in fiscal 1983. Congress, citing problems with the MCM design, instead funded only one ship in fiscal 1983 and directed the Navy to develop a second source yard (i.e., Marinette).

There are problems in the design of this class as well as indecision over engine selection.

The AVENGER was laid down on 3 June 1983, the first large mine-sweeper under construction for the U.S. Navy since the ASSURANCE was completed 25 years earlier.

Cost: The fiscal 1985 budget ships had an average construction cost of $87.4 million plus $1.8 million for outfitting and $825,000 post-delivery costs, for a total of $90 million per ship.

Design: The basic MCM design will be similar to previous MSO classes; wooden and fiberglass-reinforced plastic construction. When the MCM design was initially completed in early 1982, the ship was 217 feet overall. That figure was subsequently increased before keel laying to accommodate increased mine countermeasures equipment. One or two MNVs will be carried in addition to conventional sweep gear.

Electronics: Fitted with AN/SSN-2 precise navigation system and similar command and communications facilities as the MSH.

The MCMs will initially be fitted with the SQQ-30 variable-depth mine-hunting sonar. This equipment, an upgraded SQQ-14, has severe limitations and will be succeeded in later ships by the SQQ-32.

Engineering: To be fitted with four very-low-magnetic diesel engines for propulsion; electrical power for minesweeping gear is provided by gas turbines. A bow thruster is fitted. Maximum mine-hunting speed will be five knots.

The diesels are Waukesha L-1616 type.

This is a rendering of the current configuration of the MCM, which at one point resembled the existing Navy MSOs and, subsequently, evolved into a twin-hull (catamaran) ocean mine countermeasures ship. The current version has a mine-detecting VDS fitted forward of the bridge; aft is working space for handling MNVs and other minesweeping gear. (U.S. Navy)

A prototype Mine Neutralization Vehicle (MNV) is handled aboard an MSO by technicians from the Naval Ocean Systems Center in San Diego. The cable-controlled MNV is designed to locate, examine, and—by placing explosive charges—destroy mines. (U.S. Navy)

An MNV prototype being handled aboard an MSO. The production MNV—developed by Honeywell—will be wood-hulled with a fiberglass superstructure some 12⁵⁄₁₂-feet long; it will be propelled by two 15-hp hydraulic motors providing a speed up to six knots and will be controlled by a 5,000-foot cable. (U.S. Navy)

2 OCEAN MINESWEEPERS: "ACME" CLASS

Number	Name	FY	Builder	Laid down	Launched	Commissioned	Status
MSO 509	Adroit	54	Frank L. Sample, Jr., Boothbay Harbor, Maine	18 Nov 1954	20 Aug 1955	4 Mar 1957	**NRF-A**
MSO 511	Affray	54	Frank L. Sample, Jr., Boothbay Harbor, Maine	24 Aug 1955	18 Dec 1956	8 Dec 1958	**NRF-A**

Displacement:	720 tons light
	780 tons full load
Length:	173 feet (52.75 m) oa
Beam:	36 feet (11.0 m)
Draft:	14 feet (4.3 m)
Propulsion:	2 diesels (Packard); 2,800 bhp; 2 shafts
Speed:	14 knots
Range:	3,300 n.miles at 10 knots
Manning:	57 (5 officers + 52 enlisted) active + 26 (3 officers + 23 enlisted) reserve
Guns:	1 20-mm AA Mk 24
Radars:	SPS-53L surface search in MSO 509
	SPS-53E surface search in MSO 511
Sonars:	SQQ-14 variable depth

These ships are improved versions of the Agile and Aggressive classes. They are fitted as mine division flagships. They are operated by the Naval Reserve Force.

Class: Four ships were built to this design for the U.S. Navy (MSO 508–511) and seven for allied navies (MSO 512–518).

Design: SCB No. 45A. See previous class for design notes.

The Affray is generally similar to the earlier MSO classes, being slightly larger and slower. The forward gun is removable, with much of the space forward of the bridge taken up by the SQQ-14 variable depth sonar that is lowered through the hull. (1983, Giorgio Arra)

19 OCEAN MINESWEEPERS: "AGILE" AND "AGGRESSIVE" CLASSES

Number	Name	FY	Builder	Laid down	Launched	Commissioned	Status
MSO 427	CONSTANT	51	Fulton Shipyard Co., Antioch, Calif.	16 Aug 1951	14 Feb 1953	8 Sep 1954	**NRF-P**
MSO 433	ENGAGE	51	Colberg Boat Works, Stockton, Calif.	7 Nov 1951	18 June 1953	29 June 1954	**NRF-A**
MSO 437	ENHANCE	51	Martinolich SB Co., San Diego, Calif.	12 July 1952	11 Oct 1952	16 Apr 1955	**NRF-P**
MSO 438	ESTEEM	51	Martinolich SB Co., San Diego, Calif.	1 Sep 1952	20 Dec 1952	10 Sep 1955	**NRF-P**
MSO 439	EXCEL	51	Higgins Inc., New Orleans, La.	9 Feb 1953	25 Sep 1953	24 Feb 1955	**NRF-P**
MSO 440	EXPLOIT	51	Higgins Inc., New Orleans, La.	28 Dec 1951	10 Apr 1953	31 Mar 1954	**NRF-A**
MSO 441	EXULTANT	51	Higgins Inc., New Orleans, La.	22 May 1952	6 June 1953	22 June 1954	**NRF-A**
MSO 442	FEARLESS	51	Higgins Inc., New Orleans, La.	23 July 1952	17 July 1953	22 Sep 1954	**NRF-A**
MSO 443	FIDELITY	51	Higgins Inc., New Orleans, La.	15 Dec 1952	21 Aug 1953	19 Jan 1955	**AA**
MSO 446	FORTIFY	51	Seattle SB & DD Co., Seattle, Wash.	30 Nov 1951	14 Feb 1953	16 July 1954	**NRF-A**
MSO 448	ILLUSIVE	51	Martinolich SB Co., San Diego, Calif.	23 Oct 1951	12 July 1952	14 Nov 1953	**AA**
MSO 449	IMPERVIOUS	51	Martinolich SB Co., San Diego, Calif.	18 Nov 1951	29 Aug 1952	15 July 1954	**NRF-A**
MSO 455	IMPLICIT	52	Wilmington Boat Works Inc., Calif.	29 Oct 1951	1 Aug 1953	10 Mar 1954	**NRF-P**
MSO 456	INFLICT	52	Wilmington Boat Works Inc., Calif.	29 Oct 1951	6 Oct 1953	11 May 1954	**NRF-A**
MSO 464	PLUCK	52	Wilmington Boat Works Inc., Calif.	31 Mar 1952	6 Feb 1954	11 Aug 1954	**NRF-P**
MSO 488	CONQUEST	53	J. M. Martinac SB Corp., Tacoma, Wash.	26 Mar 1953	20 May 1954	20 July 1955	**NRF-P**
MSO 489	GALLANT	53	J. M. Martinac SB Corp., Tacoma, Wash.	21 May 1953	4 June 1954	14 Sep 1955	**NRF-P**
MSO 490	LEADER	53	J. M. Martinac SB Corp., Tacoma, Wash.	22 Sep 1953	15 Sep 1954	16 Nov 1955	**AA**
MSO 492	PLEDGE	53	J. M. Martinac SB Corp., Tacoma, Wash.	24 June 1954	20 July 1955	20 Apr 1956	**NRF-P**

Displacement:	665 tons light
	750 tons full load
Length:	172 feet (52.5 m) oa
Beam:	35 feet (10.7 m)
Draft:	14 feet (4.3 m)
Propulsion:	2 diesels (Packard except Waukesha in MSO 433, 437–438, 441–443, 448–449, 456, 488, 490)
Speed:	15.5 knots
Range:	3,300 n.miles at 10 knots
Manning:	active ships 76 (7 officers + 69 enlisted)
	NRF ships 57 (5 officers + 52 enlisted) active + 26 (3 officers + 23 enlisted) reserve
Guns:	1 40-mm AA M3 or
	1 20-mm Mk 68
Radars:	SPS-5C or SPS-53E/L surface search
Sonars:	UQS-1 or SQQ-14 variable depth

These ocean minesweepers and the newer ACME class are the survivors of the massive U.S. minesweeper construction programs started during the Korean War after shock of extensive North Korean use of Soviet-supplied mines. Large numbers of these ships were built for the U.S. Navy and several NATO navies. They are fitted for sweeping contact, magnetic, and acoustic mines but lack the capability of countering modern mines.

Of the surviving ships, three are in active Navy service and the remainder are NRF ships. The active ships serve as mine countermeasure test platforms as well as performing operational minesweeper training and exercises. The FIDELITY is based at the Navy's research center in Panama City, Fla., the two other active ships at Charleston, S.C.

Class: Fifty-eight ships of this class were built for the U.S. Navy (MSO 421–449, 455–474, 488–496); 27 more were built for allied navies (MSO 450–454, 475–487, 498–507) with the MSO 497 being cancelled.

All three ships of the similar ABILITY class (MSO 519–521) built for the U.S. Navy have been discarded. The MSO 522 was also constructed for foreign use.

Sixteen additional MSOs of this type funded in the fiscal 1966–1968 shipbuilding programs were not built.

The following U.S. ships have been discarded since the 12th edition of *Ships and Aircraft*: DASH (MSO 428), DETECTOR (MSO 429), DIRECT (MSO 430), and DOMINANT (MSO 431), all stricken on 1 October 1982. The remaining ships will be stricken as the new MCM/MSH types become available.

Classification: All MSOs originally were classified as minesweepers (AM with same hull numbers); they were changed to MSO on 7 February 1955.

Design: SCB No. 45A. These ships are of lightweight wooden construction with laminated timbers; the fittings and machinery are of stainless steel (non-magnetic) and bronze. Magnetic items are reduced to a minimum.

FEARLESS (1983, Giorgio Arra)

Electronics: These ships originally had UQS-1 mine detecting sonar; most have been refitted with the more capable SQQ-14 sonar. The latter is a variable-depth sonar, lowered on a rigid rod from the hull forward of the deck structure.

The PLUCK was test ship in the mid-1970s for the AN/SSN-2 precise navigation system fitted in the subsequent MCM and MSH classes.

Guns: As built, these ships had one 40-mm gun and two .50-cal machine guns. Most have been rearmed with provisions for mounting a 20-mm mount forward, originally a twin-barrel Mk 24 and subsequently a single-barrel Mk 68 gun. The smaller 20-mm mount was required in modernized ships to permit installation of the larger, retractable SQQ-14 sonar.

Modernization: In fiscal 1968 a program was begun to modernize the existing MSOs (SCB No. 502). New engines, communications, and sonar were installed and improved sweep gear provided. Increasing costs and shipyard delays, however, caused the program to be halted after only 13 ships had been fully modernized—MSO 433, 437, 438, 441–443, 445, 446, 448, 449, 456, 488, and 490. Subsequently, some of these features, especially the improved sonar, were fitted to several additional ships.

Operational: The NRF sweeps normally conducted only local area operations. In the second half of 1983, however, the NRF-ships EXULTANT and FEARLESS along with the active ILLUSIVE and LEADER conducted a 137-day deployment to European waters. Comprising the MCM-83 deployment, they travelled more than 12,000 miles and visited ports in six countries as well as participating in minesweeping exercises.

LEADER (1982, Giorgio Arra)

LEADER; note the floats for minesweeping gear—referred to as "pigs." (1983, Giorgio Arra)

7 MINESWEEPING BOATS

Number	Number	Number
MSB 15	MSB 28	MSB 41
MSB 16	MSB 29	MSB 51
MSB 25		

Displacement:	30.6 tons light
	41 tons full load except MSB 29 80 tons
Length:	57¼ feet (17.5 m) oa except MSB 29 82 feet (25.0 m) oa
Beam:	15⅝ feet (4.8 m) except MSB 29 19 feet (5.8 m)
Draft:	4⅓ feet (1.3 m) except MSB 29 5½ feet (1.7 m)
Propulsion:	2 diesels (Packard); 600 bhp; 2 shafts
Speed:	12 knots
Range:	360 n.miles at 12 knots
Manning:	6 or 7 (enlisted) except 11 (2 officers + 7 enlisted) in MSB 29
Guns:	several MG can be fitted
Radars:	navigation (commercial)
Sonars:	none

These are wooden-hulled minesweeping boats that were designed to be carried to assault areas aboard amphibious ships. They were used extensively in the Vietnam War, being armored and armed for sweeping rivers and channels in that conflict.

The seven surviving MSBs form Mine Division 125 at Charleston, S.C. A few others are employed by the Navy as utility and training craft.

Class: This class originally included MSB 5–54, less the MSB 24 that was not built and the MSB 29 that was built to an enlarged design in an effort to improve seakeeping qualities. All were completed 1952–1956.

The MSB 1–4 were former Army minesweepers built in 1946.

Guns: The MSBs that served in the Vietnam War were armed with several machine guns, with a raised gun tube fitted aft.

The MSB 51, with mast and navigation radar folded down, enters the docking well of the NASHVILLE (LPD 13) during exercises in the Mediterranean. RH-53D minesweeping helicopters are on the deck above. (1982, U.S. Navy, PH3 Tom Goodison)

MSB 16 (1983, Giorgio Arra)

MSB 16 (1983, Giorgio Arra)

MSB 51 (1983, Giorgio Arra)

MINESWEEPING SHRIMP BOAT

The so-called minesweeping shrimp boat (designated MSSB 1) was acquired in 1980 under contract rental to evaluate the feasibility of configuring such small fishing craft for MCM activities. The 63-foot craft had been seized by the U.S. Customs Service in February 1980 while carrying marijuana. An additional generator, MCS-type minesweeping gear, a small sonar (WQS-1), and other special equipment was installed for the craft to be evaluated.

Several other special type minesweepers have been converted from captured drug smuggling craft.

MSSB 1 (1983, Giorgio Arra)

COASTAL MINESWEEPERS

All 22 U.S. Navy coastal minesweepers of the BLUEBIRD (MSC 121, 122, 190–199, 201, 203–209) and ALBATROSS (MSC 289, 290) classes have been discarded. Two hundred twenty-two additional units were built for allied navies during the 1950s and early 1960s (MSC 60–120, 123–154, 167–189, 200, 202, 210–288, 291–315). The MSC 155–166 were cancelled.

COASTAL MINEHUNTERS

The MHC ships were intended to locate and to plot mines for mine-sweepers. The BITTERN (MHC 43), completed in 1957, was built for the purpose on a 144-foot MSC hull. The planned series production of similar MHCs was cancelled. The MHC 1–10 were converted LCT-6s; the MHC 11, 16–33, 35–42 were converted LSI (L)s; the MHC 12 and 13 converted coastal survey ships (AGSC); and the MHC 14, 34, 44–50 were converted AMS/YMS minesweepers. They were originally designated AMC(U)—coastal minesweepers (underwater locators).

INSHORE MINESWEEPERS

Two inshore minesweepers (MSI) were built for U.S. service; they survive as institute-operated research ships (see Chapter 25). Additional MSIs were built for foreign navies.

MINESWEEPING LAUNCHES

A series of 36-foot minesweeping launches (MSL) were built for sweeping mines during landing operations. They were to be carried as deck cargo by amphibious ships. A few remain as utility boats.

RIVERINE MINESWEEPING CRAFT

Several types of minesweeping craft were developed during the Vietnam War for river and channel mine-clearing operations. These were patrol minesweepers (MSR), river minesweepers (MSM), and radio-controlled drone minesweepers (MSD). All have been discarded.

SPECIAL MINESWEEPERS

The special minesweepers (MSS) were old merchant ships filled with styrofoam, fitted with over-the-side propulsion, and shock-mounted pilot house. With few crewmen aboard, they were to detonate mines laid in critical channels.

Four old Liberty-ship hulls were converted to this configuration but were designated YAG 36–39. Subsequently, in 1969 the merchant ship HARRY L. GLUCKMAN and in 1973 the landing ship WASHTENAW COUNTY (LST 1166) were modified for this role in 1969 and 1973, respectively; they were reclassified MSS 1 and 2.

MINESWEEPING DEVICES

This was a cylindrical device 251 feet long with a displacement of 3,100 tons that was to be towed through minefields; it was designed to survive mine detonations. Designated XMAP 1, the device was built at the Philadelphia Naval Shipyard in the mid-1950s, but apparently not completed. Plans for the XMAP 2 were dropped.

MINE COUNTERMEASURES SUPPORT SHIPS

Several ships were converted to mine countermeasures support ships (MCS) in the 1960s to support minesweepers and helicopters. These were the large former vehicle landing ships CATSKILL (MCS 1, ex-CM 6, ex-LSV 1), OZARK (MCS 2, ex-CM 7, ex-LSV 2), OSAGE (MCS 3, ex-LSV 3), SAUGUS (MCS 4, ex-LSV 4), and MONITOR (MCS 5, ex-LSV 5); the former tank landing ship ORLEANS PARISH (MCS 6, ex-LST 1069); and the former dock landing ship EPPING FOREST (MCS 7, ex-LSD 4).

AUXILIARY MINELAYERS

In 1949–1951 the Navy acquired 14 Army mine planters (MP series) and designated them as auxiliary minelayers, ACM 1–3, 5–9, and MMA 11–16. Six of them (3, 5–9) later went to the Coast Guard (WAGL 328–333). The missing hull numbers ACM 4 and 10 were apparently reserved for two other Army MPs that were not transferred to the Navy.

COASTAL MINELAYERS

Sixteen ships designated as coastal minelayers (MMC) were built or converted for transfer to allied navies.

24 Auxiliary Ships

Auxiliary ships are noncombatant ships that provide support to the "fighting fleet." There are a large number of different types of specialized auxiliary ships in naval service. They are listed in this chapter alphabetically, according to classification.

The U.S. Navy arranges auxiliary ships according to function with the categories being:

(1) Mobile Logistic Type Ships

Ships which have the capability to provide underway replenishment to fleet units and/or provide direct material support to other deployed units operating far from home base.

    (a) Underway Replenishment: AE, AF, AFS, AO, AOE, AOR

    (b) Material Support: AD, AR, AS

(2) Support Type Ships

A grouping of ships designed to operate in the open ocean in a variety of sea states to provide general support to either combatant forces or shore-based establishments. (Includes smaller auxiliaries which by the nature of their duties, rarely leave inshore waters.)

    (a) Fleet Support: ARS, ASR, ATA, ATF, ATS

    (b) Other Auxiliaries: AG, AGDS, AGF, AGM, AGOR, AGS, AH, AK, AKR, AOG, AOT, AP, ARC, ARL, AVM, AVT

While overly simplistic, this scheme does attempt to indicate the types of support the various auxiliaries provide to the fleet. This Navy scheme was initiated in 1978, based on a ship classification arrangement developed by the author of the present volume ten years earlier for *Jane's Fighting Ships*.

The Maritime Prepositioning Ships (MPS) are listed in this chapter as cargo ships (AK, AKR, or no hull number); the earlier, Near-Term Prepositioning Ships (NTPS) with standard naval classifications are described in this chapter. However, those merchant ships taken over for the NTPS role that have not been given standard hull numbers are listed in Chapter 8 of this volume.

Several ships officially classified as auxiliaries are listed elsewhere in this volume and are not included in the following table. These are the miscellaneous command ships CORONADO (AGF 11) and LA SALLE (AGF 3), the auxiliary submarine DOLPHIN (AGSS 555), and the training carrier LEXINGTON (AVT 16). The escort/frigate research ship GLOVER (AGDE/AGFF 1) has been reclassified as a frigate (FF 1098).

Guns: All ships operated by the Military Sealift Command are unarmed. Most Navy-manned auxiliaries have a minimal 40-mm or 20-mm self-defense armament with the major underway replenishment ships, which in wartime would provide direct support to battle groups, scheduled to receive the 20-mm Phalanx CIWS. Several of these replenishment ships also have the NATO Sea Sparrow missile system.

Operational: Auxiliary ships are operated by (1) the active Navy, (2) the Military Sealift Command (MSC) with civil service or contractor civilian crews, (3) the Naval Reserve Force (NRF) with composite active-reserve crews, or (4) by academic institutions on loan from the Navy. The MSC ships have the prefix USNS for U.S. Naval Ship and the prefix T- is appended to their hull numbers; the active and NRF ships have the prefix USS.

Underway replenishment in the forward area: The Military Sealift Command-operated fleet oiler WACCAMAW (T-AO 109) refuels the dreadnought NEW JERSEY (BB 62) off the coast of Lebanon. A large number of Navy replenishment ships as well as point-to-point cargo ships and tankers, research ships, tugs, and the maritime prepositioning ships are manned by civilian crews under the auspices of the Navy's Military Sealift Command. (1984, U.S. Navy)

Ship Type		Total Active	Navy Manned	MSC (Civilian)	NRF	Academic (Civilian)	Building-Conversion	Reserve
			Active Navy Ships					
AD	Destroyer Tender	9	9	—	—	—	—	—
AE	Ammunition Ship	13	13	—	—	—	—	—
AF	Store Ship	1	—	1	—	—	—	—
AFS	Combat Stores Ship	10	7	3	—	—	—	—
AG	Miscellaneous Auxiliary	2	—	2	—	—	—	—
AGDS	Deep Submergence Support Ship	1	1	—	—	—	—	—
AGM	Missile Range Instrumentation Ship	3	—	3	—	—	—	—
AGOR	Oceanographic Research Ship	6	1[a]	5	—	7	—	—
AGOS	Ocean Surveillance Ship	6	—	6	—	—	6	—
AGS	Surveying Ship	9	—	9	—	—	2	—
AH	Hospital Ship	—	—	—	—	—	2	1
AK	Cargo Ship	9	—	9	—	—	12	3
AKR	Vehicle Cargo Ship	9	—	9	—	—	4	—
AO	Fleet Oiler	18	7	11	—	—	2	3
AOE	Fast Combat Support Ship	4	4	—	—	—	—	—
AOG	Gasoline Tanker	3	—	3	—	—	—	—
AOR	Replenishment Oiler	7	7	—	—	—	—	—
AOT	Transport Oiler	20	—	20	—	—	5	6
AP	Transport	—	—	—	—	2[b]	—	13
AR	Repair Ship	4	4	—	—	—	—	—
ARC	Cable Repair Ship	4	—	4	—	—	—	—
ARL	Small Repair Ship	—	—	—	—	—	—	1
ARS	Salvage Ship	7	5	—	2	—	4	—
AS	Submarine Tender	12	12	—	—	—	—	—
ASR	Submarine Rescue Ship	6	6	—	—	—	—	—
ATA	Auxiliary Tug	—	—	—	—	—	—	3
ATF	Fleet Tug	12	—	7	5	—	—	10
ATS	Salvage and Rescue Ships	3	3	—	—	—	—	—
AVM	Guided Missile Ship	1	1	—	—	—	—	—

[a] Operated by the Naval Postgraduate School, Monterey, Calif.
[b] Employed as school ships by state maritime academies.

6 DESTROYER TENDERS: "SAMUEL GOMPERS" CLASS

Number	Name	FY	Launched	Commissioned	Status
AD 37	SAMUEL GOMPERS	64	14 May 1966	1 July 1967	PA
AD 38	PUGET SOUND	65	16 Sep 1966	27 Apr 1968	AA
AD 41	YELLOWSTONE	75	27 Jan 1979	28 June 1980	AA
AD 42	ACADIA	76	28 July 1979	6 June 1981	PA
AD 43	CAPE COD	77	2 Aug 1980	17 Apr 1982	PA
AD 44	SHENANDOAH	79	6 Feb 1982	17 Dec 1983	AA

Builders: AD 37-38 Puget Sound Naval Shipyard, Bremerton, Wash.
AD 41-44 National Steel & Shipbuilding, San Diego, Calif.
Displacement: AD 37-38 22,260 tons full load
AD 41-44 22,800 tons full load
Length: 643 feet (196.1 m) oa
Beam: 85 feet (25.9 m)
Draft: 22½ feet (6.9 m)
Propulsion: steam turbine; 20,000 shp; 1 shaft
Boilers: 2
Speed: 20 knots (18 knots sustained)
Range:
Manning:

	Total	Officer	Enlisted
AD 37	1,323	38	1,285
AD 38	1,487	41	1,446
AD 41	1,431	35	1,396
AD 42	1,430	35	1,395
AD 43	1,429	35	1,394
AD 44	1,431	35	1,396

Helicopters: landing area
Missiles: none
Guns: 2 40-mm machine guns Mk 19 (2 single)
2 20-mm Mk 67 (2 single)

The Navy's first post-World War II destroyer tenders, these ships are designed to support modern surface combatants, including ships with nuclear and gas turbine propulsion. The PUGET SOUND, based at Gaeta, Italy, served as flagship of the U.S. Sixth Fleet from May 1980; she is to be replaced in 1985 by the CORONADO (AGF 11). As flagship the PUGET SOUND carries approximately 225 flag personnel.

Class: The AD 39 was authorized in the fiscal 1969 shipbuilding program but was cancelled prior to the start of construction because of cost overruns in other new ship programs. The AD 40 was authorized in fiscal 1973 but was not built. An AD 45 was planned for the fiscal 1980 program but was not funded. Two additional tenders planned for fiscal 1987 and 1988 were deleted from the five-year program of January 1984.

The AD 41 and later ships are generally referred to as the YELLOWSTONE class. The SHENANDOAH was placed in commission at National Steel on 15 August 1983 but was again commissioned at Norfolk on the date shown above.

Design: The GOMPERS was SCB No. 244; subsequent ships were No. 700 in the new SCB series. These ships are similar to the L.Y. SPEAR (AS 36)-class submarine tenders.

A landing platform and hangar for DASH helicopters were provided in the AD 37 and 38. The hangar on the GOMPERS has been converted to a repair shop; the PUGET SOUND's hangar is 54⅓ feet long and 22⅓ feet wide.

The ships have two 30-ton-capacity cranes and two 6½-ton cranes.

Guns: As built the AD 37 and 38 had a single 5-inch/38-cal DP gun forward with a Mk 56 GFCS; this armament was removed and plans to install NATO Sea Sparrow missile launchers were dropped.

The SHENANDOAH, the latest in a series of destroyer tenders built to support missile-armed surface combatants. Crane arrangements differ from the earlier ships of the class. (1983, U.S. Navy)

Puget Sound (Giorgio Arra)

Acadia (1982, Giorgio Arra)

Puget Sound (Giorgio Arra)

3 DESTROYER TENDERS: "DIXIE" CLASS

Number	Name	Launched	Commissioned	Status
AD 15	PRAIRIE	9 Dec 1939	5 Aug 1940	**PA**
AD 18	SIERRA	23 Feb 1943	20 Mar 1944	**AA**
AD 19	YOSEMITE	16 May 1943	25 May 1944	**AA**

Builders:	AD 15 New York Shipbuilding, Camden, N.J.
	AD 18-19 Tampa Shipbuilding, Fla.
Displacement:	9,450 tons standard
	17,176 tons full load
Length:	530½ feet (161.8 m) oa
Beam:	73⅓ feet (22.4 m)
Draft:	25½ feet (7.8 m)
Propulsion:	steam turbines (Parsons in AD 15, Allis Chalmers in AD 18-19);
	11,000 shp; 2 shafts
Boilers:	4 (Babcock & Wilcox)
Speed:	19.6 knots

Manning:		Total	Officer	Enlisted
	AD 15	913	32	881
	AD 18	882	32	850
	AD 19	887	32	855

Helicopters:	VERTREP area
Missiles:	none
Guns:	4 20-mm Mk 68 (4 single)

The PRAIRIE is the oldest U.S. Navy ship in commission except for the relic CONSTITUTION. These ships have been modernized to support surface warships fitted with ASROC, improved electronics, etc. They were among a series of large tender-type ships begun in the late 1930s.

Class: Five destroyer tenders were built to this design (AD 14, 15, 17–19); the later NEW ENGLAND (AD 32, ex-AS 28) of this class was cancelled in 1945. The DIXIE (AD 14) was stricken on 15 June 1982 and the PIEDMONT (AD 17) was transferred to Turkey in October 1982.

Guns: As completed these ships had four 5-inch/38-cal DP guns and eight 40-mm AA guns; they were reduced up to the mid-1970s, when minimal 20-mm armament was provided.

Modernization: Various modernization programs updated these ships to support the DASH program. Manned helicopters cannot operate from these ships.

1 DESTROYER TENDER: "KLONDIKE" CLASS

Number	Name	Launched	Commissioned	Status
AD 24	EVERGLADES	28 Jan 1945	25 May 1951	AR

Builders:	Los Angeles Shipbuilding & DD, Calif.
Displacement:	8,165 tons standard
	14,700 tons full load
Length:	492 feet (150.0 m) oa
Beam:	69½ feet (21.2 m)
Draft:	27⅙ feet (8.3 m)
Propulsion:	steam turbine (General Electric); 8,500 shp; 1 shaft
Boilers:	2 (Babcock & Wilcox)
Speed:	18 knots
Manning:	approx. 850 wartime
Helicopters:	no facilities
Guns:	2 3-inch (76-mm) 50 cal AA Mk 26 (2 single)
Fire control:	1 Mk 51 gun director
	1 Mk 52 gun FCS with Mk 26 radar

This ship was built to a merchant design specifically for the tender role. Her completion was delayed after World War II. She is employed as an accommodation ship at the Philadelphia Naval Shipyard.

Class: Ten destroyer tenders were built to this configuration: the KLONDIKE class (AD 22–25) and the SHENANDOAH class (AD 26–29, 31, 36). Three additional ships were cancelled (AD 30, 33, 35). The AD 16, 20, and 21 were similar. Two ships, the KLONDIKE (AD 22) and GRAND CANYON (AD 28) were reclassified as repair ships (changed to AR) in 1960 and 1971, respectively.

The BRYCE CANYON (AD 36, ex-AV 20) was stricken on 30 June 1981; planned for sale to Pakistan.

Design: Maritime Administration C3 design.

The EVERGLADES; note merchant-style kingposts forward and former DASH facility aft. (U.S. Navy)

The destroyer tender PRAIRIE is one of several large auxiliaries of the AD/AR/AS type that were designed before World War II that continue in active Navy service. As built these ships had a destroyer's gun armament. (Giorgio Arra)

PRAIRIE (1983, Giorgio Arra)

8 + 4 AMMUNITION SHIPS: "KILAUEA" CLASS

Number	Name	FY	Launched	Commissioned	Status
T-AE 26	KILAUEA	65	9 Aug 1967	10 Aug 1968	**MSC-P**
AE 27	BUTTE	65	9 Aug 1967	29 Nov 1968	**AA**
AE 28	SANTA BARBARA	66	23 Jan 1968	11 July 1970	**AA**
AE 29	MOUNT HOOD	66	17 July 1968	1 May 1971	**PA**
AE 32	FLINT	67	9 Nov 1970	20 Nov 1971	**PA**
AE 33	SHASTA	67	3 Apr 1971	26 Feb 1972	**PA**
AE 34	MOUNT BAKER	68	23 Oct 1971	22 July 1972	**AA**
AE 35	KISKA	68	11 Mar 1972	16 Dec 1972	**PA**
AE 36	. . . . . .	86			Planned
AE 37	. . . . . .	87			Planned
AE 38	. . . . . .	88			Planned
AE 39	. . . . . .	89			Planned

Builders:	AE 26-27 General Dynamics, Quincy, Mass.
	AE 28-29 Bethlehem Steel, Sparrows Point, Md.
	AE 32-35 Ingalls Shipbuilding, Pascagoula, Miss.
Displacement:	20,500 tons full load
Length:	564 feet (172.0 m) oa
Beam:	81 feet (24.7 m)
Draft:	25¾ feet (7.8 m)
Propulsion:	steam turbine (General Electric); 22,000 shp; 1 shaft
Boilers:	3 (Foster Wheeler)
Speed:	22 knots (20 sustained)
Manning:	active ships 390 (17 or 18 officers + 372 or 373 enlisted) except 392 (18 officers + 374 enlisted) in AE 27
	T-AE 26 121 (civilian) + 35 Navy (2 officers + 33 enlisted)
Helicopters:	2 CH-46 Sea Knight
Missiles:	none
Guns:	4 3-inch (76-mm) 50-cal AA Mk 33 (2 twin) except none in T-AE 26

These are high-capability underway replenishment ships, fitted for the rapid transfer of missiles and other munitions. The KILAUEA was transferred to the Military Sealift Command on 1 October 1980; no additional transfers are planned.

The Navy has a requirement for 16 ammunition ships (AE/T-AE) to support an active fleet of 600+ ships.

Design: SCB No. 703. The KILAUEA design provides for the ship's main cargo spaces forward of the superstructure with a helicopter landing area aft. A hangar approximately 50 feet long and 15½ to 17½ feet wide is built into the superstructure. Cargo capacity is approximately 6,500 tons.

Guns: As built the ships had eight 3-inch guns in twin mounts with two Mk 56 GFCS. Their armament was reduced during the late 1970s. Two Phalanx CIWS are scheduled for installation in AE 27–29, 32.

KISKA (1983, Giorgio Arra)

KISKA (1983, Giorgio Arra)

5 AMMUNITION SHIPS: "SURIBACHI" CLASS

Number	Name	FY	Launched	Commissioned	Status
AE 21	SURIBACHI	54	2 Nov 1955	17 Nov 1956	**AA**
AE 22	MAUNA KEA	54	3 May 1956	30 Mar 1957	**PA**
AE 23	NITRO	56	25 June 1958	1 May 1959	**AA**
AE 24	PYRO	56	5 Nov 1958	24 July 1959	**PA**
AE 25	HALEAKALA	57	17 Feb 1959	3 Nov 1959	**PA**

Builders:	Bethlehem Steel, Sparrows Point, Md.
Displacement:	10,000 tons standard
	17,500 tons full load
Length:	512 feet (156.1 m) oa
Beam:	72 feet (22.0 m)
Draft:	29 feet (8.8 m)
Propulsion:	steam turbine (Bethlehem); 16,000 shp; 1 shaft
Boilers:	2 (Combustion Engineering)
Speed:	20.6 knots
Manning:	346 to 348 (16 to 18 officers + 330 enlisted)
Helicopters:	landing area only
Missiles:	none
Guns:	4 3-inch (76-mm) 50-cal AA Mk 33 (2 twin)

These ships were designed specifically for underway replenishment of munitions. The MAUNA KEA was transferred to the Naval Reserve Force on 1 October 1979 and the PYRO on 1 September 1980; however, the heavy operating tempo of the Iranian crisis of 1979–1980 led to their being returned to the active fleet on 1 June 1982.

Class: The three later ships are also referred to as the NITRO class.

Design: SCB No. 114A. Cargo capacity is 7,500 tons.

Guns: These ships were completed with eight 3-inch guns in twin mounts (see Modernization notes). The arrangement of the forward guns varies; some ships have 3-inch mounts side-by-side and others in a tandem arrangement. The Mk 56 and Mk 63 GFCS have been removed.

Modernization: All five ships were extensively modernized during the 1960s (SCB project No. 232). They were fitted to carry and transfer guided missiles; their after 3-inch gun mounts were removed and a helicopter deck installed. No hangar was provided.

MAUNA KEA—tandem gun arrangement (1983, Giorgio Arra)

HALEAKALA—side-by-side gun arrangement (1982, Giorgio Arra)

1 STORE SHIP: "RIGEL"

Number	Name	FY	Launched	Completed	Status
T-AF 58	RIGEL	53	15 Mar 1953	2 Sep 1955	**MSC-A**

Builders:	Ingalls Shipbuilding, Pascagoula, Miss.
Displacement:	7,950 tons light
	15,540 tons full load
Length:	475 feet (144.9 m) wl
	502 feet (153.1 m) oa
Beam:	72 feet (22.0 m)
Draft:	29 feet (8.8 m)
Propulsion:	steam turbine (General Electric); 16,000 shp; 1 shaft
Boilers:	2 (Combustion Engineering)
Speed:	21 knots
Manning:	115 (civilian) + 18 Navy (1 officer and 17 enlisted)

Helicopters:	landing area
Missiles:	none
Guns:	removed

The RIGEL is the last refrigerated store ship in U.S. naval service. She was assigned to MSC on 23 June 1975.

Class: Two ships of this class were constructed (AF 58 and VEGA, AF 59). They were constructed specifically for this role.

Design: SCB No. 97. Modified Maritime Administration R3-S-A4 design. Cargo capacity is 4,650 tons.

Guns: The RIGEL was completed with eight 3-inch AA guns Mk 33 in twin mounts. The two after mounts were removed for installation of a helicopter platform. The forward guns and associated Mk 56 and Mk 63 GFCS were removed when the ship was assigned to MSC.

RIGEL (1983, Giorgio Arra)

3 COMBAT STORES SHIPS: Ex-BRITISH STORES SUPPORT SHIPS

Number	Name	Launched	Completed	U.S. in Service	Status
T-AFS 8	SIRIUS	7 Apr 1966	22 Dec 1966	17 Jan 1981	**MSC-A**
T-AFS 9	SPICA	22 Feb 1967	21 Mar 1967	4 Nov 1981	**MSC-P**
T-AFS 10	SATURN	16 Sep 1966	10 Aug 1967	30 Sep 1984	**MSC**

Builders:	Swan Hunter & Wighman Richardson, Wallsend-on-Tyne, England
Displacement:	9,010 tons light
	16,792 tons full load
Length:	524 feet (159.8 m) oa
Beam:	72 feet (22.0 m)
Draft:	22 feet (6.7 m)
Propulsion:	1 diesel (Wallsend-Sulzer); 11,520 bhp; 1 shaft
Speed:	18 knots

Manning:	Civilian	Navy	Officer	Enlisted
T-AFS 8	127	43	6	37
T-AFS 9	127	43	4	39
T-AFS 10	130	45	5	40

Helicopters:	landing area except 2 CH-46 Sea Knight in T-AFS 8 (see notes)
Missiles:	none
Guns:	none

SIRIUS, as refitted with helicopter hangar facility, in 1983–1984. (1984, Giorgio Arra)

These are former Royal Navy replenishment ships, acquired by the U.S. Navy because of the increased logistics demands of maintaining two carrier battle groups in the Indian Ocean during the Iranian hostage crisis of 1979–1980. They were all previously operated as Royal Fleet Auxiliaries (RFA) with civilian crews.

The Navy has a force level goal of nine combat stores ships (AFS/ T-AFS) to support a fleet of 600 + ships. With the purchase of the third ship, the Navy dropped plans to construct an additional AFS under the fiscal 1987 shipbuilding program (at an estimated cost of $350–400 million).

Class: This was a three-ship class, their British names being LYNESS, TARBATNESS, and STROMNESS, respectively. The LYNESS was originally acquired by the U.S. government on a bare-boat charter for one year on 17 January 1981 at which time she was placed in U.S. service (named SIRUS and designated T-AFS 8); acquired on 1 March 1982.

The TARBATNESS was acquired on time charter on 30 September 1981; changed to bare-boat charter on 4 November 1981 and at that time placed in U.S. service (named SPICA and designated T-AFS 9).

The STROMNESS was acquired on 18 December 1983.

The SIRUS and SPICA were purchased under the fiscal 1982 program at a total cost of $37 million. The SATURN was purchased in fiscal 1984 for $13 million (plus $3.1 million in spare parts for the entire class).

Modernization: In U.S. service the ships are being modernized with the provision of improved communications and UNREP facilities, plus automated data processing; the T-AFS 8 has been provided with a hangar structure aft to accommodate two Sea Knight helicopters.

SIRIUS (1982, Giorgio Arra)

SPICA (1983, U.S. Navy, Lt. Don Fraiser/Lt. (jg) Dave Winkowski)

7 COMBAT STORES SHIPS: "MARS" CLASS

Number	Name	FY	Launched	Commissioned	Status
AFS 1	MARS	61	15 June 1963	21 Dec 1963	**PA**
AFS 2	SYLVANIA	62	15 Aug 1963	11 July 1964	**AA**
AFS 3	NIAGARA FALLS	64	26 Mar 1966	29 Apr 1967	**PA**
AFS 4	WHITE PLAINS	65	23 July 1966	23 Nov 1968	**PA**
AFS 5	CONCORD	65	17 Dec 1966	27 Nov 1968	**AA**
AFS 6	SAN DIEGO	66	13 Apr 1968	24 May 1969	**AA**
AFS 7	SAN JOSE	67	13 Dec 1969	23 Oct 1970	**PA**

Builders:	National Steel & Shipbuilding, San Diego, Calif.
Displacement:	16,500 tons full load
Length:	530 feet (161.6 m) wl
	581¼ feet (177.25 m) oa
Beam:	79 feet (24.1 m)
Draft:	24 feet (7.3 m)
Propulsion:	steam turbine (De Laval in AFS 1, 2, 4, 5, 7 Westinghouse in AFS 3, 6); 22,000 shp; 1 shaft
Boilers:	3 (Babcock & Wilcox)
Speed:	21 knots
Manning:	425 to 437 (24 or 25 officers + 401 to 412 enlisted)
Helicopters:	2 CH-46 Sea Knight
Missiles:	none
Guns:	4 3-inch (76-mm) 50-cal AA Mk 33 (2 twin) except 8 guns in AFS 4

These are large, built-for-the-purpose underway replenishment ships combining the capabilities of store ships (AF), store-issue ships (AKS), and aviation store ships (AVS). They do not carry bulk petroleum products as do the AOE-AOR replenishment ships.

The WHITE PLAINS is home ported in Yokosuka, Japan.

Class: Three additional ships that were originally planned in the fiscal 1977–1978 shipbuilding programs were not requested by the Administration in those years.

Design: The AFS 1-3 were SCB No. 208; the later ships were No. 705 in the later SCB series. These ships have five cargo holds (one refrigerated) with a 7,000-ton cargo capacity. A large helicopter deck is fitted with a hangar 46¾ to 51 feet in length and 16 to 23 feet wide.

Engineering: Two boilers are normally used for full-power steaming with the third shut down for maintenance.

Guns: These ships were completed with four 3-inch twin gun mounts, one pair of mounts forward and a second pair aft of the funnels. Two mounts were deleted from all ships but the WHITE PLAINS during the late 1970s; all ships lost their Mk 56 GFCS.

All are scheduled to receive two CIWS.

SAN DIEGO (1983, Giorgio Arra)

The first combat stores ship, combining the functions of an AF/AKS/AVS in a single hull. Note the empty 3-inch gun positions aft of the funnel; the twin 3-inch mounts are retained forward. (1983, Giorgio Arra)

1 HEAVY LIFT SHIP: "GLOMAR EXPLORER"

Number	Name	Launched	Completed	Status
AG 193	GLOMAR EXPLORER	14 Nov 1972	July 1973	NDRF

Builders:	Sun Shipbuilding and Dry Dock, Chester, Pa.
Displacement:	63,300 tons full load
Tonnage:	39,705 tons deadweight
	27,445 tons gross
	18,511 tons net
Length:	618¾ feet (188.7 m) oa
Beam:	115⅔ feet (35.3 m)
Draft:	46⅔ feet (14.2 m)
Propulsion:	diesel-electric (Nordberg diesels; General Electric motors); 13,200 bhp; 2 shafts
Speed:	10.8 knots
Manning:	approx. 180 (civilian)
Helicopters:	landing area
Missiles:	none
Guns:	none

The GLOMAR EXPLORER was built and operated by the Central Intelligence Agency specifically to lift the remains of a Soviet Golf-class ballistic missile submarine (SSB) that sank in the mid-Pacific in 1968. The ship lifted the forward portion of the submarine from a depth of three miles in 1974 in a clandestine operation given the code name Jennifer. (The ship's cover story was a seafloor mining operation under the aegis of millionaire Howard Hughes through the Summa Corporation for his Global Marine Development firm.)

The ship was acquired by the Navy on 30 September 1976; she was transferred to the Maritime Administration on 17 January 1977 and laid up in the National Defense Reserve Fleet in Suisun Bay, Calif.

Subsequent Navy efforts to sell the ship failed, and in 1978 she was leased to Global Marine Development, Inc., for a commercial seafloor mining venture; she was to be operated by the Lockheed Missiles and Space Company in that role. That lease was terminated in 1980, however, and the ship was returned to Navy control on 25 April 1980 and again assigned to the Maritime Administration on the same date. She remains on the Naval Register and is laid up in Suisun Bay.

There have been several studies that have proposed the ship for use as a scientific seafloor drilling ship and for other uses.

Classification: When acquired by the Navy in 1976 the GLOMAR EXPLORER was assigned hull number AG 193.

Cost: The cost of the ship at the time of construction was estimated at approximately $350 million. Certain related equipment and the cost of the HMB-1 submersible barge plus personnel brought the total project costs to some $550 million.

Design: The ship was designed specifically to lift the sunken Golf-class submarine from a depth of 16,500 feet, employing a heavy lift system including a grappling claw that could be attached to the ship clandestinely by a submersible barge (designated HMB-1). Reportedly, the barge would also be used to hide the Soviet submarine had the entire 330-foot craft been salvaged. In the event, the portion salvaged could be accommodated in a large underwater hangar or Moon Pool within the GLOMAR EXPLORER.

Name: As built, the ship was named HUGHES GLOMAR EXPLORER; changed when acquired by the Navy.

Operational: The GLOMAR EXPLORER arrived at the submarine lift site on 4 July 1974 and during the month-long operation lifted the forward portion of the submarine. The amidships section containing the three SSN-5 ballistic missiles with nuclear warheads was not salvaged. However, torpedoes were recovered, including two reported to have nuclear warheads. The remains of the submarine were studied within the GLOMAR EXPLORER; then cut apart and packaged for further analyses or jettisoned.

This was the deepest and most complex salvage operation ever undertaken.

Propulsion: Three bow and two stern thrusters are fitted with an automatic position-keeping system to permit precise maneuvering or holding directly over an object on the ocean floor.

The GLOMAR EXPLORER, as laid up in Suisun Bay, Calif. (1981, Norman Polmar)

(1) RESEARCH SHIP: CONVERTED MERCHANT SHIP

The Navy plans to convert a merchant ship for acoustic research to replace the MONOB I (YAG 61); see Chapter 25.

1 HYDROGRAPHIC RESEARCH SHIP: CONVERTED VICTORY TYPE

Number	Name	Launched	In service	Status
T-AG 164	Kingsport	29 May 1944	1 Mar 1950	**MSC-A**

Builders:	California Shipbuilding, Los Angeles, Calif.
Displacement:	7,190 tons light
	10,680 tons full load
Length:	436½ feet (133.1 m) wl
	455 feet (138.8 m) oa
Beam:	62 feet (18.9 m)
Draft:	22 feet (6.7 m)
Propulsion:	steam turbine; 8,500 shp; 1 shaft
Boilers:	2
Speed:	15.2 knots
Manning:	54 (civilian) + 15 technicians
Helicopters:	no facilities
Missiles:	none
Guns:	none

The Kingsport was built as a cargo ship and was employed in carrying military cargo until acquired by the Navy on 1 March 1950 and assigned to the Military Sea Transportation Service (retaining her original name Kingsport Victory). She continued in the cargo role as the T-AK 239 until 1961 when she was converted to a research ship to support the Project Advent defense satellite communications program. In that role the ship was renamed Kingsport and changed to T-AG 164.

The support of Project Advent and other space programs was completed in 1964 and the Kingsport was then reassigned to hydrographic research activities in support of undersea surveillance programs. She is operated by MSC in support of the Naval Electronic Systems Command; she is civilian manned.

Class: The only other AG-type ship in active naval service is the Vanguard (T-AG 194); Victory ships also survive as survey ships (AGS) and cargo ships (AK).

The Vanguard is listed with her sister ship Redstone (T-AGM 20). Two other miscellaneous auxiliary ships remaining on the Naval Register are on loan:

Classification: Changed from T-AK 239 to T-AG 164 (and renamed) on 14 November 1961.

Conversion: Conversion to a satellite communications ship included the provision of extensive communications and satellite tracking equipment, including a 30-foot parabolic communications antenna housed in a 53-foot diameter plastic radome aft of the superstructure (later removed). The ship was painted white for operations in the tropics. The conversion was SCB No. 225.

Design: Maritime Administration VC2-S-AP3 design.

Kingsport (1981, J. Jedrlinic)

Kingsport (Giorgio Arra)

SURVEYING SHIP

The small surveying ship S.P. LEE (AG 192, formerly AGS 31) was loaned to the U.S. Geological Survey in February 1974; the ship is carried on the Naval Register in a "lease" status. See Appendix B.

AUXILIARY DEEP SUBMERGENCE SUPPORT SHIP: "POINT LOMA"

Number	Name	Launched	T-AKD in service	AGDS Comm.	Status
AGDS 2	POINT LOMA	25 May 1957	29 May 1958	26 Feb 1976	**PA**

Builders:	Maryland Shipbuilding & Dry Dock, Baltimore
Displacement:	9,478 tons standard
	10,025 tons full load
Length:	465½ feet (142.0 m) oa
Beam:	74 feet (22.6 m)
Draft:	22½ feet (6.9 m)
Propulsion:	steam turbines; 6,000 shp; 2 shafts
Boilers:	2
Speed:	15 knots
Manning:	244 (14 officers + 230 enlisted) + 20 technicians
Helicopters:	no facilities
Missiles:	none
Guns:	none

The POINT LOMA was built as a "wet well" dock cargo ship (originally the POINT BARROW, T-AKD 1) to carry vehicles, supplies, and landing craft to support U.S. radar installations in the Arctic. She was assigned to MSTS upon completion and operated in that role until 1965. The ship was modified in 1965 to carry Saturn missile boosters and other space program equipment from California to Cape Kennedy and served in that role until 1970. (She also made some trips to Vietnam carrying landing craft during that period.)

The ship was laid up in 1971–1972 and then returned to general cargo work under the Military Sealift Command. She was converted in 1974–1976 to transport and support the research submersible TRIESTE. Subsequently, in the early 1980s she was fitted to instead support other submersibles and given the additional role of support ship for the operational test firings of Trident submarine missiles, being fitted with extensive tracking gear.

The POINT LOMA is operated by Submarine Development Group 1 at Point Loma (San Diego), Calif.

Classification: The classification AGDS was established on 3 January 1974. The previous TRIESTE II support ship, the modified floating dry dock WHITE SANDS (ARD 20), was briefly assigned the hull number AGDS 1.

Conversion: The ship was converted in 1974–1976 specifically for use with the TRIESTE II; she could carry, launch, recover, and service the submersible. Tankage was provided for approximately 100,000 gallons of aviation gasoline used for flotation by the TRIESTE II and the lead shot that was used by the submersible for ballast.

She was modified in 1980–1982 at the Mare Island Naval Shipyard to support the DSVs TURTLE and SEA CLIFF and to carry out deep-sea recovery operations as well as support Trident missile test launches. For the DSV support the aviation gasoline handling capability was deleted and deep-sea recovery gear was installed.

For Trident support the POINT LOMA was fitted with four missile tracking and telemetry vans; additional HF/UHF/satellite communications equipment; a variable-depth sonar tracking system; and berthing for technical support personnel.

Design: Maritime Administration S2-ST-23A design. The ship was originally ice-strengthened and winterized for Arctic supply operations. She is no longer "winterized" because of the removal of the hull steam jacket system and conversion of the firemain from dry to wet operation.

The POINT LOMA in her latest configuration. The many roles of the POINT LOMA during more than two years of service attest to the flexibility of LSD/LPD/AKD design. The crane is mounted on the port side wall. (1983, Giorgio Arra)

The bow of the POINT LOMA; the four spherical antennas are designated LASS (Launch Area Support Ship) and provide telemetry support for Trident missile flight tests in the Pacific. Several support vans are also carried. (1982, U.S. Navy)

The POINT LOMA's docking well with the stern ramp lowered. There is a traction winch at left as well as the crane for deep-ocean recovery. (1982, Giorgio Arra)

1 MISSILE RANGE INSTRUMENTATION SHIP: MARINER TYPE

Number	Name	Launched	Commissioned	Status
T-AGM 23	OBSERVATION ISLAND	15 Aug 1953	5 Dec 1958	**MSC-A**

Builders:	New York Shipbuilding, Camden, N.J.
Displacement:	13,060 tons light
	17,015 tons full load
Length:	563 feet (171.7 m) oa
Beam:	76 feet (23.2 m)
Draft:	29 feet (8.8 m)
Propulsion:	steam turbine (General Electric); 22,000 shp; 1 shaft
Boilers:	2
Speed:	20 knots
Manning:	
Helicopters:	no facilities
Missiles:	none
Guns:	none

The ship was completed for commercial service in February 1954 and after operating briefly was laid up in the National Defense Reserve Fleet in November 1954. She was transferred to the Navy on 10 September 1956 for conversion to a missile test ship for the Polaris SLBM, being commissioned in 1958; she was subsequently modified to launch the Poseidon missile. After completion of the Poseidon development program, the ship was decommissioned on 25 September 1972 and again laid up in the NDRF.

The OBSERVATION ISLAND was selected for conversion to a missile range instrumentation ship on 18 August 1977. She was fitted with the Cobra Judy phased-array radar aft and two radar spheres were installed atop her superstructure. She is operated by MSC with a civilian crew

The OBSERVATION ISLAND as a tracking ship with the Cobra Judy phased-array radar fitted amidships. (1981, Raytheon)

in support of Air Force and the National Aeronautics and Space Administration activities on the Air Force Eastern Test Range.

Class: Five Mariner-class merchant ships were acquired by the Navy, with three being converted to amphibious assault ships (AKA 112, APA 248, APA 249) and two to support ships for the Polaris program, the COMPASS ISLAND (AG 153) and OBSERVATION ISLAND. A planned third Mariner to support the Polaris effort (AG 155) was not acquired.

The COMPASS ISLAND was configured to test strategic missile submarine navigation systems. She was laid up in 1980 and stricken on 1 October 1981.

Classification: The OBSERVATION ISLAND was originally classified YAG 57 for naval service; changed to AG 154 on 19 June 1956, being listed as EAG 154 until 1 April 1968 when the ship was "reclassified" as AG 154 to avoid confusion. The ship was changed to T-AGM 23 on 1 May 1979.

Conversion: Converted to AGM configuration at the Maryland Shipbuilding & Dry Dock Co., Baltimore, Md., from 1977–1981.

Design: Maritime Administration C4-S-1A design. As an AG she was fitted with two SLBM launch tubes.

Names: Her merchant name was EMPIRE STATE MARINER.

OBSERVATION ISLAND (1981, Raytheon)

1 MISSILE RANGE INSTRUMENTATION SHIP: VICTORY TYPE

Number	Name	Launched	APA Comm.	T-AGM in service	Status
T-AGM 22	Range Sentinel	10 July 1944	20 Sep 1944	14 Oct 1971	**MSC-A**

Builders:	Permanente Metals, Richmond, Calif.
Displacement:	11,860 tons full load
Length:	436½ feet (133.1 m) wl
	455 feet (138.8 m) oa
Beam:	62 feet (18.9 m)
Draft:	23 feet (7.0 m)
Propulsion:	steam turbine (Westinghouse); 8,500 shp; 1 shaft
Boilers:	2
Speed:	17.7 knots
Manning:	68 (civilian) + 27 technicians
Helicopters:	no facilities
Missiles:	none
Guns:	none

The Range Sentinel is a former Navy amphibious transport (APA 205) converted to a missile range instrumentation ship. She served in the amphibious role in World War II, being subsequently laid up and stricken on 1 October 1958. She was reacquired from the Maritime Administration on 22 October 1969 for conversion to an AGM.

The ship operates in support of SSBN missile firings in the Atlantic.

Class: A total of eight Victory-type merchant ships served in various AGM configurations (T-AGM 1, 3-8, 22).

Classification: Changed to AGM on 26 April 1971.

Design: Maritime Administration design VC2-S-AP5.

Names: The ship's name as APA 205 was Sherburne.

1 NAVIGATION RESEARCH SHIP } **CONVERTED OILERS**
1 MISSILE RANGE INSTRUMENTATION SHIP

Number	Name	Launched	AO Comm.	T-AGM in service	Status
T-AG 194	Vanguard	22 Nov 1943	21 Oct 1947	28 Feb 1966	NDFF
T-AGM 20	Redstone	28 Feb 1944	22 Oct 1947	30 June 1966	**MSC-A**

Builders:	Marine Ship, Sausalito, Calif.
Displacement:	21,626 tons full load
Length:	595 feet (181.5 m) oa
Beam:	75 feet (22.9 m)
Draft:	25 feet (7.6 m)
Propulsion:	turbo-electric drive (General Electric); 10,000 shp; 1 shaft
Boilers:	2 (Babcock & Wilcox)
Speed:	16 knots
Manning:	76 (civilian) + 120 technicians in T-AGM 20
Helicopters:	no facilities
Missiles:	none
Guns:	none

These ships are former Mission-class oilers that were extensively converted for the missile range instrumentation role. One ship was subsequently modified for use as a navigation test ship for Trident strategic missile submarines.

Both ships initially served as Navy oilers and were then transferred to MSTS service when that service was created on 1 October 1949. The Vanguard was stricken as AO 122 on 4 September 1957; she was reacquired by the Navy on 28 September 1964 for conversion to AGM 19. The Redstone was stricken as AO 114 on 13 March 1958; reacquired by the Navy on 19 September 1964 to become AGM 20.

Redstone is assisted by a commercial tug as she departs from Cape Canaveral, Fla., in order to support a missile launch on the Eastern Test Range from Cape Kennedy. (1970, U.S. Air Force)

VANGUARD at Southampton (1984, L. &. L. van Ginderen)

The VANGUARD was assigned to the Navy's Strategic Systems Project Office[1] on 1 October 1978 for conversion to a navigation research ship to replace the COMPASS ISLAND (AG 153). She initially served as T-AGM 19 but changed to T-AG 194 on 30 September 1980.

Both ships were operated by MSC with the REDSTONE supporting Air Force and NASA activities; the VANGUARD is temporarily laid up in NDRF.

Class: A third ship of this type, the MERCURY (T-AGM 21), was stricken on 28 April 1970.

Conversions: Both ships were extensively converted to the AGM configuration at the General Dynamics yard in Quincy, Mass. A 72-foot section was installed amidships, increasing the ships' length and beam of 523½ feet and 68 feet, respectively; they were fitted with missile/space tracking systems, extensive communications equipment, and accommodations for a large technical staff. Their configurations differed as AGMs.

The VANGUARD was converted to a navigation research ship at the Todd Corporation's Brooklyn, N.Y., yard in 1979–1980.

Design: Originally these ships were Maritime Administration T2-SE-A2 design.

Names: The VANGUARD was built as the MISSION SAN FERNANDO; renamed MUSCLE SHOALS on 8 April 1965 and then VANGUARD on 1 September 1965. The REDSTONE was built as the MISSION DE PALA; changed to JOHNSTOWN on 8 April 1965 and to REDSTONE on 1 September 1965.

Operational: These ships were converted specifically to support the Apollo lunar flight program, with the MERCURY operating in the Indian Ocean, the VANGUARD in the Atlantic, and the REDSTONE in the Pacific during manned flights to the moon.

FORMER TRANSPORT TYPE

The large converted troop transports GENERAL H.H. ARNOLD (T-AGM 9, ex-AP 139) was stricken on 23 February 1982, and GENERAL HOYT S. VANDENBERG (T-AGM 10, ex-AP 145) on 8 February 1983 and temporarily laid up in NDRF. These World War II-built ships had been converted to support Air Force ICBM tests with the VANDENBERG later supporting Navy SLBM test firings. They were C4-S-A1 design.

[1]PM-1 within the Naval Material Command.

2 OCEANOGRAPHIC RESEARCH SHIPS: "GYRE" CLASS

Number	Name	FY	Launched	Delivered	Status
(AGOR 21)	GYRE	71	25 May 1973	14 Nov 1973	**Academic**
(AGOR 22)	MOANA WAVE	71	18 June 1973	16 Jan 1974	**Academic**

Builders:	Halter Marine Service, New Orleans, La.
Displacement:	950 tons full load
Length:	176 feet (53.7 m) oa
Beam:	36 feet (11.0 m)
Draft:	14½ feet (4.4 m)
Propulsion:	geared diesels (Caterpillar); 1,700 bhp; 2 shafts
Speed:	13 knots
Range:	8,000 n.miles at 10 knots
Manning:	AGOR 21 10 (civilian) + 22 scientists
	AGOR 22 15 (civilian) + 13 scientists
Helicopters:	no facilities
Missiles:	none
Guns:	none

Stern of MOANA WAVE (Giorgio Arra)

These are small "utility" research ships designed specifically for use by academic research institutions. They are operated for the Oceanographer of the Navy by Texas A&M University and the University of Hawaii, respectively; they were assigned to those institutions upon completion. The MOANA WAVE has been employed for at-sea testing of the T-AGOS towed sonar array.

Design: SCB No. 734. These ships are based on a commercial ship design. The open deck aft provides space for special-purpose vans and research equipment. A bow thruster is fitted.

Engineering: A small, 50-hp retractable propeller pod is fitted for low-speed maneuvering or station keeping during research operations, thus permitting the main engines to be shut down to reduce the interference of machinery noise and vibration with research activities.

The MOANA WAVE with her stern modified from previous configuration. (Giorgio Arra)

1 OCEANOGRAPHIC RESEARCH SHIP: "HAYES"

Number	Name	FY	Launched	Commissioned	Status
T-AGOR 16	HAYES	67	2 July 1970	21 July 1971	**MSC-A**

Builders:	Todd Shipyards, Seattle, Wash.
Displacement:	3,080 tons full load
Length:	246⁵/₁₂ feet (75.1 m) oa
Beam:	75 feet (22.9 m)
Draft:	18½ feet (5.6 m)
Propulsion:	geared diesels (General Motors); 5,400 bhp; 2 shafts
Speed:	15 knots
Range:	6,000 n.miles at 14 knots
Manning:	45 (civilians) + 30 scientists
Helicopters:	no facilities
Missiles:	none
Guns:	none

The HAYES is the Navy's largest built-for-the-purpose oceanographic research ship. This ship and the two ASR 21 submarine rescue ships are the Navy's only oceangoing catamarans.

The catamaran design provides a stable work platform with a large, open deck area; also, a center-line well makes it possible to lower research equipment into sheltered water between the two hulls. However, some sea-keeping problems were encountered with the design and it has not been repeated.

The HAYES is operated by MSC for the Office of Naval Research under the technical control of the Oceanographer of the Navy.

Design: SCB No. 726. The HAYES has two hulls, each with a 24-foot beam, spaced 27 feet apart for an overall ship beam of 75 feet. Berthing and messing spaces are located in the forward superstructure "block" while the laboratories are located aft.

Engineering: An auxiliary 165-hp diesel engine is provided in each hull to permit a "creeping" speed of 2 to 4 knots with main propulsion shut down.

The HAYES has "U.S. Naval Ship"—the designation for MSC ships—and name on the stern counters of both hulls. (1981, L. & L. van Ginderen)

The HAYES is the Firth of Clyde, Scotland. The hull design was not considered fully successful; the HAYES, however, has continued to perform useful research. (1981, L. & L. van Ginderen)

2 OCEANOGRAPHIC RESEARCH SHIPS: "MELVILLE" CLASS

Number	Name	FY	Launched	Commissioned	Status
(AGOR 14)	MELVILLE	66	10 July 1968	27 Aug 1969	**Academic**
(AGOR 15)	KNORR	66	21 Aug 1968	14 Jan 1970	**Academic**

Builders:	Defoe Shipbuilding, Bay City, Mich.
Displacement:	1,915 tons standard
	2,080 tons standard
Length:	244⁵/₆ feet (74.7 m) oa
Beam:	46⅓ feet (14.1 m)
Draft:	15 feet (4.6 m)
Propulsion:	diesel (Enterprise); 2,500 bhp; 2 cycloidal propellers
Speed:	12.5 knots
Range:	10,000 n.miles at 10 knots
Manning:	AGOR 14 23 (civilian) + 29 scientists
	AGOR 15 25 (civilian) + 25 scientists
Helicopters:	no facilities
Missiles:	none
Guns:	none

These ships were the U.S. Navy's first oceangoing ships with cycloidal propellers (see Engineering notes). They have essentially the same capabilities as the previous CONRAD class.

The MELVILLE is operated by the Scripps Institution of Oceanography and the KNORR by the Woods Hole Oceanographic Institution, both for the Office of Naval Research under the technical control of the Oceanographer of the Navy. They were assigned to those institutions upon completion.

Class: The AGOR 19 and 20 were in the fiscal 1968 program but their construction was cancelled.

Design: SCB No. 710. Although these ships have the same SCB number as the CONRAD class, they are quite different. A bow observation dome is fitted.

Engineering: These ships have a single diesel engine driving two cycloidal (vertical) propellers; the forward propeller is located just behind the bow observation dome and the after propeller is just in front of the rudder. The ships can hold a fixed position in heavy seas with winds up to 35 knots. Cycloidal propulsion—controlled by a "joystick"—allows the ship to be propelled in any direction and to turn up to 360° in their own length. This type of propulsion also allows precise station keeping and slow speeds without the use of auxiliary propulsion units. The ships have experienced some transmission system difficulties.

MELVILLE

Cycloidal propeller on the MELVILLE (Courtesy Stewart Nelson)

KNORR (L. & L. van Ginderen)

6 OCEANOGRAPHIC RESEARCH SHIPS: "CONRAD" CLASS

Number	Name	FY	Launched	In Service	Status
(AGOR 3)	ROBERT D. CONRAD	60	26 May 1962	29 Nov 1962	**Academic**
T-AGOR 7	LYNCH	62	17 Mar 1964	22 Oct 1965	**MSC-A**
(AGOR 9)	THOMAS G. THOMPSON	63	18 July 1964	4 Sep 1965	**Academic**
(AGOR 10)	THOMAS WASHINGTON	63	1 Aug 1964	17 Sep 1965	**Academic**
T-AGOR 12	DE STEIGUER	65	21 Mar 1966	28 Feb 1969	**MSC-P**
T-AGOR 13	BARTLETT	65	24 Mar 1966	15 Apr 1969	**MSC-A**

Builders:	AGOR 3 Gibbs, Jacksonville, Fla.
	AGOR 7 Marietta Manufacturing, Point Pleasant, West Va.
	AGOR 9-10 Marinette Marine, Wisc.
	AGOR 12-13 Northwest Marine Iron Works, Portland, Ore.
Displacement:	(varies) approx. 1,200 tons standard
	approx. 1,380 tons full load
Length:	196 feet (59.8 m) wl
	208⅝ feet (63.7 m) oa
Beam:	37 feet (11.3 m)
Draft:	approx. 14½ feet (4.4 m)
Propulsion:	diesel-electric (Caterpillar); approx. 1,000 bhp; 1 shaft
Speed:	13.5 knots
Range:	12,000 n.miles at 9 knots
Manning:	AGOR 3
	T-AGOR 7
	AGOR 9 22 (civilian) + 19 scientists
	AGOR 10 21 (civilian) + 17 scientists
	T-AGOR 12
	T-AGOR 13
Helicopters:	no facilities
Missiles:	none
Guns:	none

These were the U.S. Navy's first built-for-the-purpose oceanographic research ships. Three ships are operated by MSC; the CONRAD is operated by the Lamont Geological Laboratory of Columbia University, the THOMPSON by the University of Washington (state), and the WASHINGTON by the Scripps Institution of Oceanography. All are under the technical control of the Oceanographer of the Navy. The three institution-operated ships were assigned upon completion.

Class: Three other ships of this class have been transferred to other nations: the JAMES M. GILLISS (AGOR 4) to Mexico in October 1982, the CHARLES H. DAVIS (AGOR 5) to New Zealand in July 1970, and the SANDS (AGOR 6) to Brazil in July 1974.

Design: The early ships were SCB No. 185; the AGOR 12 and 13 were changed to the new series No. 710. These ships vary in detail, each with differing bridge, side structure, mast, and laboratory arrangements.

Engineering: The large stacks contain a small diesel exhaust funnel and provide space for the small, 620-ship gas turbine engine used in these ships to provide "quiet" power when noise generated by the main propulsion machinery could interfere with research activities. The gas turbine can be linked to the propeller shaft for speeds up to 6.5 knots. There is also a retractable bow propeller pod that allows precise maneuvering and can propel the ship at speeds up to 4.5 knots.

LYNCH (1973, Giorgio Arra)

Propulsion pod on rudder of the DE STEIGUER (Northwest Marine Iron Works)

DE STEIGUER (1983, Giorgio Arra)

2 OCEANOGRAPHIC RESEARCH SHIPS: CONVERTED CARGO SHIPS

Number	Name	Launched	AK in service	AGOR in service	Status
T-AGOR 8	ELTANIN	16 Jan 1957	2 Aug 1957	1962	NDRF
T-AGOR 11	MIZAR	7 Oct 1957	7 Mar 1958	1965	**MSC-P**

Builders:	Avondale Marine Ways, New Orleans, La.
Displacement:	2,036 tons light
	4,942 tons full load
Length:	262⅙ feet (79.9 m) oa
Beam:	51½ feet (15.7 m)
Draft:	22¾ feet (6.9 m)
Propulsion:	diesel-electric (Alco diesels; Westinghouse electric motors); 3,200 bhp; 2 shafts
Speed:	12 knots
Range:	
Manning:	T-AGOR 11 46 (civilians) + 15 technicians + 5 Navy (enlisted)
Helicopters:	landing area in T-AGOR 8
	no facilities in T-AGOR 11
Missiles:	none
Guns:	none

Both ships were built specifically to carry cargo for U.S. military projects in the Arctic area. They were extensively modified for oceanographic research, being assigned to MSC for operation in that role with civilian crews.

The ELTANIN was transferred to Argentina in 1972 and served as a research ship until returned to U.S. custody on 1 August 1979 and is laid up on a temporary basis in the NDRF (Norfolk) pending further disposition.

The MIZAR is operated by MSC for the Naval Electronic Systems Command.

Class: Three cargo ships were built to this design. The third ship, the MIRFAK, is laid up in the NDRF as the T-AK 271.

Classification: The ELTANIN was changed from AK 270 to AGOR 8 on 23 August 1962; the MIZAR was changed from AK 272 to AGOR 11 on 15 April 1964.

Conversion: The MIZAR was converted to an AGOR in 1964–1965, being fitted with laboratories, underwater photographic equipment, and a center well for lowering towed sensors and instruments into the sea. She has an elaborate computer-controlled hydrophone system for precise sea-floor navigation. Her center well is 23 feet long and 10 feet wide.

The ELTANIN was converted to an oceanographic research ship in 1961, being fitted with scientific equipment for Antarctic research in support of the National Science Foundation.

Design: Originally Maritime Administration C1-ME2-13a design.

Operations: After partial conversion in 1964, the MIZAR was a key participant in the search for the remains of the sunken submarine THRESHER (SSN 593). The MIZAR subsequently helped to locate the sunken USS SCORPION (SSN 589) and the Soviet Golf-class diesel submarine that sank in the mid-Pacific in 1968. She also participated in the search for the French submarine EURYDICE in the Mediterranean and the hydrogen bomb lost at sea off Palomares, Spain.

MIZAR (Giorgio Arra)

The MIZAR in her current configuration; note that the forward mast, with enclosed crow's nest, has been removed. (Giorgio Arra)

1 OCEANOGRAPHIC RESEARCH SHIP: "ACANIA"

Number	Name	Launched	In service	Status
(none)	ACANIA	29 Jan 1929	6 Aug 1971	**PA**

Builders:	Pusey and Jones, Wilmington, Del.
Tonnage:	247 tons gross
Length:	126 1/12 feet (38.4 m) oa
Beam:	21½ feet (6.6 m)
Draft:	9¼ feet (2.8 m)
Propulsion:	2 diesels (General Motors); 560 bhp; 2 shafts
Speed:	10 knots
Range:	6,500 n.miles at 10 knots
Manning:	6 + 12 students
Helicopters:	no facilities
Missiles:	none
Guns:	none

The ACANIA is operated by the Oceanography Department of the Naval Postgraduate School in Monterey, Calif. The ship was built as a private yacht and acquired by the Coast Guard in August 1942 (commissioned 26 March 1943) for use as a patrol boat, being named NELLWOOD (designated WPYc 337).

She was subsequently returned to private ownership in 1947 but later reacquired by the government. Since 1971 she has been assigned to the Naval Postgraduate School as a research vessel (designated R/V vice USS or USNS); she is not carried on the Naval Register. The ACANIA is scheduled to be retired in 1985.

For short day trips the ACANIA can embark up to some 35 students.

Design: Steel hulled.

The ACANIA cruising off Monterey Bay. (U.S. Navy, JO1 J. H. Scott)

6 + 12 OCEAN SURVEILLANCE SHIPS: "STALWART" CLASS

Number	Name	FY	Launched	In service	Status
T-AGOS 1	STALWART	79	11 July 1983	1984	**MSC-A**
T-AGOS 2	CONTENDER	79	20 Dec 1983	1984	**MSC-A**
T-AGOS 3	VINDICATOR	80	1 June 1984	1984	**MSC**
T-AGOS 4	TRIUMPH	81		1984	**MSC**
T-AGOS 5	ASSURANCE	81		1984	**MSC**
T-AGOS 6	PERSISTENT	81		1984	**MSC**
T-AGOS 7	INDOMITABLE	81		1985	Building
T-AGOS 8	PREVAIL	81		1985	Building
T-AGOS 9	ASSERTIVE	82		1985	Building
T-AGOS 10	INVINCIBLE	82		1985	Building
T-AGOS 11	DAUNTLESS	82		1985	Building
T-AGOS 12	VIGOROUS	82		1986	Building
T-AGOS 13	. . . . . .	85			Planned
T-AGOS 14	. . . . . .	85			Planned
T-AGOS 15	. . . . . .	85			Planned
T-AGOS 16	. . . . . .	86			Planned
T-AGOS 17	. . . . . .	86			Planned
T-AGOS 18	. . . . . .	86			Planned

Builders:	Tacoma Boatbuilding, Wash.
Displacement:	2,285 tons full load
Length:	224 feet (68.3 m) oa
Beam:	43 feet (13.1 m)
Draft:	15½ feet (4.6 m)
Propulsion:	4 diesel generators (Caterpillar with General Electric motors); 3,200 bhp; 2 shafts
Speed:	11 knots; array towing speed 3 knots
Range:	3,000 n.miles at 11 knots (transit) + 6,500 n.miles at 3 knots (on station)
Manning:	20 (civilian) + 10 Navy technicians
Helicopters:	no facilities
Missiles:	none
Guns:	none

STALWART on sea trials before installation of SURTASS equipment. (1984, Giorgio Arra)

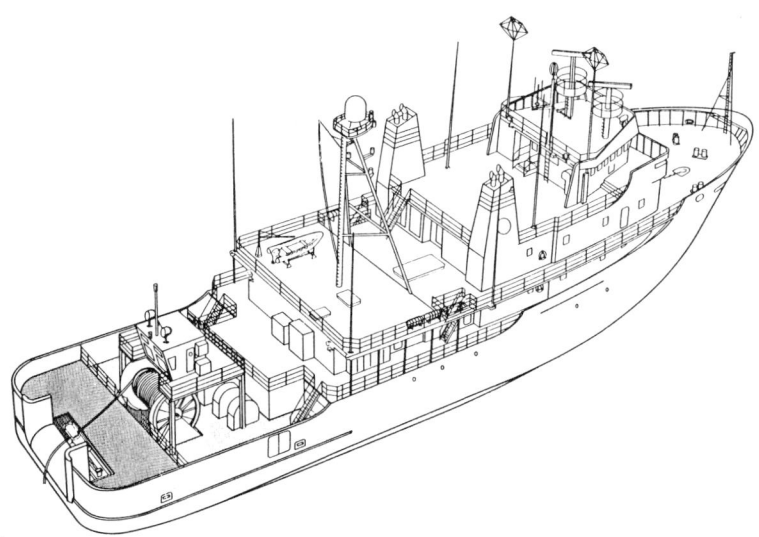

STALWART-class ocean surveillance ship

The Surveillance Towed Array Sensor System (SURTASS) is a submarine detection system towed by slow surface ships to supplement the seafloor Sound Surveillance System (SOSUS). These ships will operate where SOSUS coverage is inadequate or where the seafloor arrays are damaged or destroyed. The SURTASS data are sent via satellite link to shore facilities for processing and further transmission to ASW forces; however, the ships can provide "raw" acoustic data to ASW ships in the area. (The SURTASS concept differs from the tactical TACTAS system in that the latter are tactical hydrophone arrays towed by warships to supplement hull-mounted sonars.)

The initial Navy planned for the T-AGOS/SURTASS program called for 18 ships. This was later reduced to 12 ships because of fiscal constraints but, as indicated above, the Navy is seeking an 18-ship program.

The program has suffered from significant cost increases over original estimates and equipment failures, resulting in at least a three-year delay over the 1974 schedule.

The lead ship, the STALWART, was laid down on 18 August 1982.

Design: The T-AGOS hull is similar to that of the T-ATF 166 class.

Electronics: The SURTASS array is a flexible, tube-like structure containing numerous hydrophones towed with a 6,000-foot cable. It is neutrally buoyant when at depth, with the depth being varied to compensate for environmental conditions.

Data from the hydrophone array are generated at a very high rate. It is "preprocessed" on board the T-AGOS and sent at a much lower rate, reduced by a factor of ten, via satellite to shore stations. The data rate from ship to shore is about 32,000 bits (32 kilobits) per second.

Engineering: The four diesel generators drive two main propulsion motors. A bow-thruster powered by a 550-hp electric motor is fitted for station keeping.

Operational: Early Navy planning provided for the ships to have 90-day patrol periods plus 8 days in transit, resulting in more than 300 days at sea per year. This intensity of operations was rejected by MSC as impractical and unrealistic. A patrol duration of 60 to 74 days is now planned.

(2) SURVEY SHIPS: NEW CONSTRUCTION

Number	Name	FY	In Service	Status
T-AGS 39	. . . . . .	85		
T-AGS 40	. . . . . .	85		

These will be built-for-the-purpose ocean survey ships to replace the outdated BOWDITCH and DUTTON. Until November 1983 the Navy had planned to convert the 20-year-old merchant ships MORMACPRIDE and MORMACSCAN, completed in 1960 and 1961, respectively, to this role; both ships were laid up in NDRF (MarAd C3-S-33a type). However, congressional redirection caused the Navy to instead plan the construction of new ships. See page 271.

The ships are to conduct primarily hydrographic, magnetic, and gravity surveys.

Conversion: To be fitted with Sonar Array Survey System (SASS), a multi-beam, wide-angle precision sonar for continuous charting of a broad strip of ocean floor under the ship's track. Also provided with gravity and magnetic measuring systems.

Cost: Requested in fiscal 1985 at a cost of $245 million to construct both ships.

1 SURVEYING SHIP: "H.H. HESS"

Number	Name	Launched	In service	Status
T-AGS 38	H. H. HESS	30 May 1964	16 Jan 1976	**MSC-P**

Builders:	National Steel and Shipbuilding, San Diego, Calif.
Displacement:	3,127 tons light
	17,874 tons full load
Length:	564 feet (172.0 m) oa
Beam:	76 feet (23.2 m)
Draft:	
Propulsion:	steam turbine (General Electric); 19,250 shp; 1 shaft
Boilers:	2 (Foster Wheeler)
Speed:	20 knots
Range:	
Manning:	69 (civilian) + 14 scientists + 27 Navy technicians
Helicopters:	no facilities
Missiles:	none
Guns:	none

This ship is the former merchant ship CANADA MAIL, acquired by the Navy in 1975 for conversion to a surveying ship to replace the MICHELSON (T-AGS 23). She is operated by MSC for the Oceanographer of the Navy.

Classification: Classified as an AGS and renamed on 1 November 1976.

Conversion: Converted to a survey ship in 1975-1977.

H.H. HESS (1977, Giorgio Arra)

H. H. Hess (U.S. Navy)

4 SURVEYING SHIPS: "SILAS BENT" CLASS

Number	Name	FY	Launched	In service	Status
T-AGS 26	Silas Bent	63	16 May 1964	23 July 1965	**MSC-P**
T-AGS 27	Kane	64	20 Nov 1965	19 May 1967	**MSC-A**
T-AGS 33	Wilkes	67	31 July 1969	28 June 1971	**MSC-A**
T-AGS 34	Wyman	67	30 Oct 1969	3 Nov 1971	**MSC-A**

Builders:	T-AGS 26	American Shipbuilding, Lorain, Ohio
	T-AGS 27	Christy Corp., Sturgeon Bay, Wisc.
	T-AGS 33-34 Defoe Shipbuilding, Bay City, Mich.	
Displacement:	T-AGS 26-27	2,558 tons full load
	T-AGS 33	2,540 tons full load
	T-AGS 34	2,420 tons full load
Length:	285⅓ feet (87.0 m) oa	
Beam:	48 feet (14.6 m)	
Draft:	15 feet (4.6 m)	
Propulsion:	diesel-electric (Westinghouse diesels); 3,600 bhp; 1 shaft	
Speed:	14 knots	
Range:	12,000 n.miles at 14 knots	
Manning:	50 (civilian) + 26 scientists except 41 (civilian) + 20 scientists in T-AGS 34	
Helicopters:	no facilities	
Missiles:	none	
Guns:	none	

These ships were designed specifically for surveying operations. They differ in detail. All four ships are operated by MSC for the Oceanographer of the Navy. Several support the Navy's SOSUS program.

Design: The first two ships are SCB No. 226; the Wilkes is No. 725 in the new series and Wyman No. 728. The Keller (AGS 25) and S.P. Lee (AGS 31, later AG 192) were of a smaller design, SCB No. 214/709; see Appendix B.

Engineering: These ships have bow propulsion units for precise maneuvering and station keeping.

Kane (1979, Giorgio Arra)

WILKES (1982, Giorgio Arra)

2 SURVEYING SHIPS: "CHAUVENET" CLASS

Number	Name	FY	Launched	In service	Status
T-AGS 29	CHAUVENET	65	13 May 1968	13 Nov 1970	**MSC-P**
T-AGS 32	HARKNESS	66	12 June 1968	29 Jan 1971	**MSC**

Builders:	Upper Clyde Shipbuilders, Glasgow, Scotland
Displacement:	4,200 tons full load
Length:	393⅛ feet (119.9 m) oa
Beam:	54 feet (16.5 m)
Draft:	16 feet (4.9 m)
Propulsion:	diesel (Westinghouse); 3,600 bhp; 1 shaft
Speed:	15 knots
Range:	12,000 n.miles at 15 knots
Manning:	69 (civilian) + 12 scientists + 74 Navy technicians
Helicopters:	1 or 2 utility helicopters
Missiles:	none
Guns:	none

The CHAUVENET and HARKNESS are the largest surveying or research ships to be built specifically for those roles by the U.S. Navy. Both ships are operated by MSC for the Oceanographer of the Navy. The Navy technicians include a 19-man helicopter detachment.

Builders: These ships and the EDENTON (ATS 1)-class salvage and rescue ships were the first ships to be constructed since World War II in British yards for the U.S. Navy. Subsequently, the Navy has acquired three British-built combat stores ships (T-AFS).

Design: SCB No. 723. This is the only AGOR/AGS class with a full helicopter support capability. The hangar is 45½ feet long and 12 feet wide.

CHAUVENET (U.S. Navy)

HARKNESS (1983, Giorgio Arra)

2 SURVEYING SHIPS: VICTORY TYPE

Number	Name	Launched	In service	Status
T-AGS 21	BOWDITCH	30 June 1945	8 Oct 1958	**MSC-A**
T-AGS 22	DUTTON	8 May 1945	1 Nov 1958	**MSC-P**

Builders:	Oregon Shipbuilding, Portland
Displacement:	13,050 tons full load
Length:	455⅙ feet (138.8 m) oa
Beam:	62⅙ feet (19.0 m)
Draft:	25 feet (7.6 m)
Propulsion:	steam turbine (General Electric in T-AGS 21, Westinghouse in T-AGS 22); 8,500 shp; 1 shaft
Boilers:	2
Speed:	15 knots
Range:	
Manning:	67 (civilian) + 12 scientists + approx. 25 Navy technicians
Helicopters:	no facilities
Missiles:	none
Guns:	none

These are former Victory-type merchant ships, acquired by the Navy in 1957 and converted for seafloor charting and magnetic surveys to support the Navy's SSBN programs. They are operated by MSC for the Oceanographer of the Navy. Both ships are scheduled to be replaced in the mid-1980s.

Class: A third ship of this configuration, the MICHELSON (T-AGS 23), was stricken on 15 April 1975.

Conversion: Both ships were converted in 1957–1958; the conversion was SCB No. 179.

Design: These ships are Maritime Administration VC2-S-AP3 design.

Names: Their merchant names were SOUTH BEND VICTORY and TUSKEGEE VICTORY, respectively.

(2) HOSPITAL SHIPS: CONVERTED TANKERS

Number	Name	Launched	In service	Status
T-AH 19	MERCY		1986	Yard
T-AH 20	COMFORT		1987	Yard

Builders:	National Steel and Shipbuilding, San Diego, Calif.
Displacement:	106,600 tons full load
Length:	894 feet (272.6 m) oa
Beam:	105¾ feet (32.25 m)
Draft:	49 feet (14.9 m)
Propulsion:	steam turbines (General Electric); 24,500 shp; 1 shaft
Boilers:	2
Speed:	17.5 knots
Manning:	68 (civilian) + 21 Navy
Medical staff:	508 Navy personnel
Helicopters:	landing area

These ships are tankers being converted specifically to support the Rapid Deployment Joint Task Force. They are the first ships of the type in U.S. service since the SANCTUARY (AH 17) was decommissioned in March 1974; at that time she was serving as a naval dependents support ship.

They are to be based at U.S. ports; in crisis or wartime they would be assigned medical staffs from nearby military hospitals and go to sea within 15 days' notice.

Conversion: Both ships were converted at the National Steel and Shipbuilding yard in San Diego; the T-AH 19 conversion authorized in fiscal 1983 and the T-AH 20 in fiscal 1984.

(Earlier proposals for a hospital ship to support the RDJTF centered on conversion of the super liner UNITED STATES, laid up since her final transatlantic voyage in November 1969. The 990-foot liner, completed

DUTTON (1976, U.S. Navy)

in 1952, carried up to 2,000 passengers and was designed from the outset for conversion to a transport for 14,000 troops. As an AH she would have had 2,000–2,500 beds. She averaged 35.59 knots on her maiden transatlantic voyage, and reached 38.32 knots on her sea trials.)

Design: These ships were originally tankers.

As hospital ships they have 12 operating rooms, 4 X-ray rooms, and an 80-bed intensive care facility, with a total casualty capacity of about 1,000 patients. They are intended to accommodate a peak admission rate of 300 patients in 24 hours with surgery required by 60 percent of the admissions and an average patient stay of five days.

Maritime Administration type T8-S-100b.

Names: The merchant names of their ships were WORTH and ROSE CITY, respectively.

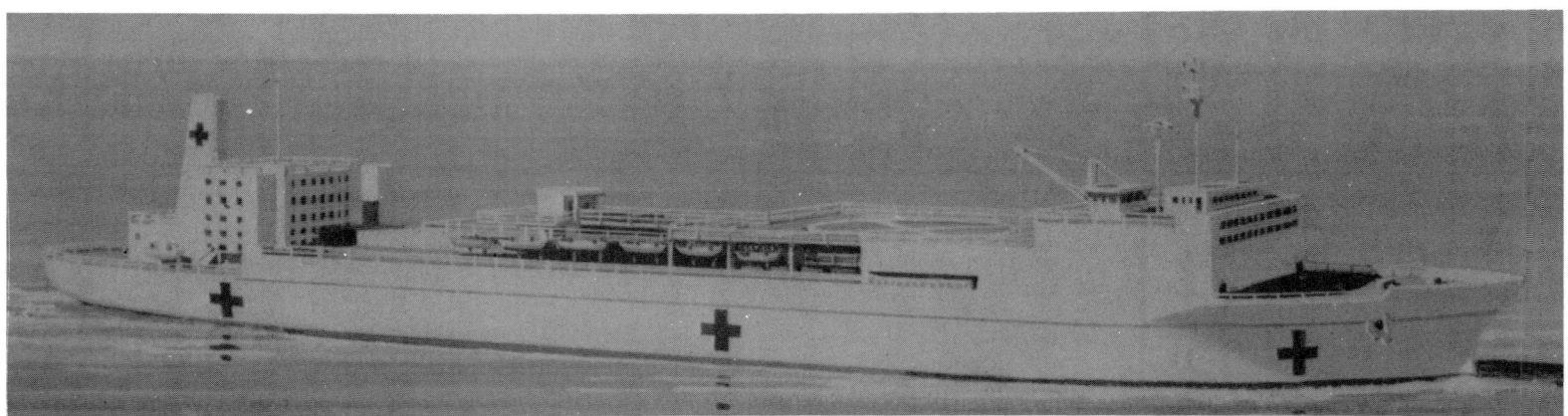

Artist's concept of MERCY configuration.

The SANCTUARY at Mayport, Fla., while configured as a dependents support ship. In this role the ship retained the AH designation but did not carry the painted crosses of a hospital ship. (1974, U.S. Navy)

1 HOSPITAL SHIP: "HAVEN" CLASS

Number	Name	Launched	Commissioned	Status
AH 17	SANCTUARY	15 Aug 1944	20 June 1945	NDRF

Builders:	Sun Shipbuilding & Dry Dock, Chester, PA.
Displacement:	11,141 tons standard
	15,400 tons full load
Length:	529 feet (161.3 m) oa
Beam:	71½ feet (21.8 m)
Draft:	24 feet (7.3 m)
Propulsion:	steam turbine (General Electric); 9,000 shp; 1 shaft
Boilers:	2 (Babcock & Wilcox)
Speed:	18.3 knots
Manning:	530 (70 officers + 460 enlisted) including medical staff
Helicopters:	landing platform

The SANCTUARY was converted while under construction to serve as a naval hospital ship. She was decommissioned from 1946 until stricken from the Navy list on 1 September 1961 and transferred to the Maritime Administration. The ship was reacquired by the Navy on 1 March 1966 and after modernization, served in the Vietnam War.

She remained in service until converted from December 1971 to December 1972 at the Hunters Point (San Francisco) Naval Shipyard to serve as a dependent support ship in conjunction with plans to base an aircraft carrier at Piraeus, Greece. She was assigned the first mixed male-female crew in the history of the U.S. Navy (excluding female medical personnel). The ship was again decommissioned on 28 March 1974 and laid up in the National Defense Reserve Fleet in the James River, Va.

During 1980 the SANCTUARY was considered for reactivation to support the prepositioning of U.S. military equipment in the Indian Ocean. Instead, the decision was made to acquire and convert two merchant ships.

Class: Six ships of this class were completed as hospital ships (AH 12–17).

Conversion: As a dependent support ship the SANCTUARY was fitted with special facilities for obstetrics, gynecology, maternity, and nursery services, and was fitted with a 74-bed hospital that could be expanded to 300 beds in 72 hours. She also had provisions for a commissary store.

Design: Maritime Administration C4-S-B2 design.

Names: Her merchant name was to have been MARINE OWL.

SANCTUARY (1973, U.S. Navy)

(5) MARITIME PREPOSITIONING SHIPS: NEW CONSTRUCTION

Name	Launched	In service	Status
2ND LT JOHN P. BOBO	Oct 1984	1985	Building
PFC DEWAYNE T. WILLIAMS	1985	1985	Building
1ST LT BALDOMERO LOPEZ	1985	1985	Building
1ST LT JACK LUMMUS	1985	1986	Building
SGT WILLIAM R. BUTTON	1985	1986	Building

Builders:	General Dynamics/Quincy, Mass.
Displacement:	40,850 tons full load
Deadweight:	22,120 tons
Length:	654½ feet (199.6 m) oa
Beam:	105½ feet (32.2 m)
Draft:	29½ feet (9.0 m)
Propulsion:	diesel; 1 shaft
Speed:	18 knots
Manning:	30 (civilian) + 8 maintenance personnel (civilian)
Flag/staff:	17 Navy (3 officers + 14 enlisted) + 3 civilian in 1 ship
Helicopters:	landing area
Missiles:	none
Guns:	none

These 5 new-construction ships, the 5 converted Maersk ships, and the 3 converted Waterman ships will form the U.S. force of Maritime Prepositioning Ships (MPS) from 1985 on. The 13 ships will be capable of carrying military supplies and stores for 3 Marine Amphibious Brigades (MAB), a total of some 46,000 troops. The ships will operate in 3 groups with each group carrying vehicles, equipment, and stores for one MAB for 30 days. Group 1: 5 Maersk ships; Group 2: 3 Waterman ships and 1 General Dynamics ship; and Group 3: 4 General Dynamics ships.

The new construction ships were classified T-AKX during planning stages. Although built specifically for the MPS role, they are technically under charter and—like the MPS conversions—are not assigned hull numbers. The first two U.S. Navy built-for-the-purpose MPS were laid down on 16 September 1983.

Design: Each of these new-construction ships will carry equipment and supplies for about a quarter of a MAB for 30 days.

These ships have 162,500 square feet of vehicle deck space and can carry 1,605,000 gallons of break-bulk petroleum products plus 81,770 gallons of potable water. A stern ramp is fitted for unloading vehicles into landing craft and onto piers, and there are five 40-ton-capacity cranes fitted.

Manning: The MPS are civilian contractor manned; the maintenance personnel will also be civilian. The staff data are for a Navy–civilian MSC team that will be assigned to one ship in each group. In addition, all ships will have berthing for a Marine "surge team" that can be embarked to assist in preparation of vehicles and unloading—up to 97 troops in these ships and the Waterman ships, and up to 77 in the Maersk ships.

An artist's view of two of the built-for-the-purpose maritime prepositioning ships unloading cargo. Note the articulated stern ramp, helicopter platform, and heavy cranes, with four of them paired for very heavy lift requirements. The prepositioning ships require secure harbors and piers to unload. (General Dynamics/Quincy)

2+3 MARITIME PREPOSITIONING SHIPS: CONVERTED MAERSK MERCHANT SHIPS

Name	Built	Acquired	Start Conv.	Delivery	In service	Status
Cpl Louis J. Hague Jr. (ex-Estelle Maersk)	1979	3 Jan 1983	3 Jan 1983	31 Aug 1984	August 1984	**MSC-MPS**
Pfc William B. Baugh Jr. (ex-Eleo Maersk)	1979	17 Jan 1983	17 Jan 1983	30 Sep 1984	1984	**MSC-MPS**
Pfc James Anderson Jr. (ex-Emma Maersk)	1979	28 Oct 1983	31 Oct 1983	Apr 1985	1985	Yard
1st Lt Alexander Bonnyman Jr. (ex-Emilie Maersk)	1980	30 Jan 1984	30 Jan 1984	Sep 1985	1985	Yard
Pvt Harry Fisher (ex-Evelyn Maersk)	1980	2 Apr 1984	2 Apr 1984	Sep 1985	1985	Yard

Builders:	Odense Staalskibsvaerft, Denmark
Displacement:	46,552 tons full load
Length:	755½ feet (230.4 m) oa
Beam:	90 feet (27.4 m)
Draft:	32¹¹/₁₂ feet (10.0 m)
Propulsion:	diesel; 1 shaft
Speed:	17.5 knots
Manning:	30 (civilian) + 20 maintenance personnel (civilian)
Flagstaff:	17 Navy (3 officers + 14 enlisted) + 3 civilian in 1 ship
Helicopters:	landing area
Missiles:	none
Guns:	none

These are former Maersk Line combination container and Roll-On/Roll-Off (RO/RO) vehicle cargo ships that were acquired by the U.S. government specifically for conversion to the MPS role. The ships were designated T-AKX during the design stage; they are technically under charter and do not have hull numbers.

Conversion: The ships were converted to each carry one-fifth of the vehicles, equipment, and supplies required by a MAB for 30 days.

During conversion a new 157½-foot midsection was added to each ship (original length 598¹/₁₂ feet with a full load displacement of 29,182 tons). In the MPS role they have 120,080 square feet of vehicle storage space and can carry up to 332 standard freight containers, 1,283,000 gallons of bulk fuels, and 65,000 gallons of potable water. Ramps and cranes provide a self-unloading capability.

The Hague, Anderson, and Fisher were converted at the Bethlehem Steel yard at Sparrows Point, Md.; the Baugh and Bonnyman at the Bethlehem Steel yard in Beaumont, Texas.

1+2 MARITIME PREPOSITIONING SHIPS: CONVERTED WATERMAN MERCHANT SHIPS

Name	Built	Acquired	Start Conv.	Delivery	In service	Status
SGT MATEJ KOCAK (ex-JOHN B. WATERMAN)	1982	15 Dec 1982	26 Aug 1983	7 Sep 1984	1984	**MSC-MPS**
PFC EUGENE A. OBREGON (ex-THOMAS HEYWARD)	1982	1 Feb 1983	5 Jan 1983	Dec 1984	1985	Yard
MAJ STEPHEN W. PLESS (ex-CHARLES CARROLL)	1982	15 May 1983	4 May 1984	April 1985	1985	Yard

Builders:	KOCAK, OBREGON Sun Shipbuilding, Chester, Pa.
	PLESS General Dynamics/Quincy, Mass.
Displacement:	48,754 tons
Length:	821 feet (250.4 m) oa
Beam:	105½ feet (32.2 m)
Draft:	32¼ feet (9.8 m)
Propulsion:	steam turbine; 1 shaft
Boilers:	2
Speed:	20 knots
Manning:	29 (civilian) + 8 maintenance personnel (civilian)
Flagstaff:	17 Navy (3 officers + 17 enlisted) + 3 civilian in 1 ship
Helicopters:	landing area
Missiles:	none
Guns:	none

These were previously container ships operated by the Waterman Corp. They were acquired specifically for conversion to the MPS role and are intended to carry one quarter of the vehicles, equipment, and supplies required by a MAB for 30 days. They were designated T-AKX during the planning stage; technically they are under charter and do not have hull numbers.

Conversion: As built these ships were 695 feet overall with a full load displacement of 38,975 tons. A 126-foot mid-body section was inserted and the ship was reconfigured for 152,524 square feet of vehicle cargo space, 540 standard cargo containers, and carry 1,544,000 gallons of bulk fuels and 94,780 gallons of potable water. The ships are fitted with vehicle ramps and cranes to provide a self-unloading capability.

All three ships were converted by the National Steel yard in San Diego, Calif.

Design: Maritime Administration C7-S-133A type.

The CHARLES CARROLL undergoing conversion at the National Steel shipyard in San Diego. (1984, Giorgio Arra)

4+4 VEHICLE CARGO/RAPID-RESPONSE SHIPS: CONVERTED SL-7 TYPE

Number	Name	Launched	In service	Status
T-AKR 287	ALGOL (ex-SEA-LAND EXCHANGE)	22 Sep 1972	June 1984	**MSC**
T-AKR 288	BELLATRIX (SEA-LAND TRADE)	30 Sep 1972	Oct 1984	**MSC**
T-AKR 289	DENEBOLA (SEA-LAND EXCHANGE)	10 May 1973	1985	Yard
T-AKR 290	POLLUX (SEA-LAND MARKET)	18 May 1973	1986	Yard
T-AKR 291	ALTAIR (SEA-LAND FINANCE)	28 Apr 1973	1985	Yard
T-AKR 292	REGULUS (SEA-LAND COMMERCE)	18 Dec 1972	1985	Yard
T-AKR 293	CAPELLA (SEA-LAND McLEAN)	9 Sep 1971	June 1984	**MSC**
T-AKR 294	ANTARES (SEA-LAND GALLOWAY)	13 May 1972	June 1984	**MSC**

Builders:	T-AKR 287, 289, 293	Rotterdamsche Dry Dock Maats, Rotterdam, Netherlands
	T-AKR 288, 291	Rheinstahl Nordseewerke, Emden, West Germany
	T-AKR 290, 292, 294	A.G. Weser, Bremen, West Germany
Displacement:	51,815 tons full load	
Length:	946⅙ ft (288.5 m) oa	
Beam:	105½ ft (32.2 m)	
Draft:	36⅔ ft (11.2 m)	
Propulsion:	steam turbines; 120,000 shp; 2 shafts	
Speed:	33 knots	
Manning:	approx. 40 (civilian) + 56—57 troops	
Helicopters:	landing area	
Missiles:	none	
Guns:	none	

These are former high-speed merchant ships of the SL-7 class built for the SeaLand Corporation in European shipyards. They are being converted to carry U.S. military cargoes with an extensive Roll-On/Roll-Off (RO/RO) capability. These are not maritime prepositioning ships but are maintained in U.S. ports, ready for rapid loading of Army or Marine equipment and sailing to crisis/war areas. They are operated by civilian charter crews.

Design: As built the SL-7 were 33-knot ships, the fastest cargo ships ever constructed for U.S. merchant service. Range is 12,200 n.miles at 27 knots.

Classification: During the planning stage these ships were designated T-AKRX. Upon acquisition they were designated T-AK and assigned hull numbers in the cargo ship (AK) series; however, upon conversion to RO/RO configuration they were changed to T-AKR but retained the AK-series hull numbers.

Conversion: Four ships are being converted with fiscal 1982 funds and four with fiscal 1984 funds; the T-AKR 287, 288, and 292 at National Steel, San Diego, Calif.; T-AKR 289 and 293 at Pennsylvania Ship-building, Chester, Pa.;[2] and T-AKR 290, 291, and 294 at Avondale Shipyards, New Orleans, La.; the first four conversions began in October 1982.

These ships are being converted to provide approximately 185,000 square feet of vehicle space plus other military equipment. A major container capability remains aft, with provisions for special racks for loading heavy material, including trucks and tanks (being lifted on off vice RO/RO). Side ports and heavy ramps are provided on both sides of the ship. Twin 35-ton-capacity cranes are fitted forward and twin 50-ton cranes aft. Through limited arcs, they can provide a combined lift of 70 and 100 tons, respectively.

A helicopter landing deck is provided amidships that can accommodate the largest U.S. military helicopters (Marine CH-53E, Army CH-47 Chinook). The four cargo decks beneath the landing deck are connected by ramps and can accommodate helicopters, the first with a height of 19½ feet and the others with 13½ feet.

In addition to the RO/RO and helicopter space, the ships can each accommodate other vehicles plus 78 35-foot flatracks and 46 20-foot containers. There is a tunnel for trucks up to 5-ton capacity in the amidships deck structure to permit passage between the forward and after cargo areas.

Satellite communications equipment is also being installed.

Names: These ships are assigned traditional Navy cargo ship names (i.e., stars and constellations), reflecting their acquisition on bare boat charter versus the time charter of MPS ships.

[2]Formerly Sun Shipbuilding and Dry Dock.

ALGOL (1984, Giorgio Arra)

Rapid-response cargo ship ALGOL (1984, National Steel and Shipbuilding)

ALGOL (stern) and BELLATRIX (bow) undergoing conversion at the National Steel yard. A paired heavy-lift crane is visible on the ALGOL. (1984, Giorgio Arra)

2 CARGO SHIPS } CONVERTED MORMAC CARGO SHIPS
1 + 2 FBM CARGO SHIPS }

Number	Name	Launched	In service	Status
T-AK 284	NORTHERN LIGHT	29 June 1961	22 Apr 1980	**MSC**
T-AK 285	SOUTHERN CROSS	23 Jan 1962	1 May 1980	**MSC**
T-AK 286	VEGA		18 Mar 1983	**MSC-A**
T-AK 296	. . . . . .			AR
T-AK 297	. . . . . .			AR

Builders:	Sun Shipbuilding and Dry Dock, Chester, Pa., except T-AK 296 at Todd Shipyards, San Pedro, Calif.
Displacement:	approx. 16,400 tons full load
Tonnage:	T-AK 284 9,361 tons gross; 12,537 tons deadweight
	T-AK 285 9,259 tons gross; 12,519 tons deadweight
	T-AK 286 18,365 tons full load
Length:	483¼ feet (147.4 m) oa except T-AK 284 487⁷/₁₂ feet (148.9 m) oa
Beam:	68 feet (20.7 m)
Draft:	31⁵/₁₂ feet (9.6 m) except T-AK 286 27 feet (8.2 m)
Propulsion:	steam turbines; 12,100 shp; 1 shaft
Boilers:	2
Speed:	21 knots
Manning:	T-AK 284 50 (civilian)
	T-AK 285 39 (civilian)
	T-AK 286 67 (civilian) + 7 Navy
Helicopters:	no facilities
Missiles:	none
Guns:	none

These were commercial cargo ships built for Moore-McCormack Lines and completed 1960–1962. After merchant service they were laid up in NDRF. The NORTHERN LIGHT and SOUTHERN CROSS were acquired by the Navy in April 1980 for use as prepositioning ships in the Indian Ocean; the VEGA was acquired in April 1981 for conversion to an FBM/SSBN supply ship to replace the VICTORIA (T-AK 281); two other ships were subsequently acquired for FBM/SSBN supply ship conversions or surveying ships. See page 262.

Conversion: The VEGA was converted to transport 16 Trident missiles and other submarine stores and supplies from U.S. ports to forward deployed submarine tenders; fitted with eight 10-ton capacity booms, four 5-ton capacity booms, and one 75-ton capacity boom. She was converted at Boland Marine and Manufacturing, New Orleans, La., from May 1982 to March 1983. The naval personnel are a security detachment.

Design: Maritime Administration C3-S-33a design. Eight ships of this design were built for commercial use. The MORMACCOVE (now T-AK 284) has a modified bow that makes her slightly longer than the other ships.

The NORTHERN LIGHT and SOUTHERN CROSS are ice strenghtened for Arctic operations.

Names: Merchant names were T-AK 284 ex-MORMACCOVE, T-AK 285 ex-MORMACTRADE, T-AK 286 ex-MORMACBAY, T-AK 296 ex-MORMAC-CAPE, and T-AK 297 ex-MORMACLAKE.

VEGA (U.S. Navy)

1 CARGO SHIP: EX-ATTACK CARGO SHIP

Number	Name	Launched	Commissioned	Status
T-AK 283	WYANDOT	28 June 1944	30 Sep 1944	NDRF

Builders:	Moore Dry Dock, Oakland, Calif.
Displacement:	7,430 tons light
	14,000 tons full load
Length:	435 feet (132.7 m) wl
	459⅙ feet (140.0 m) oa
Beam:	63 feet (19.2 m)
Draft:	24 feet (7.3 m)
Propulsion:	steam turbine (General Electric); 6,000 shp; 1 shaft
Boilers:	2 (Combustion Engineering)
Speed:	16.5 knots
Manning:	
Helicopters:	no facilities
Missiles:	none
Guns:	removed

The WYANDOT was completed as an attack cargo ship (AKA 92) of the ANDROMEDA (AKA 15) class. She was stricken from the Naval Register on 1 July 1960, but reacquired the following year because of the Berlin crisis. She was recommissioned in November 1961 and in March 1963 assigned to MSTS as a cargo ship (designated T-AK 92). She was laid up in the NDRF on 31 October 1975.

Classification: Changed from AKA 92 to AK 283 on 1 January 1969.

Design: Maritime Administration C2-S-B1 design. Cargo capacity is 4,700 tons.

Guns: The ship's original armament as an AKA consisted of one 5-inch/38-cal DP gun and eight 40-mm AA guns plus 20-mm AA weapons.

Operational: From 1947 on the WYANDOT was used primarily for supply operations in Arctic and Antarctic waters.

WYANDOT (U.S. Navy)

1 CABLE TRANSPORTER ⎤
2 FBM CARGO SHIPS ⎦ VICTORY TYPE

Number	Name	Launched	In service	Status
T-AK 280	FURMAN	6 May 1945	18 Sep 1963	**MSC**
T-AK 281	VICTORIA	28 Apr 1944	11 Oct 1965	**MSC-A**
T-AK 282	MARSHFIELD	15 May 1944	28 May 1970	**MSC-A**

Builders:	Oregon Shipbuilding, Portland, except T-AK 281
	Permanente Metals, Richmond, Calif.
Displacement:	6,700 tons light
	11,150 tons full load
Length:	455¼ feet (138.8 m) oa
Beam:	62 feet (18.9 m)
Draft:	28½ feet (8.7 m)
Propulsion:	steam turbine; 8,500 shp; 1 shaft
Boilers:	2
Speed:	17 knots
Manning:	66–69 (civilian) + Navy (security)
Helicopters:	no facilities
Missiles:	none
Guns:	none

These are former merchant ships taken over by the Navy specifically for conversion into supply ships to support FBM/SSBN tenders. With the reduction in the Navy's SSBN force and overseas basing, the FUR-MAN has been modified to transport undersea cable. All three ships are scheduled to be replaced in the 1980s.

Class: Three earlier FBM supply ships have been stricken, the ALCOR (T-AK 259), BETELGEUSE (T-AK 260), and NORWALK (T-AK 279).

Conversion: The ships were fitted to carry 16 ballistic missiles plus 430,000 gallons of black oil (for tenders), 355,000 gallons of diesel fuel, bottled gases, dry and frozen provisions, packaged petroleum products, spare parts, and torpedoes. The No. 3 hold was configured for vertical storage of 16 missiles. Also fitted for carrying radioactive waste. Conversion was SCB No. 234.

Design: Maritime Administration VC2-S-AP3 design.

Names: Former merchant names were T-AK 280 ex-FURMAN VICTORY, T-AK 281 ex-ETHIOPIA VICTORY, and T-AK 282 ex-MARSHFIELD VICTORY.

MARSHFIELD (1983, L. & L. van Ginderen)

1 ARCTIC CARGO SHIP: "ELTANIN" CLASS

Number	Name	Launched	Commissioned	Status
T-AK 271	MIRFAK	5 Aug 1957	30 Dec 1957	NDRF

Builders:	Avondale Marine Ways, New Orleans, La.
Displacement:	2,036 tons light
	4,942 tons full load
Length:	262⅛ feet (80.0 m) oa
Beam:	51½ (15.7 m)
Draft:	
Propulsion:	diesel-electric (Alco diesels; Westinghouse electric motors); 3,200 bhp; 2 shafts
Speed:	13 knots
Manning:	
Helicopters:	no facilities
Missiles:	none
Guns:	none

The MIRFAK was one of three small cargo ships built specifically for Arctic supply operations. She was operated by MSTS (later MSC) with a civilian crew until laid up in the NDRF in November 1979.

Class: Sister ships ELTANIN (AK 270) and MIZAR (AK 272) were converted to oceanographic research ships, the AGOR 8 and 11, respectively.

Design: Maritime Administration C1-ME2-13a design with strengthened hull, icebreaking prow, enclosed crows nest and control spaces, and other features for Arctic operation.

The MIRFAK in essentially her original configuration. Note the icebreaking prow and enclosed crow's nests. (U.S. Navy)

1 HEAVY-LIFT CARGO SHIP: "BROSTROM" CLASS

Number	Name	Launched	In service	Status
T-AK 267	MARINE FIDDLER	15 May 1945	10 Dec 1952	NDRF

Builders:	Sun Shipbuilding and Dry Dock, Chester, Pa.
Displacement:	22,056 tons full load
Length:	520 feet (158.6 m) oa
Beam:	71½ feet (21.8 m)
Draft:	33 feet (10.1 m)
Propulsion:	steam turbine (General Electric); 9,000 shp; 1 shaft
Boilers:	2 (Babcock & Wilcox)
Speed:	15.8 knots
Manning:	52 (civilian)
Helicopters:	no facilities
Missiles:	none
Guns:	none

The MARINE FIDDLER was built for merchant service. She was laid up from 1946 to 1952; reactivated in 1952 for commercial service but acquired instead by the Navy for MSTS operation. Converted to a heavy-lift ship in 1954. She remained in MSTS (later MSC) service until 1973 when again laid up in NDRF.

Class: The similar PVT LEONARD C. BROSTROM was stricken.

Design: Originally Maritime Administration C4-S-B1 design. She was fitted with 150-ton capacity booms, the largest in U.S. ships, for lifting locomotives, mooring buoys, and other large objects.

Names: the MARINE FIDDLER retained her merchant name in naval service.

PVT LEONARD C. BROSTROM (U.S. Navy)

2 VEHICLE CARGO SHIPS: CONVERTED "MAINE" CLASS CARGO SHIPS

Number	Name	Launched	Commissioned	Status
T-AKR 10	MERCURY	21 Dec 1976	3 June 1980	**MSC-MPS**
T-AKR 11	JUPITER	1 Nov 1975	7 May 1980	**MSC-MPS**

Builders:	Bath Iron Works, Maine
Tonnage:	13,156 tons gross
	19,172 tons deadweight
Length:	685 feet (208.9 m) oa
Beam:	102 feet (31.1 m)
Draft:	32 feet (9.75 m)
Propulsion:	steam turbine; 37,000 shp; 1 shaft
Boilers:	2
Speed:	23 knots
Manning:	42 (civilian)
Helicopters:	no facilities
Missiles:	none
Guns:	none

JUPITER (1980, U.S. Navy)

These ships were built for commercial service with the States Steamship Company. They were acquired by the Navy in 1980 for use as prepositioning ships in the Indian Ocean.

Design: Maritime Administration C7-S-95a design. These ships are RO/RO vehicle carriers, with side ports and a stern ramp for rapidly loading and unloading vehicles.

Names: Their merchant names were ILLINOIS and TYLSON LYKES, respectively. They were renamed by MSC on 14 May 1980.

The MERCURY loading Marine equipment and vehicles at Wilmington, N.C., in preparation for deploying to the Indian Ocean. (1980, U.S. Navy)

1 VEHICLE CARGO SHIP: "METEOR"

Number	Name	FY	Launched	Commissioned	Status
T-AKR 9	METEOR	63	18 Apr 1965	19 May 1967	**MSC-MPS**

Builders:	Lockheed Shipbuilding and Construction, Seattle, Wash.
Displacement:	11,130 tons standard
	21,700 tons full load
Length:	540 feet (164.7 m) oa
Beam:	83 feet (25.3 m)
Draft:	29 feet (8.8 m)
Propulsion:	steam turbines; 19,400 shp; 2 shafts
Boilers:	2
Speed:	20 knots
Manning:	47 (civilian)
Helicopters:	no facilities
Missiles:	none
Guns:	none

METEOR (1984, Giorgio Arra)

The METEOR, originally named SEA LIFT, was built specifically as a RO/RO ship for naval service. She is operated by MSC. In mid-1980 she deployed to the Indian Ocean with Marine equipment as a near-term prepositioning ship.

Classification: Authorized as T-AK 278 but changed to T-LSV 9 while under construction; changed again to vehicle cargo ship T-AKR 9 on 14 August 1969.

Design: The METEOR was one of the few ships to have an SCB (No. 236) and Maritime Administration design (C4-ST-67a) designation.

Names: Changed from SEA LIFT to METEOR on 12 September 1975 to avoid confusion with the Sealift-class tankers.

METEOR (1984, Giorgio Arra)

1 VEHICLE CARGO SHIP: "COMET"

Number	Name	Launched	In service	Status
T-AKR 7	COMET	31 July 1957	27 Jan 1958	**MSC-A**

Builders:	Sun Shipbuilding and Dry Dock, Chester, Pa.
Displacement:	7,605 tons light
	18,150 tons full load
Length:	499 feet (152.2 m) oa
Beam:	78 feet (23.8 m)
Draft:	28¾ feet (8.8 m)
Propulsion:	steam turbines (General Electric); 13,200 shp; 2 shafts
Boilers:	2 (Babcock & Wilcox)
Speed:	18 knots
Manning:	56 (civilian)
Helicopters:	no facilities
Missiles:	none
Guns:	none

The COMET was built specifically for naval service.

Classification: The COMET originally was classified T-AK 269; she was changed to vehicle cargo ship T-LSV 7 on 1 June 1963 and again to T-AKR 7 on 1 January 1969.

The LSV 1-6 were World War II-built vehicle landing ships, all of which served under other designations. The TARUS (LSV 8) was the former AK 273; she had been built as the FORT SNELLING (LSD 23).

Design: Maritime Administration C3-ST-14a design. She can accommodate several hundred vehicles in her two after holds with the two forward holds intended for general cargo.

COMET (1982, L. & L. van Ginderen)

COMET (1975, Giorgio Arra)

1 VEHICLE CARGO SHIP: "CALLAGHAN"

Number	Name	Launched	In service	Status
(none)	ADM WM. M. CALLAGHAN	17 Oct 1967	19 Dec 1967	**MSC-A**

Builders:	Sun Shipbuilding and Dry Dock, Chester, Pa.
Displacement:	24,500 tons full load
Length:	694 feet (211.6 m) oa
Beam:	92 feet (28.1 m)
Draft:	29 feet (8.8 m)
Propulsion:	2 gas turbines (General Electric); 50,000 shp; 2 shafts
Speed:	26 knots
Manning:	33 (civilian)
Helicopters:	no facilities
Missiles:	none
Guns:	none

The CALLAGHAN is technically a chartered ship rather than a Navy-owned MSC ship. The ship was designed and constructed specifically for Navy charter and is fully committed to MSC. No hull number is assigned.

Design: The ship has 167,537 square feet of vehicle storage space with four side ports and a stern ramp for rapid loading and unloading. She can off load some 750 vehicles in 27 hours.

Engineering: The CALLAGHAN was the first all-gas-turbine ship constructed for the U.S. Navy. The engines are LM 2500s, of the type used in several surface combatant classes.

ADM WM. M. CALLAGHAN (1982, L. & L. van Ginderen)

ADM WM. M. CALLAGHAN (U.S. Navy)

(18) FLEET OILERS: "HENRY J. KAISER" CLASS

Number	Name	FY	Launch	In service	Status
T-AO 187	HENRY J. KAISER	82	1985	1986	Building
T-AO 188	JOSHUA HUMPHREYS	83	1986	1987	Building
T-AO 189	. . . . . .	84		1987	Authorized
T-AO 190	. . . . . .	84		1987	Authorized
T-AO	(3 ships)	85			Planned
T-AO	(3 ships)	86			Planned
T-AO	(3 ships)	87			Planned
T-AO	(3 ships)	88			Planned
T-AO	(2 ships)	89			Planned

Builders:	Avondale Shipyards, New Orleans, LA.
Displacement:	39,400 tons full load
Length:	677½ feet (206.6 m) oa
Beam:	97½ feet (29.7 m)
Draft:	35 feet (10.7 m)
Propulsion:	diesel; 32,000 bhp; 2 shafts
Speed:	20 knots
Manning:	95 (civilian) + 21 Navy personnel
Helicopters:	landing area
Missiles:	none
Guns:	none

These fleet oilers, being built to civilian specifications, are intended for civilian (MSC) manning. The T-AO ships are manned by civil service personnel and provide UNREP support to naval forces at sea.

More than 20 ships of this design are planned for construction with the Navy's force level objective for fleet oilers (AO/T-AO) being 29 ships.

Cost: The cost for the fiscal 1985 ships average $188 million each.

Design: These are mid-size petroleum carriers with a 180,000-barrel cargo capacity. The ships have a limited UNREP capacity for dry stores as well as fuels with a tunnel for fork-lift trucks running through the superstructure to permit cargo to be carried aft to the helicopter deck.

Guns: There are provisions to mount a light gun armament (20-mm or CIWS) on the bow and after superstructure in wartime.

5 FLEET OILERS: "CIMARRON" CLASS

Number	Name	FY	Launched	Commissioned	Status
AO 177	CIMARRON	76	28 Apr 1979	10 Jan 1981	**PA**
AO 178	MONONGAHELA	76	4 Aug 1979	5 Sep 1981	**AA**
AO 179	MERRIMACK	77	17 May 1980	14 Nov 1981	**AA**
AO 180	WILLAMETTE	78	18 July 1982	18 Dec 1982	**PA**
AO 186	PLATTE	78	30 Jan 1982	16 Apr 1983	**AA**

Builders:	Avondale Shipyards, New Orleans, La.
Displacement:	26,100 tons full load
Length:	591⅓ feet (180.3 m) oa
Beam:	88 feet (26.8 m)
Draft:	33½ feet (10.2 m)
Propulsion:	steam turbine; 24,000 shp; 1 shaft
Boilers:	2
Speed:	20 knots
Manning:	198 (12 officers + 186 enlisted) except 203 (12 officers + 191 enlisted) in AO 180, 186
Helicopters:	landing platform
Missiles:	none
Guns:	2 20-mm Phalanx CIWS Mk 16 in AO 180, 186

MONONGAHELA (Giorgio Arra)

These fleet oilers are designed to provide two complete refuelings to a conventional aircraft carrier and six to eight accompanying escort ships. These five ships will eventually be assigned to the Naval Reserve Force for operation.

Classification: The AO hull numbers 182–185 were assigned to the Falcon-class transport tankers (T-AOT) and the USNS POTOMAC is T-AOT 181.

Design: SCB No. 739. These ships carry 120,000 barrels of petroleum products. They have an elliptical underwater bow for improved sea-keeping. A Vertical Replenishment (VERTREP) platform is provided, but no helicopter hangar or support facilities are installed.

Guns: Two Phalanx CIWS are planned for all ships.

Manning: Original Navy manning was to be approximately 135; it was increased to provide improved maintenance self-sufficiency for prolonged deployments.

MERRIMACK (1983, Giorgio Arra)

The PLATTE, displaying her forward- and aft-mounted Gatling guns. There is a superficial similarity between these ships and the Sealift-class T-AOTs; these UNREP ships, however, have kingposts and other fuel hose handling gear and a helicopter deck aft. (1983, Giorgio Arra)

6 FLEET OILERS: "NEOSHO" CLASS

Number	Name	FY	Launched	Commissioned	Status
T-AO 143	NEOSHO	52	10 Nov 1953	24 Sep 1954	**MSC-A**
T-AO 144	MISSISSINEWA	52	12 June 1954	18 Jan 1955	**MSC-A**
T-AO 145	HASSAYAMPA	52	12 Sep 1954	19 Apr 1955	**MSC-P**
T-AO 146	KAWISHIWI	52	11 Dec 1954	6 July 1955	**MSC-P**
T-AO 147	TRUCKEE	52	10 Mar 1955	23 Nov 1955	**MSC-A**
T-AO 148	PONCHATOULA	52	9 July 1955	12 Jan 1956	**MSC-P**

Builders:	T-AO 143	Bethlehem Steel, Quincy, Mass.
	T-AO 144–148 New York Shipbuilding, Camden, N.J.	
Displacement:	11,750 tons light	
	38,000–40,000 tons full load	
Length:	640 feet (195.2 m) wl	
	655⅔ feet (200.0 m) oa	
Beam:	86 feet (26.2 m)	
Draft:	35 feet (10.4 m)	
Propulsion:	steam turbines (General Electric); 28,000 shp; 2 shafts	
Boilers:	2 (Babcock & Wilcox)	
Speed:	20 knots	
Manning:	106 to 108 (civilian) + 21 Navy (1 officer + 20 enlisted)	
Helicopters:	landing area in T-AO 143, 144, 147	
	VERTREP area in T-AO 145, 146	
	no facilities in T-AO 148	
Missiles:	none	
Guns:	removed	

These were the first fleet oilers built for the U.S. Navy after World War II. All were originally active Navy-manned ships; AO 144 transferred to MSC for civilian manning on 2 February 1976; AO 143 on 26 May 1978; AO 145 on 17 November 1978; AO 147 on 30 January 1980; AO 146 on 1 October 1979; and AO 148 on 5 September 1980.

Design: SCB No. 82. Cargo capacity is approximately 180,000 barrels of petroleum products. Limited flag accommodations were provided for the ships to serve as flagships for service squadrons. Three ships have had a helicopter platform fitted aft; the after superstructure has been extended forward and the T-AO 143 has a deck structure forward.

Guns: As built these ships mounted four 5-inch/38-cal DP guns in single mounts plus 12 3-inch/50-cal AA guns in twin mounts. The former were removed in the late 1960s and the latter subsequently reduced until most had only four guns (two mounts) when transferred to MSC and disarmed.

TRUCKEE (Giorgio Arra)

MISSISSINEWA (Giorgio Arra)

The NEOSHO and her sister oilers have been extensively modified during their three decades of service. All guns have been removed; the after superstructure has been enlarged, and three ships have a helicopter platform aft. (1983, Giorgio Arra)

5 FLEET OILERS: "MISPILLION" CLASS

Number	Name	Launched	Commissioned	Status
T-AO 105	MISPILLION	10 Aug 1945	29 Dec 1945	**MSC-P**
T-AO 106	NAVASOTA	30 Aug 1945	27 Feb 1946	**MSC-P**
T-AO 107	PASSUMPSIC	31 Oct 1945	1 Apr 1946	**MSC-P**
T-AO 108	PAWCATUCK	19 Feb 1945	10 May 1946	**MSC-A**
T-AO 109	WACCAMAW	30 Mar 1946	25 June 1946	**MSC-A**

Builders:	Sun Shipbuilding and Dry Dock, Chester, Pa.
Displacement:	11,000 tons light
	34,750 tons full load
Length:	646 feet (197.0 m) oa
Beam:	75 feet (22.9 m)
Draft:	35½ feet (10.8 m)
Propulsion:	steam turbines (Westinghouse); 13,500 shp; 2 shafts
Boilers:	4 (Babcock & Wilcox)
Speed:	16 knots
Manning:	approx. 110 (civilian) + 21 Navy (1 officer + 20 enlisted)
Helicopters:	landing area forward
Missiles:	none
Guns:	removed

These ships were built during World War II as Navy fleet oilers. They were enlarged under the "jumbo" process in the mid-1960s to increase their cargo capacity, forming a new five-ship class. The ships were transferred from the active Navy to MSC civilian manning in 1974–1975.

Design: Originally Maritime Administration T3-S2-A3 type. They were "jumboized" in the mid-1960s with the addition of a 93-foot midsection, increasing their cargo capacity to approximately 150,000 barrels. A helicopter landing area is provided *forward*, but it is used primarily for vertical replenishment. No hangar is provided.

Guns: These ships had a designed armament of one 5-inch/38-cal DP gun, four 3-inch/50-cal AA guns, and eight 40-mm AA guns. This armament was successively reduced until only four 3-inch single mounts remained when the ships were transferred to MSC operation and completely disarmed.

MISPILLION (1982, Giorgio Arra)

PASSUMPSIC (1980, U.S. Navy)

3 FLEET OILERS: "ASHTABULA" CLASS

Number	Name	Launched	Commissioned	Status
AO 51	ASHTABULA	22 May 1943	7 Aug 1943	NDRF
AO 98	CALOOSAHATCHEE	2 June 1945	10 Oct 1945	**AA**
AO 99	CANISTEO	6 July 1945	3 Dec 1945	**AA**

Builders:	Bethlehem Steel, Sparrows Point, Md.
Displacement:	34,750 tons full load
Length:	644 feet (196.4 m) oa
Beam:	75 feet (22.9 m)
Draft	31½ feet (9.6 m)
Propulsion:	steam turbines (Bethlehem); 13,500 shp; 2 shafts
Boilers:	4 (Foster Wheeler)
Speed:	18 knots
Manning:	372 (20 officers + 352 enlisted)
Helicopters:	VERTREP area
Missiles:	none
Guns	2 3-inch (76-mm) 50-cal AA Mk 26 (2 single)

These oilers were built for naval service; they were "jumboized" to increase their cargo capacity. The ASHTABULA was Navy manned until decommissioned on 30 September 1982 and laid up in the National Defense Reserve Fleet.

Design: Originally Maritime Administration T3-S2-A1 design. The three ships were converted in the mid-1960s under the "jumbo" program (SCB No. 224); an additional 91-foot midsection was installed, increasing their cargo capacity to approximately 143,000 barrels along with a limited capacity for stores and munitions. A small VERTREP area is provided forward.

Guns: See the MISPILLION class for data on original armament.

CALOOSAHATCHEE (Giorgio Arra)

CANISTEO (1982, Giorgio Arra)

CANISTEO (Giorgio Arra)

2 FLEET OILERS: "CIMARRON" CLASS

Number	Name	Launched	Commissioned	Status
T-AO 57	MARIAS	21 Dec 1943	12 Feb 1944	NDRF
T-AO 62	TALUGA	10 July 1944	25 Aug 1944	NDRF

Builders:	Bethlehem Steel, Sparrows Point, Md.
Displacement:	25,525 tons full load
Length:	525 feet (160.1 m) wl
	553 feet (168.6 m) oa
Beam:	75 feet (22.9 m)
Draft:	31½ feet (9.6 m)
Propulsion:	steam turbines (Bethlehem); 13,500 shp; 2 shafts
Boilers:	4 (Foster Wheeler)
Speed:	18 knots
Manning:	105 (civilian)
Helicopters:	VERTREP area
Missiles:	none
Guns:	removed

TALUGA (1978, U.S. Navy)

These are the survivors of a large number of twin-screw fleet oilers constructed during World War II. Ships of this design that have been enlarged under the "jumbo" process are listed separately.

The TALUGA was transferred from active naval service to MSC on 4 May 1972 and the MARIAS on 2 October 1973. The MARIAS was laid up on 30 September 1980; the TALUGA was to be laid up in 1984.

Design: Maritime Administration T3-S2-A1 design. Cargo capacity is approximately 115,000 barrels of petroleum products. A VERTREP platform is fitted forward.

Guns: See MISPILLION class for notes on original armament.

MARIAS (Giorgio Arra)

4 + 3 FAST COMBAT SUPPORT SHIP: "SACRAMENTO" CLASS

Number	Name	FY	Launched	Commissioned	Status
AOE 1	SACRAMENTO	61	14 Sep 1963	14 Mar 1964	**PA**
AOE 2	CAMDEN	63	29 May 1965	1 Apr 1967	**PA**
AOE 3	SEATTLE	65	2 Mar 1968	5 Apr 1969	**AA**
AOE 4	DETROIT	66	21 June 1969	28 Mar 1970	**AA**
AOE 5	. . . . . .	86			Planned
AOE 6	. . . . . .	88			Planned
AOE 7	. . . . . .	89			Planned

Builders:	Puget Sound Naval Shipyard, Bremerton, Wash., except AOE 2 at New York Shipbuilding, Camden, N.J.
Displacement:	19,200 tons light
	53,600 tons full load
Length:	770 feet (234.8 m) wl
	794¾ feet (242.4 m) oa
Beam:	107 feet (32.6 m)
Draft:	39⅓ feet (12.0 m)
Propulsion:	steam turbines (General Electric); 100,000 shp; 2 shafts
Boilers:	4 (Combustion Engineering)
Speed:	27.5 knots (26 knots sustained)
Manning:	594 to 618 (23 officers + 571 to 595 enlisted)
Helicopters:	2 CH-46 Sea Knight
Missiles:	1 8-tube NATO Sea Sparrow launcher Mk 29
Guns:	2 20-mm Phalanx CIWS Mk 16 (2 multibarrel) in AOE 1, 2, 4
	4 3-inch (76-mm) 50-cal AA Mk 33 (2 twin) in AOE 3
Fire control:	1 Mk 91 missile FCS

These are the world's largest underway replenishment ships, designed to provide a carrier battle group with full fuels, munitions, dry and frozen provisions, and other supplies. (The largest foreign UNREP ship is the one-of-a-kind Soviet BEREZINA, completed in 1977, which displaces some 40,000 tons full load.)

The Navy's force goal is for 15 AOE/AOR-type ships to provide support for the planned 15 carrier battle groups within a fleet of 600+ ships.

Class: A fifth ship of this design was planned for the fiscal 1968 and subsequently the fiscal 1980 shipbuilding program, but those ships were not built. Instead the smaller and less expensive AOR design was developed.

The Navy, however, is planning the construction of at least three more AOEs to provide support for the increased number of carrier battle groups.

Design: SCB No. 196. These ships can carry 194,000 barrels of fuels, 2,100 tons of munitions, 250 tons of dry stores, and 250 tons of refrigerated stores. The ships have highly automated cargo-handling equipment. Range is 6,000 n. miles at 26 knots and 10,000 n. miles at 17 knots.

A large helicopter deck is fitted aft with a three-bay hangar for VERT-REP helicopters. Each bay is 47 to 52 feet long and 17 to 19 feet wide.

Electronics: The hull has provision for SQS-26 sonar, but it has not been installed.

Engineering: The first two ships were provided with the machinery produced for the cancelled battleship KENTUCKY (BB 66).

Guns: As built these ships were armed with eight 3-inch guns in twin mounts and associated Mk 56 GFCS. They were reduced in the mid-1970s and a NATO Sea Sparrow launcher was installed forward. The remaining 3-inch guns have been removed with two Phalanx CIWS being fitted to each ship (scheduled for AOE 3).

The DETROIT with two Phalanx CIWS fitted aft; two of the three hangar bays are open. (1983, Giorgio Arra)

The SACRAMENTO with NATO Sea Sparrow forward (3-inch gun mounts deleted); there are two missile control directors atop the bridge. (1978, Giorgio Arra)

SACRAMENTO (1978, Giorgio Arra)

7 REPLENISHMENT OILERS: "WICHITA" CLASS[3]

Number	Name	FY	Launched	Commissioned	Status
AOR 1	WICHITA	65	18 Mar 1968	7 June 1969	**PA**
AOR 2	MILWAUKEE	65	17 Jan 1969	1 Nov 1969	**AA**
AOR 3	KANSAS CITY	66	28 June 1969	6 June 1970	**PA**
AOR 4	SAVANNAH	66	25 Apr 1970	5 Dec 1970	**AA**
AOR 5	WABASH	67	6 Feb 1971	20 Nov 1971	**PA**
AOR 6	KALAMAZOO	67	11 Nov 1972	11 Aug 1973	**AA**
AOR 7	ROANOKE	72	7 Dec 1974	30 Oct 1976	**PA**

Builders:	AOR 1-6 General Dynamics, Quincy, Mass.
	AOR 7 National Steel and Shipbuilding, San Diego, Calif.
Displacement:	38,100 tons full load
Length:	659 feet (201.0 m) oa
Beam:	96 feet (29.3 m)
Draft:	33⅓ feet (10.2 m)
Propulsion:	steam turbines; 32,000 shp; 2 shafts
Boilers:	3 (Foster Wheeler)
Speed:	20 knots
Manning:	444 to 452 (20 officers + 424 to 432 enlisted)
Helicopters:	2 CH-46 Sea Knight
Missiles:	1 NATO Sea Sparrow launcher Mk 29 in AOR 3, 4, 5, 7
Guns:	2 20-mm Phalanx CIWS Mk 16 (2 multibarrel) in AOR 4-7
	2 20-mm AA Mk 67 (2 single) in AOR 7
	4 20-mm AA Mk 68 (4 single) in AOR 2, 6
Fire control:	1 Mk 91 missile FCS in AOR 3, 4, 5, 7

These are large combination petroleum-munitions UNREP ships, smaller than the AOE type but still larger than any foreign ship except the BEREZINA.

[3]Editor's note: These ships are listed out of alphabetical order before the AOG type because of the similarity of the AOE/AOR ship types.

Classification: The AOR classification was established in 1952 as fleet replenishment tanker to provide "one stop" fuel and munitions replenishment. The German war prize CONECUH, formerly the U-boat tender DITHMARSCHEN, previously designated IX 301 and then AO 110, was changed to AOR 110. The CONECUH was decommissioned in 1956 and stricken in 1960 with the designation AOR then being dropped. The WACCAMAW (AO 109) was to be similarly modified but she remained a "straight" fleet oiler. The classification AOR was established as replenishment oiler in 1964.

Design: SCB No. 707. These ships can carry 160,000 barrels of petroleum, 600 tons of munitions, 200 tons of dry stores, and 100 tons of refrigerated stores. The ships have highly automated cargo-handling equipment. The ships were built with helicopter decks but without hangars (see below). Range is 6,500 n. miles at 20 knots and 20,000 n. miles at 12 knots.

Engineering: The ships can steam at 18 knots on two boilers while the third is being maintained.

Guns: The AOR 1-6 were built with an armament two 3-inch/50-cal twin AA gun mounts aft and the Mk 56 GFCS. The 3-inch guns were removed from all ships with installation of helicopter hangars. A minimal 20-mm gun armament has been installed in some ships and all are to receive (additionally) two Phalanx CIWS.

Helicopters: The ROANOKE was built with twin helicopter hangers aft. The other ships have been similarly fitted; the hangars are each 61½ to 63 feet long and 18 to 21 feet wide.

Missiles: NATO Sea Sparrow launchers and the associated Mk 91 missile FCS are being fitted to all ships of the class (fitted atop the hangar structure, aft of the funnel).

WABASH (1983, Giorgio Arra)

The SAVANNAH with two Phalanx CIWS mounted forward of the bridge; a NATO Sea Sparrow guidance unit can be seen atop a lattice mast just ahead of the funnel. (1982, Giorgio Arra)

WABASH (1983, Giorgio Arra)

2 GASOLINE TANKERS: "ALATNA" CLASS

Number	Name	FY	Launched	In service	Status
T-AOG 81	ALATNA	55	6 Sep 1956	June 1957	**MSC**
T-AOG 82	CHATTAHOOCHEE	55	4 Dec 1956	Aug 1957	**MSC**

Builders:	Bethlehem Steel, Staten Island, N.Y.
Displacement:	5,720 tons full load
Length:	302 feet (92.1 m) oa
Beam:	61 feet (18.6 m)
Draft:	19 feet (5.8 m)
Propulsion:	diesel-electric (Alco diesels); 4,000 shp; 2 shafts
Speed:	13 knots
Manning:	40 (civilian)
Helicopters:	no facilities
Missiles:	none
Guns:	none

This two-ship class was built specifically for operation in support of U.S. military activities in the Arctic. Both ships were operated by MSTS (later MSC) until taken out of service on 8 August 1972 and laid up in the NDRF.

The ships were reacquired by the Navy on 31 July 1979 and reactivated for MSC service to replace older AOGs. It is expected that all three surviving AOGs will be replaced by new tankers under charter in the near future.

The AOGs carry petroleum products from point to point and are not fitted for underway replenishment of warships.

Design: The ships did not have an SCB number assigned; Maritime Administration T1-MET-24a design. They have ice-strengthened hulls and icebreaking prows and other features for Arctic operation (similar to T-AK 270 class). Cargo capacity is 30,000 barrels of petroleum products plus some 2,700 tons of dry cargo. A small helicopter platform was fitted aft in their original configuration.

ALATNA (1982, L. & L. van Ginderen)

ALATNA after being reacquired in 1979 and returned to service. The forward mast with protected crow's nest has been removed. (U.S. Navy)

1 GASOLINE TANKER: "TONTI" CLASS

Number	Name	Launched	In service	Status
T-AOG 78	NODAWAY	15 May 1945	7 Sep 1950	**MSC-P**

Builders:	Todd Shipyards, Houston, Texas
Displacement:	2,060 tons light
	6,000 tons full load
Length:	325⅙ feet (99.2 m) oa
Beam:	48⅙ feet (14.7 m)
Draft:	19 feet (5.8 m)
Propulsion:	diesel (Nordberg); 1,400 bhp; 1 shaft
Speed:	10 knots
Manning:	36 (civilian)
Helicopters:	no facilities
Missiles:	none
Guns:	none

The NODAWAY is the lone survivor in U.S. service of a once numerous type of small gasoline tanker. Five ships of this specific design were built as merchant tankers, all of which were acquired by the Navy in 1950 and assigned to MSTS, the predecessor of the Military Sealift Command.

Class: This class originally consisted of the T-AOG 76-80 with the AOG 64-75 being similar (BT1 design).

Design: Maritime Administration T1-M-BT2 design. Cargo capacity is 30,000 barrels.

Names: the NODAWAY was named BELRIDGE in merchant service.

(5) TRANSPORT OILERS: NEW CONSTRUCTION

Name	Launched	In service	Status
. . . . .		1985	Building
. . . . .		1985	Building
. . . . .		1985	Building
. . . . .		1985	Building
. . . . .		1986	Building

Builders:	American Shipbuilding, Tampa, Fla.
Displacement:	39,000 tons full load
Tonnage:	30,000 tons deadweight
Length:	615 feet (187.6 m) oa
Beam:	90 feet (27.4 m)
Draft:	34 feet (10.4 m)
Propulsion:	diesel; 15,300 bhp; 1 shaft
Speed:	16 knots
Manning:	28 (civilian)
Helicopters:	no facilities
Missiles:	none
Guns:	none

These are build-and-charter oilers that are being constructed specifically for naval service. They will initially be chartered by MSC for a five-year period to replace the older T-5 ships now in service. No hull numbers are assigned.

Builders: The bow sections of these ships are being built at Avondale Shipyards, New Orleans, La.

Design: Modified T-5 design with ice-strengthened hulls.

RINCON (T-AOG 77) now stricken; NODAWAY is similar. (U.S. Navy)

2 TRANSPORT OILERS: MODIFIED FALCON CLASS

Name	Launched	In service	Status
FALCON LEADER	26 Feb 1983	18 Aug 1983	**MSC**
FALCON CHAMPION	10 Sep 1983	19 Jan 1984	**MSC**

Builders:	Bath Iron Works, Maine
Displacement:	36,522 tons full load
Tonnage:	28,022 tons deadweight
Length:	666¾ feet (203.3 m) oa
Beam:	84 feet (25.6 m)
Draft:	31½ feet (9.6 m)
Propulsion:	diesel; 14,000 bhp; 1 shaft
Speed:	16 knots
Manning:	28 (civilian)
Helicopters:	no facilities
Missiles:	none
Guns:	none

These ships were built specifically for MSC and, as all T-AOT type, are operated by commercial firms under contract to MSC. No hull numbers have been assigned.

Design: Maritime Administration T6-M-136a type.

Names: Their merchant names were FALCON LEADER and FALCON CHAMPION, respectively.

4 TRANSPORT OILERS: FALCON CLASS

Number	Name	Launched	In service	Status
T-AOT 182	COLUMBIA	12 Sep 1970	15 Jan 1976	**MSC**
T-AOT 183	NECHES	30 Jan 1971	11 Feb 1976	**MSC**
T-AOT 184	HUDSON	8 Jan 1972	23 Apr 1976	**MSC**
T-AOT 185	SUSQUEHANNA	2 Oct 1971	11 May 1976	**MSC**

Builders:	Ingalls Shipbuilding, Pascagoula, Miss.
Displacement:	8,601 tons light
	45,877 tons full load
Length:	672 feet (204.9 m) oa
Beam:	89 feet (27.1 m)
Draft:	36 feet (11.0 m)
Propulsion:	diesel (Pielstick); 15,000 bhp; 1 shaft
Speed:	16.5 knots
Manning:	23 (civilian)
Helicopters:	no facilities
Missiles:	none
Guns:	none

These ships were delivered as merchant tankers in 1971 (two ships) and 1972 (two ships); they were chartered by MSC until acquired under "bareboat" charter in 1976.

Classification: These ships were designated T-AO after acquisition

The FALCON CHAMPION at launching. (Bath Iron Works)

by the Navy; changed to T-AOT on 30 September 1979. On that date the 18 tankers (T-AO) operated by MSC were changed to T-AOT as were seven ships laid up in the National Defense Reserve Fleet (T-AO 50, 67, 73, 75, 76, 78, and 134).

Design: Cargo capacity is 310,000 barrels.

Names: The merchant names for these ships were T-AOT 182 ex-FALCON LADY, T-AOT 183 ex-FALCON DUTCHESS, T-AOT 184 ex-FALCON PRINCESS, and T-AOT 185 ex-FALCON COUNTESS. They were renamed for rivers when acquired by the Navy in 1976. In naval service they are referred to as the Falcon class.

SUSQUEHANNA (1979, Giorgio Arra)

SUSQUEHANNA (U.S. Navy)

1 TRANSPORT OILER: "POTOMAC"

Number	Name	Launched	In service	Status
T-AOT 181	POTOMAC	(see notes)	12 Jan 1976	**MSC**

Builders:	Sun Shipbuilding and Dry Dock, Chester, Pa.
Displacement:	7,333 tons light
	34,800 tons full load
Length:	620 feet (189.1 m) oa
Beam:	83½ feet (25.5 m)
Draft:	34 feet (10.4 m)
Propulsion:	steam turbine; 20,460 shp; 1 shaft
Boilers:	2
Speed:	18 knots
Manning:	
Helicopters:	no facilities
Missiles:	none
Guns:	none

The POTOMAC was constructed with the mid-body and bow sections built to mate with the stern section of an earlier tanker named POTOMAC (T-AO 150). The "new" tanker was named SHENANDOAH and operated under commercial charter to MSC for several years until she was formally acquired in 1976. At that time the ship was renamed POTOMAC and designated T-AO 181.

The ship is contractor-operated by MSC with a civilian crew.

(The original POTOMAC was partially destroyed by fire on 3 October 1961, but the stern section and machinery were relatively intact; she was originally T5-S-12a type and had been launched on 8 October 1956.)

Design: Cargo capacity is 200,000 barrels.

9 TRANSPORT OILERS: SEALIFT CLASS

Number	Name	Launched	In service	Status
T-AOT 168	SEALIFT PACIFIC	13 Oct 1973	14 Aug 1974	**MSC**
T-AOT 169	SEALIFT ARABIAN SEA	26 Jan 1974	6 Feb 1975	**MSC**
T-AOT 170	SEALIFT CHINA SEA	20 Apr 1974	19 May 1975	**MSC**
T-AOT 171	SEALIFT INDIAN OCEAN	27 July 1974	29 Aug 1975	**MSC**
T-AOT 172	SEALIFT ATLANTIC	26 Jan 1974	26 Aug 1974	**MSC**
T-AOT 173	SEALIFT MEDITERRANEAN	9 Mar 1974	6 Nov 1974	**MSC**
T-AOT 174	SEALIFT CARIBBEAN	8 June 1974	10 Feb 1975	**MSC**
T-AOT 175	SEALIFT ARCTIC	31 Aug 1974	22 May 1975	**MSC**
T-AOT 176	SEALIFT ANTARCTIC	26 Oct 1974	1 Aug 1975	**MSC**

Builders:	T-AOT 168-171 Todd Shipyards, San Pedro, Calif.
	T-AOT 172-176 Bath Iron Works, Maine
Displacement:	32,000 tons full load
Length:	587 feet (179.0 m) oa
Beam:	84 feet (25.6 m)
Draft:	34⅓ feet (10.5 m)
Propulsion:	turbo-charged diesel (Pielstick); 14,000 bhp; 1 shaft
Speed:	16 knots
Manning:	30 (civilian) + 2 cadets
Helicopters:	no facilities
Missiles:	none
Guns:	none

These ships were built specifically for MSC to replace World War II-era tankers of the T2 type. The ships are contractor-operated under "bareboat" charter for MSC with civilian crews.

Design: These ships have a cargo capacity of 220,000 barrels.

Engineering: A bow thruster is fitted to assist in docking operations.

SEALIFT CHINA SEA (1982, Giorgio Arra)

1 TRANSPORT OILER: "AMERICAN EXPLORER"

Number	Name	Launched	In service	Status
T-AOT 165	AMERICAN EXPLORER	11 Apr 1958	27 Oct 1959	**MSC**

Builders: Ingalls Shipbuilding, Pascagoula, Miss.
Displacement: 31,300 tons full load
Length: 615 feet (187.6 m) oa
Beam: 80 feet (24.4 m)
Draft: 32 feet (9.75 m)
Propulsion: steam turbine (De Laval); 22,000 shp; 1 shaft
Boilers: 2 (Babcock & Wilcox)
Speed: 20 knots
Manning:
Helicopters: no facilities
Missiles: none
Guns: none

The AMERICAN EXPLORER was built for merchant use but upon completion she was acquired by the Navy. She is similar to the MAUMEE-class ships. The AMERICAN EXPLORER is contractor-operated for MSC with a civilian crew.

Design: Maritime Administration T5-S-RM2a design. Cargo capacity is 190,300 barrels of petroleum.

AMERICAN EXPLORER (1981, L. & L. van Ginderen)

3 TRANSPORT OILERS: "MAUMEE" CLASS

Number	Name	Launched	In service	Status
T-AOT 149	MAUMEE	16 Feb 1956	12 Dec 1956	**MSC**
T-AOT 151	SHOSHONE	17 Jan 1957	15 Apr 1957	**MSC**
T-AOT 152	YUKON	16 Mar 1956	17 May 1957	**MSC**

Builders: T-AOT 149, 152 Ingalls Shipbuilding, Pascagoula, Miss.
                 T-AOT 151   Sun Shipbuilding and Dry Dock, Chester, Pa.
Displacement: 32,953 tons full load
Length: 620 feet (189.1 m) oa
Beam: 83½ feet (25.5 m)
Draft: 32 feet (9.75 m)
Propulsion: steam turbine (Westinghouse); 20,460 shp; 1 shaft
Boilers: 2 (Combustion Engineering)
Speed: 18 knots
Manning:
Helicopters: no facilities
Missiles: none
Guns: none

These ships were built for naval service. All are contractor-operated for MSC with civilian crews.

Class: The POTOMAC (T-AO 150) of this class was rebuilt as the T-AO/T-AOT 181. Hull numbers AO 166–167 were reserved for planned Mission-class (T2-SE-A2) "jumbo" conversions; the T-AO 153–164 were T2-SE-A1 tankers acquired during the 1956 Suez crisis and stricken in 1957–1958.

Design: Maritime Administration T5-S-12a type. Cargo capacity is 203,200 barrels. The MAUMEE was modified in 1969–1970, being fitted with a strengthened prow and other features enabling her to transport petroleum to U.S. Arctic research sites.

YUKON (1983, Giorgio Arra)

1 TRANSPORT OILER: MISSION TYPE

Number	Name	Launched	Commissioned	Status
T-AOT 134	MISSION SANTA YNEZ	19 Dec 1943	(See notes)	NDRF

Builders:	Marine Ship Corp., Sausalito, Calif.
Displacement:	5,730 tons light
	22,380 tons full load
Length:	503 feet (153.4 m) wl
	523½ feet (159.7 m) oa
Beam:	68 feet (20.7 m)
Draft:	30⅚ feet (9.4 m)
Propulsion:	turbo-electric; 10,000 shp; 1 shaft
Boilers:	2
Speed:	16 knots
Manning:	
Helicopters:	no facilities
Missiles:	none
Guns:	none

The MISSION SANTA YNEZ is the lone survivor retained in reserve of a series of merchant tankers built late in World War II and acquired by the Navy after the war. The ship was delivered as a merchant tanker on 13 March 1944 and acquired by the Navy for use as a tanker on 22 October 1947

Class: The Mission class encompassed AO 111–137; other fleet oilers and tankers (transport oilers) of this design were in naval service during and after World War II. The SUAMICO (AO 49) class is similar (propulsion differs).

Design: Maritime Administration T2-SE-A2 design. Cargo capacity approximately 134,000 barrels of petroleum.

Guns: Unarmed when acquired by the Navy.

Names: Merchant name retained in naval service.

5 TRANSPORT OILERS: "SUAMICO" CLASS

Number	Name	Launched	Commissioned	Status
T-AOT 50	TALLULAH	25 June 1942	5 Sep 1942	NDRF
T-AOT 67	CACHE	7 Sep 1942	3 Nov 1942	NDRF
T-AOT 73	MILLICOMA	21 Jan 1943	5 Mar 1943	NDRF
T-AOT 75	SAUGATUCK	7 Dec 1942	19 Feb 1943	NDRF
T-AOT 76	SCHUYLKILL	16 Feb 1943	9 Apr 1943	NDRF

Builders:	Sun Shipbuilding and Dry Dock, Chester, Pa.
Displacement:	5,730 tons light
	22,380 tons full load
Length:	503 feet (153.4 m) wl
	523½ feet (159.7 m) oa
Beam:	68 feet (20.7 m)
Draft:	30⅚ feet (9.4 m)
Propulsion:	turbo-electric (General Electric turbine except Westinghouse in T-AOT 67 and 75); 6,000 shp; 1 shaft
Boilers:	2 (Babcock & Wilcox)
Speed:	15 knots
Manning:	
Helicopters:	no facilities
Missiles:	none
Guns:	removed

All of these ships were begun as merchant tankers but acquired by the Navy in 1942–1943 and completed as fleet oilers (AO) and Navy manned. After World War II they were employed in the tanker role by MSTS (later MSC).

All have been laid up in the NDRF.

Classification: Changed from T-AO to T-AOT on 30 September 1978 (while laid up).

Design: Maritime Administration T2-SE-A1 design. Cargo capacity is approximately 134,000 barrels.

Guns: As built this class was armed with one 5-inch/38-cal DP gun, four 3-inch/50-cal AA guns, and eight 40-mm AA guns. All ships were disarmed after World War II when employed in tanker role.

Names: Original merchant names were T-AOT 67 STILLWATER; T-AOT 73 CONESTOGA, KING'S MOUNTAIN; T-AOT 75 NEWTON; and T-AOT 76 LOUISBURG. The T-AOT 50 retained her merchant name in naval service.

MISSION SANTA YNEZ (U.S. Navy)

SCHUYLKILL (U.S. Navy)

2 TRANSPORTS: "BARRETT" CLASS

Number	Name	Launched	In service	Status
T-AP 196	EMPIRE STATE (USNS BARRETT)	27 June 1950	15 Dec 1951	**Academic**
T-AP 197	BAY STATE (USNS GEIGER)	9 Oct 1950	13 Sep 1952	Hulk
T-AP 198	STATE OF MAINE (USNS UPSHUR)	19 Jan 1951	20 Dec 1952	**Academic**

Builders:	New York Shipbuilding, Camden, N.J.
Displacement:	17,600 tons standard
	19,600 tons full load
Length:	533 feet (162.5 m) oa
Beam:	73 feet (22.3 m)
Draft:	27 feet (8.2 m)
Propulsion:	steam turbine; 13,750 shp; 1 shaft
Boilers:	2
Speed:	19 knots
Manning:	
Troops:	1,500 + 400 cabin passengers
Helicopters:	no facilities
Missiles:	none
Guns:	none

These ships were begun as passenger liners for the American President Lines; they were taken over by the Navy during construction and completed as troop transports. Placed in service in 1951–1952 with MSTS and operated by civilian crews.

All three ships were laid up in the NDRF in 1973, but quickly transferred on loan to state maritime schools, the BARRETT to the New York Maritime College, GEIGER to the Massachusetts Maritime Academy, and UPSHUR to the Maine Maritime Academy. All renamed with the prefix Training Ship (TS) by their schools with the Navy names retained on U.S. government documents.

The BAY STATE was severely damaged by fire in 1982 and has not been returned to service. Only the GEIGER and UPSHUR are retained on the NDRF roles.

Design: Maritime Administration P2-S1-DN1 design. All troop cabin, mess, and recreation spaces are fully air-conditioned. Some 1,000 additional troops can be carried (total 2,500) by converting recreation areas into high-density berthing spaces. Cabin spaces are for officers and dependents.

Engineering: The BARRETT attained 21.5 knots on trials.

Names: Merchant names were to have been T-AP 196 PRESIDENT JACKSON, T-AP 197 PRESIDENT ADAMS, and T-AP 198 PRESIDENT HAYES.

GEIGER (U.S. Navy)

6 TRANSPORTS: ADMIRAL TYPE

Number	Name	Launched	Commissioned	Status
T-AP 120	Gen Daniel I. Sultan	28 Nov 1943	23 Aug 1944	NDRF
T-AP 122	Gen Alexander M. Patch	22 Apr 1944	21 Nov 1944	NDRF
T-AP 123	Gen Simon B. Buckner	14 June 1944	24 Jan 1945	NDRF
T-AP 124	Gen Edwin D. Patrick	27 July 1944	31 Jan 1945	NDRF
T-AP 126	Gen Maurice Rose	25 Feb 1945	10 July 1945	NDRF
T-AP 127	Gen William O. Darby	4 June 1945	27 Sep 1945	NDRF

Builders:	Bethlehem Steel, Alameda, Calif.
Displacement:	9,676 tons standard
	20,120 tons full load
Length:	573 feet (174.75 m) wl
	608 1 1/12 feet (185.7 m) oa
Beam:	75½ feet (23.0 m)
Draft:	29 feet (8.8 m)
Propulsion:	turbo-electric (General Electric turbines); 18,000 shp; 2 shafts
Boilers:	4 (Combustion Engineering)
Speed:	19 knots
Manning:	500–650 (full wartime)
Troops:	4,650–5,000
Helicopters	no facilities
Missiles:	none
Guns:	removed

These ships were acquired by the Navy while under construction and placed in commission as troop transports (AP). They were transferred to the Army in 1946 for use as transports and renamed for deceased generals. They were reacquired by the Navy in 1950 but retained their Army names.

After operation by MSTS all were laid up in the NDRF.

Class: This class originally included AP 120–129.

The Admiral-type transports Gen Hugh J. Gaffey (T-AP 121) and Gen William O. Darby (T-AP 127) are employed as barrack ships, redesignated IX 507 and IX 510, respectively; see page 318.

Design: Maritime Administration P2-SE2-R1 design. The class is similar to the slightly larger General type. (These ships have kingposts forward and aft while the General type has single pole masts.)

Guns: As built an armament of four 5-inch/38-cal DP guns and eight 40-mm AA guns was fitted plus 20-mm AA guns in some ships.

Names: Original Admiral-class names were AP 120 Adm W.S. Benson, AP 122 Adm R.E. Coontz, AP 123 Adm E.W. Eberle, AP 124 Adm C.F. Hughes, AP 126 Adm Hugh Rodman, and AP 127 Adm W.S. Sims.

Gen Maurice Rose (U.S. Navy)

7 TRANSPORTS: GENERAL TYPE

Number	Name	Launched	Commissioned	Status
T-AP 110	GEN JOHN POPE	21 Mar 1943	5 Aug 1943	NDRF
T-AP 111	GEN A.E. ANDERSON	2 May 1943	5 Oct 1943	NDRF
T-AP 112	GEN W.A. MANN	18 July 1943	13 Oct 1943	NDRF
T-AP 114	GEN WILLIAM MITCHELL	31 Oct 1943	19 Jan 1944	NDRF
T-AP 117	GEN W.H. GORDON	7 May 1944	29 June 1944	NDRF
T-AP 119	GEN WILLIAM WEIGEL	3 Sep 1944	6 Jan 1945	NDRF
T-AP 176	GEN J.C. BRECKINRIDGE	18 Mar 1945	30 June 1945	NDRF

Builders:	Federal Shipbuilding and Dry Dock, Kearny, N.J.
Displacement:	11,828 tons standard
	20,175 tons full load
Length:	573 feet (174.7 m) wl
	622 7/12 feet (189.9 m) oa
Beam:	75½ feet (23.0 m)
Draft:	25½ feet (7.8 m)
Propulsion:	steam turbine (De Laval); 17,000 shp; 2 shafts
Boilers:	4 (Foster Wheeler)
Speed:	20.6 knots
Manning:	450–530 (full wartime)
Troops:	approx. 5,300
Helicopters:	no facilities
Missiles:	none
Guns:	removed

These large troop transports were acquired while under construction with some placed in partial commission for transfer to another shipyard for outfitting as a troop transport. (Full commission dates after conversion are given above.) All saw Navy service in World War II. The GORDON was turned over to the Army for use as a transport from 1949 to 1951 and was used in that role with the other ships during the Korean War (operated by MSTS). They then had periodic service until "finally" laid up, the POPE in 1970, ANDERSON in 1958, MANN and MITCHELL in 1966, GORDON in 1961, WEIGEL in 1967, and BRECKINRIDGE in 1966. All are in the NDRF.

Class: This class consisted of AP 110–119 and 176.

Design: Maritime Administration P2-S2-R2 design.

Guns: As built the ships carried four 5-inch/38-cal DP guns and eight 40-mm AA guns, with some ships also having 20-mm AA guns.

Names: AP 119 was originally named GEN C.H. BARTH; changed during construction.

(1) REPAIR SHIP: NEW DESIGN

A new class of repair ships is planned, with the first ship scheduled for the fiscal 1989 shipbuilding program. It is envisioned that several ships will be built to replace the long-serving VULCAN class.

GEN JOHN POPE (U.S. Navy)

4 REPAIR SHIPS: "VULCAN" CLASS

Number	Name	Launched	Commissioned	Status
AR 5	VULCAN	14 Dec 1940	16 June 1941	**AA**
AR 6	AJAX	22 Aug 1942	30 Oct 1943	**PA**
AR 7	HECTOR	11 Nov 1942	7 Feb 1944	**PA**
AR 8	JASON	3 Apr 1943	19 June 1944	**PA**

Builders:	AR 5 New York Shipbuilding, Camden, N.J.
	AR 6-8 Los Angeles Shipbuilding, Calif.
Displacement:	9,140 tons standard
	16,200 tons full load
Length:	520 feet (158.6 m) wl
	529⁵⁄₁₂ feet (161.5 m) oa except AR 8 530 feet (161.6 m)
Beam:	73⅓ feet (22.4 m)
Draft:	23⅓ feet (7.1 m)
Propulsion:	steam turbine (Allis Chalmers except New York Shipbuilding in AR 5); 11,000 shp; 2 shafts
Boilers:	4 (Babcock & Wilcox)
Speed:	19.2 knots

Manning:	Total	Officers	Enlisted
AR 5	836	29	807
AR 6	864	29	835
AR 7	833	30	803
AR 8	857	31	826

Helicopters:	VERTREP area
Missiles:	none
Guns:	4 20-mm Mk 67 (4 single)

These are large, highly capable repair ships although they lack the ability to support more sophisticated weapon and electronic systems.

Classification: The JASON was completed as a heavy hull repair ship (ARH 1); she was reclassified as an AR on 9 September 1957.

Design: A very small VERTREP station is provided forward. Two 20-ton capacity cranes are fitted.

Guns: As built these ships carried four 5-inch/38-cal DP guns and eight 40-mm AA guns. The 5-inch weapons were retained into the 1970s when they were beached in favor of minimal 20-mm armament.

JASON (1979, Giorgio Arra)

JASON (1979, Giorgio Arra)

JASON (1979, Giorgio Arra)

1 + 1 CABLE REPAIR SHIPS: "ZEUS" CLASS

Number	Name	FY	Launched	In service	Status
T-ARC 7	ZEUS	79	30 Oct 1982	19 Mar 1984	**MSC**
T-ARC 8	. . . . . .	86			Planned

Builders:	National Steel and Shipbuilding, San Diego, Calif.
Displacement:	8,370 tons light
	14,225 tons full load
Length:	511½ feet (156.0 m) oa
Beam:	73 feet (22.25 m)
Draft:	23⅔ feet (7.2 m)
Propulsion:	diesel-electric; 10,200 bhp; 2 shafts
Speed:	15 knots
Manning:	88 (civilian) + 6 Navy + 30 technicians
Helicopters:	no facilities
Missiles:	none
Guns:	none

The ZEUS fitting out at National Steel and Shipbuilding in San Diego. (1984, Giorgio Arra)

The ZEUS is the first cable ship built specifically for the U.S. Navy and will support SOSUS and other underwater cable activities. In addition to supporting these undersea projects, cable ships conduct special oceanographic surveys in support of the Naval Electronic Systems Command under the Oceanographer of the Navy.

Two ships of this type were planned, originally to replace the now-stricken THOR (ARC 4) and AEOLUS (ARC 3); a third ship may be subsequently constructed to provide three modern ARCs in the 1990s and beyond. (Commercial ships are also used under contract to support U.S. seafloor cable installations.)

The ZEUS was delayed because of design and construction problems; her keel was laid down 1 June 1981.

The Navy personnel are communications specialists.

Design: The ZEUS can lay up to 1,000 miles of cable in depths down to 9,000 feet. Two 1,200-hp bow and two 1,200-hp stern thrusters are fitted for station keeping while handling cables. The ZEUS and all other T-ARCs are fitted with the AN/SSN-2 precise seafloor navigation system.

The ZEUS on builder's sea trials; note side-by-side funnels. (1983, National Steel and Shipbuilding)

2 CABLE REPAIR SHIPS: "NEPTUNE" CLASS

Number	Name	Launched	Commissioned	Status
T-ARC 2	Neptune	22 Aug 1945	1 June 1953	**MSC-A**
T-ARC 6	Albert J. Meyer	7 Nov 1945	13 May 1963	**MSC-P**

Builders:	Pusey and Jones, Wilmington, Del.
Displacement:	7,400 tons full load
Length:	369 feet (112.5 m) oa
Beam:	47 feet (14.3 m)
Draft:	18 feet (5.5 m)
Propulsion:	turbo-electric; 4,000 shp; 2 shafts
Boilers:	2 (Combustion Engineering)
Speed:	14 knots
Manning:	71 (civilian) + 6 Navy personnel + 25 technicians
Helicopters:	VERTREP area in T-ARC 2
Missiles:	none
Guns:	none

These are built-for-the-purpose cable ships. Both were built as Army cable ships, the Neptune having been originally named William H.G. Bullard; both ships were completed in 1946 and laid up in Maritime Administration reserve. The Neptune was acquired by the Navy in 1953 and the Meyer in 1952 to support the SOSUS program; they were placed in Navy commission (ARC) and operated as commissioned ships (USS). The Meyer was transferred outright to the Navy and the Neptune on loan until permanently acquired in September 1966. Both were transferred to the Military Sealift Command in 1973 (changed to T-ARC).

The ships were extensively modernized 1979–1982. Both are operated by MSC with civil service personnel. The Navy personnel are communications specialists.

Design: Maritime Administration S3-S2-BP1 design. The Neptune has a helicopter platform aft, but it is used only for VERTREP.

Engineering: These were the last ships in U.S. government service with reciprocating engines; they have been reengined (see below).

Modernization: The ships have been extensively modernized, the Meyer at Bethlehem Steel, Baltimore, Md., from March 1978 to May 1980, and the Neptune at General Dynamics, Quincy, Mass., from February 1980 to February 1982. Their propulsion machinery was replaced along with all appropriate piping and wiring, and their superstructures were rebuilt.

Name: The Neptune's merchant name was William H.G. Bullard.

Albert J. Meyer (1977, Giorgio Arra)

Neptune (1975, Giorgio Arra)

1 CABLE REPAIR SHIP: "AEOLUS" CLASS

Number	Name	Launched	AKA Comm.	ARC Comm.	Status
T-ARC 3	Aeolus	29 May 1945	18 June 1945	14 May 1955	**MSC-P**

Builders:	Walsh-Kaiser, Providence, R.I.
Displacement:	7,040 tons full load
Length:	438 feet (133.6 m) oa
Beam:	58 feet (17.7 m)
Draft:	19¼ feet (5.9 m)
Propulsion:	turbo-electric (Westinghouse turbines); 6,000 shp; 2 shafts
Boilers:	2 (Wickes)
Speed:	16.9 knots
Manning:	80 (civilian) + 2 Navy technicians (enlisted)
Helicopters:	VERTREP area
Missiles:	none
Guns:	removed

The Aeolus was completed as an attack cargo ship (AKA 47). She was laid up in reserve from 1946 until converted to a cable ship in 1955. The ship was Navy manned from 1955 until 1973 when transferred to MSC for operation by civil service personnel.

Class: A sister ship, the Thor (T-ARC 4, formerly AKA 49), was stricken in 1975. The Portunus (ARC 1) was transferred to Portugal in 1959 and the Yamacraw (ARC 5) was stricken in 1965; the former ship was the converted LSM 275 and the latter ship a former Coast Guard cutter (Yamacraw/WARC 333, ex-Navy ACM 9, ex-Army Murray/MP 9).

Design: Originally Maritime Administration design S4-SE2-BE1. The Aeolus has a helicopter platform aft, but can be used only for VERTREP and as a working area.

Guns: All armament removed during ARC conversion.

Names: Named Turandot as AKA 47.

AEOLUS (1970, U.S. Navy)

AEOLUS (1970, U.S. Navy)

1 SMALL REPAIR SHIP: CONVERTED LST

Number	Name	Launched	Commissioned	Status
ARL 24 (ex-LST 963)	SPHINX	18 Nov 1944	12 Dec 1944	PR

Builders:	Bethlehem Steel, Hingham, Mass.
Displacement:	1,625 tons light
	4,100 tons full load
Length:	316 feet (96.4 m) wl
	328 feet (100.0 m) oa
Beam:	50 feet (15.25 m)
Draft:	11 feet (3.4 m)
Propulsion:	diesels (General Motors); 1,800 bhp; 2 shafts
Speed:	11.6 knots
Manning:	approx. 250 (20 officers + 130 enlisted)
Helicopters:	no facilities
Missiles:	none
Guns:	8 40-mm AA Mk 2 (2 quad)

The SPHINX is the last of several score LSTs converted to various types of repair and support ships remaining on the Naval Register. She served in World War II, the Korean War, and in Vietnam. She was laid up in reserve from 1947–1950, 1956–1967, and since 1971. She is in mothballs at the Bremerton Naval Shipyard.

Class: Thirty-nine ships were converted to the ARL configuration to repair and support landing craft in advanced areas. All converted LSTs, these ships were the ARL 1–24, 26–33, 35–41, with ARL 25 and 34 cancelled. Several of these ships survive in foreign navies.

Classification: ARL originally indicated landing craft repair ship (ARL); changed to small repair ship in 1978.

Conversion: During ARL conversion the ship was fitted with machine shops, a carpenter's shop, brass foundry, welding facilities, increased distilling capacity and fresh water storage, and additional electric power generators. Two 10-ton capacity booms were fitted forward and a 50-ton-capacity sheerleg is mounted on the port side of the deck house. A tripod mast is fitted aft, in place of the original LST pole mast. Davits are provided for two small landing craft.

Guns: The original ARL armament consisted of one 3-inch/50-cal AA gun and eight 20-mm AA guns in addition to the two 40-mm quad mounts. The SPHINX retains two Mk 51 gun directors.

The SPHINX underway off San Diego. She is the U.S. Navy's only survivor of several score LSTs converted to various repair ship and other support roles. Note the quad "forties" at her bow and stern; built-up shop and storage spaces amidships; and tripod mast. Several sister ships survive in foreign navies. (1968, U.S. Navy)

(4) SALVAGE SHIPS: "SAFEGUARD" CLASS

Number	Name	FY	Launched	Commission	Status
ARS 50	SAFEGUARD	81	12 Nov 1983	1985	Building
ARS 51	GRASP	82	21 Apr 1984	1985	Building
ARS 52	SALVOR	82	1984	1985	Building
ARS 53	GRAPPLE	83	1985	1986	Building

Builders:	Peterson Builders, Sturgeon Bay, Wisc.
Displacement:	2,900 tons full load
Length:	255 feet (77.8 m) oa
Beam:	50 feet (15.2 m)
Draft:	15 feet (4.6 m)
Propulsion:	geared diesels; 4,200 bhp; 2 shafts
Speed:	14 knots
Manning:	87 (6 officers + 81 enlisted)
Helicopters:	no facilities
Missiles:	none
Guns:	2 20-mm Mk 67 (2 single)

The salvage ship SAFEGUARD under way with a "bone in her teeth." Note the low freeboard, masts and booms forward and aft, antenna/signal mast above bridge, and twin satellite antennas alongside funnel; mooring gear is stowed under the bridge wings. (1985, L. & L. van Ginderen collection)

These ships are intended to replace the existing ARS-type ships in the salvage and towing role. The three large ATS-type tugs plus these four ships will permit the continuous peacetime deployment of one ship in the Western Pacific and one ship in the Mediterranean. No additional ships of this type are planned.

(The Navy has a national responsibility for the salvaging of all U.S. ships, both government and private, under Public Law 80-513.)

7 SALVAGE SHIPS: "ESCAPE" AND "BOLSTER" CLASSES

Number	Name	Launched	Commissioned	Status
ARS 8	PRESERVER	1 Apr 1943	11 Jan 1944	**NRF-A**
ARS 38	BOLSTER	23 Dec 1944	11 May 1945	**NRF-P**
ARS 39	CONSERVER	27 Jan 1945	9 June 1945	**PA**
ARS 40	HOIST	31 Mar 1945	21 July 1945	**AA**
ARS 41	OPPORTUNE	31 Mar 1945	5 Oct 1945	**AA**
ARS 42	RECLAIMER	25 June 1945	20 Dec 1945	**PA**
ARS 43	RECOVERY	4 Aug 1945	15 May 1946	**AA**

Builders:	Basalt Rock Co., Napa, Calif.
Displacement:	1,530 tons standard
	2,045 tons full load except ARS 8, 1,970 tons
Length:	207 feet (63.1 m) wl
	213½ feet (65.1 m) oa
Beam:	43 feet (13.1 m) except ARS 8 39 feet (11.9 m)
Draft:	13 feet (4.0 m)
Propulsion:	diesel-electric (Cooper Bessemer diesels); 3,000 bhp; 2 shafts
Speed:	16 knots except ARS 8 14.8 knots
Manning:	103 (6 officers + 97 enlisted) except 83 (4 officers + 79 enlisted) active + 47 (3 officers + 44 enlisted) reserve in ARS 38, 59 (3 officers + 56 enlisted) reserve in ARS 8
Helicopters:	no facilities
Missiles:	none
Guns:	2 20-mm Mk 68 (2 single) except Mk 67 in ARS 39, 41

These ships are fitted for salvage and towing activities. They have compressed-air diving equipment. The PRESERVER was transferred to the NRF on 1 November 1979 and the BOLSTER on 30 June 1983; they are manned by composite active-reserve crews.

Class: These classes originally included 22 ships, the ARS 5–9, 19–28 38–43, plus the cancelled ARS 44–49.

Two of these ships were converted to oceanographic ships, the AGOR 17 ex-ARS 20 and AGOR 18 ex-ARS 27; three others serve with the Coast Guard, WMEC 167 ex-ARS 9, WMEC 168 ex-ARS 26, and WMEC 6 ex-ARS 6. (See Appendix A for dates of transfer to Coast Guard.)

Guns: The original armament consisted of two or four 20-mm guns in twin mounts. After World War II most of the active ships carried a single 40-mm AA gun atop the superstructure.

CONSERVER with SKATE-class SSN (1982, Giorgio Arra)

RECLAIMER (1978, Giorgio Arra)

3 SUBMARINE TENDERS: "EMORY S. LAND" CLASS

Number	Name	FY	Launched	Commissioned	Status
AS 39	EMORY S. LAND	72	4 May 1977	7 July 1979	**AA**
AS 40	FRANK CABLE	73	14 Jan 1978	5 Feb 1980	**AA**
AS 41	McKEE	77	16 Feb 1980	15 Aug 1981	**PA**

Builders:	Lockheed Shipbuilding and Construction, Seattle, Wash.
Displacement:	13,842 tons light
	23,000 tons full load
Length:	645⅔ feet (196.9 m) oa
Beam:	85 feet (25.9 m)
Draft:	25 feet (7.6 m)
Propulsion:	steam turbine (De Laval); 20,000 shp; 1 shaft

Boilers:	2 (Combustion Engineering)		
Speed:	18 knots		
Manning:			
	Total	Officers	Enlisted
AS 39	606	51	555
AS 40	646	51	595
AS 41	626	45	581
Helicopters:	VERTREP area		
Missiles:	none		
Guns:	2 40-mm machine guns Mk 19 (2 single)		
	4 20-mm Mk 67 (4 single)		

These are improved versions of the L.Y. SPEAR-class tenders with the later ships fitted specifically to support the LOS ANGELES (SSN 688)-class attack submarines. Up to four SSNs can be supported alongside simultaneously.

Design: SCB No. 737. Submarine tenders have extensive maintenance shops for various submarine systems and equipment as well as weapon and provision storage.

EMORY S. LAND (Giorgio Arra)

FRANK CABLE (1982, Giorgio Arra)

FRANK CABLE (1979, U.S. Navy)

2 SUBMARINE TENDERS: "L.Y. SPEAR" CLASS

Number	Name	FY	Launched	Commissioned	Status
AS 36	L.Y. Spear	65	7 Sep 1967	28 Feb 1970	**AA**
AS 37	Dixon	66	20 June 1970	7 Aug 1971	**PA**

Builders:	General Dynamics, Quincy, Mass.
Displacement:	12,770 tons light
	22,628 tons full load
Length:	645⅔ feet (196.9 m) oa
Beam:	85 feet (25.9 m)
Draft:	24⅔ feet (7.5 m)
Propulsion:	steam turbines (General Electric); 20,000 shp; 1 shaft
Boilers:	2 (Foster Wheeler)
Speed:	18 knots
Manning:	AS 36 612 (51 officers + 561 enlisted)
	AS 37 623 (43 officers + 580 enlisted)
Helicopters:	VERTREP area
Missiles:	none
Guns:	4 20-mm Mk 67 (4 single)

These were the Navy's first submarine tenders designed specifically to support SSNs; they can support four submarines alongside at one time.

Class: The AS 38 of this design was authorized in the fiscal 1969 budget but was not built because of funding shortages in other ship programs.

Design: SCB No. 702.

Guns: As built these ships each had two 5-inch/38-cal DP guns. They were deleted in favor of the minimal 20-mm gun armament.

Dixon with Patrick Henry (SSN 599) alongside (1983, Giorgio Arra)

Dixon (1979, Giorgio Arra)

2 FBM SUBMARINE TENDERS: "SIMON LAKE" CLASS

Number	Name	FY	Launched	Commissioned	Status
AS 33	SIMON LAKE	63	8 Feb 1964	7 Nov 1964	**AA**
AS 34	CANOPUS	64	12 Feb 1965	4 Nov 1965	**AA**

Builders:	AS 33 Puget Sound Naval Shipyard, Bremerton, Wash.
	AS 34 Litton/Ingalls Shipbuilding, Pascagoula, Miss.
Displacement:	21,500 tons full load
Length:	643¾ feet (196.3 m) oa
Beam:	85 feet (25.9 m)
Draft:	24½ feet (7.5 m)
Propulsion:	steam turbine; 20,000 shp; 1 shaft
Boilers:	2 (Combustion Engineering)
Speed:	18 knots
Manning:	AS 33 652 (54 officers + 598 enlisted)
	AD 34 650 (53 officers + 597 enlisted)
Helicopters:	VERTREP area
Missiles:	none
Guns:	4 20-mm Mk 67 (4 single)

These tenders are designed to service FBM submarines with up to three SSBNs moored alongside simultaneously. In addition to regular AS capabilities, FBM submarine tenders also store ballistic missiles.

Class: The AS 35 of this design was authorized in fiscal 1965 but construction was deferred and the ship was not built. The ship would have provided one tender for each of five Polaris SSBN squadrons with a sixth ship in overhaul or transit. However, the Polaris SSBN program was cut from the proposed 45 to 41 submarines and only four squadrons were formed.

Design: SCB No. 238. These ships were originally built to support the Polaris missile; the SIMON LAKE was modified in 1970–1971 and the CANOPUS in 1969–1970 to support the Poseidon missile; the SIMON LAKE has subsequently been modified to handle the Trident C-4 missile (the ship is based at Kings Bay, Ga.).

Guns: Original armament of four 3-inch guns was removed.

2 FBM SUBMARINE TENDERS: "HUNLEY" CLASS

Number	Name	FY	Launched	Commissioned	Status
AS 31	HUNLEY	60	28 Sep 1961	16 June 1962	**AA**
AS 32	HOLLAND	62	19 Jan 1963	7 Sep 1963	**AA**

Builders:	AS 31 Newport News Shipbuilding, Va.
	AS 32 Ingalls Shipbuilding, Pascagoula, Miss.
Displacement:	10,500 tons standard
	18,300 tons full load
Length:	570 feet (173.8 m) wl
	599 feet (182.7 m) oa
Beam:	83 feet (25.3 m)
Draft:	24 feet (7.3 m)
Propulsion:	diesel-electric (Fairbanks-Morse diesels); 15,000 bhp; 1 shaft
Speed:	19 knots
Manning:	651 (54 officers + 597 enlisted)
Helicopters:	VERTREP area
Missiles:	none
Guns:	4 20-mm Mk 67 (4 single)

The HUNLEY and HOLLAND were the first tenders designed specifically to service fleet ballistic missile submarines. Three SBBNs can be serviced alongside simultaneously.

Design: SCB No. 194. As built they could support the Polaris missile; the HUNLEY was modified in 1973–1974 and the HOLLAND in 1974–1975 to support Poseidon-armed submarines.

As built the ships had a 32-ton-capacity hammerhead crane fitted aft. It has been replaced in both ships with amidships cranes, as in the later SIMON LAKE class. They carry 20 Poseidon missiles.

Guns: The original armament for these ships was four 3-inch/50-cal AA guns in twin mounts.

The SIMON LAKE at Kings Bay, Georgia, where the tender provides support for the SSBNs of Submarine Squadron 16, relocated from Rota, Spain. (1981, U.S. Navy, JO1 Lon Cabot)

HUNLEY (U.S. Navy)

1 FBM SUBMARINE TENDER: MODIFIED "FULTON" CLASS

Number	Name	Launched	Commissioned	Status
AS 19	PROTEUS	12 Nov 1942	31 Jan 1944	**PA**

Builders:	Moore Shipbuilding and Dry Dock, Oakland, Calif.
Displacement:	10,234 tons standard
	18,500 tons full load
Length:	564 feet (172.0 m) wl
	574½ feet (175.2 m) oa
Beam:	73 feet (22.25 m)
Draft:	25½ feet (7.8 m)
Propulsion:	diesel-electric (General Motors diesel); 11,200 bhp; 2 shafts
Speed:	18 knots
Manning:	563 (43 officers + 520 enlisted)
Helicopters:	VERTREP area
Missiles:	none
Guns:	4 20-mm Mk 68 (4 single)

The PROTEUS originally was a submarine tender of the FULTON class. She was laid up in reserve from 1947 to 1951 (reactivated for the Korean War). In 1959–1960 the PROTEUS was extensively converted to support Polaris fleet ballistic missile submarines; recommissioned 8 July 1960.

The ship is employed in general submarine support activities at Guam in the Mariana Islands, with all Polaris SSBNs having been decommissioned. She has also served as a general support ship at Diego Garcia in the early 1980s.

Conversion: The ship was converted at the Charleston Naval Shipyard to the first U.S. FBM submarine tender. A 44-foot amidships section was added amidships to provide space for additional shops and support facilities as well as vertical storage for Polaris missiles. The "insert" was six decks high and weighed about 500 tons. A thwartships travelling missile crane was installed; 20 Polaris missiles were carried. During conversion the gun battery was reduced to two 5-inch/38-cal DP guns, both forward. These guns were removed in the mid-1970s.

The conversion was SCB No. 190.

PROTEUS—before removal of forward 5-inch guns (U.S. Navy)

3 SUBMARINE TENDERS: "FULTON" CLASS

Number	Name	Launched	Commissioned	Status
AS 11	FULTON	27 Dec 1940	12 Sep 1941	**AA**
AS 17	NEREUS	12 Feb 1945	27 Oct 1945	PR
AS 18	ORION	14 Oct 1942	30 Sep 1943	**AA**

Builders:	AS 11, 17 Mare Island Navy Yard
	AS 18 Moore Shipbuilding and Dry Dock, Oakland, Calif.
Displacement:	9,734 tons standard
	18,000 tons full load
Length:	520 feet (158.6 m) wl
	529½ feet (161.5 m) oa
Beam:	73⅓ feet (22.4 m)
Draft:	25½ feet (7.8 m)
Propulsion:	diesel-electric (General Motors diesels); 11,200 bhp except AS 11
	11,500 bhp; 2 shafts
Speed:	15 knots
Manning:	AS 11 507 (51 officers + 456 enlisted)
	AS 18 509 (52 officers + 457 enlisted)
Helicopters:	VERTREP area in AS 18
Missiles:	none
Guns:	AS 11, 18 4 20-mm Mk 68 (4 single)
	AS 17 2 5-inch (127-mm) 38-cal DP Mk 30 (2 single) 4 20-mm
	Mk 24 (2 twin)

These tenders are similar to the contemporary DIXIE (AD 14)-class destroyer tenders and VULCAN (AR 5)-class repair ships. The ships have been modernized and have a limited capability to support nuclear attack submarines.

The NEREUS was decommissioned on 13 July 1971; laid up at the Bremerton Naval Shipyard.

Class: The FULTON class originally consisted of AS 11, 12, 15–19. The PROTEUS is listed separately; the SPERRY (AS 12) stricken on 30 September 1982, BUSHNELL (AS 15) on 15 November 1980, and HOWARD W. GILMORE (AS 16) on 1 December 1980. (The BUSHNELL was sunk in June 1983 as a target for submarine-launched Mk 48 torpedoes.)

Guns: As built the armament installed in these ships was four 5-inch/38-cal DP guns and eight 40-mm AA guns. The NEREUS retains one Mk 37 GFCS with Mk 25 radar.

FULTON (U.S. Navy)

NEREUS (U.S. Navy)

2 SUBMARINE RESCUE SHIPS: "PIGEON" CLASS

Number	Name	FY	Launched	Commissioned	Status
ASR 21	PIGEON	67	13 Aug 1969	28 Apr 1973	**PA**
ASR 22	ORTOLAN	68	10 Sep 1969	14 July 1973	**AA**

Builders:	Alabama Dry Dock and Shipbuilding, Mobile
Displacement:	4,950 tons full load
Length:	251 feet (76.5 m) oa
Beam:	86 feet (26.2 m)
Draft:	21¼ feet (6.5 m)
Propulsion:	diesels; 6,000 bhp; 2 shafts
Speed:	15 knots
Manning:	208 (8 officers – 200 enlisted)
Helicopters:	landing area
Missiles:	none
Guns:	2 20-mm Mk 68 (2 single)

These ships were constructed specifically to carry Deep Submergence Rescue Vehicles (DSRV) and support deep-ocean diving operations. For the latter they have the Mk II Deep Diving System that can support up to eight divers operating to depths of 1,000 feet in helium-oxygen saturation conditions. They are the Navy's only saturation diving ships and can support divers indefinitely under pressure, lowering them to the ocean floor in pressurized transfer chambers for open-sea work periods.

These ships were delayed by problems in design, construction, and fitting out.

Class: The Navy had planned to construct at least three ships of this class to support six DSRVs at three rescue unit home ports. At one point long-term planning called for ten ships as replacements for the older ASR force. However, only these two ships were funded and built. Additional ASRs are not planned.

Design: SCB No. 721. These are the Navy's largest catamaran ships, being larger than the research ship HAYES (T-AGOR 16). Each ASR hull is 26 feet wide with a separation of 34 feet between hulls. The separation facilitates the lowering and raising of DSRVs and diving chambers.

The ships have a precision three-dimensional sonar tracking system for directing DSRV operations. A helicopter deck is situated aft but is suitable primarily for VERTREP operations; limited helicopter support facilities are provided.

Accommodations are provided for a salvage staff of 14 and a DSRV operations and maintenance team of 24.

Engineering: Through-bow thrusters are fitted in each hull for maneuvering and station keeping during diving and salvage operations. (The ships are not moored when operating DSRVs.)

Guns: As built the PIGEON had two 3-inch/50-cal AA guns in two "tubs" forward on her hulls. After their removal the large mooring buoys ("spuds") were mounted in their place; previously she had two buoys forward of the bridge and two between the hulls aft.

Operational: In 1983 both ships conducted open-sea dives to 850 feet to demonstrate the ships' saturation diving capability.

The PIGEON with four anchor buoys—or "spuds"—stowed forward; her submersible and diving chamber lifting gear giving the appearance of clutter amidships; and helicopter deck aft. The Soviet Navy's new submarine salvage and rescue ships of the EL'BRUS class are much larger, displacing more than 17,000 tons full load. (1982, Giorgio Arra)

ORTOLAN (1983, Giorgio Arra)

ORTOLAN (1983, Giorgio Arra)

4 SUBMARINE RESCUE SHIPS: "CHANTICLEER" CLASS

Number	Name	Launched	Commissioned	Status
ASR 9	FLORIKAN	14 June 1942	5 Apr 1943	**PA**
ASR 13	KITTIWAKE	10 July 1945	18 July 1946	**AA**
ASR 14	PETREL	25 Sep 1945	24 Sep 1946	**AA**
ASR 15	SUNBIRD	25 June 1945	28 Jan 1947	**AA**

Builders:	ASR 9 Moore Shipbuilding and Dry Dock, Oakland, Calif.
	ASR 13–15 Savannah Machine and Foundry, Ga.
Displacement:	1,635 tons standard
	2,320 tons full load
Length:	240 feet (73.2 m) wl
	251⅓ feet (76.6 m) oa
Beam:	42 feet (12.8 m)
Draft:	14⅝ feet (4.5 m)
Propulsion:	diesel-electric (General Motors diesels except Alco in ASR 9);
	3,000 bhp; 1 shaft
Speed:	15 knots
Manning:	103 (7 officers + 96 enlisted)
Helicopters:	no facilities
Missiles:	none
Guns:	2 20-mm Mk 68 (2 single)

These are large tug-type ships fitted for salvage and helium-oxygen diving operations.

Class: Originally there were eight ships in this class, ASR 7–11, 13–15, plus the cancelled ASR 16–18.

Design: There is a pair of mooring buoys housed on both sides of the deck structure; a tripod mast aft supports three booms; and a McCann submarine rescue chamber is generally carried on the fantail.

Guns: The design armament of these ships was two 3-inch/50-cal AA guns in single mounts and two 20-mm single guns.

The FLORIKAN with the traditional fish symbol for submerged operations on her bow and a McCann submarine rescue chamber on her fantail. These ships were to have been replaced by additional PIGEON-class ASRs, but there is no near-term replacement planned for them. (1983, Giorgio Arra)

KITTIWAKE (1983, Giorgio Arra)

3 AUXILIARY TUGS: "SOTOYOMO" CLASS

Number	Name	Launched	Commissioned	Status
ATA 178 (ex-ATR 105)	TUNICA	15 June 1944	15 Sep 1944	NDRF
ATA 181 (ex-ATR 108)	ACCOKEEK	27 July 1944	7 Oct 1944	NDRF
ATA 203 (ex-ATR 130)	NAVIGATOR	26 Oct 1944	1 Jan 1945	NDRF

Builders:	ATA 178, 181 Levingston Shipbuilding, Orange, Texas
	ATA 203 Gulfport Boiler & Welding Works, Port Arthur, Texas
Displacement:	534 tons full load
Length:	133⅔ feet (40.8 m) wl
	143 feet (43.6 m) oa
Beam:	33⅝ feet (10.3 m)
Draft:	14 feet (4.3 m)
Propulsion:	diesel-electric (General Motors diesels); 1,500 bp; 1 shaft
Speed:	13 knots
Manning:	45 (5 officers + 40 enlisted)
Helicopters:	no facilities
Missiles:	none
Guns:	1 3-inch (76-mm) 50-cal AA Mk 22
	or 4 20-mm AA Mk 24 (2 twin); removed from some ships

These are the survivors of a class of small ocean-going tugs. The NAVIGATOR was laid up in 1960, TUNICA in 1962, and ACCOKEEK in 1972; all are mothballed in the NDRF.

Class: Seventy ships of this class were built, ATA 121–125, 146, 170–213, and 219–238. Deletions since the previous edition of *Ships and Aircraft* are SAMOSET (ATA 190) transferred to Haiti in October 1978, STALLION (ATA 193) to Dominican Republic in October 1980, and KEYWADIN (ATA 213) stricken on 1 June 1980.

Classification: These ships originally were classified as rescue tugs (ATR); changed to auxiliary tugs and renumbered on 15 May 1944.

Guns: As built the ships had the single 3-inch gun as well as the 20-mm weapons.

Names: Names of discarded fleet and yard tugs were assigned to these ships in 1948.

ACCOKEEK (1970, U.S. Navy)

7 FLEET TUGS: "POWHATAN" CLASS

Number	Name	FY	Launched	In service	Status
T-ATF 166	POWHATAN	75	24 June 1978	15 June 1979	**MSC-A**
T-ATF 167	NARRAGANSETT	75	12 May 1979	9 Nov 1979	**MSC-P**
T-ATF 168	CATAWBA	75	22 Sep 1979	28 May 1980	**MSC-P**
T-ATF 169	NAVAJO	75	20 Dec 1979	13 June 1980	**MSC-P**
T-ATF 170	MOHAWK	78	4 May 1980	16 Oct 1980	**MSC-A**
T-ATF 171	SIOUX	78	30 Oct 1980	12 May 1981	**MSC-P**
T-ATF 172	APACHE	78	20 Dec 1980	23 July 1981	**MSC-A**

Builders:	Marinette Marine, Wisc.
Displacement:	2,200 tons full load
Length:	225 feet (68.6 m) oa
Beam:	42 feet (12.8 m)
Draft:	15 feet (4.6 m)
Propulsion:	diesel; 4,500 bhp; 2 shafts
Speed:	15 knots
Manning:	16 (civilians) + 4 Navy (enlisted) + 20 transients
Helicopters:	VERTREP area
Missiles:	none
Guns:	none

These are ocean-going tugs based on a commercial design. They have replaced the war-built ATFs in the active fleet. The new ATF differs from the ASR and ATS types because it lacks the salvage and diving equipment of the earlier ships.

Design: SCB No. 744. These craft are easily distinguished by their side-by-side funnels and low, open sterns. The Navy personnel are communications specialists and the transients are salvage and diving specialists.

The POWHATAN, lead ship for a small class of replacements for the long-serving CHEROKEE ATFs. The newer tugs have twin funnels and a large working space aft; the POWHATAN is carrying a floating target aft. (1983, Giorgio Arra)

Navajo (1981, U.S. Navy, PH1 Corinne Kelly)

Apache (1982, Giorgio Arra)

15 FLEET TUGS: "CHEROKEE" CLASS

Number	Name	Launched	Commissioned	Status
ATF 69	Chippewa	25 July 1942	14 Feb 1943	NDRF
ATF 71	Hopi	7 Sep 1942	31 Mar 1943	NDRF
ATF 87	Moreno	9 July 1942	30 Nov 1942	NDRF
ATF 88	Narragansett	8 Aug 1942	15 Jan 1943	NDRF
ATF 91	Seneca	2 Feb 1943	30 Apr 1943	NDRF
ATF 105	Moctobi	25 Mar 1944	25 July 1944	**NRF-P**
ATF 110	Quapaw	15 May 1943	6 May 1944	**NRF-P**
ATF 113	Takelma	18 Sep 1943	3 Aug 1944	**NRF-P**
ATF 115	Tenino	10 Jan 1944	18 Nov 1944	NDRF
ATF 118	Wenatchee	7 Sep 1944	24 Mar 1945	NDRF
ATF 148	Achomawi	10 Sep 1944	11 Nov 1944	NDRF
T-ATF 149	Atakapa	11 July 1944	8 Dec 1944	NDRF
T-ATF 158	Mosopelea	7 Mar 1945	28 July 1945	NDRF
ATF 159	Paiute	4 June 1945	27 Aug 1945	**NRF-A**
ATF 160	Papago	21 June 1945	3 Oct 1945	**NRF-A**

Builders:	ATF 69, 71, 105, 148, 149, 158, 159, 160 Charleston Shipbuilding and Dry Dock, S.C.
	ATF 110, 113, 115, 118 United Engineering, Alameda, Calif.
	ATF 87, 88, 91 Cramp Shipbuilding, Philadelphia, Pa.
Displacement:	1,235 tons standard
	1,675 tons full load
Length:	195 feet (59.5 m) wl
	205 feet (62.5 m) oa
Beam:	38½ feet (11.7 m)
Draft:	15½ feet (4.7 m)
Propulsion:	diesel-electric; 3,000 bhp; 1 shaft
Speed:	16.5 knots
Manning:	71 (3 officers + 68 enlisted) in active ships
	71 active + 29 (3 officers + 29 enlisted) reserve in NRF ships
Helicopters:	no facilities
Missiles:	none
Guns:	1 3-inch (76-mm) 50-cal AA Mk 22 in most ships laid up in NDRF

These are large ocean-going tugs, many of which saw extensive combat service in World War II. Ten are laid up in the NDRF, the ATF 69, 87, and 88 since 1961; ATF 115, 118, and 148 since 1962; ATF 71 since 1964; ATF 91 since 1971; ATF 76 and 85 since 1980; and ATF 149 and 158 since 1 October 1981. The last two ships were operated by MSC with civilian crews from July 1973 and August 1974, respectively, until they were laid up.

Five ships are assigned to the Naval Reserve Force with composite

Quapaw—small-funnel type (1981, U.S. Navy)

active-reserve crews, the ATF 105, 110, 159, and 160 since 1977, and ATF 113 since 1979. None remain in active service; the last active Navy-manned ship was the SHAKORI (ATF 162), decommissioned on 29 February 1980 and transferred to Taiwan.

Class: The AT 64-76 and 81-118 were built to the same basic design (see Engineering notes). The class is officially known as the CHEROKEE (AT 66) after the loss of the NAVAJO (AT 64) in 1943 and the SEMINOLE (AT 65) in 1942. Later ships are unofficially referred to as the ABNAKI (AT 96) class. Several ships of this class serve with the U.S. Coast Guard as well as foreign navies. (See Appendix A.)

PAPAGO—large-funnel type (Giorgio Arra)

Classification: These ships all were ordered with the AT designation. The AT 66 and later ships were changed to ATF on 15 May 1944.

Design: These are steel-hulled ships. They are fitted with a 10- or 20-ton-capacity boom. Most had compressed air diving equipment.

Engineering: Ships numbered below ATF 96 have four diesels, four generators, and four electric motors driving through a gear to a single propeller shaft. The later ships have only one, very large electric motor.

The early ships also have a short, squat exhaust funnel; the later ships have waterline exhausts for their diesels and a tall, thin galley funnel (i.e., "Charlie Noble").

The TAKELMA is a small-funnel version of the long-serving CHEROKEE class. Most ATFs have only their hull number on their sides; the TAKELMA and QUAPAW have the prefix TF derived from their ATF designations. As built, these ships had a 3-inch/50-cal gun forward of the bridge; the TAKELMA carried her gun into the late 1970s. (1982, Giorgio Arra)

3 SALVAGE AND RESCUE SHIPS: "EDENTON" CLASS

Number	Name	FY	Launched	Commissioned	Status
ATS 1	EDENTON	66	15 May 1968	23 Jan 1971	**AA**
ATS 2	BEAUFORT	67	20 Dec 1968	22 Jan 1972	**PA**
ATS 3	BRUNSWICK	67	14 Oct 1969	10 Dec 1972	**PA**

Builders:	Brooke Marine, Lowestoft, England
Displacement:	3,117 tons full load
Length:	282⅔ feet (86.2 m) oa
Beam:	50 feet (15.25 m)
Draft:	15⅙ feet (4.6 m)
Propulsion:	diesels (Paxman); 6,000 bhp; 2 shafts
Speed:	16 knots
Manning:	115 (7 officers + 108 enlisted)
Helicopters:	VERTREP area
Missiles:	none
Guns:	ATS 1 4 20-mm AA Mk 24 (2 twin)
	ATS 2, 3 2 20-mm Mk 68 (2 single)

These are the only ocean-going tugs in active Navy commission. They are fitted with extensive salvage and diving capabilities. They are one of two classes of auxiliary ships to be constructed in British shipyards for the U.S. Navy, the other being the two CHAUVENET (T-AGS 29)-class ships. The more recently acquired British-built store ships (T-AFS) were constructed for RFA service.

Class: The ATS 4 was authorized in fiscal 1972 and the ATS 5 in fiscal 1973. Their construction was deferred in 1973 and plans for additional ships of the class were cancelled because of their high cost. Instead, the less capable ATF 166 class was procured.

Classification: ATF originally indicated salvage tug; changed to salvage and rescue ship on 16 February 1971.

Design: SCB No. 719. These ships have large open work spaces forward and aft. Four mooring buoys are carried (as in submarine rescue ships) to assist in four-point moors for diving and salvage activities. A 10-ton-capacity crane is fitted forward and a 20-ton-capacity crane aft. The ships have compressed air diving equipment.

Engineering: The ships have a through-bow thruster for precise maneuvering and station keeping.

BRUNSWICK with the PINTADO (SSN 672) (1980, Giorgio Arra)

BRUNSWICK (1979, Giorgio Arra)

(2) AVIATION LOGISTIC SHIPS: CONVERTED MERCHANT SHIPS

Number	Name	In service	Status
T-AVB 3	GREAT REPUBLIC	1986	Yard
T-AVB 4	YOUNG AMERICA	1986	Yard

Builders:
Displacement: 23,872 tons full load
Tonnage: 14,177 tons deadweight
Length: 602 feet (183.6 m) oa
Beam: 90 feet (27.4 m)
Draft: 29¾ feet (9.1 m)
Propulsion: steam turbine; 30,000 shp; 1 shaft
Boilers: 2
Speed: 22.3 knots
Manning: 41 (civilian) + approx. 300 Marines
Helicopters: landing area
Missiles: none
Guns: none

These ships will be converted from RO/RO-container merchant ships to provide maintenance and logistic support for Marine aircraft in forward areas. Providing peacetime support for Marine aviation, the ships will normally be based near major Marine air facilities and will be partially loaded. During a crisis the ships would be fully loaded and deployed to the forward area. The ships were bult in 1967–1969.

Class: The previous AVB 1 and 2 were tank landing ships converted to support land-based patrol aircraft from unimproved airfields and seaplanes in the Mediterranean area; they were Navy manned in the AVB role. The ALAMEDA COUNTY (LST 32) became the AVB 1 and, after she was stricken in 1962, the TALLAHATCHIE COUNTY (LST 1154) became the AVB 2.

Cost: The fiscal 1985 budget provides $42.8 million for one ship with the second ship planned for fiscal 1986.

Design: Maritime Administration C5-S-78a type. The ships are combination RO/RO and self-sustaining container ships.

Names: Original merchant names were MORMAC and MORMACSUN; changed when acqiured by Maritime Administration and laid up in NDRF.

Artist's concept of AVB conversion; note the incorrect hull number AVB 1. (U.S. Navy)

1 GUIDED MISSILE SHIP: "NORTON SOUND"

Number	Name	Launched	Commissioned	Status
AVM 1	NORTON SOUND	28 Nov 1943	8 Jan 1945	**PA**

Builders:	Los Angeles Shipbuilding and Dry Dock, Calif.
Displacement:	9,106 tons standard
	15,170 tons full load
Length:	520 feet (158.6 m) wl
	540⁵⁄₁₂ feet (164.8 m) oa
Beam:	69¼ feet (21.1 m)
Draft:	21½ feet (6.6 m)
Propulsion:	steam turbine (Allis Chalmers); 12,000 shp; 2 shafts
Boilers:	4 (Babcock & Wilcox)
Speed:	19 knots
Manning:	373 (19 officers + 354 enlisted) + 87 civilian technicians
Helicopters:	landing area
Missiles:	1 twin Mk 26 Mod 0 launcher for Standard SAM
	1 8-tube Mk 41 Vertical Launch System
Guns:	removed
Radars:	SPS-10 surface search
	SPS-40 air search
	SPS-52 3-D search
	SPY-1A multi-function (one face)

The NORTON SOUND is a test and evaluation ship for advanced weapon and electronic systems. She was originally a seaplane tender of the CURRITUCK (AV 7) class. Since 1948 she has been employed exclusively as a test and evaluation ship.

Her most recent major reconfiguration took place in 1974 when she was modified to serve as test ship for the Aegis air-defense system. One "face" of the fixed-array SPY-1 radar system was fitted on the starboard side of the superstructure, above the bridge (with a dummy "face" to port). The related Aegis fire control system and computers were installed and a twin Mk 26 missile launcher installed aft.

In 1981 an eight-tube VLS was installed forward for evaluation prior to installation in the later CG 47 and the planned DDG 51 surface combatant classes.

After World War II the battleships WYOMING (AG 17, ex-BB 32) and MISSISSIPPI (AG 128, ex-BB 41) were also used in the gunnery and, the latter ship, in the missile test roles.

Class: The class originally consisted of AV 7 and 11-13.

Classification: The NORTON SOUND was reclassified from AV 11 to AVM 1 on 8 August 1951.

Design: The ship has a large amidships hangar with an open fantail originally intended for carrying flying boats; large cranes were fitted for hoisting the flying boats from the water.

Electronics: In 1962–1964 the ship was fitted with the large SPG-59 Typhon guidance phased-array radar. After extensive testing, with cancellation of the Typhon frigate (DLGN) the radar was removed in 1966.

Guns: The ship's original armament as AV 11 consisted of 4 5-inch/38-cal DP guns, 20 40-mm AA guns, and 8 2-mm AA guns. All original armament has been removed. In 1968 the 5-inch/54-cal lightweight Mk 45 gun was installed with associated Mk 86 GFCS for at-sea evaluation. Both were subsequently removed.

Missiles: The NORTON SOUND has served as test ship for several missile and rocket programs, among them the Loon (American version of the German V-1 "buzz bomb"), Aerobee, Viking, Lark, Regulus I, Terrier, Tartar, Sea Sparrow, and Standard SAM. In 1958 the ship launched multi-stage missiles carrying low-yield nuclear warheads that were detonated some 300 miles above the earth (Project Argus).

NORTON SOUND (1979, Giorgio Arra)

NORTON SOUND (1984, Giorgio Arra)

UNCLASSIFIED MISCELLANEOUS SHIPS

These ships (designated IX) are officially considered to be Service Craft
(see Chapter 25).

25 Service Craft

The U.S. Navy operates several hundred service craft, both self-propelled and non-self-propelled. Most are at naval bases in the United States and overseas.

These craft perform a variety of fleet support services. Only the self-propelled craft are described here, as well as the Navy's miscellaneous unclassified ships (IX), which are classified as service craft. However, the submersibles and floating dry docks, also classified as service craft, are listed in subsequent chapters.

All ships and craft listed here are in service unless otherwise indicated.

Classification: Most service craft have Y-series designations, that letter having been established when these were considered yard craft; they were also known as district craft, from being assigned to naval districts. Service craft without hull designations are listed at the end of the chapter.

Guns: Service craft are not armed. The seamanship training craft (YP) can be armed with light weapons for use as harbor patrol craft while some of the utility cargo carriers (YFU) were armed for service in the Vietnam War.

Operational: Service craft are Navy-manned with a few having all-female crews.

UNCLASSIFIED AUXILIARY SHIPS

The IX ship classification, given hull numbers in 1941, reached number 301 at the end of World War II. The IX type was continued in the 300-series until the former LSMR 501 was placed in this category and classified IX with her previous hull number. Subsequent ships and craft were assigned in the 500-series.

The IX 304 was the former light cruiser Atlanta (CL 104), modified for conventional explosive tests simulating nuclear blast effects; the IX 305 was the ex-Prowess (MSF 280); the IX 307 was the instrumentation platform Brier (formerly the USCGC WLIX 299), stricken on 15 August 1982; IX 309 reclassified as YAG 61; and the classification IX 310 is assigned to two test barges linked together in use at the Naval Underwater System Center's laboratory at Lake Seneca, N.Y. (placed in service 1 April 1971).

The IX 505 was the former medium harbor tug YTM 759; the IX 509 is a former underwater explosive test barge in use at the David W. Taylor Naval Ship Research and Development Center in Maryland (built in 1942 and classified as IX on 1 December 1979).

The IX 512 is a barge employed to support the Trident missile test program; acquired from the Army (ex BD-6651) on 1 September 1983.

The IX 509 at Norfolk, Virginia. The crane at right is on board the craft. (1983, Giorgio Arra)

The large harbor tug EDENSHAW helps maneuver the frigate ANTRIM (FFG 20) into a nest of warships. The Navy has hundreds of service craft—self-propelled and towed—that support naval base operations. These small craft, rarely publicized, are invaluable to the effectiveness of the fleet. (1983, Giorgio Arra)

1 UNCLASSIFIED AUXILIARY: FORMER LST

Number	Name	Launched	Commissioned
IX 511 (ex-LST 399)	(none)	23 Nov 1942	4 Jan 1943

Builders:	Newport News Shipbuilding
Displacement:	
Length:	316 feet (96.4 m) wl
	328 feet (100.0 m) oa
Beam:	50 feet (15.25 m)
Draft:	14 feet (4.3 m)
Propulsion:	diesel (General Motors); 1,700 bhp; 2 shafts
Speed:	11.6 knots
Manning:	

Built as a tank landing ship, the LST 399 saw service in World War II, after which she was laid up until reactivated in 1952 for operation by the MSTS (manned by a Japanese civilian crew). Deactivated and stricken on 1 November 1973 and laid up in the NDRF until 25 November 1980 when reacquired by the Navy for use as a range support ship at the Pacific Missile Range, Point Mugu, Calif. Classified as IX and placed in service on 30 September 1982.

1 TEST OPERATIONS SUPPORT SHIP: FORMER LCU

Number	Name
IX 508 (ex-LCU 1618)	(none)

Builders:	
Displacement:	
Length:	135¼ feet (41.25 m) oa
Beam:	29 feet (8.8 m)
Draft:	4½ feet (1.4 m)
Propulsion:	2 geared diesels (Detroit); 2,000 bhp; 2 shafts
Speed:	11.5 knots
Manning:	13

This craft is configured to support test operations at the Naval Ocean Systems Center (NOSC) at San Diego, Calif. Formerly an LCU 1610-class landing craft completed in 1960. She served for several years in the test support role before being changed to IX 508 in December 1979.

A bow thruster is fitted.

IX 508 (1984, Giorgio Arra)

2 BARRACK SHIPS: FORMER TROOP TRANSPORTS

Number	Name	Launched	AP Comm.
IX 507 (ex-AP 121)	GEN HUGH J. GAFFEY	20 Feb 1944	18 Sep 1944
IX 510 (ex-AP 127)	GEN WILLIAM O. DARBY	4 June 1945	27 Sep 1945

These ships were built as Admiral-class troop transports (Maritime Administration P2-SE2-R1 type); both were constructed at the Bethlehem Steel yard in Alameda, Calif. The GAFFEY had been named ADM W.L. CAPPS in naval service and the DARBY had previously been named ADM W.S. SIMS. See page 294 for characteristics of the Admiral class.

The GAFFEY was stricken from the Naval Vessel Register on 9 October 1969; the ship was reacquired by the Navy on 1 November 1978 for conversion to a barracks ship; reclassified IX 507 and placed in service at the Bremerton Naval Shipyard for crews of aircraft carriers undergoing conversion and modernization.

The DARBY was reacquired from the NDRF on 27 October 1981 for similar use; the ship was modified for use as a barracks ship and then towed to Newport News Shipbuilding to house crews of aircraft carriers undergoing overhaul.

Only the accommodations and messing spaces have been rehabilitated. The ships are not capable of steaming in their current condition.

GEN WILLIAM O. DARBY at Newport News Shipbuilding (1983, Giorgio Arra)

1 RESEARCH SUPPORT SHIP: FORMER YFU

Number	Name
IX 506 (ex-YFU 82)	(none)

Builders:	Pacific Coast Engineering, Alameda, Calif.
Displacement:	900 tons full load
Length:	125 feet (38.1 m) oa
Beam:	36 feet (11.0 m)
Draft:	6 feet (1.8 m)
Propulsion:	2 diesels (General Motors); 2 shafts
Speed:	9 knots
Manning:	18 (civilian)

This former harbor utility craft was converted for use as a research platform at the NOSC facility in Long Beach, Calif. Her bow was rebuilt, with a forecastle added; a center well permits lowering test gear to depths of 900 feet. Converted in 1978–1982.

Classification: Changed from YFU 82 to IX 506 on 1 April 1978.

GEN WILLIAM O. DARBY at Newport News Shipbuilding (1983, Giorgio Arra)

IX 506 (1982, Giorgio Arra)

IX 506 (1980, U.S. Navy)

3 SELF-PROPELLED BARRACKS SHIPS: MODIFIED LST DESIGN

Number	Name	Launched	Commissioned
IX 502 (ex-APB 39)	MERCER	17 Nov 1944	19 Sep 1945
IX 503 (ex-APB 40)	NUECES	6 May 1945	30 Nov 1945
IX 504 (ex-APB 37)	ECHOLS	30 July 1945	(1 Jan 1947)

Builders:	Boston Navy Yard, Mass.
Displacement:	2,190 tons light
	4,080 tons full load
Length:	316 feet (96.4 m) wl
	328 feet (100.0 m) oa
Beam:	50 feet (15.25 m)
Draft:	11 feet (3.4 m)
Propulsion:	diesels (General Motors); 1,600 bhp; 2 shafts
Speed:	10 knots
Manning:	198 (12 officers + 186 enlisted) as APB
Troops:	approx. 900

These ships were built to provide accommodations and support for small craft. All three were completed as barracks ships (APL, later APB). They were modified in 1975–1976 to serve at shipyards for crews of ships being built or in overhaul; changed from APB to IX at that time.

Two ships were placed in commission upon original completion; the ECHOLS was placed in service. All three ships were laid up in reserve after World War II. The MERCER and NUECES were recommissioned in 1968 for service in the Vietnam War. They were rearmed at that time with two 3-inch guns (single), eight 40-mm guns (quad), and several MGs. As modified to support riverine forces in South Vietnam they had crews of 12 officers and 186 enlisted men and could accommodate 900

troops and small-craft crewmen. Both ships were again laid up in 1969–1971 until reactivated in 1975; the ECHOLS was reactivated in 1976.

Class: There were originally 14 ships of this class, APB 35–48; they were built to a modified LST design.

Classification: APL/APB 39 changed to IX 502 and APL/APB 40 to IX 503 on 1 November 1975; APL/APB 37 to IX 504 on 1 February 1976.

NUECES at San Francisco (1983, L. & L. van Ginderen)

ECHOLS at Norfolk (1976, Giorgio Arra)

1 TEST RANGE SUPPORT SHIP: CONVERTED LSMR

Number	Name	Launched	Commissioned
IX 501 (ex-LSMR 501)	ELK RIVER	21 Apr 1945	27 May 1945

Builders:	Brown Shipbuilding, Houston, Texas
Displacement:	1,100 tons full load
Length:	230 feet (70.1 m) oa
Beam:	50 feet (15.25 m)
Draft:	9⅝ feet (3.0 m)
Propulsion:	diesels; 1,400 bhp; 2 shafts
Speed:	6 knots
Manning:	71 (20 officers + 51 enlisted)

The ELK RIVER is a converted rocket landing ship employed as a test and training ship for deep-sea diving and salvage. She is operated by NOSC at San Diego.

Class: The ELK RIVER was one of several medium landing ships (LSM) completed as rocket fire support ships. All other ships of this type have been stricken, the last three having been used in the Vietnam War.

Conversion: The ship was converted to a test range support ship in 1967–1968 at Avondale Shipyards and the San Francisco Naval Shipyard. The basic 203½-foot LSMR hull was lengthened and eight-foot sponsons were added to both sides to improve the ship's stability and increase working space. A superstructure was added forward and an open center well was provided for lowering and raising equipment. The 65-ton gantry crane runs on tracks above the opening to handle small submersibles and diver-transfer chambers. An active precision positioning system is installed for position holding without mooring.

The prototype Mk II Deep Diving System (DDS) is installed in the ship. It can support eight divers operating at depths to at least 1,000 feet in helium-oxygen saturation conditions. This is the most advanced shipboard system in use today and is also installed in the two PIGEON (ASR 21)-class ships.

ELK RIVER (1968, U.S. Navy)

ELK RIVER (1983, Giorgio Arra)

1 TORPEDO TEST SHIP: FORMER CARGO SHIP

Number	Name
IX 308 (ex-AKL 17)	NEW BEDFORD

Builders:	Wheeler Shipbuilding, Long Island, N.Y.
Displacement:	700 tons
Length:	176½ feet (53.8 m) oa
Beam:	32¾ feet (10.0 m)
Draft:	10 feet (3.0 m)
Propulsion:	diesel; 1,000 bhp; 1 shaft
Speed:	13 knots
Manning:	

The NEW BEDFORD was built as an Army freight and supply ship; she was acquired by the Navy on 1 March 1950 for use as a cargo ship. The ship was later converted for torpedo testing and since 1963 has been operated by the Naval Torpedo Station, Keyport, Wash.

Classification: Originally U.S. Army FS 289; operated by Military Sea Transportation Service as T-AKL 17.

NEW BEDFORD (1973, U.S. Navy)

1 TORPEDO TEST SHIP: FORMER CARGO SHIP

Number	Name
IX 306	(unnamed)

Builders:	Higgins Industries, New Orleans, La.
Displacement:	906 tons full load
Length:	179 feet (54.6 m) oa
Beam:	33 feet (10.1 m)
Draft:	10 feet (3.0 m)
Propulsion:	diesel; 1 shaft
Speed:	12 knots
Manning:	

The IX 306 is a former Army freight and supply ship (FS 221), acquired by the Navy in January 1969 and converted to a torpedo test ship. She was placed in service in January 1969. The ship supports research activities in the Atlantic Underwater Test and Evaluation Center (AUTEC) in the Caribbean for the Naval Underwater Weapons Research and Engineering Station, Newport, R.I. The ship is manned by Navy and RCA civilian personnel.

IX 306 (1969, U.S. Navy)

1 SAILING FRIGATE: "CONSTITUTION"

Number	Name	Launched	Commissioned
(ex-IX 21)	CONSTITUTION	21 Oct 1797	1798

Builders:	Hartt's Shipyard, Boston, Mass.
Displacement:	2,200 tons
Length:	175 feet (53.4 m) gun deck
Beam:	45 feet (13.7 m)
Draft:	20 feet (6.1 m)
Masts:	fore 94 feet (28.7 m)
	main 104 feet (31.7 m)
	mizzen 81 feet (24.7 m)
Speed:	13 knots (under sail)
Manning:	49 (2 officers + 47 enlisted) as relic; up to 500 as frigate
Guns:	several smooth-bore cannon

The CONSTITUTION is the oldest U.S. ship in Navy commission. Her original commissioning date is not known; she first put to sea on 22 July 1798. She is moored as a relic at the Boston Naval Shipyard in Boston. (She is afloat, unlike HMS VICTORY, Nelson's flagship at Trafalgar, which is preserved in concrete at Portsmouth, England.)

As a sail frigate, the CONSTITUTION fought in the Quasi-War with France, against the Barbary pirates, and in the War of 1812 against Great Britain. She has been rebuilt several times and restored as much as possible to her original configuration.

No sails are fitted. Twice a year she is taken out into Boston Harbor under tow and "turned around," so that her masts do not bend from the effects of sun and wind.

Class: The CONSTITUTION was one of six sail frigates built under an act of Congress of 1794. The CONSTELLATION (36 guns) was built under the same act and broken up at Norfolk, Va., in 1852–1853 with much of her material being used to build another sailing ship of that name.

That ship served in the Navy as the IX 20 until transferred in 1954 to a private group in Baltimore, Md., where she is maintained.

Classification: The CONSTITUTION was classified as an "unclassified" ship in 1920 (IX without a hull number). She became IX 21 on 8 December 1941 and carried that classification until 1 September 1975 when it was withdrawn because, according to Navy officials, the designation "tended to demean and degrade the CONSTITUTION through association with a group of insignificant craft of varied missions and configurations."

Names: From 1917 until 1925 the ship was named OLD CONSTITUTION while the name CONSTITUTION was assigned to a battle cruiser (CC 5); that ship was never completed.

Guns: When built, the CONSTITUTION was rated as a 44-gun frigate. The actual number of guns installed has varied considerably over her long career.

1 MISCELLANEOUS AUXILIARY

Number	Name
YAG 62	(unnamed)

Builders:	
Displacement:	
Length:	120 feet (36.6 m) oa
Beam:	
Draft:	
Propulsion:	
Boilers:	
Speed:	
Range:	6,200 n.miles at 10.5 knots
Manning:	

The commercial ship DEER ISLAND was acquired on 15 March 1982 and classified as YAG 62. The craft is used for sound testing; based at Port Everglades, Fla. Built in 1966.

YAG 62 (Courtesy MAR Inc.)

CONSTITUTION (1983, L. & L. van Ginderen)

1 MOBILE LISTENING BARGE: CONVERTED WATER BARGE

Number	Name
YAG 61 (ex-IX 309)	MONOB 1

Builders:	Zenith Dredge Co, Duluth, Minn.
Displacement:	1,390 tons full load
Length:	174 feet (53.0 m) oa
Beam:	32 feet (9.75 m)
Draft:	
Propulsion:	diesel; 560 bhp; 1 shaft
Speed:	7 knots
Manning:	19 (1 officer + 18 enlisted) + technicians

The YAG 61 was originally completed in 1943 as a self-propelled water barge (YW 87). She was converted to a Mobile Noise Barge (MONOB) for acoustic research in 1969 and placed in service conducting research for the Naval Ship Research and Development Center; assigned to Port Canaveral, Fla.

Classification: Reclassified from YW 87 to IX 309 in 1969; changed to YAG 61 on 1 July 1970.

MONOB 1 (1982, U.S. Navy)

2 DIVING TENDERS

Number	Name
YDT 14 (ex-YF 294)	PHOEBUS
YDT 15 (ex-YF 336)	SUITLAND

Builders:	Erie Concrete and Steel Supply, Pa.
Displacement:	
Length:	YDT 14 132⅝ feet (40.5 m) oa
	YDT 15 132½ feet (40.4 m) oa
Beam:	30 feet (9.1 m)
Draft:	
Propulsion:	diesel (Union); 600 bhp
Speed:	
Manning:	

Both craft were converted from covered lighters built in World War II. Two non-self-propelled diving tenders (YDT) are also in service.

5 SELF-PROPELLED DREDGES

Number	Number	Number
YM 17	YM 33	YM 38
YM 32	YM 35	

These are small dredges; the YM 17 of World War II construction and the others built postwar. The YM 17, 35, and 38 are operational; the others are laid up.

3 COVERED LIGHTERS

Number	Name
YF 862	(unnamed)
YF 866	KODIAK
YF 885	KEYPORT

Builders:	YF 862, 866 Missouri Valley Bridge and Steel Co, Evansville, Ind.
	YF 885 Defoe Shipbuilding, Bay City, Mich.
Displacement:	650 tons full load
Length:	132 feet (40.2 m) oa
Beam:	30 feet (9.1 m)
Draft:	
Propulsion:	diesel; 600 bhp; 2 shafts
Speed:	10 knots
Manning:	11 (enlisted)

These are small, coastal supply craft with a 250-ton cargo capacity. They were constructed during World War II. The YF 862 and KODIAK are laid up. The KEYPORT is in service at Guam.

4 FERRYBOATS: COVERED LCU 1610 CLASS

Number	Number
YFB 88 (ex-LCU 1636)	YFB 90 (ex-LCU 1639)
YFB 89 (ex-LCU 1638)	YFB 91 (ex-LCU 1640)

Builders:	
Displacement:	~390 tons full load
Length:	134¾ feet (41.0 m) oa
Beam:	29¾ feet (9.0 m)
Draft:	6 feet (1.8 m)
Propulsion:	geared diesels (Detroit); 2,000 bhp; 2 shafts
Speed:	11 knots
Manning:	6 (enlisted)

These are former LCU 1610-class landing craft modified for use as ferryboats. Their designation was changed from LCU to YFB on 1 September 1969.

YFB 91 (1984 L. & L. van Ginderen)

2 FERRYBOATS

Number	Number
YFB 83	YFB 87

Builders:	
Displacement:	773 tons full load
Length:	180 feet (54.9 m) oa
Beam:	59 feet (18.0 m)
Draft:	
Propulsion:	diesels; 2 shafts
Speed:	
Manning:	

These are small, built-for-the-purpose ferryboats which service naval bases. Both are active.

YFB 87 (1970, U.S. Navy)

13 SPECIAL PURPOSE LIGHTERS

Number	Number
YFNX 4	YFNX 25 (ex-YFN 1224)
YFNX 7	YFNX 26 (ex-YFN 1225)
YFNX 15 (ex-YNG 22)	YFNX 30 (ex-YFN 1186)
YFNX 20	YFNX 31 (ex-YFN 1249)
YFNX 22	YFNX 32 (ex-YRBM 7)
YFNX 23 (ex-YFN 289)	YFNX 33 (ex-YFN 1192)
YFNX 24 (ex-YFN 1215)	

These are self-propelled special purpose lighters, most converted from non-self-propelled covered lighters. The YFNX 7 is in reserve; all others are in service.
All built 1943–1945.

YFNX 30 at the Naval Ocean Systems Center in San Diego. (1982, U.S. Navy)

1 REFRIGERATED COVERED LIGHTER

Number
YFR 888

Builders:	Defoe Shipbuilding, Bay City, Mich.
Displacement:	610 tons full load
Length:	132 feet (40.2 m) oa
Beam:	30 feet (9.1 m)
Draft:	
Propulsion:	diesel; 600 bhp; 2 shafts
Speed:	10 knots
Manning:	11 (enlisted)

This craft is of the same design as the Navy's surviving covered lighters (YF), but is provided with refrigerated cargo space. She is now laid up in reserve.

5 COVERED LIGHTERS (RANGE TENDER)

Number	Number	Number
YFRT 287	YFRT 451	YFRT 520
YFRT 418	YFRT 523	

Builders:	YFRT 287	Norfolk Navy Yard, Va.
	YFRT 418, 520, 523	Erie Concrete and Steel Supply, Erie, Pa.
	YFRT 451	Basalt Rock Co, Napa, Calif.
Displacement:	650 tons full load	
Length:	132½ feet (40.4 m) oa	
Beam:	30 feet (9.1 m)	
Draft:		
Propulsion:	diesel (Union except Cooper-Bessemer in YFRT 287); 600 bhp; 2 shafts	
Speed:	10 knots	
Manning:	11 (enlisted)	

These craft are used for miscellaneous support purposes. They are YF-type craft, all completed during 1941–1945 (with some originally employed in the YF role). Cargo capacity was 250 tons. The YFRT 418 is laid up in reserve; the other units are active.

Classification: The YFRT 287 and 418 originally were classified as YF, with the same hull numbers; the YFRT 523 was the YF 852.

YFR 520 with Mk 32 torpedo tubes amidships. (U.S. Navy)

6 HARBOR UTILITY CRAFT: CONVERTED LCU 1610 CLASS

Number	Number
YFU 83	YFU 100 (ex-LCU 1610)
YFU 97 (ex-LCU 1611)	YFU 101 (ex-LCU 1612)
YFU 98 (ex-LCU 1615)	YFU 102 (ex-LCU 1462)

Builders:	Defoe Shipbuilding, Bay City, Mich.
Displacement:	~390 tons full load
Length:	134¾ feet (41.0 m) oa
Beam:	29¾ feet (9.0 m)
Draft:	6 feet (1.8 m)
Propulsion:	geared diesels (Detroit); 2,000 bhp; 2 shafts
Speed:	11 knots
Manning:	6 (enlisted)

Five of these craft are converted landing craft; the YFU 83 was built to the same design specifically for the utility craft role. They carry cargo in coastal and harbor areas. All are active.

YFU 83 (1971, Defoe Shipbuilding)

9 HARBOR UTILITY CRAFT: YFU 71 CLASS

Number	Number	Number	Number
YFU 71	YFU 74	YFU 76	YFU 79
YFU 72	YFU 75	YFU 77	YFU 81
YFU 73			

Builders:	Pacific Coast Engineering Co., Alameda, Calif.
Displacement:	
Length:	125 feet (38.1 m) oa
Beam:	36 feet (11.0 m)
Draft:	7½ feet (2.4 m)
Propulsion:	diesels; 2 shafts
Speed:	8 knots
Manning:	

These craft were constructed specifically for use as coastal cargo craft in Vietnam. They were built to a modified commercial design, with 12 units (YFU 71–82) being completed in 1967–1968. Their cargo capacity is 300 tons. The YFU 71–77 and 80–82 were transferred to the U.S. Army in 1970 for use in South Vietnam; they were returned to the Navy in 1973. The YFU 82 was converted to a research craft and is listed as the IX 506. Only the YFU 73 is active.

Guns: During their Vietnam service these craft each had two or more .50-cal MG fitted.

YFU 75 (1968, U.S. Navy)

3 HARBOR UTILITY CRAFT: CONVERTED LCU 1466 CLASS

Number
YFU 50 (ex-LCU 1486)
YFU 91 (ex-LCU 1608)
YFU 94 (ex-LCU 1488)

Builders:	Defoe Shipbuilding, Bay City, Mich.
Displacement:	~360 tons full load
Length:	119 feet (36.3 m) oa
Beam:	34 feet (10.4 m)
Draft:	6 feet (1.8 m)
Propulsion:	geared diesels (Gray Marine); 675 bhp; 3 shafts
Speed:	8 knots
Manning:	6 (enlisted)

These are converted landing craft used for harbor and coastal cargo carrying. The YFU 91 is operational; the others are laid up.

13 FUEL OIL BARGES

Number	Number	Number	Number
YO 106	YO 203	YO 225	YO 264
YO 129	YO 220	YO 228	
YO 200	YO 223	YO 230	
YO 202	YO 224	YO 241	

Builders:	YO 106	Albina Engine and Machine Works, Portland, Ore.
	YO 129	Pensacola Shipyard and Engine, Fla.
	YO 200–203	Manitowoc Shipbuilding, Wisc.
	YO 220–230	Jeffersonville Boat and Machinery, Ind.
	YO 241	John H. Mathis, Camden, N.J.
	YO 264	Leatham D. Smith, Sturgeon Bay, Wisc.
Displacement:	1,400 tons full load	
Length:	174 feet (53.1 m) oa	
Beam:	32 feet (9.8 m)	
Draft:	13⅓ feet (4.1 m)	
Propulsion:	diesels; 560 bhp; 1 shaft	
Speed:	10.5 knots	
Manning:	11 (enlisted)	

These are coastal tankers with a cargo capacity of 6,570 barrels. Eleven of these craft are active with the YO 228 and 241 laid up.

Classification: The YO 264 was previously classified as a gasoline barge, YOG 105.

YO 203 (1983, Giorgio Arra)

YO 200 (1984, Giorgio Arra)

1 FUEL OIL BARGE

Number
YO 153

Builders:	Ira S. Bushey and Sons, Brooklyn, N.Y.
Displacement:	1,076 tons full load
Length:	156¼ feet (47.6 m) oa
Beam:	30⁷⁄₁₂ feet (9.3 m)
Draft:	11¾ feet (3.6 m)
Propulsion:	diesels (Fairbanks-Morse); 525 bhp; 1 shaft
Speed:	10 knots
Manning:	15 (enlisted)

The YO 153 is the only survivor in U.S. service of a class of coastal and harbor tankers. Her cargo capacity is 6,000 barrels. The craft is laid up in reserve.

1 FUEL OIL BARGE

Number	Name
YO 47	CASING HEAD

Builders:	YO 47 Lake Superior Shipbuilding, Superior, Wisc.
Displacement:	1,731 tons full load
Length:	235 feet (71.6 m) oa
Beam:	37 feet (11.3 m)
Draft:	16½ feet (5.0 m)
Propulsion:	diesels (Enterprise); 2 shafts
Speed:	9 knots
Manning:	

This is a coastal gasoline carrier built in 1941. Its cargo capacity is 10,000 barrels. The CASING HEAD is in reserve.

8 GASOLINE BARGES

Number	Number	Number	Number
YOG 58	YOG 78	YOG 87	YOG 93
YOG 68	YOG 79	YOG 88	YOG 196

Builders:	YOG 58, 87–93 R.T.C Shipbuilding, Camden, N.J.
	YOG 68 George Lawley and Sons, Neponset, Mass.
	YOG 78–79 Puget Sound Navy Yard, Bremerton, Wash.
	YOG 196 Manitowoc Shipbuilding, Wisc.
Displacement:	
Length:	174 feet (53.0 m) oa
Beam:	32 feet (9.8 m)
Draft:	
Propulsion:	diesel (General Motors except Union in YOG 58); 640 bhp except 560 in YOG 58; 1 shaft
Speed:	
Manning:	

These are self-propelled gasoline barges with a cargo capacity of 6,570 barrels. They are virtually identical to the 174-foot fuel oil barges. The YOG 78, 87, 88, and 196 are in service; the others are in reserve. The YOG 196 was formerly designated YO 196.

YOG 78 (1983, Giorgio Arra)

YOG 78 and YW 119 at Norfolk (1979, Giorgio Arra)

12 + 8 SEAMANSHIP TRAINING CRAFT: YP 676 CLASS

Number	Number	Number	Number
YP 676	YP 679	YP 683	YP 685
YP 677	YP 680	YP 684	YP 686
YP 678	YP 681		YP 687
	YP 682		

Builders:	Peterson Builders, Sturgeon Bay, Wisc.
Displacement:	134 tons full load
Length:	108 feet (32.9 m) oa
Beam:	23 feet (7.0 m)
Draft:	7⅝ feet (2.4 m)
Propulsion:	diesel (Detroit); 875 bhp; 2 shafts
Speed:	12 knots
Manning:	6 (2 officers + 4 enlisted) + 24 students

These are improved seamanship training craft, with 20 units planned for use by the Naval Academy where they will replace earlier craft.

The YP 676 was authorized in fiscal 1982 and was to deliver in September 1984. The YP 677–682 were authorized in fiscal 1983 for delivery from December 1984 through 1985; YP 683–687 were authorized in fiscal 1984 with seven more in the fiscal 1985 program.

As the new YPs are delivered, the older craft will be assigned to the Naval Officer Candidate School (see page 328), the Surface Warfare Officers School at Coronado, Calif., and the reserve COOP program (see Addenda).

YP-676 under way on trials (1984, Peterson Builders)

YP 667 (1982, Giorgio Arra)

22 SEAMANSHIP TRAINING CRAFT: YP 654 CLASS

Number	Number	Number	Number
YP 654	YP 660	YP 666	YP 672
YP 655	YP 661	YP 667	YP 673
YP 656	YP 662	YP 668	YP 674
YP 657	YP 663	YP 669	YP 675
YP 658	YP 664	YP 670	
YP 659	YP 665	YP 671	

Builders:	YP 654–663 Stephen Brothers, Stockton, Calif.
	YP 664–665 Elizabeth City Shipbuilders, N.C.
	YP 666–675 Peterson Brothers, Sturgeon Bay, Wisc.
Displacement:	71 tons full load
Length:	80⅓ feet (24.5 m) oa
Beam:	18⅓ feet (5.6 m)
Draft:	5⅓ feet (1.7 m)
Propulsion:	diesels (General Motors); 660 bhp; 2 shafts
Speed:	13.5 knots
Manning:	10 (2 officers + 8 enlisted) + 24 students

These craft are used for seamanship and navigation training at the Naval Academy in Annapolis, Md., and at the Naval Officer Candidate School and Naval Surface Warfare Officers School, both at Newport, R.I. All could be armed with machine guns and employed as harbor patrol craft.

They were built from 1965 onward, with the last three craft being authorized in FY 1977 and delivered to the Navy in 1979.

Design: These craft have wood hulls with aluminum deckhouses. The YP 655 has oceanographic research equipment installed for instructional use at the Naval Academy. The design is SCB No. 139 (later SCB No. 800 in the new series).

6 SEAPLANE WRECKING DERRICKS: YSD 11 CLASS

Number	Number	Number
YSD 39	YSD 63	YSD 74
YSD 53	YSD 72	YSD 77

Builders:	YSD 39 Norfolk Navy Yard
	YSD 53 Gulfport Boiler and Welding Works, Port Arthur, Texas
	YSD 63 Sonle Steel
	YSD 72 Omaha Steel Works
	YSD 74 Pearl Harbor Navy Yard
	YSD 77 Missouri Valley Bridge and Iron, Leavenworth, Kansas
Displacement:	270 tons full load
Length:	104 feet (31.7 m) oa
Beam:	31⅙ feet (9.5 m)
Draft:	
Propulsion:	diesels; 640 bhp; 1 shaft
Speed:	10 knots
Manning:	13–15 (enlisted)

These are small, self-propelled floating cranes completed in 1943–1944. They have 10-ton-capacity cranes. All are active. YSDs are called "Mary Anns."

(28) LARGE HARBOR TUGS: YTB 839 CLASS

Number		Status
YTB 839-840	FY 1983 program	Authorized
YTB 841-849	FY 1984 program	Authorized
YTB 850-855	FY 1985 program	Planned
YTB 856-859	FY 1986 program	Planned
YTB 860-863	FY 1987 program	Planned
YTB 864-866	FY 1988 program	Planned

Construction of these tugs was to begin in 1984.

YSD 63 (1977, Giorgio Arra)

Builders:	Marinette Marine, Wisc.
	Southern Shipbuilding, Slidell, La.
	Mobile Ship Repair, Mobile, Ala.
Displacement:	350–400 tons full load
Length:	109 feet (33.2 m) oa
Beam:	30½ feet (9.3 m)
Draft:	13½ feet (4.1 m)
Propulsion:	diesels; 2,000 bhp; 2 shafts
Speed:	12.5 knots
Manning:	11–12 (enlisted)

These tugs were completed during 1961–1975. (The similar YTB 837 and 838 were transferred to Saudi Arabia in 1975.) All of these tugs are in active service.

Design: SCB No. 147A. These and other Navy harbor tugs are used for towing and maneuvering ships in harbors and coastal waters. Their masts fold down to facilitate working alongside large ships.

The tugs are also equipped for firefighting.

75 LARGE HARBOR TUGS: YTB 760 CLASS

Number	Name	Number	Name
YTB 760	NATICK	YTB 800	EUFAULA
YTB 761	OTTUMWA	YTB 801	PALATKA
YTB 762	TUSCUMBIA	YTB 802	CHERAW
YTB 763	MUSKEGON	YTB 803	NANTICOKE
YTB 764	MISHAWAKA	YTB 804	AHOSKIE
YTB 765	OKMULGEE	YTB 805	OCALA
YTB 766	WAPAKONETA	YTB 806	TUSKEGEE
YTB 767	APALACHICOLA	YTB 807	MASSAPEQUA
YTB 768	ARCATA	YTB 808	WEMATCHEE
YTB 769	CHESANING	YTB 809	AGAWAN
YTB 770	DAHLONEGA	YTB 810	ANOKA
YTB 771	KEOKUK	YTB 811	HOUMA
YTB 774	NASHUA	YTB 812	ACCOMAC
YTB 775	WAUWATOSA	YTB 813	POUGHKEEPSIE
YTB 776	WEEHAWKEN	YTB 814	WAXAHATCHIE
YTB 777	NOGALES	YTB 815	NEODESHA
YTB 778	APOPKA	YTB 816	CAMPTI
YTB 779	MANHATTAN	YTB 817	HYANNIS
YTB 780	SAUGUS	YTB 818	MECOSTA
YTB 781	NIANTIC	YTB 819	IUKA
YTB 782	MANISTEE	YTB 820	WANAMASSA
YTB 783	REDWING	YTB 821	TONTOGANY
YTB 784	KALISPELL	YTB 822	PAWHUSKA
YTB 785	WINNEMUCCA	YTB 823	CANONCHET
YTB 786	TONKAWA	YTB 824	SANTAQUIN
YTB 787	KITTANNING	YTB 825	WATHENA
YTB 788	WAPATO	YTB 826	WASHTUCNA
YTB 789	TOMAHAWK	YTB 827	CHETEK
YTB 790	MENOMINEE	YTB 828	CATAHECASSA
YTB 791	MARINETTE	YTB 829	METACOM
YTB 792	ANTIGO	YTB 830	PUSHMATAHA
YTB 793	PIQUA	YTB 831	DEKANAWIDA
YTB 794	MANDAN	YTB 832	PETALESHARO
YTB 795	KETCHIKAN	YTB 833	SHABONEE
YTB 796	SACO	YTB 834	NEGWAGON
YTB 797	TAMAQUA	YTB 835	SKENANDOA
YTB 798	OPELIKA	YTB 836	POKAGON
YTB 799	NATCHITOCHES		

SANTAQUIN underway with mast raised; note the navigation radars above the bridge and fenders over bow and sides. (1982, Giorgio Arra)

MANISTEE with mast folded down to protect it while alongside larger ships; a water cannon for fire fighting is mounted forward of the bridge. (1983, Giorgio Arra)

6 LARGE HARBOR TUGS: YTB 752 CLASS

Number	Name	Number	Name
YTB 752	Edenshaw	YTB 757	Oshkosh
YTB 753	Marin	YTB 758	Paducah
YTB 756	Pontiac	YTB 759	Bogalusa

Builders:	YTB 752–753 Christy Corp, Sturgeon Bay, Wisc.
	YTB 756–759 Southern Shipbuilding, Slidell, La.
Displacement:	341 tons full load
Length:	85 feet (25.9 m) oa
Beam:	24 feet (7.3 m)
Draft:	13¼ feet (4.0 m)
Propulsion:	diesel; 1 shaft
Speed:	12.5 knots
Manning:	10–12 (enlisted)

These tugs were completed in 1960–1961. Their design is SCB No. 147. All are active.

Paducah and the John F. Kennedy (CV 67) (U.S. Navy)

7 SMALL HARBOR TUGS: YTL 422 CLASS

Number	Number	Number	Number
YTL 422	YTL 438	YTL 583	YTL 602
YTL 434	YTL 439	YTL 588	

Builders:	YTL 422, 434	Everett-Pacific Shipbuilding and DD, Wash.
	YTL 583, 588	Bellingham Iron Works, Wash.
	YTL 438, 439, 602	Robert Jacob, City Island, N.Y.
Displacement:	80 tons full load	
Length:	66⅙ feet (20.2 m) oa	
Beam:	17 feet (5.2 m)	
Draft:	5 feet (1.5 m)	
Propulsion:	diesel; 300 bhp; 1 shaft	
Speed:	10 knots	
Manning:	5 (enlisted)	

These are the survivors of several hundred small tugs built during World War II. The YTL 434, 588, and 602 are in service; the others are laid up.

Classification: These craft originally were classified YT with the same hull numbers. YTL originally was harbor tug, "little."

44 MEDIUM HARBOR TUGS: YTM 138 AND YTM 518 CLASSES

Number	Name	Number	Name
YTM 178	Dekaury	YTM 521	Nabigwon
YTM 189	Nepanet	YTM 524	Tutahaco
YTM 265	Hiawatha	YTM 526	Wahaka
YTM 268	Red Cloud	YTM 527	Wahpeton
YTM 359	Pawtucket	YTM 534	Nadli
YTM 364	Sassa	YTM 536	Nahoke
YTM 390	Ganadoga	YTM 542	Chegodoega
YTM 391	Itara	YTM 543	Etawina
YTM 392	Mecosta	YTM 544	Yatanocas
YTM 394	Winamac	YTM 545	Accohanoc
YTM 395	Wingina	YTM 546	Takos
YTM 397	Yanegua	YTM 547	Yanaba
YTM 398	Natahki	YTM 548	Matunak
YTM 399	Numa	YTM 549	Migadan
YTM 400	Otokomi	YTM 701	Acoma
YTM 404	Coshecton	YTM 702	Arawak
YTM 405	Cusseta	YTM 704	Moratoc
YTM 406	Kittaton	YTM 768	Apohola
YTM 413	Porobago	YTM 770	Mimac
YTM 415	Secota	YTM 776	Hiamonee
YTM 417	Taconnet	YTM 779	Pocasset

Builders:	Defoe Boiler & Machine Works, Bay City, Mich.; Gibbs Gas Engine, Jacksonville, Fla.; Pacific Coast Engineering, Oakland, Calif. Gulfport Boiler & Welding Works, Port Arthur, Texas; Consolidated SB, Morris Heights, N.Y.; Ira S. Bushey & Sons, Brooklyn, N.Y.; Coast Guard Yard, Curtis Bay, Md.; Bethlehem Steel, San Pedro, Calif.; Commercial Iron Works, Portland, Ore.
Displacement:	220–260 tons standard
	310–320 tons full load
Length:	100 feet (30.5 m) oa
Beam:	25 feet (7.6 m)
Draft:	9⁷⁄₁₂ feet (3.0 m)
Propulsion:	diesel; 1,000 bhp; 1 shaft
Speed:	14 knots
Manning:	8 (enlisted)

These are harbor tugs employed at most U.S. naval bases. Plans to construct additional YTMs (initially YTM 800–802, authorized in fiscal 1973) were dropped in favor of additional YTB construction. Most units are active, with 18 laid up in reserve. All were built in 1940–1945.

The SAGAWAMICK (YTM 522) was stricken on 15 December 1982, the TOKA (YTM 149) and MADOKAWANDO (YTM 180) on 31 January 1983; all transferred to Army. WAUBANSEE (YTM 366) stricken on 15 April 1983 and transferred to Massachusetts Maritime Academy.

Classification: These craft originally were classified as large harbor tugs (YTB) with the same hull numbers, except YTM 768 ex-YTB 502, YTM 770 ex-YTB 507, and YTM 779 ex-YTB 516.

ARAWAK (1983, Giorgio Arra)

WAHPETON (1983, Giorgio Arra)

2 MEDIUM HARBOR TUGS: YTM 760 CLASS

Number	Name
YTM 760	MASCOUTAH
YTM 761	MENASHA

Builders:	Jacobson Shipyard, Oyster Bay, N.Y.
Displacement:	~200 tons full load
Length:	85 feet (25.9 m) oa
Beam:	24 feet (7.3 m)
Draft:	11 feet (3.4 m)
Propulsion:	diesels; 2 cycloidal propellers
Speed:	12 knots
Manning:	8 (enlisted)

These tugs were built to an experimental design with cycloidal propellers that provide a high degree of maneuverability and enable them to turn 360° within their length. Both units are active.

Classification: These tugs were built as YTB 722 and 773, respectively; they were changed to YTM 760 and 761 in September 1965.

MASCOUTAH (1983, Giorgio Arra)

The MENASHA while helping to move the battleship IOWA (BB 61) from the mothball group at the Philadelphia Naval Shipyard. (1982, Giorgio Arra)

1 MEDIUM HARBOR TUG: FORMER ARMY TUG

Number	Name
YTM 750	HACKENSACK

Builders:	National Steel and Shipbuilding, San Diego, Calif.
Displacement:	470 tons full load
Length:	107 feet (32.6 m) oa
Beam:	26½ feet (8.0 m)
Draft:	14⅚ feet (4.5 m)
Propulsion:	diesel; 1,200 bhp; 1 shaft
Speed:	12 knots
Manning:	8 (enlisted)

The former U.S. Army tug LT 2089. The HACKENSACK is in service.

Class: The former Army tug LT 2077 was acquired by the Navy as the YTM 759. She was changed to IX 505 on 1 November 1975 and employed to support research activities, and was stricken on 1 December 1977. No name was assigned during naval service.

The YUMA (YTM 748 ex-LT 2078) is on loan.

6 MEDIUM HARBOR TUGS: YTM 174 CLASS

Number	Name	Number	Name
YTM 252	DEKANISORA	YTM 381	CHEPANOC
YTM 359	PAWTUCKET	YTM 382	COATOPA
YTM 380	CHANAGI	YTM 383	COCHALI

Builders:	Gulfport Boiler and Welding Works, Port Arthur, Texas
Displacement:	~200 tons full load
Length:	102 feet (31.1 m) oa
Beam:	25 feet (7.6 m)
Draft:	10 feet (3 m)
Propulsion:	diesel; 1,000 bhp; 1 shaft
Speed:	12 knots
Manning:	8 (enlisted)

Two units of this class are active (YTM 252, 380); the others are in reserve.

Classification: These tugs were originally classified YT; changed to large harbor tugs (YTB) in 1944 and reclassified as YTM on 1 February 1962. (Same hull numbers as YT/YTB/YTM.)

CHANAGI (1982, Giorgio Arra)

CHANAGI (1982, Giorgio Arra)

9 WATER BARGES

Number	Number	Number
YW 83	YW 101	YW 123
YW 86	YW 108	YW 126
YW 98	YW 113	YW 127

Builders:	YW 83	John H. Mathis, Camden, N.J.
	YW 86, 108	Zenith Dredge, Duluth, Minn.
	YW 98	George Lawley and Sons, Neponset, Mass.
	YW 101	Mare Island Navy Yard, Vallejo, Calif.
	YW 113	Marine Iron and Shipbuilding Co, Duluth, Minn.
	YW 123, 126, 127	Leathem D. Smith Shipbuilding, Sturgeon Bay, Wisc.
Displacement:	1,235 tons full load	
Length:	174 feet (53.0 m) oa	
Beam:	32 feet (9.7 m)	
Draft:	15 feet (4.6 m)	
Propulsion:	diesel; 560 bhp; 1 shaft	
Speed:	8 knots	
Manning:	22 (enlisted)	

These craft are similar to the YO/YOG types, but are employed to carry fresh water. Cargo capacity is 200,000 gallons. Three craft are in service (YW 113, 123, 127); the others are laid up.

YW 113 (1983, Giorgio Arra)

YW 119—now stricken (Giorgio Arra)

ATHENA I (foreground) and ATHENA II underway. They have yellow hulls with white superstructures. (1980, U.S. Navy)

3 RESEARCH CRAFT: "ASHEVILLE" CLASS

Number	Name	Launched	PGM Commission	To NSRDC
(ex-FG 94)	ATHENA I	8 June 1968	8 Nov 1969	21 Aug 1975
(ex-FG 98)	ATHENA II	4 Apr 1970	5 Sep 1970	3 Oct 1977
(ex-FG 100)	ATHENA III	19 June 1970	6 Feb 1971	18 Nov 1977

Builders:	Tacoma Boatbuilding, Wash.
Displacement:	approx. 265 tons full load
Length:	164½ feet (50.2 m) oa
Beam:	23¾ feet (7.2 m)
Draft:	9½ feet (2.9 m)
Propulsion:	2 diesels (Cummins), 1,750 bhp; 1 gas turbine (General Electric), 14,000 shp; 2 shafts
Speed:	16 knots on diesels; 40+ knots on gas turbines
Manning:	(civilian contractor)
Missiles:	none
Guns:	removed

These are former ASHEVILLE-class patrol combatants/gunboats, the last of a class of 17 in active U.S. naval service. Others serve with U.S. agencies and institutions and foreign navies (see page 221). The above three units were transferred on the dates indicated to the David W. Taylor Naval Ship Research and Development Center for use in various offshore experiments.

The ATHENA I has enlarged deck house forward. They carry up to 10 tons of test equipment.

Classification: When assigned to the NSRDC these ships were reclassified as service craft without specific hull designations.

Names: Their former names were PG 94 CHEHALIS, PG 98 GRAND RAPIDS, and PG 100 DOUGLAS.

1 RESEARCH SUPPORT BOAT

Number	Name
RSB-1	(ex-A.B. WOOD II)

Builders:	Bishop Marine Service
Displacement:	291 tons full load
Length:	157 feet (47.9 m) oa
Beam:	36 feet (11.0 m)
Draft:	11 feet (3.4 m)
Propulsion:	diesel; 1,530 bhp; 2 shafts
Speed:	13 knots
Manning:	5 (civilian)

This craft is operated by the Naval Surface Warfare Center at Ft. Lauderdale, Fla., to recover Space Shuttle booster rockets. The craft has a bow-thruster and is fitted with a 35-ton-capacity hydraulic telescoping boom plus winches for recovering the boosters from depths to 7,000 feet.

The craft was built in 1966 specifically to support deep-sea work and recovery operations.

RSB-1 (U.S. Navy)

RSB-1 (1983, Giorgio Arra)

2 RESEARCH SHIPS: Ex-MINESWEEPERS

Number	Name	FY	Launched	In service
(MSI 1)	COVE	56	8 Feb 1958	22 Nov 1958
(MSI 2)	CAPE	56	5 Apr 1958	27 Feb 1959

Builders:	Bethlehem Steel, Bellingham, Wash.
Displacement:	120 tons light
	240 tons full load
Length:	105 feet (32.0 m) oa
Beam:	22 feet (6.7 m)
Draft:	10 feet (3.0 m)
Propulsion:	diesel (General Motors); 650 shp; 1 shaft
Speed:	12 knots
Manning:	

The CAPE while still in Navy service at the Long Beach Naval Station. Although small, the craft has the same basic lines and arrangements of the MSO/MSC classes. (1968, U.S. Navy)

These were prototype inshore minesweepers. After several years of service in the MSI role they were assigned to research tasks. The COVE has been operated by the Johns Hopkins Applied Physics Laboratory. Since 31 July 1970; the CAPE, initially operated by APL, is now assigned to the Naval Ocean Systems Center in San Diego.

Design: SCB No. 136.

Additional MSIs have been built specifically for foreign transfer.

1 DRONE RECOVERY CRAFT: FORMER MOTOR TORPEDO BOAT

Number	Name	Launched	PT in Service
DR-1 (ex-PT 809)	RETRIEVER	7 Aug 1950	1950

Builders:	Electric Boat, Groton, Conn.
Displacement:	125 tons full load
Length:	98½ feet (30.0 m)
Beam:	26 feet (7.9 m)
Draft:	7 feet (2.1 m)
Propulsion:	4 diesel (General Motors); 4 shafts
Speed:	22–25 knots
Manning:	18–22 (1 officer + 17–21 enlisted)
Guns:	removed

The RETRIEVER was originally one of four experimental torpedo boats (PT 809–812) built as prototypes for post-World War II PT boats. After extensive trials and limited service, the PT 809 was laid up in reserve. She was subsequently reactivated and employed to carry Secret Service agents screening the presidential yacht on the Potomac River (based at the Washington Navy Yard). The craft was named GUARDIAN in that role.

In December 1974 the craft was transferred to Fleet Composite Squadron 6 at Little Creek, Va., for operation as a recovery boat for aerial drones and a control boat for surface target drone craft. She was designated DR-1 (for Drone Recovery) and named RETRIEVER on 1 July 1975.

Her crew varies with assignment.

Design: The DR-1 is all-aluminum construction. As a PT she carried four over-the-side torpedo launchers plus 20-mm and 40-mm guns.

DR-1 (1982, Giorgio Arra)

1 SURFACE EFFECT SHIP: SES-200 TYPE

Number	Name	Delivered
SES-200	. . . . . .	September 1982

Builders:	Bell Halter, New Orleans, La.
Displacement:	125 tons light
	200 tons full load
Length:	160 feet (48.8 m) oa
Beam:	39⁵/₁₂ feet (12.0 m)
Draft:	
Propulsion:	2 diesels (Allison); 3,200 bhp; 2 shafts
Lift:	2 diesels (Allison); 890 bhp; 2 fans
Speed:	32 knots on cushion in sea state 0
	27 knots on cushion in sea state 3
	16 knots off cushion in sea state 0
	14 knots off cushion in sea state 3
Range:	2,950 n.miles at 30 knots in sea state 0
	2,400 n.miles at 25 knots in sea state 3
Manning:	
Missiles:	none
Guns:	none

The SES-200 was acquired by the Navy to evaluate the mission capability of a surface effect ship of this size and design. The ship was originally delivered to the U.S. Coast Guard in September 1980 and designated WSES 1. After extensive trials, the Coast Guard ordered three similar ships (see Appendix A). Subsequently, the prototype craft was lengthened 50 feet with a midsection added to increase range and delivered to the Navy for further tests.

SES-100A and SES-100B

The experimental 100-ton surface effect ships SES-100B, built by Bell Aerospace Textron, and SES-100A, built by Aeroject-General, were stricken in 1982. The SES-100A was scrapped and the SES-100B placed on static display at the David W. Taylor Naval Ship Research and Development Center in Annapolis, Md.

1 RANGE SUPPORT SHIP (SWATH): "KAIMALINO"

Number	Name	Launched	In service
(none)	KAIMALINO	7 March 1973	1973

Builders:	Coast Guard Yard, Curtis Bay, Md.
Displacement:	228 tons full load
Length:	88⅓ feet (26.9 m) oa
Beam:	46½ feet (14.2 m)
Draft:	15¼ feet (4.65 m)
Propulsion:	2 gas turbines (General Electric); 4,400 shp; 2 shafts
Speed:	25 knots
Range:	300 n.miles at 13 knots on gas turbines
	1,000 n.miles at 4 knots on diesels
Manning:	10 (civilian) + 6 scientists

The Stable Semi-submerged Platform (SSP) KAIMALINO is an experimental craft employed in the range support role at the Naval Ocean System Center's underwater test range in Hawaii. After several years of successful trials and work activities, during 1980–1981 the KAIMALINO was modified (see Conversion notes).

The Bell-Halter SES-200 while on Navy trials. (Bell Halter)

Conversion: The KAIMALINO was modified at the Dillingham Shipyard in Hawaii in 1980–1981. The craft was enlarged from 190 to 228 tons through the addition of fiberglass buoyancy modules.

Design: The SSP is a Small Waterplane Area Twin-Hull (SWATH) craft developed to test this hull concept. The SWATH has two fully submerged, torpedo-shaped hulls, each 6½ feet in diameter, with vertical struts penetrating the water to support the superstructure and flight deck. The flight deck area is 3,400 square feet.

The SSP/SWATH concept differs from that of a catamaran, which has two conventional ship hulls joined together. The SWATH design provides a comparatively large deck area with a minimum of heave, pitch, and roll. Tests indicate that the SWATH design would be suitable for ships up to about 20,000 tons. Such a ship could operate effectively in seas up to state 10.

The KAIMALINO has a hull-stabilizing fin connecting the two submerged hulls and two small canard fins forward, one inboard on each hull. There is an opening in the craft's main deck for lowering research and recovery devices. (The opening is covered over for helicopter operations.) The beam listed above is the maximum over both hulls.

Up to 16 tons of mission equipment can be carried.

Engineering: Two T64-GE-6B aircraft-type gas turbine engines provide propulsion power. Two Detroit diesels (8V-71T) are provided for auxiliary propulsion.

Helicopters: The KAIMALINO conducted tests of the feasibility of landing helicopters on SSP/SWATH-type ships in high sea states at speeds up to 25 knots in 1976. The operations, with an SH-2F LAMPS, were completely successful.

Torpedoes: In 1982 the KAIMALINO was fitted with triple Mk 32 torpedo tubes for tests of the Mk 50 ALWT.

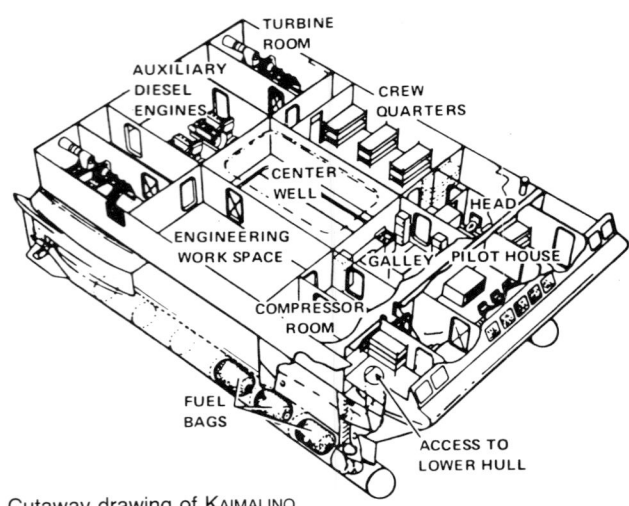

Cutaway drawing of KAIMALINO

KAIMALINO with SH-2F (1976, U.S. Navy)

The KAIMALINO off Oahu with SH-2F LAMPS helicopter from HSL-37. (1976, U.S. Navy)

KAIMALINO at Pearl Harbor (1979, Giorgio Arra)

The Navy's torpedo retrievers range from 63 feet to 102 feet. The Torpedo Weapons Retriever (TWR) shown here is 102 feet long, displaces 152 tons full load, and can reach 18 knots with four diesels. The craft can carry 17 tons of torpedoes. (1980, Giorgio Arra)

The 65-foot TR 4 has a displacement of some 35 tons fully loaded and a speed of 18.5 knots. The craft can carry four torpedoes (up to 5½ tons). The deckhouse resembles that of the PCF coastal patrol craft; a tripod mast distinguishes these craft. (1979, Giorgio Arra)

The 72-foot torpedo retriever TR 2. With a displacement of 58 tons and a speed of 18 knots, the craft can carry up to 12 tons of torpedoes. (1977, Giorgio Arra)

A stern view of a 65-foot TR showing the open, inclined stern ramp and rollers. All torpedo retrievers are diesel propelled with twin propeller shafts. (1983, Giorgio Arra)

The stern of the TR 2 shows the inclined ramp and rollers for pulling torpedoes up out of the water. Four 21-foot torpedoes can be carried side by side in these craft. (1977, Giorgio Arra)

The TR 2 at high speed. The TR 2 is designated as a 72-foot Mk 2 craft; the 72-foot Mk 1 type had no deckhouse and a smaller torpedo well. (1983, Giorgio Arra)

26 Floating Dry Docks

The Navy operates floating dry docks at several bases in the United States and overseas for the repair and maintenance of ships. These are non-self-propelled docks, but all have electrical generators to provide power for their lighting, tools, and equipment. Normally they operate with a flotilla of non-self-propelled barges that provide specialized services such as messing and berthing for ships being dry docked.

The floating docks are arranged in this chapter in alphabetical order according to their classification; they are considered service craft.

Those docks in active Navy service have their locations indicated; several others are operated by commercial firms under lease from the Navy; the Army and Coast Guard each have one dock.

Class totals are docks in U.S. government service or laid up in reserve.

Guns: No floating dry docks are armed, although many were designed to mount light anti-aircraft guns.

Operational: Active Navy docks are manned by Navy personnel and civilian employees of the Navy.

The SPARTANBURG COUNTY (LST 1192) undergoing maintenance in a floating dry dock. These docks supplement permanent docks at naval and commercial shipyards in the United States and at U.S. naval activities overseas. During a prolonged crisis or conflict they can be towed to forward areas to reduce transit time for ships requiring overhaul or repair of battle damage. (Giorgio Arra)

6 LARGE AUXILIARY FLOATING DRY DOCKS

Number	Sections	Name	Completed	Length	Width	Capacity	Construction	Status
AFDB 2	C-D-H-I	(unnamed)	1944	approx. 375 ft (114.4 m)	256 ft (78.0 m)	40,000 tons	steel	active in Subic Bay, Philippines
	A-B-E-F-G-J	(unnamed)		approx. 565 ft (172.3 m)	256 ft (78.0 m)	60,000 tons	steel	in reserve at Pearl Harbor
AFDB 4	A-B-C-D-E-F-G	(unnamed)	1944	approx. 825 ft (251.6 m)	240 ft (73.2 m)	55,000 tons	steel	in reserve at Bremerton, Wash.
AFDB 5	A-B-C-D-E-F-G	(unnamed)	1944	approx. 825 ft (251.6 m)	240 ft (73.2 m)	55,000 tons	steel	in reserve at Pearl Harbor
AFDB 7	A-B-E-G	Los Alamos	1944	approx. 475 ft (144.0 m)	240 ft (73.2 m)	30,000 tons	steel	active in Holy Loch, Scotland
	C-D			approx. 236 ft (72.0 m)	240 ft (73.2 m)	15,000 tons	steel	in reserve at Philadelphia, Pa.

These docks consist of 256- or 240-foot sections, about 80 feet wide with wing walls 83 feet high. The walls have space for accommodations, machinery, and storage. The walls fold down for towing.

The docks are assembled by the sections being connected side by side. The overall length of the assembled docks vary.

Seven of these docks were built; they were originally classified as Advanced Base Sectional Docks (ABSD) with the same hull numbers.

Manning: The Los Alamos is assigned 197 Navy personnel (5 officers + 192 enlisted).

Class: The remaining sections of the Artisan (AFDB 1) were placed on sale in 1983.

The UNREP ship White Plains (AFS 4) undergoing repairs in the Artisan (AFDB 6) at Subic Bay in the Philippines. The dock has two cranes that travel on rails along the dock's walls. (1975, U.S. Navy)

The Artisan at the Navy's Ship Repair Facility at Subic Bay; see text, above. (1978, Giorgio Arra)

5 SMALL AUXILIARY FLOATING DRY DOCKS

Number	Name	Completed	Length	Width	Capacity	Construction	Status	Notes
AFDL 1	ENDEAVOR	1943	200 ft (61 m)	64 ft (19.5 m)	1,000 tons	steel	Guantanamo Bay, Cuba	ex-AFD 1
AFDL 6	DYNAMIC	1944	200 ft (61 m)	64 ft (19.5 m)	1,000 tons	steel	Little Creek, Va.	ex-AFD 6
AFDL 10		1943	200 ft (61 m)	64 ft (19.5 m)	1,000 tons	steel	lease	ex-AFD 10
AFDL 11		1943	200 ft (61 m)	64 ft (19.5 m)	1,000 tons	steel	lease	ex-AFD 11
AFDL 12		1943	200 ft (61 m)	64 ft (19.5 m)	1,000 tons	steel	lease	ex-AFD 12
AFDL 15		1943	200 ft (61 m)	64 ft (19.5 m)	1,000 tons	steel	lease	ex-AFD 15
AFDL 16		1943	200 ft (61 m)	64 ft (19.5 m)	1,000 tons	steel	lease	ex-AFD 16
AFDL 21		1944	200 ft (61 m)	64 ft (19.5 m)	1,000 tons	steel	lease	ex-AFD 21
AFDL 22		1944	200 ft (61 m)	64 ft (19.5 m)	1,000 tons	steel	lease	ex-AFD 22
AFDL 23	ADEPT	1944	288 ft (87.8 m)	64 ft (19.5 m)	1,900 tons	steel	Subic Bay, Philippines	ex-AFD 23
AFDL 25		1944	200 ft (61 m)	64 ft (19.5 m)	1,000 tons	steel	U.S. Army	ex-AFD 25
AFDL 29		1944	200 ft (61 m)	64 ft (19.5 m)	1,000 tons	steel	lease	ex-AFD 29
AFDL 47	RELIANCE	1946	448 ft (136.6 m)	97 ft (29.6 m)	6,500 tons	steel	reserve	ex-ARD 33
AFDL 48	DILIGENCE	1956	402 ft (122.5 m)	96 ft (29.3 m)	4,000 tons	concrete	lease	

These are single section docks. Most were originally classified as Auxiliary Floating Dock (AFD) or Auxiliary Repair Dock—Concrete (ARDC).

Manning: The DYNAMIC is assigned 24 Navy personnel (1 officer + 23 enlisted). The crews for the other AFDLs are assigned to bases where they are located.

An LCU in the dry dock DYNAMIC (AFDL 6) at the Naval Amphibious Base Little Creek, Va. (1976, Giorgio Arra)

The AFDL 21 being towed by a harbor tug; note the keel blocks. (U.S. Navy)

5 MEDIUM AUXILIARY FLOATING DRY DOCKS

Number	Name	Completed	Length	Width	Capacity	Construction	Status	Notes
AFDM 1		1942	544 ft (165.8 m)	116 ft (35.4 m)	15,000 tons	steel	lease	3 sections; ex-YFD 3
AFDM 2		1942	544 ft (165.8 m)	116 ft (35.4 m)	15,000 tons	steel	lease	3 sections; ex-YFD 4
AFDM 3		1943	552 ft (168.2 m)	124 ft (37.8 m)	18,000 tons	steel	lease	3 sections; ex-YFD 6
AFDM 5	RESOURCEFUL	1943	552 ft (168.2 m)	124 ft (37.8 m)	18,000 tons	steel	Subic Bay, Philippines	3 sections; ex-YFD 21
AFDM 6	COMPETENT	1944	552 ft (168.2 m)	124 ft (37.8 m)	18,000 tons	steel	Pearl Harbor	3 sections; ex-YFD 62
AFDM 7	SUSTAIN	1945	552 ft (168.2 m)	124 ft (37.8 m)	18,000 tons	steel	Norfolk, Va.	3 sections; ex-YFD 63
AFDM 8	RICHLAND	1944	552 ft (168.2 m)	124 ft (37.8 m)	18,000 tons	steel	Guam, Marianas	3 sections; ex-YFD 64
AFDM 9		1945	552 ft (168.2 m)	124 ft (37.8 m)	18,000 tons	steel	lease	3 sections; ex-YFD 65
AFDM 10	RESOLUTE	1945	552 ft (168.2 m)	124 ft (37.8 m)	18,000 tons	steel	lease	3 sections; ex-YFD 67
AFDM 14	STEADFAST	1946	528 ft (161.0 m)	118 ft (36.0 m)	14,000 tons	steel	active	3 sections; ex-YFD 71

These are multi-section docks. All were originally classified as floating dry dock (YFD), informally known as yard floating dry docks.

Manning: The following personnel are assigned to these docks:

	Total	Officers	Enlisted
AFDM 6	149	5	144
AFDM 7	143	4	139
AFDM 10	147	5	142
AFDM 14	70	3	67

The COMPETENT (AFDM 6) at Subic Bay; note the travelling cranes on the dock walls. (U.S. Navy)

An LCU in an AFDM-type floating dry dock. (1979, Giorgio Arra)

3 AUXILIARY REPAIR DOCKS

Number	Name	Completed	Length	Width	Capacity	Construction	Status
ARD 5	WATERFORD	1942	485⅔ ft (148 m)	71 ft (21.6 m)	3,500 tons	steel	New London, Conn.
ARD 7	WEST MILTON	1943	485⅔ ft (148 m)	71 ft (21.6 m)	3,500 tons	steel	reserve
ARD 12		1943	491⅔ ft (149.9 m)	81 ft (24.7 m)	3,500 tons	steel	lease
ARD 30	SAN ONOFRE	1944	491⅔ ft (149.9 m)	81 ft (24.7 m)	3,600 tons	steel	Pearl Harbor, Hawaii
ARD 32		1944	491⅔ ft (149.9 m)	81 ft (24.7 m)	3,500 tons	steel	lease

Manning: The ARD 5 is assigned 81 Navy personnel (5 officers + 76 enlisted) and the ARD 30 is assigned 101 (5 officers + 96 enlisted).

4 + 1 MEDIUM AUXILIARY REPAIR DOCKS

Number	Name	Completed	Length	Width	Capacity	Construction	Status	Notes
ARDM 1	OAK RIDGE	1944	536 ft (163.4 m)	81 ft (24.7 m)	3,500 tons	steel	King's Bay, Ga.	ex-ARD 19
ARDM 2	ALAMOGORDO	1944	491⅔ ft (149.9 m)	81 ft (24.7 m)	3,500 tons	steel	Charleston, S.C.	ex-ARD 26
ARDM 3	ENDURANCE	1944	491⅔ ft (149.9 m)	81 ft (24.7 m)	3,500 tons	steel	Charleston, S.C.	ex-ARD 18
ARDM 4	SHIPPINGPORT	1978	492 ft (150 m)	96 ft (29.3 m)	7,800 tons	steel	New London, Conn.	FY 1975 program
ARDM 5		(1985)	492 ft (150 m)	96 ft (29.3 m)	7,800 tons	steel	building	FY 1983 program
ARDM 6		(1987)	492 ft (150 m)	96 ft (29.3 m)	7,800 tons	steel	building	FY 1984 program

The ARDM 1–3 were extensively modified from Auxiliary Repair Docks (ARD) to support ballistic missile submarines. The SHIPPINGPORT and ARDM 5 were designed specifically for this role. The ARDM 4 was built at Bethlehem Steel, Sparrows Point, Md., and the ARDM 5 at Todd Shipyards, Seattle, Wash.

The OAK RIDGE was moved from Rota, Spain, to Kings Bay, Ga., to support Submarine Squadron 16 when that unit shifted in 1979.

Manning: The ARDM 1 and 2 are each assigned 179 Navy personnel (5 officers + 174 enlisted) while the ARDM 4 is assigned 82 (5 officers + 77 enlisted).

The OAK RIDGE (ARDM 1), while at Rota, Spain, servicing an SSBN. The dock has now shifted to the submarine facility at King's Bay, Ga. (U.S. Navy)

An ARDM-type dry dock under tow. She has a ship-like bow with forward bridge structure; cranes travel along the dock walls. (U.S. Navy)

2 YARD FLOATING DRY DOCKS

Number	Completed	Length	Width	Capacity	Construction	Status	Notes
YFD 23	1943	472 ft (143.9 m)	114 ft (34.7 m)	10,500 tons	wood	lease	6 sections
YFD 54	1943	352 ft (107.3 m)	90 ft (27.4 m)	5,000 tons	wood	lease	1 section
YFD 68	1945	528 ft (160.9 m)	118 ft (36 m)	14,000 tons	steel	lease	3 sections
YFD 69	1945	528 ft (160.9 m)	118 ft (36 m)	14,000 tons	steel	lease	3 sections
YFD 70	1945	528 ft (160.9 m)	118 ft (36 m)	14,000 tons	steel	lease	3 sections
YFD 71	1945	528 ft (160.9 m)	118 ft (36 m)	14,000 tons	steel	San Diego, Calif.	3 sections
YFD 83	1943	200 ft (61.0 m)	64 ft (19.5 m)	1,000 tons	steel	U.S. Coast Guard; Curtis Bay, Md.	ex-AFDL 31

BOW DRY DOCKS

The bow dry dock program (YBD 1–4) was cancelled in 1979. These docks were to have been 104 feet long and 84 feet wide and would have permitted the partial docking of surface combatants for maintenance on SQS-23/26/53 bow sonar domes.

The program was cancelled because of reduced maintenance requirements on the sonar domes and the need to fully dock ships for other reasons. (See 11th edition of *Ships and Aircraft*, page 247, for additional details.)

27 Submersibles

Several submersibles are operated by the U.S. Navy to support search, rescue, research, and deep-ocean recovery activities. These craft have also been employed to maintain sea-floor test range and acoustic surveillance equipment.

Submarine Development Group 1 at Point Loma (San Diego) operates the rescue submersibles AVALON and MYSTIC, and the research submersibles SEA CLIFF and TURTLE. SubDevGru-1 also controls the submarines SEAWOLF (SSN 575), POGY (SSN 647), PARCHE (SSN 683), and DOLPHIN (AGSS 555); the support ship POINT LOMA (AGDS 2); the submarine rescue ships FLORIKAN (ASR 9) and PIGEON (ASR 21); and the diving-test range support ship ELK RIVER (IX 501).

Submarine Squadron 2 at the Naval Submarine Base New London (Groton, Conn.) operates the nuclear submersible NR-1 as well as a number of attack submarines.

The research submersible ALVIN is operated by the Woods Hole Oceanographic Institution in Massachusetts.

The rescue submersible AVALON mated to the after deck of the attack submarine CAVALLA (SSN 684) at Pearl Harbor. The Navy's two DSRVs provide a rescue capability for submarines disabled on the ocean floor above their collapse depth. The DSRVs can be carried by submarines and the Navy's two PIGEON (ASR 21)-class submarine rescue ships. (1981, U.S. Navy, PH1 Terry Mitchell)

NUCLEAR-PROPELLED RESEARCH VEHICLE: HTV/NR-2 DESIGN

Displacement:
Length: 153 feet (46.7 m) oa
Beam: 14½ feet (4.4 m)
Draft:
Propulsion: electric motors; 2 shafts
Reactors: 1 pressurized-water
Speed:
Operating depth: 3,000 + feet (915 + m)
Manning:

The so-called Hull Test Vehicle (HTV) was originally proposed as the NR-2 in 1976 by Admiral H. G. Rickover, then head of the Navy's nuclear-propulsion program, to provide a deep-ocean test platform for a nuclear reactor and a work submersible. Subsequently, the craft was redesignated HTV to emphasize its use of HY-130 steel. However, neither the Navy nor Congress would support the NR-2 at that time.

Since the THRESHER (SSN 593) the U.S. Navy has used HY-80 steel for submarine construction.[1] (The previous SKIPJACK/SSN 585 class apparently had some HY-80 steel.) The Soviets appear to have gone to stronger steels, even before the titanium-hull submarine Alfa, which can operate to at least 2,000 feet. The LOS ANGELES (SSN 688) was to have had HY-130 steel, but for several reasons, including weight considerations, she too was built with HY-80 steel.

Subsequently, about 1978 the Navy's leadership decided to proceed with the craft as a hull test vehicle to test the suitability of HY-130 steel for submarines.[2] But in 1983 the Navy's leadership decided that instead of constructing the nuclear-powered HTV, sections of HY-130 would be added to the conventional deep-diving research submarine DOLPHIN. In addition, the Navy has fabricated three portions of submarine hull of HY-130 steel. It is hoped that these efforts will lead to certification of HY-130. The later units of the planned SSN-21 class are to have HY-100 steel. The earlier submarines of that class, however, will be made of HY-80 steel.

[1] HY indicates high yield, with 80 indicating the steel can withstand 80,000 pounds of pressure per square inch.

[2] HY-140 was used for the small pressure capsules of the deep submergence rescue vehicles (DSRV-1 and -2).

1 NUCLEAR-PROPELLED RESEARCH SUBMERSIBLE: NR-1

Number	Name	Launched	In service
NR-1	(none)	25 Jan 1969	27 Oct 1969

Builders: General Dynamics/Electric Boat, Groton, Conn.
Displacement:
                   372 tons submerged
Length: 136⁵⁄₁₂ feet (41.6 m) oa
Beam: 12⁵⁄₁₂ feet (3.8 m)
Draft: 15¹⁄₁₂ feet (4.6 m)
Propulsion: electric motors; 2 shafts
Reactors: 1 pressurized-water
Speed: 4.6 knots surface
                   3.6 knots submerged
Operating depth: approx. 3,000 feet (915 m)
Crew: 5 (2 officers + 3 enlisted) + 2 scientists

The NR-1 was built as a test platform for a small submarine nuclear power plant. The craft has a deep-ocean research and recovery capability. The craft was funded as a nuclear-propulsion effort and was laid down on 10 June 1967. She is commanded by an officer-in-charge rather than a commanding officer.

Classification: NR-1 indicates Nuclear Research vehicle although the craft is officially listed as a submersible research vehicle.

Costs: The estimated cost of the NR-1 in 1965 was $30 million, using "state of the art" equipment. Subsequently, specialized equipment had to be developed and a hull larger than the one originally intended was designed, with congressional approval of a cost of $58 million being given in 1967. The estimated cost of the NR-1 when launched in 1969 was $67.5 million plus $19.9 million for oceanographic equipment and sensors, and $11.8 million for research and development, a total cost of $99.2 million. No final cost data have been released by the Navy.

Design: The NR-1 does not have periscopes, but instead has a fixed mast with a top-mounted television camera. The craft is fitted with external lights, a remote-control manipulator, and recovery devices.

Three bunks are provided; crew endurance is limited to 30-day missions. There is a warming oven for frozen foods and a hot-drink dispenser.

The NR-1 under tow. The submersible has been most useful for underwater search, recovery, and maintenance activities. Her superstructure and upper rudder are painted international orange. The masts are fixed. (U.S. Navy)

Electronics: Provided with forward- and side-looking sonars; a doppler sonar measures over-bottom speed.

Engineering: The NR-1 is propelled by twin propellers driven by electric motors outside of the pressure hull. Four ducted thrusters, two horizontal and two vertical, give the NR-1 a capability for precise maneuvering. Bottom wheels are installed. The craft is also fitted with lead shot ballast (22,000 pounds).

Operations: Published reports credit the NR-1 with having been used to maintain sea-floor equipment and to recover items sunk at great depths. In 1976 the NR-1 helped to recover an F-14 Tomcat fighter armed with a Phoenix missile that rolled off the deck of the carrier JOHN F. KENNEDY (CV 67) and came to rest at a depth of 1,960 feet off the coast of Scotland.

The NR-1 being helped by a harbor tug at the Naval Submarine Base New London, Conn. (1976, U.S. Navy)

The NR-1 under tow. Crewmen on the bow and on her diminutive bridge indicate the craft's small size. (U.S. Navy)

2 DEEP SUBMERGENCE RESCUE VEHICLES

Number	Name	Launched	Completed
DSRV-1	MYSTIC	24 Jan 1970	6 Aug 1971
DSRV-2	AVALON	1 May 1971	28 July 1972

Builders:	Lockheed Missiles and Space Co, Sunnyvale, Calif.
Weight:	37 tons
Length:	49⅔ feet (15 m) oa
Diameter:	8 feet (2.4 m)
Propulsion:	electric motor; 1 propeller-mounted in control shroud (see Engineering notes)
Speed:	4 knots
Operating depth:	5,000 feet (1,524 m)
Manning:	3 + 24 rescuees

These submersibles were developed after the loss of the submarine THRESHER in 1963 to provide a capability for rescuing survivors from submarines disabled on the ocean floor above their hull collapse depth. Initially 12 rescue vehicles were planned, each capable of carrying 12 survivors. Subsequently, their capability was increased to 24 survivors and the proposed number of DSRVs was reduced to six. Only two have been built and no additional units are planned. After extensive tests and evaluation, both DSRVs were declared fully operational in late 1977.

Costs: The estimated construction cost of the DSRV-1 was $41 million, and the DSRV-2 cost $23 million. The total development, construction, test, and support for these craft have cost in excess of $220 million.

Design: The DSRV consists of three interconnected personnel spheres, each 7½ feet in diameter, constructed of HY-140 steel, encased in a fiberglass-reinforced plastic shell. The forward sphere contains the vehicle's controls and is manned by the pilot and co-pilot; the center and after spheres can accommodate 24 survivors and a third crewman.

The DSRVs can mate with all U.S. submarines except the DOLPHIN and NR-1.

The DSRV is configured to be launched and recovered by a submerged attack submarine or by a PIGEON (ASR 21)-class submarine rescue ship. After launching, the DSRV can descend to the disabled submarine, "mate" with one of the submarine's escape hatches, take on board up to 24 survivors, and return to the "mother" submarine or ASR. The submersible can be air-transported in C-141 or C-5A aircraft, and ground-transported by a special trailer. It is fitted with a remote-control manipulator.

Electronics: The DSRV is fitted with elaborate search and navigation sonars, closed-circuit television, and optical viewing devices for locating a disabled submarine and mating with the hatches.

Engineering: The DSRVs have a single propeller driven by a 15-hp electric motor for forward propulsion. The propeller is in a rotating control shroud which alleviates the need for rudders and diving planes (which could interfere with a rescue mission). Four ducted thrusters, two vertical and two horizontal, each powered by a 7½-hp electric motor, provide precise maneuvering. The craft has an endurance of 5 hours at a speed of 4 knots.

Names: Names were assigned in 1977.

Operational: The DSRV rapid-deployment concept has been tested periodically from U.S. nuclear attack submarines, and in 1979 the AVALON was flown by C-5A from San Diego to Glasgow, Scotland, for deployment aboard the British SSBN REPULSE.

The AVALON being lowered onto the after deck of the CAVALLA; the pylons are transported with the DSRV and can be rapidly installed on the carrying submarine. The DSRV's mating skirt, below the craft's single access hatch, will mate with the SSN's after hatch to provide free access between the two while submerged. (1981, U.S. Navy, PH1 Terry Mitchell)

The AVALON on board the REPULSE, fitted with her mating skirt and ready for a rescue exercise. (1979, U.S. Navy)

The AVALON, mounted on a truck trailer, is eased out of a C-5A Galaxy transport at Hickam Air Force Base on Oahu. The AVALON, mounted on the trailer, will be towed to the nearby Pearl Harbor base for a submarine exercise. The mating skirt and certain other equipment are removed for carrying on the trailer. Note the propeller and circular rudder; the dark openings forward and aft are for through-hull ducted thrusters. (1981, U.S. Navy, PH1 Terry Mitchell)

The DSRV AVALON being loaded aboard the British SSBN REPULSE in the Firth of Clyde, Scotland. The DSRV can be carried by U.S. and British submarines and can mate with most of the world's submarines for rescue purposes. The DOLPHIN and NR-1 are the only U.S. submarines that are not compatible with the DSRVs.

2 RESEARCH SUBMERSIBLES: MODIFIED "ALVIN" CLASS

Number	Name	Launched	Completed
DSV-3	Turtle	11 Dec 1968	1969
DSV-4	Sea Cliff	11 Dec 1968	1969

Builders:	General Dynamics/Electric Boat, Groton, Conn.
Weight:	21 tons
Length:	26 feet (7.9 m) oa
Beam:	8 feet (2.4 m); 12 feet (3.7 m) over propeller pods
Propulsion:	electric motor; 1 propeller (see Engineering notes)
Speed:	2.5 knots
Operating depth:	Turtle 10,000 feet (3,048 m)
	Sea Cliff 20,000 feet (6,096 m)
Manning:	2 + 1 scientist

The after end of the Sea Cliff being hoisted aboard ship. Note the shrouded main propeller and two small propulsors. (1970, General Dynamics/Electric Boat)

These are small submersibles used for deep-ocean research. They were originally constructed using an HY-100 steel test sphere and an HY-100 replacement sphere originally fabricated for the Alvin. Their operating depth with the HY-100 spheres was 6,500 feet; subsequently, in 1979 the Turtle was refitted with a modified sphere providing a 10,000-foot operating depth and the Sea Cliff was fitted with a titanium sphere in 1981–1983 for 20,000-foot operations.

Classification: These craft were designated DSV-3 and DSV-4 on 1 June 1971.

Design: The original HY-100 steel spheres were seven feet in diameter. A light, fiberglass outer hull is fitted to the spheres. The craft have closed-circuit television, external lights, sonars, cameras, and hydraulic remote-control manipulators.

These craft can be transported by C-5A transports.

Engineering: A single stern propeller is fitted for ahead propulsion and two pod-mounted external electric motors rotate for maneuvering. No thrusters are fitted. Endurance is one hour at 2.5 knots and eight hours at one knot.

Names: During construction these submersibles were named the AUTEC I and II, respectively, because they were initially to be used to support the Navy's Atlantic Undersea Test and Evaluation Center (AUTEC). The names Turtle and Sea Cliff were assigned at their joint launching.

1 RESEARCH SUBMERSIBLE: "ALVIN"

Number	Name	Launched	Completed
DSV-2	Alvin	5 June 1964	1965

Builders:	General Mills Inc, Minneapolis, Minn.
Weight:	16 tons
Length:	22½ feet (6.9 m) oa
Beam:	8 feet (2.4 m); 12 feet (3.7 m) over propeller pods
Propulsion:	electric motor; 1 propeller (see Engineering notes)
Speed:	2 knots
Operating depth:	13,124 feet (4,000 m)
Manning:	1 + 2 scientists

The Alvin is operated by the Woods Hole Oceanographic Institution for the Office of Naval Research, which sponsored construction of the craft.

The Alvin accidentally sank in 5,051 feet of water on 16 October 1968 and her sphere was flooded (there were no casualties). She was raised in August 1969 and refurbished from May 1971 to October 1972, and became operational in November 1972.

Classification: Classified DSV-2 on 1 June 1971.

Design: As built, the Alvin had a single, 7-foot-diameter pressure sphere made of HY-100 steel, which gave her a 6,000-foot operating depth. She was refitted with a titanium sphere in 1971–1972, which increased her capabilities. She is fitted with a remote-control manipulator.

Engineering: See the Turtle and Sea Cliff for propulsion and maneuvering arrangement.

Operational: The Alvin made her 1,000th dive on 15 January 1980. The dive was part of NOAA studies of the intersection of the Ecuador Rift just north of the equator in the Pacific Ocean.

A dated view of the ALVIN (U.S. Navy)

The ALVIN being hoisted onto a support ship. (Woods Hole Oceanographic Institution)

1 BATHYSCAPH RESEARCH VEHICLE: "TRIESTE II"

Number	Name	Launched	Completed
DSV-1	TRIESTE II	(see comments)	1966

Builders:	Mare Island Naval Shipyard
Displacement:	84 tons surface (empty)
	300 tons submerged
Length:	78 feet (23.8 m) oa
Beam:	15 feet (4.6 m); 18¾ feet (5.7 m) over propeller pods
Propulsion:	electric motors; 3 propeller pods aft
Speed:	2 knots
Operating depth:	20,000 feet (6,096 m)
Manning:	2 + 1 scientist

The TRIESTE is the U.S. Navy's only "bathyscaph" (from the Greek for "deep boat"), designed to travel straight up and down in the water rather than maneuver like a submarine. The TRIESTE II was taken out of service on 18 May 1984. The craft's future disposition has not been determined.

The original TRIESTE was built by Auguste Piccard in Italy and launched on 1 August 1953. That vehicle was acquired by the Navy in 1958 and, piloted by Lieutenant Don Walsh, USN, and Jacques Piccard, reached a depth of 35,800 feet on 23 January 1960. The craft was rebuilt in 1963–1964 at the Mare Island Naval Shipyard, with a new sphere replacing the deep-dive Krupp chamber and a new float provided. In this configuration the craft was renamed TRIESTE II. The craft was again rebuilt in 1965–1966 and modified in 1967, all at Mare Island. Thus, the current vehicle is the "third generation-plus" bathyscaph.

Classification: The TRIESTE originally was classified as an unnumbered "submersible craft." She was assigned the hull number X 2 on 1 September 1969 and was subsequently changed to DSV 1 on 1 June 1971. (The X 1 was an unnamed midget submarine, the only craft of this type built for the U.S. Navy. That X 1 was stricken on 16 February 1973.)

Design: The TRIESTE II has a single, 7-foot-diameter pressure sphere, made of HY-120 steel. Originally rated for 12,000 feet, with the updating of certain subsystems the sphere and vehicle are now capable of 20,000-foot operations. The sphere is mounted at the bottom of a float-like hull which is filled with aviation gasoline to provide buoyancy. External lights, sonar, cameras, and a remote-control manipulator are fitted to the bottom of the float. "Leg"-like structures on each side of the sphere prevent it from sinking into the ocean floor and blocking the viewport (forward).

Engineering: The craft has three 6.5-hp electric motor pods at her stern for propulsion and limited maneuvering, and one 6.5-hp bow thruster for holding position in currents and for precise maneuvering. Her endurance is eight hours at two knots.

Names: TRIESTE was Piccard's name for the original craft.

TRIESTE II (U.S. Navy)

The TRIESTE II on the surface shows little of her hull; thrusters for maneuvering are visible forwards and aft. Her 20,000-foot depth capability permitted her to reach about 98 percent of the ocean floor. (U.S. Navy)

28 Naval Aviation

U.S. Naval Aviation operates approximately 6,300 aircraft, more than any of the world's air forces except for those of the United States, Soviet Union, and China. The generic term *naval aviation* includes the air arm of the U.S. Marine Corps, which is the only marine force in the world with a major aviation component. (Britain's Royal Marines and the Soviet Union's Naval Infantry both fly small numbers of helicopters.)

UNIT DESIGNATIONS

Naval Aviation units are designated in two systems of abbreviations— pronounceable acronyms and simpler, letter-number combinations. Thus, Training Squadron Eight is known as both TraRon-Eight and VT-8.

The V prefix for naval aircraft types and subsequently for aviation units dates from July 1920 when V was used to indicate heavier-than-air and Z for lighter-than-air blimps or airships. Thus, VF indicates fighter squadron, VA attack squadron, ZP airship patrol squadron, etc. (The last U.S. Navy airship, a Goodyear ZPG-2W, was decommissioned in 1962). Subsequently, H was introduced as the helicopter type letter in 1943 for aircraft (Sikorsky HNS-1) and for squadrons in 1944.[1]

Marine units have the letter M inserted as the second letter of unit designations.

The following are the aircraft squadron designations currently in use. Marine squadrons add a T suffix for readiness/transition units.

HC	Helicopter Combat Support
HM	Helicopter Mine Countermeasures
HMA	(Marine) Helicopter Attack
HMA/L	(Marine) Helicopter Attack/Light
HMH	(Marine) Helicopter Heavy
HML	(Marine) Helicopter Light
HMM	(Marine) Helicopter Medium
HMX	(Marine) Helicopter
HS	Helicopter Anti-Submarine
HSL	Helicopter Anti-Submarine, Light
HT	Helicopter Training
VA	Attack

VAK	Aerial Refueling
VAQ	Tactical Electronic Warfare
VAW	Carrier Airborne Early Warning
VC	Fleet Composite
VF	Fighter
VFA	Strike Fighter
VFP	Light Photographic
VMA	(Marine) Attack
VMA(AW)	(Marine) Attack (All Weather)
VMAQ	(Marine) Tactical Electronic Warfare
VMFA	(Marine) Fighter-Attack
VMFP	(Marine) Tactical Reconnaissance
VMGR	(Marine) Aerial Refueler-Transport
VMO	(Marine) Observation
VP	Patrol
VQ	Fleet Air Reconnaissance
VR	Fleet Logistics Support
VRC	Fleet Tactical Support (COD)
VRF	Aircraft Ferry
VS	Air Anti-Submarine
VT	Training
VX	Air Test and Evaluation
VXE	Antarctic Development
VXN	Oceanographic Development

Other major naval aviation organizational and installation abbreviations used in this volume are:

CVW	Carrier Air Wing
FRS	Fleet Readiness Squadron
MAG	Marine Aircraft Group
MAW	Marine Aircraft Wing
MCAF	Marine Corps Air Facility
MCAS	Marine Corps Air Station
MCCRTG	Marine Combat Crew Readiness Training Group
NAF	Naval Air Facility
NAR	Naval Air Reserve[2]
NAS	Naval Air Station
PatWing	Patrol Wing

---

[1] The H, V, and Z were also used for ship designations, hence CV for aircraft carrier, AV for seaplane tender, and AZ for airship tender; later the H was used in CVHA and CVHE to indicate helicopter carriers and in LPH, LHD, and LHA for helicopter-capable amphibious ships.

[2] Formerly Naval Air Reserve Unit (NARU); changed to NAR on 1 April 1983.

A variety of aircraft are embarked in U.S. carriers. In this view of the ENTERPRISE, when she embarked Carrier Air Wing 14, an A-7E Corsair light attack aircraft is in the foreground (others are parked in the background); at left are A-6E Intruder medium attack aircraft and EA-6B Prowler electronic warfare aircraft. The iron cross on the nose of an EA-6B helps the landing signal officer distinguish it from an A-6E during landing approach. (U.S. Navy)

ORGANIZATION

All naval aviation units belong to an administrative organization with most units also assigned to operational organizations. For example, a patrol squadron is administratively under a patrol wing while at its home base; while forward deployed the squadron would come under a different (overseas) wing or a fleet commander. Similarly, a carrier-based fighter squadron is under the fighter wing commander (administrative) while ashore and under the carrier air wing commander (operational) when aboard ship.

The administrative organization is headed by the Deputy Chief of Naval Operations (Air Warfare) and extends through the Commander Naval Air Force, Atlantic Fleet (NavAirLant) and Commander Naval Air Force, Pacific Fleet (NavAirPac) and their respective wing commanders. In addition, carrier groups and their assigned carriers are part of the naval air organization (see Chapter 3).

The following are the principal Navy air organizations:

Naval Air Force, Atlantic Fleet	Norfolk, Va.
Sea-Based ASW Wings Atlantic	Jacksonville, Fla.
Air ASW Wing 1	Cecil Field, Fla.
Helicopter ASW Wing 1	Jacksonville, Fla.
Helicopter Sea Control Wing 1	Norfolk, Va.
Tactical Wings Atlantic	Oceana, Va.
Fighter Wing 1	Oceana, Va.
Light Attack Wing 1	Cecil Field, Fla.

Medium Attack Wing 1	Oceana, Va.
Carrier AEW Wing 12	Norfolk, Va.
Patrol Wings Atlantic	Brunswick, Me.
Patrol Wing 5	Brunswick, Me.
Patrol Wing 11	Jacksonville, Fla.
Fleet Tactical Support Wing 1	Norfolk, Va.
Helicopter Tactical Wing 1	Norfolk, Va.
Naval Air Force, Pacific Fleet	North Island (San Diego), Calif.
Anti-Submarine Warfare Wing Pacific	North Island, Calif.
Fighter/Airborne Early Warning Wing Pacific	Miramar, Calif.
Light Attack Wing Pacific	Lemoore, Calif.
Medium Attack/Tactical EW Wing Pacific	Whidbey Island, Wash.
Patrol Wings Pacific	Moffett Field, Calif.
Patrol Wing 1	Kamiseya, Japan
Patrol Wing 2	Barber's Point, Hawaii
Patrol Wing 10	Moffett Field, Calif.
Fleet Air Western Pacific	Atsugi, Japan

UNIT CODES

All naval aviation organizations have letter or number-letter identification codes that are displayed on aircraft tail fins and, in some marking schemes, on wings. Navy carrier wings, Navy non-carrier wing squadrons, and Marine squadrons have individual letter codes.

The system was established in 1946 and revised on 1 June 1957 to the current fleet "split," with the first letter indicating the fleet assignment: A to M for Atlantic and N to Z for Pacific. The letters I and O are not used to avoid confusion with numerals. AF was dropped because of confusion with Air Force (used by Carrier Air Group 6, which then took code letter AE, which had previously been used by Carrier Air Group 13).

CARRIER AIR WINGS

The Navy currently has 13 active carrier air wings. During most of the 1970s the Navy had operated 13 carriers with only 12 wings. A 14th wing is scheduled to be activated about 1988 when the carrier THEODORE ROOSEVELT becomes operational. A 15th air wing may be established in the early 1990s should the Navy achieve a 15-carrier force. Alternatively, because one carrier will normally be in long-term modernization (SLEP), the Naval Air Reserve could provide the 15th wing when required.

The designation carrier air wing (CVW) was established on 20 December 1963 in place of carrier air group (CVG).[3] CAG designations reached No. 153 with several gaps in the series. The designation ASW Carrier Air Group (CVSG) was established on 1 April 1960 for aircraft assigned to ASW carriers (CVS); they were phased out in the 1960s, the last such groups being decommissioned on 30 June 1973. They were numbered from CVSG-50 to CVSG-62.

Replacement Air Groups (RAG) became Combat Readiness Air Wings

[3]The term CAG for Commander Air Group is still used to indicate the wing commander.

(CRAW) in 1963 but were phased out over the next decade, the last on 30 June 1973. Their squadrons survive, referred to as Fleet Readiness Squadrons (FRS). They provide transition training to fleet aircraft and are generally assigned to specialized (type) wings under Naval Air Force Atlantic or Pacific.

The standard carrier air wing of the 1960s and early 1970s consisted of two fighter squadrons, two light attack squadrons, one heavy (later medium) attack squadron, and detachments (later squadrons) of Airborne Early Warning (AEW), electronic warfare, and reconnaissance aircraft. In the early 1970s, with the demise of the ASW aircraft carrier (CVS), fixed-wing and helicopter ASW squadrons (VS/HS) went aboard the larger ships that could accommodate the additional planes and provide an ASW tactical control center. These squadrons now fly the S-3A Viking and SH-3D/H Sea King, respectively. Subsequently, specialized reconnaissance aircraft were phased off carrier decks in the 1970s, the active fleet's last "recce" squadrons being RVAH-7 (RA-5C Vigilante), decommissioned on 30 September 1979, and VFP-63 (RF-8G Photo Crusader), decommissioned on 30 June 1982.

Marine RF-4B Phantoms have provided a very limited photographic reconnaissance capability aboard some carriers pending the availability in the early 1980s of a Tactical Air Reconnaissance Pod System (TARPS) for the F-14A Tomcat on the larger carriers. (The Naval Air Reserve continues to operate one small RF-8G squadron.)

Thus, into the mid-1980s the standard carrier air wing consisted of:

2 fighter squadrons (VF)	24 F-14A Tomcat
2 light attack squadrons (VA)	24 A-7E Crusader
1 medium attack squadron (VA)	10 A-6E Intruder + 4 KA-6D tankers
1 EW squadron (VAQ)	4 EA-6B Prowler
1 AEW squadron (VAW)	4 E-2C Hawkeye
1 air ASW squadron (VS)	10 S-3A Viking
1 helicopter ASW squadron (HS)	6 SH-3H Sea King

In addition, forward-deployed carriers generally operate one or two EA-3B Skywarrior aircraft in the ELINT role, these being assigned from fleet air reconnaissance squadrons VQ-1 in the Pacific area and VQ-2 in the Mediterranean area.

The availability of the F/A-18 Hornet from 1982 on is being reflected in most carriers being scheduled to gain two fighter-attack squadrons (VFA) in place of the A-7E squadrons, with the MIDWAY and CORAL SEA to also have VFA squadrons in place of their F-4 Phantom fighter squadrons (VF). Further, in early 1983 Secretary of the Navy Lehman directed that several air wing variations be tested: The JOHN F. KENNEDY has an "all" F-14A Tomcat and A-6E Intruder wing, without light attack aircraft; the CONSTELLATION has two F/A-18A Hornet squadrons in place of the two A-7E Corsair units. The CORAL SEA will work up with four squadrons of F/A-18s—two Marine fighter-attack squadrons (VMFA) and two Navy strike-fighter squadrons (VFA)—plus an A-6E unit.

At the same time, range problems with the F/A-18 have led to a decision to add an eleventh A-6E to the standard Intruder squadron (now ten aircraft) with improved refueling buddy-stores to be carried by the Intruders. Eventually, A-6E aircraft with these devices will replace the KA-6D dedicated tankers, giving the carrier wings more flexibility.

NAVY SQUADRONS

Squadron assignments to carrier air wings change periodically, while the shortage of special-mission aircraft (VAQ, VAW, VS, HS) force regular shifts of these squadrons among the air wings. Similarly, Marine RF-4B, F/A-18, EA-6B, and A-6E aircraft are sometimes assigned to air wings to compensate for naval aircraft shortfalls and scheduling problems. (Marine AV-8A Harriers have also flown from carriers.)

Air Wing	Code	Ship	Squadrons	
CVW-1	AB	AMERICA	VF-33	VAQ-136
			VF-102	VAW-123
			VA-34	VS-32
			VA-46	HS-11
			VA-72	
CVW-2	NE	KITTY HAWK	VF-1	VAQ-130
			VF-2	VAW-116
			VA-145	VS-38
			VA-146	HS-2
			VA-147	

The wing was formerly aboard the RANGER.

Air Wing	Code	Ship	Squadrons	
CVW-3	AC	JOHN F. KENNEDY	VF-11	VAQ-137
			VF-31	VAW-126
			VA-75	VS-22
			VA-85	HS-7

CVW-3 was reorganized in 1983 to evaluate an all A-6E attack capability, with the KENNEDY carrying no light attack squadrons.

Air Wing	Code	Ship	Squadrons	
CVW-4		Decommissioned 1 June 1970		
CVW-5	NF	MIDWAY	VF-151	VAQ-136
			VF-161	VAW-115
			VA-56	VMFP-3 Det.
			VA-93	HS-12
			VA-115	

The MIDWAY's air wing is based at NAS Atsugi, Japan. The wing had neither VS nor HS components because of the ship's size and lack of an ASW command center until 1984 when HS-12 with six SH-3H Sea King helicopters replaced a detachment from HC-1 that had provided four SH-3G Sea Kings for SAR and utility roles. A detachment of three Marine RF-4B Phantoms from VMFP-3 provided the ship with a limited photo-reconnaissance capability until HS-12 went aboard the ship.

Air Wing	Code	Ship	Squadrons	
CVW-6	AE	INDEPENDENCE	VF-14	VAQ-131
			VF-32	VAW-122
			VA-15	VS-28
			VA-87	HS-15
			VA-176	
CVW-7	AG	DWIGHT D. EISENHOWER	VF-142	VAQ-132
			VF-143	VAW-121
			VA-12	VS-31
			VA-65	HS-5
			VA-66	

Air Wing	Code	Ship	Squadrons	
CVW-8	AJ	NIMITZ	VF-41	VAQ-135
			VF-84	VAW-124
			VA-35	VS-24
			VA-82	HS-9
			VA-86	
CVW-9	NG	RANGER	VF-24	VAQ-138
			VF-211	VAW-112
			VA-165	VS-33
			VA-192	HS-8
			VA-195	

This wing shifted in 1982 from the CONSTELLATION to the RANGER with some change of squadrons.

Air Wing	Code	Ship	Squadrons	
CVW-10		Decommissioned 20 November 1969		
CVW-11	NH	ENTERPRISE	VF-114	VAQ-133
			VF-213	VS-21
			VA-22	HS-6
			VA-94	
			VA-95	

This wing, previously aboard the AMERICA, was assigned to the ENTERPRISE when she rejoined the fleet in 1982 after her extensive modernization.

Air Wing	Code	Ship	Squadrons	
CVW-12		Decommissioned 1 June 1970		
CVW-13		CORAL SEA	VFA-131	VAQ-139
			VFA-132	VAW-127
			VMFA-314	HS-17
			VMFA-323	
			VA-55	

CVW-13 was commissioned on 1 March 1984 at NAS Oceana for assignment to the CORAL SEA after her 1983 transfer to the Atlantic Fleet and 1984–1985 modernization. The previous CVG-13 had been decommissioned on 1 October 1962. The two Marine F/A-18 squadrons will serve in the CORAL SEA until 1985 when Navy VFA-136 and VFA-137 are formed for assignment to the ship. The CORAL SEA previously carried HS-12.

Air Wing	Code	Ship	Squadrons	
CVW-14	NK	CONSTELLATION	VF-21	VAW-113
			VF-154	HS-12
			VFA-25	
			VFA-113	
			VA-196	

The CVW-14 shifted from the CORAL SEA to the CONSTELLATION in 1983 when the former ship was shifted from the Pacific to Atlantic Fleets. The wing traded A-7E Corsairs for F/A-18 Hornets in the "strike" role.

Air Wing	Code	Ship	Squadrons	
CVW-15	NL	CARL VINSON	VF-51	VAQ-134
			VF-111	VAW-114
			VA-37	VS-29
			VA-52	HS-4
			VA-105	

The VINSON took on the KITTY HAWK's CVW-15 when the newer ship shifted to the Pacific Fleet in 1983.

CVW-16	Decommissioned 30 June 1971			

CVW-17	AA	SARATOGA	VF-74	VMAQ-2 Det.
			VF-103	VAW-125
			VA-81	VS-30
			VA-83	HS-3
			VMA(AW)-533	

CVW-17 shifted from the FORRESTAL to the SARATOGA when the former ship began SLEP modernization at the Philadelphia Naval Shipyard in 1982, ending three decades of the wing operating from CVA/CV 59. At that time VF-74 and VF-103 transitioned from the F-4S Phantom to the F-14A Tomcat. A Marine A-6E squadron and a Marine EA-6B detachment joined the wing to compensate for a shortfall of Navy squadrons. VA-85, the wing's former Intruder squadron, went aboard the KENNEDY with CVW-3 to provide an all A-6E attack force.

CVW-18	Not used

CVW-19	Decommissioned 30 June 1977

CVW-20	Not used

CVW-21	Decommissioned 12 December 1975

See page 363 for CVWR-20 and -30.

In the following tables the fleet squadrons normally assigned to carrier air wings are indicated by an asterisk.

ATTACK SQUADRONS

Squadron	Aircraft	Name
*VA-12	A-7E	Clinchers (ex-Flying Ubangis)
*VA-15	A-7E	Valions
*VA-22	A-7E	Fighting Redcocks
*VA-27	A-7E	Royal Maces
*VA-34	A-6E	Blue Blasters
*VA-35	A-6E	Black Panthers
*VA-37	A-7E	Bulls
VA-42	A-6E, TC-4C	Green Pawns (AD)
VA-45	TA-4J, A-4E	Blackbirds (AD)
*VA-46	A-7E	Clansmen
*VA-52	A-6E	Knightriders
*VA-55	A-6E	Warhorses
*VA-56	A-7E	Champions
*VA-65	A-6E	Tigers
*VA-66	A-7E	Waldomen
*VA-72	A-7E	Blue Hawks
*VA-75	A-6E	Sunday Punchers
*VA-81	A-7E	Sunliners
*VA-82	A-7E	Marauders
*VA-83	A-7E	Rampagers
*VA-85	A-6E	Black Falcons
*VA-86	A-7E	Sidewinders
*VA-87	A-7E	Golden Warriors
*VA-93	A-7E	Ravens
*VA-94	A-7E	Mighty Shrikes
*VA-95	A-6E	Green Lizards
*VA-97	A-7E	Warhawks
*VA-105	A-7E	Gunslingers
*VA-115	A-6E	Eagles
VA-122	A-7E, TA-7C	Flying Eagles (NJ)
VA-127	A-4F, TA-4F/J	Cylons (NJ)
VA-128	A-6E, TC-4C	Golden Intruders (NJ)
*VA-145	A-6E	Swordsmen
*VA-146	A-7E	Blue Diamonds
*VA-147	A-7E	Argonauts
*VA-165	A-6E	Boomers
VA-174	A-7E, TA-7C	Hell Razors (AD)
*VA-176	A-6E	Thunderbolts
*VA-192	A-7E	Golden Dragons
*VA-195	A-7E	Dam Busters
*VA-196	A-6E	Milestones (ex-Main Battery)

Each carrier nominally has three attack squadrons: two light attack (VAL) or strike fighter (VFA) squadrons and one medium attack (VAM) squadron. All light and medium squadrons are designated simply VA. The A-7E squadrons have 12 aircraft and the A-6E units have 10 aircraft. In addition, the latter squadrons have 4 KA-6D tankers. During the 1984 "all-medium" wing evaluation on the KENNEDY VA-75 had 10 A-6E and 5 KA-6D aircraft and VA-85 had 14 A-6E aircraft.

Beginning in June 1984 that Navy has provided light attack squadrons to support Marine operations in the Far East. VA-105 was the first squadron to so deploy, replacing VMA-21E as the light attack squadron of Marine Aircraft Group 12; VA-37 was to deploy in December 1984. The Marines were hard pressed to meet deployment schedules because of the transition from the A-4 to AV-8B.

The Navy plans to replace all A-7Es with the F/A-18 Hornet in strike fighter squadrons (VFA). These units are listed separately.

The Intruder squadrons are scheduled to receive a fifth KA-6D because of the fuel requirements of the F/A-18 Hornet. Subsequently, development of 400-gallon external tanks for the A-6E and more reliable in-flight "buddy stores" will permit A-6E aircraft to serve in the tanker role. This will alleviate the need for specialized tankers and the squadrons will increase up to 15 A-6E (or later) aircraft. VA-55, which had been deactivated in 1975, was recommissioned in 1983 for the new CVW-13, which will also have four VFA squadrons with F/A-18s.

Atlantic Fleet A-6E squadrons are based at NAS Oceana, Va., under Commander Medium Attack Wing 1 and A-7E squadrons are at NAS Cecil Field, Fla., under Commander Light Attack Wing 1. In the Pacific the A-6E units (as well as EA-6B Prowlers) are at NAS Whidbey Island, Wash., under Commander Medium Attack/VAQ Wing Pacific. The Pacific A-7E community is at NAS Lemoore, Calif., under Commander Light Attack Wing Pacific. The MIDWAY's VA-56, 93, and 115 are based at NAF Atsugi, Japan.

The VA Fleet Readiness Squadrons (FRS) are VA-42 at Oceana and VA-128 at Whidbey Island for the A-6E; VA-122 at Lemoore and VA-174 at Cecil Field for the A-7E; VA-45 at NAS Key West, Fla., for adversary training; and VA-127 at Lemoore for adversary training. Tail codes for readiness squadrons are indicated after the squadron names in the above table. Several TC-4C Academe trainers are flown by the Intruder fleet readiness squadron.

TACTICAL ELECTRONIC WARFARE SQUADRONS

Squadron	Aircraft	Name
VAQ-33	various	Fire Birds
VAQ-34	various	
VAQ-129	EA-6B	Red Devils (ex-Vikings) (NJ)
*VAQ-130	EA-6B	Zappers
*VAQ-131	EA-6B	Lancers
*VAQ-132	EA-6B	Scorpions
*VAQ-133	EA-6B	Wizards
*VAQ-134	EA-6B	Garudas
*VAQ-135	EA-6B	Black Ravens
*VAQ-136	EA-6B	Gauntlets
*VAQ-137	EA-6B	Rooks
*VAQ-138	EA-6B	Yellow Jackets
*VAQ-139	EA-6B	Cougars

There are 10 deployable fleet tactical EW squadrons (indicated by asterisk) with a 4-plane squadron normally assigned to each carrier air wing. These squadrons all fly the EA-6B Prowler, with VAQ-132 having been the first to receive the aircraft, in July 1971. VAQ-129 provides VAQ readiness training (code NJ).

The Navy's shortfall of VAQ squadrons has led to periodic deployments of Marine VMAQ detachments aboard carriers, initially with EA-6A Intruders and now EA-6B Prowlers. VAQ-139 was established in 1983 for the newly formed CVW-13.

All active EA-6B squadrons and one of two reserve units are based at NAS Whidbey Island, Wash., except for VAQ-136, assigned to the Japan-based MIDWAY. These squadrons report administratively to Commander Medium Attack/VAQ Wing Pacific.

VAQ-33 and -34 operate under Commander Fleet Electronic Warfare Support Group (FEWSG), established in 1968 to provide ECM training for naval forces. Their aircraft simulate Soviet electronic/jamming transmissions. VAQ-33 at NAS Key West flies the EA-6A, ERA-3B/TA-3B Skywarrior, EA-4F/TA-4J Skyhawk, and P-3A Orion aircraft; VAQ-34 at the Pacific Missile Test Center Point Mugu, Calif., has six EA-7L (ex-TA-7C) Corsairs plus ERA-3B/KA-3B Skywarriors. The latter squadron was commissioned on 1 March 1983. Both squadrons use FEWSG's tail code GD; FEWSG also controls the operations of the Navy's two NKC-135 electronic warfare aircraft (see description in Chapter 29).

VAQ-33 flew the last U.S. military "Connie" (Constellation), a Lockheed NC-121K Warning Star, which was retired on 25 June 1982. These four-engine, triple-tail aircraft had served in the Navy from 1949 onward with the designations PO-1W, then WV-1 and -2, and, after 1962, EC-121; weather reconnaissance versions flew as WV-3/WC-121; and the transport version was R7V-1 and -2/C-121. The Navy's Warning Stars flew an AEW ocean barrier until mid-1965.

Some VAQ squadrons are former heavy attack squadrons (VAH), having changed their designation to VAQ when they shifted from EKA-3B Skywarriors to EA-6B aircraft in the late 1960s; other VAQs were built up from EKA-3B detachments that operated from forward-deployed carriers.

AIRBORNE EARLY WARNING SQUADRONS

Squadron	Aircraft	Name
VAW-110	E-2B/C	Firebirds (NJ)
*VAW-112	E-2C	Golden Hawks
*VAW-113	E-2B	Black Eagles
*VAW-114	E-2C	Hormel Hawgs
*VAW-115	E-2C	Sentinels (ex-Liberty Bells)
*VAW-116	E-2C	Sun Kings
*VAW-117	E-2C	Wallbangers
VAW-120	E-2C	Greyhawks (ex-Hummers) (AD)
*VAW-121	E-2C	Bluetails
*VAW-122	E-2C	Steeljaws
*VAW-123	E-2C	Screwtops
*VAW-124	E-2	Bear Aces
*VAW-125	E-2	Torchbearers (ex-Tiger Tails)
*VAW-126	E-2	Seahawks
*VAW-127	E-2C	Seabats

Each carrier air wing has a 4-plane AEW squadron flying the E-2B or E-2C Hawkeye. RVAW-110's Detachment 4 flew the Navy's last E-1B Tracers from the FRANKLIN D. ROOSEVELT (CV 42) in 1977. VAW-127 was commissioned in September 1983 for the new CVW-13 and VAW-111 was scheduled for recommissioning in 1985. All AEW squadrons are scheduled to receive the E-2C.

Fleet readiness training is provided by VAW-110 for the Pacific Fleet and by VAW-120 for Atlantic squadrons. The two readiness squadrons were designated RVAW until 1 May 1983, when they dropped the R prefix; they were the only readiness squadrons with that prefix.

West Coast squadrons are based at NAS Miramar except VAW-115 at NAF Atsugi, all under Commander Fighter/AEW Wing Pacific; East Coast units are all at NAS Norfolk under Commander Tactical Wings Atlantic.

In addition to regular carrier deployments, VAW aircraft have operated from Keflavik, Iceland, to provide AEW coverage of the Greenland-Iceland-United Kingdom (GIUK) gap, and in Operation Thunderbolt, the U.S. Customs Service effort to intercept drug smugglers off the U.S. coasts.

The current VAW structure dates from 1967, when seven AEW squadrons numbered in sequence were established. Previously VAW-11, 12, 13, and 33 provided AEW detachments to carriers while Barrier Squadron Pacific and AEW Wing Atlantic operated land-based Warning Star aircraft as part of the North American air defense efforts until 1965 (see above).

FLEET COMPOSITE SQUADRONS

Squadron	Code	Aircraft	Name
VC-1	UA	TA-4J, UH-3A, SH-3G, P-3A, VP-3A	Blue Alii
VC-5	UE	A-4E, TA-4J, SH-3G	Checkertails
VC-6	JG	none assigned	Skeeters
VC-8	GF	TA-4J, SH-3G	Redtails
VC-10	JH	TA-4J	Challengers

Composite squadrons provide utility services for the Fleet, including "dissimilar" Air Combat Maneuvering (ACM), noncombat photography, aerial target services, radar calibration, and transport with two squadrons having combat missions; VC-1 and VC-10 have TA-4J two-seat Skyhawks with the additional role of air defense for the Hawaiian Islands and Guantanamo Bay, respectively. These squadrons originated with Navy utility squadrons (VJ and later VU), being changed to fleet composite squadrons (VC) on 1 July 1965.

VC-6 at NAS Norfolk, Va., flies no aircraft, but operates air and surface target drones—the BQM-74C aerial target and QST-33 and QST-35 Septar boats. There are permanent VC-6 detachments at the Fleet Combat Training Center in Dam Neck, Va., and at the Naval Amphibious Base Little Creek, Va. Five smaller VC-6 mobile detachments operate in the Atlantic–Mediterranean areas and periodically deploy with U.S. ships operating around South America in the UNITAS exercises. The squadron has a former PT-boat, the RETRIEVER (DR-1; see Chapter 25).

VC-1 is located at Barber's Point, Hawaii; VC-5 at Cubi Point in the Philippines, with a detachment at Poro Point; VC-8 at Roosevelt Roads, P.R.; and VC-10 at Guantanamo Bay, Cuba. VC-1 flies Orions in a VIP configuration to support the Commander in Chief Pacific Fleet; note that VC-5 has single-seat A-4Es. VC-10 has been at "Gitmo" since April 1945 (originally as VJ-16, changed to VU-10 in August 1946).

VC-2 (Oceana) and VC-7 (Miramar) were decommissioned in 1980, and VC-3 (North Island) was decommissioned in 1981; the last squadron flew DC-130A Hercules to launch aerial drones.

FIGHTER SQUADRONS

Squadron	Aircraft	Name
*VF-1	F-14A	Wolfpack
*VF-2	F-14A	Bounty Hunters
*VF-11	F-14A	Red Rippers
*VF-14	F-14A	Tophatters
*VF-21	F-14A	Freelancers
*VF-24	F-14A	Renegades (ex-Fighting Red Checkertails)
*VF-31	F-14A	Tomcatters
*VF-32	F-14A	Swordsmen
*VF-33	F-14A	Tarsiers
*VF-41	F-14A	Black Aces
VF-43	various	Challengers (AD)
*VF-51	F-14A	Screaming Eagles
*VF-74	F-14A	Bedevilers
*VF-84	F-14A	Jolly Rogers
VF-101	F-14A	Grim Reapers (AD)
*VF-102	F-14A	Diamondbacks
*VF-103	F-14A	Sluggers
*VF-111	F-14A	Sundowners
*VF-114	F-14A	Aardvarks
VF-124	F-14A	Gunfighters (NJ)
VF-126	various	Bandits (NJ)
*VF-142	F-14A	Ghostriders
*VF-143	F-14A	Puckin' Dogs
*VF-151	F-4S	Vigilantes
*VF-154	F-14A	Black Knights
*VF-161	F-4S	Chargers
*VF-211	F-14A	Checkmates
*VF-213	F-14A	Black Lions

The Navy has two fighter squadrons assigned to each of 12 carriers air wings, with one other wing having strike-fighter squadrons (VFA). All FORRESTAL and later carriers have two F-14 Tomcat squadrons, a revision of the pre-1981 plan for one large carrier in addition to the MIDWAY and CORAL SEA to have F/A-18s in their fighter squadrons. The MIDWAY has the Navy's last two Phantom squadrons (VF-151 and VF-161) and the CORAL SEA has two F/A-18 strike-fighter squadrons for the fighter role. The two MIDWAY squadrons will shift to the F/A-18 in 1986. The CORAL SEA's former F-4N Phantom squadrons, VF-21 and VF-154, transitioned to the F-14A for reassignment to the CONSTELLATION.

Included in 24 F-14A fighters, organized in two VF squadrons, each large carrier is receiving three F-14A aircraft fitted with the TARPS reconnaissance package. (The Navy's last carrier-based reconnaissance squadron, VFP-63, was disestablished 30 June 1982 following a final three-plane detachment deploying aboard the CORAL SEA. The squadron flew the RF-8G Photo Crusader, which survives in one reserve squadron.)

West Coast fighter squadrons are at NAS Miramar, except for VF-151 and VF-161 at NAF Atsugi, under Commander Fighter/AEW Wing Pacific; East Coast units are at NAS Oceana under Commander Fighter Wing 1.

Fleet readiness training is provided for the F-14 by VF-101 at Oceana and VF-124 at Miramar; VF-43 at Oceana provides adversary/ACM training; and VF-126 at Miramar undertakes instrument and adversary training. The adversary training squadrons fly the TA-4J and A-4E/F Skyhawks, and T-2C Buckeyes. (VF-43 also flies the F-5E Tiger II and T-38A Talon.) The last Phantom fleet readiness squadron was VF-171 (Aces), decommissioned on 1 June 1984 with all fleet readiness training in the Phantom being undertaken by VMFAT-101 at MCAS Yuma. When VF-171 went down it flew the F-4S model. VF-121, the West Coast F-4 readiness squadron, was decommissioned on 30 September 1980; had been the Navy's first F-4 squadron.

The Navy's Fighter Weapons School (Top Gun) at Miramar flies F-5E/F and A-4E/F aircraft. The school was established in September 1969 to develop realistic adversary tactics and training for Navy fliers. It was started as VF-121 and became a separate command on 1 July 1972.

STRIKE-FIGHTER SQUADRONS

Squadron	Aircraft	Name	Notes
*VFA-25	F/A-18A	Fist of the Fleet	formerly VA-25
VFA-106	F/A-18A	Gladiators	based on VA-106
*VFA-113	F/A-18A	Stingers	formerly VA-113
VFA-125	F/A-18A	Rough Raiders	
*VFA-131	F/A-18A	Wildcats	
*VFA-132	F/A-18A	Privateers	
*VFA-136	F/A-18A		to be formed 1985
*VFA-137	F/A-18A		to be formed 1985

The Navy's strike-fighter squadrons fly the F/A-18 Hornet. The first F/A-18 squadron was Fighter Attack Squadron 125, commissioned on 13 November 1980 as the Pacific Fleet's F/A-18 readiness squadron for

Navy and Marine pilots and ground crews (tail code NJ). The squadron has a Navy commanding officer and Marine executive officer. VFA-125's first aircraft was delivered in February 1981. The squadron is located at NAS Lemoore; the second F/A-18 readiness squadron, VFA-106, was commissioned on 27 April 1984 at NAS Cecil Field as the East Coast FRS.

VFA-113 was the Navy's first F/A-18 fleet squadron, transitioning from the A-7E to F/A-18 in March 1983, followed by VA/VFA-25 later that year. Both squadrons are assigned to the carrier CONSTELLATION. The next four Navy VFA squadrons—131, 132, 136, 137—go to the CORAL SEA the first two in 1985 with the completion of the CORAL SEA's modernization, when the ship will also embark two Marine F/A-18 squadrons pending availability of VFA-136 and VFA-137.

The Marine Corps has had fighter attack squadrons (VMFA) since the introduction of the F-4 Phantom into squadron service in 1963. The designation VFA originally indicated fighter attack squadron; changed in 1983 to strike-fighter to emphasize the attack role, as most units are being converted from VA squadrons.

PATROL SQUADRONS

Squadron	Code	Name
VP-1	YB	Screaming Eagles
VP-4	YD	Skinny Dragons
VP-5	LA	Mad Foxes
VP-6	PC	Blue Sharks
VP-8	LC	Tigers
VP-9	PD	Golden Eagles
VP-10	LD	Red Lancers
VP-11	LE	Proud Pegasus
VP-16	LF	Eagles
VP-17	ZE	White Lightning
VP-19	PE	Big Red
VP-22	QA	Blue Geese
VP-23	LJ	Sea Hawks
VP-24	LR	Batmen
VP-26	LK	Tridents
VP-30	LL	Crow's Nest
VP-31	RP	Black Lightning
VP-40	QE	Fighting Marlins
VP-44	LM	Golden Pelicans
VP-45	LN	Pelicans
VP-46	RC	Grey Knights
VP-47	RD	Golden Swordsmen
VP-48	SF	Boomerangers
VP-49	LP	Woodpeckers
VP-50	SG	Blue Dragons
VP-56	LQ	Dragons

The Navy's 24 first-line patrol squadrons each fly nine P-3B/C Orion aircraft. The last active squadron with the P-3A variant was VP-44, which completed conversion to the P-3C in November 1978. All active squadrons are to convert to the P-3C by 1987.

East Coast fleet squadrons are assigned to Patrol Wing 5 at Brunswick, Me., and PatWing-11 at Jacksonville, Fla. Their Orion squadrons deploy to the Atlantic and Mediterranean areas. West Coast operational

squadrons are assigned to Patrol Wing 10 at NAS Moffett near San Francisco and PatWing-2 at Barber's Point on Oahu, Hawaii. PatWing-1 at Kamiseya, Japan, directs VP squadrons that rotate to the Western Pacific from Patrol Wings 2 and 10.

VP-30 at NAS Jacksonville and VP-31 at NAS Moffett provide Orion readiness training.

FLEET AIR RECONNAISSANCE SQUADRONS

Squadron	Code	Aircraft	Name
VQ-1	PR	P-3B, EP-3B/E, EA-3B, VA-3B	World Watchers
VQ-2	JQ	P-3A, EP-3E, EA-3B	
VQ-3	TC	EC-130Q, KC-130F	TACOMOPAC
VQ-4	HL	EC-130G/Q, KC-103F	Shadows

VQ-1 and VQ-2 provide electronic surveillance in direct support of fleet operations and carry out special reconnaissance along the borders of foreign territory. VQ-1 an NAS Agana, Guam, and VQ-2 at Rota, Spain, fly ELINT-configured Orions and Skywarriors, the latter operating from forward-deployed carriers. Their Skywarriors are the last to fly with active Navy squadrons. There are 12 land-based EP-3 Orions in the two squadrons, all converted P-3A aircraft. An eventual force of 14 new EP-3 aircraft is programmed. There is no replacement planned for the EA-3B, which is expected to be in service into the 1990s. (An ES-3 variant of the Viking was proposed as a Skywarrior replacement.)

VQ-1 was established as Electronic Countermeasures Squadron 1 at NAS Iwakuni, Japan, on 1 June 1955, initially flying P4M-1Q Mercator aircraft. VQ was changed to Fleet Air Reconnaissance Squadron on 1 January 1960. VQ-2 was commissioned on 1 September 1955 as ECM Squadron 2 at NAS Port Lyautey, Morocco, flying the P2V Neptune.

VQ-3 and VQ-4 fly specially equipped Hercules transports to provide LF/VLF communications relay to strategic missile submarines under a program known as TACAMO (Take Charge and Move Out). A follow-on TACAMO aircraft is being developed, the E-6A, based on the Boeing 707/E-3A aircraft.

FLEET LOGISTIC SUPPORT SQUADRONS

Squadron	Code	Aircraft	Name
VR-24	JM	C-1A, C-2A, CT-39G, C-130	Lifting Eagles
VRC-30	RW	C-1A, UC-12B, CT-39E	Truckin' Traders
VRC-40	CD	C-1A, CT-39E	Codfish Airlines
VRC-50	RG	C-2A, CT-39E, KC-130F, US-3A	Foo Dogs

These squadrons carry passengers and high-priority cargo in direct support of fleet operations. Overseas transport for the Navy is provided mainly by the Air Force-operated Military Aircraft Command (MAC) while transport requirements within the United States are fulfilled by the Naval Air Reserve, which regularly operates overseas as well. The VR squadrons were formerly Transport Squadrons (VR) and then Fleet Tactical Support Squadrons (VR), being changed to their current designation on 1 April 1976.

The UC-12, CT-39, and C-130 are land-based aircraft; neither the carrier-capable piston-engine C-1A nor turboprop C-2A are based aboard ship, the former because carriers store all-jet aircraft fuels and the latter because of its size. The four US-3A versions of the S-3A Viking fly long-range COD flights in the Western Pacific and Indian Ocean. (Two more are being converted.) VR-24 previously flew RH-53D Sea Stallion helicopters to provide Vertical Replenishment (VERTREP) support to the Sixth Fleet. That role has been taken over by HC-4, commissioned in 1983 at NAS Sigonella, Sicily.

VR-24 is based at Sigonella, Sicily, with its C-130s permanently based at Rota, Spain, with the squadron assigned to Fleet Air Mediterranean; VRC-30 at North Island under ASW Wing Pacific; VRC-40 at Norfolk under Fleet Tactical Support Wing 1; and VRC-50 at Cubi Point in the Philippines, under Fleet Air Western Pacific. VR-24 was previously nicknamed World's Biggest Little Airline; changed in early 1984.

VRC-30 and VRC-40 provide fleet readiness training for COD aircraft in their respective fleets.

AIRCRAFT FERRY SQUADRONS

Squadron	Code	Name
VRF-31	(none)	Storkline

VRF-31 provides pilots to transfer Navy and Marine Corps aircraft throughout the world. The squadron is based at Norfolk under Fleet Tactical Support Wing 1.

AIR ANTI-SUBMARINE SQUADRONS

Squadron	Aircraft	Name
*VS-21	S-3A	Fighting Redtails
*VS-22	S-3A	Checkmates
*VS-24	S-3A	Scouts
*VS-28	S-3A	Hukkers
*VS-29	S-3A	Dragonflies
*VS-30	S-3A	Diamond Cutters
*VS-31	S-3A	Top Cats
*VS-32	S-3A	Maulers
*VS-33	S-3A	Screwbirds
*VS-37	S-3A	Sawbucks
*VS-38	S-3A	Red Griffins
VS-41	S-3A	Shamrocks

The Navy's 11 operational air ASW squadrons each fly 10 aircraft. They are assigned to air wings aboard all carriers except the MIDWAY and CORAL SEA, which lack support capabilities and tactical ASW control centers.

VS-41 at North Island provides readiness training for the entire S-3 community (tail code NJ). VS-40 is scheduled to be established in January 1987 as an S-3A readiness squadron at Cecil Field, Fla. VS-30 was an S-2 Tracker readiness training squadron; it became an operational squadron upon transitioning to the S-3A in 1976. East Coast squadrons are assigned to Air ASW Wing 1 at Cecil Field and those on the West Coast are under ASW Wing Pacific at North Island.

TRAINING SQUADRONS

Squadron	Code	Aircraft	(Number)	Name	Training
VT-2	E	T-34C	(54)	The Doer Birds	Primary/Intermediate
VT-3	E	T-34C	(54)	Red Knights	Primary/Intermediate
VT-4	F	TA-4J	(16)	Rubber Ducks	Intermediate/Strike
		T-2C	(18)		
VT-6	E	T-28B/C	(35)	(none)	Primary/Intermediate
		T-34C	(54)		
VT-7	A	TA-4J	(33)	Eagles	Strike
VT-9	A	T-2C	(17)	Tigers	Intermediate
VT-10	F	T-2C	(27)	Cosmic Rats	Basic/Intermediate NFO
		T-39D	(7)		
VT-19	A	T-2C	(18)	Fighting Frogs	Intermediate
VT-21	B	TA-4J	(26)	Red Hawks	Strike
VT-22	B	TA-4J	(25)	King Eagles	Strike
VT-23	B	T-2C	(48)	The Professionals	Intermediate
VT-24	C	TA-4J	(25)	Bobcats	Strike
VT-25	C	TA-4J	(24)	Cougars	Strike
VT-26	C	T-2C	(51)	Tigers	Intermediate
VT-27	G	T-28B	(63)	Boomers	Primary/Intermediate
VT-28	G	T-44A	(28)	Rangers	Maritime patrol
VT-31	G	T-44A	(28)	Wise Owls	Maritime patrol
VT-41	F	T-2C	(15)		Intermediate NFO
VT-86	F	TA-4J	(9)	Sabre Hawks	Advanced NFO
		T-39D	(17)		
		T-47A	(few)		

These 19 squadrons provide fixed-wing training for Navy, Marine Corps, Coast Guard, and foreign pilots and air crewmen under the direction of the Naval Air Training Command. Single-letter tail codes indicate training wings: A for TraWing-1 (NAS Meridan), B for TraWing-2 (NAS Kingsville), C for TraWing-3 (NAS Chase Field), G for TraWing-4 (NAS Corpus Christi), E for TraWing-5 (NAS Whiting Field), and F for TraWing-6 (NAS Pensacola). TraWing-4 changed from the letter D to G in 1983.

The aircraft numbers shown in parentheses are approximate. The TA-4J, T-28B/C, and T-2C are carrier capable and enable students to practice landings aboard the training ship LEXINGTON (AVT 16) in the Gulf of Mexico.

Several new training-type aircraft are being introduced into these squadrons; see Chapter 29.

The letters T and HT (helicopter) have been used for naval aircraft since shortly after World War II; however, VT and HT were not used for squadron designations until 1 May 1960, when 17 training units were redesignated as training squadrons (VT). Note that both VT-9 and VT-26 have the nickname Tigers.

The above aircraft numbers are approximate.

AIR TEST AND EVALUATION SQUADRONS

Squadron	Code	Aircraft	Name
VX-1	JA	P-3C, EP-3A, S-3A, SH-2F, SH-3H, SH-60B	ASW Pioneers
VX-4	XF	TA-4J, F-4S, F-14A, F/A-18, TF-18	Evaluators
VX-5	XE	A-6, A-7, F/A-18	Vampires

These squadrons test and evaluate air weapon systems. VX-1 at NAS Patuxent River, Md., specializes in ASW, EW, and TACAMO systems under Sea-Based ASW Wings Atlantic; VX-4 at NAS Point Mugu, Calif., specializes in fighter weapons and tactics under Fighter/AEW Wing Pacific; and VX-5 at the Naval Weapons Center China Lake, Calif., supports air-to-surface weapons and tactics development under administrative control of Light Attack Wing Pacific. The three VX squadrons are under the operational control of the Navy's Operational Test and Evaluation Force in Norfolk, Va.

The squadrons fly a variety of operational and test aircraft.

An Aircraft Experimental and Developmental Squadron was established at NAS Anacostia, Washington, D.C., on 13 August 1942; this was the predecessor of VX-1. Two specialized development squadrons—VXE-6 and VXN-8—are numbered in the basic VX series.

ANTARCTIC DEVELOPMENT SQUADRONS

Squadron	Code	Aircraft	Name
VXE-6	XD	LC-130F/R, UH-1N	Puckered Penguins

VXE-6, home ported at Point Mugu, Calif., provides air support of U.S. Antarctic programs sponsored by the National Science Foundation. It flies Huey helicopters plus two LC-130F and five LC-130R ski-equipped

Hercules. The squadron was originally commissioned as Air Development Squadron 6 (VX-6) on 17 January 1955, specifically for Antarctic operations (Operation Deepfreeze); the squadron was subsequently redesignated VXE on 1 January 1969.

The U.S. Navy has had aviation interests in the Antarctic since 1928 when retired Commander Richard E. Byrd took 4 civilian aircraft on his first expedition to the South Pole.[4] Major Navy support began with Byrd's 1939–1940 expedition and on his 1947–1948 expedition there were 19 Navy fixed-wing aircraft and 4 helicopters, including six R4D/C-47 transports that flew from the aircraft carrier PHILIPPINE SEA (CV 47).

OCEANOGRAPHIC DEVELOPMENT SQUADRONS

Squadron	Code	Aircraft	Name
VXN-8	JB	P-3A, RP-3A/D	World Travelers

VXN-8 at Patuxent River operates one RP-3A and two RP-3D Orion aircraft in support of worldwide research projects: Project Magnet is a gravity and geomagnetic study; Project Birdseye is an ice reconnaissance and physical oceanography study; and Project Seascan is an aerial oceanographic effort. A P-3A is assigned to the squadron for training. The squadron is assigned to Tactical Support Wing 1.

HELICOPTER COMBAT SUPPORT SQUADRONS

Squadron	Code	Aircraft	Name
HC-1	UP	SH-3G, CH-53E	Pacific Fleet Guardian Angels
HC-3	SA	HH-46A, CH-46D	Packrats
HC-4	HC	CH-53E	Black Stallions
HC-5		HH-46A, CH-46D	Providers
HC-6	HW	CH-46D, UH-46D, VH-3A	Chargers
HC-11	VR	HH-46A, CH-46D	Gunbearers
HC-16	BF	HH-46A, UH-1N	Bullfrogs

Most of these squadrons provide helicopter detachments for rescue (SAR) and replenishment (VERTREP/VOD) operations in direct support of the fleet. HC-1, 3, and 11 are based at NAS North Island; HC-6 at NAS Norfolk; and HC-16 at NAS Pensacola; HC-4 was commissioned in 1983 at NAS Sigonella, Sicily and HC-5 in 1984 at NAS Agana, Guam. (HC-4 and HC-5 had existed earlier.)

HC-1's activities include providing SAR helicopters for the command ship BLUE RIDGE (LCC 19); the squadron also flies two CH-53Es for VERTREP. HC-4 flies six CH-53Es providing support to the Sixth Fleet in the Mediterranean. HC-6 uses VH-3A Sea Kings to support the CinC Atlantic Fleet. HC-16, formerly designated HCT-16, provided readiness training for Sea Knight crewmen until 1982, when HC-3 took over that role, in turn giving the Pacific Fleet's seagoing VERTREP duties to HC-5 and HC-11. HC-16 then became the readiness squadron for all

[4] While Byrd was on the expedition, Congress promoted him to rear admiral on the retired list on 21 December 1928.

UH-1N Hueys, and provides SAR helicopters for the training carrier LEXINGTON.

All helicopter utility squadrons (HU) were changed to combat support squadrons (HC) on 1 July 1965. The genesis of these squadrons was VX-3, the Navy's first helicopter squadron, established on 1 July 1946. (During World War II the U.S. Coast Guard undertook helicopter development for the Navy.) In 1948 VX-3 was split into HU-1 and HU-2, on the East and West Coasts, respectively. HC-3 was established in 1967 as the first squadron with a primary mission of vertical replenishment.

HELICOPTER MINE COUNTERMEASURES SQUADRONS

Squadron	Code	Aircraft	Name
HM-12	DH	RH-53D, CH-53E	Sea Dragons
HM-14	BJ	RH-53D	Vanguard
HM-16	GC	RH-53D	Seahawks

The Navy established HM-12 as the world's first helicopter mine countermeasures squadron on 1 April 1971 after almost 20 years of experiments with helicopters in that field. Initially flying Navy and Marine CH-53A Sea Stallions and then the specialized RH-53D, HM-12 operated off North Vietnam in November 1972–July 1973 (Operation Endsweep) and at the northern end of the Suez Canal in April 1974 (Nimbus Star) and again in July 1975 (Nimbus Stream).

Subsequently, HM-12 was designated as the Airborne Mine Countermeasures (AMCM) readiness-training squadron in 1978 with HM-14 commissioned on 12 May 1978, and HM-16 commissioned on 27 October 1978, for operational deployments. All three squadrons are based at Norfolk.

When established, HM-14 and HM-16 each had eight RH-53D helicopters with HM-12 retaining five; nine additional helicopters were used for test and evaluation at the time. Subsequently, three RH-53Ds were reassigned to VR-24 for VERTREP/VOD operations in the Mediterranean. Eight of the mine countermeasure helicopters were launched from the carrier NIMITZ for the ill-fated Tehran hostage-rescue operation in April 1980, with seven being lost. This led to reassignment of the remaining helicopters to give HM-12 four with seven each to HM-14 and HM-16.

The more capable CH-53E Super Stallion was first assigned to HM-12 in March 1983. Five of the CH-53E variants will be flown by HM-12 until the MH-53E variant is delivered to the squadron in 1987. Two of HM-12's CH-53Es provide logistics support of the Second Fleet.

HELICOPTER ANTI-SUBMARINE SQUADRONS

Squadron	Aircraft	Name
HS-1	SH-3D/G/H	Seahorses (AR)
*HS-2	SH-3H	Golden Falcons
*HS-3	SH-3H	Tridents
*HS-4	SH-3H	Black Knights
*HS-5	SH-3G/H	Night Dippers
*HS-6	SH-3H	Indians
*HS-7	SH-3H	Shamrocks
*HS-8	SH-3H	Eight Ballers
*HS-9	SH-3H	Sea Griffins
HS-10	SH-3A/H	Taskmasters (RA)
*HS-11	SH-3H	Dragon Slayers
*HS-12	SH-3H	Wyverns
*HS-15	SH-3H	Red Lions
*HS-17	SH-3H	

There are 12 operational helicopter ASW squadrons assigned to carrier air wings, each flying six SH-3H Sea Kings. HS-17 was commissioned in 1983. A thirteenth carrier squadron is planned. The SH-60F version of the Seahawk is scheduled to replace the Sea King in the 1990s, although there is serious opposition to that version by some officials within the Department of Defense.

Readiness training for these squadrons is provided by HS-1 on the East Coast at Jacksonville, and HS-10 on the West Coast at North Island. HS-1 helicopters also provide VIP transport, rescue, support, and utility services for the Commander Sixth Fleet, Commander Second Fleet (MOUNT WHITNEY/LCC 20), and Commander Middle East Force (LA SALLE/AGF 3). Atlantic HS and HSL squadrons report to Helicopter Anti-Submarine Wing 1 and the Pacific squadrons to ASW Wing Pacific.

The first helicopter ASW squadron, HS-1, was commissioned on 3 October 1951 with the Sikorsky HO4S-1 helicopter.

HELICOPTER LIGHT ANTI-SUBMARINE SQUADRONS

Squadron	Code	Aircraft	Name
HSL-30	HT	HH-2D, SH-2F	Neptune's Horsemen
HSL-31	TD	HH-2D, SH-2F	Archangels
HSL-32	HV	SH-2F	Tridents
HSL-33	TF	SH-2F	Sea Snakes
HSL-34	HX	SH-2F	Green Checkers
HSL-35	TG	SH-2F	Magicians
HSL-36	HY	SH-2F	Lamplighters
HSL-37	TH	SH-2F	Easy Riders
HSL-41	TS	SH-60B	Seahawks
HSL-42		SH-60B	
HSL-43		SH-60B	

The HSL squadrons provide detachments of ASW helicopters for deployments aboard cruisers, destroyers, and frigates. Each operational squadron has 10 to 12 aircraft. The first SH-2D LAMPS were assigned to helicopter combat support squadrons HC-4 and HC-5, which were redesignated HSL-30 and HSL-31, respectively, on 1 March 1972. These two squadrons now serve as SH-2F readiness squadrons for the Atlantic (HSL-30) and Pacific (HSL-31) squadrons; they are based at NAS Norfolk and NAS North Island, respectively. The first shipboard squadron, HSL-32, was commissioned in 1973.

HSL-41 was commissioned on 21 January 1983 at NAS North Island as the SH-60B Seahawk readiness training squadron with the first production SH-60B delivered to the squadron on 28 September 1983. Two fleet squadrons were established in 1984, HSL-42 and HSL-43.

HELICOPTER TRAINING SQUADRONS

Squadron	Code	Name	Aircraft	(Number)	Training
HT-8	E	(none)	TH-57A/B/C	(40)	Basic Helicopter
HT-18	E	(none)	TH-1, TH-57A/C	(78)	Advanced Helicopter

These squadrons provide helicopter training for Navy, Marine Corps, Coast Guard, and foreign pilots. Students first fly fixed-wing T-28 or T-34 aircraft before going into helicopters. The squadrons are numbered in the same series as VT squadrons and are part of Training Wing 5.

NAVAL AIR RESERVE

The Naval Air Reserve operates approximately 500 aircraft. These are organized into two carrier air wings and 13 maritime patrol squadrons, plus several support and transport squadrons. The Navy is in the process of upgrading the Naval Air Reserve, with F-14A Tomcat and F/A-18A Hornet aircraft entering reserve squadrons in 1984. (See Chapter 7, also see page 365 for Naval Air Reserve plan.)

All air reserve units are under the Commander Naval Air Reserve, based at New Orleans, La. The major air reserve subordinate commands are Reserve Patrol Wing Atlantic and Reserve Patrol Wing Pacific which control the VP squadrons; the Reserve Helicopter Wing which directs HAL, HC, HS, and HSL squadrons; and the Reserve Tactical Support Wing which supervises VC and VR squadrons.

Squadrons within the two reserve carrier air wings are designated in sequence based on the wing designation except for the AEW squadrons. Non-carrier air wing squadrons have designations in the standard Navy squadron numerical series. The VF, VFA, and VA squadrons are normally assigned 12 aircraft each; the VFP, VAK, VAQ, and VAW squadrons four aircraft each.

The two Reserve Carrier Air Wings (CVWR) were commissioned on 1 April 1970. There are no medium attack aircraft (A-6 Intruder) or ASW aircraft (S-3 Viking, SH-3 Sea King, or SH-60 Seahawk) assigned to these wings, although both SH-2 and SH-3 ASW helicopters are flown by the reserves.

The Naval Air Facility Washington, D.C., is located at Andrews Air Force Base in nearby Maryland.

RESERVE CARRIER AIR WINGS

Wing	Code	Squadron	Aircraft	Location
CVWR-20	AF	VF-201	F-4N	NAS Dallas, Texas
		VF-202	F-4N	NAS Dallas, Texas
		VA-203	A-7B/E	NAS Cecil Field, Fla.
		VA-204	A-7B	NAS New Orleans, La.
		VA-205	A-7B	NAS Atlanta, Ga.
		VFP-206	RF-8G	NAF Washington, D.C.
		VAK-208	KA-3B	NAS Alameda, Calif.
		VAQ-209	EA-6A	NAS Norfolk, Va.
		VAW-78	E-2B/C	NAS Norfolk, Va.
CVWR-30	ND	VF-301	F-4S, F-14A	NAS Miramar, Calif.
		VF-302	F-4S	NAS Miramar, Calif.
		VFA-303	A-7B, F/A-18A	NAS Lemoore, Calif.
		VA-304	A-7B	NAS Alameda, Calif.
		VA-305	A-7B	NAS Point Mugu, Calif.
		VAK-308	KA-3B	NAS Alameda, Calif.
		VAQ-309	EA-6A	NAS Whidbey Island, Wash.
		VAW-88	E-2B	NAS Miramar, Calif.

FIGHTER SQUADRONS

The reserve VF squadrons flew the F-4 Phantom until 1984 when VF-301 began transitioning to the F-14A Tomcat. VF-302 will receive the Tomcat in 1985, with VF-201 and VF-202 transitioning to the more capable F-4S variant.

ATTACK/STRIKE-FIGHTER SQUADRONS

The A-7B has experienced severe engine problems, limiting the flight time of the reserve Corsair squadrons. After initial congressional opposition, these squadrons began receiving the F/A-18A Hornet in 1985, with VFA-303 the first to begin transition. The squadron is training with VFA-125 at NAS Lemoore and will begin to receive its own planes in 1985–1986. VA-305 will be the second reserve F/A-18 squadron. The remaining Corsair squadrons will receive A-7E models of the Corsair as the later aircraft become available; VA-205 is the first to fly the E model.

RECONNAISSANCE SQUADRONS

Only the reserves have specialized reconnaissance squadrons (VFP), flying the RF-8G Photo Crusader, which has been discarded by the active fleet. VFP-306 was decommissioned on 1 October 1984, with TARPS-equipped F-14A Tomcats to perform reconnaissance for CVWR-30 (VF-301).

AERIAL REFUELING SQUADRONS

Only the reserves have tanker squadrons (VAK). These squadrons were changed from tactical EW squadrons (VAQ) to tanker units in October 1979, reflecting the primary role of their Skywarriors. Both VAK squadrons are based on the West Coast. The KA-3B is expected to serve in the reserves through the 1980s.

TACTICAL ELECTRONIC WARFARE SQUADRONS

The EA-6A Intruder is no longer flown by the Marine Corps. (This aircraft was never flown by Navy VAQ squadrons except for VAQ-33.)

AIRBORNE EARLY WARNING SQUADRONS

VAW-78 began to receive the E-2C variant of the Hawkeye in April 1983; VAW-88 is not scheduled to receive the C variant until the late 1980s. These squadrons have assisted in U.S. drug enforcement surveillance efforts, as have the active AEW squadrons.

COMPOSITE SQUADRONS

Squadron	Code	Aircraft	Location
VC-12	JY	TA-4J	NAS Oceana, Va.
VC-13	UX	TA-4J	NAS Miramar, Calif.

Each VC squadron flies 12 aircraft, primarily ACM training for reserve fighter and attack pilots.

PATROL SQUADRONS

Squadron	Code	Aircraft	Location
VP-60	LS	P-3B	NAS Glenview, Ill.
VP-62	LT	P-3B	NAS Jacksonville, Fla.
VP-64	LU	P-3B	NAS Willow Grove, Penna.
VP-65	PG	P-3A/B	NAS Point Mugu, Calif.
VP-66	LV	P-3B	NAS Willow Grove, Penna.
VP-67	PL	P-3A/B	NAS Memphis, Tenn.
VP-68	LW	P-3A/B	NAS Patuxent River, Md.
VP-69	PJ	P-3A/B	NAS Whidbey Island, Wash.
VP-90	LX	P-3B	NAS Glenview, Ill.
VP-91	PM	P-3B	NAS Moffett, Calif.
VP-92	LY	P-3A/B	NAS South Weymouth, Mass.
VP-93	LH	P-3B	NAF Detroit, Mich.
VP-94	LZ	P-3A/B	NAS New Orleans, La.

These squadrons each fly 9 to 12 Orion patrol aircraft. They regularly supplement active squadrons in U.S. and overseas operational deployments. They also participate in the drug surveillance effort. VP-67 was the last U.S. patrol squadron to fly the SP-2H Neptune, completing transition to the Orion in 1979. (A few survived in the active fleet in specialized roles.)

FLEET LOGISTICS SUPPORT SQUADRONS

Squadron	Code	Aircraft	Location
VR-46	JS	C-118	NAS Atlanta, Ga.
VR-48	JR	C-131	NAF Washington, D.C.
VR-51	RV	C-118	NAS Glenview, Ill.
VR-52	JT	C-118	NAS Willow Grove, Penna.
VR-55	RU	C-9B	NAS Alameda, Calif.
VR-56	JU	C-9B	NAS Norfolk, Va.
VR-57	RX	C-9B	NAS North Island, Calif.
VR-58	JV	C-9B	NAS Jacksonville, Fla.
VR-59	RY	C-9B	NAS Dallas, Texas
VR-60	RT	C-9B	NAS Memphis, Tenn.
VR-61	RS	C-9B	NAS Whidbey Island, Wash.

The VR squadrons provide transport support for active Navy and reserve activities within the United States and, on a limited basis, overseas. All are scheduled to receive the C-9B Skytrain II, military version of the commercial DC-9. VR-59 was recommissioned on 1 October 1982 from a detachment of VR-53 based at Dallas; VR-53 was changed to VR-60 on 3 October 1982; VR-54 was disestablished on 28 June 1981; and VR-61 was formed from a detachment of VR-51.

HELICOPTER LIGHT ATTACK SQUADRONS

Squadron	Code	Aircraft	Location
HAL-4	NW	HH-1K	NAS Norfolk, Va.
HAL-5	NW	HH-1K	NAS Point Mugu, Calif.

These are the Navy's only helicopter gunship squadrons. The only active U.S. Navy gunship unit was HAL-3, commissioned in April 1967 and decommissioned in 1972 after service in Vietnam; it flew UH-1E Hueys.

HELICOPTER COMBAT SUPPORT SQUADRONS

Squadron	Code	Aircraft	Location
HC-9	NW	HH-3A	NAS North Island, Calif.

The squadron's Sea King helicopters are armed and armored for combat search-and-rescue operations. They are the Navy's only combat SAR helicopters. The JVX tilt-rotor aircraft is being procured for this role

HELICOPTER ANTI-SUBMARINE SQUADRONS

Squadron	Code	Aircraft	Location
HS-75	NW	SH-3D	NAEC Lakehurst, N.J.
HS-85	NW	SH-3D	NAS Alameda, Calif.

These squadrons were to convert to the SH-2F LAMPS I; however, when this edition of *Ships and Aircraft* went to press the decision was to have the three LAMPS squadrons listed below with HS-75 and HS-85 to continue flying the SH-3.

LIGHT HELICOPTER ANTI-SUBMARINE SQUADRONS

Squadron	Code	Aircraft	Location
HSL-74	NW	SH-2F	NAS South Weymouth, Mass.
HSL-84	NW	SH-2F	NAS North Island, Calif.

HS-84 shifted from the SH-3D Sea King (as HS-84) to the LAMPS I helicopter in early 1984 to provide a stand-off ASW capability for frigates being assigned to the Naval Reserve Force. HS-74 with SH-3G Sea Kings shifts to the SH-2F in 1985 with a third SH-2F squadron (HSL-94) being formed in 1986.

NAVAL AIR RESERVE

Code	Location
6F	NAS Jacksonville, Fla.
6G	NAS Alameda, Calif.
6M	NAS Memphis, Tenn.
6S	NAS Norfolk, Va.

Non-squadron aircraft assigned to the Naval Air Reserve have number-letter tail codes. These are mostly administrative and transport aircraft.

NAVAL AIR RESERVE PLAN

	1984	1985	1986	1987	1988	1989	1990	1991	1992
VF/VFA Squadrons									
F-4S	4	3	2	1	0	0	0	0	0
F-14A	0	1	2	3	4	4	4	4	4
F/A-18	0	0	0	0	0	0	0	0	2
VA/VFA Squadrons									
A-7B	3	2	1	0	0	0	0	0	0
A-7E	2	3	4	4	4	4	4	4	4
F/A-18	1	1	1	2	2	4	4	4	6
VAW Squadrons									
E-2B	1	1	1	1	0	0	0	0	0
E-2C	1	1	1	1	2	2	2	2	2
VFP Squadrons									
RF-8G	1	1	1	1	0	0	0	0	0
VAK Squadrons									
KA-3B	2	2	2	2	2	2	2	2	2
VAQ Squadrons									
EA-6A	2	2	2	2	2	2	1	1	1
EA-6B	0	0	0	0	0	0	1	1	1
VP Squadrons									
P-3A/B	13	13	13	13	13	13	13	13	13
VR Squadrons									
C-9B	8	10	11	11	11	11	11	11	11
C-118	2	1	0	0	0	0	0	0	0
C-131H	1	1	1	1	1	1	1	1	1
VC Squadrons									
TA-4E/F/J	2	2	2	2	2	0	0	0	0
A-4M	0	0	0	0	0	2	2	2	2
HS/HSL Squadrons									
SH-2F	1	2	3	3	3	3	3	3	3
SH-3D	3	2	2	2	2	2	2	2	2
HAL Squadrons									
HH-1K	2	2	2	2	2	2	2	2	2
HC Squadrons									
HH-3A	1	1	1	1	1	1	1	1	1
HM Squadrons									
RH-53B	0	0	0	1	1	1	1	1	1

NAVAL AIR STATIONS AND FACILITIES

Code	Location
7A	NAS Patuxent River, Md.
7B	NAS Atlanta, Ga.
7C	NAS Norfolk, Va.
7D	NAS Dallas, Texas
7E	NAS Jacksonville, Fla.
7F	NAS Brunswick, Ga.
7G	NAS Whidbey Island, Wash.
7J	NAS Alameda, Calif.
7K	NAS Memphis, Tenn.
7L	NAS Pt. Mugu, Calif.
7M	NAS North Island, Calif.
7N	NAF Andrews, Wash. D.C.
7P	Naval Weapons Center China Lake, Calif.
7Q	NAS Key West, Fla.
7R	NAS Oceana, Va.
7S	NAS Lemoore, Calif.
7T	Naval Air Test Center Patuxent River, Md.
7V	NAS Glenview, Ill.
7W	NAS Willow Grove, Penna.
7X	NAS New Orleans, La.
7Y	NAF Detroit, Mich.
7Z	NAS South Weymouth, Mass.
8A	NAF Atsugi, Japan
8B	NAS Cubi Point, Philippines
8C	NAS Sigonella, Sicily
8D	Naval Station Rota, Spain
8E	Naval Station Roosevelt Roads, P.R.
8F	NAS Guantanamo Bay, Cuba
8G	NAF Mildenhall, England
8H	Okinawa
9J	Naval Station Guam, Marianas
8K	Bahrain

Aircraft assigned to various naval air stations within the United States have 7-series number-letter designations; those assigned to overseas bases are in the 8-series.

MARINE AVIATION

The Marine Aircraft Wing (MAW) is the major aviation component of the Marine Corps. There are three active and one reserve Marine Aircraft Wings that contain all fixed-wing and rotary-wing aircraft except for a few utility and cargo aircraft.

The wings vary considerably in their size and composition. A nominal air wing consists of a Marine Headquarters Wing Squadron (MWHS), Marine Air Control Group (MACG), and a Marine Wing Support Group (MWSG). The MACGs include air defense units with Hawk and Redeye anti-aircraft missiles. The accompanying table shows the nominal wing organization.

The 1st MAW is based in Japan (Iwakuni and Futema) and on Okinawa, where the wing headquarters is located. However, most of its aircraft squadrons are rotated to the Far East on a six-month basis from Marine Aircraft Group 24 at Kanohe, Hawaii, with some rotating units (detachments and squadrons) coming from the 1st and 2nd MAWs. (Marine Aircraft Group 24 is assigned to the 1st Marine Brigade on Oahu, Hawaii.) Beginning in 1984 the Navy has also provided A-7E squadrons on rotation to the 1st MAW in return for Marine F/A-18 squadrons going aboard carriers.

The 2nd MAW, with headquarters at Cherry Point, N.C., has aircraft squadrons based on the East Coast while the 3rd MAW, with headquarters at MCAS El Toro, Calif., has its squadrons on the West Coast and at Yuma, Ariz.

A Marine air wing is generally paired with a reinforced division to form a Marine Amphibious Force, an air group with a reinforced regiment to form a Marine Amphibious Brigade, and a composite squadron with a reinforced battalion to form a Marine Amphibious Unit. A composite squadron generally consists of 4 CH-53, 12 CH-46, 4 AH-1T, and 2 UH-1N helicopters deployed aboard an LHA or LPH and other amphibious ships. Additionally, AV-8 Harriers may also be assigned to the squadron, depending upon mission and aircraft and ship availability.

MARINE AIRCRAFT WINGS

Marine Aircraft Wing	Marine Aircraft Group	Squadrons
1st MAW	MAG-12 Iwakuni, Japan	VMA[a]
		VMA(AW)[b]
		Det. VMAQ-2
	MAG-15 Iwakuni, Japan	VMFA[c]
		VMFA[d]
		Det. VMFP-3
	MAG-36 Okinawa	HMM[e]
		HML[f]
		HMH[g]
		Det. VMO-1
		Det. VMO-2
		VMGR-152
2nd MAW	MAG-14 Cherry Point, N.C.	VMAQ-2
		VMAT(AW)-202
		VMA(AW)-224
		VMGR-252
		VMA(AW)-332
		VMA(AW)-533
	MAG-26 New River, N.C.	HMT-204
		HMM-261
		HMM-264
	MAG-29 New River, N.C.	HMM-266
		HMH-362
		HMH-461
		HML-167
		HMM-162
		HMM-263
		HMM-365
		HML/A-269
		HMH-464
		VMO-1
	MAG-31 Beaufort, S.C.	VMFA-115
		VMFA-122
		VMFA-251
		VMFA-312
		VMFA-333
		VMFA-451
	MAG-32 Cherry Point, N.C.	VMAT-203
		VMA-223
		VMA-231
		VMA-331
		VMA-542
3rd MAW	MCCRTG-10 Yuma, Ariz. MAG-11 El Toro, Calif.	VMFAT-101
		VMAT-102
		VMFP-3
		VMFA-314
		VMFA-323
		VMFA-531
	MAG-13 El Toro, Calif.	VMA(AW)-121
		VMA(AW)-242
		VMA-211
		VMA-214
		VMA-311
		VMA-513[h]
		VMGR-352
	MAG-16 Tustin, Calif.	HMM-161
		HMM-163
		HMM-164
		HMM-268
		HMT-301
		HMH-361
		HMH-363
		HMH-462
		HMH-465
		HMH-466
	MAG-39 Camp Pendleton, Calif.	HMA-169
		HML-267
		HMT-303
		HML-367
		HMA-369
		VMO-2
1st Marine Brigade	MAG-24 Kaneohe, Hawaii	VMFA-212
		VMFA-232
		VMFA-235
		HMM-165
		HMM-262
		HMM-265
		HMH-463
		Det. HML-367

[a] VMA-211, 214, and 311 rotate from 3rd MAW.
[b] VMA(AW)-242 rotates from 3rd MAW, and VMA(AW)-224 and 332 rotate from 2nd MAW.
[c] VMFA-212, 232, and 235 rotate from 1st Marine Brigade.
[d] VMFA-312, 333, and 451 rotate from 2nd MAW.
[e] HMM-165, 262, 265, and 364 rotate from 1st Marine Brigade.
[f] HML-267, 367, and HMA-369 rotate from 3rd MAW.
[g] HMH-361, 363, and 462 rotate from 3rd MAW.
[h] VMA-513 is based at Yuma, Ariz.

MARINE ATTACK SQUADRONS

Squadron	Code	Aircraft
VMAT-102	SC	A-4M, TA-4F
VMA(AW)-121	VK	A-6E
VMAT(AW)-202	KC	A-6E/TC-4C
VMAT-203	KD	TAV-8A, AV-8B
VMA-211	CF	A-4M
VMA-214	WE	A-4M
VMA-223	WP	A-4M
VMA(AW)-224	WK	A-6E
VMA-231	CG	AV-8A/C
VMA(AW)-242	DT	A-6E
VMA-311	WL	A-4M
VMA-331	VL	AV-8B
VMA(AW)-332	EA	A-6E
VMA-513	WF	AV-8A
VMA(AW)-533	ED	A-6E
VMA-542	CR	AV-8A/C

The Marines operate five medium (all-weather) and eight light attack squadrons, plus three readiness training units (VMAT). The A-6 squadrons generally have 10 aircraft, the AV-8 squadrons 15, and the A-4 units 19. VMA-513 was the first operational Harrier squadron, with AV-8A deliveries beginning in April 1971. The eight non-A-6 squadrons are to receive the AV-8B Harrier II, with the first squadron deliveries planned to VMA-331 in early 1985. VMAT-203 at Cherry Point received the first operational AV-8B in January 1984 with VMA-331 the first operational AV-8B squadron.

Pre-1981 planning called for these eight squadrons to receive the F/A-18 Hornet instead of the advanced Harrier; this changed with the Reagan Administration's decision to buy the advanced Harrier. The A-4 entered Marine service in 1956 and the A-6 in 1965.

MARINE ELECTRONIC WARFARE SQUADRONS

Squadron	Code	Aircraft
VMAQ-2	CY	EA-6B

The three Marine composite reconnaissance squadrons (VMCJ) were decommissioned in 1975 and their aircraft allocated to VMAQ-2 and VMFP-3. The former squadron now flies 15 EA-6B Prowlers in the EW role; the squadron previously flew the two-seat EA-6A Intruder, the only active unit to have that aircraft in squadron strength. Detachments from the squadron, assigned to the 2nd MAW, are provided to other Marine wings.

MARINE FIGHTER-ATTACK SQUADRONS

Squadron	Code	Aircraft
VMFAT-101	SH	F-4S
VMFA-115	VE	F-4S
VMFA-122	DC	F-4S
VMFA-212	WD	F-4S
VMFA-232	WT	F-4S
VMFA-235	DB	F-4S
VMFA-251	DW	F-4S
VMFA-312	DR	F-4S
VMFA-314	VW	F/A-18A
VMFA-323	WS	F/A-18A
VMFA-333	DM	F-4S
VMFA-451	VM	F-4S
VMFA-531	EC	F/A-18A

The F-4 Phantom has been flown by Marine fighter squadrons since 1961 and on 1 August 1962 those squadrons were changed from VMF(AW) to the current VMFA. Proposals to provide the F-14 Tomcat to at least four Marine squadrons were cancelled in August 1975 at the request of the Marine Corps. All Marine fighter squadrons are to transition to the F/A-18A Hornet, with VMFA-314 shifting in January 1983 and VMFA-323 and 531 later the same year. Three more squadrons—VMFA-115, 122, 251—will receive the F/A-18 in 1985–1986.

There may be a reduction to about nine squadrons in the later 1980s because of fiscal constraints.

VMFA squadrons each have 12 aircraft. VMFAT-101 provides Navy and Marine pilot-RIO transition training for the Phantom; Navy-Marine VFA-125 does F/A-18 readiness training for both services. VMFAT-101 is scheduled to transition to the F/A-18 in 1988.

MARINE TACTICAL RECONNAISSANCE SQUADRONS

Squadron	Code	Aircraft
VMFP-3	RF	RF-4B

The only active photo-reconnaissance squadron of the Navy or Marine Corps, VMFP-3 flies 21 photo versions of the Phantom. The U.S. Navy did not use the RF-4 version of the Phantom. Detachments of the VMFP-3 are provided to other wings. An RF/A-18 is planned for Marine use. The Marines took delivery of their first RF-4B in 1965.

MARINE REFUELLER-TRANSPORT SQUADRONS

Squadron	Code	Aircraft
VMGR-152	QD	KC-130F/R
VMGR-252	BH	KC-130F/R
VMGR-352	QB	KC-130F/R

Squadrons VMGR-252 and 352 fly 14 Hercules and VMGR-152 flies 8 aircraft to provide transport for Marine ground units as well as in-flight refueling for Marine aircraft. One Marine KC-130F supports the Navy-Marine Blue Angels flight demonstration team.

MARINE OBSERVATION SQUADRONS

Squadron	Code	Aircraft
VMO-1	ER	OV-10A/D
VMO-2	UU	OV-10A/D

The two observation squadrons fly the STOL-capable OV-10 Bronco. Unlike previous Marine observation aircraft, the Bronco can be heavily armed. Fifteen aircraft are assigned to each squadron—eight OV-10A and seven OV-10D. The Navy's lone light attack squadron (VAL-4) flew Broncos during the Vietnam War.

MARINE HEAVY HELICOPTER SQUADRONS

Squadron	Code	Aircraft
HMT-301	SU	CH-53A/E, CH-46E
HMH-361	YN	CH-53A/D
HMH-362	YL	CH-53D
HMH-363	YZ	CH-53A/D
HMH-461	CJ	CH-53D
HMH-462	YF	CH-53A/D
HMH-463	YH	CH-53D
HMH-464	EN	CH-53E
HMH-465	YJ	CH-53E
HMH-466	YK	CH-53E

These squadrons fly the twin-engine CH-53A/D or the three-engine CH-53E. The first of three currently planned squadrons to fly the CH-53E was HMH-464, activated at New River on 27 February 1981. Sixteen E-version helicopters will be assigned to each of the three squadrons. HMT-301 switched from the CH-46F to the CH-53E in October 1983 as the Super Stallion readiness squadron.

In the early 1980s the CH-53A/D squadrons were considered for redesignation as medium squadrons (HMM), but this was not done.

MARINE UTILITY AND ATTACK HELICOPTER SQUADRONS

Squadron	Code	Aircraft
HML/A-167	TV	AH-1T, UH-1N
HMA-169	SN	AH-1T
HML-267	UV	AH-1J, UH-1N
HML/A-269	HF	AH-1T, UH-1N
HMT-303	QT	AH-1J, UH-1N
HML-367	VT	AH-1S, UH-1N
HMA-369	SM	AH-1J, UH-1N

The Marines designate HML units as utility squadrons. Both HMA and HML squadrons each fly 24 helicopters except for 21 helicopters in the AH-1T units because of an aircraft shortage. One attack (HMA-269) and one utility (HML-167) squadron have been combined into HML/A units to facilitate the deployment of detachments of combined troop-carrying/command Huey helicopters and SeaCobra gunships (both at New River). The HML/A is a 2nd MAW designation, not formally used by Marine Corps Headquarters. HMT-204 and HMT-303 provide helicopter readiness training, with the latter squadron established in April 1982. The Huey has been in Marine service since 1964 and the SeaCobra since 1968.

MARINE MEDIUM HELICOPTER SQUADRONS

Squadron	Code	Aircraft
HMM-161	YR	CH-46E
HMM-162	YS	CH-46E
HMM-163	YP	CH-46E
HMM-164	YT	CH-46E
HMM-165	YW	CH-46E
HMT-204	GX	CH-46, CH-53
HMM-261	EM	CH-46E
HMM-262	ET	CH-46E
HMM-263	EG	CH-46E
HMM-264	EH	CH-46E
HMM-265	EP	CH-46E
HMM-266	ES	CH-46E
HMM-268	YQ	CH-46E
HMM-364		CH-46E
HMM-365	YM	CH-46E

Each medium squadron flies 12 Sea Knight helicopters, being reduced from 18 in some units. HMM-161 was the Marine Corps' first tactical helicopter squadron; it was established on 15 January 1951, flying the Sikorsky HRS-1 (CH-19). HMM-166 is scheduled to be established in fall 1985. The CH-46 is scheduled for replacement by the JVX tilt-rotor aircraft in the 1990s.

MARINE HELICOPTER SQUADRONS

Squadron	Code	Aircraft
HMX-1	MX	UH-1N, VH-1, VH-3D, CH-46E/F, CH-53D

This squadron—sometimes incorrectly called Marine Helicopter Experimental Squadron 1 or Marine Development Squadron 1—was commissioned on 1 December 1947 to develop helicopter assault tactics for the Marine Corps. The squadron, at MCAS Quantico, Va., fulfills a variety of development and operational functions, including providing helicopter transport for the President with VH-3D Sea Kings. With the President embarked, a helicopter is designated *Marine One*.

MARINE AIR RESERVE

The Marine Air Reserve consists of the 4th Marine Aircraft Wing plus a few detachments. The wing, organized similarly to the active MAWs, has some 230 aircraft and is manned by approximately 7,200 selected reservists and 2,500 active duty personnel.

In addition to the aircraft squadrons indicated for the 4th MAW, there are various wing command and support aircraft as well as a detachment of C-12 utility aircraft.

A major modernization program is underway. The two VMFA squadrons are receiving F-4J and, subsequently, will fly the F-4S versions of the Phantom. The A-4E/F squadrons will receive the A-4M and more capable helicopters are to be provided. Because of the shortage of helicopters in the active Marine units, however, in about 1988 some

CH-46E Sea Knights will be transferred to the active forces in return for CH-53A/D helicopters.

A second reserve squadron of KC-130 aircraft is being established at Stewart Air Force Base in New York State. At the end of 1983 the existing VMGR-234 had seven KC-130F and four KC-130T Hercules tankers, the latter, delivered that year, were the first factory-to-squadron aircraft assigned to the Marine air reserve. The two VMGR squadrons are to receive a total of 28 Hercules tanker-transport aircraft.

The following are the aircraft components of the 4th MAW.

Group	Squadron	Code	Aircraft	Location
MAG-41	VMFA-112	MA	F-4J	NAS Dallas, Texas
	VMFA-321	MG	F-4N	NAF Andrews, Wash., D.C.
	VMFA-134	MF	F-4N	MCAS El Toro, Calif.
	VMGR-234	QH	KC-130F/T	NAS Glenview, Ill.
	VMO-4	MU	OV-10A	NAS Atlanta, Ga.
MAG-42	VMA-124	QP	A-4E	NAS Memphis, Tenn.
	VMA-131	QG	A-4E	NAS Willow Grove, Pa.
	VMA-133	ME	A-4F	NAS Alameda, Calif.
	VMA-142	MB	A-4F	NAS Cecil Field, Fla.
	VMA-322	QR	A-4M	NAS South Weymouth, Mass.
	VMAQ-4	RM	EA-6A	NAS Whidbey Island, Wash.

MAG-46	HMA-773	MP	AH-1J	NAS Atlanta, Ga.
	HML-767	MM	UH-1N	NAS New Orleans, La.
	HML-771	QK	UH-1N	NAS South Weymouth, Mass.
	HMM-764	ML	CH-46E	MCAS El Toro, Calif.
	HMM-774	MQ	CH-46E	NAS Norfolk, Va.
MAG-49	HML-776	QL	UH-1E	NAS Glenview, Ill.
	HMH-772	MT	CH-53A	NAS Willow Grove, Pa.[a]
	HMH-777	QM	CH-53	NAS Dallas, Texas

[a] Detachments at NAS Alameda, Calif., and Dallas, Tex.

MARINE SUPPORT AIRCRAFT

Code	Aircraft	Location
5A	VP-3A	Headquarters, Marine Corps (Jacksonville, Fla.)
5B	UC-12	MCAS Beaufort, N.C.
5C	C-9B, CT-39	MCAS Cherry Point, N.C.
5D	UC-12	MCAS New River, N.C.
5F	UC-12, CT-39	MCAS Futema, Japan
5T	UC-12, CT-39	MCAS El Toro, Calif.
5Y	UC-12	MCAS Yuma, Ariz.

Three Marine A-6E Intruders from VMA (AW)–332 near Wake Island during a transPacific flight. Note the two-color paint scheme to reduce the aircraft's detectability when viewed from above or below. A two-seat, all-weather version of the F/A-18 Hornet has been proposed as a successor to the A-6E in Marine service. (U.S. Navy)

29 Naval Aircraft

This chapter describes the principal aircraft now flown by the U.S. Navy, Marine Corps, and Coast Guard.

AIRCRAFT DESIGNATIONS

Naval aircraft, with a few exceptions, are designated within the standard Department of Defense designation scheme. From 1922 until 1962 the Navy used its own designation scheme that indicated the aircraft mission, sequence of that aircraft type produced by the manufacturer, manufacturer, (hyphen) model, and modification. Thus, an AD-2N indicated the first series of attack aircraft built by Douglas, the second model, modified for night operation.

The scheme became unwieldy as the number of manufacturers of naval aircraft increased. For example, the letter F was used for Grumman (as F9F) because G was already assigned to Gallaudet; Y for Consolidated (as PBY) with C used by Curtiss and, later, Cessna and Culver as well; A for Brewster (as F2A) because B was previously assigned to Boeing and, later, Beech and Budd Manufacturing. Also, the same aircraft flown by different services had different designations. The famed Boeing B-29 Superfortress had the Navy designation P2B, the North American B-25 was used by the Navy and Marine Corps as the PBJ, and the McDonnell Phantom II entered service as the F4H in the Navy and F-110 in the Air Force.

The U.S. Air Force and Army used different designation schemes for their respective aircraft.

A new, unified scheme came into effect in October 1962 when all existing and new naval aircraft and all new Air Force planes were redesignated in a new, simplified series, almost all beginning with the series number one. The Navy-flown AD Skyraider[1] became the first plane in the new attack series, the A-1. The Navy's TF Trader started the new cargo series as C-1; the FJ Fury became the F-1; the T2V Sea Star the T-1; and the UC-1 Otter the U-1.

There was no P-1 or S-1, as the new system picked up the Navy's P2V Neptune and S2F Tracker as the P-2 and S-3, respectively. The improved P3V Orion was the obvious candidate for P-3 and the P5M Marlin, the Navy's last combat flying boat, for P-5. The designation P-4 was used, albeit briefly, for the drone versions of the Privateer (the P4Y-2K, formerly PB4Y-2). The designations P-4 and P-6 are sometimes cited as having been reserved for the P4M Mercator and the P6M Seamaster. But the last of the combination piston-turbojet Mercators were gone and the turbojet Seamaster flying boat had been cancelled before the 1962 system was established. (The next patrol aircraft would be the P-7.)

The 1962 system also introduced the mission designation of special electronic E-series aircraft. The first two planes were Navy, the WF-2 Tracer became the E-1B and the W2F-1 Hawkeye the E-2A.

Variations of the previous Air Force X (for experimental) and V (for VSTOL) designations remained, but official records differ as to which aircraft were part of the old or new series. The Marines' AV-8 Harrier is officially in the V series, but apparently the designation A-8 was avoided to reduce confusion. In the V series, however, the Ryan 'flying jeep" had already been designated XV-8. The latter program never took off, hence the "8" spot is firmly held by the successful Harrier.

Planes that were used by both services, as the Albatross seaplane (Navy UF), generally took on the Air Force numerical designation (U-16, formerly SA-16). But the Phantom was recent enough to be given a new designation, the now-familiar F-4, and not the Air Force F-110.

Helicopters proved a more confusing issue because the Army had still another designation series before 1962 in addition to those of the Navy-Marine Corps and Air Force. The Sea Knight was the Navy HRB, while the Army called the helicopter HC-1A (HC for helicopter—cargo). This became the H-46 in the new scheme. The Army's HU-1 Iroquois (HU for helicopter—utility) started the new helicopter series as H-1 with most of the Army and Air Force designations being merged to form the new H series. Navy helicopters were "stuck in" where there were gaps. The Kaman HU2K became the H-2 and the Sikorsky HSS-2 the H-3, but the Navy's HSS-1/HUS being similar to the Army-Air Force H-34 took on that designation.

---

[1] The AD had been developed with the designation BT2D—for Bomber-Torpedo/Douglas—but entered service in 1946 as the AD.

A trio of F-14A Tomcats of the carrier DWIGHT D. EISENHOWER fly escort for a Soviet Tu-20 Bear-D reconnaissance aircraft overflying the carrier during 1983 operations in the North Atlantic. "IKE" is printed below the air wing code AG. (U.S. Navy)

The 1962 aircraft designation scheme is relatively simple and, with prefix and suffix letters, can provide considerable detail. But confusion persists as the old and new schemes are mixed or written incorrectly. For example, the McDonnell Douglas F-4B Phantom is sometimes written incorrectly as F4B—which was a Boeing fighter of the 1920s. Similarly, the F4F Wildcat of World War II fame is often written incorrectly as F-4F, which is the U.S. designation used for F-4 Phantoms configured for West Germany.

Also there have been efforts to be "cute." An example is the Navy's single Fokker-Fairchild 27 which is designated UC-27—for utility-cargo—although 27 is derived from its commercial designation and not the utility or cargo aircraft series. Further, recent modifications to aircraft, which have in the past added a new suffix numeral or letter, have instead resulted in such confusing designations as the P-3C UPDATE III or EA-6B ICAP aircraft.

AIRCRAFT TYPES

The accompanying table lists the principal types of aircraft currently in use. In instances where only a particular version or model is in service the appropriate model designation is given. In the table and in the accompanying aircraft descriptions some variants are separated from the basic type because of significant differences in characteristics or equipment.

Explanation of symbols:

YTAV-8B

1st symbol— Status prefix	2nd symbol— Modified mission	3rd symbol— Basic mission	4th symbol— Aircraft type	5th symbol— Design	6th symbol— Series
J = temporary special test N = permanent special test X = experimental Y = prototype Z = planning	A = Attack C = Cargo D = Director (drone control) E = Electronics F = Fighter H = search/rescue K = tanker L = cold weather M = Missile carrier O = Observation Q = drone R = Reconnaissance S = antisubmarine T = Trainer U = Utility V = staff (VIP) W = Weather	A = Attack C = Cargo E = Electronic F = Fighter H = search/rescue M = Multipurpose O = Observation P = Patrol S = antisubmarine T = Trainer U = Utility X = research	H = Helicopter V = VSTOL or VTOL (none for conventional aircraft)	[8th VSTOL] [6th attack]	[2nd series] [5th series]

A-6E

NOTE: Letters I and O are not used to avoid confusion with numerals.

An S-3A Viking from VS-32 (foreground) and an EA-6B Prowler from VAQ-133 are prepared for launch from the waist catapults of the JOHN F. KENNEDY during operations in the North Atlantic. Blast deflectors are raised behind both aircraft. (N. Polmar)

Mission/Type	Basic Designation	Name*	Status**	Type***
Fighter	—	Kfir	N	Land
	F-4	Phantom	N-NR-MC-MCR	CV
	F-5	Tiger II	N	Land
	F-14	Tomcat	N-NR	CV
Strike Fighter	F/A-18	Hornet	N-NR-MC	CV
Attack	A-4	Skyhawk	N-NR-MC-MCR	CV
	A-6	Intruder	N-MC	CV
	A-7	Corsair	N-NR	CV
	AV-8A	Harrier	MC	VSTOL
	AV-8B	Harrier II	MC	VSTOL
Maritime Patrol	P-3	Orion	N-NR-NOAA	Land
Anti-Submarine	S-3	Viking	N	CV
Electronic Warfare	E-2	Hawkeye	N-NR	CV
	EA-3B	Skywarrior	N	CV
	KA-3B	Skywarrior	NR	CV
	EA-6A	Intruder	NR-MCR	CV
	EA-6B	Prowler	N-MC	CV
	E-6A	—	development	Land
	NKC-135	Stratotanker	N	Land
Reconnaissance	RF-4B	Phantom	MC	CV
	RF-8G	Crusader	NR	CV
Observation	OV-10	Bronco	MC-MCR	STOL
Utility	U-11A	Aztec	N	Land
	HU-25	Guardian	CG	Land
	UC-27	—	N	Land
Cargo/Transport	XV-15/JVX	—	development	VSTOL
	C-1	Trader	N	CV
	C-2	Greyhound	N	CV
	C-4	Academe	N-MC-CG	Land
	VC-10	Gulfstream II	CG	Land
	C-12	Huron	N-NR-MC-MCR	Land
	C-118	Liftmaster	NR	Land
	C-130	Hercules	N-NR-MC-MCR-CG-NOAA	Land
	C-131	Samaritan	N-NR	Land
Trainer	T-2	Buckeye	N	CV
	T-28	Trojan	N	CV
	T-34	Mentor	N	Land
	T-38	Talon	N	Land
	T-39	Sabreliner	N-MC	Land
	T-44	King Air	N	Land
	T-46	Hawk	N	CV
	T-47	—	N	Land
Helicopter	AH-1	SeaCobra	MC-MCR	
	UH-1	Huey (Iroquois)	N-NR-MC-MCR	
	SH-2	LAMPS	N-NR	
	SH-3	Sea King	N-NR-MC	
	HH-3F	Pelican	CG	
	H-46	Sea Knight	N-MC-MCR	
	HH-52	Sea Guard	CG	
	H-53	Sea Stallion	N-MC-MCR	
	H-53E	Super Stallion	N-MC	
	TH-57	SeaRanger	N	
	SH-60	Seahawk	N	
	HH-65	Dolphin	CG	
Experimental	XFV-12	—	inactive	VSTOL
	(Model 279-3)	—	development	VSTOL

* The Phantom, Corsair, and certain other aircraft were initially identified with the numeral II after their popular name; these have been discarded as the previous aircraft with that name left service use. The exception is the Tiger II.
** Status notes: N = active Navy, NR = Naval Reserve, MC = Marine Corps, MCR = Marine Corps Reserve, CG = Coast Guard, and NOAA = National Oceanic and Atmospheric Administration.
*** CV = carrier capable.

AIRCRAFT MARKINGS

Unit markings—indicating wing, squadron, or base assignment consist of letters or letter-number combinations on the rudder fin or after body of the aircraft; see Chapter 28 for codes.

Side numbers—generally on fuselage and upper right and lower left wings indicate the aircraft position in squadron or other unit. The side number sequence for carrier air wings is shown below.

Side number	Squadron		Color code
100–114	VF	fighter	insignia red
200–214	VF	fighter	orange-yellow
300–315	VA	light attack	light blue
400–415	VA	light attack	international orange
500–512	VA	medium attack	light green
513–517	VA	tanker	light green
600–603	VAW	AEW	insignia blue
604–607	VAQ	EW	maroon
610–617	HS	helicopter ASW	magenta
700–713	VS	air ASW	dark green

The wing commanders fly aircraft from one or more squadrons. Known as CAG from the outdated title Commander Air Group, the wing commander's aircraft are identified by double zero ("double nuts") instead of the squadron's normal side numbers.

Bureau numbers are assigned to all Navy and Marine Corps aircraft in sequence of their procurement. The numbers are used on the aircraft's after fuselage or tail, and on transports the last three digits are sometimes used as their side numbers. "Bureau" refers to the Bureau of Aeronautics, which directed naval aircraft procurement from 1921 to 1959, when it became the Bureau of Naval Ordnance and, subsequently, the current Naval Air Systems Command.

National insignia of the United States consists of a white star within a blue circle, with white rectangles on either side, the rectangles having a red horizontal stripe and blue border. All naval aircraft have the national insignia on both sides of the fuselage, with fixed-wing aircraft also having it on the upper left and lower right wing surfaces.

Coast Guard aircraft have the national insignia or American flag on their tail fin. Some U.S. Navy COD and other transport aircraft also have the American flag on their fin.

Coast Guard aircraft wear that service's wide orange and narrow blue stripe insignia on the forward fuselage with the Coast Guard crest on the orange stripe.

These aircraft have a four-digit side number based on their (Coast Guard) procurement sequence except for two Coast Guard executive transports, a VC-11A and VC-4A, which have the side numbers 01 and 02, respectively. Home bases for the aircraft are generally indicated, with executive aircraft 01 based at Washington's National Airport, marked "Washington".

FIGHTER AIRCRAFT

F-21A KFIR

The Navy is procuring 12 Israeli-built Kfir fighter aircraft to simulate Soviet aircraft in the adversary training of U.S. Navy and Marine Corps pilots, supplementing the F-5E/F, T-38A, and TA-4J aircraft now used in this role. Additional aircraft will be procured for this role with the principal U.S. candidates being the General Dynamics F-16 (with a Pratt & Whitney F100 engine or a General Electric F101 Derivative Fighter Engine) and the Northrop F-20 (formerly F-5G). Deliveries were to begin late in 1984. The Kfirs are being given to the U.S. Navy on a no-cost lease basis. Israel Aircraft Industries is being contracted to maintain the aircraft.

The Kfir is a refinement of the Dassault Mirage 5 design, with a more powerful engine of American origins. The aircraft was developed for the air defense and ground attack roles. This is a delta-wing, single-engine aircraft. The main wing is mounted low and aft on the fuselage. In Israeli service the Kfir has two 30-mm DEFA cannon and can carry external weapons, sensors, and fuel totalling 12,730 pounds on seven external hard points.

The Israelis are producing later variants of the aircraft, with the Kfir C2 being the first improved model, having small, detachable fore wings (canards) mounted high on the fuselage, just behind the engine intakes. *Kfir* is Hebrew for Lion Cub.

First flight (prototype) 1972; IOC 1972–1973.

Manufacturer:	Israel Aircraft Industries
Crew:	pilot
Engines:	General Electric J79-J1E turbojet; 17,900 lbst with afterburner[1]
Weights:	empty 15,873 lbs; maximum takeoff 20,514 lbs
Dimensions:	length 51 ft 1/4 in (15.55 m)
	wing span 26 ft 11½ in (8.22 m)
	wing area height 13 ft 11¼ in (4.25 m)
Speed:	maximum 1,450 mph clean (Mach 2.2 +)
Ceiling:	50,000 + ft
Range:[2]	radius approx. 250 n.miles in fighter role with 2 AAMs and external tanks
Armament:	2 30-mm DEFA cannon
Radar:	Elta EL/M-2001 X-band

[1] All thrust/horsepower data indicate highest, not continuous power.

[2] Ranges for attack and escort missions are given for hi-lo-lo-hi in most examples. Maximum or ferry ranges are usually given with empty external tanks dropped.

F-21A Kfir (Peter B. Mersky)

Israeli-built F-21A Kfir in flight after being assigned to VF-43. (U.S. Navy)

F-4 PHANTOM (formerly F4H)

The F-4 Phantom[3] is an all-weather, multi-purpose fighter flown by active and reserve Navy and Marine Corps squadrons. It was the principal first-line fighter of these services and the Air Force during the 1960s and 1970s. It has been replaced in all but three Navy carriers wings by the F-14, with the CORAL SEA flying the F/A-18 Hornet in the fighter role and the MIDWAY retaining two F-4S squadrons. The Marine Corps is replacing the F-4S in the fighter role with the F/A-18. Navy and Marine reserve fighter squadrons continue to fly the F-4N/S variants. A lengthened (62⅚-foot) RF-4B photo-reconnaissance version is also flown by the Marine Corps.

The aircraft is a two-seat, twin-engine fighter. An elongated nose houses the AWG-10 radar/fire control system with a distinctive infrared sensor mounted underneath. Four AAMs can be carried semi-recessed under the fuselage. External stores can be carried on six wing attachment points and three fuselage attachment points. The F-4 was the first naval fighter aircraft built without guns. The principal U.S. naval versions were the F-4B and F-4J, which were subsequently upgraded to the F-4N and F-4S, respectively. The F-4S has an improved wing and AWG-10A digital radar/fire control system.

McDonnell Douglas produced 5,211 aircraft for U.S. and foreign use while Japan built 138 F-4EJ variants, including 11 from parts produced by McDonnell Douglas. All production ended in 1979; the last of 1,264 delivered to the Navy and Marine Corps were completed in December 1971. The Royal Navy also flew Phantoms from carriers with the F-4K,

[3] The Roman numeral II was initially used to avoid confusion with the earlier FH-1 Phantom turbojet fighter.

Br tain's last non-VSTOL carried-based fighter. The Phantom remains in service with several foreign air forces.

First flight 27 May 1958; Navy IOC (VF-121) December 1960; F-4S IOC (VF-21) December 1979.

F-4S

Manufacturer:	McDonnell Douglas
Crew:	pilot, radar intercept officer
Engines:	2 General Electric J79-GE-10 turbojets; 17,659 lbst each with afterburner
Weights:	empty 30,776 lbs; maximum takeoff 56,000 lbs
Dimensions:	length 58 ft 3 in (17.76 m)
	wing span 38 ft 5 in (11.71 m)
	wing area 530 sq ft (49.2 m²)
	height 16 ft 3 in (4.96 m)
Speed:	maximum 1,450 mph clean at 36,000 ft (Mach 2.1)
Ceiling:	71,000 ft
Range:	radius 228 -n.miles in fighter role (A below)
	radius 136 -n.miles in attack role (B below)
	radius 334 -n.miles in attack role (C below)
	ferry approx. 1,600 n.miles with external tanks
Armament:	4 Sparrow + 4 Sidewinder AAMs + 6 500-lb bombs + 1 600-gallon tank (A) or 4 Sparrow AAMs + 8 1,000-lb bombs (B) or 5 1,000-lb bombs + 2 370-gallon tanks (C)
Radar:	AWG-10A X-band

F-4N Phantom from VMFA-323 aboard the CORAL SEA. (Lt. Pete Clayton)

F-4J Phantoms of VMFA-323 assigned to the CORAL SEA. (U.S. Navy)

F-5E/F TIGER II

The F-5E/F variants are flown by the Navy as an air combat maneuvering/adversary training aircraft. The aircraft is the penultimate design in a long series developed by Northrop primarily for Third World markets. (The much-improved F-5G has been redesignated F-20.)

The F-5E Tiger is a single-seat aircraft and the F-5F a two-seat version, both with two turbojet engines. Sidewinder AAMs can be carried on wingtips and there are one fuselage and four wing stations for ordnance.

More than 3,000 F-5 fighters and the similar T-38 Talon trainer have been built for the U.S. Air Force and some 25 foreign nations, with additional aircraft on order. The U.S. Navy has taken delivery of 17 F-5E and 6 F-5F fighters, plus several T-38s to simulate Soviet fighter aircraft. These aircraft are flown by the Navy Fighter Weapons School (Top Gun) at Miramar and VF-43 at Oceana. The naval aircraft are expected to reach the end of their service life in 1987. The aircraft is not carrier capable.

F-5E

Manufacturer:	Northrop
Crew:	pilot (2 in F-5F)
Engines:	2 General Electric J85-GE-21B turbojets; 5,000 lbst each with afterburning
Weights:	F-5E empty 9,723 lbs; maximum takeoff 24,722 lbs F-5F empty 10,576 lbs; maximum takeoff 25,152 lbs
Dimensions:	length overall F-5E 47 ft 4¾ in (14.45 m) F-5F 51 ft 4 in (15.65 m)
	wing span 26 ft 8 in (8.13 m)
	wing area 186 sq ft (17.3 m²)
	height F-5E 13 ft 4 in (4.06 m) F-5F 13 ft 1¾ in (4.01 m)
Speed:	maximum Mach 1.64 at 36,000 ft (10,975 m)
Ceiling:	service 51,800 ft (15,790 m)
Range:	radius 570 n.miles with 2 Sidewinder AAMs 1,545 n.miles with external tanks
Armament:	2 20-mm M39A2 cannon (internal) (naval training aircraft do not carry weapons)
Radar:	APQ-159 X-band pulse

F-5E Tiger II (U.S. Navy)

F-5E Tiger II (U.S. Navy)

F-14 TOMCAT

The F-14 is the standard U.S. Navy carrier-based fighter and in several respects remains the most capable fighter aircraft in service today. All aircraft carriers except the MIDWAY and CORAL SEA fly the F-14 Tomcat in the fighter role with the aircraft also being employed in the reconnaissance role with the TARPS (Tactical Air Reconnaissance Pod System).

The aircraft has variable-geometry wings that sweep back automatically during flight maneuvers; they extend for long-range flight and landings, sweeping back for high-speed flight (and carrier stowage). The two-seat aircraft is characterized by its long-range AWG-9 radar, which can detect hostile aircraft out to at least 100 miles and simultaneously track up to 24 targets, and the Phoenix missile, which can engage targets more than 60 miles away. Planned under-fuselage pallets for bombs and air-to-surface missiles have not been provided. The TARPS package can be fitted or deleted to a standard aircraft in a few hours. It contains a KS-87 frame camera, KA-99 panoramic camera, and an AN/AAD-5 infrared line scanner.

Only about 80 F-14A aircraft were originally to have been procured with subsequent aircraft to have been the F-14B with improved engines with a later F-14C to have also had upgraded avionics. Only the F-14A model, however, was produced with problems being encountered with the engine. An F-14/F101 DFE (Derivative Fighter Engine) aircraft was flight tested 1981–1982. It had maximum engine thrust of 28,500 pounds resulting in an increased radius (deck-launched intercept role) from 134 n.miles to 210 n.miles, and maximum permissible catapult weight in-

crease from 59,000 pounds to 74,000 pounds. The decision to procure 324 of the improved F-14D models with the similar F110-GE-400 engine was made in early 1984, with delivery of the first aircraft in fiscal 1987. The F-14D will also have a digital, programmable digital processor for the AWG-9 in place of the existing analog unit to improve radar/fire control performance in a jamming environment as well as improved long-range target resolution and increased reliability. First flight of the F-14D is planned for 1988.

The F-14 was originally planned for Marine Corps use, but that service turned it down, in part because of the plan to procure the AV-8A Harrier. The Navy had some 410 F-14A aircraft in early 1984 (78 aircraft were also provided to Iran). Seventy U.S. aircraft have been lost in crashes since 1970.

First flight 21 December 1970; Navy IOC (VF-124) January 1973.

F-14A

Manufacturer:	Grumman
Crew:	pilot, radar-intercept officer
Engines:	2 Pratt & Whitney TF30-P-412A turbofans; 20,900 lbst each with afterburning
Weights:	empty 39,762 lbs; normal takeoff 58,539 lbs; takeoff with 6 Phoenix AAMs 70,426 lbs
Dimensions:	length overall 62 ft 8 in (19.1 m)
	wing span 64 ft 1½ in (19.54 m) unswept
	wing span 38 ft 2½ in (11.65 m) swept back
	wing area 565 sq ft (52.49 m^2)
	height 16 ft (4.88 m)
Speed:	maximum Mach 2.4
Ceiling:	50,000 + ft
Range:	
Armament:	1 20-mm M61A1 Vulcan cannon (multibarrel; 676 rounds)
	2 Phoenix + 3 Sparrow + 2 Sidewinder AAMs + 2 300-gallon tanks or 4 Phoenix + 2 Sparrow + 2 Sidewinder AAMs + 2 300-gallon tanks
	or 6 Phoenix + 2 Sidewinder AAMs + 2 300-gallon tanks
	or 6 Sparrow + 2 Sidewinder AAMs + 2 300-gallon tanks
Radar:	AWG-9

F-14A Tomcat carrying Phoenix, Sidewinder, and Sparrow AAMs (U.S. Navy)

F-14A Tomcat fitted with TARPS (U.S. Navy)

F-14A Tomcat of VF-211 (U.S. Navy)

An F-14A Tomcat taking off from a ski-jump ramp at the Naval Air Test Center (NATC) Patuxent River, Md. (U.S. Navy)

An F-14A tomcat with six Phoenix and two Sidewinder AAMs plus a pair of external fuel tanks. (U.S. Navy)

F/A-18 HORNET

The Hornet is a strike fighter (formerly fighter/attack) aircraft that will be widely used in the fighter role by the Navy and Marine Corps, and in the attack role by the Navy, replacing the F-4 Phantom and A-7 Corsair in those respective roles. The F/A-18 has been a controversial program because of the Marine decision to procure the AV-8B Harrier instead of the F/A-18 for the attack role, rapidly increasing F/A-18 costs, and because of limited performance in some areas over the A-7. The Navy is also assigning F/A-18s to the Naval Air Reserve.

A twin-engine, single-seat aircraft, the F/A-18 is characterized by its high maneuverability, the ability to operate in either the fighter or attack role with only a change in computer software and weapon racks, and comparatively low maintenance requirements (maintenance is estimated at 10.3 man hours per flight hour average compared with 18.8 for the A-4E and 30.9 for the F-4S). The F/A-18 has wingtip positions, three fuselage stations, and four wing stations for weapons and sensor/guidance pods. A two-seat TF-18 trainer and F/A-18 for Marine combat control has been developed, and a single-seat RF/A-18 reconnaissance variant is planned.

The F/A-18 was developed as a result of congressional pressure for the Navy to obtain a lightweight fighter to complement the F-14 in carrier air wings. Congress originally directed the Navy to select the winner of the Air Force's lightweight fighter competition between the General Dynamics YF-16 and Northrop YF-17 prototypes. The Air Force selected the F-16 for production; the Navy selected the YF-17, but made major modifications, leading to the F/A-18 developed jointly by McDonnell Douglas and Northrop. (The initial order for 11 aircraft used the designation YF-18.) The aircraft has apparently failed to fully achieve its range/payload goals in the attack role.

The original Navy-Marine plan was for 1,366 aircraft. However, cutbacks in the Navy fighter and Marine attack version buys will significantly reduce the final size of the program. The following table shows the original program:

12	Marine fighter squadrons	144 aircraft
8	Marine attack squadrons	160
1	Marine photo squadron	21
1	Marine control squadron	30
6	Navy fighter squadrons	72
24	Navy attack squadrons	288
1	Navy photo squadron	36
	RDT&E aircraft	19
	readiness-training	151
	pipeline	124
	attrition	321
	Total	1366

Australia, Canada, and Spain are procuring the F/A-18 for land basing. (A proposed Northrop F-18L land-based version has not been ordered.)

First flight 18 November 1978; Navy-Marine IOC (VFA-125) February 1981; Marine IOC (VMFA-314) March 1983.

F/A-18A

Manufacturer:	McDonnell Douglas and Northrop
Crew:	pilot (2 in TF-18)
Engines:	2 General Electric F404-GE-400 turbofans; 16,000 lbst each
Weights:	fighter mission normal takeoff 33,585 lbs
	attack mission normal takeoff 48,253 lbs
Dimensions:	length overall 56 ft (17.07 m)
	wing span 37 ft 6 in (11.43 m)
	wing area 400 sq ft (37.16 m²)
	height 15 ft 3½ in (4.66 m)
Speed:	maximum Mach 1.8+
Ceiling:	50,000+ ft
Range:	radius 400+ n.miles in fighter role
	radius 550 n.miles in attack role
Armament:	1 20-mm M61 Vulcan cannon (multibarrel; 540 rounds)
	2 Sidewinder + 4 Sparrow AAMs in fighter role or 2 Sidewinder AAMs + 17,000 lbs of bombs, missiles, rockets in attack role
Radar:	APG-65 multi-mode digital

F/A-18A Hornet (McDonnell Douglas)

F/A-18 Hornet of VMFA-314 (McDonnell Douglas)

TF-18A Hornet (Robert L. Lawson)

F/A-18A Hornet with four Mk 83 1,000-pound bombs, three external fuel tanks, a Forward-Looking Infrared (FLIR) pod on the port air intake duct, a laser spot tracker and strike camera pod on the starboard duct, and Sidewinder AAMs on wingtips. (McDonnell Douglas)

ATTACK AIRCRAFT

A-4 SKYHAWK (formerly A4D)

The Skyhawk was developed in the early 1950s as a lightweight, day-light-only nuclear strike aircraft for use in large numbers from aircraft carriers. The aircraft subsequently evolved into a highly versatile attack aircraft, widely used by the Navy and Marine Corps as well as several foreign air forces. It survives in Navy service mainly as a trainer and utility aircraft (TA-4J), and with the Marines as a light-attack plane (A-4M). In addition, the Marines fly the OA-4 as a tactical control aircraft while the Navy flies the EA-4F in an EW simulation role and the A-4E/F as well as TA-4J to simulate Soviet fighter aircraft. (The MiG stand-ins are called Mongoose, a play on the NATO designation of Soviet trainers with M-series names.)

The basic Skyhawk is a single-seat, single-engine aircraft with a delta wing. (The wing does not fold for carrier stowage.) A pair of 20-mm cannon are fitted in the wing roots and there are five attachment points for up to 9,155 pounds of ordnance or external fuel tanks. The Marine OA-4M tactical control aircraft are converted TA-4F Skyhawks, retaining the J52-P-6 series engine; the single-seat A-4M has a distinctive dorsal hump housing electronic aircraft. The two-seat TA-4/OA-4/EA-4F aircraft are 42 feet 7 inches long.

A total of 2,960 A-4s were built for U.S. and foreign use of which 555 were two-seaters; the first was delivered in 1956 and the last, an A-4M for the Marine Corps, in 1979. This was one of the longest production runs of any combat aircraft in history. The Navy TA-4J variant will be replaced in the training role by the T-45 Hawk while the Marines will receive the AV-8B in place of the A-4M. The Navy-Marine Blue Angels flight demonstration team flies the A-4F. Many survive in foreign air forces, with the Israelis having used them extensively in combat as well as the Argentine Navy and Air Force during the 1982 conflict in the Falklands.

First flight 22 June 1954; Navy IOC (VA-72) 27 September 1956.

A-4M

Manufacturer:	McDonnell Douglas
Crew:	pilot (2 in TA-4J)
Engines:	1 Pratt & Whitney J52-P-408 turbojets; 11,200 lbst
Weights:	empty 10,456 lbs; maximum takeoff 24,500 lbs
Dimensions:	length 40 ft 3¾ in (12.27 m); TA-4/OA-4 variants are 42 ft 7¼ in (12.98 m)
	wing span 27 ft 6 in (8.38 m)
	wing area 260 sq ft (24.16 m²)
	height 15 ft (4.57 m); TA-4/OA-4 variants are 15 ft 3 in (4.66 m)
Speed:	maximum 670 mph at sea level; 645 mph with 4,000 lbs ordnance; cruise 483 mph
Ceiling:	42,250 ft
Range:	radius 335 n.miles with 4,000 lbs ordnance
Armament:	2 20-mm Mk 12 cannon (100 rounds each) 14 500-lb bombs or 3 1,000-lb bombs or 4 Shrike ARMs[5] or 1 2,000-lb bomb or 4 Maverick ASMs[6]
Radar:	None

[5] Anti-Radiation Missile.
[6] Air-to-Surface Missile.

TA-4J Skyhawk from VT-22 (U.S. Navy)

A-4E Skyhawk from VC-5 (U.S. Navy)

TA-4J of VC-13 with two-tone blue low visibility markings; letters and numerals in red. (Peter Mersky)

A-4F (left) and A-4M Skyhawks of VMA-133; the latter aircraft has a laser spot finder in the nose. (McDonnell Douglas)

A-6 INTRUDER (formerly A2F)

The Intruder is the Navy's carrier-based medium attack aircraft, capable of all-weather, day/night attack. One squadron is assigned to all carrier wings and it is flown by Marine medium attack squadrons. The Navy also flies the KA-6D tanker. (The EA-6A and EA-6B electronic warfare variants are listed separately.)

The Intruder is a two-seat, twin-turbojet aircraft. All weapons are carried on five attachment points, each with a 6,200-lb capacity for a maximum of 18,000 lbs of ordnance and drop tanks. The A-6E now in service has the Target Recognition Attack Multisensor (TRAM), integrating Forward Looking Infrared (FLIR), a combination laser designator/range finder, and a laser designation receiver. A capability for firing the Harpoon anti-ship missile is being provided. An improved A-6F, with new avionics and possibly the F-404 engine, has been proposed by the Navy; that model could have an IOC as early as 1988. The KA-6D tankers (some converted from A-6A) have avionics deleted from the after fuselage to provide space for reel; up to five 500-gallon drop tanks can be carried to permit the transfer of over 21,000 pounds of fuel immediately after takeoff or 15,000 pounds at a distance of 288 n.miles from the carrier. The first of four A-6A conversions flew in April 1970 (designated NA-6A as land-based test aircraft). The A-6 attack aircraft has a Sidewinder AAM capability.

More than 700 aircraft of all variants have been built for the Navy and Marine Corps with production continuing; 240 A-6A aircraft were upgraded to A-6E. Approximately 360 A-6E aircraft are currently in service with Navy and Marine attack squadrons. There are no foreign users.

First flight 19 April 1960; Navy IOC (VA-42) February 1963; KA-6D IOC (VA-176) September 1970.

A-6E

Manufacturer:	Grumman
Crew:	pilot, bombardier/navigator
Engines:	2 Pratt & Whitney J52-P-8B turbojets; 9,300 lbst each
Weights:	empty 26,600 lbs; maximum 60,400 lbs
Dimensions:	length overall 54 ft 9 in (16.69 m)
	wing span 53 ft (16.15 m)
	wing area 528.9 sq ft (49.1 m²)
	height 16 ft 2 in (4.93 m)
Speed:	maximum 644 mph at sea level
Ceiling:	service 42,400 ft
Range:	880 n.miles with combat load; ferry 2,375 n.miles
Armament:	30 500-lb bombs
	or 10 1,000-lb bombs
	or 3 2,000-lb bombs + 2 300-gallon tanks
Radar:	APQ-156 multi-mode

A-6 Intruder in landing configuration (U.S. Navy)

A KA-6D Intruder tanker landing at NAS Roosevelt Roads, Puerto Rico. Note the four external fuel tanks and hose housing below fuselage. (U.S. Navy)

A-6E Intruder of VA-128 being readied for flight at NAS Fallon, Nev. (U.S. Navy)

A-6E Intruder of VA-85 landing on FORRESTAL (U.S. Navy)

KA-6D Intruder refueling an F/A-18A Hornet (McDonnell Douglas)

A-7 CORSAIR

The Corsair[7] is a carried-based, light attack aircraft, with 24 A-7E aircraft assigned to most carrier air wings. The plane was developed specifically as a daylight attack aircraft to replace the A-4 Skyhawk. Later models have been fitted with limited night/all-weather capabilities. The plane is scheduled to be completely replaced in the Navy attack role by the F/A-18.

[7] The Roman numeral II was initially used as a suffix to avoid confusion with the earlier F4U Corsair piston fighter.

An A-7E Corsair being maintained aboard the CORAL SEA; the carrier has since shifted to F/A-18 Hornets in place of Corsairs and Phantoms. A Sidewinder AAM is fitted on the "cheek" pylon, just aft of the U.S. national insignia. (U.S. Navy)

The A-7 is a single-seat, single-engine aircraft with a high, swept-back wing configuration that closely resembles the F-8 Crusader fighter from which the attack aircraft was derived. There is an internal 20-mm Gatling gun, two fuselage cheek-position points for rockets or Sidewinder missiles, and six wing points for an aggregate of 15,000 pounds of external stores. Several two-seat TA-7C aircraft have been modified to an EA-7L jamming configuration for use in fleet exercises.

More than 1,000 A-7s were built for the Navy and Marine Corps plus 498 specifically for foreign use. A few Navy versions were TA-7C with dual controls; a proposed RA-7E with reconnaissance pods was dropped in favor of the F-14/TARPS; and an improved, twin-engine Corsair lost out in the concept stage to the F/A-18 as the new Navy attack aircraft. The A-7D model—similar to the A-7E except for engine—was produced for the U.S. Air Force.

First flight 27 September 1965; Navy IOC (VA-174) October 1966.

A-7E

Manufacturer:	LTV-Vought
Crew:	pilot (2 in TA-7C, EA-7L)
Engines:	1 Allison TF41-A-2 (Rolls-Royce Spey) turbofan; 15,000 lbst
Weights:	empty 19,111 lbs; maximum takeoff 42,000 lbs
Dimensions:	length 46 ft 1½ in (14.06 m)
	wing span 38 ft 9 in (11.8 m)
	wing area 375 sq ft (34.83 m²)
Speed:	maximum 691 mph at sea level; 646 mph at 5,000 ft with 12 500-lb bombs
Ceiling:	42,600 ft
Range:	ferry 2,485 n.miles with external tanks
Armament:	1 M61-1 Vulcan cannon (multibarrel; 1,000 rounds)
	2 Sidewinder AAMs
	32 500-lb bombs
	or 16 1,000-lb bombs
	or 6 2,000-lb bombs
Radar:	APQ-126(V) multi-mode

A pair of A-7E Corsairs of VA-86 aboard the NIMITZ. The nearer Corsair is streaming a refueling drogue from a buddy store, fitted to permit in-flight refueling of other carrier aircraft. The Corsair's successor, the F/A-18 Hornet, cannot be fitted as an in-flight tanker. The buddy store is entirely external and can rapidly be replaced by bombs or other weapons. (U.S. Navy)

A bomb-laden A-7E Corsair from CVW-3 when embarked in the KITTY HAWK; the aircraft's 00—"double nut"—number indicates it is flown by the wing commander. (Vought)

An A-7E Corsair of VA-146 landing aboard the AMERICA.

AV-8A HARRIER

The Harrier was the first VSTOL aircraft to enter first-line service with the U.S. armed forces. The British-developed Harrier was procured for three Marine attack squadrons. The Marines deemed it a success despite a high accident rate; several surviving AV-8A aircraft are being upgraded to the AV-8C, with two converted to YAV-8B prototypes for the Advanced Harrier. The Harrier is a land-based aircraft but has been extensively deployed from LHA/LPH amphibious ships, beginning with the GUAM (LPH 7) in 1972. In 1976–1977 the fleet carrier FRANKLIN D. ROOSEVELT deployed to the Mediterranean with a squadron of 14 AV-8A aircraft.

Developed from the P.1127 Kestrel VSTOL technology demonstration aircraft, the Harrier is powered by a vectored-thrust turbofan engine that exhausts through rotating nozzles. The wings do not fold. Ordnance and fuel tanks can be carried on four wing and one fuselage attachment points (in addition to gun pods) for an external payload of 4,500 pounds for short takeoff and 3,000 pounds in vertical takeoff.

The P.1127 first flew on 19 November 1960 and was evaluated by the U.S. services as the XV-6A. The AV-8A was manufactured by

McDonnell Douglas with deliveries beginning in 1971, two years after squadron delivery to the Royal Air Force. The U.S. Marines took delivery of 102 single-seat AV-8A and eight two-seat TAV-8A Harriers. One trainer and 48 single-seat aircraft have been lost in accidents. Two have been converted to AV-8C prototypes (one subsequently lost). Of the 52 surviving Harriers, 36 have been converted to C models. Variants of the Harrier serve with the Royal Navy as well as RAF (aircraft from both services, based on carriers, saw extensive combat in the 1982 war in the Falklands). Harriers are also flown from carriers by the Indian and Spanish navies.

First flight P.1127 19 November 1960, GR Mk 1 28 December 1967; Marine Corps IOC (VMA-513) January 1971.

AV-8A

Manufacturer:	British Aerospace (Kingston) and McDonnell Douglas
Crew:	pilot (2 in TAV-8A)
Engines:	1 Rolls-Royce F402-RR-402 Pegasus 11 turbofan; 21,500 lbst
Weights:	empty 12,200 lbs; gross 17,500 lbs for VTO; gross 21,489 lbs for STO; maximum 25,000+ lbs for conventional takeoff
Dimensions:	length 45 ft 6 in (13.87 m)
	wing span 25 ft 3 in (7.7 m)
	wing area 201 sq ft (18.68 m²)
	height 11 ft 3 in (3.43 m)
Speed:	maximum 637 mph at 1,000 ft (Mach 0.95)
Ceiling:	service 45,200 ft
Range:	radius 422 n.miles with 7 500-lb bombs; radius 400 n.miles with 2 AAMs and 1 hour loiter; ferry 1,800 n.miles (all STO configuration)
Armament:	2 30-mm Aden gun pods
	2 Sidewinder AAMs + 3 500-lb bombs
	or 2 Sidewinder AAMs + 3 1,000-lb bombs
Radar:	none

AV-8C (top) and AV-8B aboard an LHA; note the larger wings and landing gear housing of the AV-8B. (McDonnell Douglas)

An AV-8A Harrier of VMA-231 during 1976 Mediterranean deployment aboard the FRANKLIN D. ROOSEVELT. (U.S. Navy)

AV-8A Harrier (U.S. Navy)

AV-8A Harrier (U.S. Navy)

AV-8B HARRIER II

The AV-8B is an advanced VSTOL fighter/attack aircraft, being procured for eight Marine light attack squadrons, replacing the A-4M and, eventually, the AV-8A/C aircraft. During the Carter Administration the Department of Defense sought to have the Marines procure the F/A-18 as a replacement for the A-4M, but the Marines—with congressional support—held fast to the AV-8B program.

The AV-8B differs from previous Harrier in having a supercritical wing shape, larger trailing-edge flaps, drooped ailerons, strakes under the gun pods, redesigned engine intakes, strengthened landing gear, and a more-powerful engine, providing twice the payload of the AV-8A with up to 9,200 pounds of external stores. The aircraft carries one external 25-mm gun in twin packs faired into the under fuselage, with one fuselage and six wing points available for bombs, rockets, or missiles. The British GR Mk 5 aircraft is similar.

The Marine Corps originally planned to procure 336 operational aircraft plus four full-scale development aircraft in addition to two YAV-8B prototypes that were converted from AV-8A aircraft. This has been revised to 300 AV-8B and 28 of the two-seat TAV-8B trainers.

First flight YAV-8B on 9 November 1978; first flight AV-8B on 5 November 1981; Marine IOC January 1984.

AV-8C Harrier (McDonnell Douglas)

AV-8B

Manufacturer:	British Aerospace and McDonnell Douglas
Crew:	pilot (2 in TAV-8B)
Engines:	1 Rolls-Royce F402-RR-406 Pegasus 11 Mk 103 turbofan; 21,700 lbst
Weights:	empty 12,922 lbs; maximum takeoff VTO 19,550 lbs; maximum takeoff STO 29,750 lbs (1,200 ft/366 m takeoff run)
Dimensions:	length 46 ft 4 in (14.12 m)
	wing span 30 ft 4 in (9.25 m)
	wing area 230 sq ft (21.37 m²)
	height 11 ft 7¾ in (3.55 m)
Speed:	maximum 668 mph at sea level
Ceiling:	50,000 ft

Range:	150 n.mile radius with 12 500-lb bombs with 1 hour loiter in STO takeoff; 600 n.mile radius with 7 500-lb bombs in STO mode; ferry 2,560 n.miles with external tanks (4 300-gallon)
Armament:	1 25-mm GAU-12/U cannon (multibarrel; 300 rounds) 16 500-lb bombs or 4 Sidewinder AAMs
Radar:	none

A prototype AV-8B Harrier II takes off from the ski-jump ramp at NATC Patuxent River, Md. (McDonnell Douglas)

An AV-8B Harrier II carries 16 Mk 82 570-pound bombs during flight tests at Patuxent River, Md. The aircraft had a gross takeoff weight for the flight of 29,664 pounds. (McDonnell Douglas)

AV-8B+ HARRIER

This is a proposed fighter/attack version of the AV-8B with an air-intercept radar and improved engine. In fiscal 1982 dollars the cost increase of the AV-8B+ over the standard Advanced Harrier was estimated at approximately $2 million per aircraft in a 300-unit buy. There is no current Navy requirement or procurement plan for the fighter/attack version. However, several defense analysts and members of Congress have proposed that the Navy give serious attention to the concept.

AV-18 ADVANCED HARRIER

In 1973–1974 the U.S. and British governments considered several options and proposals for an advanced version of the Harrier, to succeed the AV-8A in U.S. Marine Corps service. One of the most promising was the AV-16A, proposed for the RAF, Royal Navy, U.S. Marine Corps, and U.S. Navy. The project died in March 1975, however, when Britain's Minister of Defence, Roy Mason, terminated the joint studies, saying that there was "not enough common ground on the Advanced Harrier for us to join in the programme with the United States." In the event, there was a great deal of commonality in the succeeding Harrier design for the RAF (GR Mk 5) and U.S. Marine Corps (AV-8B).

ANTI-SUBMARINE/MARITIME PATROL AIRCRAFT

P-2 NEPTUNE (formerly P2V)

The last P-2/P2V Neptune patrol aircraft have been retired from U.S. naval service. Three EP-2H models survived into the early 1980s, assigned to squadron VC-8 supporting target drones.

Lockheed produced 1,099 Neptunes and Kawasaki in Japan built another 89 P-2J variants (with 48 of the Lockheed aircraft assembled in Japan). In the P2V-3C model the Neptune was configured for carrier launch, but not recovery, to provide the first U.S. ship-based nuclear strike capability in the late 1940s. Several foreign nations continue to fly the Neptune.

P-3 ORION (formerly P3V)

The Orion serves in all 24 Navy patrol squadrons and the 13 reserve VP units as well as several foreign air arms. It provides long-range reconnaissance and ASW capabilities, with several squadrons now being fitted to launch the Harpoon anti-ship missile. Several specialized EP-3C Electronic Intelligence (ELINT) and RP-3 reconnaissance aircraft are also in naval service.

The aircraft was adopted from the commercial Electra. It is powered by four turboprop engines. Up to 15,000 pounds of rockets, missiles, mines, torpedoes, or nuclear depth bombs can be carried in the internal weapons bay and on ten wing pylons. They are being fitted to carry the Harpoon. (In the early 1970s some P-3B variants were fitted to carry the Bullpup AGM-12 missile.) The plane's ASW equipment includes Magnetic Anomoly Detection (MAD) and 48 external (fuselage) sonobuoy tubes plus one reloadable internal tube. The latest version is the P-3C Update III, introduced in 1984, which has an IBM Proteus signal processor system. An Update IV is being developed that will further improve EW, radar, and acoustic systems. The EP-3 aircraft has automatic electronic and communication intercept/analysis equipment to provide fleet and task force commanders with real-time intelligence. Two WP-3D are operated by the Commerce Department/NOAA. Several P-3A aircraft are on loan to the Customs Service for anti-drug surveillance. Plans to provide an in-flight refueling capability have been deferred. A few P-3A aircraft have been reconfigured as executive transports (VP-3A).

More than 500 Orions have been delivered to the Navy and Naval Reserve; additional aircraft have gone to eight other nations plus Japan producing 42 aircraft. Production continues with the Navy's goal of an all P-3C force by the late 1980s or 1990s. Additional EP-3Es are being produced to provide 14 aircraft, with replacement of the current 12 EP-3s now in service, which are converted P-3A/B aircraft, also planned.

First flight November 1959; P-3A IOC (VP-8) August 1962; P-3C IOC 1969.

P-3C

Manufacturer:	Lockheed
Crew:	command pilot, 2 pilots, flight engineer, navigator, radio operator, tactical coordinator, 3 systems operators (10); provisions for 2 additional observers
Engines:	4 Allison T56-A-14 turboprops; 4,910 ehp each[8]
Weights:	empty 61,491 lbs; normal takeoff 135,000 lbs; maximum takeoff 142,000 lbs
Dimensions:	length 116 ft 10 in (35.61 m)
	wing span 99 ft 8 in (30.37 m)
	wing area 1,300 sq ft (120.77 m²)
	height 33 ft 8½ in (10.29 m)
Speed:	maximum 473 mph at 15,000 ft; cruise 380 mph at 25,000 ft; loiter 230 mph (with two engines shut down)
Ceiling:	service 28,300 ft
Range:	radius 1,346 n.miles with 13 hours on station

Armament:	weapons bay	wing points
	8 Mk 46 torpedoes	+ 4 Mk 46 torpedoes
	or 2 2,000-lb mines	+ 4 Mk 46 torpedoes
	or 4 1,000-lb mines	+ 4 Mk 46 torpedoes
	or 8 Mk 46 torpedoes	+ 16 5-inch rockets

Radar:	APS-115 I-band (APS-80 in P-3B, APS-20 in EP-3B/E)

[8] Estimated horsepower.

P-3B of VP-31 (U.S. Navy)

EP-3E Orion of VQ-2 (U.S. Navy)

P-3C Orion of VP-4 (U.S. Navy)

WP-3D Orion of National Oceanic and Atmospheric Administration (NOAA)

RP-3D Orions assigned to VXN-8; fuselage markings include international orange trim and words U.S. Navy Oceanographic Office, with American flag on tail fin. (U.S. Navy)

S-3 VIKING

The S-3A is the Navy's carrier-based ASW aircraft, with one ten-plane squadron serving aboard all carriers except the MIDWAY and CORAL SEA. The Viking replaced the S2F/S-2 Tracker, although that plane served aboard only specialized ASW carriers.

The aircraft was designed to be within the approximate dimensions of the piston-engine Tracker but to be faster and to carry more advanced ASW equipment. The internal weapons bay, sized to hold four Mk 44/46 torpedoes, can carry 2,400 pounds of weapons. There are also two wing pylons. ASW systems include the ASQ-81 MAD, Forward-Looking Infrared (FLIR), and 60 sonobuoys in fuselage tubes. The wings and tail fin fold for carrier stowage. The S-3B is planned for limited production with an improved acoustic processor, improved radar (APS-137), and Harpoon anti-ship missile capability. Six preproduction S-3A aircraft have been modified to a US-3A cargo configuration for operation from carriers in the Western Pacific and Indian Ocean. These planes have two pilots, a loadmaster, and room for five passengers. The production of 20 ES-3 ELINT aircraft to replace the carrier-capable EA-3B was cancelled, while a Lockheed-proposed KS-3 tanker to succeed the KA-6D was dropped.

The last of 187 S-3A aircraft was completed in 1978. Up to 160 are planned for upgrading to S-3B in addition to a production run of 82 to 103 new aircraft; the first two modifications are to complete in 1985.

First flight 21 January 1972; Navy IOC (VS-41) February 1974.

S-3A

Manufacturer:	Lockheed
Crew:	2 pilots, tactical coordinator, systems operator
Engines:	2 General Electric TF34-GE-400 turbofans; 9,275 lbst each
Weights:	empty 26,783 lbs; maximum takeoff 52,539 lbs
Dimensions:	length 53 ft 4 in (16.26 m)
	wing span 68 ft 8 in (20.93 m)
	wing area 598 sq ft (55.56 m²)
	height 22 ft 9 in (6.94 m)
Speed:	maximum 506 mph at sea level; cruise 400+ mph; loiter 240 mph at 20,000 ft
Ceiling:	40,000 ft
Range:	patrol 2,300+ n.miles; ferry 3,000+ n.miles
Armament:	*weapons bay* *wing points*
	4 Mk 46 torpedoes + 6 500-lb bombs
	or 4 500-lb bombs + 6 500-lb bombs
Radar:	APS-116

S-3A Viking of VS-21 (Lockheed)

US-3A Viking COD aircraft with cargo pods fitted. (Lockheed)

S-3A Viking of VS-28 (Robert L. Lawson)

S-3A Viking of VS-29; note that the tail fin folds in addition to wings for shipboard stowage; the only fixed-wing carrier aircraft that do not have folding wings are the F-14 Tomcat (whose wings sweep back), A-4 Skyhawk, and AV-8 Harrier. (Lockheed)

ELECTRONIC WARFARE AIRCRAFT

E-2 HAWKEYE (formerly W2F)

The Hawkeye is a carrier-based Airborne Early Warning (AEW) aircraft developed specifically for carrier operation. The E-2C variant is considered by many authorities as the most capable radar warning and aircraft control plane now in service. A four-plane squadron is provided to each carrier, having replaced the piston-engine WF/E-1 Tracer in active squadrons and the two reserve AEW units.

The Hawkeye's most distinctive feature is the 24-foot diameter, saucer-like radome for the APS-120/125 UHF radar. The radome revolves freely in the airstream at the rate of six revolutions per minute. It provides sufficient lift to offset its own weight in flight and can be lowered to facilitate handling the aircraft aboard ship. The E-2C represents primarily an avionics upgrade over the previous E-2A/B variants (which had the APS-96 radar). One of the prototype E-2A aircraft was modified to a YE-2C configuration and subsequently employed as a trainer (TE-2C). The APS-125 in the E-2C has an effective aircraft detection range of some 240 n.miles with an over-land/water capability; the aircraft can simultaneously track more than 250 air targets and control up to 30 interceptors.

More than 100 E-2 aircraft have been built for the Navy, and production is continuing. The aircraft has also been produced for Egypt, Israel, and Japan.

First flight 21 October 1960; first flight E-2C 20 January 1971; Navy IOC (VAW-11) January 1964.

E-2C

Manufacturer:	Grumman
Crew:	2 pilots, combat information center officer, air controller, radar operator or technician (5)
Engines:	2 Allison T56-A-422 turboprops; 4,591 shp each
Weights:	empty 37,678 lbs; maximum takeoff 51,569 lbs
Dimensions:	length 57 ft 7 in (17.56 m)
	wing span 80 ft 7 in (24.58 m)
	wing area 700 sq ft (65.03 m²)
	height 18 ft 4 in (5.59 m)
Speed:	maximum 375 mph; cruise 310 mph
Ceiling:	30,800 ft
Range:	radius 200 -n.miles with 6 hours on station; ferry 1,525 n.miles
Armament:	none
Radar:	APS-125 (APS-120 in early E-2C aircraft)

TE-2C Hawkeye of VAW-120 (U.S. Navy)

E-2C Hawkeye of VAW-112 (Grumman)

E-2C Hawkeye of VAW-126 (U.S. Navy)

E-6A TACAMO

This aircraft will replace the EC-130 in the TACAMO (Take Charge And Move Out) role of providing VLF signal relay to strategic missile submarines at sea. The E-6A will be a naval version of the Boeing 707 aircraft, which also serves as the airframe for the EC-135/E-3 AWACS (Airborne Warning and Control System).

The aircraft was developed under the designation EXC. The Navy had proposed a competition of available airframes; however, only Boeing responded with the modified 707/EC-137/E-3 design. In the TACAMO role the E-6A will have the same VLF equipment as the EC-130Q with over 30,000 feet of trailing wire antenna. Normal mission duration will be about 15 hours. All crew training and maintenance support are to be provided by Boeing.

The Navy plans to procure 15 E-6A aircraft, including one research and development aircraft that will be later upgraded to full operational capability. The first two aircraft are to be delivered in 1987 and the last one in 1991.

First flight in 1986; IOC in fiscal 1988.

E-6A

Manufacturer:	Boeing
Crew:	4 flight crew + 5 mission crew + 8 relief crew seats
Engines:	4 General Electric/SNECMA CFM-256
Weights:	gross take off 342,000 lbs

Dimensions:	length 152 ft 11 in (46.61 m)
	wing span 148 ft 4 in (45.23 m)
	wing area 4,590 sq ft (426.41 m²)
	height 42 ft 5 in (12.92 m)
Speed:	530 mph
Ceiling:	29,000+ ft
Range:	radius 1,000 n.miles with 6 hours loiter
Radar:	APS-133

Retouched photo of EC-135/E-3 airframe fitted with CFM-56 engines for E-6A TACAMO role given Navy markings; squadron markings of VQ-3 or VQ-4 are missing. (Boeing)

EA-3B/KA-3B SKYWARRIOR (formerly A3D-2Q)

The Skywarrior is the oldest combat aircraft remaining in naval service. It was developed as a long-range, carrier-based nuclear strike aircraft. The Skywarrior survived its intended successor, the A3J/A-5 Vigilante, now in service as the EA-3B flown by several active electronic squadrons (VAQ/VQ) and the KA-3B flown by two Naval Reserve tanker squadrons (VAK). A few aircraft are also used in the VIP transport configuration (TA-3B and VA-3B, the former with dual controls).

The aircraft has a twin turbojet configuration with an internal weapons bay. In the strike role the internal weapons bay could hold up to 12,800 pounds of nuclear or conventional weapons. The EA-3B has the weapons bay modified to carry four sensor operators and ELINT equipment and the KA-3B to carry fuel tanks and refueling gear. The latter can lift 34,178 pounds of fuel (5,026 gallons) of which about two-thirds can be transferred to other aircraft. As built, a twin, remote/radar-control 20-mm gun turret was fitted in the tail. The Navy took delivery of 282 Skywarriors: 2 XA3D-1 prototypes, 1 YA3D-1 prototype, 49 A3D-1 and 164 A3D-2 strike aircraft, 30 reconnaissance aircraft (RA-3B), 24 electronic aircraft (EA-3B), and 12 training aircraft (TA-3B). Several strike and recce aircraft were converted to EA-3A, ERA-3B, and EKA-3B, the last a combination tanker-jammer aircraft. The Air Force flew the similar B-66 Destroyer in the bomber, electronic, reconnaissance, and weather roles.

First flight 22 October 1952; Navy IOC A3D-1/A-3A (VAH-1) March 1956; first flight A3D-2Q/EA-3B prototype 10 December 1958.

EA-3B

Manufacturer:	Douglas
Crew:	pilot, navigator, 4 electronic systems operators, additional crewman (optional)
Engines:	2 Pratt & Whitney J57-P-10 turbojets; 12,400 lbst each
Weights:	empty 41,193 lbs; loaded 61,593 lbs; maximum takeoff 78,000 lbs
Dimensions:	length 74 ft 4 in (23.27 m)
	wing span 72 ft 6 in (22.10 m)
	wing area 812 sq ft (75.44 m²)
	height 22 ft 8 in (6.9m)
Speed:	maximum 640 mph at sea level, 610 mph at 10,000 ft; cruise 459 mph
Ceiling:	41,300 ft service
Range:	radius 1,200 -n.miles
Armament:	removed
Radar:	ASB-1B

One of two dual-control TA-3B Skywarriors based at NAF Andrews for use by the Secretary of the Navy and the Chief of Naval Operations. (U.S. Navy) is flying from the cockpit.

EA-3B Skywarrior of VQ-1 (U.S. Navy)

ERA-3B Skywarrior of VAQ-33 (U.S. Navy)

EA-6A INTRUDER (formerly A2F-1H)

This version of the Intruder has a built-in Electronic Countermeasures (ECM) suite to detect and jam hostile radars, primarily for suppressing anti-aircraft missile systems. The aircraft was developed specifically for Marine Corps use. It was replaced in active Marine service by the more capable EA-6B Prowler beginning in 1977. It is flown by Navy VAQ-33 and remains in service with Naval Reserve and Marine Corps Reserve squadrons.

The aircraft is similar to the basic A-6 aircraft, with a distinctive pod atop the tail fin and up to five jamming pods and two fuel tanks carried on one fuselage and six wing pylons.

Twenty-one aircraft were built for the Marine Corps plus 6 A-6A conversions.

First flight 26 June 1963; IOC 1965.

EA-6A

Manufacturer:	Grumman
Crew:	pilot, electronic systems operator/navigator
Engines:	2 Pratt & Whitney J52-P-8 turbojets; 9,300 lbst each
Weights:	empty 28,643 lbs; maximum takeoff 58,833 lbs
Dimensions:	length 55 ft 3 in (16.84 m)
	wing span 53 ft (16.15 m)
	wing area 528.9 sq ft (49.1 m²)
	height 16 ft 3 in (4.95 m)
Speed:	maximum 563 mph; cruise 450 mph
Ceiling:	service 40,000 ft
Range:	
Armament:	none
Radar:	APQ-92 search and APQ-112 track

EA-6A Intruder of VAQ-309 (Peter Mersky)

EA-6B PROWLER

The EA-6B is a modified Intruder with significantly more EW/ECM capabilities than the EA-6A. Four-plane VAQ squadrons flying the Prowler are normally assigned to each aircraft carrier.

The Prowler has the basic Intruder configuration with an enlarged cockpit with four crewmen. There is a distinctive electronics pod atop the tail fin, and up to five jamming pods or fuel tanks can be carried on fuselage and wing pylons. The weight of internal avionics/EW equipment totals 8,000 pounds in addition to 950 pounds being carried on each of five pylons; normally five ALQ-99 pods are carried, each with two jamming transmitters. A KA-6H tanker based on the enlarged EA-6B airframe was proposed as a successor to the KA-6D but none were procured. The EA-6B has undergone a number of EW system upgrades since the original configuration with these modifications being given the designations EXCAP (Expanded Capability) first delivered in 1973, ICAP (Improved Capability) first delivered in 1976, and ICAP II first delivered in 1984. These upgrades respond to changing foreign radar/SAM threats. By 1979 all earlier aircraft updated to ICAP configuration; the ICAP II became operational in 1984; and an ADVCAP (Advanced Capability) is planned for an IOC of 1990. The EA-6B name was changed from Intruder to Prowler in February 1972. Over 70 aircraft were in service in early 1984.

First flight 25 May 1968; IOC (VAQ-132) July 1971; the EA-6B continues in production.

EA-6B[9]

Manufacturer:	Grumman
Crew:	pilot, navigator, 2 electronics system operators
Engines:	2 Pratt & Whitney J52-P-408 turbojets; 11,200 lbst each
Weights:	empty 32,162 lbs; normal takeoff 54,461 lbs; maximum takeoff 65,000 lbs

[9] Normal takeoff weight, speed, ceiling, and range with five jamming pods mounted.

Dimensions:	length 59 ft 10 in (18.24 m)
	wing span 53 ft (16.15 m)
	wing area 528.9 sq ft (49.1 m²)
	height 16 ft 3 in (4.95 m)
Speed:	maximum 613 mph at sea level; cruise 483 mph
Ceiling:	service 41,000 ft
Range:	700 n.miles
Armament:	none
Radar:	APQ-129

EA-6B Prowler with five jamming pods mounted; three pods and two external fuel tanks are normal for most missions. (U.S. Navy)

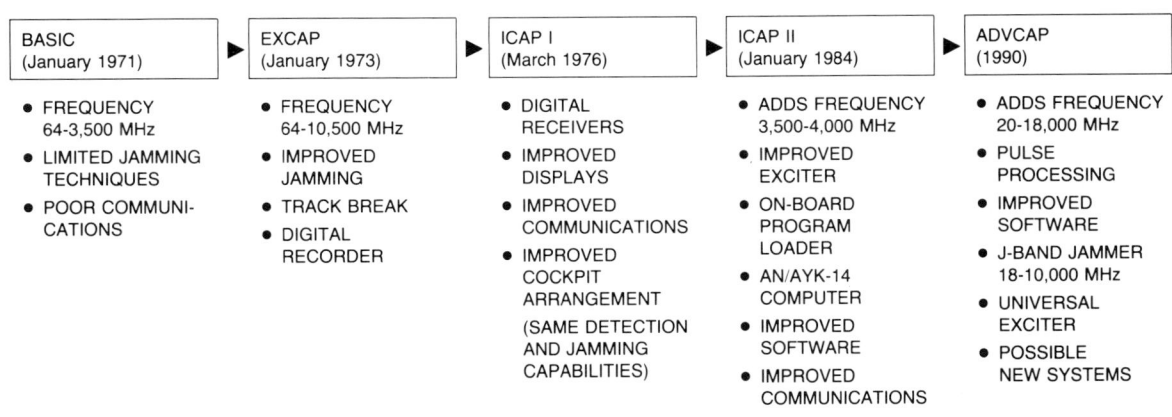

BASIC (January 1971)	EXCAP (January 1973)	ICAP I (March 1976)	ICAP II (January 1984)	ADVCAP (1990)
• FREQUENCY 64-3,500 MHz	• FREQUENCY 64-10,500 MHz	• DIGITAL RECEIVERS	• ADDS FREQUENCY 3,500-4,000 MHz	• ADDS FREQUENCY 20-18,000 MHz
• LIMITED JAMMING TECHNIQUES	• IMPROVED JAMMING	• IMPROVED DISPLAYS	• IMPROVED EXCITER	• PULSE PROCESSING
• POOR COMMUNICATIONS	• TRACK BREAK	• IMPROVED COMMUNICATIONS	• ON-BOARD PROGRAM LOADER	• IMPROVED SOFTWARE
	• DIGITAL RECORDER	• IMPROVED COCKPIT ARRANGEMENT (SAME DETECTION AND JAMMING CAPABILITIES)	• AN/AYK-14 COMPUTER	• J-BAND JAMMER 18-10,000 MHz
			• IMPROVED SOFTWARE	• UNIVERSAL EXCITER
			• IMPROVED COMMUNICATIONS	• POSSIBLE NEW SYSTEMS

EA-6B Electronic Countermeasure Modifications

EA-6B Prowler of VAQ-131 (U.S. Navy)

EC-121 WARNING STAR (formerly WV)

The last military Constellation, a Navy NC-121K Warning Star assigned to VAQ-33, was retired on 25 June 1982. The aircraft, originally designated PO-1 and then WV-2, was acquired as part of the Navy's seaward extension of the Distant Early Warning (DEW) line established in the early 1950s to warn of Soviet bomber attack. Starting in 1954 a total of 142 Warning Stars was delivered. Various models of the Lockheed Constellation and "Super Connie" were flown by the Navy and Air Force, the former also using the R7V transport.

NKC-135A STRATOTANKER

The Navy's Fleet Electronic Warfare Support Group (FEWSG) operates two of these aircraft in the electronic warfare simulation/jamming role in support of weapons development and fleet exercises. They are the largest aircraft currently in service with Navy markings although they are flown by McDonnell Douglas personnel.

These are modified Boeing 707 airframes. Both were built for the Air Force as KC-135A tanker aircraft with standard in-flight refueling equipment. They were modified by the Air Force for research work, with refueling equipment removed. Further modifications by the Navy included removal of some of the body fuel cells to provide equipment bays, replacement of the weather track radar with a sea search unit, provision of wing pylons of electronic pods, and an electronic warfare office/navigator station in the cargo cabin area. Each has about 12,500 pounds of electronic equipment on board and on two wing pylons, providing a greater jamming capability than any other aircraft now flying.

The aircraft retain their Air Force serial numbers; they entered naval service on 9 December 1977 (No. 563596) and 15 May 1978 (No. 553134). The U.S. Air Force flies a number of EC-135 aircraft in special electronic configurations (with others used in the airborne command post and radio relay roles; the Israeli Air Force flies similar converted 707s in these roles). Previously the Navy flew two EB-47E Stratofortresses in this role.

A third large aircraft is being procured for FEWSG activities.

NKC-135A

Manufacturer:	Boeing
Crew:	2 pilots, electronic warfare officer/navigator
Engines:	4 Pratt & Whitney J57-P-59W turbojets; 13,750 lbst each
Weights:	empty 123,000 lbs; maximum 270,000 lbs
Dimensions:	length 134 ft 6 in (40.99 m)
	wing span 130 ft 10 in (39.88 m)
	wing area 2,433 sq ft (225.7 m²)
	height 41 ft 8 in (12.69 m)
Speed:	maximum 530 mph at 25,000 ft
Ceiling:	approx. 41,000 ft
Range:	approx. 4,400 n.miles
Armament:	none
Radar:	navigation radar

The NKC-135A Stratolifter is the largest aircraft currently in U.S. naval service. Assigned to FEWSG, the aircraft is flown by civilian contractor personnel in support of fleet exercises and electronic warfare development programs. (Robert L. Lawson)

RECONNAISSANCE AIRCRAFT

RF-4B PHANTOM (formerly F4H-1P)

The Marine Corps has one squadron of RF-4B photo-reconnaissance aircraft. These are similar to the carrier-capable F-4B Phantom, lengthered to 62⅚ feet and fitted with internal cameras, infrared detector, and APQ-102 Side Looking Aircraft Radar (SLAR).

An RF-4B of VMFP-3 assigned to the carrier MIDWAY; the reconnaissance version of the Phantom is one of the few U.S. Marine Corps aircraft not flown by the Navy. (U.S. Navy)

RF-8G CRUSADER (originally F8U-1P)

The Navy's only remaining Crusaders are RF-8G photo-reconnaissance aircraft flown by one reserve squadron. The aircraft was a first-line carrier from the mid-1950s into the late 1970s.

Up to six internal cameras are fitted; no other reconnaissance sensors are provided. The Crusader was the first U.S. production aircraft to achieve more than 1,000 mph in level flight, and it established several speed records. The latter included a record flight across the United States in an F8U-1P by then-Major John Glenn, later astronaut, senator, and presidential candidate.

A total of 1,222 F8U/F-8 Crusaders were built for the U.S. Navy plus 42 for the French Navy. Seventy-three of the original RF-8A (formerly F8U-1P) photo planes were remanufactured in the late 1960s to extend their service life, being redesignated RF-8G.

First flight XF8U-1 25 March 1955; Navy IOC (VC-3 and VF-32) March 1957.

RF-8G

Manufacturer:	Vought (LTV)
Crew:	pilot
Engines:	1 Pratt & Whitney J57-P-420 turbojet; 18,000 lbst with afterburner
Weights:	empty 16,796 lbs; loaded 27,822 lbs
Dimensions:	length 55 ft 6½ in (16.93 m)
	wing span 35 ft 8 in (10.87 m)
	wing area 375 sq ft (34.84 m²)
	height 15 ft 9 in (4.8 m)
Speed:	983 mph at 35,000 ft; 673 mph at sea level
Ceiling	51,800 ft
Range:	radius 640 n.miles
Armament:	none
Radar:	navigation radar

An RF-8G Crusader from reserve squadron VFP-306. Only one reserve squadron now flies the Crusader in U.S. service. There is a single camera port on the starboard side; two on the port side. No armament is provided. The reserve squadrons now have low-visibility markings. (U.S. Navy)

RF-8G Crusader of VFP-306 (Peter Mersky)

OBSERVATION AIRCRAFT

OV-10D BRONCO

The Bronco was developed during the Vietnam War as a multi-purpose Counterinsurgency (COIN) aircraft. It was flown in Vietnam by the Navy and Marine Corps, with the Navy units being subsequently disbanded. The Short Take-Off and Landing (STOL) operating characteristics have permitted limited flight operations from LHA/LPH-type ships without the use of catapults or arresting gear.

With the removal of the second seat the OV-10 can carry 3,200 pounds of cargo or five troops or two litter patients plus a medical attendant. Nineteen OV-10A aircraft were modified to the Night Observation Gunship System (NOGS)—two YOV-10D and 15 OV-10D. These have Forward-Looking Infrared (FLIR) and laser target designators, and a three-barrel cannon mounted in an under-fuselage turret. The turret can be removed and five attachment points provided for gun pods, rockets, bombs, or fuel tanks.

The Navy and Marine Corps took delivery of 117 aircraft from 1965 to 1977, with others going to the U.S. Air Force and foreign services.

First flight 16 July 1965; Marine Corps IOC (HML-267) February 1968.

OV-10D

Manufacturer:	Rockwell International
Crew:	pilot, observer
Engines:	2 Garrett-AiResearch T76-G-420/421 turboprops; 1,040 shp each
Weights:	empty 6,893 lbs; loaded 9,908 lbs; maximum 14,444 lbs
Dimensions:	length 41 ft 7 in (12.67 m)
	wing span 44 ft (13.41 m)
	wing area 291 sq ft (27.03 m²)
	height 15 ft 1 in (4.62 m)
Speed:	maximum clean 281 mph at sea level
Ceiling:	service 24,000 ft
Range:	radius 198 n.miles with full weapons load; ferry 1,200 n.miles
Armament:	1 20-mm M-97 cannon (multibarrel)
	3,600 lbs bombs, rockets
Radar:	none

OV-10D Bronco on helicopter carrier OKINAWA (U.S. Marine Corps)

OV-10A Bronco (U.S. Navy, PHC John Francavillo)

UTILITY AIRCRAFT

U-11A AZTEC

These aircraft are used for logistics support at naval bases. Aztec is the commercial name. They are slightly longer than the standard commercial aircraft.

U-11A

Manufacturer:	Piper
Crew:	pilot + 4 passengers
Engines:	2 Avco Lycoming O-540-A3D5 flat-six pistons; 250 hp each
Weights:	empty 3,183 lbs; maximum takeoff 5,200 lbs
Dimensions:	length 31 ft 3¾ in (9.83 m)
	wing span 37 ft 3¾ in (11.37 m)
	wing area 207 ft (19.23 m²)
	height 10 ft 1 in (3.07 m)
Speed:	maximum 215 mph at sea level; cruise 206 mph at 3,850 ft
Ceiling:	service 17,600 ft
Range:	cruise approx. 800–1,300 n.miles[10]
Radar:	weather radar

[10] Varies significantly with fuel carried in place of passengers.

U-11A Aztec (U.S. Navy)

OV-10D Bronco

HU-16 ALBATROSS (formerly JR2F/UF)

All of these twin-engine, amphibian utility aircraft have been retired from U.S. military service, the last being a Coast Guard HU-16E retired on 10 March 1983. The last Navy Albatross was retired in 1976.

Following the first flight in 1947, the Albatross entered service with the Navy (JR2F/UF), Air Force (SA-16), and Coast Guard. The Coast Guard operated 88 aircraft from 1951 on. The designation was changed to HU-16 in 1962.

HU-25A GUARDIAN

The Guardian is an all-weather, medium-range search and surveillance aircraft employed by the Coast Guard. It replaces the HU-16 Albatross and HC-131 Samaritan aircraft.

This aircraft is a modification of the French-developed commercial Falcon 20G. It has two turbofan engines mounted in nacelles outboard of the after fuselage, an arrangement similar to the T-39 Sabreliner. In addition to crew and passengers, 3,200 pounds of rescue supplies are carried. A galley and toilet are provided.

Forty-one aircraft were produced for the Coast Guard by the Guardian Jet Corporation, a jointly owned subsidiary of Dassault Breguet and Pan American. Coast Guard IOC February 1982; 30 aircraft were in service at the end of 1983 with the last of the 41 aircraft delivered in 1984.

HU-25A

Manufacturer:	Guardian Jet
Crew:	2 pilots, drop master, avionics man, air crewman (5) + 3 passengers + 4 litters
Engines:	2 Garrett AiResearch ATF3-6-2C turbofans; 5,538 lbst each
Weights:	empty 19,000 lbs; maximum takeoff 33,510 lbs
Dimensions:	length 56 ft 3 in (17.15 m)
	wing span 53 ft 6 in (16.30 m)
	wing area 450 sq ft (41.80 m²)
	height 17 ft 5 in (5.32 m)
Speed:	maximum 531 mph at 40,000 ft
Ceiling:	service 42,000 ft
Range:	2,250 n.miles with 30 minutes on station
Radar:	APS-127 search/weather radar

HU-25A Guardian (U.S. Coast Guard)

HU-25A Guardian (U.S. Coast Guard)

UC-27

The Navy has acquired one Fokker 27 light transport.

The aircraft, with a high wing mounting two engine nacelles, is a Dutch-designed transport in versions capable of carrying 28 to 60 passengers. A maritime patrol version has also been developed. The single U.S. Navy F-27F is used in support of the Atlantic Underwater Test and Evaluation Center (AUTEC); it is operated by Imperial Aviation and based at West Palm Beach Airport, Fla.

In commercial and military/coast guard use in several nations, more than 200 F27s have been produced in the United States by a joint Fairchild-Fokker venture in addition to the Dutch production. The Maritime Enforcer version is fitted for electronic surveillance and can carry two Exocet AM-39 or Harpoon anti-ship missiles. The designation UC-27 is non-standard.

First flight (commercial F27) 24 November 1955.

UC-27

Manufacturer:	Fairchild and Fokker (Netherlands)
Crew:	2 pilots, air crewman + 40 passengers
Engines:	2 Rolls-Royce Dart Mk 529-7E turboprops; 1,910 shp each
Weights:	empty 25,660 lbs; maximum takeoff 42,000 lbs
Dimensions:	length 77 ft 2 in (23.53 m)
	wing span 95 ft 2 in (29.02 m)
	wing area 754 sq ft (70.04 m²)
	height 27 ft 7 in (8.41 m)
Speed:	cruise 215 mph
Range:	850 n.miles

UC-27 when assigned to the Naval Air Development Center (U.S. Navy)

CARGO/TRANSPORT AIRCRAFT

C-1A TRADER (formerly TF-1)

The Trader is a Carrier On-board Delivery (COD) aircraft developed to carry high-priority freight and passengers between aircraft carriers at sea and land bases.[11] The plane was derived from the S2F/S-2 Tracker ASW aircraft.

The cargo plane has twin reciprocating engines and closely resembles the Tracker's high-wing, single-tail configuration. Cargo capacity is limited by conventional side-door loading; the Trader's internal cargo capacity is 90 cubic feet. Because the Navy has removed the high-octane fuel for reciprocating engines from carriers to reduce fire hazard, these planes cannot be refueled aboard ship.

Grumman produced a total of 87 Traders for the U.S. Navy, with about 30 remaining in service. A few were configured as electronic training aircraft (designated TF-1Q and, after 1962, EC-1A). These planes will be replaced by new-production C-2A aircraft.

C-1A

Manufacturer:	Grumman
Crew:	2 pilots + 7 passengers
Engines:	2 Wright R1820-82 radial pistons; 1,525 hp each
Weights:	loaded 27,000 lbs
Dimensions:	length 42 ft (12.8 m)
	wing span 69 ft 8 in (21.23 m)
	wing area 485 sq ft (45.1 m²)
	height 16 ft 4 in (4.98 m)
Speed:	334 mph
Ceiling:	
Range:	1,200 n.miles
Radar:	none
Payload:	3,500 lbs cargo or passengers

[11] Prior to the TF-1/C-1A the Navy used mainly converted TBF/TBM Avenger torpedo bombers in the COD role.

C-2A GREYHOUND

The Greyhound is a second generation built-for-the-purpose COD aircraft, having been derived from the E-2 Hawkeye AEW aircraft.

The cargo aircraft has the E-2's wings, power plant, and tail configuration, but a larger fuselage and rear-loading ramp. This last feature permits the carrying of high-cube cargo, including some aircraft engines. Cargo capacity is 675 cubic feet.

Nineteen C-2A models were originally procured. In the late 1970s the Navy developed a plan to produce 24 new COD aircraft beginning in fiscal 1983 to replace the existing C-1A and, eventually, C-2A aircraft. The principal candidate for the new COD—designated VCX for planning purposes—was a variant of the S-3A Viking, with one having been modified to a US-3A COD configuration. (Five additional Vikings have been remade into CODs.) The decision, however, was to procure 39 additional C-2 aircraft, with eight per year to be delivered in 1985–1988, plus seven aircraft in 1989. Twelve of the original 19 remain in service.

C-2A

Manufacturer:	Grumman
Crew:	2 pilots, flight engineer + 39 passengers or 20 litters
Engines:	2 Allison T56-A-8A turboprops; 4,050 shp each
Weights:	empty 31,250 lbs; loaded 54,382 lbs
Dimensions:	length 56 ft 8 in (17.27 m)
	wing span 80 ft 7 in (24.57 m)
	wing area 700 sq ft (65.03 m²)
	height 15 ft 11 in (4.85 m)
Speed:	maximum 352 mph at 30,000 ft; cruise 296 mph at 30,000 ft
Ceiling:	28,800 ft
Range:	1,440 n.miles
Radar:	navigation radar
Payload:	10,000 lbs cargo or passengers

The VRC-40 flight line of C-1A Traders. (Peter Mersky)

C-2A Greyhound (Grumman)

C-2A Greyhound loading cargo (Grumman)

C-2A Greyhound of VR-24 (U.S. Navy)

C-4 ACADEME

The Coast Guard operates one VC-4A as an executive transport and the Navy and Marine Corps fly several TC-4C trainers for A-6 Intruder bombardier/navigators.

The trainer is a modified Grumman Gulfstream I executive transport, a low-wing, twin turboprop aircraft with the long nacelles common to Rolls-Royce engines. The TC-4C variants have a simulated A-6 cockpit with pilot and bombardier/navigator positions in the aft section of the cockpit. Four identical bombardier/navigator training consoles are located forward of the A-6 cockpit. An A-6 DIANE (Digital Integrated Attack Navigation Equipment) is provided.

Grumman produced 200 Gulfstream I commercial aircraft plus the similar Coast Guard VC-4A and 9 modified TC-4C aircraft for the Navy and Marine Corps. Although officially named Academe in military service, the Coast Guard uses the commercial name Gulfstream I for its VIP aircraft; based at the large Coast Guard air station at Elizabeth City, N.J., the aircraft was accepted on 19 March 1963. First flight Gulfstream I on 14 August 1958; TC-4C June 1967.

TC-4C

Manufacturer:	Grumman
Crew:	2 pilots, 2 instructors + 5 students
Engines:	2 Rolls-Royce Dart Mk 529-8X turboprops; 2,210 shp each
Weights:	empty 24,575 lbs; loaded 36,000 lbs
Dimensions:	length 67 ft 10¾ in (20.69 m), VC-4A 63 ft 9 in (19.43 m)
	wing span 78 ft 4 in (23.87 m)
	wing area 610.3 sq ft (185.99 m²)
	height 23 ft 4 in (7.10 m)
Speed:	maximum 365 mph at 15,000 ft; cruise 250 mph
Ceiling:	service 30,000 ft
Range:	996 n.miles at 5,000 ft; 1,721 n.miles at 30,000 ft
Radar:	APN-153, DIANE

VC-4A Gulfstream I (U.S. Coast Guard)

TC-4C Academe of VA-128; note FLIR pod under nose radome (U.S. Navy)

C-9B Skytrain II and CT-39G Sabreliner (McDonnell Douglas, Harry Gann)

VC-11 GULFSTREAM II

The Coast Guard has one Gulfstream II flown in the executive transport role. The only C-11 in government service, the plane was acquired in 1969 and is based in Washington, D.C.

This is a swept-wing, T-tail aircraft, with engine nacelles mounted on the after fuselage, resembling the T-39 Sabreliner configuration.

VC-11

Manufacturer:	Grumman
Crew:	2 pilots, 2 crewmen (4) + 12 passengers
Engines:	2 Rolls-Royce Mk 511-8 turbofans; 11,400 lbst each
Weights:	59,500 lbs loaded
Dimensions:	length 79 ft 11 in (24.35 m)
	wing span 68 ft 10 in (21.00 m)
	wing area 793.5 sq ft (73.72 m²)
	height 24 ft 6 in (7.47 m)
Speed:	maximum 588 mph
Ceiling:	43,000 ft
Range:	2,930 n.miles
Radar:	navigation radar

C-9B SKYTRAIN II

The C-9B is a military version of the commercial DC-9 series 32 transport. The plane is convertible to the cargo or transport role.

This sleek-looking, swept-wing transport has a T-tail with the turbofan engines in nacelles mounted on the after fuselage.

All Skytrains are flown by Naval and Marine Reserve units. The U.S. Air Force flies the C-9A Nightingale in the medical evacuation role and the VC-9C as an executive transport. The Navy-Marines had 19 aircraft as of mid-1984.

First flight DC-9 series 30 on 1 August 1966.

C-9B

Manufacturer:	McDonnell Douglas
Crew:	2 pilots, crew chief, 2 attendants (5) + 90 passengers
Engines:	2 Pratt & Whitney JT8D-9 turbofans; 14,500 lbst each
Weights:	empty 59,706 lbs in cargo configuration; empty 65,283 lbs empty in transport configuration; 110,000 lbs maximum takeoff
Dimensions:	length 119 ft 4 in (36.37 m)
	wing span 93 ft 5 in (28.47 m)
	wing area 1,000.7 sq ft (92.97 m²)
	height 27 ft 6 in (8.38 m)
Speed:	maximum 576 mph; cruise 504 mph
Ceiling:	service 37,000 ft
Range:	2,538 n.miles with 10,000 lbs cargo
Radar:	weather radar
Payload:	32,444 lbs cargo or passengers

VC-11A Gulfstream II; this is the commercial name. (U.S. Coast Guard)

UC-12B HURON

The Navy and Marine Corps use this military version of the Super King Air 200 for transport and utility purposes.

The aircraft's twin turboprop engines are mounted far forward on the low wing; the aircraft has a T-tail compared with the conventional tail configuration of the smaller T-44A King Air trainer.

More than 2,800 aircraft of this basic design have been produced, most for civilian use. This is the only aircraft flown by the U.S. Army, Navy, Marine Corps, and Air Force (plus the Army National Guard and Marine Corps Reserve). The Navy and Marine Corps purchased 66 aircraft in the UC-12B configuration with 48 more planned.

UC-12B

Manufacturer:	Beech
Crew:	2 pilots + 8 passengers
Engines:	2 Pratt & Whitney PT6A-41 turboprops; 850 shp each
Weights:	empty 7,869 lbs; loaded 12,500 lbs
Dimensions:	length 43 ft 9 in (13.34 m)
	wing span 54 ft 6 in (16.61 m)
	wing area 303 sq ft (28.15 m²)
	height 14 ft 6 in (4.42 m)
Speed:	maximum cruise 310 mph; cruise 261 mph
Ceiling:	31,000 ft
Range:	1,760 n.miles
Radar:	none
Payload:	2,000 lbs cargo or passengers

UC-12B Huron assigned to NAS New Orleans (U.S. Navy)

C-117 SKYTRAIN (formerly R4D)

All of these twin-engine transports have been retired from Navy and Marine Corps service. The last C-117 flown by the U.S. Marine Corps was retired on 28 June 1982 and the last Navy "Gooney Bird" was retired on 1 July 1982.

Developed as the commercial Douglas DC-3, the aircraft was the most widely used by U.S. and foreign military services in World War II, being known as the Dakota and Skytrain, and, informally, Gooney Bird. Douglas military production totaled 10,048 aircraft from 1938 to 1945 plus about 2,000 built in the USSR as the Li-2 and several in Japan. The U.S. naval versions were designated R4D, changed to C-47 in 1962 and after rebuilding C-117. Six took off from the carrier PHILIPPINE SEA (CV 47) in 1947 to land in the Antarctic.

C-118B LIFTMASTER (formerly R6D-1)

Naval Reserve squadrons continue to fly the C-118B transport pending the availability of additional C-9B Skytrains. At least one C-118 is configured as a VIP transport. All are to be retired by 1985.

This is a conventional, four-engine transport that had wide commercial and military service, designated DC-6A in the former role.

C-118B

Manufacturer:	Douglas
Crew:	2 pilots, navigator, flight engineer, crewman (5) + 76 passengers or 60 litters + 6 attendants
Engines:	4 Pratt & Whitney R-2800-52W radial pistons; 2,500 hp each
Weights:	empty 54,995 lbs; loaded 103,000 lbs; maximum takeoff 112,000 lbs
Dimensions:	length 107 ft (32.61 m)
	wing span 117 ft 6 in (35.81 m)
	wing area
	height 28 ft 8 in (8.74 m)
Speed:	303 mph at 16,700 ft
Ceiling:	21,900 ft
Range:	2,000 n.miles with maximum cargo
Radar:	
Payload:	31,611 lbs cargo or passengers

C-118 Liftmaster (U.S. Navy)

C-118 Liftmaster (U.S. Navy)

C-130 HERCULES (formerly GV-1)

The Hercules or "Herk" is the most widely flown military transport in the West. The Navy flies the C-130 as a logistics aircraft and the EC-130 as a VLF strategic communications aircraft under the TACAMO (Take Charge And Move Out) program; the Marine Corps uses the KC-130 as a tactical transport and aerial tanker; and the Coast Guard employs the HC-130 as a long-range search and surveillance aircraft.

The C-130 is a four-engine cargo aircraft has a high wing with the main landing gear in pods to provide a clear fuselage cargo space. A KC-130F conducted carrier landings and takeoffs from the FORRESTAL in 1963 without the use of arresting gear or catapults. The Navy has several ski-fitted LC-130F/R aircraft flown by VXE-6. The Navy EC-130G/Q TACAMO aircraft have the AN/USC-13 airborne VLF communications suite with a trailing wire antenna over 30,000 feet in length. (The Navy's DC-130 drone carriers have been discarded.)

The Marine KC-130F/R/T aircraft can accommodate removable aluminum tanks for 3,600 gallons of fuel in the cargo area; two refueling drogues can be streamed simultaneously. One Marine KC-130 is equipped as a maintenance center to support the Navy-Marine Blue Angels flight demonstration team, carrying a crew of 7 and 30 maintenance personnel.

The Coast Guard HC-130B/E/H aircraft carry air-droppable rescue and salvage gear. The HC-130H provides an increased range, flare launchers, and other improved features over the C-130B aircraft they are replacing. (Only one HC-130E is in service; see Appendix A for Coast Guard aircraft strength.)

The Hercules is also widely used by the U.S. Air Force, with more than 50 other nations employing the military versions. Through the end of 1983 Lockheed had produced 1,700 military and commercial Hercules. Production continues of the HC-130H for the Coast Guard and KC-130T for the Marine Corps Reserve.

KC-130R

Manufacturer:	Lockheed (Georgia)
Crew:	2 pilots, navigator, flight engineer, radio operator/loadmaster (5 + 92 troops
Engines:	4 Allison T56-A-15 turboprops; 4,591 shp each
Weights:	empty 75,368 lbs; loaded 109,744 lbs; maximum takeoff 155,000 lbs
Dimensions:	length 99 ft 5 in (30.32 m) wing span 132 ft 7 in (40.42 m) wing area 1,745 sq ft (162.12 m²) height 38 ft 3 in (11.66 m)
Speed:	maximum 348 mph at 19,000 ft; cruise 331 mph
Ceiling:	25,000 ft
Range:	radius 2,564 n.miles with maximum payload; radius 1,000 n.miles in tanker role with 32,140 lbs of fuel for transfer
Radar:	APN-59B
Payload:	26,913 lbs cargo or passengers

An EC-130 Hercules TACAMO aircraft of VQ-4 streaming VLF wire antennas. (U.S. Navy)

KC-130 Hercules of VMGR-252 refueling an A-4E of VC-5 (U.S. Navy)

HC-130B Hercules (U.S. Coast Guard)

C-131 SAMARITAN (formerly R4Y)

The Navy flies a small number of C-131F/G aircraft in the transport role with a few configured as VIP transports (VC-131). All Coast Guard HC-131A aircraft have been discarded.

This is a twin-engine, low-wing transport that saw considerable commercial service with the designations Convair 340 (F) and 440 (G). The 340 (a stretched model 240) flew for the first time on 5 October 1951 and the prototype 440 first flew on 6 October 1955.

C-131G

Manufacturer:	Convair
Crew	2 pilots, flight engineer + 44 passengers or 21 litters + 3 attendants
Engines:	2 Pratt & Whitney R-2800-52W radial pistons; 2,500 hp each
Weights:	loaded 53,200 lbs
Dimensions:	length 79 ft 2 in (24.14 m)
	wing span 105 ft 4 in (32.08 m)
	wing area 920 sq ft (85.5 m²)
	height 28 ft (8.53 m)
Speed:	316 mph
Ceiling:	service 24,900 ft
Range:	2,000 n.miles
Radar:	none

C-131 Samaritan (U.S. Navy)

XV-15A/JVX PROGRAM

The XV-15A is a tilt-rotor technology demonstration aircraft. Developed by Bell Helicopter Textron, the XV-15A will be scaled up to a military cargo-transport aircraft and produced by Bell and Boeing Vertol under a program designated JVX for Joint Service Advanced Vertical Lift Aircraft. This will be the only new naval aircraft in development in the 1980s.

The XV-15 has twin rotor-engine nacelles mounted on a connecting wing; the nacelles rotate to a horizontal position for conventional aircraft flight and are vertical for vertical take-off and landing or hover. Rolling takeoffs and landings are also possible. Thus, the design has the advantages of both a conventional aircraft and a helicopter.

Bell produced two XV-15A aircraft, with the first flight on 3 May 1977, under NASA and Army sponsorship. Subsequently the Navy-Marine Corps gave support to the project. The XV-15s have achieved their flight demonstration goals in extensive testing by NASA and the services, with one being airlifted to the Paris air show in 1982 in a C-5A Galaxy transport, where it performed for international audiences. In a key XV-15 evaluation, one aircraft flew 54 landings and takeoffs from the helicopter carrier TRIPOLI (LPH 10) in August 1982. Although the XV-15A was not intended for shipboard operation, the tests were successful with only minor difficulties. Tilt-rotor technology is now considered sufficiently mature for a scaled-up aircraft to be produced for military service.

The Navy-Marine Corps have the lead in developing the JVX. The Marine Corps is looking at the JVX to replace the CH-46 Sea Knight and CH-53A/D Sea Stallion beginning in the early 1990s. At this writing the proposed force levels and roles for the JVX are: Marine Corps—552 for amphibious/vertical assault; Navy—50 for combat search and rescue (replacing Naval Air Reserve HH-3A helicopters); and Air Force—200 for special operations (supplementing HH-53 and HH-60D helicopters, and C-130 transports).

The Army has largely withdrawn from the JVX program because of financial problems facing the service; several high-costs systems are being procured at this time, including large numbers of the UH-60 Black Hawk and AH-64 Apache helicopters. The Army had planned to buy 284 JVX aircraft for corps-level aeromedical evacuation, and as Special Electronic Mission Aircraft (SEMA), in the latter role replacing two helicopter and three fixed-wing aircraft types (EH-1, EH-60, RV-1, RC-12, OV-10).

The Navy and Marine Corps were given the lead in the JVX program on 27 December 1982 and were committed to paying for 50 percent of development costs, the Army 34 percent, and the Air Force 16 percent. The Navy's current plans for the JVX are restricted to the combat SAR role, a role now assigned to the Naval Reserve. This is a narrow view of the potential for naval use of a VSTOL aircraft with the planned JVX characteristics. The Navy's own Sea-Based Air Master Study conducted in the mid-1970s recommended the development of three VSTOL aircraft designs, the first being a Type A subsonic aircraft that could carry out the Marine's medium assault role plus Navy ASW, AEW, COD, and SAR roles. (The Type B was to be a supersonic fighter/attack VSTOL aircraft, and the Type C an eventual replacement for the LAMPS III antisubmarine helicopter.)

The Marines' need to develop a replacement for the aging CH-46 and CH-53A/D helicopters led to initiation of the HXM medium helicopter requirement (sometimes referred to as V/HXM, to indicate a possible VSTOL candidate). The JVX will fulfill this requirement with a scaled-up XV-15 having a gross takeoff weight possibly as high as 40,000 pounds and twin, side-by-side rotors with a diameter of 38 feet powered by General Electric T700 engine. This aircraft will be able to carry 24 combat-loaded troops or 10,000 pounds of cargo, including an HMMWV vehicle, on external sling, with a cruise speed of at least 250 mph, and a dash speed of 316–345 mph with a 700-n.mile radius. The plane's unrefueled endurance will be ten hours in the ferry configuration (i.e., from the continental United States to Hawaii or across the Atlantic). This ferry range is vital if the aircraft is to be self-deployable to potential crisis spots, where it can marry up with units of the Rapid Deployment Force or other ground troops.

Being fully capable of VSTOL operation and hovering, the JVX will probably be the first "aircraft" to replace a helicopter.

For the near term the Navy's only interests in the JVX are for use by the Marine Corps for the V/HXM requirement plus the small combat SAR effort. Marine development and operational testing will begin with the initial production aircraft in fiscal 1991–1992 with series deliveries to start in fiscal 1993. The aircraft will be produced by a teaming of Bell with Boeing Vertol to take advantage of the latter's extensive experience in manufacturing large helicopters (CH-46, CH-47, etc.).

The Marine Corps program calls for 18 active and 2 reserve squadrons of 15 aircraft each, requiring:

combat requirement	290 aircraft
support requirement	20
RDT&E	2
training	40
pipeline (10.6 % of above)	37
life-cycle attrition	163
Total	552

The Navy plans for 50 JVX aircraft—10 to replace HH-3A Sea Kings in reserve squadron HC-9, 10 for active squadrons, and the remainder for test, training, etc.

The current Navy-Marine schedule calls for JVX flight testing to start in August 1987 with a Marine IOC of 1991.

XV-15A with engine nacelles in high-speed position (Bell Textron)

XV-15A on board TRIPOLI (U.S. Navy, R. Stewart)

XV-15A with engine nacelles in takeoff/landing position (U.S. Navy)

XV-15A

Manufacturer:	Bell
Crew:	2 pilots
Engines:	2 Avco Lycoming LTC1K-4K turboshafts; 1,800 shp each
Weights:	empty 9,670 lbs; loaded 13,000 lbs; maximum takeoff 15,000 lbs
Dimensions:	length 42 ft 2 in (12.83 m)
	span (over engine nacelles) 35 ft 2 in (10.72 m)
	height 15 ft 4 in (4.67 m)
	rotor diameter 25 ft (7.62 m)
	aircraft width (including rotor blades) 57 ft 2 in (17.4 m)
Speed:	maximum 382 mph at 17,000 ft; cruise 230–350 mph
Ceiling:	29,000 ft
Range:	
Radar:	none

TRAINING AIRCRAFT

T-2 BUCKEYE (formerly T2J)

The Buckeye is used by the Navy for undergraduate jet pilot training with a few aircraft also flown by fleet readiness squadrons for spin recovery training.

The aircraft has straight wings, generally with wing tip tanks fitted, with the twin engines buried in the bottom of the fuselage. Wing pylons can be fitted. The Buckeye is carrier capable. The aircraft's service life is being extended from 7,500 to 12,000 hours, at considerable cost, pending availability of the T-45 Hawk for the training role.

The Navy had 214 T-2B/C aircraft in service in 1983, with 202 assigned to training squadrons (VT), 6 in fleet readiness squadrons (VF) for spin recovery training, and 6 assigned to the Naval Test Pilots School at NAS Patuxent River.

T-2C

Manufacturer:	North American Rockwell
Crew:	pilot, student
Engines:	2 General Electric J85-GE-4 turbojets; 2,950 lbst each
Weights:	empty 8,115 lbs; maximum takeoff 13,179 lbs
Dimensions:	length 38 ft 4 in (11.67 m)
	wing span 38 ft 2 in (11.62 m)
	wing area 255 sq ft (23.69 m²)
	height 14 ft 10 in (4.51 m)
Speed:	maximum 522 mph at 25,000 ft
Ceiling:	40,400 ft
Range:	909 n.miles
Armament:	up to 640 lbs of bombs or rockets on 2 wing stations + wingtip tanks
Radar	none

T-2C Buckeyes of VT-23 (U.S. Navy)

T-28 TROJAN

All of these piston-engine primary trainers were to have been retired by the end of 1984. The Navy had about 100 T-28B/C variants in service at the beginning of 1983. The Trojan was carrier capable.

T-34C MENTOR

The Mentor is the Navy's primary and basic flight training aircraft.

The low-wing, turboprop C model has replaced the earlier piston-engine aircraft in Navy service. The plane is not carrier capable.

About 330 T-34C aircraft are in service and on order with a Navy requirement for some 450 aircraft. IOC 1976.

T-34C

Manufacturer:	Beech
Crew:	pilot, student
Engines:	1 Pratt & Whitney of Canada PT6A-25 turboprop; 400 shp
Weights:	empty 2,940 lbs; maximum gross 4,300 lbs
Dimensions:	length 28 ft 8½ in (8.75 m)
	wing span 33 ft 3⅞ in (10.16 m)
	wing area 179.6 sq ft (16.69 m²)
	height 9 ft 7 in (2.92 m)
Speed:	maximum 257 mph at 5,335 ft; cruise 247 mph at 5,335 ft
Ceiling:	30,000 ft
Range:	740 n.miles
Radar:	none

T-34C Mentor (Beech)

T-38A TALON

The T-38 is the standard U.S. Air Force trainer, flown in small numbers by the Navy for test-pilot proficiency and air combat maneuver training.

The T-38 is closely related to the design of the Northrop F-5 Freedom Fighter and F-5E/F/G (now F-20) Tiger II aircraft.

From 1958 to 1972 Northrop produced 1,187 T-38s for U.S. and foreign service.

T-38A

Manufacturer:	Northrop
Crew:	pilot, student
Engines:	2 General Electric J85-GE-5A/J turbojets; 3,850 lbst each with afterburner
Weights:	empty 7,594 lbs; maximum takeoff 12,000 lbs
Dimensions:	length 46 ft 10 in (14.13 m)
	wing span 25 ft 43 in (7.7 m)
	wing area 170 sq ft (15.80 m²)
	height 12 ft 11 in (3.92 m)
Speed:	maximum cruise 630 mph at 40,000 ft; economical cruise 594 mph above 40,000 ft
Ceiling:	53,600 ft
Range:	1,140 n.miles
Radar:	none

T-38A Talon of VF-43 (Robert L. Lawson)

T-39D SABRELINER (formerly T3J-1)

The T-39D is used to train bombardier/navigators and radar intercept officers. In addition, 18 CT-39E/G aircraft are employed to transport high-priority cargo and passengers.

The low, swept-wing configuration of the T-39 has two turbojet engine nacelles mounted on the after fuselage. The aircraft is not carrier capable. The T-39D is similar to the Air Force T-39B. The CT-39 aircraft carry a crew of three and seven passengers. These were modified commercial Sabreliner series 40 (E) and 60 (G) aircraft, acquired specifically for the transport role and never used as trainers. One T-39D was fitted as the test bed for the F/A-18 Hornet's APG-65 radar.

First flight modified commercial Sabreliner September 1958, T-39A June 1960, T-39D December 1962.

T-39D

Manufacturer:	North American Rockwell
Crew:	pilot, pilot/instructor + 4 students
Engines:	2 Pratt & Whitney J60-P-3A turbojets; 3,000 lbst each
Weights:	loaded 17,760 lbs
Dimensions:	length 43 ft 9 in (13.33 m)
	wing span 44 ft 5 in (13.53 m)
	wing area 342.6 sq ft (31.83 m²)
	height 16 ft (4.88 m)
Speed:	maximum 540 mph at 20,000 ft; cruise 436 mph at 40–45,000 ft
Ceiling:	service 42,000 ft
Range:	1,195 n.miles; ferry 1,505 n.miles
Radar:	APQ-94 in T-39D

CT-39G Sabreliner of VR-24 (U.S. Navy)

T-39D Sabreliner (U.S. Navy)

T-44A KING AIR

The T-44 was procured as a replacement for the TS-2/US-2 Tracker in the multi-engine training role.

The aircraft is a modification of the commercial Air King 90, with a straight wing mounting twin turboprop engines relatively far forward, with a conventional tail configuration. The aircraft can be configured as a transport carrying two pilots and three passengers. During development the military version was designated VTAM(X).

From 1977 on the Navy took delivery of 61 T-44A aircraft, all being assigned to VT-21 and VT-31. The U.S. Army procured unpressurized versions as the U-21A while the Air Force obtained one as the LC-6A for special missions.

T-44A

Manufacturer:	Beech
Crew:	2 pilots, instructor + 2 students, 2 passengers
Engines:	2 Pratt & Whitney of Canada PT-6A-34B turboprops; 550 hp each
Weights:	empty 6,326 lbs; maximum takeoff 9,650 lbs
Dimensions:	length 35 ft 6 in (10.82 m)
	wing span 50 ft 3 in (15.32 m)
	wing area 293.9 sq ft (27.3 m²)
	height 14 ft 3 in (4.33 m)
Speed:	cruise 276 mph at 15,000 ft
Ceiling:	service 29,500 ft
Range:	1,265 n.miles
Radar:	air search

T-44A King Air assigned to Training Wing 4 (tail code changed from D to G in 1983) (U.S. Navy)

T-45A HAWK

The Hawk is being procured as the Navy's basic undergraduate jet training aircraft, replacing the T-2C and TA-4J. The aircraft is a variant of British Aerospace's Hawk trainer. Despite using this off-the-shelf aircraft, the first flight of a naval Hawk is taking place *five* years from time of decision. The Navy had planned to procure 253 carrier-compatible T-45A trainers and 54 land-based T-45B variants. Congress has directed, however, that they all be "wet" (i.e., carrier-capable) T-45A models. (Details of the revised all-wet program were not decided when *Ships and Aircraft* went to press.) Twelve British Hawk T Mk 1 aircraft may be loaned to the U.S. Navy for interim use.

Developed by Hawker Siddeley Aviation before it was merged into British Aerospace, the Hawk entered RAF service in 1976. Since then, more than 200 have been built. The U.S. Navy's aircraft "system" was originally designated VTX-TS, the VTX for a new training aircraft and TS for Training System, i.e., the simultaneous development of simulators and other training devices. The American Hawks will have a small ventral fin, arresting hook, and modified wing, landing gear, and speed brakes. Endurance is approximately four hours.

First flight of T-45B was scheduled for February 1987, with IOC in 1988; T-45A flight tests were to begin in December 1988 with IOC in 1991. The first two land-based T-45B aircraft were to be British-assembled with the remaining 52 aircraft being assembled by McDonnell Douglas at Long Beach with deliveries from 1988 to 1990. The first T-45As were to be produced alongside the last T-45Bs. First flight T Mk 1 on 21 August 1974.

T-45

Manufacturer:	British Aerospace and McDonnell Douglas
Crew:	pilot, student
Engines:	1 Rolls-Royce Turbomeca Adour Mk 851 turbofan; 5,200 lbst
Weights:	empty 8,756 lbs; gross takeoff 12,440 lbs
Dimensions:	length 36 ft 7¾ in (11.17 m)
	wing span 30 ft 9¾ in (9.39 m)
	wing area 179.6 sq ft (16.69 m²)
	height 13 ft 1¼ in (3.99 m)
Speed:	maximum 645 mph
Ceiling:	50,000 ft
Range:	ferry 1,600 n.miles (with external tanks)
Radar:	none

Hawk trainer (British Aerospace courtesy J.W.R. Taylor)

The prototype T-47A in flight. (Cessna)

T-47A

The T-47A is entering Navy service to replace the T-39D. The aircraft is a modified commercial Cessna Citation II. The naval aircraft has a shortened wing and extended leading edge devices.

Fifteen aircraft are planned with deliveries in 1984–1985 to Training Wing 6, with phaseout of the T-39D by May 1985. The first flight of a Citation II (Model 550) occurred on 31 January 1977.

T-47A

Manufacturer:	Cessna
Crew:	pilot, instructor + 3 students
Engines:	2 Pratt & Whitney JT15D-5 turbofans; 2,500 lbst each
Weights:	empty 9,035 lbs; maximum 15,000 lbs
Dimensions:	length 47 ft 11 in (14.61 m)
	wing span 46 ft 6 in (14.18 m)
	height 14 ft 10 in (4.51 m)
Speed:	cruise 443 mph; maximum 483 mph
Ceiling:	43,000 ft
Range:	approx. 1,700 n.miles
Radar:	APQ-159

HELICOPTERS

AH-1 SEACOBRA

The SeaCobra is a specialized gunship helicopter that evolved from the widely used Huey series. It is flown by the Marine Corps's attack helicopter squadrons.

The SeaCobra has a narrow (38-inch) fuselage providing minimal cross section with stub wings for carrying rocket packs or gun pods, a nose turret with a 20-mm three-barrel cannon, and tandem seating for a gunner (forward) and pilot. The T model was formerly designated AH-

1J (Improved), having been changed in August 1975. The 56 AH-1J SeaCobras are being fitted with the Army-developed Hellfire missile; the 49 AH-1T helicopters have been fitted with the TOW anti-tank missile and AIM-9 Sidewinder AAM, for a total of 1,000 pounds of weapons. The new AH-1T models will be fitted with the General Electric T700 engine, permitting a weapons load of 3,000 pounds.

The Marines plan to procure 44 of the T700 Models (AH-1T +); the protoype flew on 16 November 1983.

First flight (AH-1G) 7 September 1965; IOC AH-1J January 1971; AH-1T October 1977.

AH-1T

Manufacturer:	Bell
Crew:	pilot, gunner
Engines:	Pratt & Whitney twin-pack T-400-WV-402 turboshaft; 2,050 shp (total)
Weights:	empty 8,014 lbs; loaded 14,000 lbs
Dimensions:	fuselage length 48 ft 2 in (14.86 m)
	overall length 58 ft (17.68 m)
	height 13 ft 8 in (4.15 m)
	main rotor diameter 48 ft (14.63 m)
Speed:	maximum 207 mph
Ceiling:	service 12,450 ft
Range:	227 n.miles

Armament:	AH-1T (T400)	AH-1T (T700)
	1 20-mm cannon (475 rounds)	1 20-mm cannon (750 rounds)
	8 TOW missiles	8 TOW missiles
		38 2.75-inch rockets
		2 Sidewinder AAMs

An AH-1J SeaCobra with standard Marine markings but not organizational markings. The AH-1T has low-visibility combat markings; the word "Marines" is barely visible on the fuselage. Note the twin skids and stub wings. (Bell Helicopter Textron)

UH-1 HUEY (IROQUOIS)

The Huey series, whose name is derived from the earlier HU-1E designation, is the most widely used military helicopter in the Western world.

The Huey is flown by the Navy in the training (TH-1L), combat rescue (HH-1K), and utility roles, and by the Marines in the assault and utility roles. (The TH-1L is being replaced by the TH-57C SeaRanger.) More than 9,000 Hueys have been produced for U.S. and foreign service.

First flight (XH-40) 22 October 1956; Marine IOC (VMO-1) March 1964.

A Marine AH-1T SeaCobra, with 2.75-inch rocket pods, in action during the American assault on Grenada in October 1983. The M197 nose turret, the same as in the AH-1J, has a three-barrel, 20-mm Gatling gun, the lightweight version of the M61 gun system. A laser designator is fitted. (Department of Defense)

UH-1N

Manufacturer:	Bell
Crew:	2 pilots; crewman + 12 to 15 troops
Engines:	2 United Aircraft of Canada PT6 turboshafts; 900 shp each
Weights:	empty 5,549 lbs; maximum 10,500 lbs
Dimensions:	fuselage length 42 ft 5 in (12.93 m)
	overall length 57 ft 3 in (17.47 m)
	height 14 ft 5 in (4.39 m)
	main rotor diameter 48 ft 2 in (14.7 m)
Speed:	126 mph
Ceiling:	15,000 ft; 12,900 ft hover in ground effect
Range:	250 n.miles
Armament:	various combinations of machine guns and rockets can be mounted

TH-1L Huey from HT-8 (U.S. Navy)

A UH-1E Huey landing aboard the assault ship TRIPOLI (LPH 10) during exercises off the coast of South Korea. (U.S. Navy, PH1 D. Brockschmidt)

UH-1N Huey from VXE-6 painted in international orange (U.S. Navy, Robert L. Lawson)

SH-2F LAMPS I (formerly HU2K)

The LAMPS (Light Airborne Multi-Purpose System) is a ship-based helicopter integrated with ASW ships for submarine attack and over-the-horizon targeting of ship-launched cruise missiles. The Navy's need for ship-based ASW helicopters in the early 1970s led to the conversion of 20 single-engine HU2K/UH-2 Seasprite utility helicopters to the SH-2D configuration and another 85 to the SH-2F variant. (Subsequently, the surviving D models were upgraded to F, the last in 1983.) Two additional Seasprites were converted to a YSH-2E configuration.

The SH-2 LAMPS are employed to localize and attack submarine contacts initially made by surface ASW ships. The helicopters have no sonobuoy analysis capability. They are fitted with the LN66 radar, a 15-sonobuoy dispenser, and AN/ASQ-81 MAD (Magnetic Anomaly Detection). The General Electric T700 engine of the SH-60B was being considered for new production helicopters but when this edition went to press old and new had the T58.

In addition to the surviving SH-2F helicopters, the Navy is purchasing 48 new SH-2F helicopters to operate from ASW ships that cannot carry the larger SH-60B LAMPS III. Those ships are (one helicopter per ship): TRUXTUN (CGN 35), 9 BELKNAP (CG 26) class, 6 BROOKE (FFG 1) class, GLOVER (FF 1098), 48 KNOX (FF 1040) class, and 6 GARCIA (FF 1040) class. The four VIRGINIA (CGN 38)-class cruisers have had their LAMPS hangar deleted. Originally 65 "new" SH-2Fs were planned.

One hundred ninety UH-2 utility helicopters were built through 1965. The 48 new SH-2F helicopters being produced by Kaman will be the first helicopters built by that firm in 15 years and the first of this series manufactured in an ASW configuration. About 90 "old" SH-2F helicopters were in service in early 1984. First flight 2 July 1959; Navy IOC (HU-2) December 1962.

SH-2F

Manufacturer:	Kaman
Crew:	2 pilots, systems operator
Engines:	2 General Electric T58-GE-8F turboshaft; 1,350 shp each
Weights:	empty 6,953 lbs; maximum 12,800 lbs (13,500 lbs beginning with 28th new production SH-2F)
Dimensions:	fuselage length 38 ft 4 in (11.69 m)
	overall length 52 ft 7 in (16.04 m)
	height 15 ft 6 in (4.73 m)
	main rotor diameter 44 ft (13.42 m)
Speed:	maximum 165 mph; cruise 150 mph
Ceiling:	22,500 ft; 18,600 ft hover in ground effect
Range:	420 n.miles; operating radius approx. 35 -n.miles
Armament:	1 Mk 50 or 2 Mk 46 ASW torpedoes

An SH-2F LAMPS from HSL-34 based aboard the MOINESTER (FF 1097). The main landing gear is retracted; the tail wheel was moved forward from the D to F models. The sonobuoy dispenser is outlined on the port side, under the engine nacelle. (U.S. Navy, PH1 Douglas P. Tesner)

An SH-2F from HSL-37 lands aboard a U.S. ship in the Sea of Japan during the search for debris from the Korean flight 007 airliner shot down by Soviet forces on 1 September 1983. A Soviet stern trawler-factory ship steams in the background. (U.S. Navy)

SH-3 SEA KING (formerly HSS-2)

The Sea King has been the U.S. Navy's standard carrier-based ASW helicopter since the early 1960s and should serve into the 1990s, when it is scheduled to be replaced by the SH-60F Blackhawk. The helicopter is also flown by the U.S. Coast Guard (see below) and Air Force, and several foreign services. The Marine Corps flies the VH-3D as a presidential transport (squadron HMX-1).

The Navy flies the SH-3D/H variants in the ASW role, the latter all converted from earlier models. They have ASQ-13 dipping sonar, sonobuoys in the SH-3H, APN-130 doppler radar, ASQ-81 MAD, and ECM systems. The dipping sonar has a 450-foot operating depth. Two Sea Kings were used to test sensors for the SH-60B (designated YSH-3J). The RH-3A was used briefly in the MCM role. The Sea King has a "boat" hull, but does not normally alight on the water (unlike the Coast Guard HH-3F, described below). The Naval Air Reserve also flies the HH-3A combat rescue variant. The helicopter is flown by several foreign services as well as by the U.S. Air Force.

Approximately 100 SH-3Hs were available to the Navy in early 1984; all are being upgraded under a Service Life Extension Program (SLEP); another 26 SH-3D types are being modified to the SH-3H configuration. A number of SH-3G utility helicopters are also in Navy service, the survivors of a number of SH-3A variants with ASW equipment removed.

First flight XHSS-2 11 March 1959; Navy IOC (HS-1) June 1961.

SH-3H

Manufacturer:	Sikorsky
Crew:	2 pilots, 2 systems operators
Engines:	2 General Electric T58-GE-10 turboshafts; 1,400 shp each
Weights:	empty 13,465 lbs; maximum takeoff 21,000 lbs
Dimensions:	fuselage length 54 ft 9 in (16.69 m)
	overall length 72 ft 8 in (22.15 m)
	height 16 ft 10 in (5.13 m)
	main rotor diameter 62 ft (18.9 m)
Speed:	maximum 166 mph; cruise 136 mph
Ceiling:	service 14,700 ft; 10,500 ft hover in ground effect
Range:	540 n.miles
Armament:	2 Mk 46 torpedoes

An SH-2F from HSL-37 based aboard the TRIPPE (FF 1075) refuels while hovering over the DEWEY (DDG 45) off the coast of Brazil. A streamed Magnetic Anamoloy Detection (MAD) device is stowed on the starboard side of the helicopter; the radome is visible under the nose. (U.S. Navy)

An SH-3D Sea King from HS-4 embarked in the RANGER; a lightweight torpedo is visible under the starboard sponson/wheel housing; a rescue winch is fitted above the starboard door. (U.S. Navy)

A VH-3D from HMX-1 with a white top and United States of America on the fuselage, indicating the helicopter is assigned to transport the President. (U.S. Navy)

An SH-3D from HS-5 embarked in the INDEPENDENCE lowering a dipping sonar while operating in the Mediterranean. (U.S. Navy)

An SH-3G from VC-5 hovering near the wrecked Philippine frigate DATU KALAN-TIAW, beached at Calayan Island in the Philippines. (U.S. Navy, PH1 Felimon Barbante)

HH-3F PELICAN

This version of the Sea King was built specifically for the U.S. Coast Guard SAR role. It is similar to the HH-3E Jolly Green Giant rescue version flown by the U.S. Air Force. They carry droppable rescue supplies and have modified boat-type hulls and sponson-floats for water operations.

Forty of these helicopters were built for the Coast Guard with 37 remaining in service in early 1984.

Coast Guard IOC 1968.

HH-3F

Manufacturer:	Sikorsky
Crew:	2 pilots, 1 or 2 crewmen + 15 passengers or 8 litters
Engines:	2 General Electric T58-GE-5 turboshafts; 1,500 shp each
Weights:	22,050 lbs maximum
Dimensions:	fuselage length 57 ft 3 in (17.45 m)
	overall length 73 ft (22.25 m)
	height 18 ft 1 in (5.51 m)
	main rotor diameter 62 ft (18.9 m)
Speed:	maximum 162 mph; cruise 125 mph
Ceiling:	11,000 ft; 4,100 ft hover in ground effect
Range:	400 n.miles
Armament:	none

HH-3F helicopters at the Coast Guard Air Station in Astoria, Ore. (U.S. Coast Guard)

A Coast Guard HH-3F Pelican hovering while lowering rescue sling. Note the radome and the different sponson configuration. (U.S. Coast Guard)

CH-46 SEA KNIGHT (formerly HRB)

The CH-46 is the Marines' principal assault helicopter and is flown by the Navy in the Vertical Replenishment (VERTREP) role.

The Sea Knight has a tricycle landing gear and small, wheel-housing sponsons aft, distinguishing it from the similar, widely flown CH-47 Chinook cargo helicopter. The helicopter has a rear ramp for rapid loading and unloading of cargo, including small vehicles. The Marines are upgrading 273 CH-46A/D troop helicopters to the CH-46E, beginning in 1977. Provided in the upgrade are improved engines, crash attenuating seats for pilots, a more survivable fuel system, and an improved rescue winch. The Navy flies UH-46 and HH-46 variants.

The Navy and Marine Corps took delivery of 624 Sea Knights from 1961 to 1977. First flight (YHC-1A) 22 April 1958; Marine IOC (HMM-265) June 1964.

A UH-46D Sea Knight from HC-6 is caught by a camera during replenishment operations in the eastern Mediterranean. The Sea Knight is the most numerous helicopter currently in Navy-Marine service (U.S. Navy, JOC Kirby Harrison)

Marines race aboard a CH-46E from HMT-301 on the assault ship TARAWA. (U.S. Navy)

CH-46E

Manufacturer:	Boeing Vertol
Crew:	2 pilots, crewman + 25 troops
Engines:	2 General Electric T58-GE-16 turboshafts; 1,870 shp each
Weights:	empty 15,198 lbs; maximum 24,300 lbs
Dimensions:	fuselage length 45 ft 8 in (13.92 m)
	overall length 84 ft 4 in (25.72 m)
	main rotor diameters 25 ft 6 in (7.81 m)
	height 16 ft 8 in (5.08 m)
Speed:	maximum 161 mph; cruise 158 mph
Ceiling:	9,400 ft
Range:	radius 75 n. miles; ferry 600 n.miles
Armament:	2 .50-cal MG (with 22 troops and 4 crew)

HH-52A SEA GUARD (formerly HU2S-1G)

This is a commercial helicopter adopted by the Coast Guard for the SAR mission. The H-52 series is not flown by any other U.S. military service. It is being replaced by the HH-65A Dolphin.

Designated S-62 by Sikorsky, the helicopter is flown by several nations in a commercial configuration. It has a boat hull for amphibious operation, but suffers from single-engine operation. Some have been fitted with Forward-Looking Infrared (FLIR) detection systems.

The Coast Guard acquired 99 of these helicopters with 71 remaining in service in early 1984. First flight 14 May 1958; Coast Guard IOC January 1963.

HH-52A

Manufacturer:	Sikorsky
Crew:	2 pilots, crewman + 6 passengers
Engines:	1 General Electric T58-GE-8B turboshaft; 1,250 shp
Weights:	empty 5,083 lbs; maximum 8,100 lbs
Dimensions:	fuselage length 44 ft 7 in (13.59 m)
	overall length 45 ft 6 in (13.87 m)
	height 16 ft (4.88 m)
	main rotor diameter 53 ft (16.17 m)
Speed:	maximum 109 mph; cruise 98 mph
Ceiling:	11,200 ft; 12,200 ft hover in ground effect
Range:	radius 150 n.miles with 20-minute loiter; 475 n.miles
Armament:	none

An HH-52A Pelican painted in international orange, the color used for Coast Guard helicopters carried aboard icebreakers. (U.S. Coast Guard)

HH-52A based at Coast Guard Air Station San Francisco (U.S. Coast Guard)

CH-53A/D SEA STALLION

The CH-53A/D is the Marine Corps' heavy assault helicopter, now being succeeded in the heavy-lift role by the CH-53E (see below). The Navy employs the RH-53D as a VERTREP and mine countermeasures helicopter (to be succeeded by the MH-53E). Eight of the latter were used in the aborted April 1980 attempt to rescue hostages from the American embassy in Tehran; seven of those helicopters were destroyed in the operation.

The helicopters have large cargo compartments with a stern ramp. The RH-53D variants are similar to the CH-53A/D but with upgraded T64-GE-415 engines and automatic flight controls for sustained low-level flight. The MCM versions have provisions for two swivel .50-caliber MG and can stream Mk 103 cutters for countering contact mines, Mk 104 acoustic countermeasures, Mk 105 hydrofoil sled for countering magnetic mines, Mk 106 which is the sled with acoustic sweep equipment added, and the AN/SPU-1 Magnetic Orange Pipe (MOP) for countering shallow-water mines. The sled weighs about 6,000 pounds and is 27 feet long and 13 feet wide; the MOP is 33 feet long, 10 inches in diameter, and weighs 1,000 pounds (filled with polystyrene). The AQA-14 dipping/towed sonar is also available for the RH-53D. Refueling in flight five times from KC-130 tankers, an RH-53D has made an 18½-hour flight across the United States.

The Navy and Marine Corps took delivery of 384 helicopters with others going to the U.S. Air Force and foreign services; these included 30 RH-53D models (another six MCM versions went to Iran).

First flight (CH-53A) 14 October 1964; Marine Corps IOC (HMH-463) November 1966.

CH-53D

Manufacturer:	Sikorsky
Crew:	2 pilots, crewman + 38 troops or 24 litters + 4 attendants (7 crewmen in RH-53D)
Engines:	2 General Electric T64-GE-413 turboshafts; 3,925 shp each
Weights:	empty 23,628 lbs; loaded 34,958 lbs; maximum 42,000 lbs
Dimensions:	fuselage length 67 ft 2 in (20.48 m)
	overall length 88 ft 3 in (26.92 m)
	height 24 ft 11 in (7.59 m)
	main rotor diameter 72 ft 3 in (22.04 m)
Speed:	maximum 196 mph; cruise 173 mph
Ceiling:	21,000 ft; 13,400 ft hover in ground effect
Range:	540 n.miles; ferry 886 n.miles
Armament:	none

An RH-53D from HM-12 lifts a MOP minesweeping device; external tanks are fitted to the fuselage sponsons, and there are rear-view mirrors on the nose to assist in handling sweep gear. (U.S. Navy)

An RH-53D Sea Stallion prepares to lift a Mk 105 hydrofoil sweep sled from the amphibious ship RALEIGH (LPD 1). (U.S. Navy)

A Marine CH-53 Sea Stallion from HMH-361 lifts supplies from the TARAWA during an amphibious exercise. (U.S. Marine Corps)

An RH-53D Sea Stallion prepares to start up aboard the INCHON (LPH 12). (U.S. Navy)

CH-53E/MH-53E SUPER STALLION

Developed specifically for the U.S. Navy and Marine Corps, this is the heaviest lift helicopter in service outside of the Soviet Union. It is entering Marine and Navy service as the CH-53E and will be flown by the Navy as the MH-53E in the VERTREP and MCM roles.

These helicopters can lift 16 tons of external load. They have the same basic configuration as the Sea Stallion, but with three engines, a seven-blade main rotor (vice six in the CH-53A/D), larger rotor blades, in-flight refueling probe, and improved transmission. Two 650-gallon external tanks can be fitted to the sponsons. The CH-53E can lift 93 percent of the heavy equipment in a Marine division compared with 38 percent for the CH-53D. The MH-53E can handle the MCM equipment listed for the RH-53D plus the ALQ-166 Lightweight Magnetic Sweep (LMS). It will be capable of night operations with a six-hour mission capability. (The RH-53D can operate only in daylight.)

The current program is for 103 CH-53E helicopters to be procured for the Marine Corps and 35 MH-53E for the Navy. First flight YCH-53E 1 March 1974, CH-53E 13 December 1980, MH-53E 1 September 1983 (a CH-53E in the MCM configuration flew on 23 December 1981); Marine IOC (CH-53E) (HMH-464) February 1981; Navy IOC (MH-53E) 1987.

CH-53E

Manufacturer:	Sikorsky
Crew:	2 pilots, crewman + 55 troops
Engines:	3 General Electric T64-GE-416 turboshafts; 4,380 shp each
Weights:	empty 33,226 lbs; maximum 73,500 lbs
Dimensions:	fuselage length 73 ft 4 in (22.33 m)
	overall length 99 ft ½ in (30.18 m)
	height 27 ft 9 in (8.46 m)
	main rotor diameter 79 ft (24.08 m)
Speed:	maximum 195 mph; cruise 172 mph
Ceiling:	18,500 ft; 9,500 ft hover in ground effect
Range:	radius 50 n.miles with 16 tons external cargo; radius 500 n.miles with 10 tons external cargo; ferry 1,000 n.miles
Armament:	none

A CH-53E Super Stallion from newly established HC-4 prepares to refuel from a C-130 Hercules tanker of the New York Air National Guard off the coast of Sicily. (U.S. Navy, JOC Kirby Harrison)

CH-53E Sea Stallion. More than 60 helicopters of this type had been delivered by early 1984 for Navy and Marine use; all Navy CH-53E models will be reconfigured to MH-53E. (Sikorsky)

The three-engine CH-53E is the largest helicopter in Western military service. The third engine is visible just under the main rotor hub on the port side. This helicopter has low-visibility Marine markings. (Sikorsky)

TH-57 SEARANGER

The SeaRanger is a training version of the commercial Bell 206 Jet-Ranger series. The Navy purchased 40 off-the-shelf commercial aircraft as the TH-57A in 1968; subsequently, 89 improved TH-57C models were ordered in the early 1980s. The latter will replace the TH-1L Hueys now in the training role.

The JetRanger was originally designed to compete in a U.S. Army 1961 light observation helicopter competition. Bell lost that competition, but the Model 206 was commercially successful and was later produced in large numbers for the Army as the OH-58 Kiowa. The Navy's TH-57A were fitted with dual controls; the TH-57C models have improved avionics and controls. Their designation was changed from TH-57A to TH-57C in February 1983.

IOC 1968; the first TH-57C was delivered in November 1982.

TH-57A

Manufacturer:	Bell
Crew:	1 pilot + 4 students
Engines:	1 Allison T63-A-700 turboshaft; 317 shp
Weights:	empty 1,464 lbs; maximum 3,000 lbs
Dimensions:	fuselage length 32 ft 7 in (9.94 m)
	overall length 41 ft (12.5 m)
	height 9 ft 7 in (2.91 m)
	main rotor diameter 35 ft 4 in (10.78 m)
Speed:	maximum 138 mph; cruise 117 mph
Ceiling:	18,900 ft; 13,600 ft hover in ground effect
Range:	300 n.miles
Armament:	none

TH-57A SeaRanger from HT-8 (U.S. Navy)

The prototype TH-57A SeaRanger displays the classic Bell light helicopter configuration. (Bell Helicopter Textron)

SH-60B SEAHAWK (LAMPS III)

The Seahawk is the helicopter component of the Navy's ship-based LAMPS III ASW and over-the-horizon targeting system.[12] The Seahawk is adopted from the UH-60A, the U.S. Army's basic transport helicopter. (It is also flown by the Army in EW versions and by the Air Force as the HH-60D special operations Black Hawk.)

The SH-60B carries 2,000 pounds of avionics including the ESM sensor of the SLQ-32 found aboard most U.S. surface warships. It also has a 25-sonobuoy dispenser, APS-124 radar, FLIR, and ASQ-81 MAD. No dipping sonar is fitted; the planned carrier-based SH-60F will have the AQS-13F dipping sonar, with a 1,500-foot cable, but certain other ASW equipment deleted, including MAD and sonobuoys. Early plans called for an SH-60B crew of four. The IBM Corporation was the prime contractor for the LAMPS III/SH-60B, the first time that the airframe manufacturer did not perform this role for a U.S. Navy helicopter.

The Navy plans to procure 200 operational helicopters in addition to six prototypes; in theory these are to provide two helicopters per ship to the following: Ticonderoga (CG 47) class, 4 Kidd (DDG 993) class, 31 Spruance (DD 963) class, and 61 Oliver Hazard Perry (FFG 7) class. However, these 200 SH-60B models will be far too few to fill the "deck spots" of these ships.

The planned procurement of the SH-60F is:

6 helicopters per carrier	90	helicopters
training (25 percent of above)	22	
pipeline (15 percent of above)	17	
attrition (about 2 percent of		
90 + 22 for 20 years)	46	
Total	175	

In addition to a U.S. Army and Air Force procurement of more than 1,000 helicopters, the Philippines is purchasing the UH-60 while several other nations have expressed interest. Spain will buy the SH-60B while Japan is planning to produce the SH-60B for shipboard use.

First flight YUH-60 17 October 1974, SH-60B December 1979; Navy IOC (HSL-41) September 1983, SH-60F IOC 1986.

---

[12] The SH-2 was the LAMPS I helicopter; the LAMPS II was a study effort.

SH-60B

Manufacturer:	Sikorsky
Crew:	pilot, copilot/airborne tactical officer, sensor operator
Engines:	2 General Electric T700-GE-401 turboshafts; 1,713 shp each
Weights:	empty 13,648 lbs; loaded 19,500 lbs in ASW role, 18,000 lbs in Harpoon targeting role, 21,000+ lbs in utility role
Dimensions:	fuselage length 50 ft (15.26 m) overall length 64 ft 10 in (19.76 m) height 17 ft 2 in (5.23 m) main rotor diameter 53 ft 8 in (16.36 m)
Speed	maximum cruise 151 mph
Ceiling:	
Range:	radius 50 n.miles with 3 hours loiter; radius 150 n.miles with 1 hour loiter
Armament:	2 Mk 46 or Mk 50 ASW torpedoes

An SH-60B during shipboard evaluation. Two dummy torpedoes are fitted with the MAD antenna visible outboard of the torpedo. (U.S. Navy)

An SH-60B Seahawk, navalized version of the UH-60 Black Hawk which is replacing the Huey as the U.S. Army's principal troop-carrying helicopter. The naval variant, which is extensively modified, has an electrically folding main rotor and folding tail, with the tail wheel strengthened and moved forward. Note the sonobuoy dispenser on the port side which holds 25 buoys. (Sikorsky)

HH-65A DOLPHIN

The French-designed Dolphin is being procured by the Coast Guard to replace the aging HH-52A in the short-range SAR role.

Developed by Aerospatiale as model SA 366G Dauphin, the helicopter was selected in a Coast Guard competition in 1979. The helicopter has a fan-in-fin *fenestron* tail rotor. The U.S. Coast Guard version has droppable rescue equipment and an infrared search system. Several nations fly the helicopter in the military role with other variants which are fitted with anti-ship missiles and ASW equipment. Maximum mission endurance is almost four hours.

The Coast Guard is procuring 90 Dolphins, with deliveries from late 1983 to January 1987. The deliveries were delayed from a planned IOC of July 1982 because of engine problems. First flight SA 360 2 June 1972.

HH-65A

Manufacturer:	Aerospatiale
Crew:	2 pilots, crewman + 3 passengers
Engines:	2 Avco Lycoming LTS101-750A-1 turboshafts; 680 shp each
Weights:	empty 4,188 lbs; maximum 8,400 lbs
Dimensions:	fuselage length 37 ft 6 in (11.43 m) overall length 43 ft 9 in (13.33 m) height 12 ft 9 in (3.89 m) main rotor diameter 39 ft 2 in (11.9 m)
Speed:	maximum 175 mph; cruise 145 mph
Ceiling:	6,700 ft hover in ground effect
Range:	radius 165 n.miles with 30 minutes loiter; maximum 410 n.miles
Armament:	none

An HH-65A Dolphin based at the Coast Guard Air Station Mobile, Ala. (Aerospatiale)

HH-65A Dolphin (U.S. Coast Guard)

EXPERIMENTAL AIRCRAFT

VSTOL DEVELOPMENT AIRCRAFT

McDonnell Douglas is designing a single-engine, supersonic VSTOL aircraft for the naval strike-fighter mission. The aircraft is designated 279-3 by the firm. If the design effort is successful, production of the lead aircraft could begin in the early 1990s.

The aircraft's engine, modified from that of the AV-8B, would have vectored thrust with four exhaust nozzles. The aircraft will have a canard wing forward with the main wing at approximately the center of the fuselage. An estimated 41 percent of the aircraft's structural weight (3,866 pounds) would be made of composite material, about 15 percent more than in the AV-8B. Up to 11 store stations are proposed for bombs, rockets, and missiles.

The model 279-4 would be a two-place aircraft.

Manufacturer:	McDonnell Douglas
Crew:	pilot
Engines:	1 modified Rolls-Royce Pegasus 11 turbofan
Weights:	empty approx. 19,500 lbs; gross takeoff approx. 46,000 lbs in STO mode with 400-ft takeoff run, approx. 29,840 lbs in VTO mode
Dimensions:	length 56 ft (17.07 m)
	wing span 35 ft 9 in (10.9 m)
	wing area 428 sq ft (130.4 m²)
	height 17 ft 4 in (5.28 m)
Speed:	Mach 2 at altitude
Ceiling:	
Range:	
Armament:	1 25-mm cannon (multibarrel) (400 rounds)
	18,000 lbs of missiles, bombs, or rockets

QUIET SHORT-HAUL RESEARCH AIRCRAFT

The NASA-sponsored Quiet Short-Haul Research Aircraft (QSRA) a modified de Havilland of Canada C-8A Buffalo STOL aircraft, conducted landing and takeoff trials aboard the KITTY HAWK in 1980. This was the third four-engine aircraft to fly from U.S. aircraft carriers, being preceded by the Lockheed C-130 Hercules and Vought-LTV XC-142 VSTOL aircraft.

No further QSRA carrier operations are planned. See the 12th edition of *Ships and Aircraft* for details and additional photographs.

NASA's Quiet Short-Haul Research Aircraft during 1980 carrier landing tests aboard the USS KITTY HAWK off San Diego. (NASA)

An artist's concept of the proposed Model 279-3 supersonic naval VSTOL strike-fighter. (McDonnell Douglas drawing by Maron Horonzak)

XFV-12A

The XFV-12A was conceived as a high-performance VSTOL fighter for shipboard operation. The prototype XFV-12A was to have begun flying in 1978 after an extensive NASA-Navy test program. However, the prototype has been delayed and has never flown, resulting in the cancellation of procurement.

The aircraft has a thrust-augmented wing design to allow vertical and short takeoffs and landings. The unusual configuration features a delta wing aft with vertical stabilizers and small canard wings forward. Engine exhaust is diverted through nozzles in the wing and canards to achieve vertical flight. To reduce cost and lead times, the single aircraft built made extensive use of F-4 Phantom and A-4 Skyhawk components, with an engine developed from that of the F-14 Tomcat.

The single XFV-12A prototype is in storage at the NASA facility in Langley, Va.; there are no plans to further test the prototype. See the 12th edition of *Ships and Aircraft* for characteristics.

The XFV-12A being "flight tested" while tethered at the NASA Langley, Va., research center. The aircraft has not been test flown and proved a practical failure. (National Aeronautics and Space Administration)

XFV-12A (Rockwell International)

XFV-12A (Rockwell International)

30 Weapons

NAVAL GUNS

The principal guns now being installed in U.S. Navy and Coast Guard ships are the 5-inch Mk 45 lightweight gun (CG 47 class and planned for the DDG 51 class), the 76-mm Mk 75 OTO Melara (FFG 7 and WMEC 901 classes, and retrofitted in the WHEC 715 class), and the 20-mm Mk 16 Phalanx CIWS (warships, amphibious ships, and major underway replenishment ships). The 5-inch guns are considered primarily shore-bombardment weapons, the 76-mm guns are anti-aircraft weapons, and the CIWS are for defense against attacking anti-ship missiles.

The Navy's shipboard firepower is being dramatically increased by the reactivation of the four IOWA (BB 61)-class battleships. Two of these ships, each armed with nine 16-inch/50-cal guns and twelve 5-inch guns, were in commission when this edition of *Ships and Aircraft* went to press, with at least one more dreadnought to follow them into service.

Beyond the battleships, however, there has been a steady decline of naval guns as older cruisers and destroyers have been decommissioned with newer ships generally having fewer guns of smaller caliber. All cruisers armed with 8-inch and 6-inch guns have been retired, as have all of the 5-inch gunned FRAM destroyers and all but one of the 18 destroyers of the FORREST SHERMAN (DD 931) class, which carried up to three 5-inch guns.

5-inch guns. The OLIVER HAZARD PERRY (FFG 7) class of frigates, the largest surface combatant class built by the U.S. Navy since World War II, is armed with the 76-mm gun while the ships they replace had 5-inch weapons. The only Navy ships now in production with 5-inch guns are the Aegis cruisers of the TICONDEROGA (CG 47) class. These ships are intended for AAW/ASW defense of carrier battle groups and are rarely expected to be in a position to employ their guns in shore bombardment.

As originally planned the new ARLEIGH BURKE (DDG 51) class of guided missile destroyers was to have only two Phalanx CIWS. Subsequently, the design was revised to provide an additional 76-mm OTO Melara gun. Continued criticism, however, led to another revision, providing a single 5-inch Mk 45 gun in addition to the two CIWS.[1]

The 5-inch/54-cal Mk 45 for the TICONDEROGA and BURKE classes is capable of engaging air or surface targets. The gun mount is unmanned,

with the gun crew all stationed below deck. The mount stows up to 20 rounds of ready service ammunition that can be fired quickly by a single man at the below-deck control console. The magazine can be reloaded while the gun is firing without interrupting the firing sequence. The maximum rate of fire is 16–20 rounds per minute with fixed ammunition. Firing Rocket Assisted Projectiles (RAP) and other separated ammunition reduces the firing rate.

The older active cruisers, destroyers, and frigates have the single 5-inch/54-cal Mk 42 gun mount. Several different mods are in service, most of which are limited to engaging surface targets. The guns may be fired by local or remote control. Maximum firing rate is 36 rounds per minute.

The nuclear cruiser LONG BEACH (CGN 9) has World War II-era 5-inch/38-cal Mk 30 gun mounts. These were fitted in the LONG BEACH and other all-missile cruisers during the 1960s as defense against small craft and aircraft. The gun has a rate of fire of up to 20 rounds per minute.

Twin 5-inch/38-cal Mk 28 gun mounts are fitted in the IOWA-class battleships. As these ships are reactivated the 5-inch battery is being reduced from ten twin mounts to six.

6-inch and 8-inch guns. Prior to the recommissioning of the battleship NEW JERSEY (BB 62) in December 1982, the largest guns in the active fleet were of 5-inch caliber. The last U.S. active ship with 6-inch/47-cal guns was the cruiser-flagship OKLAHOMA CITY (CG 5), which was retired in December 1979, while the last active ship with 8-inch/55-cal guns was the NEWPORT NEWS (CA 148), decommissioned and stricken in July 1978. The only warships in service today in foreign navies with guns larger than 5-inch are in the Soviet Navy. The ten SVERDLOVS mount from six to twelve 6-inch guns (a total of 108 guns). Some of these ships are in reduced commission. (Following completion of the SVERDLOV program in 1954, the Soviet Navy produced destroyers with 130-mm or smaller guns until 1959; the large number of Soviet warships built in the 1960s and 1970s had 76.2-mm or smaller guns. The warships now emerging from Soviet yards, however, have introduced larger, highly advanced gun systems, including 130-mm/70-cal guns in the SOVREMENNYY-class destroyers, the SLAVA-class cruisers, and apparently the later KIROV-class battle cruisers.)

The U.S. Navy's plan to install the 8-inch/55-cal Mk 71 Major Caliber Lightweight Gun (MCLWG) in the 31 SPRUANCE (DD 963)-class destroy-

---

[1] These mark numbers for the gun *mount*; see table for designation of actual guns.

The Tomahawk cruise missile has given a new dimension to the striking power of U.S. surface combatants and submarines. Previously only aircraft carriers and strategic missile submarines had a long-range strike capability; with Tomahawk a variety of ships have a long-range anti-ship and conventional or nuclear land attack capability. Here the NEW JERSEY (BB 62) fires a Tomahawk from one of her *starboard* launchers during trials off San Clemente, Calif. (1983, U.S. Navy)

Turret/Mount[a]	Gun Barrel(s)	Crew	Turret/Mount Weight	Rate of Fire[b]	Maximum Ranges[c]	Ammunition Weights[d]	Ships/Class
16"/50 cal (406 mm) triple turret	Mk 7 Mod 0	79	1,700 tons	2 rpm	40,185 yds AP 41,622 yds HC	2,700 lbs AP 1,900 lbs HC	BB 61
8"/55 cal (203 mm) triple turret	Mk 16 Mod 0	45	451 tons	10 rpm	30,100 yds AP 31,350 yds HC @41° elevation	335 lbs AP 260 lbs HC	CA 134
8"/55 cal (203 mm) Mk 71 single mount (MCLWG)	Mk 39 Mod 2	6	172,895 lbs	12 rpm; guided projectiles 6 rpm	31,408 yds	260 lbs HC	(program cancelled)
5"/38 cal (127 mm) Mk 24 single mount	Mk 12 Mod 1	15	33,100 lbs	18 rpm	17,306 yds @ 45° 32,250 ft @ 85°	55 lbs	CV 9, 16, CG 10
5"/38 cal (127 mm) Mk 28 twin mount	Mk 12 Mod 1	27	153,000– 169,000 lbs	18 rpm	17,306 yds @ 45° 32,250 ft @ 85°	55 lbs	BB 61
5"/38 cal (127 mm) Mk 30 single mount	Mk 12 Mod 1	17	~45,000 lbs	20 rpm	17,306 yds @ 45° 32,250 ft @ 85°	55 lbs	CGN 9, FFG 1, FF 1040, FF 1098, AS 15, AS 17
5"/38 cal (127 mm) Mk 32 twin mount	Mk 12 Mod 1	27	~120,000 lbs	18 rpm	17,306 yds @ 45° 32,250 ft @ 85°	55 lbs	CA 134
5"/54 cal (127 mm) Mk 42 single mount	Mk 18 Mod 0	14	Mod 1–6 ~145,000 lbs Mod 10 139,000 lbs	20 rpm	25,909 yds @ 47° 48,700 ft @ 85°	70 lbs	Mod 7 and 10 in DD 931; Mod 10 in CGN 35, CG 26, DDG 37, 31, 2, FF 1952
5"/54 cal (127 mm) Mk 45 single mount		6	47,820 lbs	16–20 rpm	25,909 yds @ 47° 48,700 ft @ 85°	70 lbs	CGN 38, CGN 36, CG 47, DD 963, LHA
3"/50 cal (76 mm) Mk 22 single mount	Mk 21 Mod 0	11	7,510–8,310 lbs	20 rpm	14,041 yds @ 45° 29,367 ft @ 85°	7 lbs	auxiliaries
3"/50 cal (76 mm) Mk 26 single mount	Mk 21/22	11	9,210–10,130 lbs	20 rpm	14,041 yds @ 45° 29,367 ft @ 85°	7 lbs	auxiliaries
3"/50 cal (76 mm) Mk 27 twin mount	Mk 22	12	30,960–31,700 lbs	50 rpm	14,041 yds @ 45° 29,367 ft @ 85°	7 lbs	CA 134
3"/50 cal (76 mm) Mk 33 twin mount	Mk 22	12	~33,000 lbs	50 rpm	14,041 yds @ 45° 29,367 ft @ 85°	7 lbs	CA 134, DD 931, FF 1037, AGF 3, amphibious ships, auxiliaries
76 mm/62 cal Mk 75 single mount	Mk 75	4	13,680 lbs	75–85 rpm	~21,000 yds @ 45° ~39,000 ft @ 85°	14 lbs	FFG 7
40 mm/60 cal Mk 1 twin mount	Mk 1 Mod 0	5–9	13,000 lbs	160 rpm	11,000 yds @ 42° 22,800 ft @ 90°	1.5 lbs 1.9 lbs	LST
40mm/60 cal Mk 2 quad mount	Mk 1 Mod 0	11	23,800–25,500 lbs	160 rpm	11,000 yds @ 42° 22,800 ft @ 90°	1.5 lbs 1.9 lbs	BB 61, LSD, auxiliaries
40mm/60 cal Mk 3/M3 single mount	M1	4–5	2,264 lbs	160 rpm	11,000 yds @ 42° 22,800 ft @ 90°	1.5 lbs 1.9 lbs	LST, MSO, ARS
40 mm Mk 64 single mount	Mk 19	1			2,400 yds		amphibious, small combatants, auxiliaries
20 mm/70 cal Mk 10 single mount	Mk 2/4	2	700–1,100 lbs	450 rpm	4,800 yds @ 35° 10,000 ft @ 90°	0.2 lbs	MSO, auxiliaries
20 mm Mk 67 single mount	Mk 16 Mod 5	1		800 rpm	3,300 yds	0.75 lbs	CGN 25, LHA, auxiliaries
20 mm Mk 68 single mount	Mk 16 Mod 5	1		800 rpm	3,300 yds	0.75 lbs	MSO, auxiliaries

Turret/Mount[a]	Gun Barrel(s)	Crew	Turret/Mount Weight	Rate of Fire[b]	Maximum Ranges[c]	Ammunition Weights[d]	Ships/Class
20 mm/76 cal Mk 15 CIWS six-barrel Phalanx "Gatling" gun	M61	—	~12,000 lbs	3,000 rpm	1,625 yds		planned for ~250 ships
81 mm mortar Mk 2[e]		2	580 lbs	10 rpm trigger mode; 18 rpm drop-fire mode	2,200 yds	10.85 lbs	PCF, PTF
40 mm MG Mk 19		1	77 lbs	350–400 rpm	2,400 yds	0.75 lbs	various

[a] See text for definitions of mount and turret.
[b] Rounds-per-minute per barrel.
[c] Maximum range at 45° elevation unless otherwise indicated.
[d] AP = Armor Piercing; HC = High Capacity.
[e] Mk 2 Mod 0 mounted "piggy-back" with .50-cal MG.

ers as well as possibly in some future ship classes died with the cancellation of the gun project by Secretary of Defense Harold Brown in July 1978. A prototype gun had been successfully evaluated in the SHERMAN-class destroyer HULL (DD 945) from 1975 to 1979. Characteristics of the Mk 71 are provided in the accompanying table because of historical interest.

The Mk 71 MCLWG is a comparatively small and lightweight mount. It could automatically fire 75 rounds from the ready service loader. The maximum rate of fire is 12 rounds per minute.

The two mothballed DES MOINES (CA 134)-class ships have three triple turrets with 8-inch guns.

3-inch guns. The large number of 3-inch/50-cal anti-aircraft guns fitted from the early 1950s onward in surface combatants, amphibious ships, and fleet auxiliaries have been entirely removed from the active warships and auxiliaries; a few are retained in amphibious ships. The guns were generally ineffective and difficult to maintain. Instead, amphibious ships and auxiliaries have been refitted with the Phalanx CIWS and/or Sea Sparrow point-defense missiles. Small 40-mm grenade-firing MGs or 20-mm guns are also provided for defense against small craft or swimmers making terrorist attacks. The surviving 3-inch guns in active ships are twin mounts (Mk 33) or single mounts (Mk 34). These are open or shielded (unarmored) mounts. They have two open, drum-type magazines for each barrel, which are hand loaded. The maximum rate of fire is 50 rounds per barrel per minute.

Several older types of 3-inch gun mounts are in mothballed ships.

76-mm guns. The PERRY-class frigates and PEGASUS (PHM 1)-class hydrofoil missile craft as well as Coast Guard cutters have the 76-mm/62-cal Mk 75 gun mount. The gun system was designed by the OTO Melara firm in Italy and is generally identified by the firm's name.

The 76-mm gun is specifically designed for ships as small as 200 tons and is capable of engaging air or surface targets. It is remotely controlled with a small, unmanned mount and can fire up to 85 rounds per minute.

20-mm Phalanx CIWS. The Phalanx Close-In Weapon System (CIWS) is intended to defeat attacking anti-ship missiles. The installation of

Phalanx CIWS followed by several years the appearance of similar rapid-fire gun systems, of larger caliber, in Soviet surface warships.

The Phalanx underwent initial at-sea tests in the destroyer KING (DDG 41, then DLG 10) from August 1973 to March 1974, with operational suitability tests in the destroyer BIGELOW (DD 942) from November 1976 to 1978. Production was initiated in December 1977. The first operational gun was fitted in 1980 to the aircraft carrier CORAL SEA (CV 43). A year later the Japanese destroyer KURAMA became the first foreign ship to mount the Phalanx; several foreign navies have followed.

The Phalanx CIWS is a totally integrated system that includes the AN/VPS-2 search and track radar, gun, magazine, weapon control unit, and associated electronics, all fitted into a single unit 15 feet high and weighing about 6 tons. Thus, it is suitable for small combat craft (and is fitted in Saudi Arabian and Israeli missile craft) as well as larger warships. The U.S. Navy plans to fit the Phalanx in more than 250 ships, from single guns in frigates to four mounts in IOWA-class battleships.

The CIWS is designated both Mk 15 and Mk 16, with the 20-mm gun designated Mk 26. The gun is a six-barrel Gatling gun, adopted from the Air Force M61 Vulcan gun series used in several types of aircraft and ground mounted for airfield defense.[2] The gun is hydraulically powered with a theoretical firing rate of 3,000 rounds per minute, a very low dispersion rate, and a 900-round magazine. Later guns have a larger magazine, and the earlier weapons will be upgraded. The frigate RENTZ (FFG 46) in June 1984 became the 100th U.S. Navy ship to have the Phalanx installed.

The gun fires a depleted-uranium bullet or penetrator manufactured from the waste product of nuclear energy programs. The depleted uranium penetrator is 2.5 times heavier than steel. The diameter of the penetrator is only 12.75 millimeters and is fired in a nylon sabot with an aluminum pusher that imparts spin to the projectile. The sabot and pusher break away after the round leaves the muzzle with a velocity of

[2] The CIWS is sometimes referred to—incorrectly—as the Vulcan-Phalanx. The designation Mk 15 and Mk 16 are used by the U.S. Navy. The latter is used in this edition, based on the official publication *Armament of Naval Ships of the United States* (1 January 1984), published by the Naval Sea Systems Command.

1,000 feet per second. The built-in J-band, pulse-doppler radar combines several functions and follows the bullets in flight to make corrections for the next burst being fired. Early Navy analyses indicated that about 200 rounds would be fired per gun in each engagement against a missile.

All engagement functions are performed automatically with a high-speed digital computer. When active the CIWS will engage any incoming, high-speed target unless the operator holds fire. Reaction time for the CIWS is less than two seconds from the time the threat is detected and identified.

40-mm gun. Several small combatants have the automatic, remote-control 40-mm/60-cal Mk 3 Mod 7 Bofors cannon. This weapon may be set for full- or semi-automatic fire, being rated up to 160 rounds per minute.

A few earlier mods of the single 40-mm gun survive, while some laid up ships, including the battleships MISSOURI (BB 63) and WISCONSIN (BB 64), have the quad 40-mm/60-cal Mk 2 mount. These older guns are hand loaded with four-round clips.

40-mm machine gun. Numerous auxiliaries, small combatants, and Coast Guard cutters have the 40-mm Mk 19 grenade launcher. This is usually fitted to the Mk 64 machine gun mount. The launcher is manually fired and shoots high-velocity 40-mm grenades from linked belts. The launcher has a cyclic rate of fire of 325 to 375 rounds per minute, with the rounds configured in an armor-piercing shape, having been initially designed to counter lightly armored vehicles. (The Mk 19 can also be mounted on vehicles and in helicopters.)

40-mm saluting gun. The 40-mm Mk 11 gun mount is found in aircraft carriers, cruisers, missile destroyers, amphibious ships, and auxiliaries. This weapon is for saluting only and has no combat capability.

20-mm guns. The similar single-barrel 20-mm Mk 67 and Mk 68 cannon are fitted on auxiliary and amphibious ships and on Coast Guard cutters for close-in defense against surface craft. These are refinements of the Oerlikon design.

81-mm mortar. Several small combatants mount the 81-mm mortar Mk 2 Mod 0 or 1. The Mod 0 is generally mounted on a tripod while the Mod 1 is fitted piggy-back above a .50-caliber M2 flexible machine gun. The mortar may be fired by the trigger or drop-fire mode. The trigger firing allows the gunner to fire at near horizontal positions. The rate of fire is up to 10 rounds per minute with the trigger method and 18 rounds with the drop-fire mode.

This weapon is especially useful for illumination.

Classification. Guns are classified by inside barrel diameter and gun-barrel length. Diameters traditionally were listed in inches for weapons larger than one-inch diameter, and in millimeters for smaller weapons. Thus, a 5-inch/38-caliber gun has a barrel length of 190 inches. The Italian-designed OTO Melara 76-mm gun retains its metric measurement in U.S. naval service.

Nomenclature. According to the Navy, "A mount is an assembled unit which includes the gun barrel (or barrels), housing(s), slide(s), carriage, stand, sight, elevating and training drives, ammunition hoists, and associated equipment. Mounts include guns from 20-mm caliber up to but not including 6-inch caliber. . . . A mount differs from a turret in that a mount does not have a barbette structure."

"Mounts are designated as single-purpose [SP], dual-purpose [DP], or antiaircraft [AA], depending upon the elevation of which they are capable and the types of targets they are designed to take under fire."

The unmanned, unarmored mounting for the 8-inch Mk 71 MCLWG is considered a mount (rather than a turret).

An open-mount Mk 24 Mod 11 5-inch gun on an ALBANY (CG 10)-class cruiser; these weapons remain on mothballed ESSEX (CV 9)/HANCOCK (CV 19)-class carriers. (U.S. Navy)

A 2 700-pound bullet from a 16-inch gun aboard the battleship Iowa (BB 61) streaks toward the horizon during firing trials in the Gulf of Mexico. (1984, Litton/Ingalls Shipbuilding)

The A and B triple 16-inch turrets of the New Jersey. Proposals to replace the after 16-inch turret with a vertical launch missile system or Harrier VSTOL facility have been dropped. (U.S. Navy, PH2 Gary Ballard)

Crewmen load powder charges for the NEW JERSEY's 16-inch guns. (U.S. Navy, PHC Terry Mitchell)

Triple 8-inch turrets of a SALEM (CA 139)-class cruiser. (U.S. Navy)

The HULL (DD 945) mounting the Mk 71 8-inch major caliber lightweight gun. The ship is significantly smaller than the SPRUANCE (DD 963)-class destroyers that were intended to carry the gun in place of their forward 5-inch weapon. (Giorgio Arra)

As built the IOWA (BB 61)-class battleships carried ten Mk 28 twin 5-inch gun mounts. This was the NEW JERSEY in 1968; the missile-like cannisters are chaff launchers. The first two IOWAS had Mod 0 mounts; the second two ships Mod 2. (U.S. Navy)

Workmen rehabilitate 5-inch guns on the IOWA (BB 61) during preparations for her reactivation; the gun shield has been removed. (U.S. Navy)

Mk 30 Mod 94 5-inch mount on the TALBOT (FFG 4). The Mk 30—as evidenced by its high mod number—was one of the guns most widely used by the U.S. Navy during World War II. (Giorgio Arra)

Mk 42 Mod 9 5-inch gun on the MOINESTER (FF 1097). The gun crew earned an E for gunnery excellence. (Giorgio Arra)

Mk 33 Mod 0 twin 3-inch gun mount on the SPIEGEL GROVE (LSD 32). These open mounts have been difficult to maintain and have limited effectiveness; belatedly, the number aboard amphibious and auxiliary ships has been reduced. (U.S. Navy)

Mk 45 Mod 0 5-inch gun on the helicopter carrier TARAWA (LHA 1). The LHAs are the only amphibious ships now in service to carry 5-inch guns. (U.S. Navy)

Ammunition handling for a Mk 33 Mod 0 twin 3-inch mount. (U.S. Navy)

Rear view of a Mk 33 Mod 13 single 3-inch mount on the MOUNT WHITNEY; the ammunition handling space is severely restricted. (U.S. Navy)

The Mk 75 76-mm OTO Melara gun dominates the forward portion of the Pegasus (PHM 1). The Mk 75 is the main gun battery of the Oliver Hazard Perry (FFG 7) class as well as several Coast Guard cutters.

Mk 7 40-mm gun being fitted to a PB Mk III. (U.S. Navy)

Mk 33 Mod 13 twin 3-inch gun mount on the Mount Whitney (LCC 20). (Giorgio Arra)

Mk 2 quad 40-mm AA mount in combat; fitted to more than a thousand ships in World War II, the "quad forties" are now found only in the mothball fleet. (U.S. Navy)

81-mm mortar mounted "piggy-back" with .50-cal machine gun on a PCF. (U.S. Navy)

Mk 19 machine gun/grenade launcher fitted on a tripod mount. This weapon fires belted 40-mm grenades that can penetrate light armor out to 2,200 meters. (U.S. Marine Corps)

Mk 7 40-mm gun fitted to a PB Mk III. (U.S. Navy)

Mk 67 Mod 1 20-mm single gun mount on BAINBRIDGE (CGN 25). (N. Polmar)

M2 .50-cal twin machine gun mounted on PBR Mk II. (U.S. Navy)

The Phalanx CIWS was designed to be rapidly "bolted on" to ships of virtually any size. (General Dynamics/Pomona)

Phalanx CIWS firing. The Phalanx installation is officially designated as the Mk 16 "group" and is known as the Phalanx, *not* Vulcan-Phalanx. The ammunition drum below the barrels is manually reloaded in the open, a shortcoming of the weapon. The Phalanx will be installed in all active surface combatant classes except DDG 37, DDG 2, DD 933, and FFG 1. (General Dynamics/Pomona)

Phalanx CIWS on the NEW JERSEY during firing trials; the "dish" radar antenna is from an adjacent Mk 37 GFCS. (U.S. Navy, PHC Terry Mitchell)

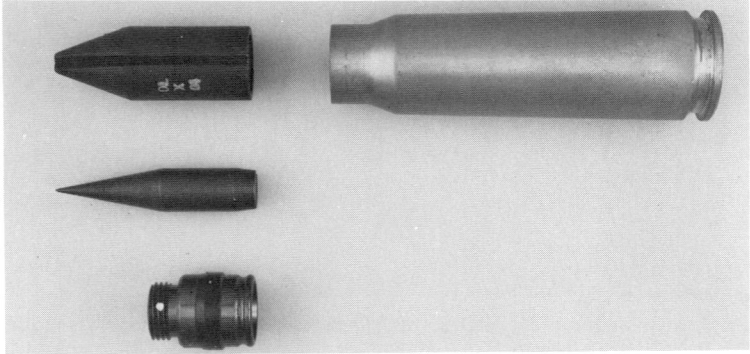

The 20-mm Phalanx round, showing the sabot that falls away after firing, the sub-caliber penetrator or "bullet" of depleted uranium, the pusher, and 20-mm shell casing. (General Dynamics/Pomona).

NAVAL MINES

The U.S. Navy has three mine procurement programs underway: the CAPTOR (Encapsulated Torpedo), which is an advanced anti-submarine weapon that can be laid by aircraft, surface ships, or submarines; the improved Quickstrike mine which is an air-delivered, fuzed bomb; and the Submarine-Launched Mobile Mine (SLMM), which is launched from submarine torpedo tubes and travels several thousand yards to its target area. The Quickstrike and SLMM are anti-surface ship mines.

In addition, bomb modification kits are being procured. Several older types of mines, most aircraft-laid, also remain in service.

CAPTOR. The Mk 60 CAPTOR, which became operational in 1979, is the Navy's principal anti-submarine mine. It is a deep-water weapon, normally laid by aircraft or submarine. Upon being laid, the CAPTOR is anchored to the ocean floor. It accoustically detects passing submarines, ignoring surface ships; upon detecting a hostile submarine the CAPTOR launches a Mk 46 Mod 4 torpedo.

The mine has suffered from significant development and operational problems. These have led to several production delays. A potential problem is the relatively small, 96-pound warhead of the Mk 46 torpedo.

Quickstrike. The Mk 65 Quickstrike mine is the latest in a series of aerial bombs modified for use against surface ships in shallow-water, i.e., laid on the bottom to continental shelf depths (about 600 feet). The Mk 65 is a 2,390-pound bomb with a thin-wall mine casing. The mine is normally laid by low-flying A-6E and A-7E carrier-based aircraft.

Several earlier Quickstrike mines are available, the Mk 62 converted from the Mk 82 500-pound bomb, the Mk 63 converted from the Mk 83 1,000-pound bomb, and the Mk 64 converted from the Mk 84 2,000-pound bomb. These are also shallow-water mines that are used against surface ships.

A stockpile goal of approximately 80,000 Quickstrike weapons was identified in 1982 by a Navy official. The Quickstrike is a follow-on program to the Destructor bomb-to-mine program.

SLMM. The Mk 67 SLMM is a torpedo-like mine that permits covert mining by submarines in waters that are inaccessible to other means of delivery. This is also a shallow water, bottom mine for use against surface ships. Some outdated Mk 37 torpedoes were modified to an SLMM configuration for test and evaluation purposes.

A Navy official in 1982 listed the Navy's SLMM acquisition plan for 895 mines, although subsequent program schedules have called for larger numbers (see below).

The following is the Navy's procurement schedule for these three types of mines:

One new mine program has been cancelled, the Medium Depth Mine. Development of the long-delayed Medium Depth Mine (MDM) was cancelled in late 1981 because of high costs, according to Navy spokesmen. Other, classified reasons have also been given by the Navy. Congress had strongly backed the mine and directed the Navy to support the program, which one member of Congress described as "critical."

The MDM was an ASW mine intended for use on the continental shelf. During its development the mine was designated PRAM (Propelled Ascent Mine) and then IWD (Intermediate Water Depth) mine prior to MDM. The MDM was to have weighed about 2,500 pounds and was to have been delivered by aircraft and submarines.

Several older mines remain in service and are listed in the accompanying table.

Most naval mines can be set with several influence combinations (e.g., magnetic, acoustic) and with counters that will permit a certain number of ships or submarines to pass before detonating. Timers allow a delay in activating the mines, to allow the planting submarine to depart the area or to neutralize the mine after a specific period.

The principal U.S. means of minelaying is by aircraft. The Navy's carrier-based A-6E, A-7E, and S-3A aircraft and the land-based P-3 patrol/ASW aircraft are configured for minelaying. The Department of Defense considered the possibility of employing C-130, C-141, and C-5 cargo aircraft in the minelaying role under a program called CAML (Cargo Aircraft Minelaying), but the effort has not been pursued. With the CAML rig fitted, a C-130 could carry 16 2,000-pound mines.

The Air Force's B-52D Stratofortress was the most capable minelaying aircraft, but all 80 aircraft of that type have been retired.

U.S. submarines are configured to launch the SLMM and CAPTOR as well as several older mines. However, mines can be carried by submarines only at the expense of torpedoes, SUBROC, Harpoon, or other internally stowed weapons. Submarines at sea when a mining

AIRCRAFT MINE CAPACITIES

Aircraft	Wing Pylons		Weapons Bay
A-6 Intruder	5 2,000-lb		—
A-7 Corsair II	6 2,000-lb		—
S-3 Viking	2 2,000-lb	+	4 500-lb
P-3 Orion	10 500-lb	+	8 500-lb
		or	
	8 1,000-lb	+	3 1,000-lb
		or	
	6 2,000-lb	+	1 2,000-lb

	fiscal 1982*	fiscal 1983*	fiscal 1984*	fiscal 1985**	fiscal 1986**	fiscal 1987**	fiscal 1988**
CAPTOR	400	300	300	475	600	493	(none)
Quickstrike	n/a	n/a	600	559	743	743	777
SLMM	101	266	242	280	290	284	266

n/a = not available.
 * Actual.
 ** Planned.

decision was made would have to return to port, unload some or all of their other weapons, load mines, and then undertake the mining mission. Depending upon how many mines were carried, they could be required to return to port and rearm before undertaking anti-submarine or anti-shipping operations. Alternatively, during a period of crisis some sub-marines could be pre-loaded with mines, again at the expense of other weapons. Also, the Los Angeles (SSN 688)-class submarines are not fitted to carry mines.

No U.S. surface ships are employed to lay mines except in exercises for minesweepers or swimmers.

Designation	Type[a]	Targets	Weight	Explosive	Length	Delivery Platform	Notes
Mk 52	shallow-bottom	submarines surface ships	1,000 lbs	625 lbs	7$\frac{5}{12}$ ft (2.3 m)	aircraft	
Mk 55	shallow-bottom	submarines	2,120 lbs (Mod 3)	1,290 lbs	9½ ft (2.9 m)	aircraft	
Mk 56	medium-moored	submarines	2,135 lbs	360 lbs	11½ ft (3.5 m)	aircraft	
Mk 57	medium-moored	submarines	2,059 lbs	340 lbs	10$\frac{1}{12}$ ft (3.1 m)	submarine	
Mk 60 CAPTOR	deep-moored	submarines	2,000 lbs	96 lbs	12$\frac{1}{6}$ ft (3.7 m)	aircraft, submarine	with Mk 46 Mod 4 torpedo
Mk 67 SLMM	shallow-bottom	surface ships	1,765 lbs		13$\frac{5}{12}$ ft (4.1 m)	submarine	modified Mk 37 torpedo (self-propelled)
Destructor series							
Mk 36	shallow-bottom	surface ships	531 lbs CF[b] 570 lbs LD[c]			aircraft	modified Mk 82 bomb
Mk 40	shallow-bottom	surface ships	985 lbs CF[b] 1,105 lbs LD[c]			aircraft	modified Mk 83 bomb
Mk 41	shallow-bottom	surface ships	2,093 lbs CF[b]			aircraft	modified Mk 84 bomb
Quickstrike series							
Mk 62	shallow-bottom	surface ships	500 lbs			aircraft	modified Mk 82 bomb
Mk 63	shallow-bottom	surface ships	1,000 lbs			aircraft	modified Mk 83 bomb
Mk 64	shallow-bottom	surface ships	2,000 lbs		12½ ft (3.8 m)	aircraft	modified Mk 84 bomb
Mk 65	shallow-bottom	surface ships	2,390 lbs		10$\frac{2}{3}$ ft (3.3 m)	aircraft	new design; "thin wall"

[a] Shallow mines are laid to a maximum depth of approximately 600 ft; medium-depth mines to a maximum of about 1,000 ft; and deep-water to about 3,000 ft (CAPTOR).
[b] Fixed Conical Fin tail assembly.
[c] Extending Low Drag tail assembly.

A Mk 55 mine is rolled off the frigate Meyerkord (FF 1058) during a mining exercise off the coast of southern California. Special mine rails were fitted to the ship's helicopter deck for the exercise. (U.S. Navy)

Mk 55 mine (left) with fins fitted and Mk 52 without fins; HBX 3 is the explosive used in the mines. (U.S. Navy)

Mk 60 CAPTOR mine fitted with parachute pack. (U.S. Navy)

Mk 56 mine fitted on A-4 Skyhawk attack aircraft. (U.S. Navy)

An inert Mk 55 mine loaded on an S-3 Viking ASW aircraft. (U.S. Navy)

MISSILES

The missiles currently available or under development for the Navy and Marine Corps for use from aircraft, surface ships, and submarines are listed below. (Ground- and vehicle-launched missiles used by the Marine Corps are not listed.)

The missiles are arranged alphabetically by their popular names. All missiles in U.S. service or advanced development have letter-number designations explained in the accompanying table. There is a single series for missiles and a separate series for rockets. Of the weapons described here, the ASROC RUR-5A is the only one from the latter designation series; also listed is the ABRS rocket being considered for naval use.

ABRS

The ABRS (Assault Ballistic Rocket System) is being proposed for installation on the Navy's NEWPORT (LST 1179)-class landing ships to provide fire support for amphibious assaults. The unguided rocket and launcher are adopted from the U.S. Army's Multiple Launch Rocket System (MLRS).

Under current proposals each LST would be fitted with two 12-rocket launch systems on the ship's after deck. Up to 156 reloads could be provided in 12-rocket containers. Earlier proposals by the Vought Corporation proposed the ABRS for backfit to the SPRUANCE-class destroyers and the concept of a full LST 1179 conversion to a "rocket monitor," carrying several ABRS launchers. No procurement decision has been made by the Navy.

The U.S. Army's Multiple Launch Rocket System (MLRS) is being considered for Navy shipboard use as the Assault Ballistic Rocket System. This photo of the Army self-propelled unit shows the 12-rocket launcher pod; it can be rapidly reloaded from six-round containers. (Vought)

IOC:	(undetermined for U.S. Navy)
Manufacturer:	Vought
Weight:	686 lbs
Length:	12 ft 11 in (3.94 m)
Span:	(ballistic)
Diameter:	8.9 in (227 mm)
Propulsion:	solid-propellant rocket
Range:	10+ n.miles
Guidance:	(ballistic)
Warhead:	352 lb conventional (644 M77 grenades)
Platforms:	landing ships (LST 1179)

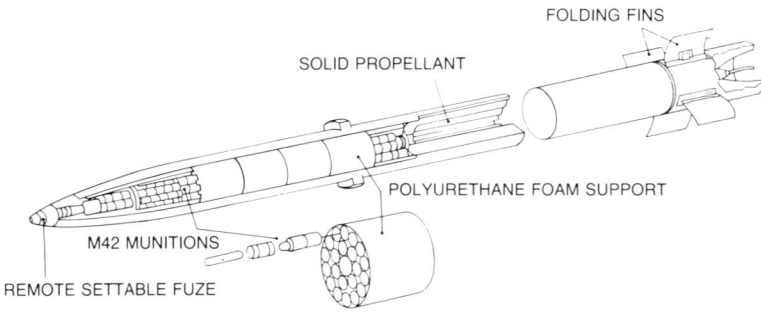

ABRS/MLRS round showing M42 submunitions.

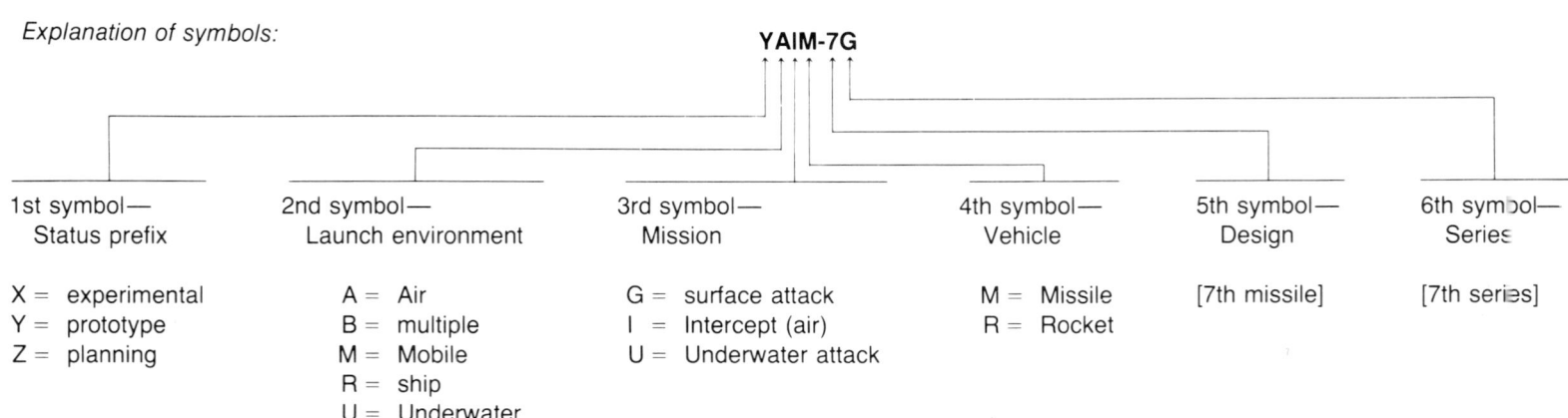

Explanation of symbols:

YAIM-7G

1st symbol— Status prefix	2nd symbol— Launch environment	3rd symbol— Mission	4th symbol— Vehicle	5th symbol— Design	6th symbol— Series
X = experimental	A = Air	G = surface attack	M = Missile	[7th missile]	[7th series]
Y = prototype	B = multiple	I = Intercept (air)	R = Rocket		
Z = planning	M = Mobile	U = Underwater attack			
	R = ship				
	U = Underwater				

AMRAAM AIM-120A

The Advanced Medium-Range Air-to-Air Missile is being developed jointly by the Navy and Air Force to succeed the Sparrow AAM. The missile is planned to have high resistance against enemy ECM and have a "snap-down" capability to engage low-flying aircraft and possibly anti-ship missiles.

It is anticipated that production of the missile could total some 20,000 weapons for U.S. use—13,000 for the Air Force and 7,000 for the Navy—plus allied requirements. The Hughes Aircraft Company is also studying the possible use of the missile from surface ships (Sea AMRAAM).

Flight tests were scheduled to begin in 1984.

IOC:	1986
Manufacturer:	Hughes
Weight:	200–350 lbs
Length:	
Span:	
Diameter:	
Propulsion:	solid-fuel rocket
Range:	
Guidance:	command-inertial; active terminal radar homing
Warhead:	30–50 lbs conventional
Platforms:	fighter aircraft (F-14, F/A-18)

ASROC RUR-5A

The ASROC—Anti-Submarine Rocket—is a ship-launched, ballistic ASW weapon that can be fitted with a conventional Mk 44/46 homing torpedo or a nuclear depth bomb. From the early 1960s onward ASROC was fitted to all U.S. Navy cruisers, destroyers, and frigates until the advent of the PERRY-class frigates. The ASROC is short range only; almost continuous proposals for an Extended-Range (ER) ASROC have been deferred.

A Vertical-Launch ASROC (VLA), however, is being developed, with about double the standard ASROC range, for firing from the VLS being installed in the CG 59, DDG 51, and DD 963 classes. This weapon would also be suitable for launch from modified ASROC launchers. (The Navy had originally sought to combine the replacement for ASROC and SUBROC in a single weapon; this proved too difficult, however, and the VLA will be surface launched and the ASW Stand-Off Weapon submarine launched.)

The standard ASROC is fired from an eight-tube box launcher (Mk 16) and from Mk 10 and Mk 26 surface-to-air missile launchers. It is used by 11 foreign navies.

The ASROC was tested on only one occasion with a nuclear warhead, being fired from the destroyer AGERHOLM (DD 826) on 11 May 1962 in the Pacific.

IOC:	1961
Manufacturer:	Honeywell
Weight:	1,000 lbs
Length:	15 ft (4.6 m)
Span:	(ballistic)
Diameter:	12¾ in (324 mm)
Propulsion:	solid-propellant rocket
Range:	approx. 6 n.miles
Guidance:	ballistic (terminal acoustic homing with Mk 46 torpedo)
Warhead:	conventional (Mk 46 Mod 1 in U.S. Navy) or nuclear depth bomb (W44)
Platforms:	cruisers destroyers frigates

ASROC fired from the frigate BROOKE (FFG 1) (U.S. Navy)

ASROC fired from the frigate Bowen (FF 1097) (U.S. Navy)

ASW STAND-OFF WEAPON

The ASW Stand-Off Weapon (SOW) is intended to replace the submarine-launched SUBROC anti-submarine weapon beginning in the early 1990s. Whereas SUBROC is a nuclear-only weapon, the ASW SOW may have both a nuclear and conventional capability, in the latter configuration carrying the Mk 50 ALWT (Advanced Lightweight Torpedo).[3] The ASW SOW should be capable of ranges out to at least the second convergence zone (approximately 60 miles), or double the range of the SUBROC.

The ASW SOW would be launched from standard 21-inch submarine torpedo tubes. The missile would be encapsulated, with the capsule shed when it reaches the surface, after which the missile travels through the air on a ballistic trajectory to the target. Over the target the warhead or torpedo would be released.

[3] This would be akin to the Soviet use of SS-N-15 (nuclear) and SS-N-16 (conventional) weapons from submarines.

During the concept stage the Navy envisioned a common ASW stand-off weapon for surface ships and submarines. The technical and program difficulties proved too great, however, and the surface-launched weapon became the Vertical-Launch ASROC (VLA). Boeing has used the name Seahawk for the weapon.

IOC:	approx. 1990
Manufacturer:	Boeing
Weight:	approx. 2,700 lbs
Length:	approx. 21 feet (6.4 m)
Span:	(ballistic)
Diameter:	approx. 21 inch (533 mm) encapsulated
Propulsion:	solid-propellant rocket
Range:	approx. 60–90 n.miles
Guidance:	ballistic (terminal acoustic homing with Mk 50 ALWT torpedo)
Warhead:	nuclear
	or Mk 50 ALWT torpedo
Platforms:	submarines (planned for SSN 594 and later classes)

An artist's concept of the ASW SOW; note folding tail stabilizing fins and change in diameter of front section. (Boeing)

HARM anti-radiation missile launched from an A-7E Corsair about to strike a target ship off Point Mugu, Calif. (U.S. Navy)

HARM AGM-88A

The HARM—High-speed Anti-Radiation Missile—was developed by the Naval Weapons Center at China Lake, Calif., for attacking hostile radars. The missile is a successor to the Shrike AGM-45A and Standard-ARM AGM-78D missiles, providing greater range, increased velocity, more frequency coverage, and additional flexibility in reacting to threats through an on-board computer. With respect to the last, HARM will automatically calculate threat priorities and engage the one that poses the greatest threat to friendly aircraft.

The first production missiles were delivered in December 1982. A production run of some 8,000 missiles is planned for the U.S. Navy with Air Force and foreign use also planned.

IOC:	1984–1985
Manufacturer:	Texas Instruments
Weight:	796 lbs
Length:	13 ft 7 in (4.17 m)
Span:	3 ft 8 in (1.13 m)
Diameter:	approx. 10 in (253 mm)
Propulsion:	solid-propellant rocket
Range:	approx. 80 n.miles
Guidance:	radar homing
Warhead:	145 lbs conventional
Platforms:	fighter aircraft (F/A-18)
	attack aircraft (A-6, A-7)

HARM on A-7E Corsair attack aircraft (U.S. Navy)

HARPOON AGM/RGM-84

The Harpoon was the first U.S. Navy missile designed for shipboard launch against surface targets since the Regulus I, which was deployed in the 1950s, primarily for the strategic attack role. The missile was initially conceived for aircraft use against surfaced Soviet Echo-class cruise missile submarines. Subsequently, the missile was developed for air, surface, and submarine launch against surface targets.

The missile is carried in most U.S. surface combatant classes, being launched from surface-to-air missile launchers (Mk 11, 13), vertical launchers (Mk 41), ASROC box launchers (Mk 29), and canisters (Mk 140, Mk 141). In shipboard (and submarine) launch the missile has a rocket booster fitted. Submarines can launch the Harpoon encapsulated from standard 21-inch torpedo tubes. The capsule rises to the surface and the missile ignites, leaving the canister. The P-3C and A-6E aircraft can carry the Harpoon; the S-3A and A-7E have conducted flight tests with Harpoon, and it is planned for the S-3B aircraft.

Several foreign navies employ the Harpoon from surface ships, with the Royal Navy using the underwater-launched Sub-Harpoon.

From June 1982 onward the U.S. Navy has taken delivery of the Block 1B Harpoon with improved radar guidance and a lower flight altitude. The subsequent 1C version, delivered from 1984, has improved guidance and burns a higher-density fuel, resulting in an increase in range, possibly to 80 n.miles. The maximum Harpoon flight velocity is Mach 0.85.

IOC:	1977 surface ships and submarines
	1979 aircraft (P-3C)
	1981 aircraft (A-6E)
Manufacturer:	McDonnell Douglas
Weight:	1,168 lbs for air launch
	1,470 lbs for Mk 11 or Mk 13 launch
	1,530 lbs for Mk 140, Mk 141 or SSN launch
Length:	12 ft 6 in (3.8 m) for air launch
	15 ft 2 in (4.6 m) for surface/submarine launch
Span:	3 ft (0.9 m)
Diameter:	13 ft 4 in (338 mm)
Propulsion:	turbojet (Teledyne CAE J402-CA-400); 600 lbst + solid-propellant booster for surface/submarine launch
Range:	60 n.miles
Guidance:	active radar
Warhead:	510 lbs conventional
Platforms:	attack aircraft (A-6E)
	patrol aircraft (P-3C)
	submarines (SSN 594 and later classes)
	cruisers
	destroyers
	frigates
	small combatants (PHM)

Harpoon underwater launch from HMS CHURCHILL (McDonnell Douglas)

A sailor prepares a Harpoon missile fitted to the wing of a P-3C Orion patrol aircraft. (McDonnell Douglas)

Harpoon on P-3C Orion (McDonnell Douglas)

Harpoon cannisters being fitted to the missile cruiser Long Beach (CGN 9) (McDonnell Douglas)

Harpoon being fired from the ASROC launcher of the frigate Badger (FF 1071) (McDonnell Douglas)

HELLFIRE AGM-114

The Hellfire (derived from Helicopter-Launched Fire and forget) is an anti-tank missile planned for use from Marine attack helicopters. The missile is intended to replace the wire-guided TOW, with the Hellfire being a free-flight weapon with a longer range which permits launch-and-leave tactics. The missile was developed by the Army.

The Hellfire is modular, allowing a variety of sensors to be fitted. The Marines will use the laser-guided variant. The target can be designated for helicopters by ground-based or airborne laser designators.

The Marines intend to first fit the missile to the AH-1J SeaCobra, followed by the AH-1T models.

IOC:	1986
Manufacturer:	Rockwell International
Weight:	95 lbs
Length:	5 ft 4 in (1.625 m)
Span:	1 ft 1 in (0.33 m)
Diameter:	7 in (178 mm)
Propulsion:	solid-propellant rocket
Range:	
Guidance:	laser
Warhead:	conventional
Platforms:	helicopters (AH-1J/T)

HELLFIRE missiles on Marine AH-1J SeaCobra (Bell Helicopter Textron)

LRDMM

The proposed LRDMM (Long-Range Dual-Mode Missile) was envisioned as a long-range (over 100-mile) missile for launching from Aegis ships. The missile would have been used against incoming anti-ship missiles launched at long ranges, attack bomber aircraft, and electronic jamming aircraft. At one point it was also envisioned that the airframe could be used for the ASW Stand-Off Weapon (SOW).

The project was not pursued because of technical difficulties and uncertainty over how to conduct the outer air battle to defend battle groups against attacking Soviet cruise missile aircraft. See listing for Standard SM-3.

MAVERICK AGM-65

This is an air-to-surface missile derived from an Air Force anti-tank missile for use by Marine aircraft in the close air support role and by the Navy in the anti-ship role.

The Marines will use the AGM-65E laser-guided version, compatible with air- and ground-based laser designators. The Navy's AGM-65F will combine the Imaging Infrared (I²R) of the Air Force AGM-65D missile with the warhead and propulsion sections of the AGM-65E. These Mavericks will have a 300-pound penetrating blast warhead in place of the 125-pound shaped charge used for attacking tanks in the Air Force versions.

The Maverick missile is also used by the Iranian, Israeli, and Swedish air forces. More than 30,000 missiles have been built. The first Navy launch of an AGM-65F occurred in September 1983 from an A-7E aircraft, successfully striking a discarded destroyer.

IOC:	Marine Corps
	Navy
Manufacturer:	Hughes
Weight:	637 lbs
Length:	8 ft 2 in (2.49 m)
Span:	2 ft 4½ in (0.72 m)
Diameter:	12 in (305 mm)
Propulsion:	solid-propellant rocket
Range:	12 n.miles
Guidance:	AGM-65E laser
	AGM-65F infrared
Warhead:	300 lb high explosive
Platforms:	attack aircraft (A-4M, A-6E, A-7E)

The AGM-65F version of the Maverick air-to-surface missile mounted on an A-7 Corsair. (Hughes)

MRASM AGM-109

The MRASM (Medium-Range Air-to-Surface Missile) was a joint Navy-Air Force program to develop an air-launched missile with a 250-n.mile range for delivering submunitions against runways. Originally to be a (shortened) variant of the Tomahawk, during early development significant changes were made to most components, reducing the commonality with Tomahawk. The Navy's interest in MRASM was minimal while the Air Force's position was divided: the Tactical Air Command (TAC) had limited interest while the Strategic Air Command (SAC) envisioned the MRASM as a useful weapon for the B-52G strategic bomber. The situation was further complicated by the Department of Defense decision in 1983 to retire 90 of the approximately 150 available B-52G bombers.

The MRASM program was terminated by Congress in 1983. Other weapons that could be adopted to the MRASM role at that time included the Air Force GBU-15, an air-launched glide bomb, and the Navy's Harpoon, while the Air Force Advanced Cruise Missile (ACM)—a "stealth" weapon—could be used by strategic aircraft. Also being planned is an Army-Air Force effort to develop a common Joint Tactical Missile System (JTACMS) that could be ground launched and carried by strategic and tactical aircraft for "deep attack."

The designation AGM-109H was intended for the Air Force airfield attack weapon and AGM-109L for a projected Navy anti-ship and land-attack version.

PENGUIN II

The Penguin II is a surface-to-surface missile developed by the Norwegian Navy that has undergone extensive evaluation for small craft by the U.S. Navy. The Norwegians have also developed an air-launched version. The missile has several unusual features, including an indirect flight path to target. It is operated in a fire-and-forget mode. The Penguin is fired from a stage/launcher container that weighs 1,100 pounds. Many Penguin components are American made.

The U.S. Navy has no procurement plans for the Penguin. However, Congress has proposed that the Navy consider the missile for use on the SH-60B helicopter.

The original Penguin became operational on Norwegian fast attack boats in 1972; it is also used by the Greek, Swedish, and Turkish navies. The improved Mk II became operational in 1979 and the Mk III has been developed for launch from F-16 strike fighters of the Norwegian Air Force.

IOC:	(undetermined for U.S. Navy)
Manufacturer:	Kongsberg Vaapenfabrikk (Norway)
Weight:	726 lbs
Length:	9 ft (3.0 m)
Span:	4 ft 7 in (1.4 m)
Diameter:	11 in (280 mm)
Propulsion:	solid-propellant rocket + solid-propellant booster
Range:	17 n.miles
Guidance:	inertial + infrared terminal
Warhead:	264 lb conventional
Platforms:	small combatants (PB)
	helicopters

PHOENIX AIM-54

The Phoenix was developed for long-range fleet air defense against attacking Soviet bomber aircraft. It is the most sophisticated and longest-range air-to-air missile in service with any nation. The missile can be carried only by the F-14 fighter with the AWG-9 radar/fire control system; the AWG-9 is capable of simultaneously guiding all six Phoenix missiles that can be carried by an F-14.

The AIM-54A, with analog electronics, has been replaced in U.S. service with the AIM-54C, which has a digital system to allow software programming for more rapid target discrimination, improved beam attack, better resistance to electronic countermeasures, longer range, increased altitude, and increased reliability. The AIM-54A was compromised by having been provided to the Iranian Air Force prior to the fall of the Shah in 1979. The AIM-54B was an interim model, similar to the 54A without the earlier missile's liquid cooling system; it did not go into production. The missile's design range was 60 n.miles; intercepts have been made out to at least 110 n.miles. The A and C models have a combined 85 percent success rate.

A second production source is being considered by the Navy.

Hughes Aircraft Company proposed a shipboard short-range defensive missile system in the 1970s based on the Phoenix/AWG-9.

IOC:	1974
Manufacturer:	Hughes
Weight:	985 lbs
Length:	13 ft (4.0 m)
Span:	3 ft (0.9 m)
Diameter:	15 in (380 mm)
Propulsion:	solid-propellant rocket
Range:	110 n.miles
Guidance:	semiactive radar in cruise phase; active terminal radar homing
Warhead:	135 lbs conventional
Platforms:	fighter aircraft (F-14)

Penguin being launched by a PBR Mk III; note the open missile cannister, fire control dome, and telemetry antennas. (U.S. Navy)

Phoenix being launched by F-14A Tomcat fighter (Hughes)

POSEIDON (C-3) UGM-73

The Poseidon SLBM was derived from the Polaris missile, with increased strike capability through a Multiple Independently targeted Reentry Vehicle (MIRV) warhead, the first strategic missile of any nation to have that feature. The Poseidon MIRV can carry up to 14 RVs, with 8 to 10 being a common loadout. The RVs can be directed at specific targets within range of the warhead's "footprint." The missile range is reduced when the larger numbers of RVs are carried.

The Poseidon replaced the Polaris A-2/A-3 missiles in the 31 LAFAYETTE (SSBN 726)-class submarines. Subsequently, the last 12 submarines of that class have received the Trident C-4 missile in place of the Poseidon. Procurement of the missile has ceased.

IOC:	1971
Manufacturer:	Lockheed
Weight:	65,000 lbs
Length:	34 ft (10.4 m)
Span:	(ballistic missile)
Diameter:	74 in (1.9 m)
Propulsion:	2-stage solid-propellant rocket
Range:	approx. 2,500 n.miles with reduced number of RVs
Guidance:	inertial
Warhead:	nuclear (W68); 8 to 14 RVs
Platforms:	strategic missile submarines (SSBN 616)

Poseidon test missile (within transport cannister) being loaded into the JAMES MADISON (U.S. Navy)

Poseidon test launch from the JAMES MADISON (SSBN 627) (U.S. Air Force)

RAM RIM-116A

The Rolling Airframe Missile (RAM) is being developed to provide a rapid-reaction, short-range missile for shipboard defense using off-the-shelf components. The RAM is the first Navy shipboard fire-and-forget missile and the only Navy missile that rolls during flight (i.e., is not stabilized in flight).

The RAM has the infrared seeker from the Army's Stinger missile and the rocket motor, fuze, and warhead from the Sidewinder AAM. The missile is supersonic. The RAM missile can be fired from a specialized, 24-missile launcher (Ex-31) or in two of the eight cells of the NATO Sea Sparrow launcher (five missiles per cell). The Ex-31 uses the mount and elevation/train assemblies from the Phalanx CIWS.

The missile is co-sponsored by Denmark and West Germany. The first RAM engineering missiles were delivered in September 1981.

IOC:	1988
Manufacturer:	General Dynamics/Pomona
Weight:	154 lbs
Length:	9 ft 2 in (2.79 m)
Span:	1 ft 5 in (431.8 mm)
Diameter:	5 in (127 mm)
Propulsion:	solid-propellant rocket
Range:	4+ n.miles
Guidance:	dual mode—passive RF acquisition and mid-course guidance with IR terminal or passive RF all the way[4]
Warhead:	25 lb conventional
Platforms:	various surface ships

[4] RF = Radio Frequency and IR = Infrared.

RAM missile and launcher (General Dynamics/Pomona)

SEA SPARROW RIM-7

The Sea Sparrow is an adaption of the Sparrow AAM employed as an anti-ship missile defense system. The concept was developed in the 1960s to counter the threat from Soviet anti-ship weapons and is fired from the eight-tube box Mk 25 launcher of the Basic Point Defense Missile System (BPDMS) or the Mk 29 launcher of the NATO Sea Sparrow Missile (NSSM). The RIM-7H and -7M missiles are used in this role.

The Sea Sparrow launchers are fitted in ships that do not have Tartar/ Terrier/Standard missile capabilities. The launchers are not automatically reloaded, and many ships do not have any reloads on board. Several foreign navies employ the Sea Sparrow in the missile-defense role. The following data apply to the RIM-7H. See listing for Sparrow missile for additional data.

Sea Sparrow fired from the helicopter carrier GUADALCANAL (LPH 7); the debris is from the break-through covering of the launch cell. (U.S. Navy)

IOC:	1969 (RIM-7M in 1983)
Manufacturer:	Raytheon
Weight:	450 lbs
Length:	12 ft (3.7 m)
Span:	3 ft 4 in (1.0 m)
Diameter:	8 in (203 mm)
Propulsion:	solid-propellant rocket
Range:	approx. 10 n.miles
Guidance:	radar homing
Warhead:	90 lb conventional
Platforms:	aircraft carriers
	destroyers
	frigates
	command ships (LCC)
	amphibious ships (LHA, LPH)
	auxiliaries (AOE, AOR)

Sea Sparrow on loading rail aboard the frigate ROARK (FF 1053) (Giorgio Arra)

SHRIKE AGM-45

The Shrike is an anti-radiation missile designed to home on hostile radars. The missile was developed for the U.S. Navy and was used in the Vietnam War from 1964 onward. There are more than a dozen variants reflecting changes in the guidance seeker to counter different electronic threats. The Shrike suffers from a short range and is being replaced by the HARM.

The missile was developed by the Naval Weapons Center, China Lake, Calif. It is also used by the U.S., British, and Israeli air forces, with the RAF having used them (ineffectively) in the 1982 Falklands conflict.

Loading a Sea Sparrow into a test launcher. The missile's fins are fixed and do not retract when in the launcher. (U.S. Navy)

IOC:	1963
Manufacturer:	Texas Instruments
Weight:	390 lbs
Length:	10 ft (3.0 m)
Span:	3 ft (0.9 m)
Diameter:	8 in (203 mm)
Propulsion:	solid-propellant rocket
Range:	approx. 10 n.miles
Guidance:	passive radar homing
Warhead:	145 lb conventional
Platforms:	fighter aircraft (F/A-18)
	attack aircraft (A-4M, A-6E, A-7E)

Shrike anti-radiation missile on F-4E Phantom (U.S. Navy)

Shrike ARM (top) and Standard-ARM on F-4G Phantom (U.S. Navy)

SIAM

The Defense Advanced Research Projects Agency (DARPA) is sponsoring the development of technology for the SIAM (Self-Initiating Anti-aircraft Missile) for use from a submerged submarine against an ASW fixed-wing aircraft or helicopter. The weapon would be launched from special tubes in the submarine and home on the attack. The towed acoustic arrays now used by submarines could detect low-flying aircraft to initiate SIAM launch.

The concept is not new, with one earlier U.S. Navy experiment using variants of the Sidewinder missile being dubbed "Subwinder." The Royal Navy and Vickers have developed the SLAM (Submarine-Launched Air Missile) in which the submarine surfaces or at least broaches its sail to extend a six-tube Blowpipe missile launcher. The SIAM concept calls for missile launch while the submarine remains completely submerged.

Ford Aerospace was contracted by DARPA to demonstrate the feasibility of the concept. During the Ford work, test vehicles were successfully launched against QH-50 drone helicopters. The future of this project was not determined when this edition went to press. The following characteristics are tentative.

IOC:	undetermined
Manufacturer:	undetermined
Weight:	approx. 150 lbs
Length:	approx 8 ft 4 in (2.5 m)
Span:	5¾ in (147 mm)
Diameter:	5¾ in (147 mm)
Propulsion:	solid-propellant rocket
Range:	
Guidance:	radar and infrared homing
Warhead:	conventional
Platforms:	proposed for submarines (SSBN, SSN)

The first test firing of a SIAM technology demonstration missile, fired against flares mounted on a QH-50C drone helicopter hovering at 1,500 feet above the White Sands Missile Range, N.M. This 1980 ground-launched test flight was nondestructive with the flares mounted on a rack extending away from the helicopter. (U.S. Army)

SIDEWINDER AIM-9

The Sidewinder is possibly the most widely used missile outside of the Soviet Union with more than 110,000 missiles having been produced for 27 nations in addition to the United States. Developed by the naval research center at China Lake, Calif., the Sidewinder is a simple, effective, infrared-homing missile.

The AIM-9H and -9L variants are in use as is the AIM-9M, which is currently in production. The -9H has solid state guidance in lieu of vacuum tube electronics of the previous version; the -9L has all-aspect detection and launch capability, with increased seeker sensitivity; and the -9M missile has improved resistance to electronic countermeasures and can engage targets against hot backgrounds. An AIM-9C with a modified anti-radiation seeker is called Sidearm. Missile speed is in excess of Mach 2.

The Sidewinder has been used extensively (and very successfully) in recent conflicts by Britain and Israel.

IOC:	1956 (AIM-9H in 1973, AIM-9L in 1978, AIM-9M in 1983)
Manufacturer:	Raytheon and Ford Aerospace
Weight:	88 lbs for AIM-9H
	86½ lbs for AIM-9L/M
Length:	9 ft 6 in (2.9 m)
Span:	2 ft ¾ in (0.63 m) for AIM-9H
	2 ft 1 in (0.635 m) for AIM-9L/M
Diameter:	5 in (127 mm)
Propulsion:	solid-propellant rocket
Range:	approx. 10 n.miles
Guidance:	infrared homing
Warhead:	25 lbs conventional for AIM-9H
	20.8 lbs conventional for AIM-9L/M
Platforms:	fighter aircraft (F-4, F-14, F/A-18)
	attack aircraft (A-6E, A-7E)

Sidewinder being attached to the "cheek" fuselage pylon of an F-8 Crusader fighter. (U.S. Navy)

Sidewinder fitted on F/A-18A from VFA-125 (U.S. Navy, PH1 Richard J. Boyle)

TA-4J Skyhawk from VC-10 firing a Sidewinder AAM (U.S. Navy)

Sidearm missile fitted to AH-1 SeaCobra. (U.S. Navy, S. Wyatt)

SPARROW III AIM-7

The Sparrow is an all-weather, medium-range AAM. It has been adopted for surface launch in the Sea Sparrow variants for use in the anti-ship missile defense role.

The AIM-7F and AIM-7M are in wide U.S. Navy service with the latter currently in production. The -7F has an improved, semi-active doppler radar homing system with a smaller solid-state seeker than earlier versions; the -7M has an advanced monopulse seeker with improved resistance to electronic countermeasures, new autopilot, and new fuze. Missile speed is reportedly in excess of Mach 3.5.

More than 40,000 missiles have been produced for U.S. and foreign air forces. In addition to the two U.S. producers, the Sparrow is manufactured in Japan by Mitsubishi. The following data are for the AIM-7F model.

IOC:	1958 (AIM-7F in 1976, AIM-7M in 1983)
Manufacturer:	Raytheon and General Dynamics/Pomona
Weight:	500 lbs
Length:	12 ft (3.7 m)
Span:	3 ft 4 in (1.1 m)
Diameter:	8 in (203 mm)
Propulsion:	solid-propellant rocket
Range:	approx. 30 n.miles
Guidance:	semiactive radar homing
Warhead:	88 lbs conventional
Platforms:	fighter aircraft (F-4, F-14, F/A-18)

Sparrow III launched by an F-4B Phantom (U.S. Navy)

Sparrow III being fitted to F-14A Tomcat (U.S. Navy)

STANDARD-ARM AGM-78

This is an Anti-Radiation Missile (ARM) adopted from the Standard RIM-66A surface-to-air missile. It was also employed briefly by the U.S. Navy as an interim surface-to-surface missile pending availability of the Harpoon. The Standard-ARM is obsolescent and is being replaced by the HARM.

Models -78A through -78D were developed, with some sub-variants to respond to changes in Soviet radars. The missile speed is about Mach 2. The Standard-ARM was used by the U.S. Navy and Air Force in Vietnam, and by the Israeli Air Force.

IOC:	1968
Manufacturer:	General Dynamics/Pomona
Weight:	1,799 lbs
Length:	14 ft 10¾ in (4.57 m)
Span:	3 ft 6 in (1.1 m)
Diameter:	13 in (330 mm)
Propulsion:	solid-propellant rocket
Range:	15 n.miles
Guidance:	passive radar homing
Warhead:	215 lbs conventional
Platforms:	attack aircraft (A-4, A-6, A-7)

STANDARD (SM-1 MR) RIM-66B

The Standard series of surface-to-air missiles was developed as replacements for the 3-T missiles, the trouble-plagued Talos, Terrier, and Tartar. Initially the MR (Medium Range) missiles were to replace the Tartar and the ER (Extended Range) missiles the Terrier and Talos. However, various modifications and production blocks of Standard missiles have blurred model distinctions.

Some 30 foreign warships are fitted with Standard missile launchers.

The SM-1 MR is the oldest Standard type remaining in service, being a single-stage, relatively short-range weapon.

IOC:	1970
Manufacturer:	General Dynamics/Pomona
Weight:	1,100 lbs
Length:	14 ft 8 in (4.5 m)
Span:	3 ft 6 in (1.1 m)
Diameter:	13½ in (342 mm)
Propulsion:	solid-propellant rocket
Range:	15–20 n.miles
Guidance:	semiactive radar homing
Warhead:	conventional
Platforms:	cruisers
	destroyers
	frigates

STANDARD (SM-2 MR) RIM-66C

This missile has increased range, the addition of mid-course guidance, and enhanced resistance to electronic countermeasures compared with the SM-1 MR version. It is intended specifically for use aboard Aegis missile cruisers.

IOC:	1981
Manufacturer:	General Dynamics/Pomona
Weight:	1,400 lbs
Length:	14 ft (4.3 m)
Span:	3 ft 6 in (1.1 m)
Diameter:	13½ in (342 mm)
Propulsion:	solid-propellant rocket
Range:	approx. 40 n.miles in early missiles; up to 90 n.miles in later missiles
Guidance:	semiactive radar homing
Warhead:	conventional
Platforms:	cruisers (CG 47)

Standard-MR SM-2 firing from the guided missile ship NORTON SOUND (AVM 1) (U.S. Navy)

STANDARD (SM-2 ER) RIM-67B

The SM-2 ER version of the Standard has mid-course guidance, an inertial reference system, and improved resistance to electronic countermeasures. Significantly larger than the MR missiles, this missile will have a nuclear version. Approval of development of a missile with the W81 nuclear warhead—designated SM-2(N)—was approved in 1979. This is a two-stage missile that can reach an altitude of approximately 80,000 feet.

Production of the less capable SM-1 ER missile ended in 1974.

IOC:	1981
Manufacturer:	General Dynamics/Pomona
Weight:	2,900 lbs
Length:	26 ft 2 in (7.9 m)
Span:	5 ft 3 in (1.6 m)
Diameter:	13½ in (342 mm)
Propulsion:	solid-propellant rocket + solid-propellant booster
Range:	approx. 65 n.miles
Guidance:	inertial with semiactive radar homing
Warhead:	conventional (nuclear W81 in development)
Platforms:	cruisers
	destroyers

Standard-ER firing from the cruiser WAINWRIGHT (CG 28) (U.S. Navy)

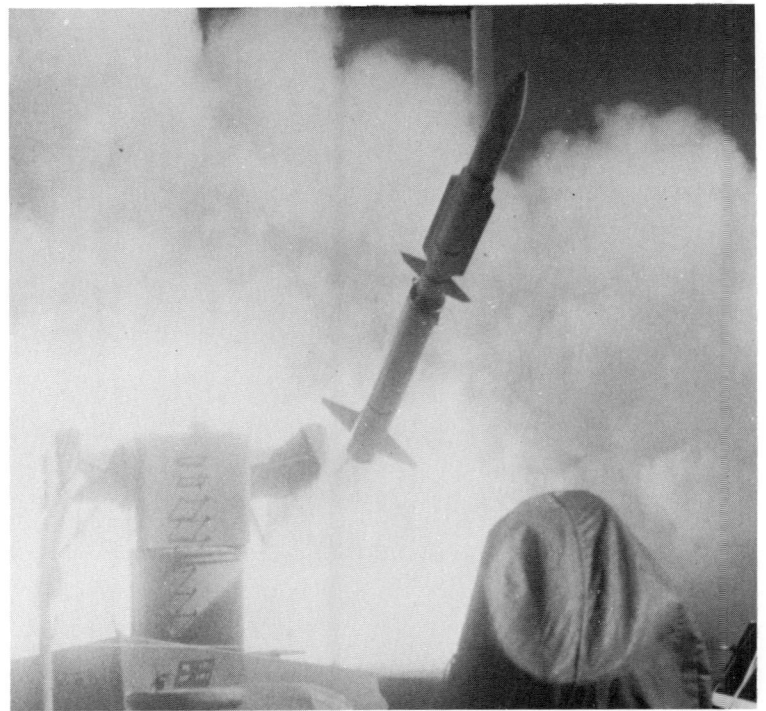

Standard-ER/SM-2 firing from the cruiser LONG BEACH (CGN 9) (U.S. Navy)

STANDARD (SM-3)

A Standard SM-3 missile is under consideration to provide a very-long-range missile for intercepting Soviet stand-off jamming aircraft and possibly missile-carrying aircraft at ranges greater than possible with the SM-2 ER. This is similar to the concept of the LRDMM (see above); a concept called Thor was similar.

STINGER FIM-92

The Stinger is an advanced, shoulder-held surface-to-air missile that resembles the World War II-era bazooka rocket launcher. The missile was placed aboard several U.S. naval ships in the eastern Mediterranean beginning in the winter of 1983–1984 in reaction to threatened terrorist attacks against U.S. ships. (The Soviet Navy similarly uses the shoulder-held SA-7 Grail missile, formerly Strela, in various ships.)

Originally designated Redeye II, the missile is tube-launched with four pop-out vanes at the front and four folding fins at the rear.

The Stinger is used by the U.S. Marine Corps, Army, and Air Force as well as by several foreign services, with the British having scored successes with the missile in the 1982 war in the Falklands. The missile is replacing the Redeye in U.S. service. An improved Stinger-POST (Passive Optical Seeker Technique), with increased resistance to countermeasures, entered production in fiscal 1984.

IOC:	1982 (U.S. Army)
Manufacturer:	General Dynamics/Pomona
Weight:	34.5 lbs (missile and launch tube)
Length:	5 feet (1.5 m)
Span:	8 inches (203 mm)
Diameter:	2¾ inches (527 mm)
Propulsion:	solid-propellant rocket
Range:	approx. 3 n.miles (effective range is probably less)
Guidance:	infrared homing
Warhead:	conventional
Platforms:	various ships

Stinger shoulder-fired missile (U.S. Army)

Stinger missile in flight with fins extended (U.S. Army)

SUBROC UUM-44A

The SUBROC (Submarine Rocket) is a rocket-propelled nuclear depth bomb that can be launched from standard 21-inch submarine torpedo tubes. After being launched the missile streaks to the surface, leaves the water, and then releases the nuclear depth bomb to parachute down to the water.

The weapon is analog and hence not compatible with U.S. attack submarines having the Mk 117 digital fire control system. Thus, only about 25 submarines of the PERMIT (SSN 594) and later classes carry the weapon. The remaining missiles are wearing out rapidly and all will probably be discarded prior to the replacement ASW Stand-Off Weapon becoming available in the early 1990s.

IOC:	1964
Manufacturer:	Goodyear
Weight:	4,000 lbs
Length:	21 ft (6.4 m)
Span:	(ballistic)
Diameter:	21 in (533 mm)
Propulsion:	solid-propellant rocket + booster
Range:	approx. 25 n.miles
Guidance:	inertial
Warhead:	nuclear (W55)
Platforms:	submarines (SSN 594 and later classes with Mk 113 analog fire control system)

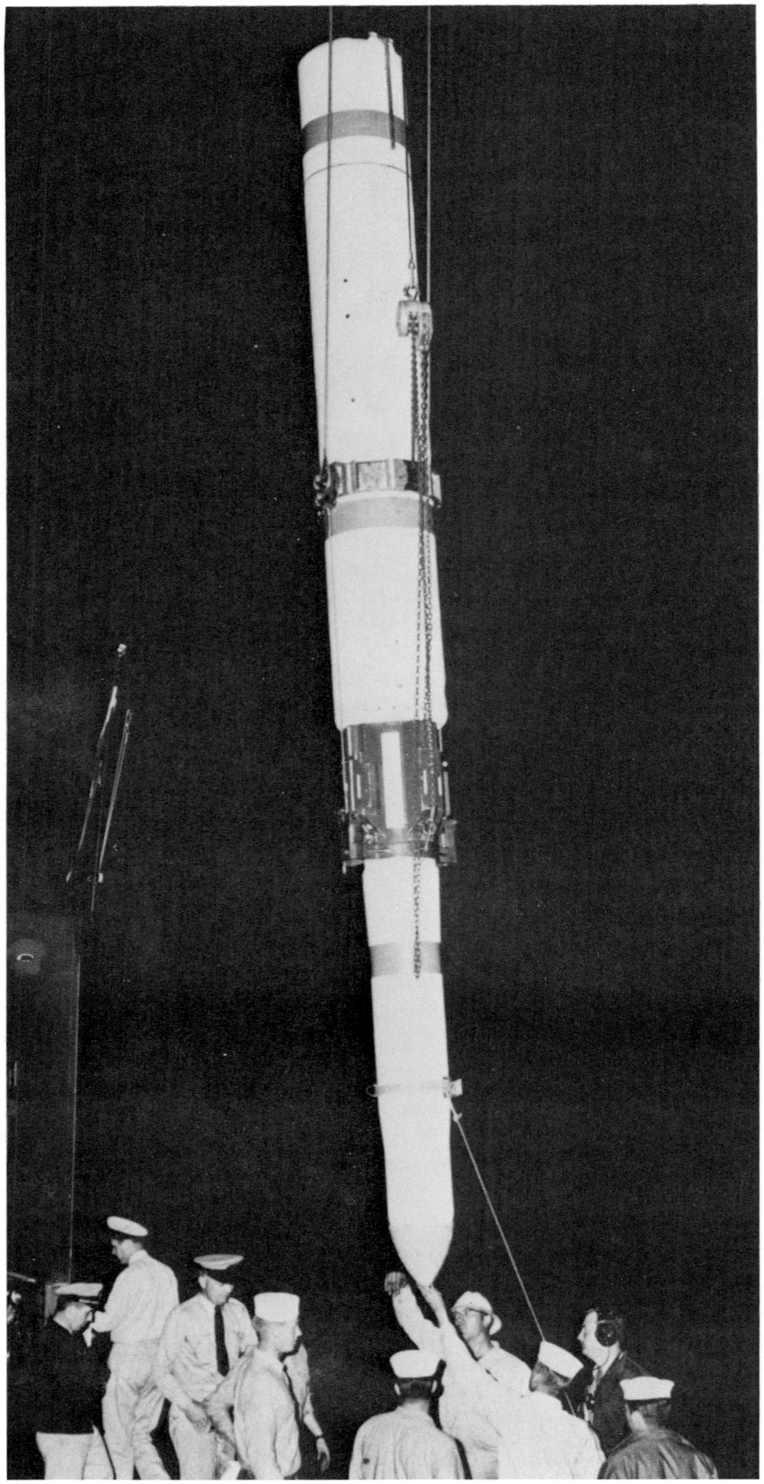

Night loading of SUBROC missile aboard the attack submarine PERMIT (SSN 594) (Goodyear)

SUBROC firing from submerged submarine; this weapon is being rapidly phased out of service as SSNs are being provided with a digital fire control system. The demise of the SUBROC leaves the U.S. Navy without a nuclear ASW weapon pending availability of the ASW Stand-Off Weapon. (U.S. Navy)

TARTAR RIM-24

The Tartar was the U.S. Navy's first surface-to-air missile developed specifically for use on destroyer and smaller warships. It was one of the 3-T missiles which, along with the Terrier and now-discarded Talos, evolved from the Bumblebee Program of World War II. The RIM-24B and -24C versions are in U.S. and foreign service, with U.S. ships being refitted with the Standard-MR series.

IOC:	1960
Manufacturer:	General Dynamics/Pomona
Weight:	1,300 lbs
Length:	15 ft (4.6 m)
Span:	3 ft 6 in (1.1 m)
Diameter:	13½ in (342 mm)
Propulsion:	solid-propellant rocket
Range:	10 + n.miles
Guidance:	semiactive radar homing
Warhead:	conventional
Platforms:	cruisers
	destroyers
	frigates

Tartar SAMs on the destroyer ROBISON (DDG 12) (Giorgio Arra)

TERRIER RIM-2

The Terrier was the first of the 3-T missiles to enter service and is retained by the U.S. Navy in limited numbers primarily because of the nuclear capability of the BTN (Beam-riding, Terrier, Nuclear) version. It is the only Navy SAM with a nuclear warhead pending development of the Standard SM-2(N). Other Terrier ships have been refitted with the Standard missile.

The Terrier was intended for installation in cruisers (including the DLG/DLGN-type frigates) but was fitted in two aircraft carriers, the KITTY HAWK (CV 63) and CONSTELLATION (CV 64), and one destroyer, the GYATT (DDG 1, ex-DD 712). The missile was eliminated from later carrier designs because of high carrier construction costs; the missile was also proposed for battleship installation in the late 1940s. It has been removed from the KITTY HAWK.

Conventional Terriers were in service with the Dutch and Italian navies; they have been replaced by the Standard-ER SM-1.

IOC:	1955 (BTN in 1962)
Manufacturer:	General Dynamics/Pomona
Weight:	3,000 lbs
Length:	26 ft 2 in (7.9 m)
Span:	3 ft 6 in (1.1 m)
Diameter:	13½ in (342 mm); booster 18 in (456 mm)
Propulsion:	solid-propellant rocket + solid-propellant booster
Range:	20–40 n.miles (varies with version)
Guidance:	radar beam riding
Warhead:	conventional or nuclear (W45)
Platforms:	aircraft carriers (CV 64)
	cruisers
	destroyers (DDG 37, ex-DLG 6)

Terrier launching from the cruiser LEAHY (CG 16) (U.S. Navy)

TOMAHAWK BGM-109

The Tomahawk is a long-range cruise missile developed for both surface and submarine launch against both surface ship and land targets. It was initially known as the Sea-Launch Cruise Missile (SLCM), but in 1979 the Navy began using the terms Tomahawk Land-Attack Missile (T-LAM) and Tomahawk Anti-Ship Missile (T-ASM) to distinguish the principal variants.[5]

The missile is being deployed in Armored Box Launchers (ABL) on battleships and some SPRUANCE-class destroyers. It will also be carried in the vertical launchers (Mk 41) of later TICONDEROGA-class cruisers, BURKE-class destroyers, and most of the SPRUANCES. It can also be fired from 21-inch submarine torpedo tubes and, in the later LOS ANGELES class, from vertical launch tubes. The missile has a high subsonic speed.

An air-launched Tomahawk competed unsuccessfully with the Boeing Air-Launched Cruise Missile (ALCM) for use on B-52 strategic bombers. The Ground Launched Cruise Missile (GLCM) version, however, was selected as a theater nuclear weapon for deployment in Western Europe under Air Force control.

The following table lists the Tomahawk versions identified when this edition went to press. The AGM series were part of the cancelled MRASM program, described on page 440. Warheads from the discarded Bullpup missile are used in several variants.

Model	Service	Launch mode	Type	Warhead
BGM-109A	USN	ship/sub	LAM	nuclear (W80); IOC 1984
BGM-109B	USN	ship/sub	ASM	conventional (1,000-lb Bullpup)
BGM-109C	USN	ship/sub	LAM	conventional (1,000-lb Bullpup)
BGM-109D	USN	ship/sub	LAM	conventional (bomblets)
BGM-109E	USN	ship/sub	ASM	conventional; concept idea
BGM-109F	USN	ship/sub	LAM	conventional; concept idea
BGM-109G	USAF	ground	LAM	nuclear (W84); IOC 1983
AGM-109C	USN	air	LAM	conventional
AGM-109H	USAF	air	LAM	conventional (airfield attack munitions)
AGM-109I	USN	air	LAM/ASM	conventional
AGM-109J	USN	air	LAM	conventional

The program was delayed more than one year in the early 1980s because of test and production problems. The MERRILL (DD 976) was fitted with the first Tomahawk installation in October 1982 for at-sea evaluation; the battleship NEW JERSEY was the second ship, receiving the Tomahawk in March 1983. The GUITARRO (SSN 665) was the first submarine armed with Tomahawk; after serving as Tomahawk test ship, she was armed with the T-ASM version in March 1983.

In late 1983 McDonnell Douglas was selected as a second source to produce the missile.

IOC:	1984 T-ASM in surface ships
	1983 T-ASM in submarines

[5] The dash has now been dropped and the missiles are designated simply TLAM and TASM.

	1986 T-LAM in surface ships and submarines
	1984 T-LAM(N) in surface ships and submarines
Manufacturer:	General Dynamics/Convair
	McDonnell Douglas
Weight:	2,650 lbs + 550-lb booster
	+ 1,000-lb capsule for submarine launch
Length:	18 ft 2 in (5.55 m) for T-ASM + 2 ft (0.6 m) booster
Span:	8 ft 8 in (2.6 m)
Diameter:	21 in (533 mm)
Propulsion:	turbofan + solid-propellant booster
Range:	T-ASM 250+ n.miles
	T-LAM(N) 1,350 n.miles
	T-LAM(C) 500–700 n.miles
Guidance:	active radar homing in T-ASM (same as Harpoon SSM)
	inertial and TERCOM (Terrain Contour Matching) in T-LAM
Warhead:	1,000 lb conventional in T-ASM and T-LAM nuclear (W80) in T-LAM(N)
Platforms:	attack submarines
	battleships
	cruisers
	destroyers

Tomahawk test launched from an underwater capsule simulating the vertical launch tube of a LOS ANGELES (SSN 688)-class submarine. (General Dynamics/Pomona)

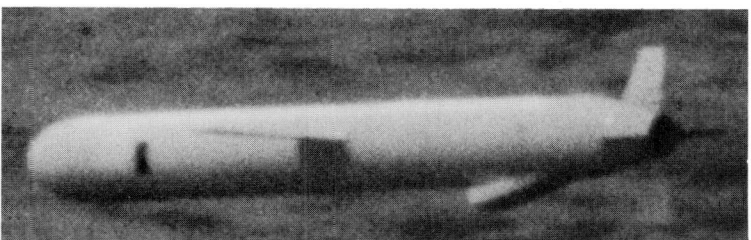

Tomahawk missile in flight with wings, tail fins, and air-intake scoop extended. (U.S. Navy)

Tomahawk missile in flight (U.S. Navy)

Tomahawk T-ASM (subsequently TASM) variant about to strike target ship (U.S. Navy)

TOW MGM-71

The TOW—for Tube-launched, Optically tracked, Wire-guided—is an anti-tank missile fired from Army and Marine Corps helicopters as well as from ground and vehicle mounts. The AH-1T is the only Marine helicopter fitted with TOW.

Improved versions, designated Improved TOW (ITOW) and TOW2, have an upgraded warhead and an upgraded warhead plus higher impulse motor, respectively. The missile has a high subsonic speed.

IOC:	1970
Manufacturer:	Hughes and Emerson Electric
Weight:	54 pounds
Length:	3 ft 8 in (1.1 m)
Span:	3 ft 9 in (1.1 m)
Diameter:	6 in (152 mm)
Propulsion:	solid-fuel rocket + solid-fuel booster
Range:	1.5 n.miles (2 n.miles for TOW2)
Guidance:	optical/wire
Warhead:	8 lb conventional (shaped charge)
Platforms:	helicopters (AH-1T)

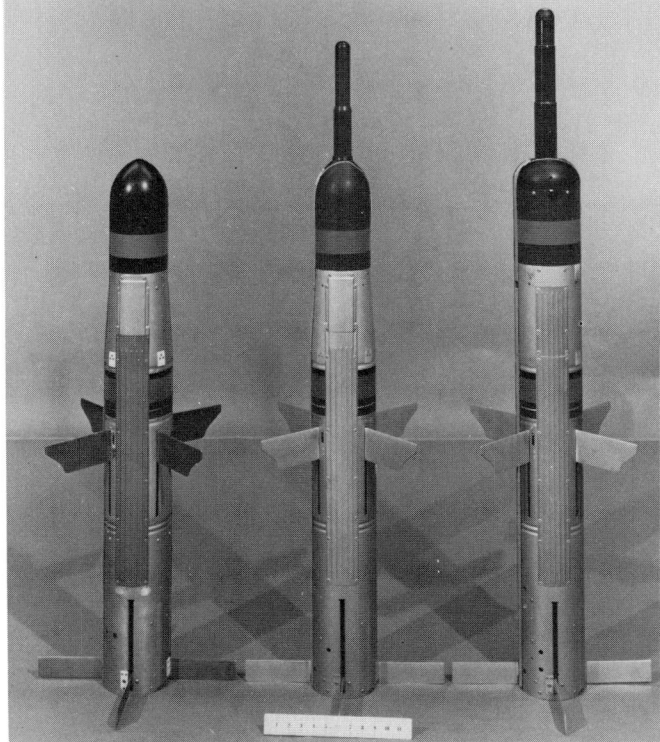

TOW missiles, from left: the basic TOW, the Improved TOW, and TOW 2; the TOW and I-TOW have 5-inch diameter warheads; the TOW 2 has a 6-inch warhead; spikes provide improved stand-off detonation against armored vehicles. (Hughes)

TOW missile fired from a jeep-mounted launcher; note the control wires; the after fins of the missile have not fully extended. (U.S. Marine Corps)

TRIDENT I (C-4) UGM-96

The Trident SLBM evolved from the Department of Defense STRAT-X study of the late 1960s that proposed an advanced SLBM with a range of 6,000 n.miles to be carried in a new class of submarine. Subsequently, the Navy proposed a two-phase program: The Trident C-4 (also called Trident I) based on an Extend-range Poseidon (EXPO) missile with a range of some 4,000 n.miles, and the later Trident D-5 (II) to be developed at a later date with the longer range.

The C-4 missile has a MIRV warhead with eight Mk 4 independently targeted reentry vehicles. It has double the yield and twice the accuracy of the previous Poseidon C-3 missile. The weapon was designed to carry the Mk 500 Evader *Maneuvering* Reentry Vehicle (MaRV) warhead; this was designed to overcome ballistic missile defenses and is not being developed. The C-3 is a three-stage missile. After it reaches a certain altitude an aerospike extends from the nose. This spike cuts the friction of the air flowing past the missile, extending its range by about 300 miles.

Twelve LAFAYETTE-class submarines have been refitted with the Trident missile and the first eight OHIO (SSBN 726)-class submarines will have the missile. This missile is being procured by the Royal Navy for a new class of submarines to succeed that country's four Polaris-missile submarines.

IOC:	1979
Manufacturer:	Lockheed
Weight:	65,000 lbs
Length:	34 ft (10.4 m)
Span:	(ballistic)
Diameter:	74 in (1.9 m)
Propulsion:	3-stage solid-propellant rocket
Range:	approx. 4,000 n.miles
Guidance:	inertial
Warhead:	nuclear (W76); 8 RVs
Platforms:	strategic missile submarines (SSBN 616, 726)

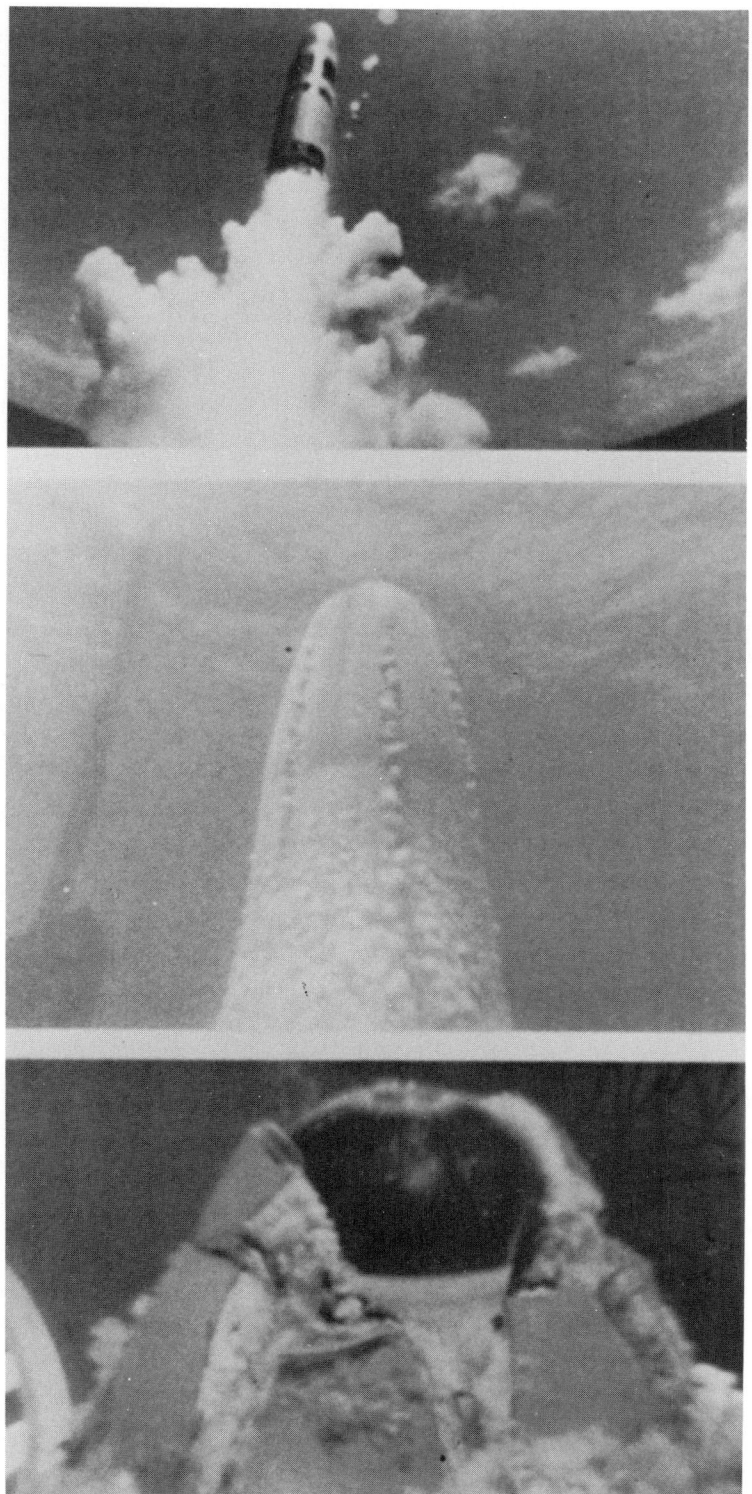

Trident C-4 launch from submarine JOHN C. CALHOUN (SSBN 630) (U.S. Air Force)

Underwater launch sequence of Trident C-4 missile. (Courtesy Los Alamos National Laboratory)

Trident C-4 re-entry vehicles photographed from a P-3C Orion at an altitude of 20,000 feet and about 15 miles from the point of impact. The timed exposure was about 40 seconds in duration. The lights at right are burning debris from the re-entry. (U.S. Navy)

TRIDENT II (D-5)

The longer-range Trident D-5 missile was approved for development in September 1981 and will be deployed in the ninth OHIO-class submarine (the SSBN 734) in 1990. Subsequently the first eight submarines of that class will be refitted to fire the D-5. Submarines configured to fire the D-5 missile will not be able to launch the C-4.

The D-5 can carry 75 percent more payload than the C-4. The later missile will probably carry eight of the Mk 5 RVs. The first D-5 test flight is scheduled for 1987. (The W87 warhead is also planned for the MX Peacekeeper missile.)

IOC:	1990
Manufacturer:	Lockheed
Weight:	approx. 126,000 lbs
Length:	44 ft (13.4 m)
Span:	(ballistic)
Diameter:	83 in (2.1 m)
Propulsion:	3-stage solid-propellant rocket
Range:	approx. 6,000 n.miles
Guidance:	inertial
Warhead:	nuclear (W87); probably 8 RVs
Platforms:	submarines (SSBN 726)

VERTICAL LAUNCH ASROC (VLA)

This program is described under the ASROC listing; see page 435.

WALLEYE AGM-62

The Walleye is an unpowered glide bomb. However, it is listed in the missile designation series and is operationally considered as such against surface ships and hardened ground targets. It is locked onto the target before launch by the pilot or bombardier/navigator who aligns the target on a television display in the cockpit. The aircraft can immediately depart the area after launch with the missile gliding toward the preselected TV target image.

A nuclear version was used by the Air Force (not the Navy, as stated in the previous edition).

The missile is being phased out of service. It is used by the U.S. and Israeli air forces.

Walleye ASM (U.S. Navy)

IOC:	1967
Manufacturer:	Martin and Hughes
Weight:	1,100 lbs for Walleye I
	2,000 lbs for Walleye II
Length:	11 ft 3 in (3.4 m) for Walleye I
	13 ft (4.0 m) for Walleye II
Span:	3 ft 9 in (1.1 m) for Walleye I
	4 ft 3 in (1.3 m) for Walleye II
Diameter:	15 in (380 mm) for Walleye I
	18 in (456 mm) for Walleye II
Propulsion:	none (a ram air turbine provides electrical power for guidance and controls)
Range:	14 n.miles for Walleye I
	30 n.miles for Walleye II
Guidance:	electro-optical (television)
Warhead:	850 lbs conventional in Walleye I
	2,000 lbs conventional in Walleye II
Platforms:	fighter aircraft (F-4)
	attack aircraft (A-4, A-7)

Walleye I ASM on A-7 Corsair; the pod on the outer pylon is for the missile data link. The Walleye has a cover on the optical seeker in the nose. (U.S. Navy)

MISSILE LAUNCHING SYSTEMS

Designation	Missiles	Type	Operational	System Weight[a]	Ships/Class
Mk 10 Mod 0	40 Terrier/Standard-ER	twin	1960	275,875 lbs	DDG 37–46
Mk 10 Mod 1	40 Terrier/Standard-ER	twin	1961	277,436 lbs	CGN 9
Mk 10 Mod 2	80 Terrier/Standard-ER	twin	1961	450,857 lbs	CGN 9
Mk 10 Mod 3	40 Terrier/Standard-ER	twin	1961	284,665 lbs	CV 64 (starboard)
Mk 10 Mod 4	40 Terrier/Standard-ER	twin	1961	284,665 lbs	CV 64 (port)
Mk 10 Mod 5	40 Terrier/Standard-ER	twin	1962	287,516 lbs	CG 16–24, CGN 25 (forward)
Mk 10 Mod 6	40 Terrier/Standard-ER	twin	1962	274,938 lbs	CG 16–24, CGN 25 (aft)
Mk 10 Mod 7	60 Terrier/Standard-ER/ASROC	twin	1964	361,994 lbs	CG 26–34, CGN 35
Mk 10 Mod 8	60 Terrier/Standard-ER/ASROC	twin	1967	364,197 lbs	CGN 35
Mk 11 Mod 0	42 Tartar/Standard-MR/Harpoon	twin	1962	165,240 lbs	DDG 2–14
Mk 11 Mod 1	42 Tartar/Standard-MR	twin	1962	165,240 lbs	CG 10–11 (starboard)
Mk 12 Mod 0	42 Tartar/Standard-MR	twin	1962	165,240 lbs	CG 10–11 (port)
Mk 12 Mod 1	52 Talos	twin	1962	~700,000 lbs	CG 10–11 (forward and aft)
Mk 13 Mod 0	40 Tartar/Standard-MR	single	1962	132,561 lbs	DDG 15–24
Mk 13 Mod 1	40 Tartar/Standard-MR	single	1967	135,079 lbs	DDG 31–34
Mk 13 Mod 2	40 Tartar/Standard-MR	single	1968	135,079 lbs	DDG 35–36
Mk 13 Mod 3	40 Tartar/Standard-MR	single	1974	135,012 lbs	CGN 36–37
Mk 13 Mod 4	40 Tartar/Standard-MR/Harpoon	single	1978	134,704 lbs	FFG 7
MK 16 Mods 1 to 6	8 ASROC[b]	8-tube		47,782 lbs	cruisers, destroyers, frigates; some modified to launch Harpoon or Standard-ARM missiles (Mk 112 launcher box)
Mk 22 Mod 0	16 Tartar/Standard-MR	single	1966	92,395 lbs	FFG 1–6
Mk 25 Mod 1	8 Sea Sparrow BPDMS	8-tube	1967	32,081 lbs	carriers, frigates, amphibious ships
Mk 26 Mod 0	24 Standard-MR/ASROC	twin	1976	162,028 lbs	CGN 38–41, AVM 1
Mk 26 Mod 1	44 Standard-MR/ASROC	twin	1976	208,373 lbs	CGN 38–41, CG 47–58
Mk 26 Mod 2	64 Standard-MR/ASROC	twin		254,797 lbs	CGN 42 design
Mk 29 Mod 0	8 NATO Sea Sparrow	8-tube	1974	24,000 or 28,000 lbs[c]	carriers, destroyers, frigates, amphibious ships, auxiliaries; NATO Sea Sparrow (Mk 132 launcher box)
Mk 41	61 Standard/Harpoon/Tomahawk/ASROC	vertical	development	~188,000 lbs	CG 59, DDG 51, DD 963
Mk 41	29 Standard/Harpoon/Tomahawk/ASROC	vertical	development	~94,000 lbs	DDG 51
Mk 140 Mod 0[d]	4 Harpoon	4-tube	1976	9,000 lbs	PHM 1–6
Mk 141 Mod 1[d]	4 Harpoon	4-tube	1977	13,000 lbs	cruisers, destroyers
Ex-31	24 RAM	24-tube	development	11,700 lbs	undetermined

[a] Does not include missiles and hydraulic fluids; missiles are included for Mk 16, 25, 29, 140, and 141.
[b] Does not include reloads available in some ships.
[c] One-director and two-director systems, respectively.
[d] These are launcher and not system designations.

Mk 29 NATO Sea Sparrow launcher with two Mk 76 directors (right) on KITTY HAWK (CV 63) (Giorgio Arra)

Mk 29 NATO Sea Sparrow launcher in the Spanish frigate DESCUBIERTA; the Spanish Navy makes extensive use of the U.S. combat systems and U.S. ship designs. (Stefan Terzibaschitsch)

Mk 26 Mod 0 launcher in the NORTON SOUND launching a test missile. (U.S. Navy)

Mk 10 Mod 0 twin Terrier/Standard-ER launcher on the FARRAGUT (DDG 37). Behind each opening is a 20-round circular or "Coke bottle" horizontal magazine; some Mk 10 mods have three and four 20-round magazines. Missile fins are manually fitted within the launch system. The two angled deck tube ends are for jettisoning dud missiles over the side. (Giorgio Arra)

Mk 13 Mod 4 launcher in an OLIVER HAZARD PERRY (FFG 7)-class frigate firing a Harpoon SSM. (U.S. Navy)

Mk 16 ASROC launcher in the frigate MOINESTER. The angled deckhouse face behind the launcher indicates an ASROC reload capability; the A and chevron indicate three excellence awards for the ASROC crew. (Giorgio Arra)

Mk 41 eight-tube VLS module being installed in the NORTON SOUND (Litton/Ingalls)

An eight-tube module of a Mk 41 VLS being installed in the NORTON SOUND in 1981. The VLS, which can fire ASROC Harpoon, Standard, and Tomahawk missiles, will be fitted in ships of the CG 47, DDG 51, and DD 963 classes. (Litton/Ingalls)

Mk 13 Mod 4 launcher on the JACK WILLIAMS (FFG 24) in the loading position. (Giorgio Arra)

NUCLEAR WEAPONS

The U.S. Navy has nuclear weapons available for three of the four major warfare areas, with new nuclear weapons under development in those three categories: Anti-Submarine Warfare (ASW), Anti-Air Warfare (AAW), and strike or land attack. The Navy has no nuclear weapons available for Anti-Surface Warfare (ASUW) except for air-dropped bombs and, under certain conditions, some ASW and AAW weapons could be used against surface ships.

During the past decade the number of nuclear weapons in the fleet has declined significantly and in some areas, especially ASW and AAW, the weapons now available are outdated and suffer from limited effectiveness.

Nuclear weapons appear to provide three major offensive advantages over conventional weapons in war at sea. First, whereas multiple hits with high-explosive weapons would probably be required to sink a cruiser or aircraft carrier, a single nuclear weapon, of even small size, would suffice. Second, defense against nuclear weapons would require a 100 percent effectiveness since a single penetrating missile or "leaker" could destroy the target. And, third, less accuracy is required for a nuclear weapon to be effective.

In the AAW role the nuclear-armed defensive missile could deter concentrated air attacks against U.S. ships as nuclear bursts might force attacking bombers to separate to greater distances, reducing the concentration of their missiles and thus enabling conventional defending systems to have a greater effectiveness. In ASW operations a nuclear weapon could compensate for the target submarine's area of uncertainty or the limited effectiveness of conventional ASW weapons. This could be especially true against high-speed and deep-diving submarines, which may give the ASW unit only a single, brief attack opportunity before the enemy submarine is beyond attack range or has itself launched an attack.

Another consideration is the potential use of high-altitude bursts of nuclear weapons to create Electromagnetic Pulse (EMP) effects that would severely degrade electronic systems of ships and aircraft over large ocean areas. Underwater nuclear bursts could similarly degrade sonar effectiveness, creating a condition known as "blue out" over some acoustic frequencies.

Finally, being able to use tactical nuclear weapons would ease magazine constraints in surface warships and, especially, submarines. For example, if a submarine carries a weapons load of 15 percent nuclear and 85 percent conventional, with the use of conventional weapons only part of its weapons load is usable while in a nuclear situation all would be available.

There are thus several tactical advantages to the employment of nuclear weapons at sea. Of course, there are also military as well as political reasons for not employing even tactical nuclear weapons (TAC-NUC). But such weapons do exist and, in marked contrast to the current U.S. naval TACNUC situation, the Soviet Navy has increased the types and probably the numbers of nuclear weapons in service during the past decade. Soviet exercises and professional writings continue to stress the potential use of tactical nuclear weapons at sea. (In addition to stressing the offensive aspects of nuclear war at sea, modern Soviet warships down to missile craft of the Osa class are configured to operate in a nuclear environment with survivability features that are not now found in any U.S. surface combatants.)

The decline in Navy tactical nuclear weapons is matched by what many authorities and analysts have considered a limited understanding of tactical and technical TACNUC considerations in the U.S. Navy. Several efforts are underway, however, to improve the U.S. Navy's TACNUC offensive and defensive capabilities.

Strategic Attack. Nineteen strategic missile submarines are at sea with the Poseidon C-3 missile and 16 are armed with the Trident C-4. All of these missiles have Multiple Independently targeted Re-entry Vehicle (MIRV) warheads:

	Warhead	SSBN 616 class	SSBN 726 class
Submarines		31	4
Poseidon C-3	W68	304	—
Trident C-4	W76	192	96

Additional Trident SSBN 726-class submarines are being completed at the rate of one per year, each carrying 24 missiles. Beginning with the ninth submarine these will carry the improved Trident D-5 missile. Subsequently, the earlier submarines will be rearmed with the D-5.

The number of submarines and missiles will decline from the late 1980s onward as the older, SSBN 726-class units are retired after 30 years of service. The SSBN force will reach a nadir of some 17 or 18 submarines (408–432 missiles), with a currently planned end strength of 20 submarines (480 missiles). Although the number of submarines and missiles will be far below the 1967–1980 strength of 41 Polaris/Poseidon missiles (656 missiles), the range, accuracy, and megatonnage of the Trident force will be considerable.

The Tomahawk Land-Attack Missile or T-LAM(N), being deployed from 1984 onward, is carried by surface warships in Armored Box Launchers (ABLs) or Vertical Launch Systems (VLS), as well as in submarines, fired from torpedo tubes and, in the later Los Angeles (SSN 688) class, from the vertical launch tubes. Up to 250 surface ships and submarines of the following classes may be fitted to carry the T-LAM(N): BB 61, CG 47, DDG 51, DD 963, and SSN 688 plus the next generation attack submarine (SSN-21).

The ability to strike targets ashore with nuclear weapons from surface ships and submarines previously existed with the Regulus cruise missile, in service from 1954 to 1965, and with 16-inch projectiles for Iowa-class battleships, which were available from 1956 to 1961. (Although both the Regulus and nuclear 16-inch projectiles have been phased out of U.S. service, the Soviets have retained similar nuclear systems, the SS-N-3 and -12 Shaddock cruise missiles and apparently the 6-inch/152-mm nuclear projectiles, the latter being fired from their Sverdlov-class light cruisers and possibly newer warship classes.)

The nuclear T-LAM uses much of the same missile technology as in other Tomahawk variants, including the controversial Ground-Launched Cruise Missile (GLCM) being deployed in European NATO countries (The Navy's T-Lam, however, uses a different nuclear warhead from that in the GLCM. The Air Force's ALCM cruise missile has the same W80-series warhead used in the nuclear T-LAM.) Thus the T-LAM(N) "buys in" on large-scale missile programs.

Strike/Anti-Surface Warfare. Several nuclear bombs are available for naval aircraft: the B43, which entered service in 1961 and has several configurations with a maximum explosive force of about one megaton; the B57, available since 1963 in bomb and depth bomb configurations up to about 20 kilotons; and the B61, which came into service in 1963 and has yields up to some 500 kilotons. There are several configurations of these bombs with differing yields, and some later nuclear weapons have variable yields.

The carrier-based A-7E Corsair attack plane can carry any one of the bombs while the all-weather A-6E Intruder can carry two bombs. There has been no public indication of whether the F/A-18 Hornet, which is replacing the F-4 and A-7 aboard carriers, has been fitted to deliver nuclear weapons.

Periodically there have been proposals to provide a nuclear warhead for the Harpoon anti-ship missile. However, there has never been a formal program to develop the weapon and it is unlikely there will be one.

Anti-Submarine Warfare. The Navy has nuclear ASW weapons that can be launched from air, surface, and submarine platforms. The B57 nuclear depth bomb is carried by the S-3A and P-3B/C ASW aircraft and SH-3D/H helicopters. The weapon has been in the inventory since 1964 and is becoming dated. At this time no replacement is planned.

Approximately 160 cruisers, destroyers, and frigates carry the ASROC (Anti-Submarine Rocket), a short-range weapon that can carry either a conventional Mk 46 torpedo or a W44 nuclear warhead. This weapon, in service since 1961, also suffers from age as well as range limitations.

The number of ASROC-armed ships will continue to decline as older ASW frigates are retired and their Perry-class replacements do not have ASROC. Several proposals to develop a longer-range ASROC were aborted as were efforts to develop a common ASW stand-off weapon for surface ships and submarines.

A vertical-launch version of the existing ASROC is under development and, if pursued, would enable the Ticonderoga and Burke classes built with VLS, as well as the refitted Spruance-class ships, to have the Vertical-Launch ASROC (VLA) for relatively close-in use.

The submarine situation is even more tenuous with the outdated SUBROC (Submarine Rocket) now carried by only some 25 attack submarines still fitted with the Mk 113 analog torpedo fire control system. The SUBROC, with the W55 warhead, also entered service in 1964.

An ASW Stand-Off Weapon (SOW) is being developed and should be available for all Permit and later SSNs by about 1990. This weapon will have more than twice the approximately 25-n.miles range of SUBROC, permitting attacks against hostile submarine contacts out to about the third convergence zone. At this time only a nuclear depth bomb is definitely planned as the warhead, but efforts are underway to also fit the Mk 50/ALWT torpedo to the weapon.

The Navy's only nuclear torpedo, the Mk 45 ASTOR, has been phased out of service because of the effectiveness of the conventional Mk 48 (see Torpedoes, below). The ASTOR—for Anti-Submarine Torpedo— was carried by SSNs and SSBNs.

Anti-Air Warfare. A few guided missile cruisers and destroyers are armed with the Terrier BTN (Beam-riding, Terrier, Nuclear) missile. Like most U.S. naval nuclear weapons, the Terrier is outdated, having entered the fleet in 1962 with the W45-1 warhead. As a beam-riding weapon, the Terrier is limited to radar line-of-sight ranges and the system suffers from major maintenance problems.

A replacement is under development, the Standard SM-2(N) with the W81 warhead. This weapon, which will be compatible with the TICONDEROGA and other missile ship classes, will provide a longer-range and more flexible air defense for surface forces. The Navy's other anti-aircraft missile with a nuclear warhead, the Talos, was phased out of the fleet in 1980.

There have been periodic proposals to provide a nuclear warhead to the Phoenix air-to-air missile carried by the F-14 fighter, but there is currently no program for this concept.

Pair of B61 bombs on dolly. The B61-3 and -4 model bombs are currently in production. (Courtesy Los Alamos National Laboratory)

Warhead	Weapon System	IOC/Status
B43	aerial bomb	1961; outdated
W44	ASROC	1961
W45	Terrier SAM	1962; being phased out
W55	SUBROC	1964; being phased out
B57	aerial bomb/depth bomb	1963
B61	aerial bomb	1968
W68	Poseidon (C-3) SLBM	1970
W76	Trident (C-4) SLBM	1979
W80	Tomahawk T-LAM(N)	1984
W81	Standard SM-2(N) SAM	development
W87	Trident (D-5) SLBM	development

Only two U.S. missile systems have been fully tested to the detonation of their nuclear warhead—a Polaris A-2 fired from the ETHAN ALLEN (SSBN 608) on 6 May 1962, and this ASROC fired from the destroyer AGERHOLM (DD 826) on 11 May 1962. (U.S. Navy)

TORPEDOES

The U.S. Navy has three torpedoes in service: the lightweight Mk 46 used by aircraft and surface ships, and in mines; the heavy weight Mk 48 carried in all submarines but the DARTER (SS 576); and a few Mk 37 torpedoes retained for the DARTER. All three torpedoes are intended primarily for the anti-submarine role although the Mk 37 and 48 can be used against surface ships. Replacements are being developed for the Mk 46 and Mk 48 torpedoes, the Mk 50 ALWT (Advanced Lightweight Torpedo) and the Mk 48 ADCAP (Advanced Capability), respectively.

The current heavy and lightweight torpedoes have severe limitations related to the current weapon programs, technical issues, and the nature of the Soviet submarine threat. The following table outlines the problems with U.S. torpedoes that have been identified publicly. It must be acknowledged that the Mk 48 is *the best* heavy torpedo currently in service with any navy, but the requirements placed on that weapon are severe.

U.S. TORPEDO LIMITATIONS

Torpedo	Program	Technical	Threat
Mk 46	long interval until successor	small warhead limited range if ship launched	Soviet submarines (1) high speeds (2) large size (3) double hull (4) anechoic coatings to reduce sonar effectiveness (6) use of decoys (7) under ice operations
Mk 48	limited procurement	limited loadout in submarines	Soviet submarines (1) high speeds (2) anechoic coatings (3) use of decoys (4) under ice operations

By some criteria U.S. torpedoes have lagged behind the potential threat since the appearance of the first Soviet nuclear-powered submarines in the late 1950s. In a 1981 congressional colloquy between a senator and the Deputy Chief of Naval Operations (Surface Warfare), Vice Admiral William H. Rowden, the senator noted that new Soviet submarines of the Alfa class can travel at "40-plus knots and could probably outdive most of our anti-submarine torpedoes." He then asked what measures were being taken to redress this particular balance.

The admiral replied, "We have modified the Mark 48 torpedo . . . to accommodate to the increased speed and to the diving depth of those particular submarines." The admiral was less confident of the Mark 46 used by aircraft, helicopters, and surface ships: "We have recently modified that torpedo to handle what you might call the pre-Alfa. . . ."

In addition to the relatively high speeds of modern Soviet submarines, i.e., 43 knots for the Alfa SSN, about 35–40 knots for the Papa SSGN, with higher speeds expected for later submarines, Soviet undersea craft are difficult targets for several reasons. The large, double hull and mul-

tiple compartments of Soviet submarines could reduce the effectiveness of the small Mk 46 and planned Mk 50 warheads. Both heavy and light torpedo effectiveness could also suffer from the Soviet use of anechoic coatings on their submarine hulls that degrade torpedo acoustic guidance, and the extensive use of acoustic decoys. Finally, the Mk 48's capability is reduced in the under-ice environment of the Arctic ice pack.

Navy officials also consider the number of Mk 48s being procured as insufficient for a major conflict. The original Navy procurement goal was about 4,000 submarine torpedoes. But that number has been reduced by more than one-quarter by the Department of Defense. If one subtracts the torpedoes used for trials and training, and those weapons in overhaul, there are hardly enough available for one "ship full" of all attack and strategic missile submarines.

Finally, the number of torpedoes that can be carried in U.S. submarines is limited. In SSNs the number is constrained by the need to carry SUBROC in some units (and later the ASW SOW), Harpoons, and some variations of the Tomahawk; in SSBNs there are few reload spaces and some are devoted to MOSS decoys.

Submarines carry only the Mk 48 torpedo while about 25 attack submarines also carry the SUBROC, a rocket-propelled depth charge with a nuclear warhead (see page 449); the diesel submarine DARTER carries the Mk 37.

Surface ships have the Mk 46 torpedo as an ASW weapon, launched by (1) over-the-side Mk 32 torpedo tubes, (2) LAMPS helicopters, or (3) ASROC. U.S. destroyers had "long" torpedo tubes for launching heavy anti-ship torpedoes until the late 1950s, when it was decided they would carry only the lightweight torpedoes to counter submarines. For a brief period in the 1960s the Mk 48 was intended for tube-launch from surface warships to provide a long-range, wire-guided ASW torpedo. Several cruiser/frigate (DLG/DLGN) and escort classes were fitted with handling gear and 21-inch tubes in their stern counter or after deck house. However, this aspect of the Mk 48 program was cancelled and only Mk 32 tubes for lightweight torpedoes have been retained.

ASW Helicopters and Aircraft carry the Mk 46 torpedo, external on the SH-2F, SH-3H, and SH-60B helicopters, and in internal weapon bays in the S-3A and P-3 fixed-wing aircraft.

Procurement schedule for torpedoes put forth in January 1984 was:

fiscal 1982*	fiscal 1983*	fiscal 1984**	fiscal 1985**
228 Mk 46	440 Mk 46	1,200 Mk 46	1,565 Mk 46
144 Mk 48-4	144 Mk 48-4	144 Mk 48-4	144 Mk 48-4

* Actual.
** Proposed.

The Mk46 numbers include new NEARTIP torpedoes and conversions. The Reagan Administration's fiscal 1985 program originally consisted of 144 new Mk 48 Mod 4 torpedoes plus 23 ADCAP modification kits; in May 1984 the request was cut to 51 new torpedoes. The Congress instead funded 108 new Mk 48s plus the kits.

MK 37 TORPEDO

The predecessor as the standard U.S. Navy submarine torpedo, the Mk 37 is retained only for the diesel-electric submarine DARTER. The Mk 37 was the standard Navy submarine-launched ASW torpedo for about 20 years. During that period older Mk 16 steam-driven torpedo was used for the anti-ship role (retired in 1975).

The principal developers of the Mk 37 were Westinghouse Electric (Sharon, Pa.); Harvard Underwater Sound Laboratory (Cambridge, Mass.); and Ordnance Research Laboratory of Pennsylvania State University. Engineering development began in 1946 and was produced by the Naval Ordnance Plant, Forest Park, Ill. When introduced in 1956 the Mk 37 was also tube-launched from surface combatants.

The Mk 37 is a two-speed torpedo. It is launched with guide rails to permit firing from 21-inch torpedo tubes, with the shorter length permitting more to be carried aboard submarines than a full-size 21-inch/21-foot torpedo. All Mod 3 torpedoes were Mk 37 Mod 0 refurbished and reissued as the Mod 3.

The Mk 37 is used by several foreign navies with some discarded Mk 37s being fitted with improved engines and guidance for transfer to foreign navies as the NT-37C.

All torpedo data are based on published information.

Mk 37 Mod 3

IOC:	1967
Weight:	1,430 lbs
Diameter:	19 in (481 mm)
Length:	11¼ ft (3.4 m)
Propulsion:	electric
Speed:	40+ knots
Range:	approx. 8,800 yards
Guidance:	wire; active/passive acoustic
Warhead:	330 lbs high explosive (HBX-3)
Platforms:	submarine (SS 576)

MK 46 LIGHTWEIGHT TORPEDO

The Mk 46 is a lightweight torpedo intended for use against submarines by helicopters, aircraft, and surface ships, and is fitted in the CAPTOR deep-water mine. The lightweight torpedo concept dates to the late 1940s when it was envisioned that future convoys would be protected from submarine attack by helicopters with dipping sonar and airships (blimps) with towed sonar. For this application, light weight (initially a maximum of 350 pounds) became a primary consideration for ASW torpedoes. In addition, the concept would require large numbers of torpedoes, hence cost was also an important factor in torpedo design. Subsequently, surface combatants were fitted with "short" torpedo tubes for these torpedoes and the ASROC was fitted with the short torpedo.

The first lightweight ASW torpedo to enter fleet service was the Mk 43 Mod 1 (260 pounds) in 1951, and later Mod 3, followed by the Mk 44 Mod 0 (425 pounds) introduced in 1957, followed by the Mod 1. The Mk 46 is thus the third generation of lightweight ASW torpedoes.

The Mk 46 was developed by the Naval Ordnance Test Station (Pasadena, Calif.) and Aerojet General (Azusa, Calif.). Subsequent production was undertaken at the Naval Ordnance Plant (Forest Park, Ill.) and

Honeywell (Minneapolis, Minn.) as well as Aerojet. The Mk 46 has a higher speed, twice the range, deeper operating depth, and better acoustic performance than its predecessor, the Mk 44. Propulsion was provided with a thermal piston engine, with the Mod 0 using a solid propellant grain and the Mod 1 having a liquid monopropellant fuel, the latter providing improved performance. There was no Mod 3 torpedo.

The Mod 4 version of the Mk 46 is especially configured for the CAPTOR (Encapsulated Torpedo) naval mine.

In 1981 Secretary of Defense Harold Brown stated that "because the existing Mk 46 torpedo will not meet the submarine acoustic and countermeasures threat through the early 1980s, we have budgeted for a new version called the Near-Term Torpedo Improvement Program (NEARTIP)." This program includes modification kits for earlier Mk 46s as well as new torpedo procurement. The NEARTIP or Mod 5 has an improved sonar transducer, new guidance and control group, and engine improvements.

The Mk 46 is widely used by foreign navies.

IOC:	Mod 0 1966
	Mods 1/2 1967
	Mod 5 1979
Weight:	Mod 0 568 lbs
	Mods 1/2 508 lbs
Diameter:	12.75 inches (324 mm)
Length:	8½ feet (2.6 m)
Propulsion:	Mod 0 piston engine (solid propellant)
	Mods 1/2 cam engine (liquid monopropellant) contrarotating propellers
Speed:	approx. 45 knots maximum
Range:	approx. 8,000 yards
Guidance:	active/passive acoustic homing
Warhead:	approx. 95 lbs high explosive
Platforms:	Mod 0 aircraft (P-3B/C, S-3A, SH-2F, SH-3D/H, SH-60B)
	Mods 1/2 cruisers, destroyers, frigates
	Mod 4 mines (CAPTOR)

MK 48 HEAVY TORPEDO

This is the latest weapon in a long series of heavy torpedoes, 21 inches (533 mm) in diameter with a length up to 21 feet. U.S. submarines have had 21-inch diameter torpedo tubes since the R (SS 78) class, first completed in 1918.

The immediate predecessor of the Mk 48 was the Mk 37, which remains in limited U.S. Navy service. The Mk 48 also replaced the Mk 45 ASTOR (Anti-Submarine Torpedo), the U.S. Navy's only nuclear torpedo, in service from 1958 to 1977 with a W34 warhead. The long range and improved guidance of the Mk 48 made it as effective with a large conventional warhead as the Mk 45 in most situations. Also, the Mk 48's anti-surface ship capability was considered sufficient to cancel the purely anti-surface Mk 47.

Development of the Mk 48 began in the early 1960s as the Navy-sponsored RETORC (Research Torpedo Configuration) research project of the Applied Research Laboratory of Pennsylvania State University and the Westinghouse Electric Corp. (Baltimore, Md.). The project was initially designated Ex-10. This effort led to the Mk 48 Mod 0 torpedo with a turbine propulsion system. This was subsequently refined into the Mk 48 Mod 2.

In 1967 the Gould firm (Cleveland, Ohio)[6] and Naval Surface Warfare Center (White Oak, Md.) began developing the Mod 1 with a redesigned acoustic homing guidance and a piston (swashplate) engine. The torpedo uses an Otto fuel that contains its own oxidizer for combustion. After evaluation of the two versions, the Mod 1 was selected for production by Gould for fleet use.

From the outset the Mk 48 had a guidance wire that spins out simultaneously from the submarine and the torpedo to permit the submarine to exercise control over the "fish," at least during the initial stages of its run. The Mod 3 introduced several improvements including TELE-COM (Tele-Communications) to provide two-way data transmissions between submarine and torpedo, thus the torpedo can transmit acoustic data back to the submarine for processing.

The Mod 4 version was upgraded to provide more capability against the Alfa-class SSN.

The Mk 48 is also used in Australian and Dutch submarines.

Mk 48 Mods 1/3/4

IOC:	1972
Weight:	3,450 lbs
Diameter:	21 inches (533 mm)
Length:	19⅙ feet (5.8 m)
Propulsion:	piston engine (liquid monopropellant fuel); pump-jet
Speed:	maximum 55 knots
Range:	approx. 35,000 yards
Guidance:	wire + active/passive acoustic homing
Warhead:	approx. 650 lbs high explosive (PBXN-103)
Platforms:	submarines (SSBN/SSN)

MK 48 ADCAP

The Mk 48 ADCAP (Advanced Capability) version was developed from 1978 onward to counter the Alfa and other advanced Soviet submarines. The ADCAP performance requirements were to: (1) improve target acquisition range, (2) reduce the effect of enemy countermeasures, (3) minimize shipboard constraints such as warmup and reactivation time, and (4) enhance effectiveness against surface ships.

The principal changes to the Mk 48 to meet these requirements were made to the torpedo's acoustic transducer (guidance) and control system. The higher-powered active sonar enables the torpedo to search a much greater volume of water to attain a target submarine. And the sonar is electrically steered, reducing the need for the torpedo to maneuver while searching. The torpedo retains the Gould (swashplate) motor with a larger fuel capacity.

[6] Formerly the Clevite Corporation.

The ADCAP program has suffered delays and severe cost increases. In 1982 the Chief of Naval Operations, Admiral Thomas B. Hayward, said that the problems included the following: (1) the original R&D program being significantly under estimated; (2) the scope of effort increasing because of the evolving Soviet submarine threat; (3) an attempt being made to accelerate the IOC; (4) too little emphasis being placed on cost control; and (5) the prime contractor (Hughes) being new to torpedo business and underestimating the effort required.

The estimated IOC for ADCAP is 1986.

MK 50 ADVANCED LIGHTWEIGHT TORPEDO

The Advanced Lightweight Torpedo (ALWT) is being developed as a successor to the Mk 46 to provide an improved kill capability against modern Soviet submarines. Nevertheless, it still suffers from many of the shortcomings of the Mk 46. The ALWT program was initiated in August 1975 with a design competition subsequently being held between Honeywell (Ex-50 design) and McDonnell Douglas (Ex-51). The former was selected to develop the torpedo. During the competition the torpedo was designated Mk XX.

Special features of the Mk 50 include the AKY-14 programmable digital computer. The maximum weight of the torpedo will be 800 pounds, with a length and diameter similar to the Mk 46 to permit carriage by existing helicopters and the S-3A Viking.

Mk 50 ALWT

IOC:	1990 estimated
Weight:	approx. 800 lbs
Diameter:	12¾ in (324 mm)
Length:	9½ feet (2.9 m)
Propulsion:	Stored Chemical Energy Propulsion System (SCEPS); pump-jet
Speed:	approx. 50+ knots
Range:	
Guidance:	active/passive acoustic homing
Warhead:	approx. 100 lbs conventional (shaped charge)
Platforms:	ASW aircraft
	ASW helicopters
	surface ships

REGAL ADVANCED TORPEDO PROJECT

The REGAL is a program of the Defense Advanced Research Projects Agency (DARPA) to develop and demonstrate the technological feasibility of a remotely guided lightweight torpedo. REGAL is an acronym for Remotely Guided Autonomous Lightweight torpedo. The weapon would have an integrated acoustic array and signal processing capability. Upon entering water the acoustic array and torpedo separate with the array, descending to a preset depth while the torpedo conducts a slow-speed target search, being wire guided by the array. The project was to transition to the Navy late in 1983.

Mk 32 triple 12.75-inch torpedo tubes on the destroyer DEWEY (DDG 45) being trained outboard in preparation for firing. The size of these tubes and the constraints of P-3/S-3 aircraft weapon bays have restricted the development of succeeding torpedoes for surface ship and aircraft use. (U.S. Navy, PH2 K. Brewer)

Mk 48 torpedo being loaded in the strategic missile submarine STONEWALL JACKSON (SSBN 634). (U.S. Navy, Comdr. G. I. Peterson)

An SH-3D Sea King releases a Mk 46 helicopter; the parachute restraining clamps are falling below the torpedo. (U.S. Navy)

Mk 48 torpedo (Gould)

Rear of Mk 48 torpedo showing propulsor and (top) guide for control wire. (Gould)

Four Mk 46 Mod 1 torpedoes in the weapons bay of a P-3 Orion aircraft. Parachute packs are fitted to the tails of the torpedo. (U.S. Navy)

Mk 48 Mod 1 torpedoes are readied for loading in an attack submarine at Port Canaveral, Fla. (U.S. Air Force)

Mk 46 torpedo fitted to an SH-3D Sea King helicopter; note the contra-rotating propellers. (U.S. Navy)

31 Electronics

ELECTRONIC DESIGNATIONS

Most U.S. Navy electronic systems are identified by the joint electronics type designation system illustrated below. This was formerly called the joint Army-Navy nomenclature system, and the three letter-plus-number designations are still prefixed by the AN/ of the World War II era. In this volume the AN/ is generally omitted. Electronic systems designated in various mark (Mk) series do not have the AN prefix.

ELECTRONIC WARFARE SYSTEMS

Electronic Warfare (EW) consists of efforts to detect, locate, exploit, reduce, or prevent an enemy's use of the electromagnetic spectrum, and actions that retain one's own use of the electromagnetic spectrum. There are several divisions of EW:

- Electronic warfare Support Measures (ESM)
- Signal Intelligence (SIGINT)
- Electronic Countermeasures (ECM)
- Electronic Counter-Countermeasures (ECCM).

Because EW deals with electromagnetic energy and not just electronics, also included are infrared, laser, and optical systems. Radiation produced by nuclear weapons, however, is usually classified as nuclear effects and not EW.

Electronic Warfare Support Measures

Electronic warfare support measures are the portion of EW that seeks to detect, intercept, locate, record, and analyze enemy electromagnetic radiations. Thus, ESM provides the information required to conduct

Explanation of symbols:

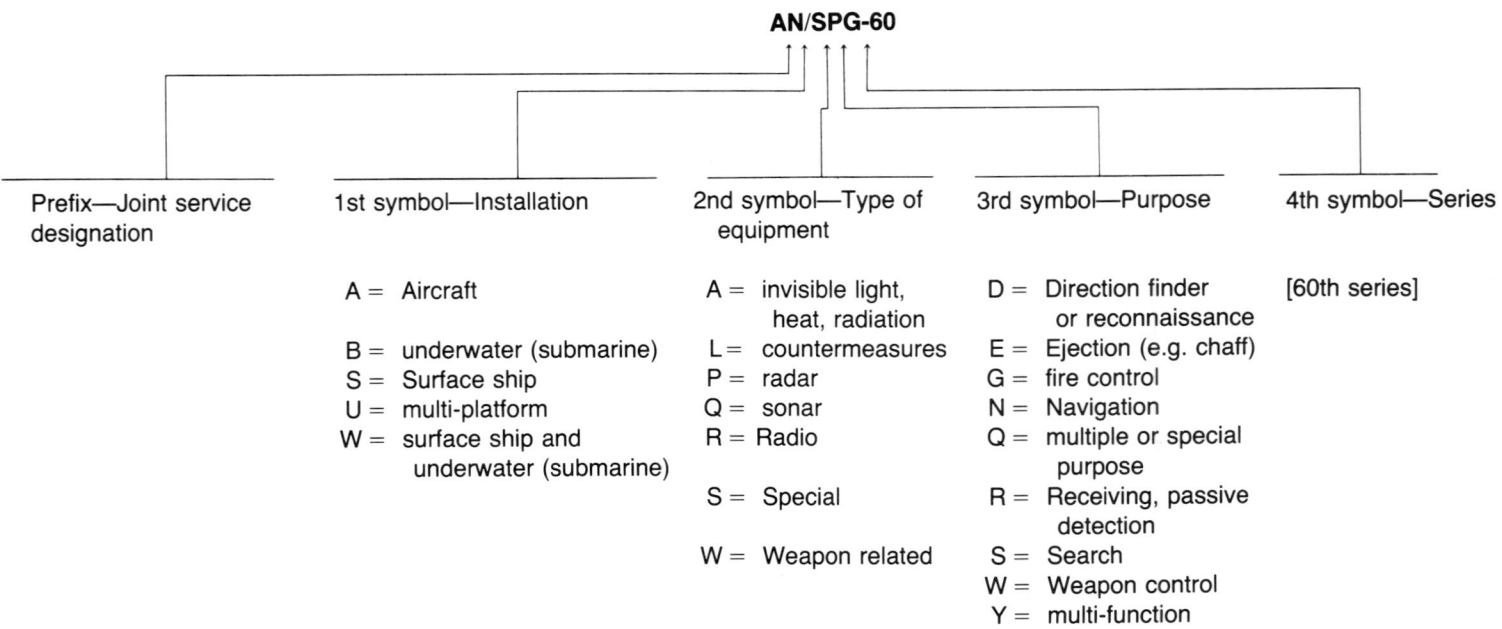

AN/SPG-60

Prefix—Joint service designation	1st symbol—Installation	2nd symbol—Type of equipment	3rd symbol—Purpose	4th symbol—Series
	A = Aircraft	A = invisible light, heat, radiation	D = Direction finder or reconnaissance	[60th series]
	B = underwater (submarine)	L = countermeasures	E = Ejection (e.g. chaff)	
	S = Surface ship	P = radar	G = fire control	
	U = multi-platform	Q = sonar	N = Navigation	
	W = surface ship and underwater (submarine)	R = Radio	Q = multiple or special purpose	
		S = Special	R = Receiving, passive detection	
		W = Weapon related	S = Search	
			W = Weapon control	
			Y = multi-function	

Electronics have a major role in naval systems; the forest of antennas above the Mississippi (CGN 40) and South Carolina (CGN 37) reveal only a portion of the electronic components of their combat systems. Information on electronics must be included in any meaningful discussion of modern warships and aircraft. (1982, Giorgio Arra)

electronic countermeasures and counter-countermeasures for immediate threat recognition. Generally passive, ESM seeks to detect the enemy through "listening" to his radio and radar emissions.

The U.S. Navy has a variety of ESM systems that are used in ships, submarines, aircraft, and ashore. ESM offers a number of obvious tactical advantages: it permits the ESM collection platform to remain electronically silent; and it can detect a hostile radar's transmissions beyond the radar detection range because the radar requires much of its power to return a signal to the transmitter after it detects a target.

There are highly specialized—and highly classified—ESM systems, such as the ALR-series receivers in the Navy's EA-3B Skywarrior and

EP-3E Orion aircraft that support fleet operations. The reported EA-3B ESM/surveillance systems include:
- ALQ-40 ECM receiver
- APA-69 radar spectrum analyzer
- APR-25 radio spectrum analyzer
- ASB-1B search radar.

The venerable Skywarrior, which first entered Navy squadron service as a carrier-based nuclear strike aircraft in 1956 and began service in the EA-3B version in 1959, is expected to continue in service into the 1990s. In the mid-1970s the Navy proposed to convert 20 S-3A Viking ASW aircraft to the carrier-based VQ/ESM role to replace the Skywarriors; however, the decision was made to retain the Vikings as the anti-submarine role and the aging Skywarriors carry on in two electronic reconnaissance squadrons (VQ) and EW training squadrons (VAQ), along with the EP-3E ESM-configured Orions in the VQ units.

The principal EP-3 ESM/surveillance systems are reported as:

- AAR-37 infrared receiver
- ALD-8 direction finder
- ALQ-76 jammer
- ALQ-78 ECM receiver
- ALQ-108 IFF jammer
- ALQ-110 radio signal collector
- ALQ-132 infrared countermeasures set
- ALR-52 frequency-measuring receiver
- ALR-60 communications intercept and recording
- APS-20 surveillance radar.

Other ESM capabilities are incorporated into multi-function systems. For example, according to published Navy material, a LOS ANGELES (SSN 688)-class submarine has the following equipment for the collection of Electromagnetic Intelligence (ELINT), including Acoustic Intelligence (ACINT) and Communications Intelligence (COMINT):

- BQQ-5 sonar system that has a passive classification processor that can continuously evaluate low-frequency acoustic data from sonars
- BQS-15 sonar detecting/ranging set
- BRD-7 radio direction finder
- WLR-8 receiver that can detect enemy fire control radars as well as radio communication frequencies (reportedly having a 50 MHz to 18 GHz frequency range)
- WLR-9 acoustic intercept receiver that can detect active search sonars and acoustic-homing torpedoes
- WLR-10 countermeasures.

Several of these equipment are multi-purpose, especially the BQQ-5 system and the BQS-15, which are the submarine's tactical sonars, the former having both active and passive modes. Additional ESM equipment can be installed for special collection missions.

Electronic surveillance and collection equipment have special design characteristics, among them:

Wide-spectrum or bandwidth capability: Because the frequency of a foreign radar may not be known before it operates, a wide bandwidth must be covered. With modern technology, this means a frequency spectrum from 30 MHz to 50 GHz. This range is too large for a single receiver; thus several receivers with different tuning ranges must be used or a single receiver in which different tuning units can be inserted to cover the frequency range.

Wide dynamic range: The ESM receiver must be able to receive very weak signals and very strong signals. The receiver may be at different distances from different signals at the same time, and widely dissimilar signals could impair both collection and analysis unless the equipment is designed specifically for the role.

Unwanted signal rejection: The ability to reject unwanted signals—also called narrow band-pass—is desirable because it enables the receiver to discriminate between the target frequency and signals at other, nearby frequencies.

Good angle-of-arrival measurement: The ability of a receiver to accurately take bearings on a distant transmitter permits different bearings (taken by the same or by several surveillance platforms) to be plotted to give the precise location of the transmitter. Airborne, shipboard, or ground-based digital computers can be programmed to rapidly perform this function.

The receiver should be designed to immediately alert the operator to the presence of a signal of possible interest, to sort out the signal of interest, and to analyze the signal. The alerting and sorting are particularly important because an airborne ESM platform may be exposed to the signal for a short time compared with a ship or shore facility, or the signal may be on the air for only a very short time. The current trend in ESM is to automatically record the intercepted signal for later analysis and, if appropriate, for reproduction for use in EW libraries.

The submarine is an excellent ESM platform because it is difficult for an enemy to detect her by radar and visual means or even by acoustic sensors under some conditions. And, of course, a submarine is not impeded by surface weather. Submarines are particularly useful in gaining acoustic intelligence on enemy submarines, and modern nuclear-powered submarines in particular are quiet and have essentially unlimited underwater endurance. The periodic press reports of U.S. and Soviet submarines "scraping" one another in close encounters in northern waters suggest that U.S. submarines are used in such surveillance missions in areas such as the Arctic and Norwegian Sea. An ACINT capability is also found in the Navy's seafloor sound surveillance system. In addition to providing a peacetime warning system of Soviet submarine movements, the SOSUS networks in the Atlantic, Pacific, and regional seas can record data on surface ship and submarine noise characteristics.

Aircraft—especially the Navy's specialized EA-3B Skywarriors and EP-3 Orions from Fleet Air Reconnaissance Squadrons 1 and 2, based at Agana, Guam, and Rota, Spain, respectively—have long conducted ESM missions along the peripheries of the Soviet Union, Mainland China, and North Korea. These aircraft, with the EA-3Bs being carrier capable, also provide electronic surveillance of surface ships and submarines. The primary advantage of aircraft ESM platforms is their altitude, permitting them to detect distant electronic emissions, including those originating inside enemy territory.

Aircraft—and surface ships—also are used to stimulate enemy radars and communications as they near enemy territory. In turn, this stimulation permits the aircraft or ship to then record the electromagnetic responses of an enemy, that is, which of their radars they turn on, which of their communications channels they use, and so forth.

Signal Intelligence

Signal Intelligence (SIGINT) includes the collection of intelligence information for Navy and national requirements, including all Communications Intelligence (COMINT), Electronic Intelligence (ELINT), Acoustic Intelligence (ACINT), and telemetry intelligence. By executive order, the National Security Agency (NSA) is the national program manager for the collection, analysis, and dissemination of SIGINT. The platforms and personnel involved in SIGINT, however, belong to the armed services, and some systems obviously have both ESM and SIGINT collection capabilities. Thus, the actual operation of SIGINT activities are conducted by the services and, in wartime, the operational control of some dedicated SIGINT platforms would be assigned to tactical commanders.

Surface warships are used extensively for SIGINT activity. The U.S. destroyers TURNER JOY (DD 951) and MADDOX (DD 731) were on the De Soto SIGINT patrols off the North Vietnamese coast in August 1964 when they were attacked by motor torpedo boats in the Gulf of Tonkin incidents. Because of the hostile nature of the North Vietnamese and the guerrilla war then going on, destroyers were deemed the appropriate ESM platforms.

In the supposedly more benign environment of international waters off North Korea, the U.S. Navy carried naval and National Security Agency teams on board the "passive" SIGINT surveillance ships BANNER (AGER 1) and PUEBLO (AGER 3), while the LIBERTY (AGTR 5) was used in 1967 to monitor Israeli communications during the Six-Day War. The United States and Soviet Union had long believed that such ships operated by the two super powers were immune to hostile actions by the Third World. Attacks on the PUEBLO and LIBERTY demonstrated, however, that a super power's ships are not immune. The U.S. Navy has ceased to operate such "passive" intelligence ships, although more than 50 of these intelligence collectors are still active in the Soviet Navy (designated AGI by NATO).

Land-based aircraft, satellites, and land facilities also provide SIGINT collection of foreign naval activities.

Electronic Countermeasures

Electronic Countermeasures (ECM) are intended primarily to (1) detect threats to friendly forces and (2) inhibit or degrade the effectiveness of enemy weapons and sensors. Most surface warships, submarines, and combat aircraft have ECM systems to help protect them against hostile detection and attack. In addition, there are specialized ECM aircraft that assist other aircraft in penetrating heavily defended areas.

Different ECM techniques are used to reduce the effectiveness of enemy radars. The three basic techniques are: (1) to interfere with the radar through jamming and deception; (2) to change the electrical properties of the air between the radar and (friendly) target, mainly through chaff; and (3) to change the reflective properties of the (friendly) target through radar-absorbing materials or paint and through electronic and mechanical echo (blip) enhancers or decoys.

Although the above discussion concentrated on ECM techniques against radar, to some extent the concepts are usable against electromagnetic communications and sonar. For example, the properties of shipboard noise can be reduced. Modern U.S. surface warships use the PRAIRIE and Masker systems of creating small air bubbles around a ship's hull and wake to reduce her acoustic signature. Advanced submarine hull designs reduce noises created by submarine movement while special internal mountings reduce propulsion and auxiliary machinery noises. Of course, surface ships and, especially, submarines can slow or stop to reduce their self-generated noises.

Torpedo countermeasures also include decoys to replace the ship or submarine target in the torpedo's target-acquisition process. U.S. surface combatants have the T-Mk-6 Fanfare torpedo countermeasure device and, in the newer ships, the SLQ-25 Nixie. These are towed

devices. The effectiveness of Nixie was demonstrated in the 1982 war off the Falklands when a Nixie being towed by the British carrier HERMES attracted and was blown up by a British ASW torpedo launched against a suspected Argentine submarine contact.

U.S. attack submarines are reported to carry acoustic device countermeasure Mk 23 that will decoy homing torpedoes while ballistic missile submarines also can launch the Mk 70 MOSS (Mobile Submarine Simulator) from torpedo tubes to simulate a full-size submarine to hostile sonar.

There are a large number of threat warning and countermeasure systems in U.S. surface ships and submarines, mostly numbered in the SLQ and WLR series. The latest surface ship ECM equipment is the highly publicized SLQ-32 "design-to-cost" EW suite. Variations of this system are scheduled to be installed in most Navy surface ships in the 1980s.

There are three variants of the SLQ-32 with modular "building blocks" for different types of ships. The (V)1 variant for frigates, some amphibious ships (LSD, LPD, LST), and auxiliary ships (AE, AFS) provides warning, identification, and bearing of radar-guided cruise missiles and their launch platforms.

The (V)2 variant for guided-missile destroyers (DDG), frigates (FF/FFG), and the SPRUANCE (DD 963)-class large destroyers has the (V)1 capability and expanded ESM capabilities. The (V)3 configuration for cruisers (CG/CGN), large amphibious ships (LCC, LHA, LPH), and auxiliaries (AOE, AOR) has the (V)1 and (V)2 capabilities and the means to counter or deceive missile guidance radars. The (V)3 has a quick-reaction mode that permits the initiation of jamming against a target signal before its characteristics are fully analyzed. This feature could be particularly useful against "pop-up" submarine-launched missiles or those fired by missile craft hiding in coastal shore "clutter." The IOWAS are receiving the (V)3 version.

The SLQ-32 and other ECM systems are used in conjunction with Rapid Blooming Offboard Chaff (RBOC) or Super RBOC launchers that fire either semi-automatically or on manual direction from a ship's ECM operators. (The infrared decoys and flares can also be fired in response to detections by threat warning devices.) The SLQ-32 reportedly experienced problems during early fleet exercises, which, coupled with maintenance difficulties and questions about its ability to handle high-angle missile attacks, demonstrates the complexity of the ECM situation.

Several other, lesser EW sets are in current Navy use, principally the WLR-1, 6, 8, 9, 10, 11, 12, and SLR-12 threat warning systems; ULQ-6 deception repeater; and the SLQ-17 and BLR-14 countermeasure systems. The SLQ-17 used in carriers includes the WLR-8 and provides computer-controlled warning and jamming capabilities. The BLR-14—dubbed the Submarine Acoustic Warfare System (SAWS)—provides an integrated receiver, processor, display, and countermeasure launch system for submarines.

The principal naval ECM aircraft is the EA-6B Prowler, flown by the Navy and Marine Corps. The EA-6B is easily distinguished from the A-6 Intruder, from which it was developed, by the housing atop its tail fin and up to five jammer pods carried on its wings and fuselage. The pods are ALQ-99 tactical jammers, each with an exciter/processor and a minicomputer to detect, identify, and jam a broad spectrum of hostile radars. The aircraft also has the ALQ-100 multi-band track breaking system and ALQ-92 communications jammer. The EA-6B is probably the most capable EW aircraft in the West (although Grumman has provided these systems in the Air Force's EF-111A).

The basic EA-6B aircraft has had its frequency coverage extended through a series of updates (see Chapter 29).

The EA-6B aircraft are designed to provide ECM support for strike aircraft attacking defended targets. The strike aircraft can themselves carry chaff, ECM pods, and radar-homing missiles to further enhance their survivability. The Navy plans to provide each carrier air wing with four EA-6B Prowlers, while the Marine Corps has one squadron with about 15 ECM aircraft, with the reserves still flying the EA-6A Intruder.

Electronic countermeasures are costly, not only in resources (especially for research and development), but because of tactical uncertainties and limitations that they impose. For example, it may be undesirable to employ ECM against an enemy's communications for by doing so one denies communications intercept to one's own side. Or, firing chaff and decoys to defend against a possible enemy missile attack can degrade one's own radar effectiveness.

Also, ECM produces "soft kills." It is not always possible for the ECM operator to determine if his efforts were successful. Further, ESM/SIGINT/ECM/ECCM are undertaken with a continuous interaction. Those who allocate resources are not anxious to spend funds on an ECM system, for example, that may counter a threat that the intelligence community predicts will be present in the future. Somehow, it seems easier to buy a new ship, or missile, or aircraft rather than develop a new "black box" to counter a possible threat.

Electronic Counter-Countermeasures

Electronic Counter-Countermeasures (ECCM) are those actions taken to retain the effectiveness of one's own use of the electromagnetic spectrum against hostile electronic warfare efforts.

The following table lists the major submarine electronic warfare systems in surface ships and submarines that have been identified publicly.

Designation	Purpose	Manufacturer	Platforms
ALR-600	radar warning	General Instrument	65-ft PB
BLQ-3/4/5	acoustic jammer	General Electric	submarines
BLQ-8	acoustic system	Bendix, Aerojet	submarines
BLR-1/10	acoustic warning	(various)	submarines
BLR-13	ECM receiver	Kollmorgan	submarines
BLR-14 SAWS[a]	threat warning, processor, countermeasure launcher	Sperry	submarines
BLR-15	ESM receiver	Kollmorgan	submarines
BRD-6/7	radio direction finder	Sanders	submarines
SLQ-17	DECM[b]	Hughes	aircraft carriers
SLQ-25 Nixie	towed torpedo countermeasure	Aerojet	surface ships
SLQ-32(V)1	radar warning (H/I/J bands)	Raytheon	AE, AFS, LKA, LSD, LST
SLQ-32(V)2	radar warning (B through J bands)	Raytheon	DD, DDG, FF, FFG
SLQ-32(V)3	radar warning (B through J bands); ECM (H/I/J bands)	Raytheon	AOE, AOR, BB, CG, CGN, DDG 37, LHA, LPH
SLR-12			surface ships
SRD-19 Diamond	radio direction finder	Sanders	surface ships
SSQ-74 Outboard[c]	electronic deception	ITT Avionics	surface ships
SSQ-82 Mute	shipboard emitter monitor and control		surface ships
ULQ-6	deception repeater	General Instrument	surface ships
WLR-1	radar warning	(various)	surface ships
WLR-6 Waterboy	radar warning, signal collection	GTE Sylvania	surface ships, submarines
WLR-8	radar warning	GTE Sylvania	carriers, submarines
WLR-8(V)4/5	radar warning	GTE Sylvania	submarines
WLR-9	sonar receiver	Norden	submarines
WLR-10	ECM receiver	Astro Labs	submarines
WLR-11	radar warning	ARGO Systems	surface ships
T-Mk 6 Fanfare	towed torpedo countermeasure		surface ships
Mk 23	torpedo decoy		SSN
Mk 70 MOSS	Mobile Submarine Simulator	Gould	SSBN
Mk 107	target acquisition	IBM	PHM

[a] Submarine Acoustic Warfare System.
[b] Deceptive ECM.
[c] Also SSQ-72; designated SSES (Ships Signal Exploitation System).

SHIPBOARD RADAR

U.S. Navy shipboard radars are used principally for surface and air search, height finding, weapons fire control, target illumination, and aircraft control. In a few radars two functions can overlap, with some advanced radars, such as the SPY-1, providing multi-function capabilities in a single system.

Search Radar

In general, search radars use broad beams and sweep through 360° to indicate the presence of targets, but they cannot provide precise target location. The most widely used radar in the Navy is the SPS-10 surface search, found in most surface combatants, amphibious ships, and auxiliaries. Its 11-foot wide antenna has been a familiar sight on U.S. and allied ships since late 1953. It is generally considered a horizon-range radar, although significantly longer range detections are made.

Several hundred of the G-band SPS-10s are in use. The improved SPS-55, similar to the SPS-10 but with higher resolution, is being fitted in newer U.S. naval ships, while the existing SPS-10s are scheduled to be replaced by the solid-state SPS-67(V) using the same antenna. The only other major surface search radars in U.S. service are the X-band BPS-series that are used in submarines for surface navigation. The newer SSNs and Trident SSBNs have the BPS-15 on masts that retract into the sail structure.

There are a number of two-dimensional (2-D) air search radars in Navy use, and efforts under way to reduce the inventory to a few, advanced sets. The oldest sets still in service are the SPS-29 and the similar SPS-37, introduced to the fleet in 1958 and 1960, respectively.

These B-band sets are found in a few of the early CHARLES F. ADAMS (DDG 2) class, some older missile cruisers, and the now-decommissioned destroyers of the FORREST SHERMAN (DD 931/DDG 31) class. There is also the dated SPS-43A, that entered service in 1962, which is found in several aircraft carriers and older missile cruisers.

The SPS-29/37/43 use the same antenna, with the SPS-37A and SPS-43A having a larger antenna that provides longer detection ranges. For example, the SPS-37A is reported to have an effective detection range against aircraft of about 300 miles vice 230 miles for the SPS-37. The DDG 2-14 are receiving SPS-40C/D radars while the BELKNAP (CG 26) and LEAHY (CG 16) cruiser classes with older radars are being refitted with the SPS-49. Ironically, the nuclear-propelled BAINBRIDGE (CGN 25) emerged from her modernization several years ago with an SPS-37 still mounted aft (and an equally dated SPS-39D radar forward).

The SPS-40 is a widely used B-band 2-D air search radar capable of very long detection ranges. It is fitted in about 125 cruisers, destroyers, and frigates, amphibious ships, and large SACRAMENTO (AOE 1)-class UNREP ships. Older SPS-40 radars are being upgraded to the -40C/D configuration, which uses solid-state electronics to increase reliability from about 80 hours Mean Time Between Failure (MTBF) to some 200 hours.

The most effective rotating 2-D air search radar in the U.S. Navy is the SPS-49, a C-band radar. It was evaluated in 1965 on board the experimental destroyer GYATT (DD 712) and an advanced version was installed in the cruiser DALE (CG 19) in 1975. This radar features high reliability, with MTBF said to exceed 300 hours. It is a very long-range radar and has a narrow beam, which helps to counter hostile jamming efforts.

This radar is replacing SPS-37A and SPS-43A radars in cruisers and aircraft carriers, and supplements the SPY-1A radar in the TICONDEROGA (CG 47)-class Aegis cruisers. It is also installed in the OLIVER HAZARD PERRY (FFG 7)-class frigates and the modernized IOWA (BB 61)-class battleships.

Also being installed in aircraft carriers, missile destroyers, frigates, and helicopter carriers for air search are the SPS-58/65 radars. These D-band, pulse-doppler radars are used for both search and target acquisition for the Sea Sparrow point-defense missile systems. The SPS-65 can "share" the SPS-10 antenna while the SPS-58 has its own 16-foot antenna. These radars have no integral display but use those of the ships' Naval Tactical Data Systems (NTDS).

The LN-66 and CRP-series commercial navigation radars have been mounted in several surface combatants, aircraft carriers, and auxiliary ships, with the LN-66 also fitted in the SH-2F LAMPS I helicopter.

Three-Dimensional Radar

Three-dimensional (3-D) E-band air search radars are necessary to provide accurate altitude information for surface-to-air missile systems and directing fighter aircraft. The Royal Navy's lack of 3-D radars provided major problems in task force defense in the 1982 conflict off the Falklands.

A few of the older SPS-39 radars, first deployed in the early 1960s, remain. They have been replaced by the SPS-48 and SPS-52 radars. Another outdated height-finding radar, the SPS-30, has left the active fleet. The last ship to operate with the SPS-30 was the carrier CORAL SEA (CV 43) into 1983, with the set removed during the ship's 1983–1984 overhaul.

The SPS-48, a radar first deployed in 1962, is found in carriers, missile cruisers, missile destroyers, and the two command ships of the BLUE RIDGE (LCC 19) class. The older SPS-48A sets are being upgraded with Automatic Detection and Tracking (ADT) features and are designated SPS-48C. This radar is more capable than the SPS-52 and can support the Standard SM-2 long-range missile.

The SPS-52 is an improved SPS-39. Since 1963 it has been installed in several aircraft carriers, missile cruisers, missile destroyers, the six BROOKE (FFG 1)-class frigates, and the five TARAWA (LHA 1)-class helicopter carriers. The LHAs also use this radar for aircraft control. It is credited with a range of 60 miles against small, high-speed aerial targets, and out to much greater distances against large, high-flying aircraft. The sets in the older ships are being modified to improve reliability and performance.

Fire Control Radar

The narrow-beam fire control radars are keyed to specific targets by the ships' search radars. In addition, most anti-aircraft missiles require radar reflections from the target on which to home. These reflections are generally provided by "searchlight" radars, so called because of their target illumination role and, to some extent, their resemblance to giant searchlights. Some older anti-aircraft missiles also require a radar beam to "ride" or follow to the target aircraft. The only beam-riding missile remaining in U.S. service is the Terrier BTN.

U.S. Navy narrow-beam control radars operate in the G/I/J-bands. The oldest set in widespread use is the Mk 35 (predating the AN designations), which is mounted on the Mk 56 Gunfire Control System (GFCS) in several older surface combatant and amphibious ships.

The SPG-49 was the Talos track/illuminating G-band radar, used in conjunction with the diminutive SPW-2 Talos guidance system. These have been removed from the cruiser LONG BEACH (CGN 9).

The SPG-51 is a pulse-doppler, G-band tracking/illumination radar used with the Tartar/Standard-MR missile in cruisers, destroyers, and frigates. In ships armed with the larger, Terrier/Standard-ER missile, the SPG-55 illumination and guidance G-band radar is provided. Most ships have 2 radar sets for each missile launcher, thus a double-end missile cruiser with four SPG-55s could simultaneously engage up to 4 aerial targets.

Most of the Navy's destroyers and frigates built since the mid-1950s have the Mk 68 GFCS with the SPG-53 radar for directing their 5-inch guns. The newest radar of this type is the SPG-60, which provides gun control data and permits Standard-MR missile tracking with the addition of an illuminator to the Mk 86 GFC. The SPG-60 is a monopulse radar, and is combined with the SPQ-9, a high-resolution, short-range, track-while-scan radar in the Mk 86 weapon control system. Thus, a single fire control system can serve several functions. The X-band SPG-60 is credited with a nominal range of some 50 miles. The Separate Target Illumination Radar (STIR) using the SPG-60 antenna mount is found in the FFG 7 class to provide 2 missile control channels for the Mk 86.

The Mk 86 system can simultaneously track up to 120 incoming targets in a track-while-scan mode.

The SPQ-9, working in X-band frequencies, operates from a minimum of 150 yards out to 20 miles with the high scan rate of 60 revolutions per minute to detect and track incoming missiles as well as surface targets. The Mk 86 system with the SPG-60/SPQ-9 combination is found in new missile cruisers, the Spruance-class destroyers, and the Tarawa class, while the Aegis-armed Ticonderoga class has the SPQ-9 with a modified Mk 86 (Mod 9).

The Aegis missile ships have four Mk 99 missile control directors that use the SPG-62 illumination channel to provide radar reflections for Standard missiles.

One other significant U.S. fire control radar is the Target Acquisition System (TAS) Mk 23. This is a rapidly rotating, spin-stabilized linear array antenna linked to a shipboard AN/UYK-20 computer to provide rapid detection and weapons direction against low-flying missiles and aircraft. It operates in the D band and is credited with a range of 20 n.miles against anti-ship missiles and 90 n.miles against aircraft. The system can simultaneously track up to 54 targets. TAS Mk 23 was evaluated in the frigate Downes (FF 1070) from 1975 until recent replacement of the ship's NATO Sea Sparrow with a Phalanx CIWS.

The TAS Mk 23 is now being installed in Spruance-class destroyers and several of the Sacramento (AOE 1) and Wichita (AOR 1) replenishment ships, beginning with the Seattle (AOE 3) in April 1980.

Phased-Array Radar

Conventional radars that mechanically rotate or train in a vertical plane cannot provide sufficiently rapid coverage to cope with high-speed and multiple aircraft or missile threats. There is also a delay in coordinating azimuth from a 2-D search radar and altitude from a height-finding radar. Rather, the "aiming" of a radar beam electronically through the energizing of individual radar elements out of phase can "point" a radar very rapidly. By using a large number of elements greater beam focusing is achieved, creating a very narrow, high-resolution beam. Because the aim can be changed quickly (i.e., faster than by mechanical means), large angular areas can be searched rapidly.

The U.S. Navy used phased-array radars operationally in World War II, the first being the Mk VIII (CXEM) main battery fire control radar in battleships and cruisers. Phased-array technology was applied to several naval radars after the war, including the SPS-26/39/42 series, and the improved SPS-48 and SPS-52, all E-band radars. These radars are Frequency Scan (FRESCAN) radars that rotate mechanically in azimuth while pointing of the beam in elevation is controlled by varying the frequency of the signal.

The SPS-26 was laboratory tested in 1953 and the first set went to sea in the frigate Norfolk (DL 1) in 1957 and the nuclear radar picket submarine Triton (SSRN 586) in 1959. The SPS-39 was the production model of the radar with the similar SPS-42 being configured for integration with shipboard NTDS. The SPS-48 is a sophisticated, long-range FRESCAN radar.

In the late 1950s development began of the large "billboard" SPS-32/33 frequency scan radars. The SPS-32 was a very-long-range FRESCAN 2-D radar that scanned in azimuth with detection ranges of 400 miles reported against large aerial targets under ideal conditions. Each of the four SPS-32 billboard antennas was 40 feet wide and 20 feet wide. The SPS-33 provided 3-D multiple-target tracking in azimuth and elevation. The latter used FRESCAN in elevation and phase scan or energy switching in azimuth. Each of four SPS-33 antenna faces was 25 feet by 20 feet. The SPS-33 was generally used for tracking and the SPS-32 for search.

This SPS-32/33 combination—a total of 8 fixed antennas—was installed in the Navy's first two nuclear surface warships, the Long Beach and Enterprise (CVAN 65), both completed in 1961 although the radars installations were not completed until 1962. The sets were too large for subsequent nuclear surface ships, the SPS-32 radar weighing about 48½ tons and the SPS-33 about 120 tons. During subsequent service the radars were plagued by maintenance and reliability problems, and they have been replaced during overhauls by conventional radars.

The next major Navy development in this effort was the SPG-59 phased-array radar intended for the aborted Typhon missile frigate program. This technology instead formed the base for the Aegis SPY-1 S-band radar, whose development formally began in the late 1960s. The SPY-1 (one radar "face") began operation at the RCA-development facility in Cherry Hill, N.J., in 1973, followed a year later by a SPY-1 in the missile test ship Norton Sound (AVM 1). The SPY-1 is now being installed in the Ticonderoga class and is planned for the Arleigh Burke (DDG 51)-class destroyers.

The SPY-1 combines the azimuth and height search, target acquisition, classification, and tracking functions and can provide command guidance to ship-launched missiles. The replacement of several different radars with the single SPY-1 results in the reduction or elimination of several complex interfaces between specialized radars, speeds up all functions, and provides a very large target-handling capability. The SPY-1 radar—consisting of the antenna, transmitter, signal processor, control groups, and auxiliary equipment—employs 4 fixed antennas and operates in the S-band. The antennas each contain 4,480 separate radiating elements in an octagonal face only 12½ feet across. This small size facilitates ship design with the Ticonderoga having 2 antennas on a forward deck house (facing forward and to starboard) and 2 on an after deck house (facing aft and to port). These 4 antennas each cover a 90° quadrant from the horizon to zenith for total scanning around the ship.

Control of the SPY-1 is exercised by four UYK-7 digital computers that schedule and direct the beams, necessary because the SPY-1 can project hundreds of pencil-thin radar beams in rapid sequence, far too many for manual control or coordination. Beam steering is a mathematical problem that requires the calculations of a computer system. Indeed, computer capacity is a practical limitation on the number of targets that the SPY-1 can handle at one time. When a target is detected the computers automatically schedule several more beams to "dwell" on the target within a second of the initial detection, thus initiating a track. Hundreds of targets can thus be identified and tracked simultaneously, out to ranges on the order of 200 miles.

In earlier missile ships the surface-to-air missiles had to be guided all the way from launch to the target. Missile ships could thus be characterized by the number of guidance channels, i.e., separate guidance radars available. The modern Standard missiles have an "autopilot" that is set just prior to launch. The SPY-1 continuously tracks both the missiles in flight and targets, and the missile guidance can be updated while in flight. Specific radar guidance is required only for the few seconds before the missile intercepts. With this concept the TICONDEROGA's four guidance radars can handle perhaps 20 separate targets simultaneously. This provides a vast improvement over previous AAW ship capabilities.

The SPY-1 radar is also highly resistant to electronic countermeasures. It has frequency diversity and can "sense" jamming and automatically shift to different frequencies where less interference is present. Also, digital signal-processing techniques are employed to counter or suppress jamming as well as sea clutter. The latter feature is vital for an effective defense against sea-skimming missiles whose radar return is often lost to conventional radars because of sea clutter masking the target's signal.

There are four versions of the SPY-1:

SPY-1 Development model fitted in the NORTON SOUND since 1974.

SPY-1A Production radar provided in 12 TICONDEROGA-class ships (CG 47–58); the four antenna faces are divided between the forward and after deckhouses.

SPY-1B Production radar with upgraded antenna, improved transmitter and signal processor for increased effectiveness against low flying and small radar-cross section missiles, and enhanced ECM resistance; introduced in CG 59.

SPY-1C Designation not used.

SPY-1D Single deckhouse version for the ARLEIGH BURKE class.

The Aegis system is not inexpensive and the SPY-1 radars are a major contribution to the cost. Compared with alternative radar systems, however, the SPY-1 offers overwhelming superiority in several performance categories. Further, the system appears to be easier to maintain and more suitable for shipboard installation than the previous SPS-32/33 radars. The latter feature made it feasible to install the Aegis/SPY-1 in the SPRUANCE hull, resulting in a minimal increase in ship displacement to produce the TICONDEROGA-class cruisers.

The Mk 92 weapon control system in the PERRY-class frigates, installed in conjunction with the SPG-60 radar, has been proposed for modification to a phased-array configuration by Sperry, its manufacturer. This would, if successful, provide a significant increase in AAW/ASMD effectiveness of the PERRY class. The cost of the upgraded system was estimated in 1984 at $100 million for the lead ship and $70 million for follow-on ships, plus development costs. Further, the ability of the "tight" PERRY-class ships to accommodate the equipment and possible additional personnel is questionable.

Led by Sperry lobbying, there has been an effort in Congress to force the Navy to accept the phased-array radar in the single ship added to the FY 1985 budget.

Aircraft Control Radar

Aircraft control radars are unique to aviation ships (CV/CVN/LHA/LHD/LPH) and are designated in the SPN-series, referred to as "spin" radars. They are used to guide aircraft into the proper approach pattern or glide path to the ship. The SPN-41, -42, -43, and -44 are currently in service.

Radar Improvements

The newer radars entering U.S. Navy service, and modifications to existing sets, permit improvements in logistics, maintenance, and operations. The last is reflected in such features as automatic detection and tracking, increased ranges, enhanced resistance to enemy countermeasures, and improved reliability. Thus, to some extent, the Navy's radars are improving to help counter an increasing and changing threat from the Soviet Union and several Third World nations.

At this time only the Aegis/SPY-1 is capable of countering the "high threat" weapons that will exist in the Soviet Union in the late 1980s and beyond. The improvements to the SPS-48 and SPS-49, however, should provide improved capabilities for area defense in non-Aegis ships. Also, integrated and automatic detection and tracking systems now being fitted to non-Aegis ships will enhance the effectiveness of other radars.

The following are the principal radars in U.S. surface ships and submarines. Fire control radars were assigned mark (Mk) numbers beginning in 1941. This series ran through Mk 47 with the next radar initiating the SPG series. Subsequently, later versions of some earlier radars were given the SPG prefix, as SPG-34.

Weapon Designation Radars

Several aircraft carriers, missile destroyers, frigates, and helicopter carriers have the SPS-58/65 air search radars to support quick-reaction missile defense systems. These L-band, pulse-doppler radars are used for both search and target acquisition for the Sea Sparrow point-defense missile systems. The SPS-65 can "share" the SPS-10 antenna while the SPS-58 has its own 16-foot antenna. These radars have no integral display but use those of the ships' Naval Tactical Data Systems (NTDS). These sets will be phased out in favor of the TAS Mk 23.

In addition, numbered in different (non-radar) series are several other weapon control radars: the Mk 23 Target Acquisition System (TAS) for the NATO Sea Sparrow launcher Mk 29; the Mk 91 fire control radar for the NATO Sea Sparrow; the Mk 92/94 weapon FCS adopted from the Dutch M28 system; and the Mk 115 director/illuminator for the basic Sea Sparrow launcher Mk 25.

The Mk 23, intended for automatic reaction/target designation of incoming sea-skimming missiles, has a maximum range of almost 100 miles and a minimum designation range of 20 miles. Up to 54 missiles can be tracked simultaneously with a two-second scan rate. The Mk 23 first went to sea in the frigate DOWNES (FF 1071) in 1975.

The Mk 91 fire control radar for the NATO Sea Sparrow has side-by-side receiving and transmitting antennas; it typically has targets designated automatically by the SPS-58/65 radars or the Mk 23 TAS.

The Mk 92/94 is a combined tracking and illuminating incorporating two antennas, one for air and surface target tracking. The Mod 2 version, in the PERRY-class frigates, is combined with the STIR radar to provide a second missile guidance channel in those ships. The Mod 1/5 versions are for gun control only (Mod 1 in PEGASUS/PHM 1 class, except that the lead ship has Mk 94 prototype, BEAR/WMEC 901 class, and planned for HAMILTON/WHEC 715 class); Mod 0/2 versions can control guns or missiles (Mod 2 in PERRY class).

The Mk 115, associated with the Sea Sparrow BPDMS, is a director/

illuminator adopted from the older Mk 51 gun director mount. It also has side-by-side antennas.

The Phalanx CIWS has a built-in AN/VPS-2 J-band pulse-doppler radar employing a single transmitter with separate search and tracking radars mounted above the actual Gatling gun. The radar operates autonomously and provides tracking of both incoming targets and outgoing bullets, detects the angular error between them, and automatically corrects gun aim.

The frequency bands shown below are the original ones assigned for most radars; see the Frequency Spectrum table (see page 487).

Sailor holding towed "fish" for SLQ-25 Nixie with towing cable in foreground. (Aerojet General)

SLQ-32(V)3 antenna on the Aegis cruiser YORKTOWN (CG 48); two Mk 36 Rapid Blooming Offboard Chaff (RBOC) launchers are mounted forward of the antenna. (N. Polmar)

SLQ-17A(V) antenna on the carrier ENTERPRISE (CVN 65) (Hughes)

SLQ-32(V)1 antenna on the frigate MOINESTER (FF 1097) (Giorgio Arra)

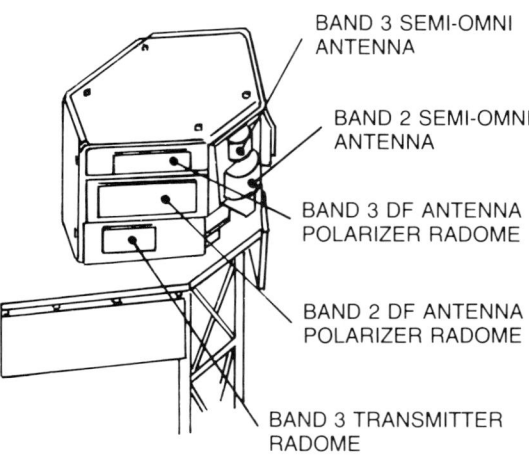

BAND 3 SEMI-OMNI
ANTENNA

BAND 2 SEMI-OMNI
ANTENNA

BAND 3 DF ANTENNA
POLARIZER RADOME

BAND 2 DF ANTENNA
POLARIZER RADOME

BAND 3 TRANSMITTER
RADOME

SLQ-32 EW system

Mk 35 radar affixed to the Mk 56 GFCS aboard the aircraft carrier MIDWAY (CV 41). The 48-inch-diameter dish provides acquisition and tracking for 3-inch and 5-inch guns. The only guns now mounted in active U.S. aircraft carriers are the Phalanx CIWS plus saluting batteries. (U.S. Navy)

Mk 25 radar atop Mk 37 GFCS (right) and Mk 13 radar atop Mk 38 gun director on the battleship NEW JERSEY (BB 62). (U.S. Navy)

BPS-15 radar on the HAWKBILL (SSN 666) (Giorgio Arra)

SPG-15C radar, part of the Mk 74 missile FCS, on the frigate BROOKE (FFG 1). (Giorgio Arra)

SPS-10 antenna over SPS-37 radar on the destroyer EDSON (DD 946) (Giorgio Arra)

SPS-52 3-D radar antenna on the frigate BROOKE (FFG 1) (Giorgio Arra)

SPG-35A radar atop Mk 68 GFCS (N. Polmar)

SPS-55B on the destroyer FARRAGUT (DDG 37) (Giorgio Arra)

SPG-49B "searchlight" radars for Talos illuminating and tracking in the CHICAGO (CG 11), now stricken. A diminutive SPW-2 radar is shown above the pair of SPG-49B radars. (Giorgio Arra)

SPG-60 below SPQ-9A antennas on Virginia (CGN 38)-class cruiser (Lockheed)

SPS-67(V) antenna (United Technologies/Norden)

SPS-64(V)9 antenna (Raytheon)

SPS-10 antenna over SPS-40D on the frigate Lang (FF 1060) (Giorgio Arra)

SPS-48C 3-D radar antenna (Giorgio Arra)

STIR radar antenna on the frigate FAHRION (FFG 22) (Giorgio Arra)

SPQ-9A antenna dome on the NASSAU (LHA 4); an SPG-60 radar is mounted below the dome and a Tactical Air Navigation (TACAN) pod atop the mast. (Giorgio Arra)

Reverse side of SPY-1A antenna during assembly (RCA)

SPS-6 air search radar atop SPS-10 surface search radar on the THOMASTON (LSD 28) (N. Polmar)

SPS-52 3-D radar on the destroyer LAWRENCE (DDG 4) (U.S. Navy)

SPS-49 radar antenna on the frigate JACK WILLIAMS (FFG 24) (Giorgio Arra)

SPS-10 antenna over SPS-29 on the destroyer SOMERS (DDG 34) (Giorgio Arra)

SPY-1A antenna production line; the third antenna in line has almost all blocks of radiating elements installed; the fourth antenna "face" is essentially complete. Variants of the SPY-1 are being fitted to the CG 47 and DDG 51 classes, with one antenna having been installed in the missile ship NORTON SOUND (AVM 1). (RCA)

SPS-48A radar on the destroyer JOHN PAUL JONES (DDG 32) (Giorgio Arra)

Mk 92 multi-function radar housing on hydrofoil missile craft HERCULES (PHM 2) (Boeing)

Designation	Purpose	Operational	Band	Manufacturer	Platforms (class)	Notes
Mk 13	radar for Mk gun director (range and bearing)		X	Western Electric	BB 61, CA 134	none in active ships
Mk 25	radar for Mk 37 GFCS (conical scanning)		X	Western Electric	BB 61, CA 134, CV	none in active ships
Mk 34/SPG-34	radar for Mk 57 gun director and Mk 63 GFCS (conical scanning)		X	Western Electric	BB 61, CA 134, LST	none in active ships
Mk 35	radar for Mk 56 GFCS		X	General Electric	BB 61, CA 134, CG 10, CGN 9, FF	
BPS-5	surface search and navigation	1953	X	Lockheed	submarines	
BPS-11	surface search and navigation		X	Western Electric	submarines	
BPS-12/14	surface search and navigation		X	Fairchild	submarines	modified BPS-5
BPS-15	surface search and navigation		X	Sperry	submarines	
CRP-series	short-range navigation		X		various ships	
LN-66	short-range navigation		X		various ships	also in SH-2F helicopter
SG-6	surface search and navigation		X		BB 61, CA 134	none in active ships
SPG-50	radar for Mk 63 GFCS		X		CA 134	updated SPG-34
SPG-51/C/D	radar for Mk 74 missile FCS; Tartar/Standard-MR illumination and tracking	1960	G	Raytheon	CG 10, CGN 36, CG 38, DDG 2, DDG 31, DDG 993, FFG 1	pulse-doppler radar
SPG-53A/B/F	radar for Mk 68 GFCS		X	Western Electric	CG 26, DDG 2, DDG, 31, DDG 37	modified SPG-48
SPG-55B/F	Terrier/Standard-ER illumination and guidance		J	Sperry	CG 16, CG 26, CGN 9, CGN 25, CGN 35	replaces SPQ-5
SPG-60	radar for MK 86 missile/GFCS; Standard-MR tracking and illumination		X	Lockheed	CGN 36, CGN 38, DDG 993, DD 963, LHA 1	pulse-doppler radar; see STIR (below)
SPG-62	Standard SM-2 illuminator (Aegis)		X	Raytheon	AVM 1, CG 47	Mk 99 missile FCS component
SPQ-9A	radar for Mk 86 GFCS; surface search and weapons control	1970	X	Lockheed	CG 47, CGN 36, CGN 38, DDG 993, DD 963, LHA 1	high-resolution, pulse-doppler; track-while-scan
SPS-6B/C/D/E	air search	1950	L	Bendix Westinghouse	AOE 1, BB 62, CA 134, LSD 28	mod C/E in active ships
SPS-8A	height finding	1955	S	General Electric	BB 61, CA 134	none in active ships
SPS-10B to F	surface search and navigation	1953	G	GTE Sylvania Raytheon	most combatant, amphibious, auxiliary ships	
SPS-12C	air search	1953	L	RCA	AVT 16, CA 134	
SPS-29B/C/E	long-range air search[a]	1958	B	Westinghouse	DDG 31, DDG 37	
SPS-30	height finding	1962	F	General Electric	CG 10	last active ship was CV 43
SPS-37/A	long-range air search[a]	1960	B	Westinghouse	CGN 25, CV, DD, DDG 2, DDG 37	
SPS-39A	3-D search	1960	E	Hughes	CGN 25, DDG 2	
SPS-40/B	air search	1961	B	Lockheed	CGN 35, CGN 36, CGN 38, DDG 2, DDG 3, LCC, amphibious ships	
SPS-43A	long-range air search[a]	1962	B	Hughes Westinghouse	CA 134, CG 10, CV	SPS-43A in carriers replaced by SPS-49
SPS-48/A/B/C/E	3-D search	1962	E	ITT Gilfillan	CG, CGN, CV, CVN, DDG, LCC	FRESCAN radar
SPS-49	long-range air search	1965[b]	C	Raytheon	CV, CVN, BB, CG, CGN, FFG 7	narrow-beam; very long range
SPS-52A/B/C	3-D search	1963	E	Hughes	DDG 2, FFG 1, LHA 1	improved SPS-39A; FRESCAN
SPS-53	surface search	1967	X	Sperry	BB 61, MSO, auxiliary ships	navigation radar
SPS-55	surface search		I	Cordion	BB 61, CG 47, DD, FFG 7	slotted array
SPS-58/65	low-level threat detection		D	Westinghouse	AOE, AOR, CV, CVN, FF, LCC, LHA, LPH	pulse-doppler radar; can use SPS-10 antenna
SPS-67(V)	surface search/navigation			Norden	surface ships	successor to SPS-10
SPW-2A/B	Talos missile guidance		C	Sperry	CG 10	none in active ships
SPY-1/A/D	Aegis multi-function, long-range radar		F	RCA	AVM 1, CG 47, DDG 51	fixed array antennas
STIR	Separate Target Illumination Radar	1974	X		FFG 7	modified SPG-60
Mk 23 TAS	Target Acquisition System		D	Hughes	AOE, AOR, CV, CVN, DD 963	pulse-doppler radar
Mk 91	weapon direction radar for NATO Sea Sparrow		X			
MK 92	weapon direction radar			Sperry	FFG 7, PHM 1	Mk 94 prototype in PHM 1
MK 115	weapon direction radar for Sea Sparrow BPDMS				various ships	
Phalanx	weapon direction radar for Phalanx CIWS		ku		various ships	built into Phalanx CIWS

[a] The SPS-29/37/43 use the same antenna; the SPS-37A and SPS-43A use a larger antenna.
[b] See text above.

SPS-58/SPS-65 antenna (Westinghouse)

SHIPBOARD SONAR

Sonar is the U.S. Navy's principal means for detecting and targeting submarines. Essentially all Navy surface combatants and submarines are fitted with sonars; anti-submarine aircraft employ expendable sonobuoys; some ASW helicopters use dipping sonars as well as sonobuoys; many sea mines have sonars; mine countermeasure forces use sonars to detect mines; and the United States makes extensive use of seafloor Sound Surveillance Systems (SOSUS). These sonars are passive or active with some equipment operating in both modes.

No active U.S. aircraft carriers are equipped with sonar.

Hull Mounted Sonar

Surface ship sonars vary considerably in type and installation. The principal hull-mounted sonars in the U.S. Navy today are the SQS-23, SQS-26/53 series, and SQS-56. These sonars had their origins in the early 1950s, when the first Soviet post-World War II submarines began going to sea in large numbers.

The SQS-23 passive/active mode sonar became operational from 1958 onward in modernized war-built FRAM destroyers, modernized FORREST SHERMAN-class destroyers, and the newer COONTZ (DLG 9/DDG 37) and CHARLES F. ADAMS classes. Initially, the sonar domes were fitted under the hull, in the traditional position of sonars. However, one FORREST SHERMAN, the BARRY (DD 933), and the last five of the CHARLES F. ADAMS-class ships (DDG 20–24) have bow-mounted SQS-23 domes. Moving the sonar forward to the bow has the advantage of placing the sonar as far as possible from own-ship machinery and propeller noises. The bow sonar also necessitates special care in maneuvering with tugs or pulling alongside a pier, and in dry docking the ship.

The SQS-23 is range limited, with a direct-path active range of some 10,000 yards—intended to be compatible with the ASROC weapon. In an effort to improve the capability of ships with the SQS-23, the several ships with that sonar are being fitted with a second (passive) dome under the Performance And Integration Retrofit (PAIR). At sea since the mid-1970s, this arrangement is designated SQQ-23 and is reported to be highly effective.

An even larger sonar, with perhaps double the 36-kilowatt power of the SQS-23, was sought by the late 1950s as it became evident that the Soviets would continue to improve their submarines, especially with the advent of nuclear propulsion. In 1958 the Navy awarded contracts for competitive models of the larger and more capable SQS-26.

In the early 1960s, the SQS-26 became the standard ASW ship sonar, providing a nominal direct-path range of 20,000 yards. Significantly, delays in delivery and technical problems caused the SQS-26 not to be approved for service use until November 1968. By that time more than a score of ships had been fitted with the sonar: the BRONSTEIN (DE 1037), GARCIA (DE 1040), BROOKE (DEG 1), and BELKNAP (DLG 26) classes, and the TRUXTUN (DLGN 35). The sonars were of limited effectiveness during this period while the ships long-range ASW delivery capability was limited to the short range of ASROC and the short-lived Drone Anti-Submarine Helicopter (DASH) program.

The large SQS-26 next went into the subsequent 46 ships of the KNOX (DE 1052) class and the two nuclear cruisers of the CALIFORNIA (CGN

Band Designations

Current Frequency Designations Used by USA and NATO	A		B	C				D		E	F	G	H	I	J		K		L	M	
Wavelength (cm)	300	200	150	100	75	60	50	40	30	20	15	10	6	5	3.75	3	2	1.5	1	0.75	0.6	0.5	0.4	0.3
Frequency (GHz)	0.1	0.15	0.2	0.3	0.4	0.5	0.6	0.75	1	1.5		3	5	6	8.0	10	15	20	30	40	50	60	70	100
Previous Frequency Designations*	VHF			UHF				L		S		C		X	K_u	K	K_a		Millimeter		
Frequency Designations (WW II)		P		L			S		C	X			K		Q	V	

36) class. With these installations a number of improvements were made to the SQS-26. An advance was made with addition of a digital interface with the Mk 116 fire control system resulting in the new designation SQS-53. This sonar went into the SRUANCE-class ASW destroyers and the class variations, the KIDD (DDG 993) and TICONDEROGA designs, as well as the VIRGINIA (CGN 38)-class nuclear cruisers. A new digital solid-state display was substituted to become the SQS-53B sonar. A continuing improvement program will provide a solid state, digital transmitter and receiver.

This latest version, the SQS-53C, is being procured for back fit in these ships and for the ARLEIGH BURKE-class destroyers. (A total of 109 of these sets are now planned for shipboard installation.)

However, the SQS-53 has not been provided to the latest ASW frigates of the OLIVER HAZARD PERRY class. The severe cost and size constraints imposed by the Chief of Naval Operations when they were designed led to the small, higher-frequency and thus shorter-range SQS-56 being developed for this large class. Use of the SQS-56 has saved perhaps 600 tons of displacement in the FFG 7, while requiring far less electrical power than the 66 kilowatts of the SQS-53. The loss, however, is effective range, with the SQS-56 being capable of detections only on the order of five miles—far too little for effective use of ship-based ASW helicopters.

Other factors in the decision to reduce the OLIVER HAZARD PERRY-class sonar effectiveness were the availability of large numbers of SQS-26/53 sonars in other ASW ships and the potential of towed array sonars being installed in the FFG 7 class.

Variable Depth and Towed Array Sonar

During the 1950s the U.S. Navy developed two additional types of surface ship sonars: Variable Depth Sonar (VDS) and Towed Array Sonar (TAS). The VDS is lowered over the stern of the ship to place the sonar dome below the near-surface thermal layers that reflect sonar beams.

The principal U.S. Navy ships now using VDS are the KNOX-class frigates. They can use either their hull-mounted SQS-26 or the SQS-35 VDS, or radiate a sonar beam on one and receive its echo on the other. The VDS "fish" can be towed at relatively high speeds and can be operated down to depths of several hundred feet. It is mechanically retracted and stowed on a cradle within the stern of the ship.

The towed arrays have been more successful and are planned for much wider use in the fleet. The Tactical Towed Array Sonars (TACTAS) consist of a passive (hydrophone) system in a cable towed behind the ship. By using convergence zone detection techniques, TACTAS has long-range capabilities against Soviet submarines, especially when employed by screening ships away from the noisy task force center.[2]

The SQR-15/16 were the first long-range arrays, fitted in frigates for evaluation and subsequent operational service. The improved SQR-18/19 arrays were for tactial use from surface combatants. These later

TACTAS, however, can be used only at slow speeds (although the array can be towed or reeled in or out while the ship is at high speeds).

Few details of the arrays have been made public. The SQR-19 array has a nominal diameter of 3¼ inches and is towed at the end of a 5,600-foot cable. The array section weighs about 10,000 pounds, with the shipboard electronics weighing 12,900 pounds and the array handling equipment another 16,800 pounds.

In the KNOX-class frigates the current SQR-18A TACTAS is attached to the VDS towing body to facilitate handling. The improved SQR-19 TACTAS, which has encountered delays because of contractual and technical difficulties, is now in production. It is planned for the SPRUANCE and OLIVER HAZARD PERRY classes, and eventually the ARLEIGH BURKE class. This array is specifically intended for use with the SH-60B LAMPS III helicopter. The system was also planned for the TICONDEROGA-class Aegis cruisers. However, since the Aegis cruisers will operate in the center of carrier task groups, often in close proximity to other ships, the effectiveness of TACTAS may be limited in those ships. (The PERRY-class ships being assigned to the NRF will instead have the SQR-18A and carry SH-2F helicopters.)

A few older frigates carry the SQR-15 towed array.

Another towed surface ship sonar is the Surveillance Towed Array System (SURTASS) being fitted in the new T-AGOS ocean surveillance ships. These will provide long-range detection in areas where SOSUS is unavailable or limited. The SURTASS/T-AGOS system will have the means of providing tactical data to warships, but their primary purpose will be to transmit data via satellites to processing stations ashore.

Submarine Sonar

A submarine operating in the ocean depths is in the ideal sonar position: below the surface wave action and in the environment of the opposing submarine. Further, in the relative calm of the depths, the submarine can maneuver at very slow speeds, which enhances the submarine's own sonar effectiveness and reduces her vulnerability to passive acoustic detection. Thus, the submarine becomes a natural hunter of other submarines.

The PERMIT (SSN 594) and STURGEON (SSN 637) classes were built with the BQQ-2 sonar suite, which included a large, 15-foot-diameter bow sphere mounting the BQR-7 conformal array of passive hydrophones plus the active/passive BQS-11/12/13 sonars. The various sonars complemented each other. For example, the BQR-7 searched in azimuth (i.e., horizontally) while the BQS-11/12/13 series could form beams in elevation/depression.

The BQQ-2 was a predominately analog sonar that used mechanical steering to direct passive listening and active "pinging" beams. This beam steering used a set of switches similar in concept to a television channel selector switch. Each beam had its own switch, with the "channels" representing direction. The large number of hydrophones in the BQQ-2 enabled essentially continuous bearing coverage. While the submarines had several processors to display acoustic signals from these hydrophones, the interpretation, correlation, and classification of the signals were done manually. These sets have mostly been upgraded to the BQQ-5 configuration.

---

[2] If the ocean depth is sufficient, sound will travel down and back to the surface at an annulus about 30 miles away, i.e., to the first convergence zone. An advanced passive sonar system can be effective out to two convergence zones or some 60 to 70 miles.

The BQQ-5 series in the Los Angeles class is a digital system that integrates the bow-mounted sonar array, the conformal or hull array, and the towed array. A computer type of signal processor is used to select the hydrophones and steer the beams. With this method the number of beams that can be formed is limited only by computer capacity. Also the digital BQQ-5 suffers far less from internal noises than its predecessor, the BQQ-2 with manual switching, thus enhancing the detection of weaker acoustic signals. And, the BQQ-5 digital computer's processing allows a reduction in the number of normal watchstanders. The BQQ-5B and -5C now being procured have improved display consoles and capabilities.

Strategic missile submarines (SSBN) employ sonar for defensive purposes. The Lafayette (SSBN 616)-class submarines have the BQR-7 and BQR-21 passive sonars. The BQR-21 DIMUS (Digital Multi-beam Steering), also found in a few SSNs, is a highly capable set. These sets are not integrated as are the components of the BQQ-2/5 suites. However, the new Ohio (SSBN 726)-class Trident submarines have essentially the BQQ-5 suite without the active set (redesignated BQQ-6). (See table for installation details.)

The active component of the BQQ-5 is required in SSNs to provide accurate range measurements for their offensive weapons and in those situations where passive sonar is limited. The cost of the active capability, however, is considerable. The typical power needed to achieve 10,000-yard detections with an active sonar is about one-half million watts, while a nominal passive sonar requires less than one-half watt of power for similar detection ranges. Also, the active sonar could be up to ten times heavier than a passive set. But the accuracy of active sonar is needed for non-homing weapons, for shallow-water operations, and against very quiet submarines.

The more modern U.S. submarines also have towed passive arrays that are streamed out as the craft travels slowly in the depths. In addition to submarine and surface ship detection, according to recent congressional testimony, the towed array can also be used for aircraft detection in conjunction with submarine-launched anti-aircraft missiles should those weapons be developed for U.S. submarines. (The Soviet Navy is reported to be developing such weapons.)

Some special-purpose sonars are also fitted in submarines, such as upward-looking ice-detecting sets. While these are usually mounted on the hull or the sail structure, the BQR-19 is a mast-mounted sonar used by SSBNs for collision avoidance and other special applications.

A final submarine sonar type in limited U.S. use is PUFFS, originally an acronym for Passive Underwater Fire-control Feasibility System. The PUFFS concept provides for high-accuracy passive ranging through the correlation of signals received by multiple arrays fitted to the submarine. The older Darter (SS 576) has the BQG-4 PUFFS, easily recognized by three fin-like domes on the upper deck. Later PUFFS and Micro-PUFFS systems have the passive arrays fitted flush with the submarine's hull (apparently three hydrophones on each side).

Seafloor Arrays

Beyond using their own sonars, ASW forces can be guided to potential surface or undersea targets by seafloor acoustic systems, generally known as SOSUS in the U.S. Navy. During World War II, limited acoustic arrays were installed on the ocean floor near harbors. Immediately after the war the U.S. Navy began development of deep-ocean arrays. By 1948 arrays were being tested at sea and by 1951 the first SOSUS arrays were being implanted. Also termed Project Caesar, the first set of operational hydrophones was installed at Sandy Hook, south of Manhattan, followed in 1952 by a deep-water (1,200-foot) installation off Eleuthra in the Bahamas. That year the CNO directed the establishment of six arrays in the western Atlantic, all to be ready by the end of 1956. The first arrays in the Pacific were operational in 1958. Overseas installations followed.

Initially a number of Naval Facilities (NAVFAC) were established as the shore terminals for SOSUS, with NAVFACs being located along both U.S. coasts, in the Caribbean, Iceland, and Japan as well as at other overseas locations. Subsequently the seafloor hydrophones have been replaced, and the NAVFACs in the United States and Caribbean have been consolidated as more capable arrays and computers have been developed.

Acoustic data from the NAVFACs and Regional Evaluation Centers (REC) are provided through the Ocean Surveillance Information System (OSIS) to the Atlantic, Pacific, and European area Fleet Command Centers (FCCS) and to the Naval Ocean Surveillance Information Center (NOSIC), in Suitland, Md., near Washington, D.C., as well as to the National Command Authorities (NCA). Thus, SOSUS information is provided at several levels—to tactical as well as theater and national commanders—and for technical evaluation.

Little was said about SOSUS until the 1960s when Secretary of Defense Robert S. McNamara publicly discussed how SOSUS could guide ASW aircraft to submarine contacts. The sonar search range of submarines would be enhanced through SOSUS coordination, if tactical communication links between submarines and SOSUS terminals were used.

Published sources cite detection ranges of "hundreds" of miles by SOSUS, with arrays reported in the Atlantic and Pacific areas, as well as some regional seas. Several update programs have been announced, especially related to computer capability which can more rapidly provide data with an improved Signal-to-Noise Ratio (SNR).

The obvious vulnerabilities of SOSUS in wartime, as well as some coverage limitations, have led to the T-AGOS/SURTASS program, as well as to proposals for smaller arrays that could be planted by surface ships or aircraft. The latter has been an on-again, off-again program identified by such acronyms as MSS (Moored Surveillance System) and RDSS (Rapidly Deployable Surveillance System). This form of sonar would probably be quite useful, in view of increased Soviet naval operating areas and the growing Third World submarine forces.

Dipping Sonar

The Navy's SH-3 Sea King ASW helicopters are fitted with the AQS-13 active "dipping" sonar. This sonar is generally used in areas where ship-generated noises are high (e.g., near a carrier battle group) and passive sonar or sonobuoy effectiveness is limited. The aging SH-3 Sea Kings will require replacement by the end of this decade, with the SH-60F variant of the Seahawk with AQS-13F proposed for this role.

Mine Warfare

Another significant use of sonar in ASW is mine warfare, with the U.S. Navy's CAPTOR (encapsulated torpedo) being fitted with sonar to detect hostile submarines passing through the "attack envelope" of the mine's Mk 46 homing torpedo. The Mk 60 uses a passive sonar initially to detect targets and an active acoustic set to identify the hostile submarine before launching an acoustic-homing Mk 46 torpedo.

Sonar is also used in mine countermeasures with high-resolution sonars in minesweepers (now the SQQ-14 with the SQQ-30/32 in development), helicopters (AQS-14), and submarines to detect mines; seafloor navigation with sonar to determine bottom contours; and possibly over-the-horizon targeting of surface ships through detection of their machinery noises.

Airborne MCM is undertaken by RH/MH-53 helicopters employing the AQS-14 towed sonar.

Sonar Concepts

While surface ships rely heavily on active as well as passive sonar, the U.S. Navy tends generally to emphasize the passive sonar. This is especially in submarines and the seafloor SOSUS complex. Fundamentally, passive sonars seek to detect the sounds radiated by a submarine—the signal—in a background of undesired sound—the noise. The key principle of passive sonar is the relationship between the signal and the noise, normally expressed as the Signal-to-Noise Ratio (SNR).

As submarines become quieter, the signal has gone down. At the same time the background noise has increased. In addition to marine life, this noise includes military, commercial, and recreation shipping, offshore oil drilling, and so on. Thus, much of the current effort in sonar technology seeks to counter this decreasing SNR. The noise produced by submarines is both narrow band and broad band. Reciprocating and rotating machineries generate the narrow band emissions. For a submarine with alternating current electrical systems the frequencies and amplitude of many of these emissions are independent of the ship's speed. Sounds in the broad band spectrum can be caused by the flow of water over the hull, the turbulence of fluids in internal piping (such as steam in a nuclear plant), and mechanical friction. Propeller noises are both narrow band and broad band, with the sounds due to cavitation, when it occurs, dominating the broad band spectrum.

Several actions are possible to Soviet submarine designers to reduce these passive "signatures," in turn causing the American scientific-technical community to work harder on the SNR. Of course, in wartime passive sonar operation could be frustrated by the extensive use of decoys and noisemakers, the detonation of weapons in the ocean, and by submarine tactics. In particular, SOSUS seems vulnerable to a number of active and passive countermeasures. Soviet publications indicate that SOSUS positions are well known.

Active sonars are less vulnerable than passive sonars to the SNR problem but have the vulnerability of announcing the presence of the searching surface ship or submarine (or helicopter with dipping sonar). Soviet submarines are known to use anechoic (sonar-absorbing) coatings to reduce the effectiveness of active sonar.

Thus, there is a see-saw battle between improvements in sonar, especially improving the SNR, while the Soviets are developing quieter submarines and employing tactics to reduce their vulnerability to detection.

Designation	Purpose	Operational	Manufacturer	Platforms	Notes
BQG-4 PUFFS[a]	passive fire control	1963	Sperry	SS 576	three fin domes
BQQ-2	active/passive sonar system	1960	Raytheon	SSN 594, SSN 597, SSN 637, SSN 671, SSN 685	includes BQR-7 and BQS-6; being upgraded to BQQ-5
BQQ-5	active/passive sonar system	1976	IBM	SSN 688 plus older SSN updates	improved, digital BQQ-2
BQQ-6	passive sonar system	1981	IBM	SSBN 726	passive BQQ-5
BQR-2B	passive detection	1955	EDO	see BQS-4	component of BQS-4
BQR-7	passive detection	1955	EDO, Raytheon	see BQQ-2	conformal hydrophone array
BQR-15	passive detection	1974	Western Electric	SSN 608, SSBN 616	includes towed array and BQF-23 signal processor
BQR-19	short-range rapid-scanning	1970	Raytheon	SSN 598, SSN 608	
BQR-21	passive detection		Honeywell	SSN/SSBN	Digital Multi-beam Steering (DIMUS)
BQR-23	passive detection			SSBN	
BQS-4	active/passive sonar system	1955	EDO	SS, older SSN	
BQS-8/14/20	mine/under-ice detection	1960	EDO, Hazeltine	newer SSN	
BQS-11/12/13	active/passive bow sonar for BQQ-5			newer SSN	
BQS-15				newer SSN	replaces BQS-6 in BQQ-2/5
SQQ-14	mine detection and classification		EDO	MSO	cable-lowered from hull
SQQ-23	active/passive detection	1972	Sperry	CG 16, CGN 9, CGN 25, DDG 2, DDG 37	modified SQS-23; two domes for Performance and Integration Retrofit (PAIR)
SQQ-30	mine detection and classification			MCM	limited capability
SQQ-32	mine detection and classification			MCM, MSH	
SQR-15	passive towed array			FF	

Designation	Purpose	Operational	Manufacturer	Platforms	Notes
SQR-18A TACTAS	passive towed array	1978	EDO	FF	Tactical Towed Array Sonar; attached to SQS-35 body
SQR-19	passive towed array		General Electric	CG 47, DDG 997, DD 963, FFG 7	improved TACTAS for LAMPS III ships
SQS-23	active/passive detection	1958	Sangamo	CG, CGN, DDG, CV 66, modified DD 931	being upgraded to SQQ-23 PAIR
SQS-26	active/passive detection	1962	General Electric	CG 26, CGN 36, FF 1037, FF 1040, FF 1052, FF 1098, FFG 1	AXR, BX, CX modifications
SQS-35 IVD	Independent Variable Depth Sonar; active/passive	1968	EDO	FF 1052	
SQS-53	active/passive detection	1975	General Electric	CG 47, CGN 38, DD 963, DDG 51	SQS-26CX with digital interface for Mk 116 underwater FCS
SQS-56	active/passive detection	1977	Raytheon	FFG 7	
SURTASS	long-range passive detection	1984		T-AGOS	Surveillance Towed Array Sonar System

SQS-35 Variable Depth Sonar (VDS) installation in stern of the frigate FRANCIS HAMMOND (FF 1067). Subsequent installation of towed arrays in this class uses the handling gear and "fish" of the SQS-35 to mount the towed array. (U.S. Navy)

This is a rare view of a submarine sonar dome—in this view a 15-foot diameter BQS-6 sphere that was subsequently fitted with transducers and installed in a PERMIT (SSN 594)-class submarine. The opening in the sphere at right provides access from the submarine's pressure hull to the sonar. (U.S. Navy)

The towed "fish" of the SQS-35 VDS aboard the frigate VALDEZ (FF 1096) (U.S. Navy)

The frigate McCLOY (FF 1038) is the smallest ship to have SQS-26 bow-mounted sonar. The dome partially floods when at sea and has some dampening effects on ship motion. The SQS-26 and its successor SQS-53 have active and passive listening modes. (U.S. Navy, Ed Dowling)

The structure immediately aft of the sail on the DARTER (SS 576) is the amidships dome for the BQG-4 PUFFS. No other U.S. submarines now have this configuration. (Giorgio Arra)

SONOBUOYS

Naval aircraft employ expendable short-duration sonobuoys for the localization of submarines. Generally, sonobuoys are employed after an initial submarine contact is gained by other means. However, there are sonobuoy barrier tactics, in which a string of sonobuoys is periodically planted ahead of a task force. The Navy's S-3A Viking, P-3 Orion, SH-2F LAMPS I, and SH-60B Seahawk LAMPS III all launch and monitor sonobuoys, as does the SH-3H variant of the Sea King. Five types of ASW sonobuoys are now in production:

- SSQ-36 thermal recording buoy
- SSQ-41 Jezebel OMNI (Omni-directional)
- SSQ-53 DIFAR (Directional Finding And Ranging)
- SSQ-62 DICASS (Directional Command Active Sonobuoy System)
- SSQ-77 VLAD (Vertical Line Array DIFAR).

The older SSQ-50 and SSQ-57 are also in service.

Sonobuoys are used in a complementary manner. Of the newer ones, the SSQ-41 passive, omnidirectional buoys are laid in patterns to obtain initial, large-area target data. (The -41A has a frequency range of 10 to 6,000 Hz while the -41B range is 10 to 20,000 Hz.)

The SSQ-57 is also used passively for initial detection, after which the SSQ-53 DIFAR is employed to use active echo ranging to determine a target's exact bearing. Several specialized buoys are also in use. The SSQ-36 provides data on thermal conditions from the surface down to 1,000 feet to assist the aircraft processor in analyzing the buoy data being transmitted to the ASW aircraft or helicopter, while the SSQ-71 is a two-way acoustic communications buoy launched by aircraft.

The current sonobuoys operate to relatively shallow depths. For example, the SSQ-53A operates at depths of 90 to 1,000 feet. However, there are much deeper sound channels that could be exploited for submarine detection, and new sonobuoys are intended to make use of long-range sound propagation in the deep ocean. The SSQ-77, now in production, is a deep-searching sonobuoy with a long-line array, as is the SSQ-79 Steered Vertical Line Array (SVLA). The -77 has a frequency range of 10 to 2,400 Hz. Also in the offing is the SSQ-75 Expendable Reliable Acoustic Path Sonobuoy (ERAPS), which will actively seek very quiet submarines.

All current sonobuoys are of a standard "A"-size that fits launch chutes on board ASW aircraft—36 inches in length and 4⅞ inches in diameter.

The SSQ-75, however, will be larger and will probably be carried as an external store. But, at the same time, efforts are being made to reduce sonobuoy size with dwarf "B" versions of the SSQ-53/77/79 being developed that will permit three sonobuoys to be carried in a standard "A"-size launcher.

A pair of Mk 70 Mobile Submarine Simulator (MOSS) decoys are loaded on board a submarine. (U.S. Navy)

Designation	Purpose	Manufacturer	Production start	Weight	Hydrophone depth
SSQ-36	bathythermograph (water temperature profile)	Sparton			none
SQQ-41A	omnidirectional passive detection	Hermes, Magnavox, Sparton	1964	15.7 pounds	60 or 300 feet
SQQ-41B			1975	16.6 pounds	60 or 1,000 feet
SQQ-47A/B	active explosive echo ranging		1965	23 pounds	60 or 800 feet
SQQ-50/A CASS	Command Active Sonobuoy System		1969	38 pounds	60 or 1,500 feet
SQQ-53 DIFAR	passive directional	Magnavox, Sparton	1967	18.4 pounds	90 feet
SQQ-53A			1974	22.5 pounds	90 or 1,000 feet
SQQ-57	passive in restricted waters	Hermes, Sparton			
SQQ-62 DI-CASS	Directional Command Active Sonobuoy System	Raytheon	1978	39 pounds	60 or 1,500 feet
				27 pounds	1,000 feet
SQQ-77 VLAD	passive vertical Line Array DIFAR	Sparton			none
SQQ-86	communications link buoy				

An SH-3D Sea King ASW helicopter lowering an AQS-13 dipping sonar (U.S. Navy)

Sailors load sonobuoys into the dispenser of P-3 Orion ASW aircraft. Sonobuoys are carried by fixed-wing ASW aircraft and helicopters. Retardation fins ("rotor-chute"), shown folded here, extend in flight to slow the descent of sonobuoys; upon entering the water the hydrophone is released and descends to a prede-termined depth, connected by wire to the floating buoy that then transmits signals to the aircraft. (U.S. Navy)

Sonobuoys being loaded into a helicopter. (U.S. Navy)

A   Coast Guard

The U.S. Coast Guard is a separate military service under the Department of Transportation. The service is responsible for the enforcement of U.S. laws in coastal waters and on the high seas subject to the jurisdiction of the United States.

At the direction of the President, the Coast Guard can become a part of the Navy (as during both World Wars) or it can operate in a war zone while remaining an independent service (as during the Korean and Vietnam Wars).

The Coast Guard was established on 4 August 1790 as the Revenue Marine of the Department of the Treasury. Subsequently, it became the Revenue Cutter Service and, from 1915, the Coast Guard. The service incorporated the Lighthouse Service in 1939. The Coast Guard was transferred from the Treasury Department to the newly established Department of Transportation in 1967.

OPERATIONS

The principal peacetime missions of the Coast Guard are: (1) recreational boating safety; (2) search and rescue; (3) aids to navigation (maintaining almost 400 lighthouses and some 13,000 minor navigational lights); (4) merchant marine safety; (5) environmental protection; (6) port safety; and (7) enforcement of laws and treaties.

The last mission comprises the enforcement of the nation's customs and immigration laws, including the prevention of smuggling and narcotics, and also the enforcement of fisheries laws, including international treaties related to the 200-mile national economic zone. This mission in particular, aggravated by the mass exodus of Cubans in May–June 1980, has created major operational problems for the Coast Guard.

VESSELS

The Coast Guard uses the term *vessels* for all watercraft operated by the service. Within that classification, the term *cutter* is used for ships that have "an assigned personnel allowance and that [have] installed habitability features for the extended support of a permanently assigned crew." In practice, this includes 65-foot tugs and larger vessels, except ferries. Cutters are generally identified by their length.

All smaller Coast Guard vessels are referred to as *boats*, including barges, yachts, and ferryboats.

The Coast Guard vessel designation scheme is derived from that of the U.S. Navy (see Chapter 9). All Coast Guard designations are prefixed by the letter W (*unofficially* for White-painted ships). The larger cutters are numbered in a single, sequential series that was initiated in 1941–1942. Cutters less than 100 feet in length and boats have hull numbers with the first two digits indicating the vessel's length overall.

The cutter designations currently in use for oceangoing vessels and other major types are:

WAGB	Icebreaker
WAGO	Oceanographic cutter
WHEC	High Endurance Cutter (multi-mission; 30 to 45 days at sea without support)
WIX	Training cutter
WLB	Offshore buoy tender (full sea-keeping capability; medium endurance)
WLI	Inshore buoy tender (short endurance)
WLIC	Inland construction tender (short endurance)
WLM	Coastal buoy tender (medium endurance)
WLR	River buoy tender (short endurance)
WLV	Light Vessel
WMEC	Medium Endurance Cutter (multi-mission; 10 to 30 days at sea without support)
WPB	Patrol Boat (multi-mission; 1 to 7 days at sea without support)
WSES	Surface Effect Ship

The Coast Guard uses the term *icebreaker* for a variety of vessels with the following categories:

Type A	GLACIER	(WAGB 4)
Type B	MACKINAW (WAGB 83) and Wind class (WAGB 281)	
Type C	Bay class (WTGB 140)	
Type D	medium harbor tugs (WYTM)	
Type E	small harbor tugs (WYTL)	
Type P	Polar (WAGB 10) class	

Cutter names are prefixed by USCGC for U.S. Coast Guard Cutter.

The Coast Guard also operates several hundred small lifeboats and patrol boats. These are mostly 44-, 40-, 30-, and 22-foot unnamed craft.

Most cutters are painted white, with the larger icebreakers painted red and buoy tenders and habor tugs painted black (superstructures remain white).

The Coast Guard insignia, a narrow blue and wide orange stripe with the Coast Guard shield superimposed on the latter, is carried on the bows of all vessels except lightships.

The Coast Guard cutter RUSH (WMEC 723) maneuvers with a carrier battle group during exercises in the North Pacific in April 1983. There are increasing efforts to integrate the Coast Guard into peacetime naval operations, while at the same time naval forces are helping the Coast Guard's efforts to halt drug smuggling into the United States. On the horizon are the aircraft carriers ENTERPRISE (CVN 65), MIDWAY (CV 41), and CORAL SEA (CV 43). (U.S. Navy)

Type	Class/Ship	Length	Active	Building	Reserve	Commissioned	Notes
WHEC 715	HAMILTON	378	12	—	—	1967–1972	to be modernized
WHEC 41	OWASCO	254	—	—	5	1945–1946	
WHEC 379	UNIMAK	311	1	—	—	1943	ex-Navy AVP
WHEC 31	Secretary	327	4	—	—	1936–1937	
WMEC 901	BEAR	270	5	8	—	1983	
WMEC 615	RELIANCE	210	16	—	—	1964–1969	
WMEC 6	ESCAPE	213	3	—	—	1943–1944	ex-Navy ARS
WMEC 76	UTE	205	5	—	—	1940–1945	ex-Navy ATF
WMEC 38	STORIS	230	1	—	—	1942	ex-WAGB type
WMEC 62	BALSAM	180	3	—	—	1942–1945	ex-WLB type
WSES 2	Sea Bird	150	3	—	—	1982–1983	surface effect ships
WPB	Cape	95	25	—	—	1953–1959	
WPB	Point	82	53	—	—	1960–1970	
WAGB	Polar	399	2	—	—	1976–1978	
WAGB 4	GLACIER	310	1	—	—	1955	ex-Navy AGB
WAGB 281	Wind	269	2	—	—	1943–1945	ex-Navy AGB
WAGB 83	MACKINAW	290	1	—	—	1944	
WIX 327	EAGLE	295	1	—	—	1936	training bark
WLB 62	BALSAM	180	30	—	—	1942–1945	being modernized
WLM	coastal buoy tenders		13	—	—		
WLI	inland buoy tenders		6	—	—		
WLIC	inland construction tenders		18	—	—		
WLR	river buoy tenders		18	—	—		
WTGB	harbor icebreakers		9	—	—		ex-WYTM type
WYTM	medium harbor tugs		8	—	—		
WYTL	small harbor tugs		14	—	—		

AVIATION

The Coast Guard air arm operates 166 aircraft based at 27 air stations in the continental United States, Hawaii, Alaska, and Puerto Rico. In addition, the service's HAMILTON (WHEC 715) and BEAR (WMEC 901) classes and icebreakers regularly operate helicopters, while some of the other cutter classes have landing decks but cannot support helicopters.

Coast Guard aviators are Navy trained, with specialized training being given at the Coast Guard Aviation Training Center in Mobile, Ala.

Two major aircraft procurement programs are under way: 41 HU-25A Guardian Medium-Range Search (MRS) aircraft are being acquired to replace the HU-16 Albatross amphibian and HC-131 Samaritan, and 90 HH-65A Dolphin Short-Range Recovery (SRR) helicopters are being acquired to replace the HH-52A Sea Guard helicopters. Both of the new aircraft are of French design and are not being flown by any other U.S. military service. (See Chapter 29 for details of aircraft.) The Coast Guard's HH-52A was also unique to the service, but historically most Coast Guard aircraft have been of the same type as flown by the Navy. Additional HC-130H Hercules will replace earlier "Herkes."

Cutters of the BEAR class are intended to operate Navy SH-2F LAMPS I helicopter in wartime, although the availability of those helicopters and of cutters to support them is questionable. The larger HAMILTON-class cutters are also to be modified to support the SH-2F.

The following table lists the aircraft currently in Coast Guard service with the numbers in parentheses indicating aircraft in reserve or storage. No aircraft are flown by the Coast Guard Reserve.

Number	Type	Mission
1	VC-4A Gulfstream I	executive transport
1	VC-11A Gulfstream II	executive transport
4 (3)	HC-130B Hercules	Long-Range Search (LRS)
1	HC-130E Hercules	Long-Range Search (LRS)
18	HC-130H Hercules	Long-Range Search (LRS)
33	HU-25A Guardian	Medium-Range Search (MRS)
37 (3)	HH-3F Pelican	Medium-Range Recovery (MRR)
71	HH-52A Sea Guard	Short-Range Recovery (SRR)

PERSONNEL

Uniformed Coast Guard personnel operate all cutters and boats as well as aircraft. Medical personnel are provided by the U.S. Public Health Service on assignment to the Coast Guard.

Active duty Coast Guard strength in the fall of 1984 was 4,597 officers, 1,389 warrant officers, and 26,425 enlisted men and women.

Coast Guard strength has thus declined since 1980, when there were approximately 4,800 officers, 1,400 warrants, and 32,000 enlisted men and women on active duty. During that period the number of cutters in service has increased while the number of aircraft has remained essentially the same.

In addition, the Coast Guard has 12,000 selected reservists who attend periodic drills as well as summer active duty training, and 6,000 non-drilling ready reserves.

As of early 1983 the Coast Guard had approximately 130 women officers (with 35 assigned to cutters) and 1,750 enlisted women (with 85 assigned to cutters). Women have served in Coast Guard cutters since the fall of 1977 when the GALLANTIN (WHEC 721) and MORGENTHAU (WHEC 722) each embarked two female officers and ten enlisted women. These were the first U.S. combat ships to have female crew members permanently assigned. Subsequently, women were assigned to other cutters and since 1979 they have commanded Cape-class patrol boats.

Coast Guard personnel have Navy-style ranks with the Commandant having the rank of full admiral with the Deputy Commandant being a vice admiral.

To most Americans small patrol craft seen on inland and coastal waters—such as this 41-footer—symbolize the Coast Guard. However, the service is in many respects the most versatile of the U.S. military services, in peacetime as well as in war. (1983, Giorgio Arra)

12 HIGH ENDURANCE CUTTERS: "HAMILTON" CLASS

Number	Name	Builder	Laid down	Launched	Commissioned	Status
WHEC 715	HAMILTON	Avondale Shipyards, New Orleans, La.	4 Jan 1965	18 Dec 1965	20 Feb 1967	**AA**
WHEC 716	DALLAS	Avondale Shipyards, New Orleans, La.	7 Feb 1966	1 Oct 1966	1 Oct 1967	**AA**
WHEC 717	MELLON	Avondale Shipyards, New Orleans, La.	25 July 1966	11 Feb 1967	22 Dec 1967	**PA**
WHEC 718	CHASE	Avondale Shipyards, New Orleans, La.	15 Oct 1966	20 May 1967	1 Mar 1968	**AA**
WHEC 719	BOUTWELL	Avondale Shipyards, New Orleans, La.	12 Dec 1966	17 June 1967	14 June 1968	**PA**
WHEC 720	SHERMAN	Avondale Shipyards, New Orleans, La.	13 Feb 1967	23 Sep 1967	23 Aug 1968	**PA**
WHEC 721	GALLANTIN	Avondale Shipyards, New Orleans, La.	17 Apr 1967	18 Nov 1967	20 Dec 1968	**AA**
WHEC 722	MORGENTHAU	Avondale Shipyards, New Orleans, La.	17 July 1967	10 Feb 1968	14 Feb 1969	**PA**
WHEC 723	RUSH	Avondale Shipyards, New Orleans, La.	23 Oct 1967	16 Nov 1968	3 July 1969	**PA**
WHEC 724	MUNRO	Avondale Shipyards, New Orleans, La.	18 Feb 1970	5 Dec 1970	10 Sep 1971	**PA**
WHEC 725	JARVIS	Avondale Shipyards, New Orleans, La.	9 Sep 1970	24 Apr 1971	30 Dec 1971	**PA**
WHEC 726	MIDGETT	Avondale Shipyards, New Orleans, La.	5 Apr 1971	4 Sep 1971	17 Mar 1972	**PA**

Displacement:	2,716 tons standard
	3,050 tons full load
Length:	350 feet (106.7 m) wl
	378 feet (115.2 m) oa
Beam:	42¾ feet (13.0 m)
Draft:	20 feet (6.1 m)
Propulsion:	CODOG: 2 gas turbines (Pratt & Whitney), 28,000 shp; 2 diesels (Fairbanks Morse), 7,200 shp; 2 shafts
Speed:	29 knots
Range:	14,000 n.miles at 11 knots; 2,400 n.miles at 29 knots
Manning:	148–165 (13–16 officers + 132–151 enlisted)
Helicopters:	1 HH-3F Pelican or HH-52A Sea Guard can be embarked (see notes)
Guns:	1 5-inch (127-mm) 38-cal DP Mk 30
	2 40-mm Mk 19 (2 single)
	2 20-mm Mk 67 (2 single)
ASW weapons:	6 12.75-inch (324-mm) torpedo tubes Mk 32 (2 triple)
Radar:	SPS-29D air search
	2 SPS-64(V)6 surface search
Sonars:	SQS-38 keel-mounted
Fire control:	1 Mk 1 target designation system
	1 Mk 56 gun FCS
	1 Mk 309 torpedo control panel
	1 Mk 35 radar

The propulsion machinery is CODOG (Combination Diesel Or Gas turbine). A 350-hp bow propeller pod is fitted.

Modernization: All of these cutters are scheduled to be updated under a Fleet Rehabilitation and Modernization (FRAM) program. The principal changes will be:

5-inch/38-cal DP gun	replaced by 76-mm OTO Melara Mk 76
Mk 56 GFCS	replaced by Mk 92 FCS
SPS-29 air search radar	replaced by SPS-40 air search radar
flight deck	upgraded to accommodate SH-2F LAMPS I
communications	upgrade
—	installation of SQR-4 and SQR-17 sonobuoy receiving set
—	installation of helicopter landing aids

Names: The first nine ships of this class were named for Secretaries of the Treasury; the last three ships honor Coast Guard heroes.

These are the largest cutters in Coast Guard service except for the Polar-class icebreakers.

Anti-submarine: As completed, the earlier ships of this class were fitted with two ahead-firing hedgehogs. They have been removed.

Class: Originally 36 ships of this class were proposed. Planning for additional ships was deferred in favor of retaining older cutters and then was dropped with construction of the smaller BEAR-class cutters.

Design: The superstructures of these ships are fabricated largely of aluminum. They are fitted with oceanographic and meteorological facilities.

The helicopter hangars are used as balloon shelters.

Electronics: The original keel-mounted SQS-36 sonar has been replaced by the SQS-38, a hull-mounted version of the SQS-35 variable-depth sonar.

Engineering: These were the largest U.S. combat ships to have gas-turbine propulsion until completion of the SPRUANCE (DD 963) in 1975. The gas turbines are FT-4A, marine versions of the J75 aircraft engine.

MIDGETT (1983, Giorgio Arra)

The Munro is about to take aboard a Navy SH-2F LAMPS helicopter during operations in the Sea of Japan following the downing of a Korean airliner by Soviet fighter aircraft. These cutters have helicopter platforms, but their hangars are suitable only for supporting weather balloons. (1983, U.S. Navy)

The Mellon and the other cutters of this class are scheduled to be modernized; while their combat potential will be improved, some critics feel that retention of the 5-inch/38-cal gun would provide more capability than the planned 76-mm OTO Melara weapon. (1983, Giorgio Arra)

5 HIGH ENDURANCE CUTTERS: "OWASCO" CLASS

Number	Name	Builder	Laid down	Launched	Commissioned	Status
WHEC 41	CHAUTAUQUA	Western Pipe & Steel, San Pedro, Calif.	22 Dec 1943	14 May 1944	4 Aug 1945	CGR
WHEC 65	WINONA	Western Pipe & Steel, San Pedro, Calif.	8 Nov 1944	22 Apr 1945	15 Aug 1946	CGR
WHEC 67	MINNETONKA	Western Pipe & Steel, San Pedro, Calif.	26 Dec 1944	21 Nov 1945	20 Sep 1946	CGR
WHEC 69	MENDOTA	Coast Guard Yard, Curtis Bay, Md.	1 June 1943	29 Feb 1944	2 June 1946	CGR
WHEC 70	PONTCHARTRAIN	Coast Guard Yard, Curtis Bay, Md.	1 July 1943	29 Apr 1944	28 July 1945	CGR

Displacement:	1,563 tons standard
	1,913 tons full load
Length:	254 feet (77.4 m) oa
Beam:	43 feet (13.1 m)
Draft:	17 feet (5.2 m)
Propulsion:	turbo-electric (Westinghouse turbines); 4,000 shp; 2 shafts
Boilers:	2 (Foster Wheeler)
Speed:	18.4 knots
Range:	12,000 n.miles at 10 knots; 6,000 n.miles at 18.4 knots
Manning:	139 (13 officers + 126 enlisted)
Helicopter.	no facilities
Guns:	1 5-inch (127-mm) 38-cal DP Mk 30
ASW weapons:	removed
Radar:	1 SPS-29D
	1 SPS-62(V)1
Fire control:	1 Mk 52 gun FCS
	1 Mk 26 radar

These are relatively short, beamy ships, built as heavily armed "gunboats" for ocean escort.

The CHAUTAUQUA, MENDOTA, and PONTCHARTRAIN were decommissioned in 1973, and the WINONA and MINNETONKA in 1974. They were to be stricken but were instead laid up in reserve. The WINONA and MINNETONKA are at Alameda, Calif., the others at Curtis Bay, Md.

Armament: As built these cutters were to mount four 5-inch guns in twin mounts, eight 40-mm AA guns in quad mounts, and four 20-mm AA guns plus depth charge racks. Some of the ships completed after the war were never fitted with full armament. The two-island superstructure was intended to permit a floatplane to be stowed amidships; however, none is believed to have carried an aircraft.

Class: There were originally 13 ships in this class, WPG 39–44 and WPG 64–70.

Classification: All were completed as gunboats (WPG); all 13 were changed to high endurance cutters (WHEC) on 1 May 1966.

Names: Names changed during construction were WHEC 67 ex-SUNAPEE and WHEC 70 ex-OKEECHOBEE.

MINNETONKA (1970, U.S. Coast Guard)

The CHAUTAUQUA with a hedgehog in the B position forward of the bridge. (1968, U.S. Coast Guard)

1 HIGH ENDURANCE CUTTER: "CASCO" CLASS

Number	Name	Builder	Laid down	Launched	AVP Comm.	USCG Comm.	Status
WHEC 379 (ex-AVP 31)	UNIMAK	Associated Shipbuilders, Seattle, Wash.	15 Feb 1942	27 May 1942	31 Dec 1943	14 Dec 1948	**AA**

Displacement:	1,766 tons standard
	2,800 tons full load
Length:	300 feet (91.4 m) wl
	310¾ feet (94.7 m) oa
Beam:	41 feet (12.5 m)
Draft:	13½ feet (4.1 m)
Propulsion:	diesels (Fairbanks Morse); 6,080 shp; 2 shafts
Speed:	18 knots
Range:	20,000 n.miles at 10 knots
Manning:	132 (12 officers + 120 enlisted)
Helicopters:	no facilities
Guns:	1 5-inch (127-mm) 38-cal DP Mk 30 (1 × 1)
	2 40-mm machine gun Mk 19 (2 single)
ASW weapons:	removed
Radar:	2 SPS-64(V)1/6
Fire control:	removed

The UNIMAK is the only survivor in U.S. service of 34 BARNEGAT (AVP 10)-class seaplane tenders built during World War II (four were completed as torpedo-boat tenders and one as an amphibious force flagship). The UNIMAK and 17 sister ships were transferred to the Coast Guard in 1946–1948 (WAVP/WHEC 370–387). She operated as a training cutter (WTR) from 1956 until her decommissioning in May 1974. The ship had been scheduled for transfer to South Vietnam (as had other ships of this class), but with the fall of the Saigon government she was laid up in reserve; she was recommissioned as a WHEC in August 1977 to support the 200-mile U.S. offshore resource zone.

Armament: The UNIMAK has carried a variety of armament during her Navy and Coast Guard service. An ASW hedgehog and two Mk 32 triple tubes had been removed prior to her decommissioning in 1974.

Class: Ships of this class continue to serve in the navies of Ethiopia, the Philippines, and Vietnam.

Classification: The ship was built as the Navy AVP 31. Her classification was changed to WAVP 31 upon transfer to the Coast Guard and to WHEC 379 on 1 May 1966. Subsequently, she was changed to WTR 379 on 28 November 1969 but was recommissioned in 1977 as WHEC.

Names: CASCO was the Coast Guard class name.

The UNIMAK and the Navy's NORTON SOUND (AVM 1) are the last seaplane tenders in U.S. service. Note the weather balloon hangar aft; the cluttered fantail is not suitable for helicopter operations. The hedgehog shown in the B position in front of the bridge has been deleted. (1970, U.S. Coast Guard)

4 HIGH ENDURANCE CUTTERS: "SECRETARY" CLASS

Number	Name	Builder	Laid down	Launched	Commissioned	Status
WHEC 31	BIBB	Charleston Navy Yard	15 Aug 1935	14 Jan 1937	19 Mar 1937	**AA**
WHEC 33	DUANE	Philadelphia Navy Yard	1 May 1935	3 June 1936	16 Oct 1936	**AA**
WHEC 34	INGHAM	Philadelphia Navy Yard	1 May 1935	3 June 1936	6 Nov 1936	**AA**
WHEC 37	TANEY	Philadelphia Navy Yard	1 May 1935	3 June 1936	24 Oct 1936	**AA**

Displacement:	2,216 tons standard
	2,656 tons full load
Length:	308 feet (93.9 m) wl
	327 feet (99.7 m) oa
Beam:	41 feet (12.5 m)
Draft:	15 feet (4.6 m)
Propulsion:	steam turbines (Westinghouse); 6,200 shp; 2 shafts
Boilers:	2 (Babcock & Wilcox)
Speed:	19.8 knots
Range:	8,000 n.miles at 10.5 knots; 4,000 n.miles at 19.8 knots
Manning:	124–136 (13–15 officers + 110–121 enlisted)
Helicopters:	no facilities
Guns:	1 5-inch (127-mm) 38-cal DP Mk 30
	2 40-mm machine guns Mk 19 (2 single)
ASW weapons:	removed
Radar:	2 SPS-64(V)1/6
Fire control:	removed

These are large cruising cutters, the largest ships in Coast Guard service prior to the HAMILTON class. The DUANE and INGHAM were built in the same dry dock at the Philadelphia Navy Yard.

Armament: These ships carried a variety of armament during their long service lives. During early World War II their main battery was three 5-inch/51-cal guns. Into the 1960s they carried an ASW armament of one hedgehog and two Mk 32 triple torpedo tubes.

Class: Seven ships of this class were built; one ship, the ALEXANDER HAMILTON (WPG 34), was sunk by a German submarine in 1942. Three additional ships were authorized, but their construction was deferred in 1941 in favor of the OWASCO (WPG 39) class.

The SPENCER (WPG/WHEC 36) served as a stationary steam-propulsion training ship at the Coast Guard Yard, Curtis Bay, Md., from 23 January 1974 until decommissioned on 15 December 1980; she was sold/stricken the following year. CAMPBELL (WHEC 32) was stricken on 1 April 1982.

Classification: Early in World War II these ships were classified as gunboats (WPG 31–37). In 1944–1945 six ships were reclassified as amphibious force flagships and carried an AGC prefix with their Coast Guard hull numbers, except that the DUANE was changed to AGC 6 in the Navy designation sequence. All were retained on the Coast Guard roles and were not transferred to the Navy.

After the war all reverted to their WPG classifications. All were changed to high endurance cutters (WHEC) on 1 May 1968.

Names: These ships were named for Secretaries of the Treasury. Originally full names were used, but in 1942 they were shortened to surnames only; these ships were formerly GEORGE M. BIBB, GEORGE W. CAMPBELL, WILLIAM J. DUANE, SAMUEL D. INGHAM, JOHN C. SPENCER, and ROGER B. TANEY.

INGHAM (1980, Robert L. Scheina)

The BIBB underway, showing the graceful if dated lines of this class. An SPS-29 radar was previously mounted on the tripod mast in most of this class; an SPS-64 navigation-search radar is carried forward. (1983, Giorgio Arra)

5 + 8 MEDIUM ENDURANCE CUTTERS: "BEAR" CLASS

Number	Name	Builder	Laid down	Launched	Commissioned	Status
WMEC 901	BEAR	Tacoma Boatbuilding, Tacoma, Wash.	23 Aug 1979	25 Sep 1980	4 Feb 1983	**AA**
WMEC 902	TAMPA	Tacoma Boatbuilding, Tacoma, Wash.	3 Apr 1980	19 Mar 1981	16 Mar 1984	**PA**
WMEC 903	HARRIET LANE	Tacoma Boatbuilding, Tacoma, Wash.	15 Oct 1980	6 Feb 1982	1984	**PA**
WMEC 904	NORTHLAND	Tacoma Boatbuilding, Tacoma, Wash.	9 Apr 1981	7 May 1982	1985	Building
WMEC 905	SPENCER (ex-SENECA)	Robert E. Derecktor, Middletown, R.I.	26 June 1982		1985	Building
WMEC 906	SENECA (ex-ESCANABA)	Robert E. Derecktor, Middletown, R.I.	16 Sep 1982		1985	Building
WMEC 907	ESCANABA (ex-TAHOMA)	Robert E. Derecktor, Middletown, R.I.	1 Apr 1983		1985	Building
WMEC 908	TAHOMA (ex-SPENCER)	Robert E. Derecktor, Middletown, R.I.	28 June 1983		1986	Building
WMEC 909	...... (ex-ARGUS)	Robert E. Derecktor, Middletown, R.I.			1986	Building
WMEC 910	...... (ex-TAHOMA)	Robert E. Derecktor, Middletown, R.I.			1986	Building
WMEC 911	...... (ex-ERIE)	Robert E. Derecktor, Middletown, R.I.			1987	Building
WMEC 912	...... (ex-McCULLOCH)	Robert E. Derecktor, Middletown, R.I.			1987	Building
WMEC 913	...... (ex-EWING)	Robert E. Derecktor, Middletown, R.I.			1987	Building

Displacement:	1,820 tons full load
Length:	255 feet (77.8 m) oa
	270 feet (82.3 m) oa
Beam:	38 feet (11.6 m)
Draft:	13¾ feet (4.2 m)
Propulsion:	2 diesels; 7,000 bhp; 2 shafts
Speed:	19.5 knots
Range:	3,850 n.miles at 19.5 knots
	6,370 n.miles at 15 knots
	10,250 n.miles at 12 knots
Manning:	99 (11 officers + 88 enlisted)
Helicopters:	1 HH-3 or HH-52 or HH-65
Guns:	1 76-mm/62-cal AA Mk 75
ASW weapons:	none
Torpedoes:	none
Radars:	2 SPS-64(V)1/6
Sonars:	none
Fire control:	Mk 92 weapons control system

These are multi-purpose cutters. However, they lack ASW weapons and sensors for employment in traditional Coast Guard wartime combat missions without extensive modification. They have also been criticized for their slow speed.

Thirteen ships are currently planned. The first four were ordered from Tacoma Boatbuilding with the remainder planned for procurement from the Tacoma yard; however, the Coast Guard was forced in competitive bidding to order the remainder from a yard in Rhode Island operated by Robert E. Derecktor.

The BEAR was not delivered to the Coast Guard until late in 1983.

Aircraft: A helicopter hangar and landing deck are provided; the ships can handle any of the Coast Guard's helicopters as well as the Navy's SH-2F LAMPS I.

Class: The lead ship was authorized in fiscal 1976, WMEC 902–904 in fiscal 1977, and WMEC 905–913 in fiscal 1980. The class is officially known as the Famous class, but generally referred to as the BEAR class.

Costs: The estimated cost per ship is $65 million (fiscal 1982).

Design: Design criteria for this class included 14-day law enforcement patrols in areas out to 400 miles from base. Active fin stabilizers are fitted.

The SLQ-32(V)2 EW system is fitted in these ships, the first Coast Guard cutters to be completed with a contemporary EW suite since World War II. These ships are designed to be fitted with the following military systems in wartime: SH-2F LAMPS I anti-submarine helicopter, two Harpoon anti-ship quad missile launchers, one 20-mm Phalanx CIWS, Tactical Towed Array Sonar (TACTAS), and chaff launchers. The ships seem unlikely, however, to accommodate simultaneously all or even most of these systems, in part because of the number of additional personnel required as well as the probable lack of available systems during a conflict.

Accommodations are provided for 109 personnel.

Names: The Coast Guard initially named all 13 ships of the class. Subsequently, these prematurely awarded names for WMEC 905 and later ships were withdrawn and those cutters were renamed, as indicated above.

The BEAR with helicopter hangar extended. (1983, U.S. Coast Guard)

BEAR (1983, U.S. Coast Guard)

The BEAR underway; note the foreshortened forecastle; the 76-mm OTO Melara gun and associated Mk 92 GFCS; and satellite antennas forward of the mast and at the after end of the hangar. (1983, U.S. Coast Guard)

The BEAR with her helicopter hangar retracted; the hangar extends along the tracks visible on the helicopter deck. SLQ-32(V)2 EW antennas are visible behind the bridge. (1983, U.S. Coast Guard)

16 MEDIUM ENDURANCE CUTTERS: "RELIANCE" CLASS

Number	Name	Launched	Commissioned	Status
WMEC 615	RELIANCE	25 May 1963	20 June 1964	AA
WMEC 616	DILIGENCE	20 July 1963	26 Aug 1964	AA
WMEC 617	VIGILANT	24 Dec 1963	3 Oct 1964	AA
WMEC 618	ACTIVE	21 July 1965	17 Sep 1966	AA
WMEC 619	CONFIDENCE	8 May 1965	19 Feb 1966	PA
WMEC 620	RESOLUTE	30 Apr 1966	8 Dec 1966	PA
WMEC 621	VALIANT	14 Jan 1967	28 Oct 1967	AA
WMEC 622	COURAGEOUS	18 Mar 1967	19 Apr 1968	AA
WMEC 623	STEADFAST	24 June 1967	25 Sep 1968	AA
WMEC 624	DAUNTLESS	21 Oct 1967	10 June 1968	AA
WMEC 625	VENTUROUS	11 Nov 1967	16 Aug 1968	PA
WMEC 626	DEPENDABLE	16 Mar 1968	22 Nov 1968	AA
WMEC 627	VIGOROUS	4 May 1968	2 May 1969	AA
WMEC 628	DURABLE	29 Apr 1967	8 Dec 1967	AA
WMEC 629	DECISIVE	14 Dec 1967	23 Aug 1968	AA
WMEC 630	ALERT	19 Oct 1968	4 Aug 1969	AA

Builders:	WMEC 615–617	Todd Shipyards, Houston, Texas
	WMEC 618	Christy Corp, Sturgeon Bay, Wisc.
	WMEC 619, 625, 628–629	Coast Guard Yard, Curtis Bay, Md.
	WMEC 620–624, 626–627, 630	American Shipbuilding, Lorain, Ohio
Displacement:	950 tons standard	
	1,007 tons full load except WMEC 616–619 970 tons	
Length:	210½ feet (64.2 m) oa	
Beam:	34 feet (10.4 m)	
Draft:	10½ feet (3.2 m)	
Propulsion:	2 turbo-charged diesels (Alco); 5,000 shp; WMEC 615–619 additionally have 2 gas turbines (see notes); 4,000 shp; 2 shafts	
Speed:	18 knots	
Range:	6,100 n.miles at 14 knots (WMEC 615–619 at 13 knots); 2,700 n.miles at 18 knots (WMEC 615–619 2,100 n.miles)	
Manning:	64–76 (8–10 officers + 54–66 enlisted)	
Helicopters:	none assigned	
Guns:	1 3-inch (76-mm) 50-cal Mk 22	
	2 40-mm machine guns Mk 19 (2 single)	
ASW weapons:	none	
Radars:	2 SPS-64(V)1	

These are search-and-rescue ships. They can land helicopters but have no hangar.

Classification: These ships were originally classified as patrol craft (WPC); changed to WMEC with same hull numbers on 1 May 1966. The RELIANCE was changed to WTR on 27 June 1975 (the TR indicating Training of Reserves); she reverted to WMEC on 16 August 1982.

Design: The RELIANCE design has a small island superstructure with 360° visibility from the bridge to facilitate helicopter operations and towing. The ALERT was fitted with the Canadian-developed "Beartrap" helicopter hauldown system.

Engineering: The first five cutters were built with CODAG (Combination Diesel And Gas turbine) plants to provide experience in operating mixed propulsion plants. Those cutters have a high acceleration rate from all stop, or with their engines shut down can be at full speed in a few minutes; they can make 15.25 knots on gas turbines alone. The cost factor influenced the decision to make the remaining ships all-diesel.

VALIANT (1982, Giorgio Arra)

DILIGENCE with HH-52A Sea Guard coming aboard off the New England coast. (1979, U.S. Coast Guard)

3 MEDIUM ENDURANCE CUTTERS: FORMER SALVAGE SHIPS

Number	Name	Launched	Navy ARS Comm.	Status
WMEC 6 (ex-ARS 6)	ESCAPE	22 Nov 1943	20 Nov 1943	**AA**
WMEC 167 (ex-ARS 9)	ACUSHNET	1 Apr 1943	5 Feb 1944	**AA**
WMEC 168 (ex-ARS 26)	YOCONA	8 Apr 1944	3 Nov 1944	**PA**

Builders:	Basalt Rock, Napa, Calif.
Displacement:	1,557 tons standard
	1,745 tons full load
Length:	213½ feet (65.1 m) oa
Beam:	39 feet (12.8 m)
Draft:	15 feet (4.9 m)
Propulsion:	diesels; 3,000 shp; 2 shafts
Speed:	15.5 knots
Range:	20,000 n.miles at 7 knots; 9,000 n.miles at 15.5 knots
Manning:	77 (9 officers + 68 enlisted)
Helicopters:	no facilities
Guns:	2 40-mm machine guns Mk 19 (2 single)
Radars:	2 SPS-64

These are former Navy salvage ships; two were permanently transferred to the Coast Guard after World War II and the ESCAPE transferred on loan on 4 December 1980.

Classification: Upon transfer to the Coast Guard, these ships were classified as tugs (WAT 167 and WAT 168, respectively). Changed to WMEC on 1 May 1966, with the ACUSHNET subsequently modified to handle environmental data buoys and changed to oceanographic cutter (WAGO 167) in 1969; she has been redesignated as WMEC in 1978.

Names: Two ships were renamed in Coast Guard service; former Navy names were SHACKLE (ARS 9) and SEIZE (ARS 26). The ex-ARS 6 retains her Navy name.

The ESCAPE, on loan from the Navy to Coast Guard, retains her Navy ARS hull number with her Coast Guard WMEC designation. Two sister ships have higher Coast Guard hull numbers. (U.S. Coast Guard)

5 MEDIUM ENDURANCE CUTTERS: FORMER FLEET TUGS

Number	Name	Launched	Navy ATF Comm.	Status
WMEC 76 (ex-ATF 76)	UTE	24 June 1942	31 Dec 1942	**AA**
WMEC 85 (ex-ATF 85)	LIPAN	17 Sep 1942	29 Apr 1943	**AA**
WMEC 153 (ex-ATF 153)	CHILULA	1 Dec 1944	5 Apr 1945	**AA**
WMEC 165 (ex-ATF 66)	CHEROKEE	10 Nov 1939	26 Apr 1940	**AA**
WMEC 166 (ex-ATF 95)	TAMAROA	13 July 1943	9 Oct 1943	**AA**

Builders:	WMEC 76, 85	United Engineering, Alameda, Calif.
	WMEC 153	Charleston Shipbuilding and Dry Dock, S.C.
	WMEC 165	Bethlehem Steel, Staten Island, N.Y.
	WMEC 166	Commercial Iron Works, Portland, Ore.
Displacement:	1,731 tons full load	
Length:	205 feet (62.5 m) oa	
Beam:	38½ feet (11.7 m)	
Draft:	17 feet (5.2 m)	
Propulsion:	diesel-electric (General Motors diesels); 3,000 shp; 1 shaft	
Speed:	16.2 knots	
Range:	15,000 n.miles at 8 knots; 6,500 n.miles at 16.2 knots	
Manning:	76 (6 officers + 70 enlisted)	
Helicopters:	no facilities	
Guns:	1 3-inch (76-mm) 50-cal AA Mk 22	
	2 40-mm machine guns Mk 19 (2 single)	
Radars:	2 SPS-64	

These are former Navy fleet tugs. Three ships were transferred to the Coast Guard after World War II (ex-ATF 153, 165, 166); the UTE and LIPAN were transferred on loan on 30 September 1980. The two later ships were operated by the Navy's Military Sealift Command with civilian crews at the time of transfer (designated T-ATF).

Classification: These ships were classified ATF by the Navy; upon transfer to the Coast Guard the first three ships became WAT, with two having new hull numbers assigned. All three were changed to WMEC on 1 May 1966.

Names: The TAMAROA was named ZUNI in Navy service. The others retain their Navy names.

LIPAN—with 3-inch gun removed (1981, U.S. Coast Guard)

The Tamaroa is one of several Navy tug-type ships in Coast Guard service as multi-purpose cutters. Again, those on loan retain Navy hull numbers; permanent transfers have Coast Guard numbers. The Coast Guard excellence awards and service ribbons adorn the bridge wings—the letters DC indicating damage control. (1983, Giorgio Arra)

MEDIUM ENDURANCE CUTTERS: FORMER AUXILIARY TUGS

The former Navy tugs Modoc (WMEC 194, ex-ATA 194) and Comanche (WMEC 202, ex-ATA 202) were stricken in 1980 and transferred to the Maritime Administration for disposal. See the 12th edition of *Ships and Aircraft* for details.

1 MEDIUM ENDURANCE CUTTER: "STORIS"

Number	Name	Launched	Commissioned	Status
WMEC 38	Storis	4 Apr 1942	30 Sep 1942	**PA**

Builders:	Toledo Shipbuilding, Ohio
Displacement:	1,715 tons standard
	1,925 tons full load
Length:	230 feet (70.1 m) oa
Beam:	43 feet (13.1 m)
Draft:	15 feet (4.6 m)
Propulsion:	diesel-electric (Cooper Bessemer diesels); 1,800 shp; 2 shafts
Speed:	14 knots
Range:	22,000 n.miles at 8 knots; 12,000 n.miles at 14 knots
Manning:	72 (9 officers + 63 enlisted)
Helicopters:	no facilities
Guns:	1 3-inch (76-mm) 50-cal AA Mk 22
	2 40-mm machine guns Mk 19 (2 single)
Radars:	2 SPS-64

The Storis was built specifically for offshore icebreaking and patrol in the Greenland area. She has been employed in Alaskan service for search, rescue, and law enforcement since 1949.

Classification: The Storis originally was classified WAG 38; she was changed to WAGB 38 on 1 May 1966. Subsequently she was reclassified as a medium endurance cutter (WMEC) on 1 July 1972 to emphasize her role in law enforcement off the Alaskan fishing grounds.

Guns: As built, the Storis carried two 3-inch guns and four 20-mm guns plus ASW weapons.

Names: The ship was initially named the Eskimo, but was changed during construction to Storis.

Storis in Alaskan waters (1979, U.S. Coast Guard)

3 SES CUTTERS: SEA BIRD CLASS

Number	Name	Commissioned	Status
WSES 2	Sea Hawk	16 Oct 1982	**AA**
WSES 3	Shearwater	16 Oct 1982	**AA**
WSES 4	Petrel	June 1983	**AA**

Builders:	Bell Halter, New Orleans, La.
Displacement:	105 tons light
	150 tons full load
Length:	110 feet (33.5 m) oa
Beam:	39 feet (11.9 m)
Draft:	5 feet 6 in (1.7 m) on cushion
	8 feet 3 in (2.5 m) off cushion
Propulsion:	2 diesels (Allison 16V149TI); 3,200 bhp; 2 shafts
Lift:	2 diesels (Allison 8V92TI); 890 bhp; 2 fans
Speed:	33 knots on cushion in sea state 0
	30 knots on cushion in sea state 3
	19 knots off cushion in sea state 0
	15 knots off cushion in sea state 3
Range:	1,000 n.miles on cushion in sea state 3
Manning:	18 (2 officers + 16 enlisted)
Helicopters:	no facilities
Guns:	2 .50-cal machine guns (2 single)
Radars:	2 navigation (Decca 914)
Sonars:	none

All three acquired by the Coast Guard primarily for use in the drug enforcement role. They were obtained after evaluation of a prototype ship, the DORADO (designated WSES-1); she was commissioned in the Coast Guard in 1981 and, after extensive trails, transferred to the Navy. (See Chapter 25.)

Mission endurance is seven days.

SEA HAWK (foreground) and SHEARWATER (U.S. Coast Guard)

SEA HAWK at high speed (U.S. Coast Guard)

SEA HAWK (foreground) and SHEARWATER (Bell Aerospace Textron)

PATROL BOATS

4 + 12 PATROL BOATS: ISLAND CLASS

Number	Name	Number	Name
WPB 1301	FARALLON	WPB 1309	AQUIDNECK
WPB 1302	MANITOU	WPB 1310	MUSTANG
WPB 1303	MATAGORDA	WPB 1311	NAUSHON
WPB 1304	MAUI	WPB 1312	SANIBEL
WPB 1305	MONHEGAN	WPB 1313	EDISTO
WPB 1306	NUNIVAK	WPB 1314	SEPELO
WPB 1307	OCRACOKE	WPB 1315	MATINICUS
WPB 1308	VASHON	WPB 1316	NANTUCKET

Builders:	Bollinger Shipyard, Lockport, La.
Displacement:	
Length:	109 feet (33.24 m)
Beam:	
Draft:	
Propulsion:	diesel; 6,000 bhp; 2 shafts
Speed:	29.5 knots
Range:	
Manning:	16 (2 officers + 14 enlisted)
Guns:	1 20-mm Mk 16
	2 .50-cal machine guns (2 single)
Radars:	SPS-64

The Coast Guard is constructing this class for offshore surveillance and for search and rescue operations. The contract for these boats was originally awarded in May 1984 to the Marine Power and Equipment Co., Seattle, Wash., for 16 boats; however, a U.S. District Court set aside the award because of irregularities in the procurement process. The Bollinger contract was awarded August 1984.

The design is based on an existing patrol boat to minimize cost and risk. The Marine Power boats were to have been a modification of a Korean design. The boats will be steel-hulled with an aluminum deck and superstructure. Under the Bollinger contract of August 1984 the lead boat was to be delivered in July 1985 with the others to follow at 45-day intervals. The FARALLON was delivered on 4 August 1985.

The first four boats are assigned to Patrol Boat Squadron 1 at Miami, Fla. The next four will go to Patrol Boat Squadron 2 at Roosevelt Roads, Puerto Rico.

25 PATROL BOATS: CAPE CLASS

Number	Name	Number	Name
(A Series)		WPB 95313	CAPE MORGAN
WPB 95300	CAPE SMALL	WPB 95314	CAPE FAIRWEATHER
WPB 95302	CAPE HIGGON	WPB 95316	CAPE FOX
WPB 95303	CAPE UPRIGHT	WPB 95317	CAPE JELLISON
WPB 95304	CAPE GULL	WPB 95318	CAPE NEWAGEN
WPB 95305	CAPE HATTERAS	WPB 95319	CAPE ROMAIN
WPB 95306	CAPE GEORGE	WPB 95320	CAPE STARR
WPB 95307	CAPE CURRENT	(C Series)	
WPB 95308	CAPE STRAIT	WPB 95321	CAPE CROSS
WPB 95309	CAPE CARTER	WPB 95322	CAPE HORN
WPB 95310	CAPE WASH	WPB 95324	CAPE SHOALWATER

Number	Name	Number	Name
WPB 95311	CAPE HEDGE	WPB 95326	CAPE CORWIN
(B Series)		WPB 95328	CAPE HENLOPEN
WPB 95312	CAPE KNOX	WPB 95332	CAPE YORK

Builders:	Coast Guard Yard, Curtis Bay, Md.
Displacement:	105 tons full load
Length:	95 feet (29.0 m) oa
Beam:	19 feet (5.8 m)
Draft:	6 feet (1.8 m)
Propulsion:	diesels (Cummins); 2,300 shp; 2 shafts
Speed:	A and B series 20 knots
	C series 21 knots
Range:	A series 2,600 n.miles at 9 knots; 460 n.miles at 20 knots
	B series 3,000 n.miles at 9 knots; 460 n.miles at 20 knots
	C series 2,800 n.miles at 9 knots; 500 n.miles at 21 knots
Manning:	14–17 (1 officer + 13–16 enlisted)
Guns:	removed (see notes)
Radars:	SPS-64(V)1

These are 95-foot cutters employed for port security, search and rescue, and patrol. The A series was constructed in 1953, the B series in 1955–1956, and the C series in 1958–1959. (Nine additional C-series cutters were transferred to South Korea in 1968.)

Plans to discard this class in favor of new construction were dropped and they were modernized instead. All are active.

Class: CAPE CORAL (WPB 95301) stricken on 6 June 1983.

Design: These are steel-hulled cutters. As built, the principal difference in the series was that the last group had less electronic equipment.

Guns: During the 1970s these cutters each carried two .50-cal MG or an 81-mm mortar mounted "piggyback" with a .50-cal MG. Only small arms are now carried.

Modernization: All modernized from 1977 through 1983. They have been fitted with new engines, improved electronics, and modified superstructures; their accommodations also have been upgraded. The designation R series is used in some documents for the modernized boats.

CAPE KNOX (top) and POINT BARNES; these two classes can be distinguished by their superstructures and the first two digits of their hull numbers, which indicate length. (1972, U.S. Coast Guard)

CAPE HORN with awning spread aft and benches for entertaining guests. (1980, Robert L. Scheina)

53 PATROL BOATS: POINT CLASS

Number	Name	Number	Name
(A Series)		WPB 82353	POINT MONROE
WPB 82302	POINT HOPE	WPB 82354	POINT EVANS
WPB 82311	POINT VERDE	WPB 82355	POINT HANNON
WPB 82312	POINT SWIFT	WPB 82356	POINT FRANCIS
WPB 82314	POINT THATCHER	WPB 82357	POINT HURON
(C Series)		WPB 82358	POINT STUART
WPB 82318	POINT HERRON	WPB 82359	POINT STEELE
WPB 82332	POINT ROBERTS	WPB 82360	POINT WINSLOW
WPB 82333	POINT HIGHLAND	WPB 82361	POINT CHARLES
WPB 82334	POINT LEDGE	WPB 82362	POINT BROWN
WPB 82335	POINT COUNTESS	WPB 82363	POINT NOWELL
WPB 82336	POINT GLASS	WPB 82364	POINT WHITEHORN
WPB 82337	POINT DIVIDE	WPB 82365	POINT TURNER
WPB 82338	POINT BRIDGE	WPB 82366	POINT LOBOS
WPB 82339	POINT CHICO	WPB 82367	POINT KNOLL
WPB 82340	POINT BATAN	WPB 82368	POINT WARDE
WPB 82341	POINT LOOKOUT	WPB 82369	POINT HEYER
WPB 82342	POINT BAKER	WPB 82370	POINT RICHMOND
WPB 82343	POINT WELLS	(D Series)	
WPB 82344	POINT ESTERO	WPB 82371	POINT BARNES
WPB 82345	POINT JUDITH	WPB 82372	POINT BROWER
WPB 82346	POINT ARENA	WPB 82373	POINT CAMDEN
WPB 82347	POINT BONITA	WPB 82374	POINT CARREW
WPB 82348	POINT BARROW	WPB 82375	POINT DORAN
WPB 82349	POINT SPENCER	WPB 82376	POINT HARRIS
WPB 82350	POINT FRANKLIN	WPB 82377	POINT HOBART
WPB 82351	POINT BENNETT	WPB 82378	POINT JACKSON
WPB 82352	POINT SAL	WPB 82379	POINT MARTIN

Builders:	Coast Guard Yard, Curtis Bay, Md.
Displacement:	A series 67 tons full load
	C series 66 tons full load
	D series 69 tons full load
Length:	83 feet (25.3 m) oa
Beam:	17⅙ feet (5.2 m)
Draft:	5¾ feet (1.8 m)
Propulsion:	diesel; 1,600 shp; 2 shafts
Speed:	A series 23.5 knots
	C series 23.7 knots
	D series 22.6 knots
Range:	A and C series 1,500 n.miles at 8 knots
	D series 1,200 n.miles at 8 knots
Manning:	8–10 (0–2 officers + 8–10 enlisted)
Guns:	2 .50-cal MG (2 single)
	or 1 81-mm mortar Mk 2/1 .50-cal MG
	removed from some cutters
Radars:	SPS-64(V)1

These are 82-foot cutters used for port security, and search and rescue. The A series was constructed in 1960–1961, the C series in 1961–1967, and D series in 1970. (Twenty-six Point-class cutters were transferred to South Vietnam in 1969–1970.) All Coast Guard units are active.

Design: These are steel-hulled cutters with aluminum superstructures. There are no noticeable differences among the various series of the Point class.

Guns: The mortars and MGs are being replaced by small arms.

Names: The WPB 82301–82344 were assigned geographical point names in January 1964; later cutters were named as built.

POINT HURON with rubber motor launch on after deck. (1983, L. & L. van Ginderen)

POINT BROWER (1983, Giorgio Arra)

ICEBREAKERS

2 ICEBREAKERS: POLAR CLASS

Number	Name	Launched	Commissioned	Status
WAGB 10	POLAR STAR	17 Nov 1973	19 Jan 1976	**PA**
WAGB 11	POLAR SEA	24 June 1975	23 Feb 1978	**PA**

Builders:	Lockheed Shipbuilding, Seattle, Wash.
Displacement:	10,430 tons standard
	13,190 tons full load
Length:	399 feet (121.6 m) oa
Beam:	83½ feet (25.5 m)
Draft:	33½ feet (10.2 m)
Propulsion:	CODOG: 6 diesels (Alco), 18,000 bhp; 3 gas turbines (Pratt & Whitney), 60,000 shp; 3 shafts
Speed:	18 knots
Range:	28,000 n.miles at 13 knots; 16,000 n.miles at 18 knots
Manning:	139 (14 officers + 125 enlisted) + 10 scientists
Helicopters:	2 HH-52A Sea Guard
Guns:	2 40-mm machine guns Mk 19 (2 single)
Radars:	2 SPS-64

These are the largest icebreakers in service outside of the Soviet Union. Several ships were originally planned in this class as replacements for the Wind-class icebreakers. No additional ships are planned, in part because of the higher-than-anticipated costs.

Design: These ships have conventional icebreaker hull forms. A hangar and flight deck are fitted aft and two 15-ton-capacity cranes are abaft the hangar. Arctic and oceanographic laboratories are provided.

Engineering: CODOG (Combination Diesel Or Gas turbine) propulsion is provided, with diesel engines for cruising and rapid-reaction gas turbines available for surge-power requirements. The gas turbines are FT-4A-12s. Controllable-pitch propellers allow propeller thrust to be reversed with reversing the direction of shaft rotation. Both ships have experienced problems with their controllable-pitch propellers and control systems.

The original design provided for a speed of 21 knots; not achieved.

The POLAR SEA (foreground) and POLAR STAR steam together in the Strait of Juan de Fuca between Canada and the United States. An HH-52A Sea Guard sits on the helicopter deck of the POLAR STAR. Early Polar-class designs had a single funnel. (1978, U.S. Coast Guard)

POLAR SEA (1983, L. and L. van Ginderen)

POLAR STAR (1983, L. and L. van Ginderen)

The POLAR SEA, one of two Polar-class icebreakers, the first ships of this type built in the United States in two decades. U.S. research and military interests in the polar regions are supported by four Coast Guard-operated icebreakers. The Polar ships have had engineering problems. (1982, U.S. Coast Guard)

1 ICEBREAKER: "GLACIER"

Number	Name	Launched	AGB Comm.	WAGB Comm.	Status
WAGB 4	GLACIER	27 Aug 1954	27 May 1955	30 June 1966	**PA**

Builders:	Ingalls Shipbuilding, Pascagoula, Miss.
Displacement:	6,406 tons standard
	8,775 tons full load
Length:	309½ feet (94.4 m) oa
Beam:	74 feet (22.6 m)
Draft:	29 feet (8.8 m)
Propulsion:	diesel-electric (10 Fairbanks-Morse diesels, 2 Westinghouse electric motors); 21,000 shp; 2 shafts
Speed:	17.5 knots
Range:	29,000 n.miles at 12 knots; 12,000 n.miles at 17.5 knots
Manning:	229 (14 officers + 215 enlisted)
Helicopters:	2 HH-52A Sea Guard
Guns:	2 40-mm machine guns Mk 19 (2 single)
Radars:	2 SPS-64

GLACIER (top) and BURTON ISLAND (WAGB 283) (1975, U.S. Coast Guard)

The GLACIER was the largest icebreaker constructed in the United States prior to completion of the POLAR STAR. She was active in the U.S. Navy as AGB 4 from 1955 until she was transferred to the Coast Guard in 1966 (stricken from the Navy on 1 July 1966, the day after transfer to the Coast Guard).

The GLACIER was given an extensive overhaul at the Southwest Maine shipyard at Terminal Island (Long Beach, Calif.) in 1983–1984. The ship is expected to be in service through the 1980s.

Guns: As built, the GLACIER mounted two 5-inch DP guns, six 3-inch AA guns, and four 20-mm AA guns. The lighter weapons were removed prior to transfer to the Coast Guard, and the twin 5-inch gun mount was removed in 1969.

GLACIER (U.S. Coast Guard)

2 ICEBREAKERS: WIND CLASS

Number	Name	Launched	Commissioned	Status
WAGB 281 (ex-AGB 6)	WESTWIND	31 Mar 1943	18 Sept 1944	**GL**
WAGB 282	NORTHWIND	25 Feb 1945	28 July 1945	**AA**

Builders:	Western Pipe and Steel, San Pedro, Calif.
Displacement:	3,500 tons standard
	6,515 tons full load
Length:	269 feet (82.0 m) oa
Beam:	63½ feet (19.4 m)
Draft:	29 feet (8.8 m)
Propulsion:	diesel-electric (Enterprise diesels); 10,000 shp; 2 shafts
Speed:	16 knots
Range:	38,000 n.miles at 10.5 knots; 16,000 n.miles at 12.5 knots
Manning:	131 (14 officers + 117 enlisted) in WAGB 281
	157 (15 officers + 142 enlisted) in WAGB 282
Helicopters:	1 or 2 HH-52A Sea Guard
Guns:	2 40-mm machine guns Mk 19 (2 single)
Radars:	2 SPS-64

The Wind-class icebreakers were the principal U.S. icebreakers for more than three decades. Originally seven ships were in this class, with two built for the Navy and the remaining five to Coast Guard specifications. Three of the latter ships served with the Soviet Navy after World War II.

Class: The accompanying table lists all seven Wind-class ships and their service.

Design: The two Navy-sponsored ships had reduced armament (guns and ASW weapons) as originally built compared with Coast Guard ships. The Navy ships were also among the first to be constructed with a helicopter platform.

Engineering: As built, these ships had a third propeller shaft forward capable of delivering 3,300 shp for backing down in heavy ice. The bow shafts were removed because of continued propeller losses in heavy ice operations. Both ships were built with Fairbanks Morse diesels; the WESTWIND was re-engined in 1973–1974 and the NORTHWIND in 1974–1975, both with Enterprise diesels. (Funnel heightened.)

Guns: As built, some of the Coast Guard design ships had up to four 5-inch DP guns, 12 40-mm AA guns, and several 20-mm AA guns. The postwar-built Navy ships were equipped with one 5-inch gun and lighter weapons. Into the 1960s, the NORTHWIND had two 5-inch guns and the other ships each had one 5-inch gun; all guns were removed 1969–1970.

The WESTWIND is one of two survivors of a class of versatile and capable icebreakers that served in the U.S. and Soviet navies as well as in the Coast Guard. As built, some carried up to four 5-inch guns and twin mounts plus a dozen 40-mm guns in quad mounts; the survivors—as do other Coast Guard icebreakers—have a pair of 40-mm machine gun/grenade launchers. An HH-52A Sea Guard rests on the WESTWIND's helicopter deck. She and the NORTHWIND were re-engined in 1973–1974 and 1974–1975, respectively; taller funnels were fitted, distinguishing them from earlier ships of the class. (1974, U.S. Coast Guard)

Original No./Name	USSR Name	Postwar U.S. Navy	Coast Guard No./Name	Stricken
AG 88 BURTON ISLAND	. . . . . .	AGB 1 BURTON ISLAND (1946–1966)	WAGB 283 BURTON ISLAND	197€
AG 89 EDISTO	. . . . . .	AGB 2 EDISTO (1947–1965)	WAGB 284 EDISTO	197€
WAG 278 NORTHWIND	SEVERNI VETER (1945–1951)	AGB 5 STATEN ISLAND (1951–1966)	WAGB 278 STATEN ISLAND	197€
WAG 279 EASTWIND	. . . . . .	—	WAGB 279 EASTWIND	1972
WAG 280 SOUTHWIND	KAPITAN BELUSOV (1945–1950)	AGB 3 ATKA (1950–1966)	WAGB 280 SOUTHWIND	1974
WAG 281 WESTWIND	SEVERNI POLIUS (1945–1951)	(ABG 6 WESTWIND)[a]	WAGB 281 WESTWIND	(active)
WAG 282 NORTHWIND (II)	. . . . . .	—	WAGB 282 NORTHWIND	(active)

[a] The WESTWIND was assigned a U.S. Navy hull number but was actually transferred directly from the USSR to the Coast Guard.

1 ICEBREAKER: "MACKINAW"

Number	Name	Launched	Commissioned	Status
WAGB 83	MACKINAW	4 Mar 1944	20 Dec 1944	**GL**

Builders:	Toledo Shipbuilding, Ohio
Displacement:	5,252 tons full load
Length:	290 feet (88.4 m) oa
Beam:	75 feet (22.9 m)
Draft:	19 feet (5.8 m)
Propulsion:	diesel-electric (Fairbanks Morse diesels. Westinghouse electric motors); 10,000 shp aft + 3,000 shp forward; 2 shafts aft + 1 shaft forward
Speed:	18.7 knots
Range:	41,000 n.miles at 9 knots; 10,000 n.miles at 18.7 knots
Manning:	127 (10 officers + 117 enlisted)
Helicopters:	none assigned
Guns:	none

The MACKINAW was designed and constructed specifically for Coast Guard use on the Great Lakes.

Classification: The ship originally was classified WAG 83; she was changed to WAGB on 1 May 1966.

Design: The MACKINAW has many of the features of the Wind class; however, being designed for the Great Lakes, the ship is longer and wider than the oceangoing ships with significantly less draft. Two 12-ton-capacity cranes are fitted. The ship has a clear deck aft for a helicopter, but no hangar is provided.

Name: Originally named MANITOWOC.

MACKINAW (1983, U.S. Coast Guard)

TRAINING CUTTERS

1 TRAINING BARK: "EAGLE"

Number	Name	Launched	Coast Guard Comm.	Status
WIX 327	EAGLE	13 June 1936	Jan 1946	**TRA-A**

Builders:	Blohm and Voss, Hamburg, Germany
Displacement:	1,816 tons full load
Length:	231 feet (90 m) wl
	295 feet (89.9 m) over bowsprit
Beam	39⅛ feet (11.9 m)
Draft:	17 feet (5.2 m)
Masts	fore and main 150⅓ feet (45.7 m)
	mizzen 132 feet (40.2 m)
Propulsion:	auxiliary diesels (M.A.N.); 700 bhp; 1 shaft
Speed:	up to 18 knots under sail; 10.5 knots on auxiliary diesels
Allowance:	65 (19 officers + 46 enlisted) + 195 cadets
Guns:	none

The EAGLE is the former German naval training bark HORST WESSEL. Taken by the United States as a reparation after World War II, she was acquired in January 1946 at Bremerhaven and assigned to the Coast Guard. Based at New London, Conn., she has been employed to train Coast Guard cadets on summer practice cruises.

Class: The ALBERT LEO SCHLAGETER (launched 1937) was also taken over by the United States in 1945 but was sold to Brazil in 1948 and re-sold to Portugal in 1962; a third ship of this basic design, the GORCH FOCK (1933), was taken over by the Soviet Union in 1946 and renamed the TOVARISH. A later ship of the same general design, also named the GORCH FOCK, was built at the same German yard for the West German Navy (launched 1958).

Design: The EAGLE is steel-hulled. She carries up to 21,350 square feet of sail.

The EAGLE with sails spread. When the Coast Guard orange-and-blue hull stripes and words *Coast Guard* were applied to cutters the EAGLE was exempted; they were applied in 1976 in preparation for the U.S. bicentennial celebration and Operation Sail in New York Harbor that year. (1983, U.S. Coast Guard)

BUOY TENDERS

3 MEDIUM ENDURANCE CUTTERS 31 SEAGOING BUOY TENDERS	"BALSAM" CLASS

Number	Name	Number	Name
WLB 62	BALSAM	WLB 389	BITTERSWEET
WLB 277	COWSLIP	WLB 390	BLACKHAW
WLB 290	GENTIAN	WLB 392	BRAMBLE
WLB 291	LAUREL	WLB 393	FIREBRUSH
WMEC 292	CLOVER	WLB 394	HORNBEAM
WMEC 295	EVERGREEN	WLB 395	IRIS
WLB 296	SORREL	WLB 396	MALLOW
WLB 297	IRONWOOD	WLB 397	MARIPOSA
WMEC 300	CITRUS	WLB 399	SAGEBRUSH
WLB 301	CONIFER	WLB 400	SALVIA
WLB 302	MADRONA	WLB 401	SASSAFRAS
WLB 303	TUPELO	WLB 402	SEDGE
WLB 305	MESQUITE	WLB 403	SPAR
WLB 306	BUTTONWOOD	WLB 404	SUNDEW
WLB 307	PLANETREE	WLB 405	SWEETBRIER
WLB 308	PAPAW	WLB 406	ACACIA
WLB 309	SWEETGUM	WLB 407	WOODRUSH
WLB 388	BASSWOOD		

Builders:	WLB 62, 290–291, 296, 302–303, 389, 392–393, 395–397, 399–400, 406–407 Zenith Dredge Co, Duluth, Minn. WLB 277, 292, 295, 300–301, 305–309, 388, 390, 394, 401–405 Marine Iron and Shipbuilding Co, Duluth, Minn. WLB 297 Coast Guard Yard, Curtis Bay, Md.
Displacement:	935 tons standard 1,025 tons full load
Length:	180 feet (54.9 m) oa
Beam:	37 feet (11.3 m)
Draft:	13 feet (4.0 m)
Propulsion:	diesel-electric; 1,000 bhp in WLB 62–303 series except WLB 297, others 1,200 shp; 1 shaft
Speed:	WLB 62–303 series (except WLB 297) 12.8 knots; others 15 knots
Manning:	53 (6 officers + 47 enlisted)
Guns:	2 40-mm Mk 19 machine guns (2 single) in most tenders; others are unarmed

These tenders service navigation buoys and other aids to navigation in coastal waters. They were completed in 1942–1945 with several sub-types. All are active or are undergoing modernization.

Class: The EVERGREEN was refitted as an oceanographic cutter in 1973 and reclassified WAGO; she was changed to WMEC on 1 May 1982.

The CITRUS and CLOVER were changed to WMEC in June 1979 and February 1980 to replace the MODOC (WMEC 194) and COMANCHE (WMEC 202), respectively.

The COWSLIP (WLB 277) was stricken on 23 March 1973 (sold); she was repurchased by the Coast Guard in January 1981 and recommissioned in November 1981. The BLACKTHORN (WLB 391) was rammed and sunk on 28 January 1980.

Design: The WLB 62, 296, 300, 390, 392, 402–404 have strengthened hulls for icebreaking.

Engineering: The WLB 277, 389, 394, and 295 are fitted with controllable-pitch, bow-thrust propellers.

Guns: As completed, these tenders had one 3-inch AA gun and two or four 40-mm AA guns.

Modernization: Fourteen ships are to receive SLEP modernization, being fitted with new main engines, electronics, and other systems plus improved habitability. The SORREL was the first ship, with her 16-month SLEP being completed in January 1983.

Names: The ACACIA originally was named the THISTLE.

The CITRUS in white employed as a medium endurance cutter; a Navy ATF is in the background. (1982, Giorgio Arra)

BLACKHAWK (1983, Giorgio Arra)

1 COASTAL BUOY TENDER: "HOLLYHOCK" CLASS

Number	Name
WLM 212	FIR

Builders:	
Displacement:	989 tons full load
Length:	175 feet (53.3 m) oa
Beam:	34 feet (10.4 m)
Draft:	12 feet (3.7 m)
Propulsion:	diesels; 1,350 bhp; 2 shafts
Speed:	12 knots
Manning:	40 (5 officers + 35 enlisted)

This tender was originally classified WAGL; she was changed to coastal tender (WLM) on 1 January 1965. Launched in 1939.

The F R is the survivor of three large, built-for-the-purpose buoy tenders. (1969, U.S. Coast Guard)

3 COASTAL BUOY TENDERS: RED CLASS

Number	Name	Number	Name
WLM 685	RED WOOD	WLM 688	RED CEDAR
WLM 686	RED BEECH	WLM 689	RED OAK
WLM 687	RED BIRCH		

Builders:	Coast Guard Yard, Curtis Bay, Md.
Displacement:	471 tons standard
	512 tons full load
Length:	157 feet (47.8 m) oa
Beam:	33 feet (10.1 m)
Draft:	6 feet (1.8 m)
Propulsion:	diesels; 1,800 bhp; 2 shafts
Speed:	12.8 knots
Manning:	33–35 (4–5 officers + 29–32 enlisted)

RED CEDAR (1975, Giorgio Arra)

These buoy and navigation aid tenders have strengthened steel hulls for light icebreaking and are fitted with bow thrusters. WLM 685–686 were launched in 1964, WLM 687 in 1965, WLM 688 in 1970, and WLM 689 in 1971.

Armament: No coastal or small buoy tenders are armed.

RED BEECH (1970, U.S. Coast Guard)

7 COASTAL BUOY TENDERS: WHITE CLASS

Number	Name	Number	Name
WLM 540	WHITE SUMAC	WLM 545	WHITE HEATH
WLM 542	WHITE BUSH	WLM 546	WHITE LUPINE
WLM 543	WHITE HOLLY	WLM 547	WHITE PINE
WLM 544	WHITE SAGE		

Builders:	
Displacement:	435 tons standard
	600 tons full load
Length:	133 feet (40.5 m) oa
Beam:	31 feet (9.4 m)
Draft:	9 feet (2.7 m)
Propulsion:	diesels (Union); 600 bhp; 2 shafts
Speed:	9.8 knots
Manning:	19–22 (1–2 officers + 18–21 enlisted)

All of these tenders are converted Navy self-propelled lighters (YF). All were launched in 1943.

WHITE BUSH (1969, U.S. Coast Guard)

1 INLAND BUOY TENDER ⎱ "COSMOS" CLASS
4 INLAND CONSTRUCTION TENDERS ⎰

Number	Name	Number	Name
WLIC 293	Cosmos	WLIC 315	Smilax
WLIC 298	Rambler	WLIC 316	Primrose
WLI 313	Bluebell		

Builders:	Dubuque Boat & Boiler, Iowa, except Bluebell Burchfield Boiler, Tacoma, Wash.
Displacement:	178 tons full load
Length:	100 feet (30.5 m) oa
Beam:	24 feet (7.3 m)
Draft:	5 feet (1.5 m)
Propulsion:	diesels; 600 bhp; 2 shafts
Speed:	10.5 knots
Manning:	14 (1 officer + 13 enlisted)

All formerly WLI; 4 changed to inland construction tenders (WLIC) on 1 October 1979. Cosmos launched in 1942, others in 1944, except Bluebell in 1945.

Buckthorn (1970, U.S. Coast Guard)

Rambler (1983, U.S. Coast Guard)

1 INLAND BUOY TENDER: "BUCKTHORN"

Number	Name
WLI 642	Buckthorn

Builders:	Mobile Ship Repair, Ala.
Displacement:	200 tons full load
Length:	100 feet (30.5 m) oa
Beam:	24 feet (7.3 m)
Draft:	4 feet (1.2 m)
Propulsion:	diesels; 600 bhp; 2 shafts
Speed:	11.9 knots
Manning:	17 (1 officer + 16 enlisted)

The Buckthorn was launched in 1963.

2 INLAND BUOY TENDERS: BERRY CLASS

Number	Name
WLI 65303	Blackberry
WLI 65304	Chokeberry

Builders:	Dubuque Boat & Boiler, Iowa
Displacement:	68 tons full load
Length:	65 feet (19.8 m) oa
Beam:	17 feet (5.2 m)
Draft:	4 feet (1.2 m)
Propulsion:	diesel; 220 bhp; 1 shaft
Speed:	9 knots
Manning:	5 (enlisted)

These tenders were launched in 1946.

2 INLAND BUOY TENDERS: IMPROVED BERRY CLASS

Number	Name
WLI 65400	Bayberry
WLI 65401	Elderberry

Builders:	
Displacement:	68 tons full load
Length:	65 feet (19.8 m) oa
Beam:	17 feet (5.2 m)
Draft:	4 feet (1.2 m)
Propulsion:	diesels; 400 bhp; 2 shafts
Speed:	11.3 knots
Manning:	10 (enlisted)

Both tenders were launched in 1954.

BAYBERRY (1979, U.S. Coast Guard)

10 INLAND CONSTRUCTION TENDERS: "ANVIL" CLASS

Number	Name	Number	Name
(A series)		(C series)	
WLIC 75301	ANVIL	WLIC 75306	CLAMP
WLIC 75302	HAMMER	WLIC 75307	WEDGE
(B series)		WLIC 75308	SPIKE
WLIC 75303	SLEDGE	WLIC 75309	HATCHET
WLIC 75304	MALLET	WLIC 75310	AXE
WLIC 75305	VISE		

Builders:	
Displacement:	145 tons
Length:	75 feet (22.9 m) oa, except C series 76 feet (23.2 m) oa
Beam:	22 feet (6.7 m)
Draft:	4 feet (1.2 m)
Propulsion:	diesels; 600 bhp; 2 shafts
Speed:	A series 8.6 knots
	B series 9.1 knots
	C series 9.4 knots
Manning:	9–10 (1 officer in some tenders + 9 enlisted)

These tenders were launched in 1962–1965.

WEDGE with crane barge (1971, U.S. Coast Guard)

1 RIVER BUOY TENDER: "SUMAC"

Number	Name
WLR 311	SUMAC

Builders:	Peterson and Haecker, Blair, Neb.
Displacement:	478 tons full load
Length:	115 feet (35.0 m) oa
Beam:	30 feet (9.1 m)
Draft:	6 feet (1.8 m)
Propulsion:	diesels; 2,250 bhp; 3 shafts
Speed:	10.6 knots
Manning:	23 (1 officer + 22 enlisted)

The SUMAC was launched in 1943.

1 RIVER BUOY TENDER: "DOGWOOD"

Number	Name
WLR 259	DOGWOOD

Builders:	
Displacement:	310 tons
Length:	114 feet (34.7 m) oa
Beam:	26 feet (7.9 m)
Draft:	5 feet (1.5 m)
Propulsion:	diesels; 2,800 bhp; 2 shafts
Speed:	11 knots
Manning:	19 (enlisted)

The DOGWOOD was launched in 1940.

1 RIVER BUOY TENDER: "LANTANA"

Number	Name
WLR 80310	LANTANA

Builders:	Peterson and Haecker, Blair, Neb.
Displacement:	235 tons full load
Length:	80 feet (24.4 m) oa
Beam:	30 feet (9.1 m)
Draft:	6 feet (1.8 m)
Propulsion:	diesels; 945 bhp; 3 shafts
Speed:	10 knots
Manning:	20 (1 officer + 19 enlisted)

The LANTANA was launched in 1943.

4 INLAND CONSTRUCTION TENDERS: "PAMLICO" CLASS

Number	Name	Number	Name
WLIC 800	PAMLICO	WLIC 802	KENNEBEC
WLIC 801	HUDSON	WLIC 803	SAGINAW

Builders:	Coast Guard Yard, Curtis Bay, Md.
Displacement:	416 tons
Length:	160 feet (48.8 m) oa
Beam:	30 feet (9.1 m)
Draft:	4 feet (1.2 m)
Propulsion:	diesels; 1,000 bhp; 2 shafts
Speed:	10 knots
Manning:	13 (enlisted)

These tenders were all launched in 1976.

KENNEBEC (1982, Giorgio Arra)

9 RIVER BUOY TENDERS: "GASCONADE" CLASS

Number	Name	Number	Name
WLR 75401	GASCONADE	WLR 75406	KICKAPOO
WLR 75402	MUSKINGUM	WLR 75407	KANAWHA
WLR 75403	WYACONDA	WLR 75408	PATOKA
WLR 75404	CHIPPEWA	WLR 75409	CHENA
WLR 75405	CHEYENNE		

Builders:	
Displacement:	141 tons full load
Length:	75 feet (22.9 m) oa
Beam:	22 feet (6.7 m)
Draft:	4 feet (1.2 m)
Propulsion:	diesels; 600 bhp; 2 shafts
Speed:	7.6–8.7 knots
Manning:	18–20 (enlisted)

These tenders were launched in 1964–1971.

CHEYENNE with buoy barge (1971, U.S. Coast Guard)

6 RIVER BUOY TENDERS: "OUACHITA" CLASS

Number	Name	Number	Name
WLR 65501	OUACHITA	WLR 65504	SCIOTO
WLR 65502	CIMARRON	WLR 65505	OSAGE
WLR 65503	OBION	WLR 65506	SANGAMON

Builders:	
Displacement:	143 tons
Length:	65½ feet (20.0 m) oa
Beam:	21 feet (6.4 m)
Draft:	5 feet (1.5 m)
Propulsion:	diesels; 600 bhp; 2 shafts
Speed:	10.5 knots
Manning:	19–23 (enlisted)

These tenders were launched in 1960–1962.

OSAGE (U.S. Coast Guard)

TUGS

7 + ICEBREAKING TUGS: BAY CLASS

Number	Name	Commissioned
WTGB 101	KATAMI BAY	8 Jan 1979
WTGB 102	BRISTOL BAY	5 Apr 1979
WTGB 103	MOBILE BAY	6 May 1979
WTGB 104	BISCAYNE BAY	8 Dec 1979
WTGB 105	NEAH BAY	18 Aug 1980
WTGB 106	MORRO BAY	25 Jan 1981
WTGB 107	PENOBSCOT BAY	1984

Builders:	WTGB 101–106 Tacoma Boatbuilding, Wash.
	WTGB 107 Bay City Marine, Wisc.
Displacement:	662 tons full load
Length:	140 feet (42.7 m) oa
Beam:	37 feet (11.3 m)
Draft:	12 feet (3.7 m)
Propulsion:	diesel-electric; (Fairbanks-Morse diesels; Westinghouse electric drive); 2,500 bhp; 1 shaft
Speed:	14.7 knots
Manning:	17 (3 officers + 14 enlisted)

These are the largest tugs to be constructed specifically for the Coast Guard. They are designed to provide general towing and support services and can break through ice 20 inches thick; they are fitted with a hull air lubrication system for operations in ice areas.

Additional ships may be built.

Classification: These tugs were originally designated WYTM. The KATAMI BAY was changed to WTGB on 5 February 1979; the others were changed to WTGB upon completion.

The MORRO BAY at Norfolk. (1981, L. and L. van Ginderen)

8 MEDIUM HARBOR TUGS: "MANITOU" CLASS

Number	Name	Number	Name
WYTM 71	APALACHEE	WYTM 93	RARITAN
WYTM 72	YANKTON	WYTM 96	CHINOOK
WYTM 73	MOHICAN	WYTM 98	SNOHOMISH
WYTM 91	MAHONING	WYTM 99	SAUK

Builders:	
Displacement:	370 tons full load
Length:	110 feet (33.5 m) oa
Beam:	27 feet (8.2 m)
Draft:	11 feet (3.3 m)
Propulsion:	diesel-electric; 1,000 bhp; 1 shaft
Speed:	11.2 knots
Manning:	20 (1 officer + 19 enlisted)

The YTM 91 and 92 were launched in 1939; the others in 1943.

BRISTOL BAY (1979, U.S. Coast Guard)

APALACHEE (1983, Giorgio Arra)

14 SMALL HARBOR TUGS: 65-FT CLASS

Number	Name	Number	Name
WYTL 65601	CAPSTAN	WYTL 65608	PENDANT
WYTL 65602	CHOCK	WYTL 65609	SHACKLE
WYTL 65603	SWIVEL	WYTL 65610	HAWSER
WYTL 65604	TACKLE	WYTL 65611	LINE
WYTL 65605	TOWLINE	WYTL 65612	WIRE
WYTL 65606	CATENARY	WYTL 65614	BOLLARD
WYTL 65607	BRIDLE	WYTL 65615	CLEAT

Builders:	
Displacement:	72 tons full load
Length:	65 feet (19.8 m) oa
Beam:	19 feet (5.8 m)
Draft:	7 feet (2.1 m)
Propulsion:	diesel; 400 bhp; 1 shaft
Speed:	9.8–10.5 knots
Manning:	10 (enlisted)

These tugs were launched in 1961–1967.

CHOCK (1983, Giorgio Arra)

FERRIES

1 FERRY

Number	Name
(none)	TIDES

Builders:	
Displacement:	744 tons full load
Length:	185 feet (56.3 m) oa
Beam:	55 feet (16.8 m)
Draft:	9 feet (2.7 m)
Propulsion:	diesel-electric; 1,350 bhp
Speed:	12 knots
Manning:	(civilian)

The TIDES is assigned to Governors Island, N.Y. She is a former commercial ferry, launched in 1946.

1 FERRY

Number	Name
(none)	GOVERNOR

Builders:	Moore Drydock, Oakland, Calif.
Displacement:	1,600 tons standard
Length:	242⅔ feet (74.0 m) oa
Beam:	65½ feet (20.0 m)
Draft:	14 feet (4.3 m)
Propulsion:	
Speed:	
Manning:	

The GOVERNOR is undergoing conversion and will be assigned Governor's Island, New York, off the southern tip of Manhattan. The island has been the site of a major Coast Guard station since 1966.

The ship was built in 1954 and as the CROWN CITY was used by the Navy in San Diego; she was subsequently sold to the State of Washington, renamed KULSHAN, and employed in the Puget Sound area. She was acquired by the Coast Guard in 1982 and rehabilitated by the Coast Guard yard at Curtis Bay from late 1982 until early 1985.

2 FERRIES

Number	Name
(ex-FB 812)	LT SAMUEL S. COURSEN
(ex-FB 813)	PVT NICHOLAS MINUE

Builders:	John H. Mathis, Camden, N.J.
Displacement:	869 tons full load
Length:	172 feet (52.4 m) oa
Beam:	48 feet (14.6 m)
Draft:	14 feet (4.3 m)
Propulsion:	diesel-electric; 1,000 bhp
Speed:	12 knots
Manning:	(civilian)

These ferries are used to transport personnel and vehicles between lower Manhattan and Governors Island, N.Y. Both are former U.S. Army ferries built in 1955. They do not have Coast Guard hull numbers.

LT SAMUEL S. COURSEN (1974, U.S. Coast Guard)

LIGHTSHIPS

2 LIGHTSHIPS

Number	Name
WLV 612	LIGHTSHIP I
WLV 613	LIGHTSHIP II

Builders:	Coast Guard Yard, Curtis Bay, Md.
Displacement:	WLV 612–613 607 tons full load
Length:	128 feet (39.0 m) oa
Beam:	30 feet (9.1 m)
Draft:	11 feet (3.4 m)
Propulsion:	diesel; 550 shp; 1 shaft
Speed:	11 knots
Allowance:	18 (1 officer + 17 enlisted)

These are the last of a long line of lightships operated by the Coast Guard. These ships are in reserve at Boston, Mass. All lightships have been replaced by fixed installations.

The WLV 612 launched in 1950; WLV 613 in 1952. Coast Guard lightships exchanged names according to location, but their hull numbers remain constant.

Design: These are steel-hull ships with two 55-foot masts.

The former LIGHTSHIP NANTUCKET, one of the last of a disappearing ship type. The Coast Guard operates almost 400 lighthouses and more than 13,000 minor lights in U.S. coastal and inland waters. (1976, U.S. Coast Guard)

PATROL BOATS

44-foot patrol boat 44396 (1983, L. and L. van Ginderen)

41-foot patrol boat 41338 (1983, Giorgio Arra)

52-foot patrol boat 52313 (1970, U.S. Coast Guard)

The Coast Guard operates several hundred small patrol and rescue craft, such as these clustered around a Point-class cutter as Coast Guardsmen prepared to escort the Trident submarine OHIO (SSBN 726) into Bangor, Wash., in 1982. The smaller craft are unnamed and hence are not rated as cutters. (1982, U.S. Coast Guard, M.W. Rodrigues)

B National Oceanic and Atmospheric Administration

The National Oceanic and Atmospheric Administration (NOAA) conducts ocean surveys and other research and surveying activities for the U.S. government. These activities are of a nonmilitary nature. However, NOAA maps and charts are used by the armed forces, and during time of war or national crisis the NOAA oceanographic and hydrographic research ships can be expected to operate with the Navy, either as a separate service or integrated into the Navy.

NOAA is an agency of the Department of Commerce with the ships operated by the National Ocean Survey. Prior to the establishment of NOAA in 1970, the National Ocean Survey was a division of the Environmental Services Science Administration from 1965. Before that the ships were operated by the Coast and Geodetic Survey (since 1878, and the Coast Survey from 1834, and the Survey of the Coast from 1807).

Ten NOAA research and survey ships at the NOAA Pacific Marine Center in Seattle, Wash. (1976, NOAA)

SHIPS

Oceanographic and hydrographic research and survey ships are listed on the following pages. In addition, the National Marine Fisheries Service of NOAA operates a dozen fisheries research ships.

NOAA ships are classified by their "Horsepower Tonnage," the numerical sum of the vessel's shaft horsepower plus gross tonnage. Class I ships are 5501–9000 HPT, Class II are 3501–5500 HPT, Class III are 2001–3500 HPT, Class IV are 1001–2000 HTP, Class V are 501–1000 HPT, and Class VI are up to 500 HPT.

These ships are designated by a three-digit number preceded by the letter R for Research and S for Survey, with the first digit indicating the HPT class.

The following table lists the NOAA research and survey ships, their HPT class, current hull number, and previous designation.

Armament: NOAA ships are unarmed.

Class	No.	Name	Former No.
I	R101	OCEANOGRAPHER	OSS 01
I	R102	DISCOVERER	OSS 02
I	R103	RESEARCHER	OSS 03
I	S132	SURVEYOR	OSS 32
II	S220	FAIRWEATHER	MSS 20
II	S221	RAINIER	MSS 21
II	S222	MT. MITCHELL	MSS 22
III	S328	PEIRCE	CSS 28
III	S329	WHITING	CSS 29
III	S330	MCARTHUR	CSS 30
III	S331	DAVIDSON	CSS 31
IV	S492	FERREL	ASV 92
V	S590	RUDE	ASV 90
V	S591	HECK	ASV 91

AVIATION

The NOAA Research Flight Facility owns three aircraft, one de Havilland Twin Otter and two Lockheed WP-3D Orions. Several commercial aircraft are on lease to NOAA and several Army helicopters are on loan to the agencies.

The WP-3D Orions have 8-man crews: 2 pilots, 1 flight engineer, 1 navigator, 1 mission scientist, 1 camera operator, 1 flight director, and 1 chief scientist; passenger scientists can be embarked in these aircraft.

PERSONNEL

NOAA has 400 commissioned officers, of whom approximately 120 are assigned to ships. Ninety licensed civil service personnel and about 625 unlicensed personnel are also assigned to ships. Medical officers are provided to ships when necessary from the U.S. Public Health Service.

2 RESEARCH SHIPS: "OCEANOGRAPHER" CLASS

Number	Name	Launched	Commissioned	Status
R101	OCEANOGRAPHER	18 Apr 1964	13 July 1966	PR
R102	DISCOVERER	29 Oct 1964	29 Apr 1967	**PA**

Builders:	Aerojet-General Corp, Jacksonville, Fla.
Displacement:	3,959 tons light
Length:	303⅓ feet (92.4 m) oa
Beam:	52 feet (15.8 m)
Draft:	18½ feet (5.6 m)
Propulsion:	diesel-electric (4 diesels); 5,000 bhp; 2 shafts
Speed:	18 knots
Manning:	R101 14 officers + 63 civilians + 30 scientists
	R102 13 officers + 66 civilians + 24 scientists

These are NOAA's largest ships. They have graceful, yacht-like lines. The OCEANOGRAPHER is laid up in temporary reserve.

Design: Maritime Administration S2-MET-MA62a design.

Engineering: These ships have a 400-hp through-bow thruster.

DISCOVERER (1978, NOAA)

OCEANOGRAPHER; note randome aft of the funnel. (1978, NOAA)

1 SURVEY SHIP: "SURVEYOR"

Number	Name	Launched	Commissioned	Status
S132	SURVEYOR	25 Apr 1959	30 Apr 1960	**PA**

Builders:	National Steel Co, San Diego, Calif.
Displacement:	3,150 tons light
Length:	292⅓ feet (88.8 m) oa
Beam:	46 feet (14.0 m)
Draft:	18 feet (5.5 m)
Propulsion:	steam turbine (De Laval); 3,200 shp; 1 shaft
Boilers:	2 (Combustion Engineering)
Speed:	16 knots
Manning:	12 officers + 64 civilians + 16 scientists

Design: Maritime Administration S2-S-RM28a design. A helicopter platform has been fitted aft.

Engineering: The SURVEYOR is the only steam-powered ship in NOAA service. There is a 200-hp electric auxiliary propulsion motor installed aft.

SURVEYOR; note helicopter platform aft. (1977, NOAA)

1 RESEARCH SHIP: "RESEARCHER"

Number	Name	Launched	Commissioned	Status
R103	RESEARCHER	5 Oct 1968	8 Oct 1970	**AA**

Builders:	American Shipbuilding Co, Lorain, Ohio
Displacement:	2,875 tons light
Length:	278¼ feet (84.8 m) oa
Beam:	51 feet (15.5 m)
Draft:	16¼ feet (5.0 m)
Propulsion:	2 diesels; 3,200 bhp; 2 shafts
Speed:	16 knots
Manning:	13 officers + 55 civilians + 14 scientists

Design: Maritime Administration S2-MT-MA74a design. Fitted with a bow sonar dome.

Engineering: The RESEARCHER is fitted with a 450-hp, 360° retractable bow thruster for precise maneuvering and "creeping" speeds up to seven knots.

MT. MITCHELL at Norfolk, Virginia (1981, L. and L. van Ginderen)

RESEARCHER; note helicopter platform aft. (NOAA)

FAIRWEATHER; note survey launches on after deck. (1978, NOAA)

3 SURVEY SHIPS: "FAIRWEATHER" CLASS

Number	Name	Launched	Commissioned	Status
S220	FAIRWEATHER	15 Mar 1967	2 Oct 1968	**PA**
S221	RAINIER	15 Mar 1967	2 Oct 1968	**PA**
S222	MT. MITCHELL	29 Nov 1966	23 Mar 1968	**AA**

Builders:	Aerojet-General Corp, Jacksonville, Fla.
Displacement:	1,798 tons light
Length:	231 feet (70.4 m) oa
Beam:	42 feet (12.8 m)
Draft:	13⅝ feet (4.2 m)
Propulsion:	2 diesels; 2,400 bhp; 2 shafts
Speed:	14.5 knots
Manning:	12 officers + 57 civilians + 4 scientists

Design: Maritime Administration S1-MT-MA72a design.
Engineering: These ships have a 200-shp through-bow thruster.

2 SURVEY SHIPS: "PEIRCE" CLASS

Number	Name	Launched	Commissioned	Status
S328	PEIRCE	15 Oct 1962	6 May 1963	**AA**
S329	WHITING	20 Nov 1962	8 July 1963	**AA**

Builders:	Marietta Manufacturing Co, Point Pleasant, W.Va.
Displacement:	760 tons light
Length:	164 feet (50.0 m) oa
Beam:	33 feet (10.1 m)
Draft:	10 feet (3.0 m)
Propulsion:	diesels; 1,600 bhp; 2 shafts
Speed:	12.5 knots
Manning:	8 officers + 33 civilians + 2 scientists

Design: Maritime Administration S1-MT-59a design.

PEIRCE (1983, Giorgio Arra)

WHITING (NOAA)

2 SURVEY SHIPS: "McARTHUR" CLASS

Number	Name	Launched	Commissioned	Status
S330	MCARTHUR	15 Nov 1965	15 Dec 1966	**PA**
S331	DAVIDSON	7 May 1966	10 Mar 1967	**PA**

Builders:	Norfolk Shipbuilding and Dry Dock Co, Va.
Displacement:	995 tons light
Length:	175 feet (53.3 m) oa
Beam:	38 feet (11.5 m)
Draft:	11½ feet (3.5 m)
Propulsion:	diesels; 1,600 bhp; 2 shafts
Speed:	13 knots
Manning:	8 officers + 30 civilians + 2 scientists

Design: Maritime Administration S1-MT-MA70a design.

McARTHUR (1978, NOAA)

1 SURVEY SHIP: "FERREL"

Number	Name	Launched	Commissioned	Status
S492	FERREL	4 Apr 1968	4 June 1968	**AA**

Builders:	Zigler Shipyard, Jennings, La.
Displacement:	363 tons light
Length:	133¼ feet (40.5 m) oa
Beam:	32 feet (9.7 m)
Draft:	7 feet (2.1 m)
Propulsion:	diesels; 750 bhp; 2 shafts
Speed:	10.6 knots
Manning:	5 officers + 14 civilians

The FERREL conducts near-shore and estuarine-current surveys. She employs data collection buoys in her work; there is a large open buoy stowage area aft as well as a comprehensive workshop.

Design: Maritime Administration S1-MT-MA83a design.

Engineering: Fitted with a 100-hp through-bow thruster.

FERREL (NOAA)

2 SURVEY SHIPS: "RUDE" CLASS

Number	Name	Launched	Commissioned	Status
S590	RUDE	17 Aug 1966	29 Mar 1967	**AA**
S591	HECK	1 Nov 1966	29 Mar 1967	**AA**

Builders:	Jacobson Shipyard, Oyster Bay, N.Y.
Displacement:	214 tons light
Length:	90 feet (27.4 m) oa
Beam:	22 feet (6.7 m)
Draft:	7 feet (2.1 m)
Propulsion:	diesels; 800 bhp; 2 shafts
Speed:	11.5 knots
Manning:	S590 13 officers + 8 civilians
	S591 12 officers + 8 civilians

These ships work as a pair using wire drags to locate underwater navigational hazards. One commanding officer is assigned to the two vessels; he normally rides one ship and the executive officer the other.

Design: Maritime Administration S1-MT-MA71a design. Side-scanning sonar is installed.

Engineering: The propellers on these ships are protected by shrouds, similar to Kort nozzles. Auxiliary propulsion provides 70 hp to each propeller for slow-speed dragging operations.

NATIONAL GEOLOGICAL SURVEY

The National Geological Survey is a separate agency within the NOAA organization. It operates one major survey ship, the former USNS S.P. LEE.

1 SURVEY SHIP: "S.P. LEE"

Number	Name	FY	Launched	In service
(none)	S.P. LEE	65	19 Oct 1967	2 Dec 1968

Builders:	Defoe Shipbuilding, Bay City, Mich.
Displacement:	1,297 tons full load
Length:	208⅓ feet (63.5 m) oa
Beam:	39 feet (11.9 m)
Draft:	14⅙ feet (4.3 m)
Propulsion:	diesel-electric; 1,000 bhp; 1 shaft
Speed:	12 knots
Range:	12,000 n.miles at 12 knots
Manning:	approx. 55

HECK (1977, NOAA)

The S. P. LEE at Wellington. (1983, L and L. van Ginderen)

The ship was built as a naval surveying ship and placed in service with the Military Sealift Command upon completion in 1968 (designated T-AGS 31). Although intended to operate under the Oceanographer of the Navy, the ship was assigned to support the Naval Underwater Research and Development Center in San Diego. (In this role the ship conducted acoustic tests in the Atlantic, Mediterranean, and Pacific.)

The LEE was reclassified as a miscellaneous research ship (T-AG 192) on 25 September 1970. She was taken out of service on 29 January 1973 and transferred on indefinite loan to the National Geological Survey on 27 February 1974. The ship is in active service.

Class: The LEE and a sister ship, the KELLER (T-AGS 25), were built to a modified CONRAD (AGOR 3) design. The KELLER was transferred to Portugal on 21 January 1972.

NATIONAL MARINE FISHERIES

The National Marine Fisheries is a separate agency of NOAA which operates several fisheries research ships. They are listed below in order of NOAA hull number.

The DAVID STARR JORDAN is one of the several research ships of NOAA's National Marine Fisheries Service. (1984, Giorgio Arra)

Number	Name	Displacement	Length	Speed	Completed	Status/Remarks
R223	MILLER FREEMAN	1,920 tons	215 ft	14 knots	1968	
R332	OREGON II	952 tons	170 ft	12 knots	1967	
R342	ALBATROSS IV	1,089 tons	187 ft	12 knots	1962	
R441	GEORGE B. KELEZ	936 tons	176½ ft	10.5 knots	1944	Built as a U.S. Army FS-type ship; commissioned by NOAA in March 1975.
R443	TOWNSEND CROMWELL	652 tons	163 ft	11.5 knots	1963	
R444	DAVID STARR JORDAN	993 tons	171 ft	11.5 knots	1965	
R445	DELAWARE II	758 tons	155 ft	11.5 knots	1968	
R446	CHAPMAN	520 tons	127 ft	11 knots	1980	
R551	OREGON	373 tons	100 ft	9.3 knots	1949	
R552	JOHN N. COBB	250 tons	93 ft	9.3 knots	1950	
R663	MURRE II	295 tons	86 ft	8 knots	1943	Conducts fishery research and carries cargo in southeast Alaskan waters.
R680	VIRGINIA KEY	90 tons	65 ft	9 knots	1952	

C Advanced Technology Ships

The U.S. Navy has been a world leader in the development of advanced-technology surface ships and craft. However, of several ship and vehicle designs developed and periodic proposals and programs for series production, only two classes of advanced-technology craft have been series produced for the U.S. Navy: six hydrofoil missile ships (PHM) in the 1970s and a planned class of more than 100 air cushion landing craft (LCAC) begun in the 1980s. These two series are described in this volume in Chapters 22 and 20, respectively.

In addition, the U.S. Navy is evaluating a Surface Effect Ship (SES) that has been procured in small numbers by the Coast Guard, while the Navy is examining the possible use of advanced-technology hull forms in a new series of mine hunters (MSH) and multi-purpose patrol boats (PBM) with advanced-technology configurations. Navy considerations to acquire additional ocean surveillance ships (T-AGOS) with SWATH configurations have been dropped.

Four advanced-technology hull forms have been developed and evaluated by the U.S. Navy during the past two decades:

Hydrofoils use submerged foils or wing-like structures to lift the hull

The world's largest military hydrofoil was the research ship PLAINVIEW (AGEH 1), shown here at high speed in Puget Sound, Wash. The CH-46A Sea Knight was used to demonstrate the feasibility of transferring personnel between helicopters and high-speed craft. Note the Mk 32 triple torpedo tubes on the PLAINVIEW's amidships deck. (1972, U.S. Navy)

The U.S. Navy evaluated three Patrol Air Cushion Vehicles (PACV) in the Vietnam conflict, where the high-speed craft successfully operated in the Mekong Delta. The three craft were subsequently evaluated by the Coast Guard in U.S. waters, being designated as *Hover* craft. At left is the Navy's PACV-1 and, at right is the Coast Guard's HOVER 01. (1968, U.S. Navy; 1970, U.S. Coast Guard)

above the water to achieve high speed and stability. Several prototype hydrofoil combat craft have been built and, as noted above, six PEGASUS (PHM 1)-class hydrofoil missile craft are in service.

In addition to the ships and craft listed here, during the 1960s the Navy experimented with landing vehicles (LVHX) and landing craft (LCVP(H)) fitted with hydrofoils. The latter craft were given the nicknames HIGH POCKET and HIGH LANDER.

Small Waterplane Area Twin Hull (SWATH) craft have twin, torpedo-shaped hulls that are fully submerged to provide a very high degree of ship stability. The twin hulls accommodate machinery, with the main structure being above water. Unlike the other advanced-technology designs, these are not high-speed craft. A range support craft has been built to this configuration, the KAIMALINO (see Chapter 25).

Surface Effect Ships (SES) ride on a "bubble" of air that is contained by flexible "skirts" forward and aft and rigid sidewalls. These sidewalls penetrate the water surface, providing stability in rough water. The Coast Guard's three SES cutters are described in Appendix A.

Air Cushion Vehicles (ACV) similarly ride on a bubble of air that is entirely contained by flexible skirts, permitting them to operate above the water and to operate at high speeds over marshes and ground. As noted above, the LCAC is in series production for the Navy.

The following are brief listings of the various prototype advanced-technology ships and craft developed by the U.S. Navy. Most are described in more detail in previous editions of *Ships and Aircraft*. In addition, there have been scores of major studies for employing advanced-technology ships in a variety of roles, including forward-deployment store ships, aircraft carriers, and underway replenishment ships.

In the following tables data on full load displacement, length overall (of hull and not over foils for hydrofoils), and maximum speed are given. Where craft have undergone modifications, the later displacement and length are given.

HYDROFOILS

Number	Name/Designation	Displacement	Length	Speed	Completed	Status/Remarks
—	DENISON	80 tons	104 ft	62 knots	1960	Maritime Administration test craft developed with Navy assistance; built by Grumman-Jakobson's Shipyard; disposed of after trials.
—	FRESH-1	20 tons	47 ft	84 knots	1963	In storage since 1964 following Navy evaluation.
PCH 1	HIGH POINT	110 tons	115 ft	45 knots	1963	In Navy service; see Chapter 22. Evaluated by Coast Guard as WMEH 1.
PGH 1	FLAGSTAFF	67 tons	74⅓ ft	40 + knots	1968	Grumman competitive prototype for PHM; to Coast Guard for evaluation (WPBH 1) and subsequently stricken.
PGH 2	TUCUMCARI	57 tons	71¾ ft	40 + knots	1968	Boeing competitive prototype for PHM; wrecked on reef in November 1972 and stricken in October 1973.
AGEH 1	PLAINVIEW	320 tons	212 ft	50 knots	1969	The world's largest hydrofoil; stricken after evaluation by Navy; fitted with Mk 32 torpedo tubes.

SMALL WATERPLANE AREA TWIN HULL CRAFT

Number	Name/Designation	Displacement	Length	Speed	Completed	Status/Remarks
—	KAIMALINO	228 tons	88 ft	25 knots	1973	In Navy service; see Chapter 25 for details.

SURFACE EFFECT SHIPS

Number	Name/Designation	Displacement	Length	Speed	Completed	Status/Remarks
—	XR-1	17 tons		34 knots	1963	Disposed of after evaluation by Navy; several x-craft variants.
—	SES-100A	110 tons	80 ft	75+ knots	1972	Scrapped after evaluation by Navy.
—	SES-100B	100 tons	77¾ ft	91.9 knots	1972	Following Navy evaluation placed on static display at Naval Ship Research and Development Center, Annapolis, Md.
—	SES-200	200 tons	160 ft	32 knots	1982	In Navy service; evaluated by Coast Guard as WSES-1; see Chapter 25.

SES-100A (1974, Aerojet General)

SES-100B (1974, Bell Aerospace)

AIR CUSHION VEHICLES

Number	Name/Designation	Displacement	Length	Speed	Completed	Status/Remarks
—	SKMR-1	20 tons	65½ ft	70 knots	1963	Bell Aerospace research craft; disposed of after Navy evaluation.
—	PACV 1	8.5 tons	38¾ ft	60 knots	1965	British-developed SR.N5 hovercraft built by Bell; evaluated by U.S. Navy and used in combat in Vietnam in 1966–1969; to Coast Guard for evaluation in 1969 for evaluation as HOVER 01, 02, 03; all stricken.
—	PACV 2	8.5 tons	38¾ ft	60 knots	1965	
—	PACV 3	8.5 tons	38¾ ft	60 knots	1965	
—	JEFF-A	162.5 tons	100 ft	50 knots	1977	Aerojet-General competitive prototype for LCAC; disposed of after trials.
—	JEFF-B	160 tons	87 ft	50 knots	1977	Bell Aerospace competitive prototype for LCAC; continues in test status; see Chapter 20.

D Shipyards

There are some 200 shipyards and ship-repair yards in the United States. There are 32 privately owned yards and 8 government-owned yards that can be considered major shipyards, having the facilities and work force to construct or convert oceangoing naval ships (defined as one or more shipbuilding positions that can accommodate a ship at least 475 feet in length and 68 feet in beam.) In addition, the Coast Guard operates a single shipyard.

PRIVATE SHIPYARDS

All U.S. Navy ship construction begun since 1969 has been done in private yards. More than 100 Navy ships and large craft are currently under construction in 15 of these private yards. These and 3 other yards are engaged in Navy conversion work. (These 18 yards are indicated by asterisks in the following list). About three-quarters of the dollar value of Navy new construction is done by 4 of the yards—Bath Iron Works, General Dynamics/Electric Boat, Litton/Ingalls, and Newport News. Six yards, including some doing Navy construction, are building about 15 commercial ships.

More than 70,000 workers are employed in private yards building these naval ships, with another 10,000 workers in the private shipyards engaged in naval repair and overhaul work. By dollar value about one-third of the Navy's overhaul and conversion work is done in private yards and two-thirds in naval shipyards.

The 32 major privately owned shipyards are listed below, with asterisks indicating yards currently engaged in Navy or Coast Guard programs.

ADDSCO Industries Inc., Mobile, Ala.
*Avondale Shipyards Inc., New Orleans, La.
*Bath Iron Works Corp., Bath, Maine
*Bay Shipbuilding Corp., Sturgeon Bay, Wisc.
*Bethlehem Steel Corp., Beaumont, Texas
 Bethlehem Steel Corp., San Francisco, Calif.
*Bethlehem Steel Corp., Sparrows Point, Md.
 Coastal Dry Dock and Repair Corp., Brooklyn, N.Y.[1]
 Equitable Shipyards Inc., Madisonville, La.
 FMC Corporation, Portland, Ore.
 Fraser Shipyards, Superior, Wisc.

*General Dynamics/Electric Boat Division, Groton, Conn.
*General Dynamics/Quincy Shipbuilding Division, Quincy, Mass.
*Litton Industries/Ingalls Shipbuilding Division, Pascagoula, Miss.
 Levingston Shipbuilding Co., Orange, Texas
*Lockheed Marine/Shipbuilding Division, Seattle, Wash.
 Marathon LeTourneau Co., Gulf Marine Division, Brownsville, Texas
 Marine Power & Equipment Co., Seattle, Wash.
*Marinette Marine Corp., Marinette, Wisc.
*National Steel & Shipbuilding Co., San Diego, Calif.
*Newport News Shipbuilding, Newport News, Va.
*Norfolk Shipbuilding & Drydock Corp., Norfolk, Va.
*Pennsylvania Shipbuilding Co., Chester, Pa.
*Tacoma Boatbuilding Co., Tacoma, Wash.
*Tampa Shipbuilding, Tampa, Fla.
 Texas Gulfport Shipbuilding Co., Port Arthur, Texas
 Todd Shipyards Corp., Galveston, Texas
 Todd Shipyards Corp., Houston, Texas
*Todd Pacific Shipyards Corp., Los Angeles (Long Beach), Calif.
 Todd Pacific Shipyards Corp., San Francisco, Calif.[2]
*Todd Pacific Shipyards Corp., Seattle, Wash.
 Triple A Shipyards, Hunters Point, San Francisco, Calif.[3]

In addition to these major shipyards, the Bell Aerospace-Halter facility is producing surface effect ships and air cushion vehicles for Navy and Coast Guard use; the small Peterson yard is producing ships for the Navy, and the Robert E. Derecktor yard is building Coast Guard cutters. These yards are described below.

Four major shipyards have recently closed down, continuing the trend of a diminishing number of yards in the United States. The American Shipbuilding Co. closed its yards in Chicago, Ill., and Toledo, Ohio, in 1982, and its yard in Lorain, Ohio, in 1983. (The firm continues to operate the Tampa Shipbuilding firm and a yard in Nashville, Tenn.). The Maryland Shipbuilding & Dry Dock Co. in Baltimore, Md., closed down in 1984.

The Boeing Company previously produced a number of hydrofoil prototypes plus the Navy's six PEGASUS (PHM 1)-class missile craft. The Boeing facility is no longer producing naval craft.

[1] Facilities are part of the former New York Naval Shipyard.

[2] Formerly Bethlehem Steel shipyard.
[3] Facilities are part of the former San Francisco Naval Shipyard/Hunters Point.

All but 3 of the private yards as well as the 8 naval shipyards are considered to be working at below their peacetime optimum workload. The 3 yards working at near their maximum peacetime capacity are the General Dynamics/Electric Boat, Lockheed Marine, and Newport News shipyards. The size of the largest dry dock *or* ship construction facility is indicated below (listed as dry dock size); in addition, floating dry docks are in use at several private and naval shipyards. Commercial yard employment is as of mid-1983. Only Navy and Coast Guard programs are discussed.

Avondale Shipyards

Established in 1938, this yard has produced destroyers, frigates, and landing ships and craft for the Navy as well as building the entire HAM-ILTON (WHEC 715) class of large cutters for the Coast Guard. From October 1982 until January 1983 the Avondale drydocked the battleship IOWA (BB 61) as the initial phase of her reactivation (completed at Litton/Ingalls). In 1983 the yard was selected as a second source for the WHIDBEY ISLAND (LSD 41) class.

The yard was acquired by the Ogden Corp. in 1959.

Avondale is located at Westwego, La., just above New Orleans on the Mississippi River.

Recent Navy programs:	LSD, T-AO construction
	T-AKR conversion
Yard area:	177 acres
Maximum dry dock size:	1,200 × 126 feet
	1,020 × 174 feet
Current work force:	5,175

Bath Iron Works

Bath Iron Works has been a major builder of destroyer-type ships. It built 24 of the OLIVER HAZARD PERRY (FFG 7)-class frigates and in 1982 the yard was selected as a second souce for the TICONDEROGA (CG 47)-class cruisers.

The Bath shipyard was founded in 1884 on the Kennebec River, about 10 miles from Popham, Mass., where in 1607 the first ship was built by European settlers in the New World. The yard subsequently built small iron and then steel ships. It began building torpedo boats for the Navy in 1896 and later constructed destroyers. A second facility was completed at nearby Portland, Maine, in 1983.

Bath Iron Works merged with the floor manufacturing firm of Congoleum-Nairn in 1967.

Recent Navy programs:	CG, FFG construction
Yard area:	91 acres
Maximum dry dock size:	850 × 136 feet (floating dry dock at Portland)
	720 × 130 feet (Bath)
Current work force:	7,725

Bell Halter

This facility has become the nation's leading producer of air cushion craft, currently building the LCAC landing craft for the Navy, having recently delivered 4 surface effect ships for Navy evaluation and Coast Guard use.

The parent firm is Bell Aerospace Textron, originally founded in 1935 to produce aircraft. Since 1958 the firm has been a leader in the development of air cushion vehicles and surface effect ships. The firm subsequently joined with Halter Marine Inc. to form Bell Halter, with facilities in New Orleans.

Recent Navy work:	LCAC
Yard area:	
Maximum dry dock size:	
Current work force:	750

Bethlehem Steel/Beaumont

This Bethlehem Steel yard's only current Navy work is cargo ship conversions. Established in 1917, the yard built minesweepers for the Navy in World War II in addition to merchant ships. Bethlehem Steel acquired the yard in 1947. After the war it continued to build merchant ships and, subsequently, offshore drilling rigs.

Beaumont, Texas, is on the Naches River, some 70 miles east of Houston.

Recent Navy work:	T-AK conversion
Yard area:	103 acres
Maximum dry dock size:	800 × 96 feet
Current work force:	1,150

Bethlehem Steel/Sparrows Point

One of several shipyards owned by Bethlehem Steel, the yard previously produced large numbers of auxiliary and amphibious ships for the Navy. The yard was established in 1891 and was taken over by Bethlehem in 1916. In the 1970s it constructed supertankers. The yard's Navy work now consists only of conversions of maritime prepositioning ships.

Sparrows Point is located at Baltimore, Md., on the Patapsco River at the upper end of Chesapeake Bay.

Recent Navy programs:	T-AK conversion
Yard area:	199 acres
Maximum dry dock size:	1,200 × 192 feet
Current work force:	1,550

General Dynamics/Electric Boat

This is the largest submarine construction yard outside of the Soviet Union, with a current production capability rated at one Trident SSBN and three attack submarines (SSNs) per year. The yard produces only submarines, although in the 1960s it did build several commercial submersibles as well as the Navy's NR-1 nuclear-propelled research submersible.

The yard traces its history to 1899 when it completed the submarine HOLLAND (SS 1). The present facility at Groton, Conn., was begun in 1911 to build diesel engines for submarines with the first submarines built there being 4 undersea craft for Peru in the 1920s. The first U.S. submarine built at Electric Boat was the CUTTLEFISH (SS 171), completed in 1934. The yard launched the world's first nuclear submarine, the NAUTILUS (SSN 571), in 1954.

The General Dynamics/Electric Boat yard at Groton, Conn., is the West's largest submarine construction facility, although smaller than Soviet submarine yards. Except for commercial submersibles and foreign submarines, Electric Boat has built only submarines for the U.S. Navy. In the center of this photograph are the Trident submarine OHIO (SSBN 726) in the flooded dock, the keel (circle) of the GEORGIA (SSBN 729), and the MICHIGAN (SSBN 727), out of water. The Trident construction "shec" is at right. (1979, U.S. Navy)

Ccmponents of SSNs and SSBNs are manufactured at the firm's facility at Quonset Point, R.I., and are barged to the Electric Boat yard.

The Electric Boat firm became a division of the General Dynamics Corp in 1952.

The yard is located on the Thames River at Groton, Conn. The Thames River enters Long Island Sound.

Recent Navy programs:	SSBN, SSN construction
Yard area:	123 acres
Maximum dry dock size:	617 × 96 feet (pontoon graving dock)
Current work force:	21,000 at Groton + 5,500 at Quonset Point

General Dynamics/Quincy

This is the former Fore River shipyard, which previously produced aircraft carriers, battleships, and nuclear-propelled cruisers. The yard was founded at the beginning of the century. Its first carrier was the famed LEXINGTON (CV 2), and the last capital ships were the carrier PHILIPPINE SEA (CV 47), completed in 1946, and the battleship MASSACHUSETTS (BB 59), in 1942. During the 1960s the yard also built several nuclear attack submarines.

Currently the yard is engaged in conversions of maritime prepositioning ships.

The Bethlehem Steel Corp., previous owner of this yard, closed the facility in 1964 and sold it to the General Dynamics Corp. The work force was expected to increase to some 5,100 during 1984.

Recent Navy programs:	T-AK
Yard area:	187 acres
Maximum dry dock size:	936 × 143 feet
Current work force:	2,400

Litton Industries/Ingalls Shipbuilding

The Litton/Ingalls shipbuilding complex consists of two adjacent shipyards, providing a highly diversified shipbuilding and repair capability. Along with Newport News Shipbuilding, the Litton/Ingalls complex may be considered the most capable and flexible shipyard in the United States. (However, Ingalls no longer builds nuclear ships and its largest naval ships have been LHD/LHA helicopter carriers compared with the CVN type built at Newport News.)

The West Bank facility was built in the 1960s specifically for modular and horizontal construction of high-technology ships. At that time, it was the most advanced shipyard in the United States and the only completely new shipyard built in the country since World War II. The yard immediately won contracts for the Navy's Forward Deployment Logistic (FDL) ships, TARAWA (LHA 1)-class helicopter carriers, and SPRUANCE (DD 963)-class destroyers to be built in the new facility. The West Bank yard's single assembly facility is equivalent to six conventional inclined ways in terms of ships delivered per year.

The older East Bank facility was acquired by Litton Industries in 1961. Previously known as the Ingalls Shipbuilding Co., it has produced a variety of ships for the Navy, including nuclear attack submarines in the 1960s and early 1970s.

The yard now produces the TICONDEROGA-class cruisers and the new LHD helicopter carriers as well as commercial offshore drilling rigs. The yard also rehabilitated the battleship IOWA (BB 61) in 1983–1984.

The yards are located at Pascagoula, Miss., near the city of Biloxi on the Mississippi Sound off the Gulf of Mexico.

Recent Navy programs:	BB modernization
	CG, LHD construction
Yard area:	788 acres (551 currently in use)
Maximum dry dock size:	800 × 173 feet (West Bank)
	690 × 85 feet (East Bank)
	650 × 90 feet (East Bank)
Current work force:	10,200

Lockheed Marine

The yard, formerly known as the Puget Sound Bridge and Dredging Co., was one of the West Coast's oldest shipbuilding facilities, having begun operations in 1889. It was acquired by the Lockheed Aircraft Corp. in 1959, being subsequently known as Lockheed Shipbuilding & Construction Co., and from 1983 as Lockheed Marine/Shipbuilding Division.

The yard has most recently built submarine tenders, frigates, and amphibious ships for the Navy and the two Polar-class icebreakers for the Coast Guard. It was the lead yard for the WHIDBEY ISLAND-class dock landing ships.

The yard is located in Seattle, Wash., on Puget Sound's Elliot Bay.

Parent organization:	Lockheed
Recent Navy programs:	LSD construction
Yard area:	121 acres
Maximum dry dock size:	690 × 90 feet
Current work force:	3,000

Marinette Marine

This yard is one of several small, inland shipyards in the United States. It has long produced small ships and craft for the Navy.

Located at Sturgeon Bay, Wisc., the yard is on an inlet of Green Bay, about 40 miles northeast of the city by that name. The bay is connected by canal to Lake Michigan.

Recent Navy programs:	MCM, T-ATF construction
Yard area:	
Maximum dry dock size:	1,100 × 136 feet
Current work force:	800

National Steel and Shipbuilding

National Steel, sometimes known by the initials NASSCO, has produced a number of auxiliary ships as well as tank landing ships for the Navy. Its recent SAN DIEGO-class merchant tankers (188,500 deadweight tons) are the largest ships ever built on the West Coast.

The yard was acquired by Morrison-Knudson Co. in 1961.

The yard is located in San Diego, Calif., adjacent to the naval base. The yard operates a large graving dock (687 feet × 90 feet) at the base.

The number employed at the yard decreased sharply in 1982–1983, down from 6,000 in one year.

Recent Navy programs:	T-ARC, AS construction
	T-AH, T-AK, T-AKR conversion
Yard area:	97 acres
Maximum dry dock size:	980 × 170 feet
Current work force:	3,450

Newport News Shipbuilding

Newport News Shipbuilding is one of the two most capable shipyards in the United States. It is the only yard currently constructing nuclear-propelled surface ships and one of only two constructing submarines. The yard now builds NIMITZ (CVN 68)-class carriers and attack submarines for the Navy but is seeking to additionally construct Trident SSBNs. Its current construction capability is rated at two SSNs per year.

The yard was founded in 1886 and has built a variety of ship types for the Navy. It constructed the last nuclear-propelled cruisers and before that built battleships, the last being the INDIANA (BB 58), completed in 1942. The yard has built all U.S. aircraft carriers since the ENTERPRISE (CVN 65), laid down in 1958; 23 carriers have been built by the yard and 3 CVNs are now under construction. A new facility for constructing submarines is being developed. (Beyond naval programs, Newport News has a large commercial shipbuilding effort underway.)

The Newport News Shipbuilding and Dry Dock Co. was acquired by the Tenneco Corp. in 1968.

The yard is located at Newport News, Va., near the Norfolk Naval

The sprawling West Bank shipyard at the Litton/Ingalls complex in Pascagoula, Miss., was the first modern American shipyard to assemble ships using production lines with horizontal conveyors and a floating launch mechanism. Here the Aegis missile cruiser VINCENNES (CG 49) is shown in the final stages of assembly; portions of two sister ships are visible at right. (1984, Litton/Ingalls Shipbuilding)

The destroyer ELLIOTT (DD 967) is towed off the syncrolift platform at the Todd San Pedro yard. The ship's keel is nine feet above the deck; note the two tractors under the stern, one of which can tow the ship across the moveable rails to a work bay. Todd and other U.S. shipyards have invested considerable resources in modernization despite a shrinking shipbuilding market. (1984, Todd Shipyards)

Shipyard and Norfolk Naval Base. It is at the mouth of the James River at the entrance to Hampton Roads.

Recent Navy programs:	SSN, CVN construction
Yard area:	435 acres (275 currently in use)
Maximum dry dock size:	1,600 × 246 feet
Current work force:	28,250

Pennsylvania Shipbuilding

This is the former Sun Shipbuilding and Dry Dock Co., a major builder of commercial and naval cargo-type ships. The yard has been taken over by the Pennsylvania Shipbuilding Co. (an affiliate of Paden, Inc.) in 1982.

Established in 1920 at Chester, Pa., which is west of Philadelphia on the Delaware River, the yard has mainly constructed merchant ships.

Recent Navy programs:	T-AKR conversion
Yard area:	172 acres
Maximum dry dock size:	1,000 × 195 feet
Current work force:	1,250

Peterson Builders

Long a builder of small ships and craft, this yard is currently engaged in programs for the U.S. Navy and recently completed a series of 390-ton missile craft (PGG) for Saudi Arabia.

The yard is inland, located on Sturgeon Bay, Wisc., and connected to Lake Michigan by canal.

Recent Navy programs:	MCM, ARS construction
Yard area:	
Maximum dry dock size:	360 × 36 feet
Current work force:	650

Robert E. Derecktor

The firm took over an existing yard at Middletown, R.I., to construct the BEAR (WMEC 901)-class Coast Guard cutters.

Middletown is near Newport, on Narragansett Bay.

Recent Navy/CG programs:	WMEC construction
Yard area:	
Maximum dry dock size:	450 × 96 feet
Current work force:	800

Tacoma Boatbuilding

A long-time producer of small ships and craft for the U.S. Navy, the yard also built PGM-type patrol craft for South Korea and a series of 815-ton missile craft (PCG) for Saudi Arabia. Yard employment was more than 2,000 in 1983.

The yard is at Tacoma, Wash., south of the city of Seattle on Puget Sound.

Recent Navy/CG programs:	T-AGOS, WMEC, WTGB construction
Yard area:	45 acres
Maximum dry dock size:	650 × 400 feet
Current work force:	1,400

Todd Pacific Shipyards (San Pedro)

This yard, formerly the Los Angeles Shipbuilding and Dry Dock Co., was operated by Todd Pacific Shipyards for the government from 1943 after the yard lagged in producing Navy ships. Todd purchased the yard in 1945. Naval construction in the postwar period included destroyers. The yard subsequently became a major builder of escort ships/frigates for the Navy. Future Navy work is uncertain as the PERRY-class production run is coming to an end. The work force has declined from 5,800 in mid-1983.

In 1983–1984 the yard's construction and repair capability was expanded by an estimated 250 percent with the addition of a syncrolift facility. The lifting platform is 655 feet long and 106 feet wide and can accommodate ships up to 780 feet in length displacing up to 22,000 tons; the platform lifts ships from the water after which they are towed on rails by a tractor to adjacent work areas. This facility makes the Todd San Pedro yard the most capable commercial shipbuilding and repair yard on the West Coast.

The yard is at San Pedro, Calif., a southern suburb of Los Angeles on San Pedro Bay. The yard is near the Long Beach Naval Shipyard.

Recent Navy programs:	FFG, ARDM construction
Yard area:	90 acres
Maximum dry dock size:	800 × 87 feet
Current work force:	2,500

Todd Pacific Shipyards (Seattle)

The site of shipbuilding since the 1890s, this yard built the battleship NEBRASKA (BB 14), completed in 1907, and a variety of other merchant and naval vessels. Under an unusual contract with the Electric Boat Co. the yard constructed submarines before World War I. A varied construction program followed with Todd taking control of the yard in 1916 (at the time, the Seattle Construction and Dry Dock Co.). As Todd Pacific-Tacoma, the yard produced escort carriers (CVE) and destroyers during World War II, with destroyer and frigate construction continuing after the war.

The current program of construction of PERRY-class frigates for the U.S. and Australian navies is being completed resulting in a severe drop in employment from approximately 4,500 in mid-1983.

The yard is in Seattle, Wash., on the northwest corner of Harbor Island in Elliot Bay.

Recent Navy programs:	FFG construction
Yard area:	47 acres
Maximum dry dock size:	600 × 96 feet
Current work force:	1,200

The Todd Pacific Shipyard facility in the center of Seattle, Wash., is typical of the U.S. shipyards performing both naval and commercial work. Eight OLIVER HAZARD PERRY (FFG 7)-class frigates are visible in this view plus several commercial ships. With the end of the frigate program the Todd Seattle and San Pedro yards are working far below capacity—as are most U.S. shipyards. (Todd Shipyards/Camera Craft)

NAVAL SHIPYARDS

There are 8 naval shipyards in operation. Naval shipyards reached a post-World War II peak in 1961 when there were 11 active government yards with 101,000 employees. Subsequently, the naval shipyards in Boston, New York (Brooklyn), and San Francisco (Hunter's Point) have closed down.[4]

The naval shipyards now undertake only modernization, overhaul, and repair work. The last ships built by naval shipyards were the DRUM (SSN 677) by Mare Island, SAND LANCE (SSN 660) by Portsmouth, BLUE RIDGE (LCC 19) by Philadelphia, and DETROIT (AOE 4) by Puget Sound, all delivered in 1970–1972. The Mare Island and Puget Sound yards are credited with being able to resume construction activities in the near term if necessary.

Some 77,000 civilians are employed in the naval shipyards. A minimum number of naval personnel are assigned to these yards, mainly for command and administrative functions.

The table at the bottom of this page indicates the areas of shipyard specialization.

Charleston Naval Shipyard

The yard primarily supports submarines, with the remaining yard capability allocated mostly to destroyer-size and smaller surface ships. It was established in 1901.

The yard is located on the Cooper River, just north of the city of Charleston, S.C. The river empties into the Atlantic Ocean.

Yard area:	1,980 acres
Maximum dry dock size:	750 × 140 feet
Current work force:	60 Navy + 8,640 civilian

Long Beach Naval Shipyard

This yard specializes in surface ship work and modernized the battleships NEW JERSEY (BB 62) and MISSOURI (BB 63) from 1981 onward. Congress authorized funds to build the yard in 1940 and the yard was formally established in February 1943—the last U.S. naval shipyard to be opened. The yard is the closest government yard to the San Diego naval complex and provides support to the large number of surface ships based there.

[4] A portion of the former New York Naval Shipyard facilities are operated by the Coastal Dry Dock Corp., doing commercial and naval overhaul and repair work; the yard has built some tankers since being retired from naval use. Part of the Hunter's Point facilities are operated by Triple A Shipyards.

The yard is located in the Los Angeles suburb of Long Beach, on San Pedro Bay.

Yard area:	204 acres
Maximum dry dock size:	1,003 × 142 feet
Current work force:	45 Navy + 6,770 civilian

Mare Island Naval Shipyard

This yard is the leading submarine yard on the West Coast. While concentrating on SSNs and SSBNs, it also undertakes modernization and overhaul of surface combatants and auxiliary ships.

Established in 1854, the yard previously constructed battleships as well as lesser naval vessels and submarines. The last dreadnought built on the West Coast, the CALIFORNIA (BB 44), was completed at Mare Island in 1921.

Located across the Napa River from Vallejo, Calif., the yard is on San Pablo Bay, a part of the greater San Francisco Bay area. It is 35 miles northeast of San Francisco. During World War II landfills at the northern end of Mare Island made it a peninsula.

Yard area:	4,071 acres
Maximum dry dock size:	741 × 92 feet
Current work force:	60 Navy + 10,240 civilian

Norfolk Naval Shipyard

The Norfolk yard specializes in surface ship work, especially the overhaul of nuclear aircraft carriers as well as nuclear submarines. The Norfolk area contains the Navy's largest base complex and is headquarters for the U.S. Atlantic Fleet as well as the NATO Supreme Allied Commander Atlantic.

Ship construction at this site began in 1767, and it was established as a naval shipyard in 1801. The yard has built warships up to battleship and carrier size, the last being the ALABAMA (BB 60), completed in 1942, and TARAWA (CV 40), in 1946.

The Norfolk yard is on the Elizabeth River, just south of Hampton Roads, Va. With Newport News and Portsmouth, Norfolk comprises the port complex of Hampton Roads.

Yard area:	801 acres
Maximum dry dock size:	1,092 × 143 feet
Current work force:	150 Navy + 13,270 civilian

Pearl Harbor Naval Shipyard

The yard provides overhauls for surface ships and submarines. It adjoins the naval base, which includes a submarine base, supply depot, and

NAVAL SHIPYARD SPECIALIZATION

	Charleston	Long Beach	Mare Island	Norfolk	Pearl Harbor	Philadelphia	Portsmouth	Puget Sound
Strategic Missile Submarines	●		●				●	●
Attack Submarines	●		●	●	●		●	●
Aircraft Carriers		●		●		●		●
Guided Missile Ships	●	●		●	●	●		●
Surface Nuclear Ships			●					●

An SSBN undergoing overhaul at the Newport News Shipbuilding and Dry Dock yard in Virginia. The Newport News yard is the largest in the West and one of only two U.S. yards now building nuclear ships. (1983, Giorgio Arra)

other facilities. The base is adjacent to the headquarters of the U.S. Pacific Fleet and Pacific Command.

A treaty with King Kalakaua of Hawaii in 1887 gave the United States exclusive rights to use Pearl Harbor as a coaling station, but it was not so used until 1908. A naval yard was later built, with the first dry dock completed in 1919. No major construction has been done at the yard.

Pearl Harbor is an inlet on the southern coast of the Hawaiian island of Oahu. The shipyard is on the eastern side of the inlet, adjacent to Hickam Air Force Base. It is the only shipyard in the Hawaiian Islands.

Yard area:	354 acres
Maximum dry dock size:	1,088 × 135 feet
Current work force:	55 Navy + 6,870 civilian

Philadelphia Naval Shipyard

The yard specializes in the overhaul and modernization of surface combatants, being especially qualified to support advanced missile and electronic systems. The yard has also performed the SLEP modernizations on the carriers SARATOGA (CV 60) and FORRESTAL (CV 59).

Established in 1801, the yard was originally located at the foot of Federal Street in Philadelphia. All yard activities were moved to League Island between 1862 and 1876. The yard has constructed a variety of ships up to battleship and aircraft carrier size, the last of those types being the WISCONSIN (BB 64) and NEW JERSEY, both completed in 1944, and the VALLEY FORGE (CV 45), in 1946. The yard reactivated the NEW JERSEY during the Vietnam War (1968).

The yard is joined to the South Philadelphia mainland, at the junction of the Delaware and Schuylkill rivers, which empty into Delaware Bay.

Yard area:	828 acres
Maximum dry dock size:	1,092 × 150 feet
Current work force:	115 Navy + 11,160 civilian

Portsmouth Naval Shipyard

Long one of the Navy's principal submarine construction yards, the yard now performs almost exclusively submarine overhauls. An early site of colonial shipbuilding, the first warship launched in North America was built at Portsmouth in 1690 for the Royal Navy. From 1775 the then-private yard built warships for the Continental Navy, becoming a naval shipyard in 1800.

Although generally described as being in Portsmouth, N.H., the yard is actually on Seavey Island at Kittery, Maine, near the mouth of the Piscataqua River.

Yard area:	266 acres
Maximum dry dock size:	741 × 91⅕ feet
Current work force:	100 Navy + 8,455 civilian

Puget Sound Naval Shipyard

This yard can accommodate the Navy's largest ships and serves as the principal carrier overhaul and modernization yard on the West Coast. It can support nuclear carriers and nuclear submarines, including SSBNs. The yard is also a site for mothballed naval ships.

The shipyard was founded in 1891.

The yard is in the city of Bremerton, Wash., about 15 miles west of the city of Seattle. It is on Puget Sound.

Yard area:	1,081 acres
Maximum dry dock size:	1,152 × 180 feet
Current work force:	235 Navy + 11,860 civilian

COAST GUARD SHIPYARDS

The U.S. Coast Guard operates a small shipyard at Curtis Bay, Md. The yard performs primarily overhaul and conversions of Coast Guard craft, having previously built small cutters, the largest being the RELIANCE (WMEC 615) as well as the Navy SWATH ship KAIMALINO.

The yard is located in a suburb of Baltimore.

Yard area:	
Maximum dry dock size:	350 feet
Current work force:	270 Coast Guard + 800 civilian

Todd/Seattle
Lockheed Marine
Puget Sound NSY
Tacoma Boatbuilding
Boeing

Marinette Marine
Peterson Builders
Bay City

Bath Iron Works
Portsmouth NSY
General Dynamics/Quincy
Robert E. Derecktor
General Dynamics/Electric Boat
Penn Shipbuilding
Philadelphia NSY
Bethlehem/Sparrows Point
Curtis Bay USCG Yard
Newport News
Norfolk NSY

Mare Island NSY

Todd/San Pedro
Long Beach NSY

National Steel

Charleston NSY

Pearl Harbor NSY

Bethlehem/Beaumont

Bell Textron
Avondale

Litton/Ingalls

E Reading List

Material on the contemporary U.S. Fleet may be found in several books and periodicals. In addition, the annual hearings of the armed services and appropriations committees of the Senate and House of Representatives are most informative sources of information on the U.S. Navy and related activities, if one has the patience to wade through the several thousand pages of hearings produced every year.

One name has dominated the list of books on U.S. naval subjects published during the past few years, that of Dr. Norman Friedman of the Hudson Institute. In addition to the books listed below, he has written a number of important professional papers in this area.

Several highly useful professional papers in this area have also been produced by the Center for Naval Analyses.

BOOKS

Jan S. Breemer, *U.S. Naval Developments* (Annapolis, Md.: Nautical and Aviation, 1983). This volume provides a discussion of U.S. Navy post-World War II policy and technical developments.

Norman Friedman, *Naval Radar* (Annapolis, Md.: Naval Institute Press, 1981).

_____ , *Submarine Design and Development* (Annapolis, MD.: Naval Institute Press, 1984).

_____ , *U.S. Aircraft Carriers* (Annapolis, Md.: Naval Institute Press, 1983).

_____ , *U.S. Cruisers* (Annapolis, Md.: Naval Institute Press, 1984).

_____ , *U.S. Destroyers* (Annapolis, Md.: Naval Institute Press, 1982).

_____ , *U.S. Naval Weapons* (Annapolis, Md.: Naval Institute Press, 1983).

U.S. Navy, *United States Naval Aviation 1910–1980* (Washington, D.C.: Government Printing Office, 1981). A detailed chronology of U.S. naval aviation—ships and aircraft.

PERIODICALS

The Hook. Monthly journal of the Tailhook Association, with detailed historical and contemporary descriptions of U.S. carrier aviation.

Naval Aviation News.* A most useful publication of the Navy's air organizations—the Deputy CNO (Air Warfare) and Naval Air Systems Command—produced six times per year.

Naval Institute *Proceedings*. Monthly magazine of the Navy's professional society, with a broad spectrum of articles on the Navy, Marine Corps, and Coast Guard. The annual May Naval Review of the *Proceedings* as well as the occasional special issue on an aspect of naval warfare or the Coast Guard or Marine Corps provides an in-depth look at an issue not available elsewhere.

Naval War College Review. The monthly magazine of the Naval War College provides perceptive views of U.S. naval issues.

Navy Times. Weekly, privately published newspaper stressing naval personnel matters, but with discussions of naval policy.

Sea Power. The monthly journal of the Navy League provides a useful perspective on contemporary naval and maritime issues.

Surface Warfare.* Published every second month, this is a most informative magazine produced under the auspices of the Deputy CNO (Surface Warfare).

The periodicals *Journal of Electronic Defense* and *Military Electronics* provide coverage of the important field of electronic warfare.

ANNUALS

The naval annuals *Jane's Fighting Ships* (London: Jane's Yearbooks) and *Flottes de Combat* (Paris: Editions Maritimes & d'Outre-Mer) are also of interest to those seeking information on the U.S. Navy. The latter volume, edited by Jean Labayle Couhat, is published every second year in French and in alternate years in an English-language edition prepared by A.D. Baker III (Annapolis, Md.: U.S. Naval Institute).

* Available through the Government Printing Office.

Ship Name and Class Index

(Harbor and service craft with designation prefixes Y and WY are not indexed.)

Ship Designation Index

Addenda

NAVAL RESERVE

Planning for the Naval Air Reserve and Naval Reserve Force is in a state of flux as continued increases and improvements are being made. The following represents the latest force level planning for NRF surface ships when this edition went to press. The original plan to provide the NRF with 16 ships of the OLIVER HAZARD PERRY (FFG 7) class was increased by two ships in mid-1984. (The latest Naval Air Reserve plan is shown on page 365.)

	1984	1985	1986	1987	1988	1989
DD 931 class	1	1	1	1	1	1
FFG 7 class	3	5	9	12	16	18
FF 1052 class	6	6	6	7	8	8
MCM type	0	0	1	3	8	8
MSH type	0	0	0	0	1	2
MSO type	18	17	17	13	9	5
YP/trawler*	0	6	12	18	22	22

* Under this Craft of Opportunity Program (COOP), to begin in fiscal 1985, commercial trawlers and YP-type seamanship training craft will be fitted with limited mine countermeasure capabilities, including side scanning sonar and sweep gear.

In addition, current Navy planning provides for the NRF to continue to operate two LSTs. These are to be joined in the early 1990s by an additional LST, one LSD, and one LPD.

The four NRF-operated fleet tugs (ATF) will be phased out in late 1984 and 1985. The future of the two NRF-operated salvage ships (ARS) is uncertain; the transfer of ships of the new ARS 50 class to the NRF is also under consideration.

Two large repair ships (AR) will be transferred to the NRF. Also, the five AO 177-class ships are planned for eventual assignment to the reserves beginning in fiscal 1988, after the oilers are modernized.

Finally, assignment of the battleship WISCONSIN (BB 64) to the NRF has been considered but rejected.

STRATEGIC MISSILE SUBMARINES

The number of SSBNs in commission is declining; the older Poseidon submarines are being retired as the new Trident submarines are completed in order for the United States to remain within the SALT agreement of 950 missiles. Furthermore, the rate of decline will accelerate as the remaining Poseidon SSBNs reach the end of their 30-years service life. The SSBN force will reach a nadir of between 15 and 17 boats in the late 1990s. The force will then increase to the current goal of 20 Trident submarines: 10 in the Pacific, based at Bangor, Washington; and 10 in the Atlantic, based at Kings Bay, Georgia.

The SAM RAYBURN (SSBN 635) was decommissioned in 1985. The Navy is seeking funds from Congress to employ her as a dockside nuclear training ship.

The NATHAN HALE (SSBN 623) and ANDREW JACKSON (SSBN 619) have been tentatively selected for decommissioning during 1986.

OHIO CLASS

SSBN 730	HENRY M. JACKSON	comm. 6 Oct 1984
SSBN 732	ALASKA	launched 12 Jan 1985
		comm. 25 Jan 1986

SUBMARINES

The development of the SSN-21 SEAWOLF class is delayed because of redesign requirements and problems with the SUBACS sensor-weapons control system. The lead ship not expected to be authorized until at least fiscal 1990, with a completion date of 1996. The current estimated cost for 30 submarines is $38 *billion,* with the lead ship costing $2 *billion.*

The redesign includes placing the 30-inch torpedo tubes amidships, four angled to port and four to starboard, and not in the more efficient bow position originally proposed.

The Submarine Advanced Combat System (SUBACS) is under development for the later units of the LOS ANGELES (SSN 688) class and the SEAWOLF class attack submarines. The original SUBACS program provided for three versions: (2) SUBACS Basic, to be installed in the SSN 688 class beginning with the SSN 751; (2) SUBACS A for the SSN 688 class beginning with the SSN 760 and the SSN-21; and (3) SUBACS B for eventual fit to all of the SSN-21 type.

In 1985, however, major technical and management problems in the SUBACS program—which led to large cost overruns—forced the Navy to restructure the effort. Under the revised plan the SSN 751 and later ships will be provided with a modified SUBACS Basic with the SSN-21 class being fitted with a combined A/B version (designated the B version).

The SUBACS problems can be expected to contribute to delays in the SSN-21 program. The prime contractor for the development of SUBACS was IBM; the problems with the program are expected to preclude that firm from participation in the later development and production efforts.

LOS ANGELES CLASS

SSN 710	AUGUSTA	comm. 19 Jan 1985
SSN 717	OLYMPIA	comm. 17 Nov 1984
SSN 718	HONOLULU	comm. 6 July 1985
SSN 719	PROVIDENCE	launched 4 Aug 1984
		comm. 27 July 1985
SSN 720	PITTSBURGH	launched 8 Dec 1984
		comm. 23 Nov 1985
SSN 721	CHICAGO	launched 13 Oct 1984
SSN 722	KEY WEST	launched 20 July 1985
SSN 723	OKLAHOMA CITY	launched 4 November 1985
SSN 724	LOUISVILLE	launched 14 December 1985

STURGEON CLASS

The last nine units of this class are slightly longer; six of these submarines, beginning with the CAVALLA (SSN 684), were to be modified to carry a single lockout chamber-hangar for swimmers and a Swimmer Delivery Vehicle (SDV). Only one chamber-hangar exists, with others planned for fabrication in the late 1980s.

ETHAN ALLEN CLASS

The SAM HOUSTON (SSN 609) and JOHN MARSHALL (SSN 611) were converted at the Puget Sound Naval Shipyard from October 1983 to late 1985. The $16 million conversion of the two ex-SSBNs include provisions for carrying passengers and equipment. Also included were fittings for two lockout chamber-hangars to be installed on the deck (aft of the sail), each of which can accommodate a Swimmer Delivery Vehicle (SDV). The hangars, however, will not be available in sufficient numbers for these submarines and the six modified STURGEON-class SSNs until the early 1990s. The two ex-SSBNs will probably be retired about 1990.

GEORGE WASHINGTON CLASS

The GEORGE WASHINGTON was decommissioned as the SSN 598 on 24 January 1985 and the PATRICK HENRY as the SSN 599 on 25 May 1984. Both began the deactivation process several months earlier. (As SSNs their missile fire control system was deleted and concrete was placed in their missile tubes.)

The ROBERT E. LEE (SSN 601) was decommissioned on 30 September 1983 and was stricken on 15 January 1984.

NAUTILUS

The NAUTILUS (SSN 571) arrived at the New London, Connecticut, memorial site in 1985 after being decommissioned at the Mare Island Naval Shipyard.

AIRCRAFT CARRIERS

NIMITZ CLASS

CVN 71	THEODORE ROOSEVELT	launched 27 Oct 1984
CVN 72	ABRAHAM LINCOLN	laid down 3 Nov 1984

FORRESTAL CLASS

The FORRESTAL (CV 59) underwent SLEP from January 1983 through July 1985. The INDEPENDENCE (CV 62) entered the Philadelphia Naval Shipyard in April 1985 for a 28-month SLEP modernization.

CRUISERS

TICONDEROGA CLASS

CG 49	VINCENNES	comm. 6 July 1985
CG 50	VALLEY FORGE	launched 29 Sep 1984
		comm. 18 Jan 1986
CG 51	THOMAS S. GATES	laid down 23 Aug 1984
		launched 14 Dec 1985
CG 52	BUNKER HILL	laid down 11 Jan 1984
		launched 13 Apr 1985
		comm. 20 Sep 1985
CG 53	MOBILE BAY	laid down 5 June 1984
		launched 12 Oct 1985
CG 54	ANTIETAM	laid down 15 Nov 1984
CG 55		laid down 18 Mar 1985
CG 56		laid down 22 July 1985

BELKNAP CLASS

BELKNAP (CG 26) modified to serve as Sixth Fleet Flagship effect 1 June 1986.

DESTROYERS

SPRUANCE CLASS

MOOSBRUGGER (DD 980) fitted with improved SQS-53B in 1982.

FRIGATES

OLIVER HAZARD PERRY CLASS

FFG 9	WADSWORTH	to Naval Reserve Force
FFG 16	CLIFTON SPRAGUE	to Naval Reserve Force
FFG 37	CROMMELIN	comm. 18 June 1983
FFG 48	VANDEGRIFT	comm. 24 Nov 1984
FFG 49	ROBERT G. BRADLEY	comm. 11 Aug 1984
FFG 50	JESSE L. TAYLOR	comm. 1 Dec 1984
FFG 51	GARY	comm. 17 Nov 1984
FFG 52	CARR	comm. 27 July 1985
FFG 53	HAWES	comm. 8 Feb 1985
FFG 54	FORD	comm. 29 June 1985
FFG 55	ELROD	laid down 21 Nov 1983
		launched 12 May 1984
		comm. 6 July 1985
FFG 56	SIMPSON	laid down 27 Feb 1984
		launched 31 Aug 1984
FFG 57	REUBEN JAMES	laid down 19 Nov 1983
		launched 8 Feb 1985
FFG 58	SAMUEL B. ROBERTS	launched 8 Dec 1984
FFG 60	RODNEY M. DAVIS	laid down 8 Feb 1985
		launched 11 Jan 1986
FFG 61	INGRAHAM	

KNOX CLASS

FF 1055	HEPBURN	to Naval Reserve Force
FF 1058	MEYERKORD	to Naval Reserve Force
FF 1061	PATTERSON	to Naval Reserve Force
FF 1072	BLAKELY	to Naval Reserve Force

AMPHIBIOUS SHIPS

WHIDBEY ISLAND CLASS

LSD 41	WHIDBEY ISLAND	comm. 9 Feb 1985

LANDING CRAFT

LANDING CRAFT AIR CUSHION

Lockheed Shipbuilding, Seattle, Washington, selected as second source for LCAC production.

LCU 1610 CLASS

LCU 1680 and LCU 1681 are being built by Moss Point Marine of Escatawpa, Mississippi; to complete in late 1986.

LANDING VEHICLES

In 1985 the designation LVT was changed to AAV for Assault Amphibious Vehicle (e.g., AAV7A1 vice LVTP-7A1).

In 1985 the secretary of the navy cancelled the Marine Corps's planned follow-on tracked vehicle designated LVT(X), the successor to the AAV 7/LVTP-7 series.

PATROL SHIPS AND CRAFT

MULTI-MISSION PATROL CRAFT

The Navy is considering a class of approximately six multi-mission patrol craft (PCM) to supplement the PEGASUS (PHM 1) class for operations in the Caribbean area. The proposed ships would have PHM-type weapons/surveillance capabilities plus an ASW capability, probably the AQS-13-series dipping sonar and a towed array. Construction would begin in the late 1980s.

FAST PATROL BOATS

All remaining PTF-type boats have been discarded.

MINE COUNTERMEASURES SHIPS AND CRAFT

CRAFT OF OPPORTUNITY PROGRAM

The Navy is modifying 22 small craft to a minesweeper configuration under the Craft Of Opportunity Program (COOP)—10 former seamanship training craft (YP) and 12 former fishing craft. The ten older YP training craft are from the U.S. Naval Academy. They are intended for harbor clearance, supplementing the larger MSH and MCM classes.

The first three units are former fishing craft named TIKI, DIXIE, and ROBIN GALE III. The first two craft are assigned to Seattle, and the third to Galveston, Texas. All three were placed in service during 1985.

The Naval Reserve Force will operate the COOP effort. Each minesweeper will be assigned four crews of nine enlisted men each, the crews being designated as Blue, Gold, Red, and Green. The crews will rotate training on the craft. In wartime or during mobilization, the crews would rotate operating the craft. Plans call for at least three additional craft to be similarly operated in an emergency.

Along the Atlantic and Gulf coasts the COOP units will be controlled by Mine Squadron 2; the Pacific coast units will be under Mine Group 1 in Seattle, Washington.

AUXILIARY SHIPS

ACOUSTIC RESEARCH SHIP

The catamaran oceanographic research ship HAYES (T-AGOR 16) is being converted into an acoustic research ship under the fiscal 1986 program.

OCEAN SURVEILLANCE SHIPS

T-AGOS 4	TRIUMPH	launched 7 Sep 1984
T-AGOS 5	ASSURANCE	launched 12 Jan 1985
T-AGOS 6	PERSISTENT	launched 6 Apr 1985
T-AGOS 7	INDOMITABLE	launched 16 July 1985
T-AGOS 8	PREVAIL	launched 7 Dec 1985

FLEET OILERS

T-AO 187 through 190 to be built by Avondale Shipyards, New Orleans, Louisiana; T-AO 191 and 192 to be built by Pennsylvania Shipbuilding, Chester, Pennsylvania.

T-AO 187	HENRY J. KAISER	launched 5 Oct 1985

SURVEILLANCE SHIP

The landing craft repair ship SPHINX (ARL 24) has been modified to serve as an intelligence surveillance ship, being reactivated in 1985 and recommissioned on 30 March 1985. She will be employed in the surveillance role off the coast of Nicaragua; in this role the SPHINX has a crew of 191 (11 officers + 180 enlisted)

SALVAGE SHIPS

ARS 50	SAFEGUARD	comm. 17 Aug 1985
ARS 51	GRASP	comm. 14 Dec. 1985
ARS 52	SALVOR	launched 28 July 1984
ARS 53	GRAPPLE	launched 8 Dec 1984

FLEET TUGS

ATF 105	MOCTOBI	laid up in reserve 1985
ATF 110	QUAPAW	laid up in reserve 1985

AUXILIARY CRANE SHIPS

In addition to various standard types of merchant ships laid up in a "ready reserve" status with the National Defense Reserve Fleet, eight cargo ships are being modified to serve as auxiliary crane ships. These ships will provide the capability of unloading themselves and other cargo ships onto piers or into lighters when major port facilities are not available.

The eight ships, of the C5 and C6 cargo configurations, will be laid up in the NDRF in the James River, Virginia. They are being converted under the aegis of the Military Sealift Command are are designated T-ACS although they will remain under Maritime Administration and not Navy/MSC custody.

The lead ship conversion was the SS PRESIDENT HARRISON, renamed KEYSTONE STATE (T-ACS 1). The ship, a C6-S-1 of 17,782 deadweight tons, was converted from March 1983 to May 1984 (see photos). The seven other T-ACS conversions are funded in the fiscal 1984–1989 shipbuilding and conversion programs.

SERVICE CRAFT

SEAMANSHIP TRAINING CRAFT

YP 688 under construction

SUBMERSIBLE SUPPORT CRAFT

The catamaran submersible support ship Lulu was transferred to the Navy in late 1984. The Lulu—named for the mother of oceanographer-physicist Allyn Vine—was previously used to support the research submersible ALVIN at the Wood's Hole Oceanographic Institution, Mass. (That craft was named for Dr. Vine.) In naval service the Lulu will operate with Submarine Development Group I in San Diego, Calif.

Name	Built
Lulu	1964

Builders:	
Displacement:	460 tons
Length:	105 feet (32.0 m) oa
Beam:	48 feet (14.6 m)
Draft:	11 feet (3.3 meters)
Propulsion:	diesels (1 forward + 2 aft); 2 shafts
Speed:	6.5 knots
Range:	2,000 n.miles at 6 knots
Manning:	9 (civilian) + 10 submersible operation/support + 8 scientists

NAVAL AVIATION

Helicopter Combat Support Squadron 8 established on 1 December 1984 with CH-46D Sea Knight helicopters; to support VERTREP operations off Virginia Capes and to deploy to Sixth Fleet.

Patrol Squadron 68 (Naval Air Reserve) transferred from NAS Patuxent River, Maryland, to NAF Washington (Andrews AFB, Maryland)

Marine Medium Helicopter Squadron 166 was established in September 1985 with CH-46E Sea Knight helicopters.

NAVAL AIRCRAFT

F-16N

The secretary of the navy announced in 1985 that the Navy would procure 14 General Dynamics F-16 Fighting Falcon fighters in the F-16N variant as a naval adversary training aircraft. These aircraft, flown by the U.S. Air Force and several allied nations, will succeed the F-21A Kfir. (The F-16 has been flown extensively in combat by the Israeli Air Force.)

The F-16 was a competitor with the Northrop YF-17 for the U.S. Air Force lightweight fighter role. The F-16 was selected, with the Navy selecting a heavily modified F-17 design for the fighter-attack role, that plane evolving into the F/A-18 Hornet.

V-22 OSPREY

The production JVX tilt-rotor aircraft will be designated V-22 and given the name Osprey. The Marine Corps version will be the MV-22, the Navy search-and-rescue version will be the HV-22, and the Air Force transport version will be the CV-22.

T-45A GOSHAWK

This aircraft will be named Goshawk

WEAPONS

PENGUIN II

The Penguin II missile is being evaluated by the Navy for use from the SH-60B Seahawk helicopter in the air-to-surface role.

SKIPPER II AGM-123A

The Skipper is a propelled, laser-guided bomb made up of off-the-shelf components. The Naval Weapons Center at China Lake in California created the missile in an effort to produce a low-cost weapon with a short development time. Development began in January 1980.

The missile uses a 1,000-pound warhead which is a Mk 83 general-purpose bomb and the propulsion motor of the Shrike ARM; the laser guidance and control sections are from the Air Force Paveway II (unpowered) laser-guided bomb. The Skipper had an IOC in 1985 and is launched from A-6E Intruder aircraft.

COAST GUARD

HAMILTON CLASS

The East Coast cutters of this class will be modernized at the Bath Iron Works yard and the West Coast cutters at the Todd Pacific shipyard in Seattle, Washington. The first cutter began conversion in October 1985.

BEAR CLASS

WMEC 902	Tampa	laid down 12 Apr 1980 (correction)
WMEC 903	Harriet Lane	comm. 20 Sep 1984
WMEC 904	Northland	comm. 17 Dec 1984
WMEC 905	Spencer	launched 16 June 1984
WMEC 906	Seneca	launched 16 June 1984
WMEC 907	Escanaba	launched 24 Aug 1985
WMEC 908	Tahoma	launched 24 Aug 1985
WMEC 909	Campbell	laid down 10 Aug 1984
WMEC 910	Thetis	laid down 24 Aug 1984
WMEC 911	named Forward	
WMEC 912	named Legare	
WMEC 913	named Mohawk	

SHIPYARDS

The decision was made to close the General Dynamics shipyard at Quincy, Massachusetts, in October 1985, one year after the yard's centennial celebration. When the decision was made to close, the yard had 4,200 employees. The yard was shut down because of the failure to obtain Navy shipbuilding contracts. (There was no commercial work available).

Ironically, the Israeli Navy had selected the GD/Quincy yard in 1984 to construct three diesel-electric submarines, but the U.S. chief of naval operations prohibited the yard from participating in the submarine project.

The Iowa (BB 61) off New York City. Note the amidships arrangement of the Tomahawk armored box launchers and Harpoon cannisters; the second set of Phalanx CIWS is fitted forward of the Harpoons; the forward set is just visible on the bridge wings. Plans to provide these ships with a large number of vertical-launch tubes for Tomahawk missiles have been dropped. (1984, Giorgio Arra)

Maritime prepositioning ship Pvt Harry Fisher. Note the various radar and communications antennas atop the bridge; the height of the helicopter platform; and the stowed stern vehicle unloading ramp. Heavy-lift cranes reduce the dependence on port facilities. (1985, Bethlehem Steel)

Launcher for Rolling Airframe Missile (RAM) fitted to stern of the destroyer DAVID R. RAY (DD 971) for missile evaluation. (1985, Jurgen Zeitlhofer)

Auxiliary crane ship KEYSTONE STATE (T-ACS 1) (1984, Giorgio Arra)

The destroyer CONOLLY (DD 979) showing the paired four-missile Tomahawk ABLs forward of the bridge, alongside the ASROC launcher. The "A" and three chevrons on the ASROC "box" indicates four ASW excellence awards for the ship. (1985, Jurgen Zeitlhofer)

A U.S. Air Force F-16 carrying Sidewinder missiles on its wing tips and a centerline fuel tank; the aircraft also has four under-wing stores pylons. The Navy will procure the F-16N version of this aircraft for adversary training. (U.S. Air Force)

The vehicle cargo/rapid-response ship ALGOL (T-AKR 287) at sea after conversion from an SL-7 cargo liner. Note the portside opening, twinned heavy-lift cranes, and large amidships open deck area. (1984, National Steel and Shipbuilding)

A P-3A Orion has been fitted with a phased-array radar forward of the vertical stabilizer to collect telemetry data on the Pacific Missile Range beyond the distances possible with ground-based instrumentation. This aircraft and the P-3 at right are operated by the Navy missile test center at Pt. Mugu, Calif. (U.S. Navy)

Stern angle of the salvage ship SAFEGUARD (ARS 50) at speed. (1985, L. & L. van Ginderen collection)

The last World War II-built LST on the Navy List is back in commission. Seen here at San Diego in September 1985 before transferring to the Atlantic, the SPHINX (ARL 24) is reportedly being employed as a surveillance ship. Her after superstructure has been enlarged, a helicopter platform fitted, and most of the lift gear removed. The quad 40-mm guns are retained. (1985, Giorgio Arra)